JOSH HOWARD P

SASQUATCH

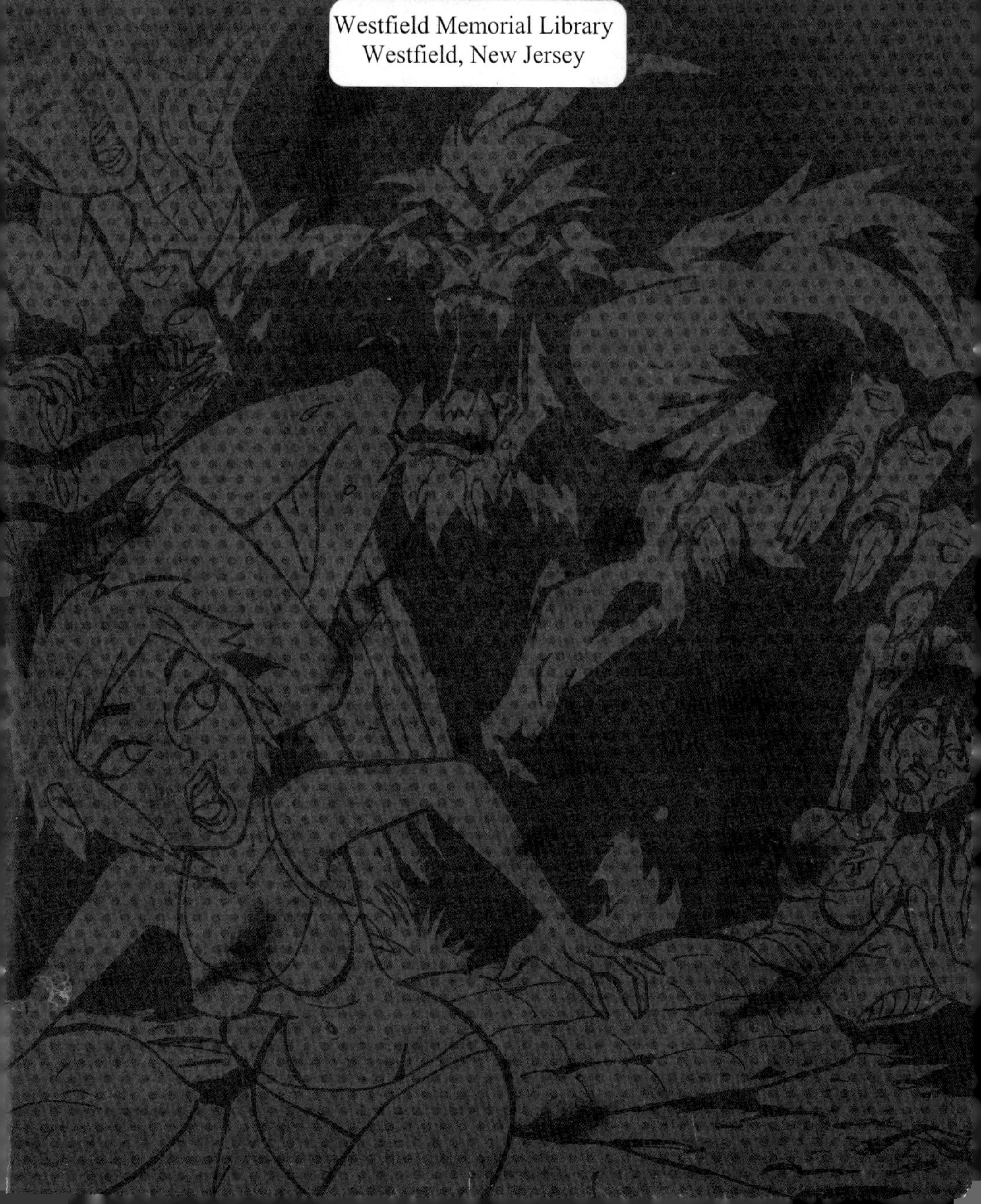

A Viper Comics Trade Paperback Original

Published by Viper Comics
9400 N. MacArthur Blvd., Suite 124-215
Irving, TX 75063

First edition: April 2007
ISBN10: 0-9777883-8-5
ISBN13: 978-0-9777883-8-5

Cover Illustration: Josh Howard
Cover Design: Jim Resnowski
Page 1 Illustration: Josh Howard

Editors: Josh Howard & Jim Resnowski
Assistant Editors: Jason M. Burns & Jessie Garza

JESSIE GARZA PRESIDENT & PUBLISHER
JIM RESNOWSKI EDITOR-IN-CHIEF & CREATIVE DIRECTOR
JASON M. BURNS ASSISTANT PUBLISHER

VIPER COMICS   WWW.VIPERCOMICS.COM   EST. 2001

Printed in the USA.

Special Thanks to Loren Coleman. Visit Loren on the web at
www.lorencoleman.com and www.cryptomundo.com.

CONTENTS

HOW IT ALL STARTED

When other kids were reading *Cat in the Hat* and *Run, Spot, Run*, I was reading things like *Unexplained Mysteries* and the *Search for Bigfoot*. Even at that young age, the idea of unknown phenomena and mysterious creatures was something I was inexplicably drawn to. But time, age, and experience have a way of weeding out all the nonsense, and things like Loch Ness Monster begin to seem more and more ridiculous. However, while UFOs and Mothman lost their luster, one area of the unknown continued to hold my interest - Bigfoot, otherwise known as Sasquatch.

Flash forward to July, 2006. The Viper crew and I had begun the long drive home from San Diego Comic-Con. In the wee hours of the morning conversations can go almost anywhere, and they usually do. Somehow Pat Bussey and I got on the subject of Sasquatch. For those unaware, Pat enjoys giving me unending grief for my fascination with all things Bigfoot. But all the joking around led to us talking about doing our own takes on Sasquatch in comic form. Naturally we began to talk about getting our other friends involved, wondering what it would be like if we were to put together some sort of dream project. Viper head honcho Jessie Garza overheard our insane ranting, and before the end of the trip, a Sasquatch anthology was officially on the schedule for 2007.

Of course, that was only the beginning. What we envisioned was fairly ambitious for a relatively small publisher like Viper. When we began the long process of recruiting talent, we had no idea how it would be received or if there would be any interest at all. Much to my surprise, most everyone we asked was entirely enthusiastic about joining up. It seemed I wasn't alone in my obsession. What follows is probably the most diverse collection of stories about one subject ever compiled. From World War II to the War on Terror, from UFOs to Santa Claus, no ground is left uncovered. Prepare to laugh, cry, and be utterly horrified.

Josh Howard
March, 2007

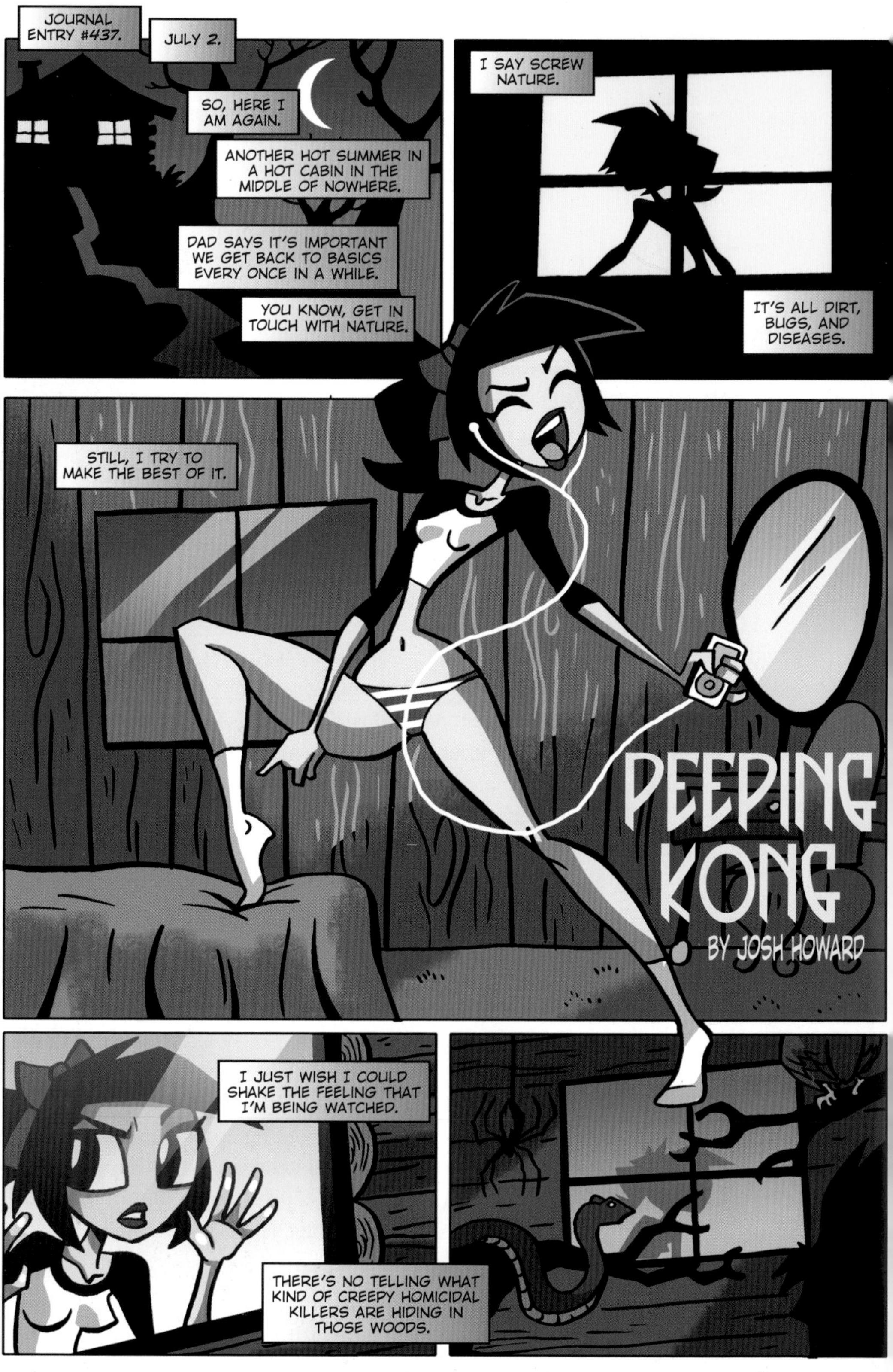
JOURNAL ENTRY #437.
JULY 2.
SO, HERE I AM AGAIN.
ANOTHER HOT SUMMER IN A HOT CABIN IN THE MIDDLE OF NOWHERE.
DAD SAYS IT'S IMPORTANT WE GET BACK TO BASICS EVERY ONCE IN A WHILE.
YOU KNOW, GET IN TOUCH WITH NATURE.
I SAY SCREW NATURE.
IT'S ALL DIRT, BUGS, AND DISEASES.
STILL, I TRY TO MAKE THE BEST OF IT.
PEEPING KONG
BY JOSH HOWARD
I JUST WISH I COULD SHAKE THE FEELING THAT I'M BEING WATCHED.
THERE'S NO TELLING WHAT KIND OF CREEPY HOMICIDAL KILLERS ARE HIDING IN THOSE WOODS.

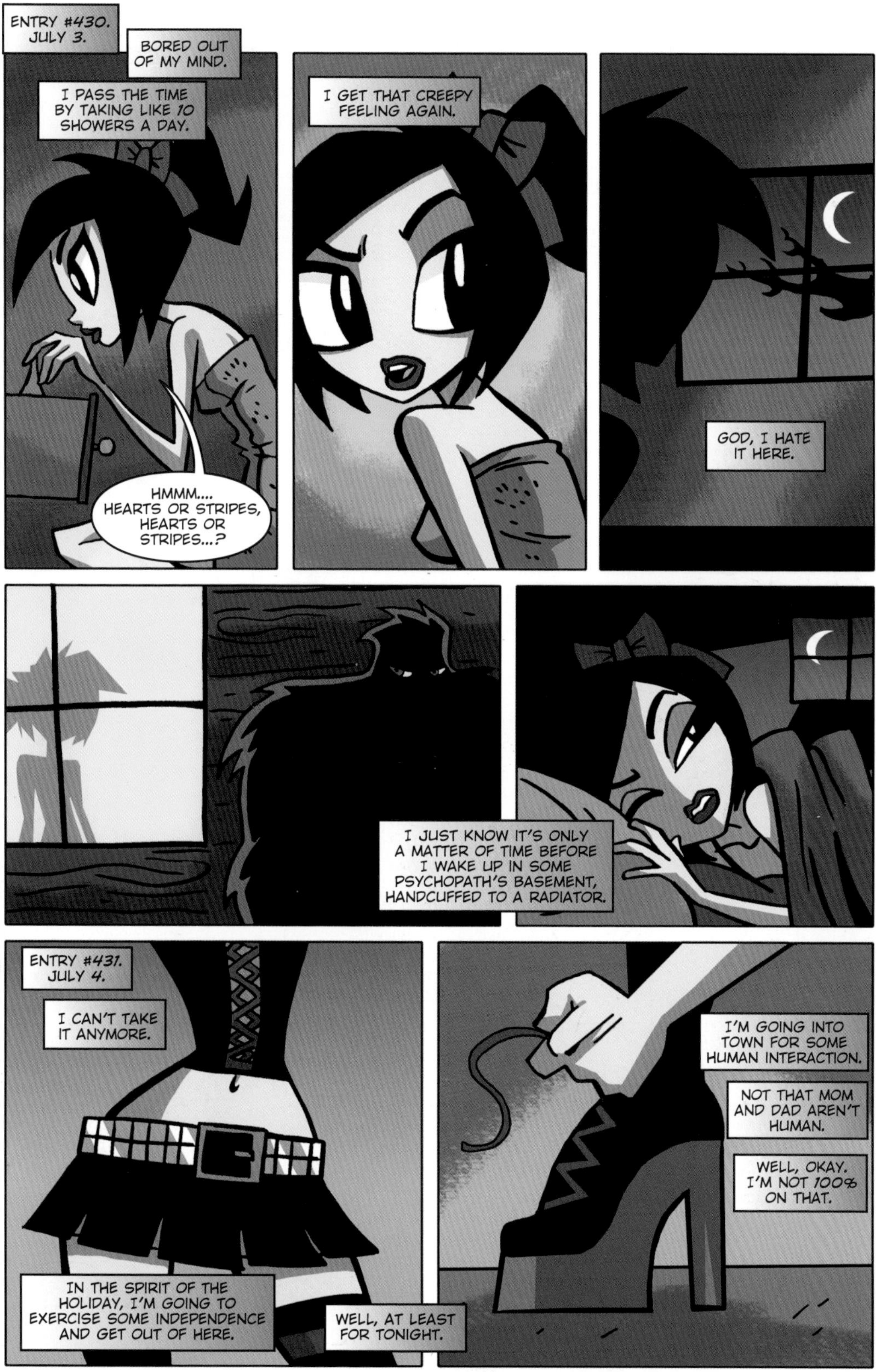
ENTRY #430.
JULY 3.
BORED OUT OF MY MIND.
I PASS THE TIME BY TAKING LIKE 10 SHOWERS A DAY.
HMMM.... HEARTS OR STRIPES, HEARTS OR STRIPES...?
I GET THAT CREEPY FEELING AGAIN.
GOD, I HATE IT HERE.
I JUST KNOW IT'S ONLY A MATTER OF TIME BEFORE I WAKE UP IN SOME PSYCHOPATH'S BASEMENT, HANDCUFFED TO A RADIATOR.
ENTRY #431.
JULY 4.
I CAN'T TAKE IT ANYMORE.
IN THE SPIRIT OF THE HOLIDAY, I'M GOING TO EXERCISE SOME INDEPENDENCE AND GET OUT OF HERE.
WELL, AT LEAST FOR TONIGHT.
I'M GOING INTO TOWN FOR SOME HUMAN INTERACTION.
NOT THAT MOM AND DAD AREN'T HUMAN.
WELL, OKAY. I'M NOT 100% ON THAT.

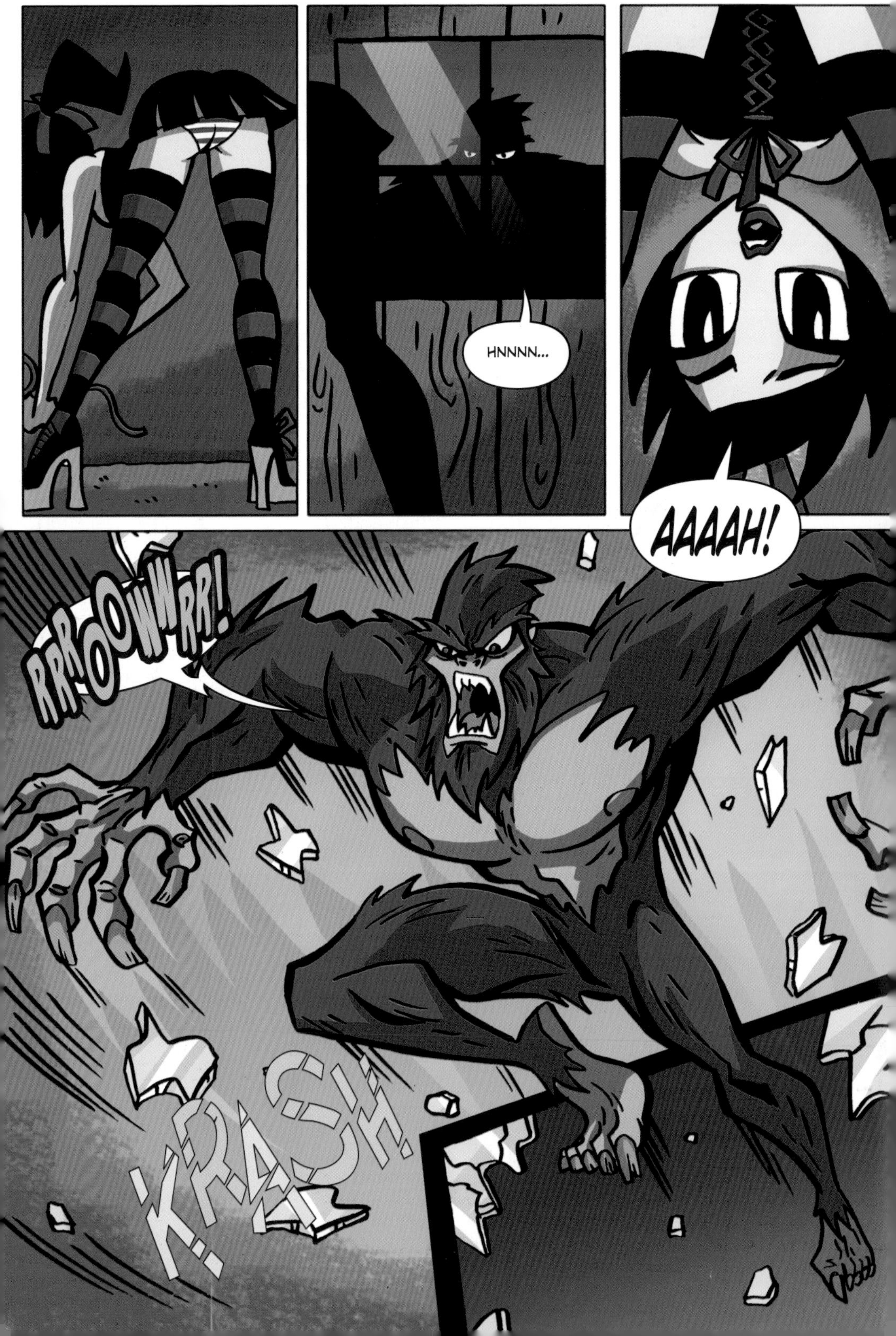
HNNNN...
AAAAH!
RRROOWWRR!
KRASH!

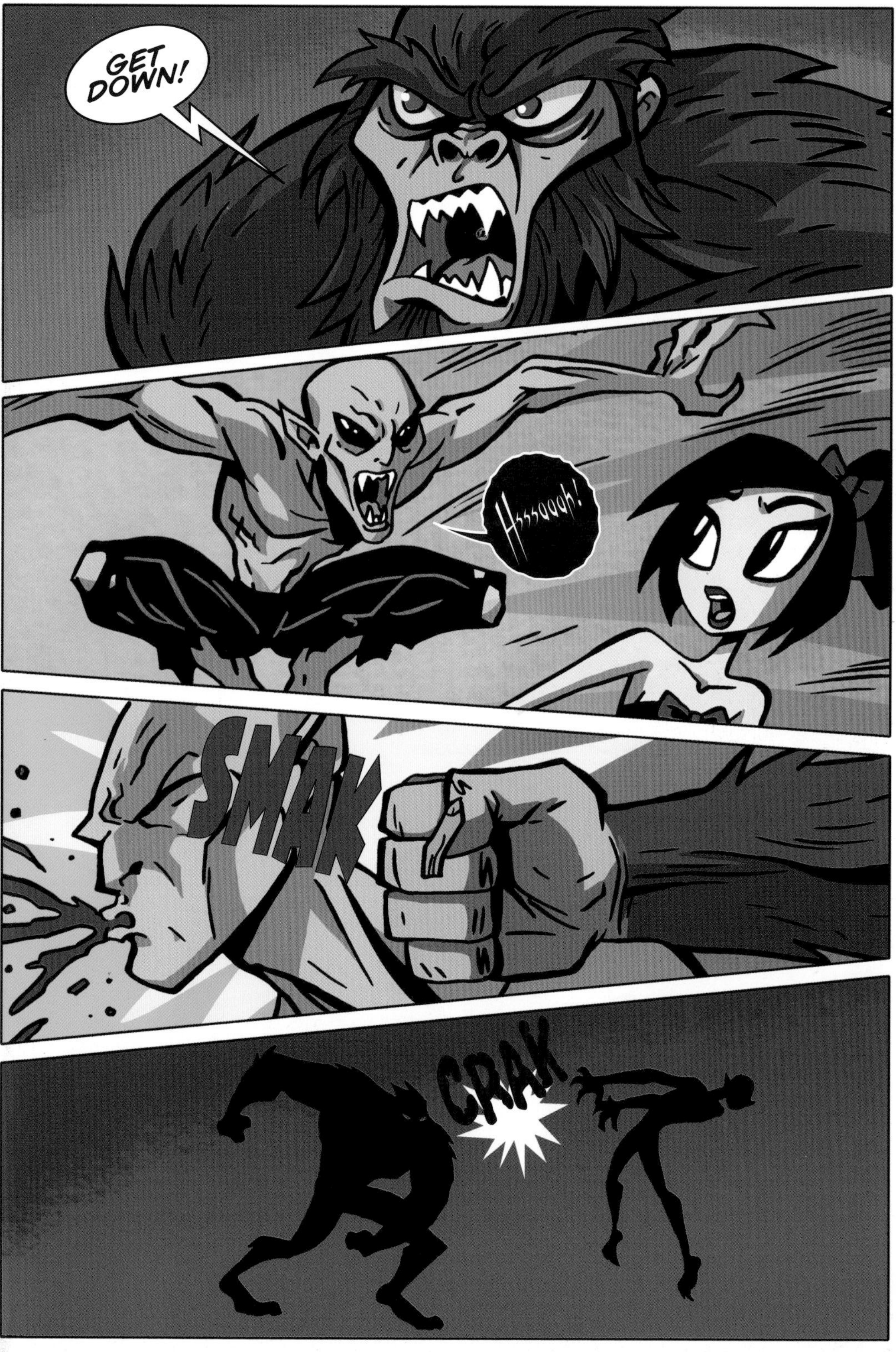
GET DOWN!
Hsssaaah!
SMAK
CRAK

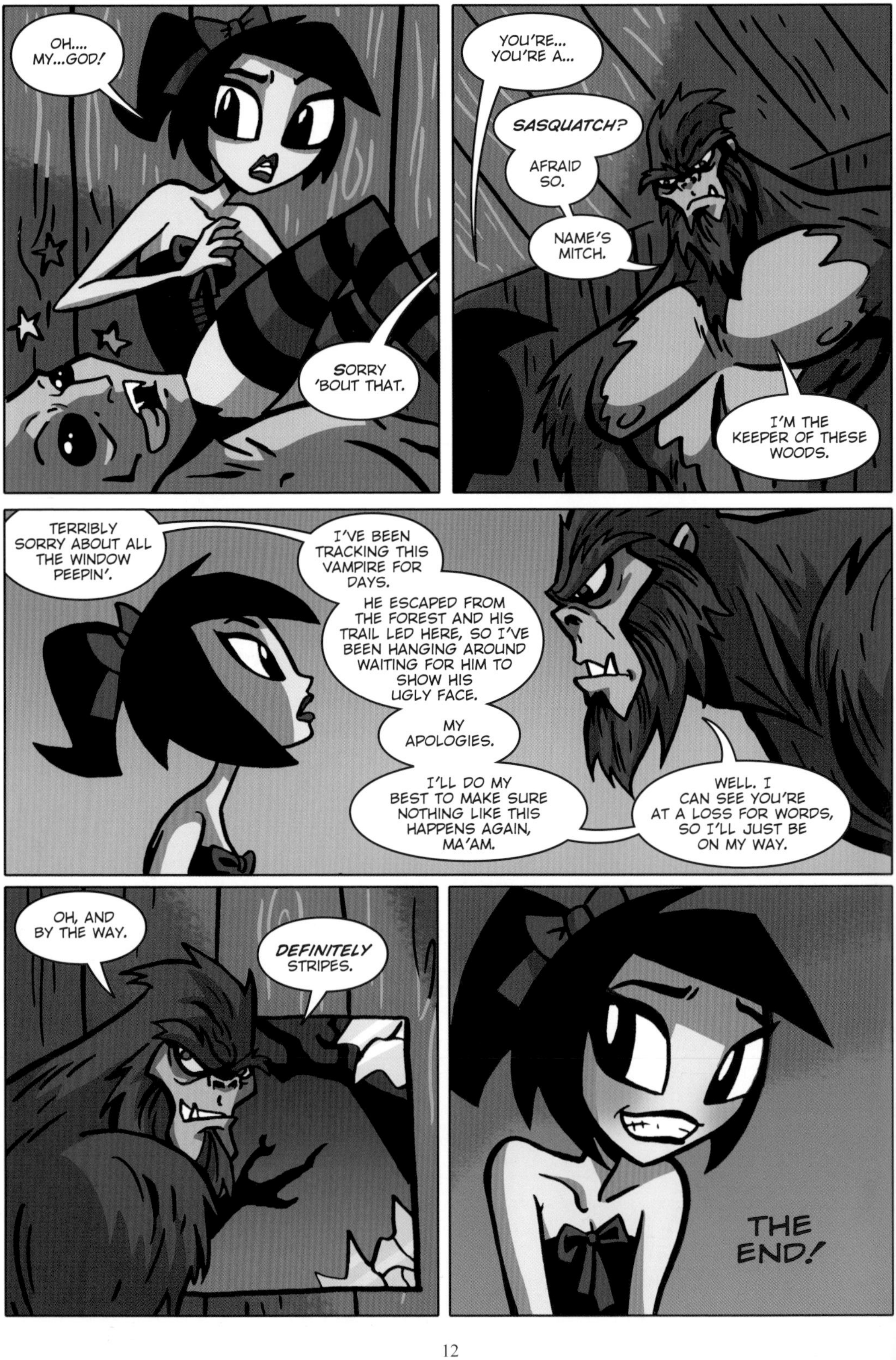
OH.... MY...GOD!
SORRY 'BOUT THAT.
YOU'RE... YOU'RE A...
SASQUATCH?
AFRAID SO.
NAME'S MITCH.
I'M THE KEEPER OF THESE WOODS.
TERRIBLY SORRY ABOUT ALL THE WINDOW PEEPIN'.
I'VE BEEN TRACKING THIS VAMPIRE FOR DAYS.
HE ESCAPED FROM THE FOREST AND HIS TRAIL LED HERE, SO I'VE BEEN HANGING AROUND WAITING FOR HIM TO SHOW HIS UGLY FACE.
MY APOLOGIES.
I'LL DO MY BEST TO MAKE SURE NOTHING LIKE THIS HAPPENS AGAIN, MA'AM.
WELL. I CAN SEE YOU'RE AT A LOSS FOR WORDS, SO I'LL JUST BE ON MY WAY.
OH, AND BY THE WAY.
DEFINITELY STRIPES.
THE END!

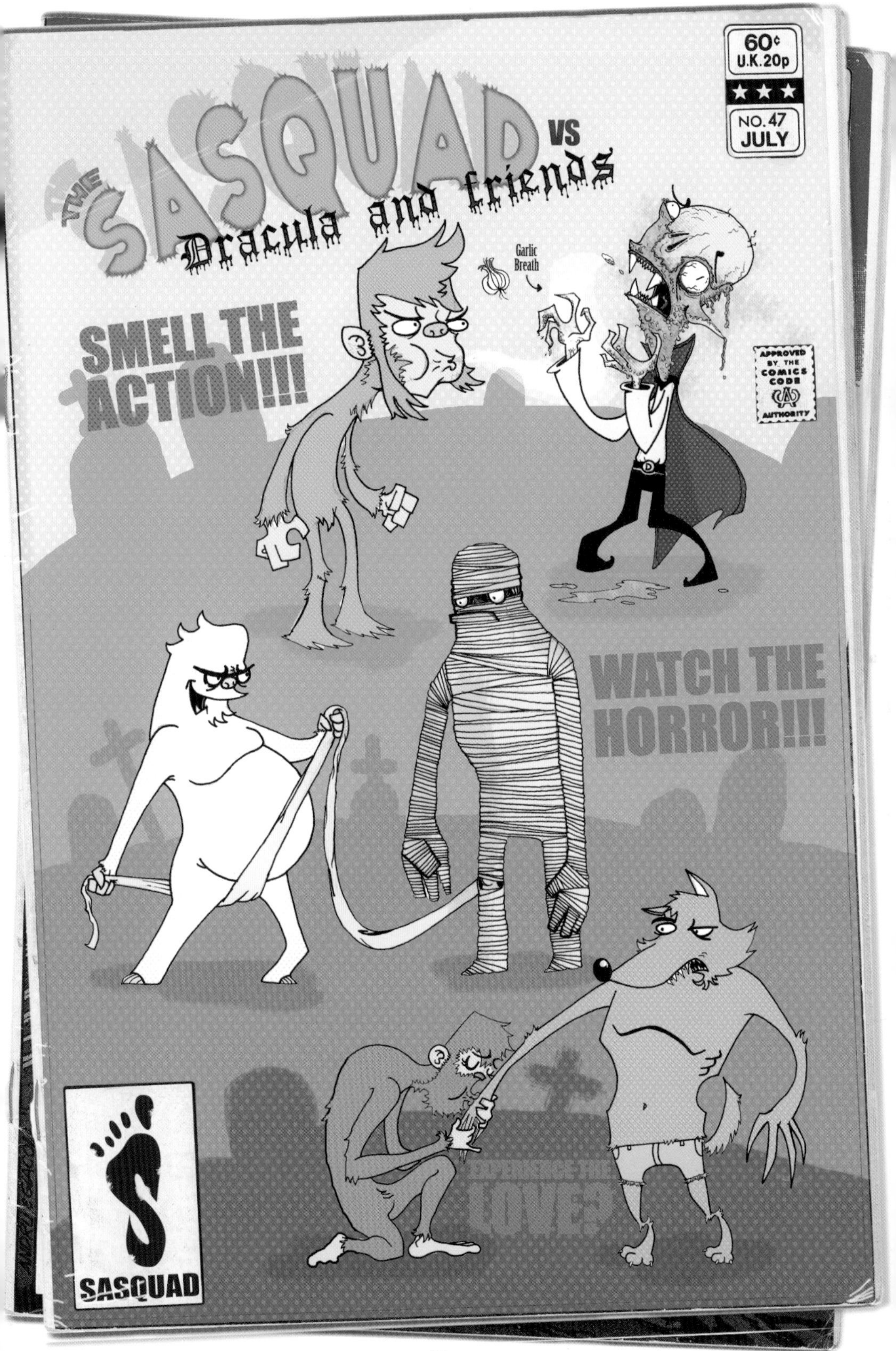
60¢
U.K.20p
NO.47
JULY
THE SASQUAD VS
Dracula and friends
Garlic Breath
SMELL THE ACTION!!!
APPROVED BY THE COMICS CODE AUTHORITY
WATCH THE HORROR!!!
EXPERIENCE THE LOVE?
SASQUAD

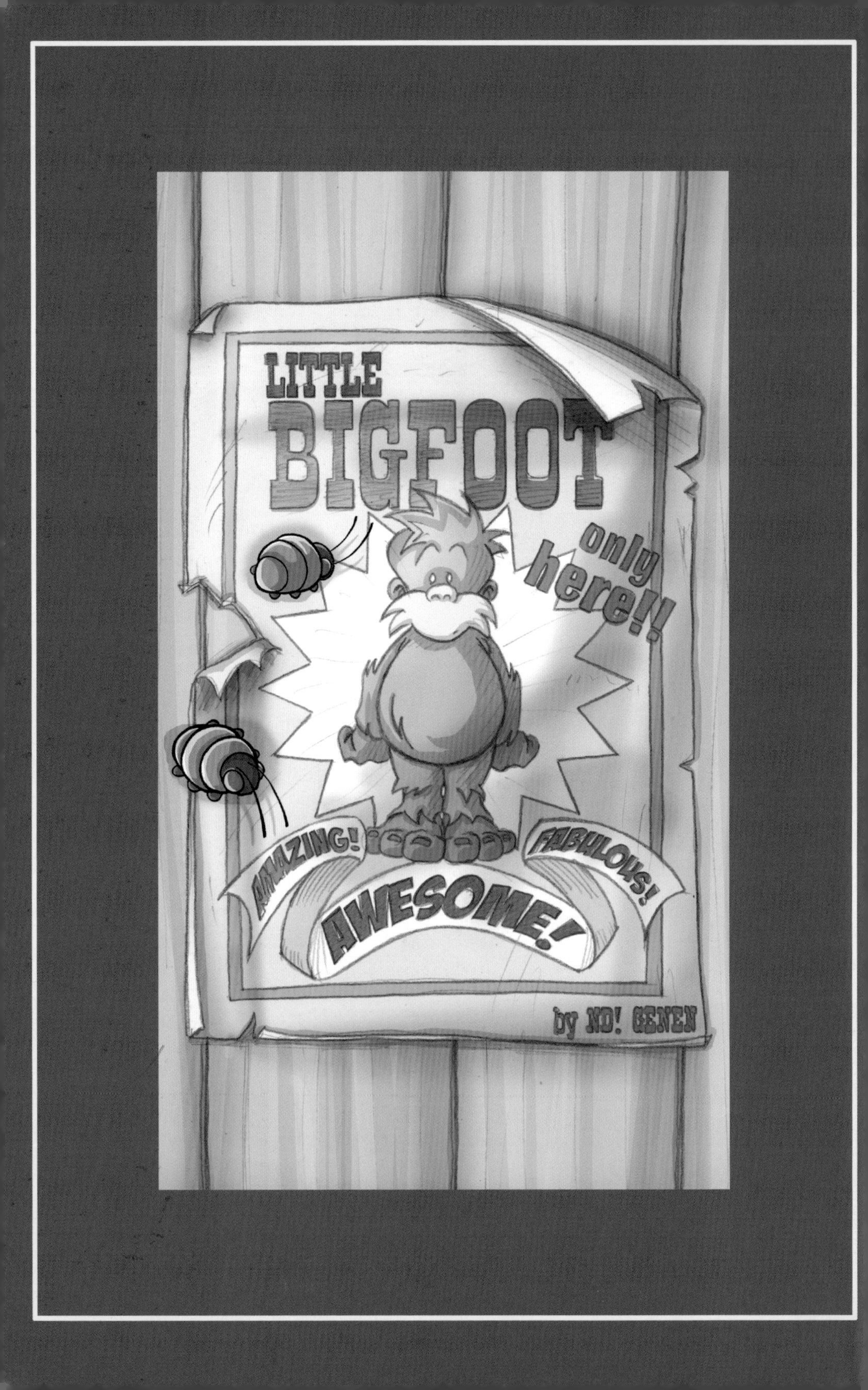
LITTLE BIGFOOT
only here!!
AMAZING!
FABULOUS!
AWESOME!
by NO! GENEN

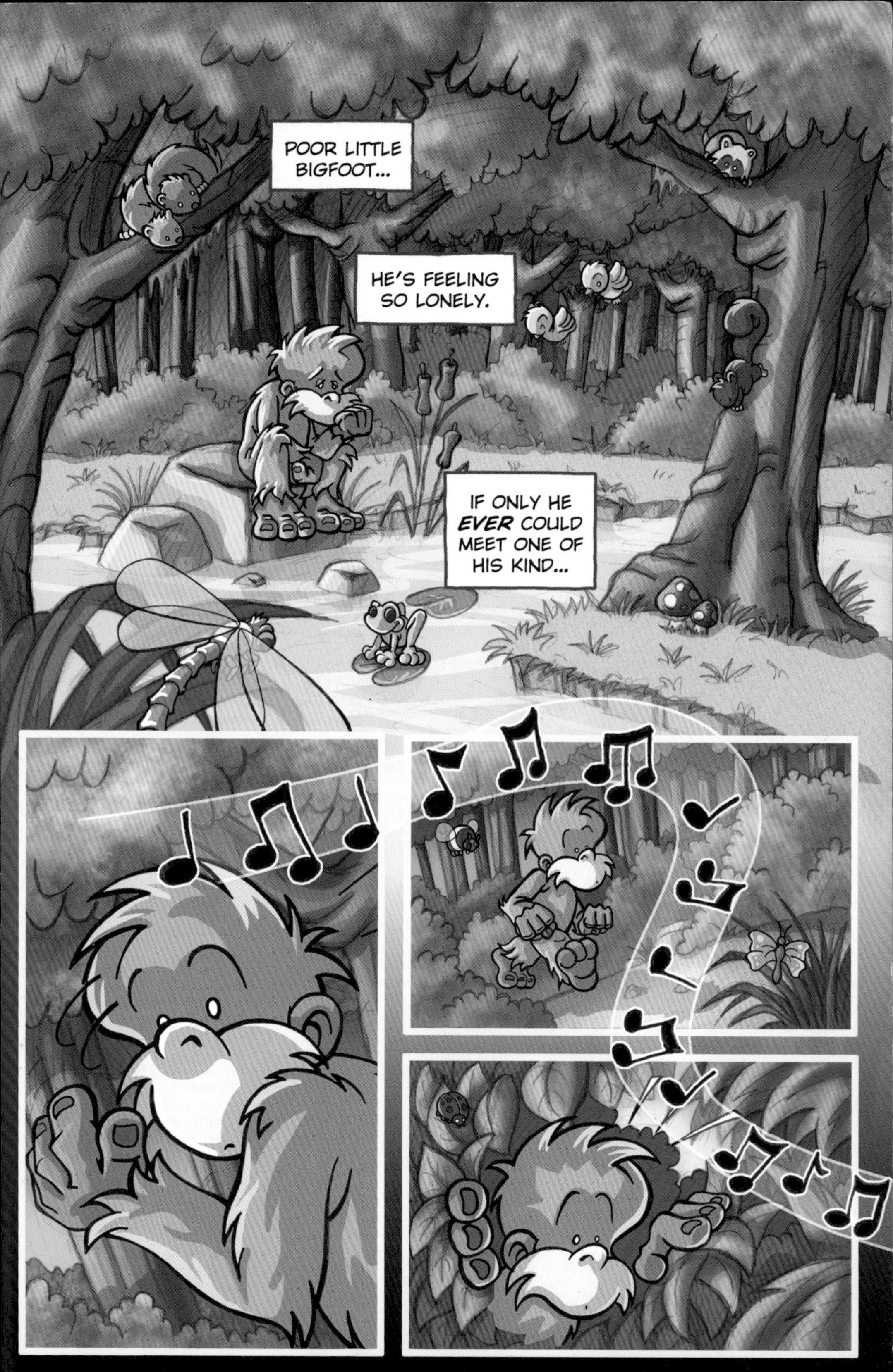
POOR LITTLE BIGFOOT...
HE'S FEELING SO LONELY.
IF ONLY HE EVER COULD MEET ONE OF HIS KIND...

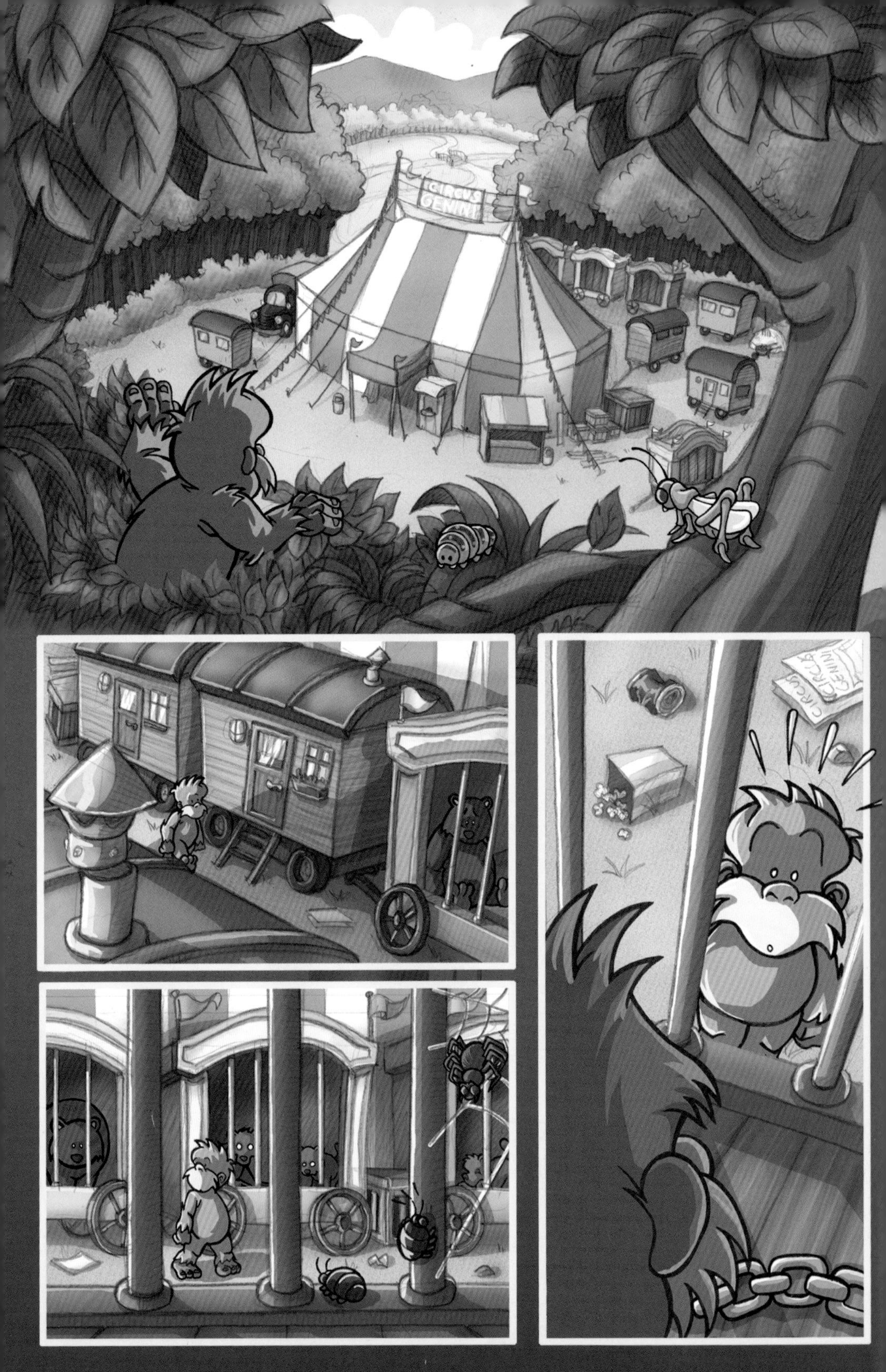
CIRCUS
GENINI
CIRCUS
GENINI
CIRCUS

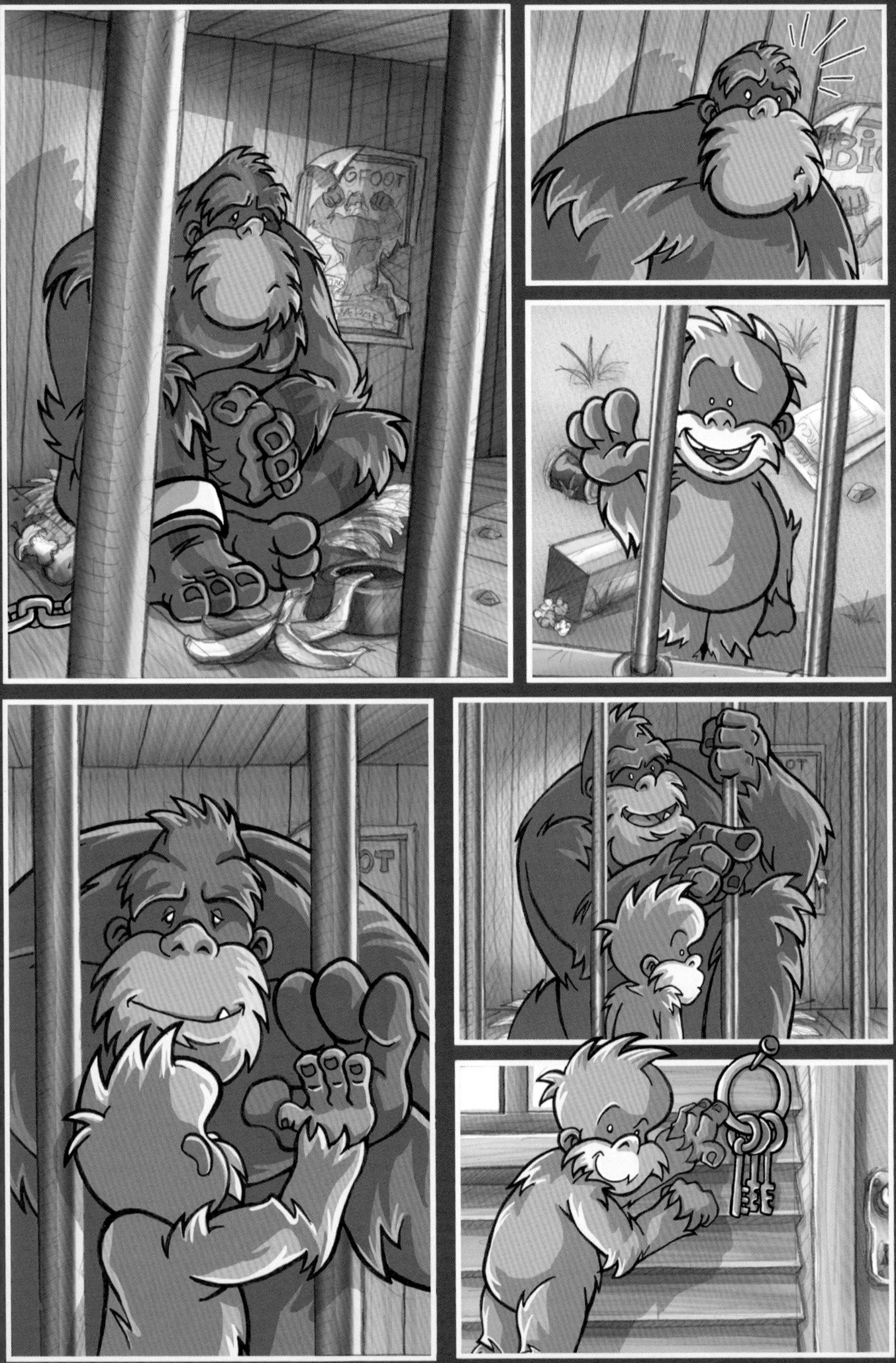

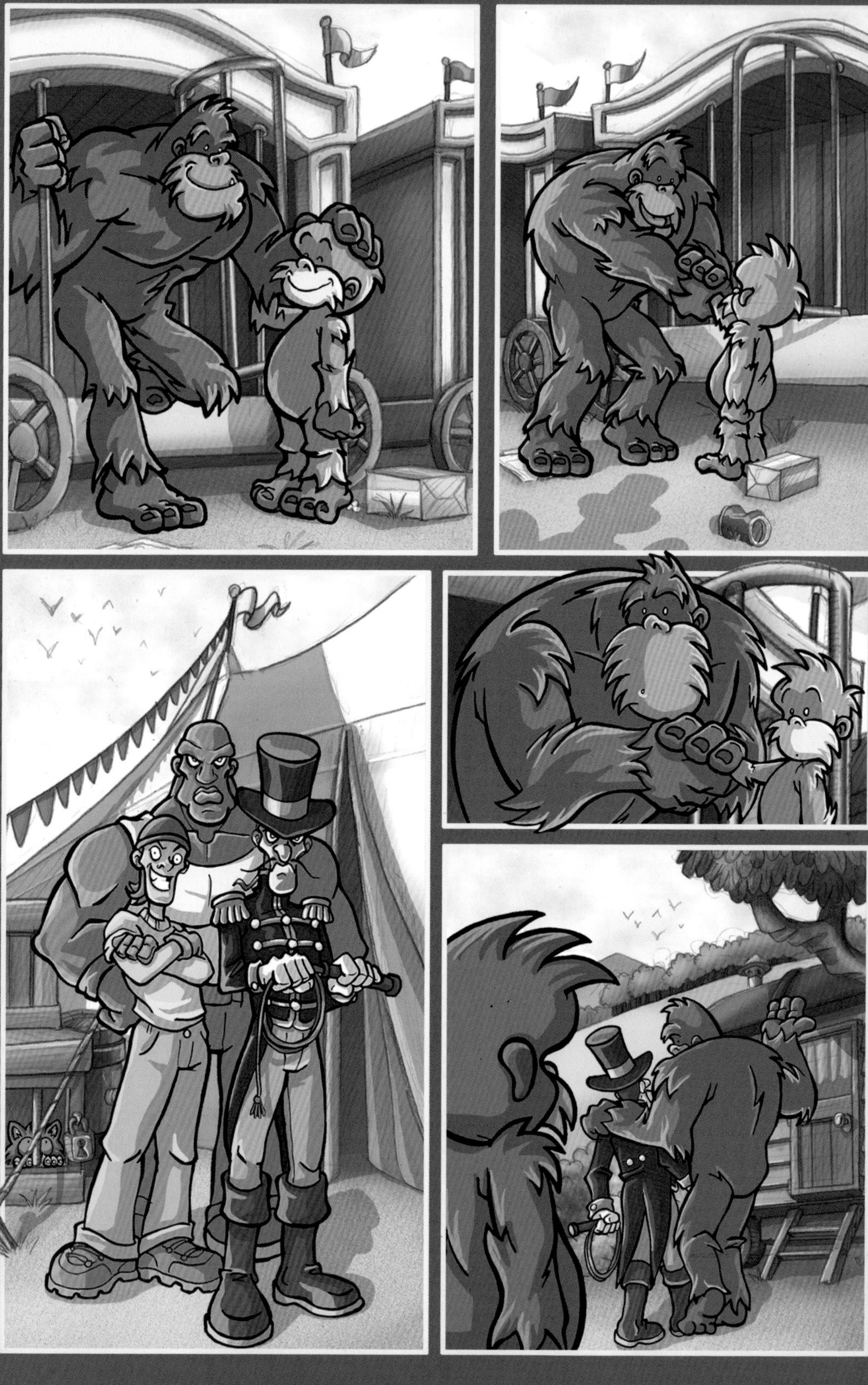

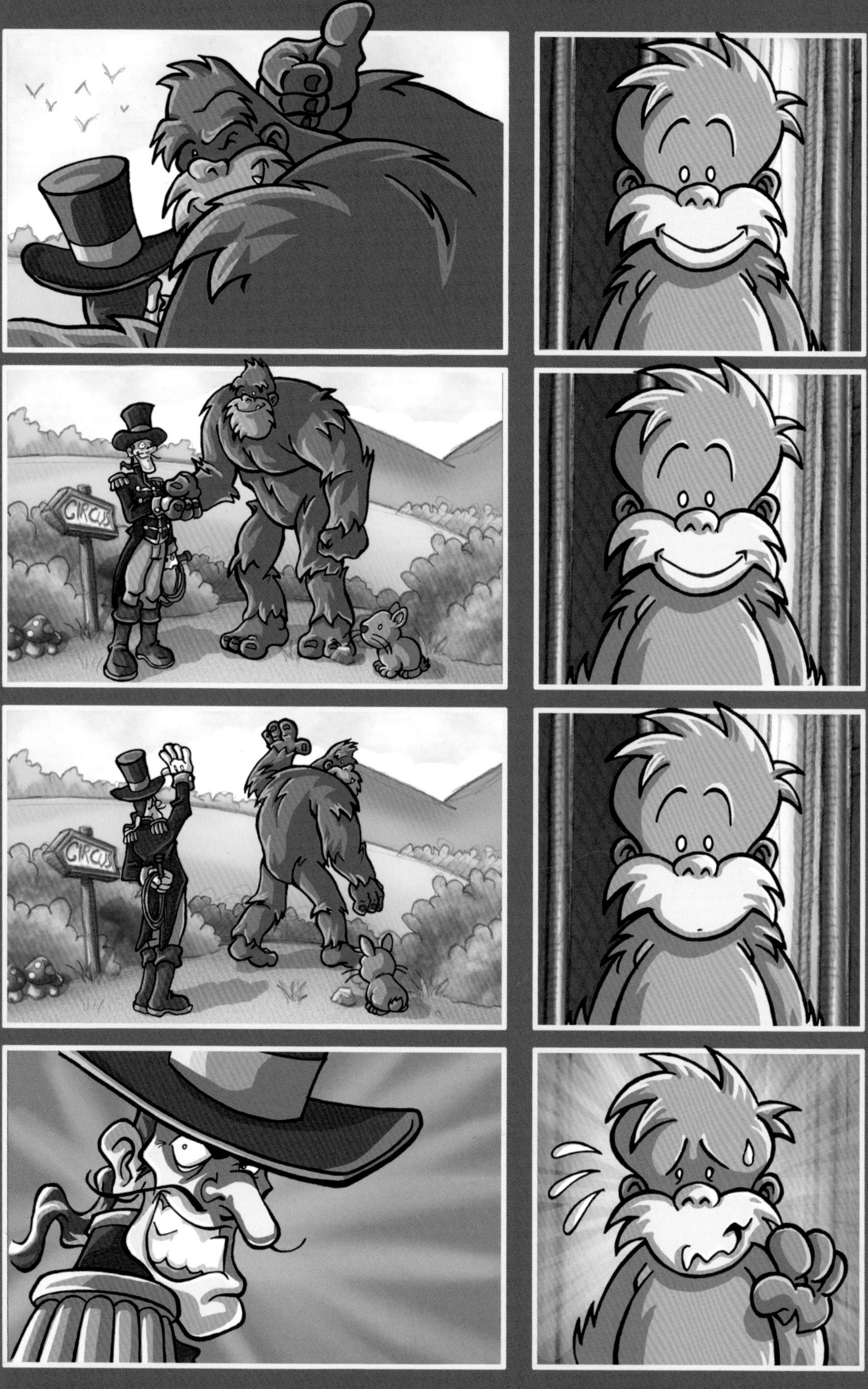
CIRCUS

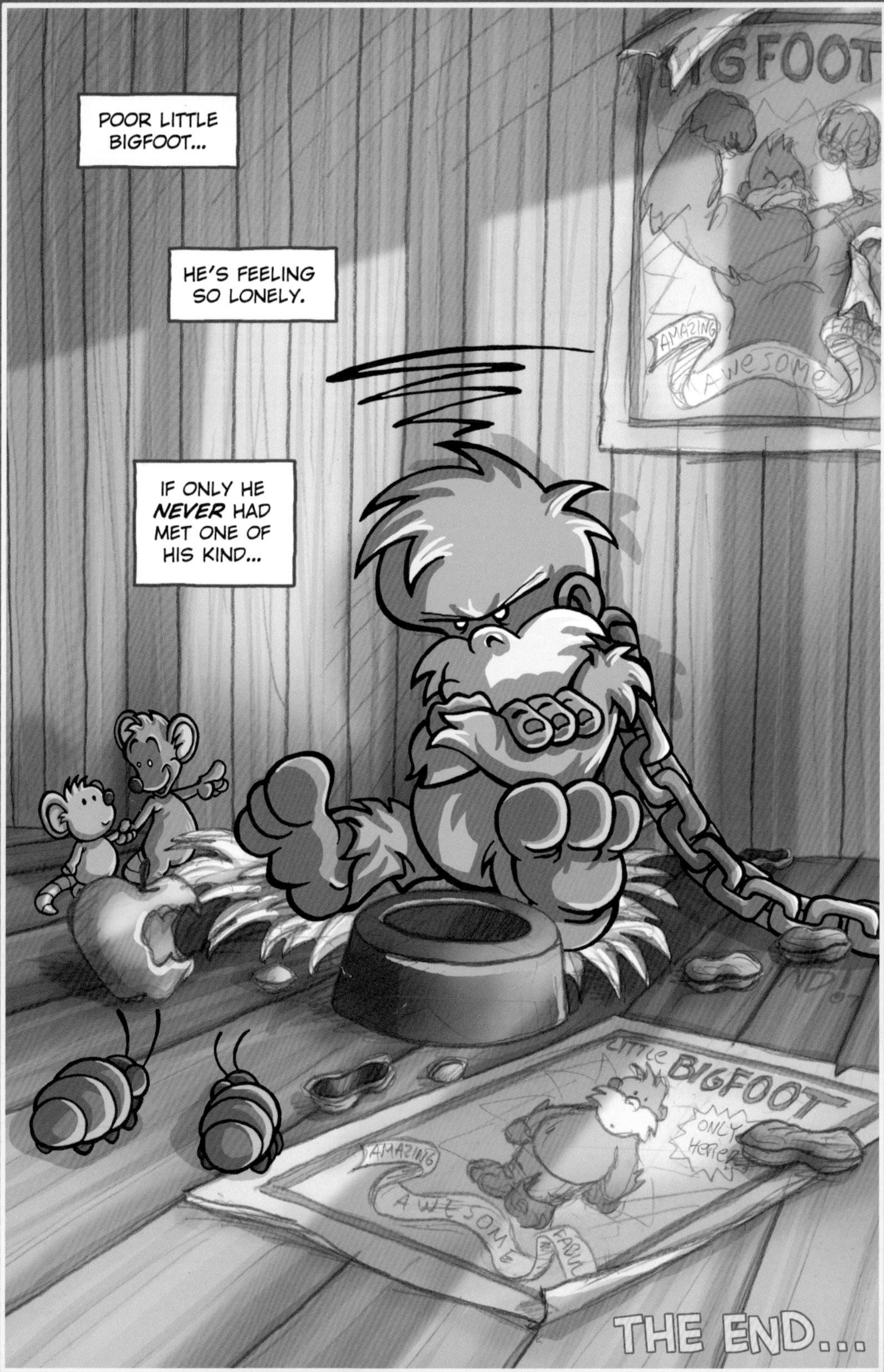
POOR LITTLE BIGFOOT...
HE'S FEELING SO LONELY.
IF ONLY HE *NEVER* HAD MET ONE OF HIS KIND...
BIGFOOT
AMAZING
AWESOME
LITTLE BIGFOOT
ONLY HERE!
AMAZING
AWESOME
THE END...

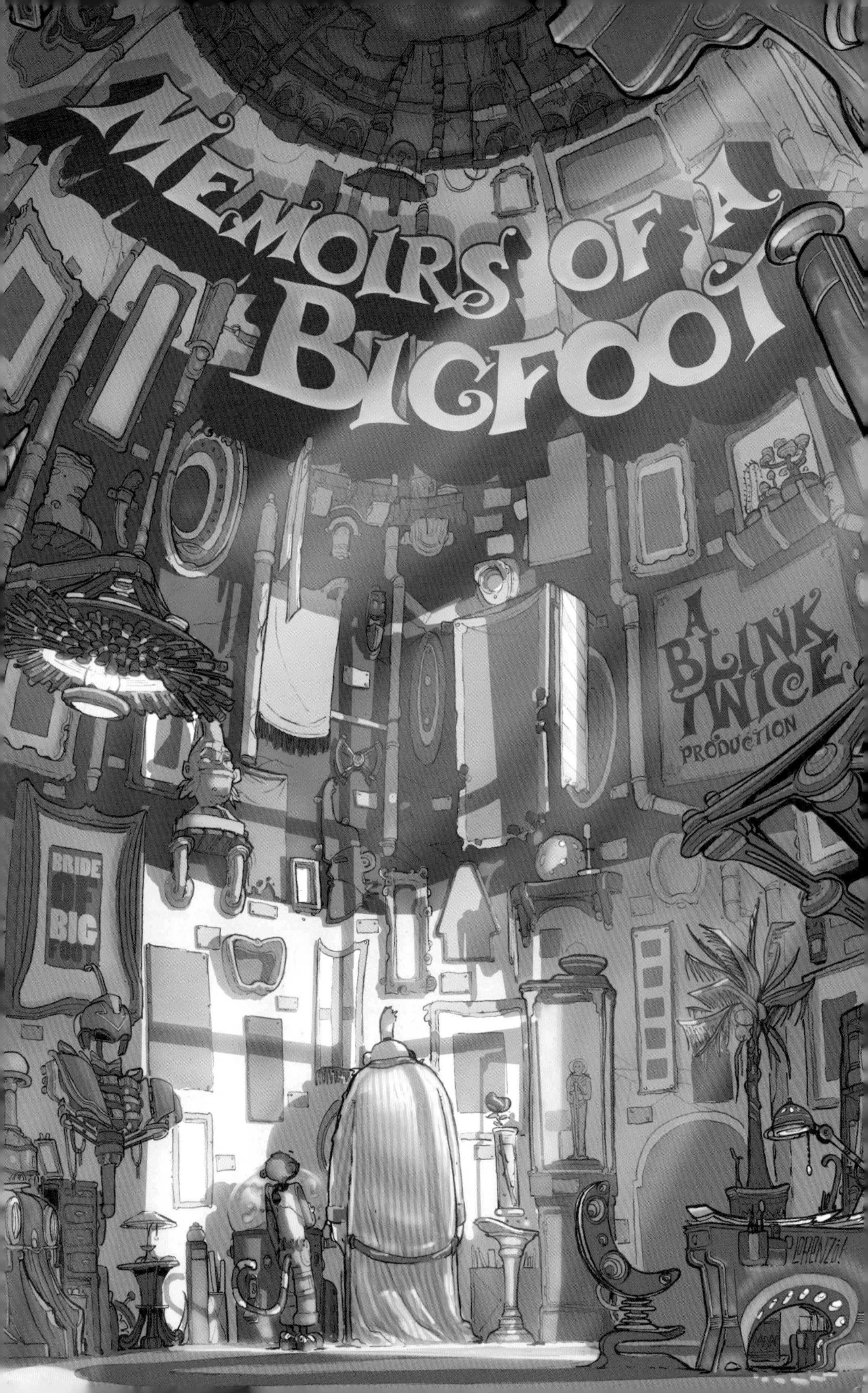
MEMOIRS OF A BIGFOOT
A BLINK TWICE PRODUCTION
BRIDE OF BIG FOOT
LORENZO!

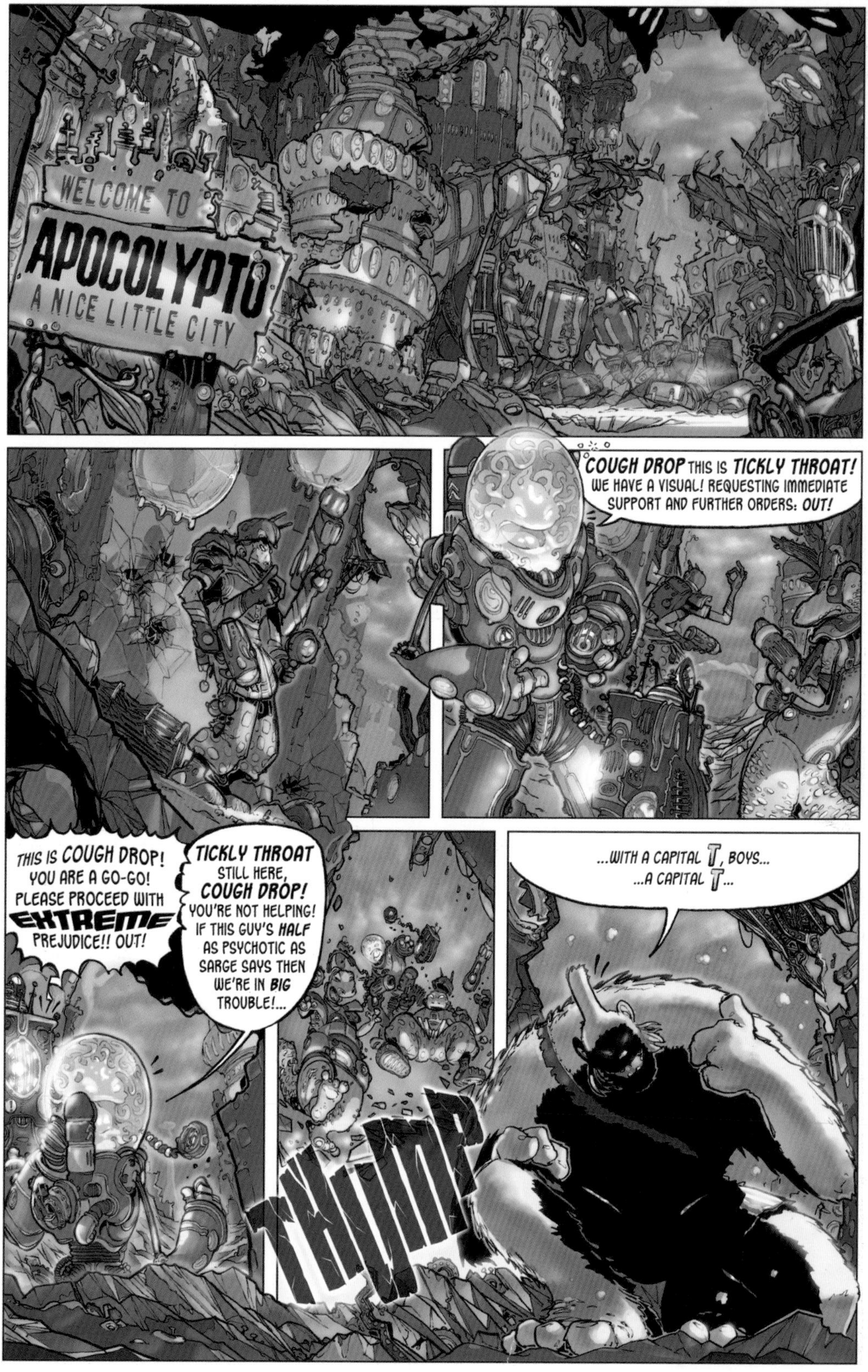
WELCOME TO
APOCOLYPTO
A NICE LITTLE CITY
COUGH DROP THIS IS TICKLY THROAT! WE HAVE A VISUAL! REQUESTING IMMEDIATE SUPPORT AND FURTHER ORDERS: OUT!
THIS IS COUGH DROP! YOU ARE A GO-GO! PLEASE PROCEED WITH EXTREME PREJUDICE!! OUT!
TICKLY THROAT STILL HERE, COUGH DROP! YOU'RE NOT HELPING! IF THIS GUY'S HALF AS PSYCHOTIC AS SARGE SAYS THEN WE'RE IN BIG TROUBLE!...
...WITH A CAPITAL T, BOYS... ...A CAPITAL T...
THWUMP

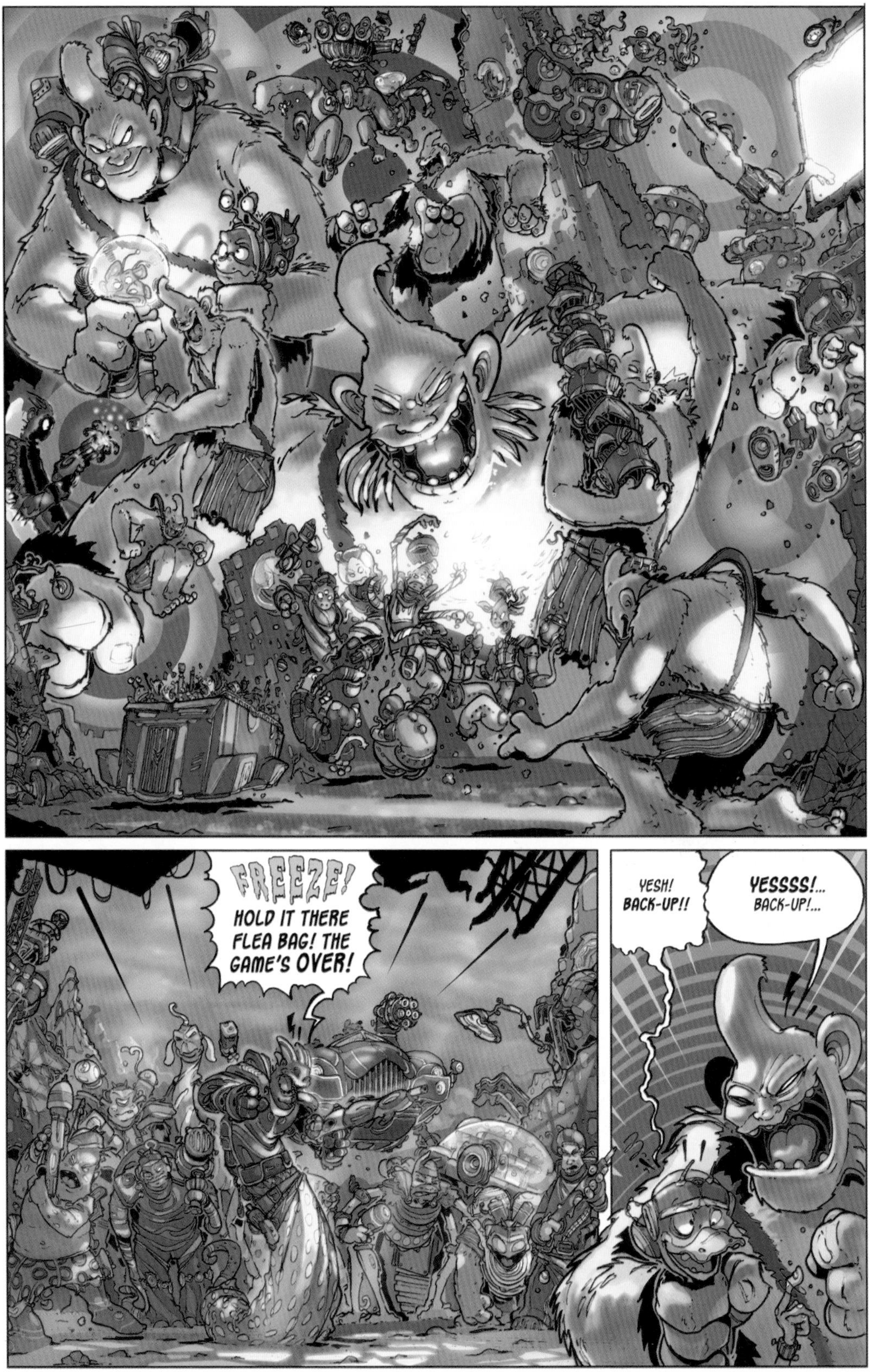
FREEZE!
HOLD IT THERE FLEA BAG! THE GAME'S OVER!
YESH! BACK-UP!!
YESSSS!... BACK-UP!...

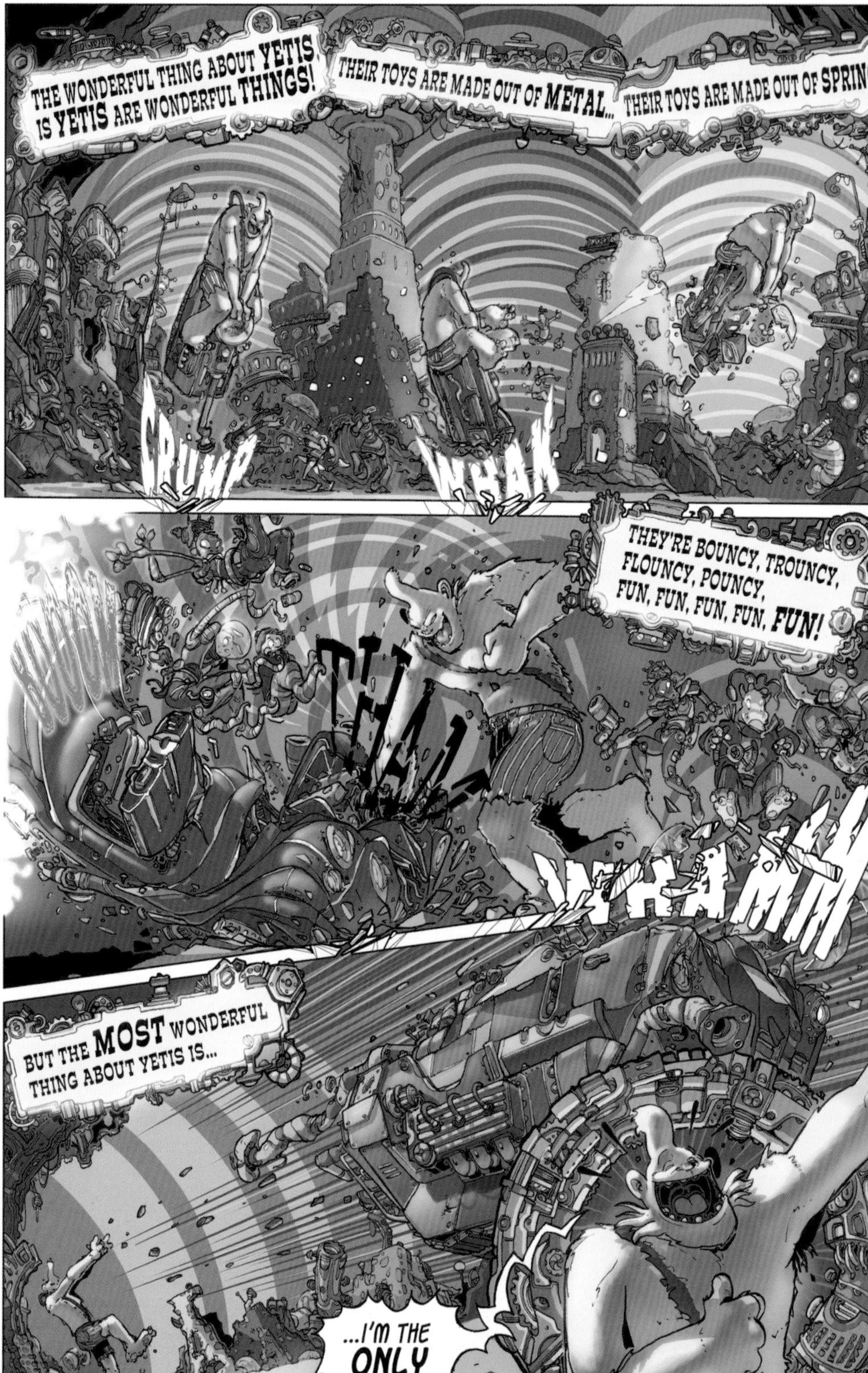
THE WONDERFUL THING ABOUT YETIS IS YETIS ARE WONDERFUL THINGS!
THEIR TOYS ARE MADE OUT OF METAL...
THEIR TOYS ARE MADE OUT OF SPRINGS!
CRUMP
WHAK
THEY'RE BOUNCY, TROUNCY, FLOUNCY, POUNCY, FUN, FUN, FUN, FUN, FUN!
THAK
WHAMM
BUT THE MOST WONDERFUL THING ABOUT YETIS IS...
...I'M THE ONLY ONE!

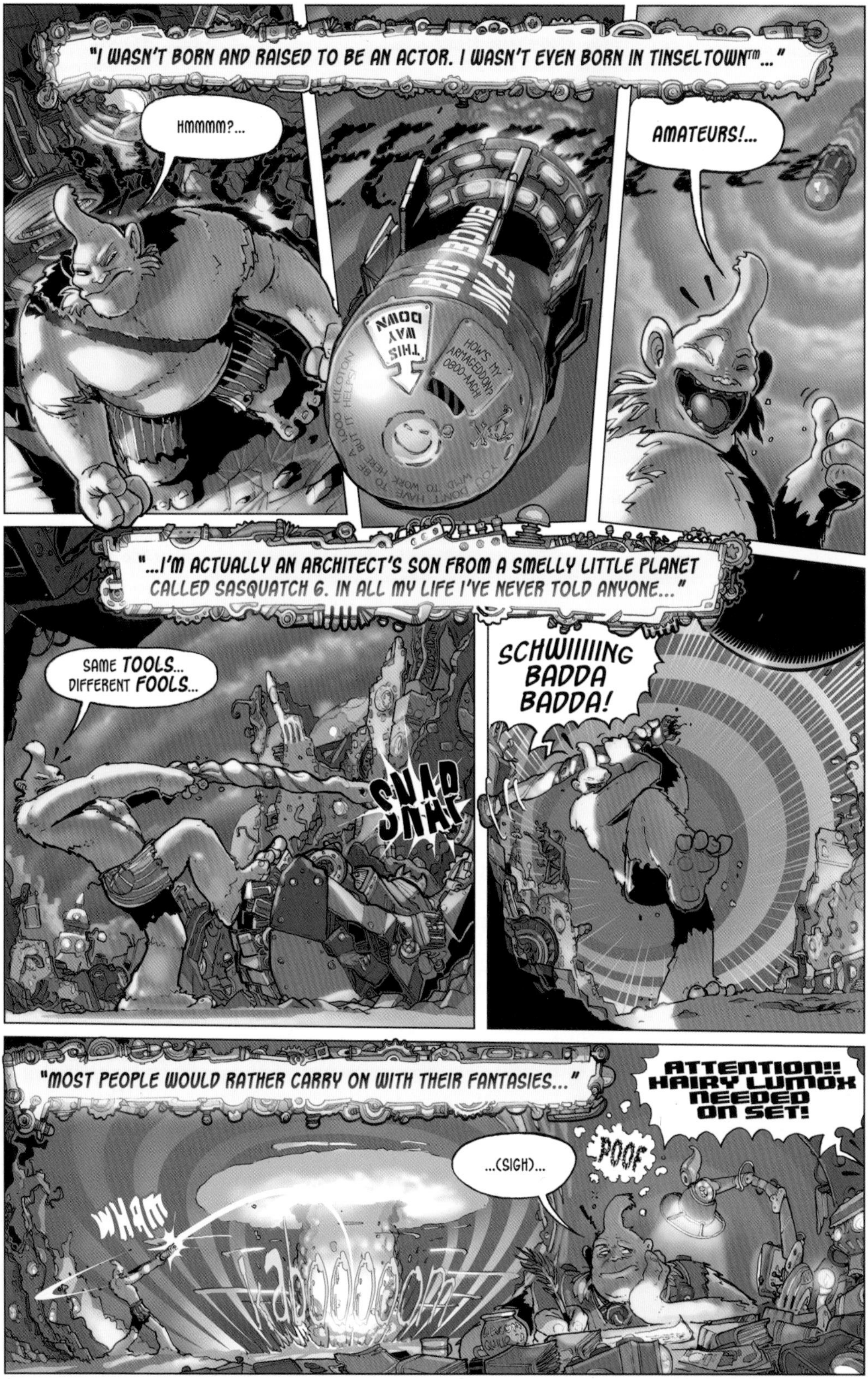
"I WASN'T BORN AND RAISED TO BE AN ACTOR. I WASN'T EVEN BORN IN TINSELTOWN™..."
HMMMM?...
THIS WAY DOWN
HOW'S MY ARMAGEDDON? 0800-AAGH!
AMATEURS!...
"...I'M ACTUALLY AN ARCHITECT'S SON FROM A SMELLY LITTLE PLANET CALLED SASQUATCH 6. IN ALL MY LIFE I'VE NEVER TOLD ANYONE..."
SAME TOOLS... DIFFERENT FOOLS...
SCHWIIIIING BADDA BADDA!
"MOST PEOPLE WOULD RATHER CARRY ON WITH THEIR FANTASIES..."
ATTENTION!! HAIRY LUMOX NEEDED ON SET!
...(SIGH)...
POOF

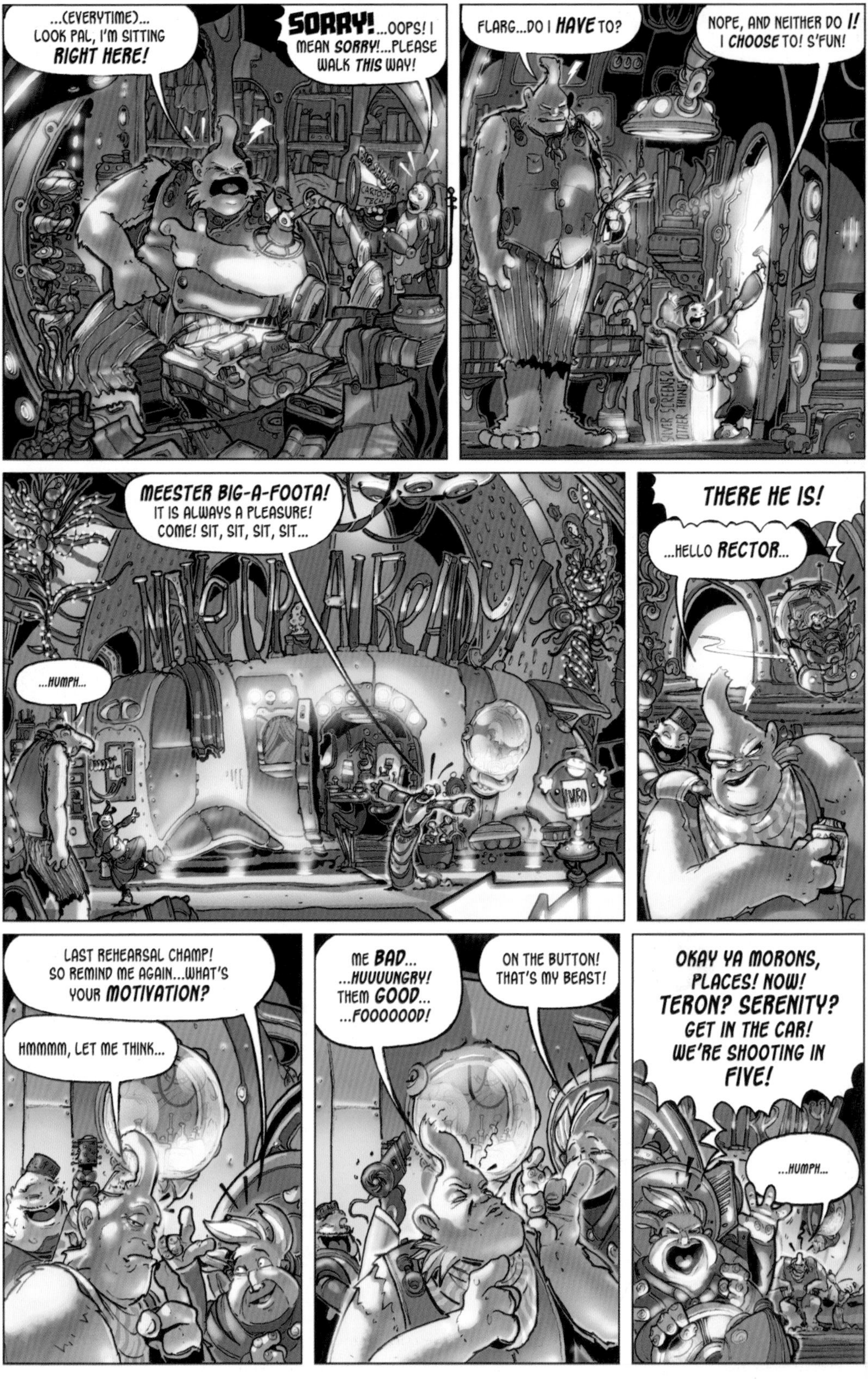

...(EVERYTIME)... LOOK PAL, I'M SITTING **RIGHT HERE!**
SORRY!...OOPS! I MEAN *SORRY!*...PLEASE WALK *THIS* WAY!
CARTOON TECH
FLARG...DO I **HAVE** TO?
NOPE, AND NEITHER DO ***I!*** I ***CHOOSE*** TO! S'FUN!
MEESTER BIG-A-FOOTA! IT IS ALWAYS A PLEASURE! COME! SIT, SIT, SIT, SIT...
...HUMPH...
THERE HE IS!
...HELLO **RECTOR**...
LAST REHEARSAL CHAMP! SO REMIND ME AGAIN...WHAT'S YOUR ***MOTIVATION?***
HMMMM, LET ME THINK...
ME ***BAD***... ...*HUUUUNGRY!* THEM ***GOOD***... ...*FOOOOOOD!*
ON THE BUTTON! THAT'S MY BEAST!
OKAY YA MORONS, PLACES! NOW! TERON? SERENITY? GET IN THE CAR! WE'RE SHOOTING IN FIVE!
...HUMPH...

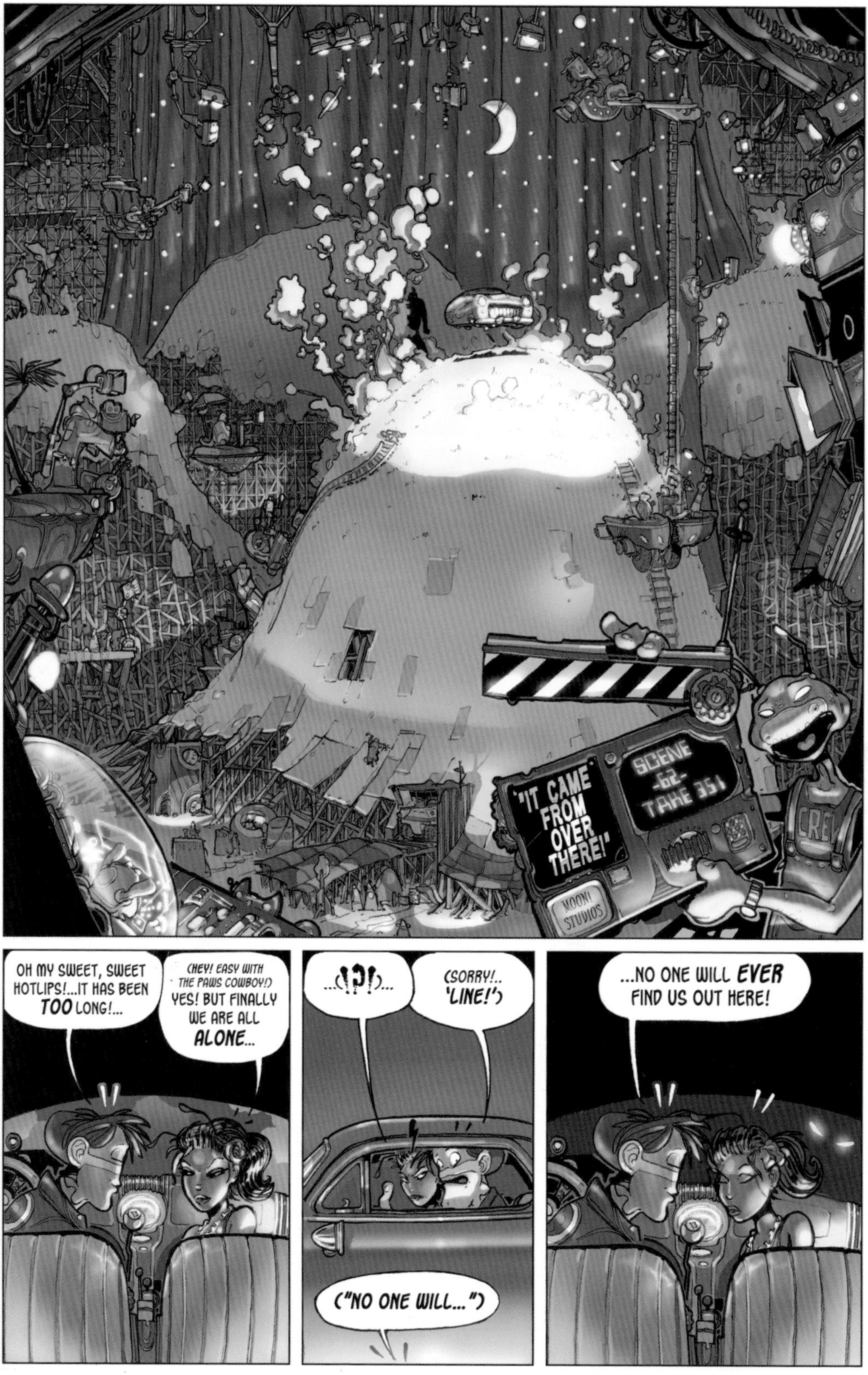
"IT CAME FROM OVER THERE!"
SCENE -62- TAKE 351
MOONI STUDIOS
OH MY SWEET, SWEET HOTLIPS!...IT HAS BEEN TOO LONG!...
(HEY! EASY WITH THE PAWS COWBOY!) YES! BUT FINALLY WE ARE ALL ALONE...
...¡?!...
(SORRY!.. 'LINE!')
("NO ONE WILL...")
...NO ONE WILL EVER FIND US OUT HERE!

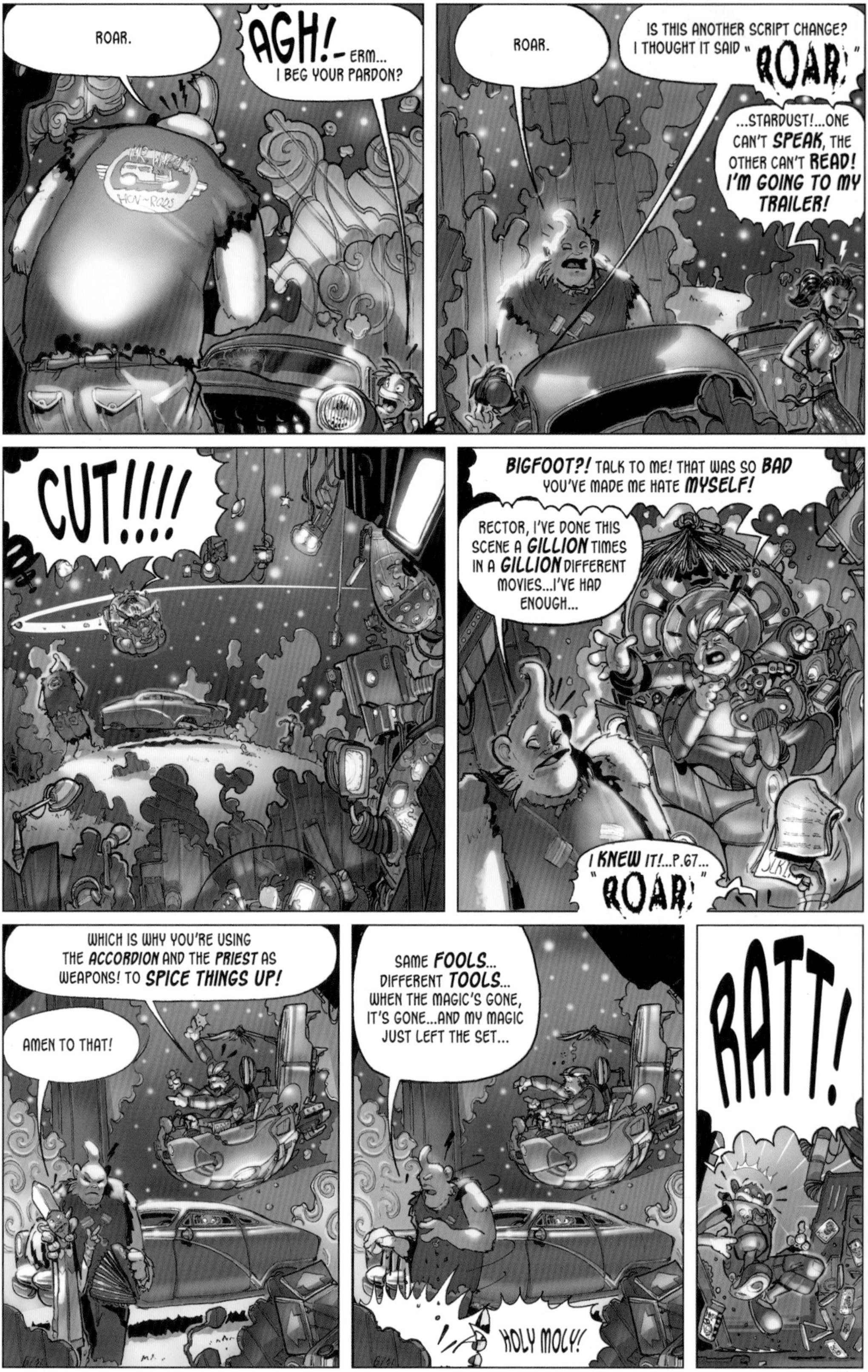
ROAR.
AGH!–ERM... I BEG YOUR PARDON?
ROAR.
IS THIS ANOTHER SCRIPT CHANGE? I THOUGHT IT SAID "ROAR!"
...STARDUST!...ONE CAN'T SPEAK, THE OTHER CAN'T READ! I'M GOING TO MY TRAILER!
CUT!!!!
BIGFOOT?! TALK TO ME! THAT WAS SO BAD YOU'VE MADE ME HATE MYSELF!
RECTOR, I'VE DONE THIS SCENE A GILLION TIMES IN A GILLION DIFFERENT MOVIES...I'VE HAD ENOUGH...
I KNEW IT!...P.67... "ROAR!"
WHICH IS WHY YOU'RE USING THE ACCORDION AND THE PRIEST AS WEAPONS! TO SPICE THINGS UP!
AMEN TO THAT!
SAME FOOLS... DIFFERENT TOOLS... WHEN THE MAGIC'S GONE, IT'S GONE...AND MY MAGIC JUST LEFT THE SET...
HOLY MOLY!
RATT!

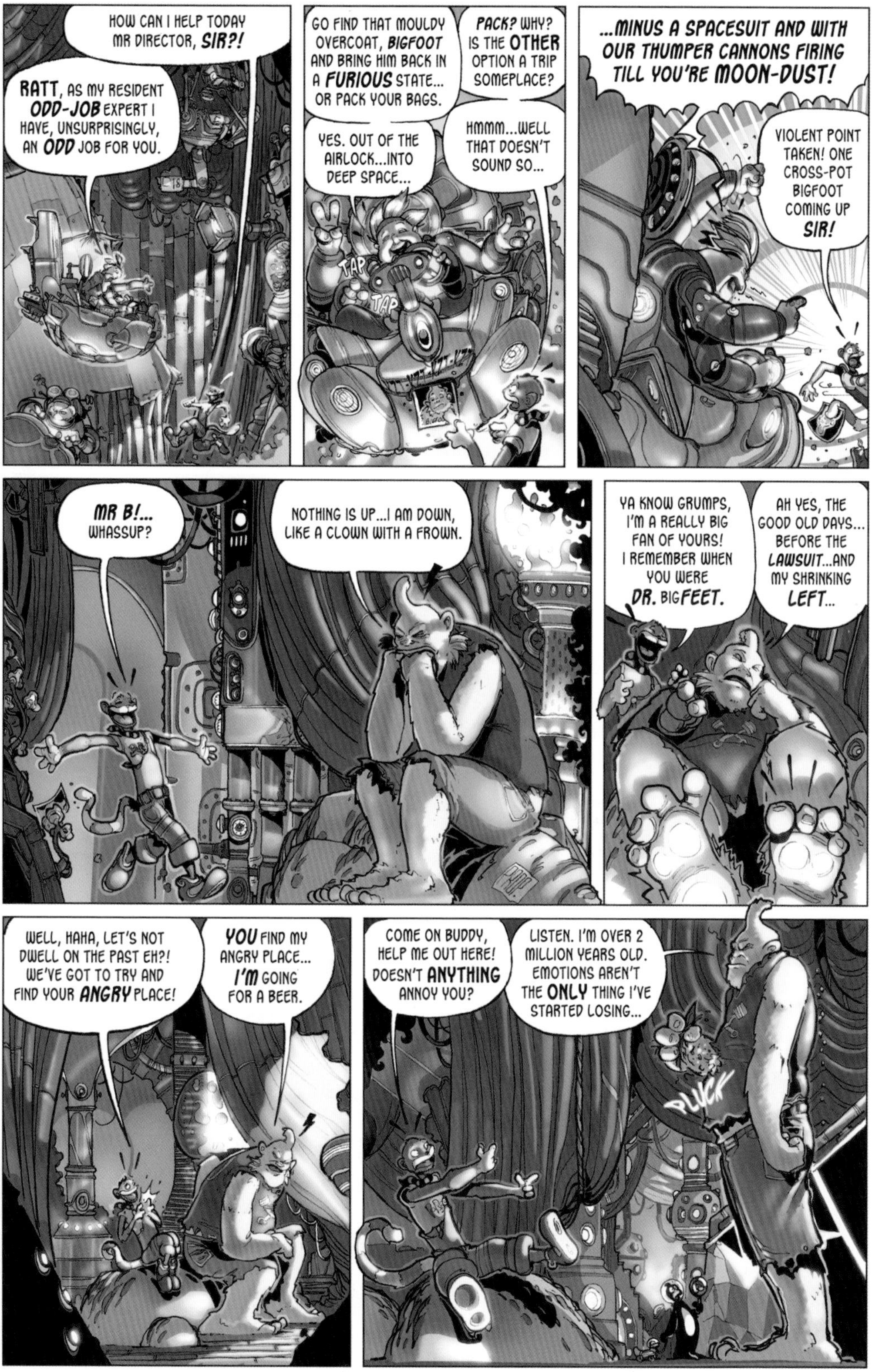
HOW CAN I HELP TODAY MR DIRECTOR, SIR?!
RATT, AS MY RESIDENT ODD-JOB EXPERT I HAVE, UNSURPRISINGLY, AN ODD JOB FOR YOU.
GO FIND THAT MOULDY OVERCOAT, BIGFOOT AND BRING HIM BACK IN A FURIOUS STATE... OR PACK YOUR BAGS.
PACK? WHY? IS THE OTHER OPTION A TRIP SOMEPLACE?
YES. OUT OF THE AIRLOCK...INTO DEEP SPACE...
HMMM...WELL THAT DOESN'T SOUND SO...
TAP
TAP
...MINUS A SPACESUIT AND WITH OUR THUMPER CANNONS FIRING TILL YOU'RE MOON-DUST!
VIOLENT POINT TAKEN! ONE CROSS-POT BIGFOOT COMING UP SIR!
MR B!... WHASSUP?
NOTHING IS UP...I AM DOWN, LIKE A CLOWN WITH A FROWN.
YA KNOW GRUMPS, I'M A REALLY BIG FAN OF YOURS! I REMEMBER WHEN YOU WERE DR. BIGFEET.
AH YES, THE GOOD OLD DAYS... BEFORE THE LAWSUIT...AND MY SHRINKING LEFT...
WELL, HAHA, LET'S NOT DWELL ON THE PAST EH?! WE'VE GOT TO TRY AND FIND YOUR ANGRY PLACE!
YOU FIND MY ANGRY PLACE... I'M GOING FOR A BEER.
COME ON BUDDY, HELP ME OUT HERE! DOESN'T ANYTHING ANNOY YOU?
LISTEN. I'M OVER 2 MILLION YEARS OLD. EMOTIONS AREN'T THE ONLY THING I'VE STARTED LOSING...
PLUCK

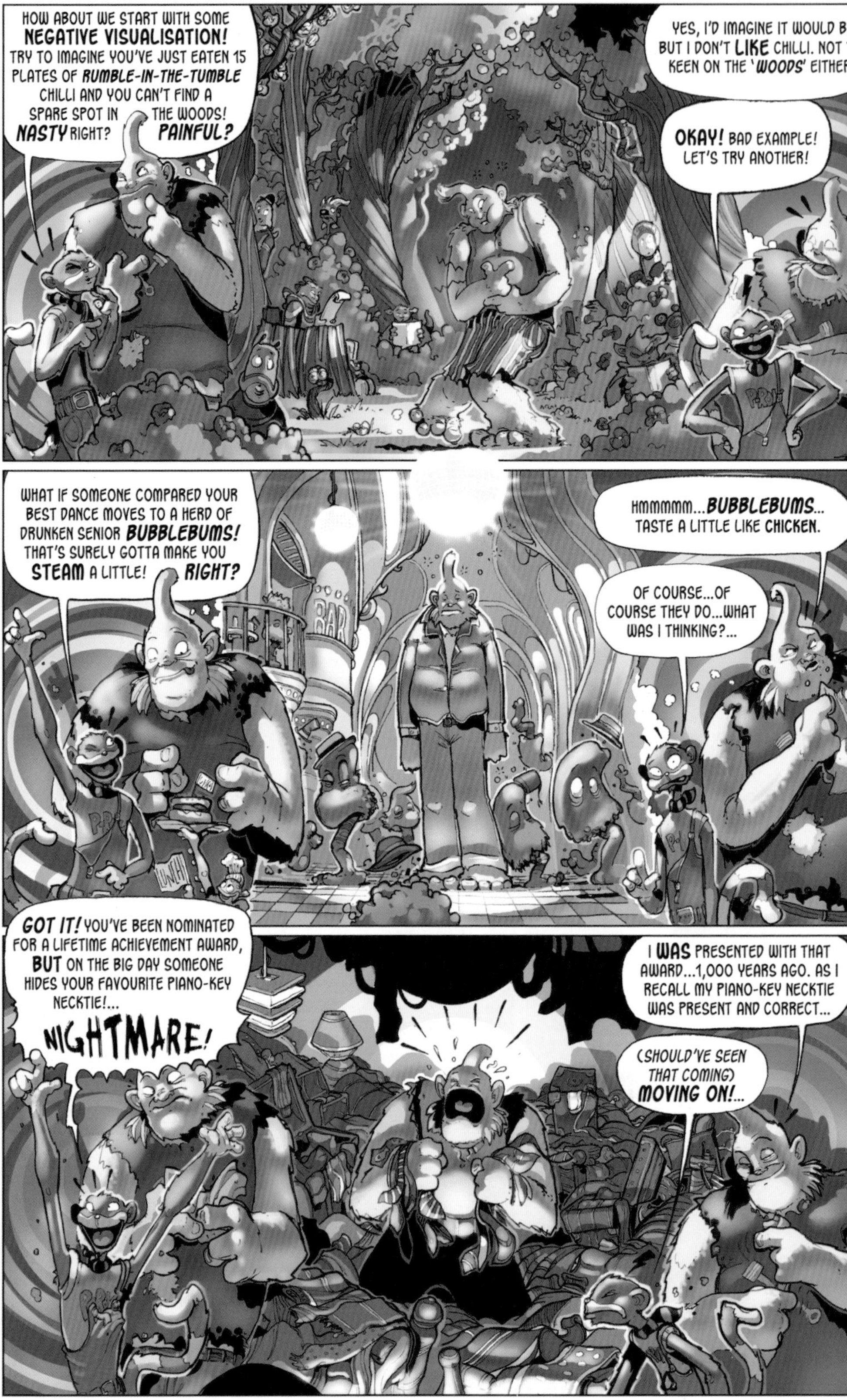
HOW ABOUT WE START WITH SOME NEGATIVE VISUALISATION! TRY TO IMAGINE YOU'VE JUST EATEN 15 PLATES OF RUMBLE-IN-THE-TUMBLE CHILLI AND YOU CAN'T FIND A SPARE SPOT IN THE WOODS! NASTY RIGHT? PAINFUL?
YES, I'D IMAGINE IT WOULD BE. BUT I DON'T LIKE CHILLI. NOT TOO KEEN ON THE 'WOODS' EITHER...
OKAY! BAD EXAMPLE! LET'S TRY ANOTHER!
WHAT IF SOMEONE COMPARED YOUR BEST DANCE MOVES TO A HERD OF DRUNKEN SENIOR BUBBLEBUMS! THAT'S SURELY GOTTA MAKE YOU STEAM A LITTLE! RIGHT?
HMMMMM...BUBBLEBUMS... TASTE A LITTLE LIKE CHICKEN.
OF COURSE...OF COURSE THEY DO...WHAT WAS I THINKING?...
BAR
GOT IT! YOU'VE BEEN NOMINATED FOR A LIFETIME ACHIEVEMENT AWARD, BUT ON THE BIG DAY SOMEONE HIDES YOUR FAVOURITE PIANO-KEY NECKTIE!...
NIGHTMARE!
I WAS PRESENTED WITH THAT AWARD...1,000 YEARS AGO. AS I RECALL MY PIANO-KEY NECKTIE WAS PRESENT AND CORRECT...
(SHOULD'VE SEEN THAT COMING) MOVING ON!...

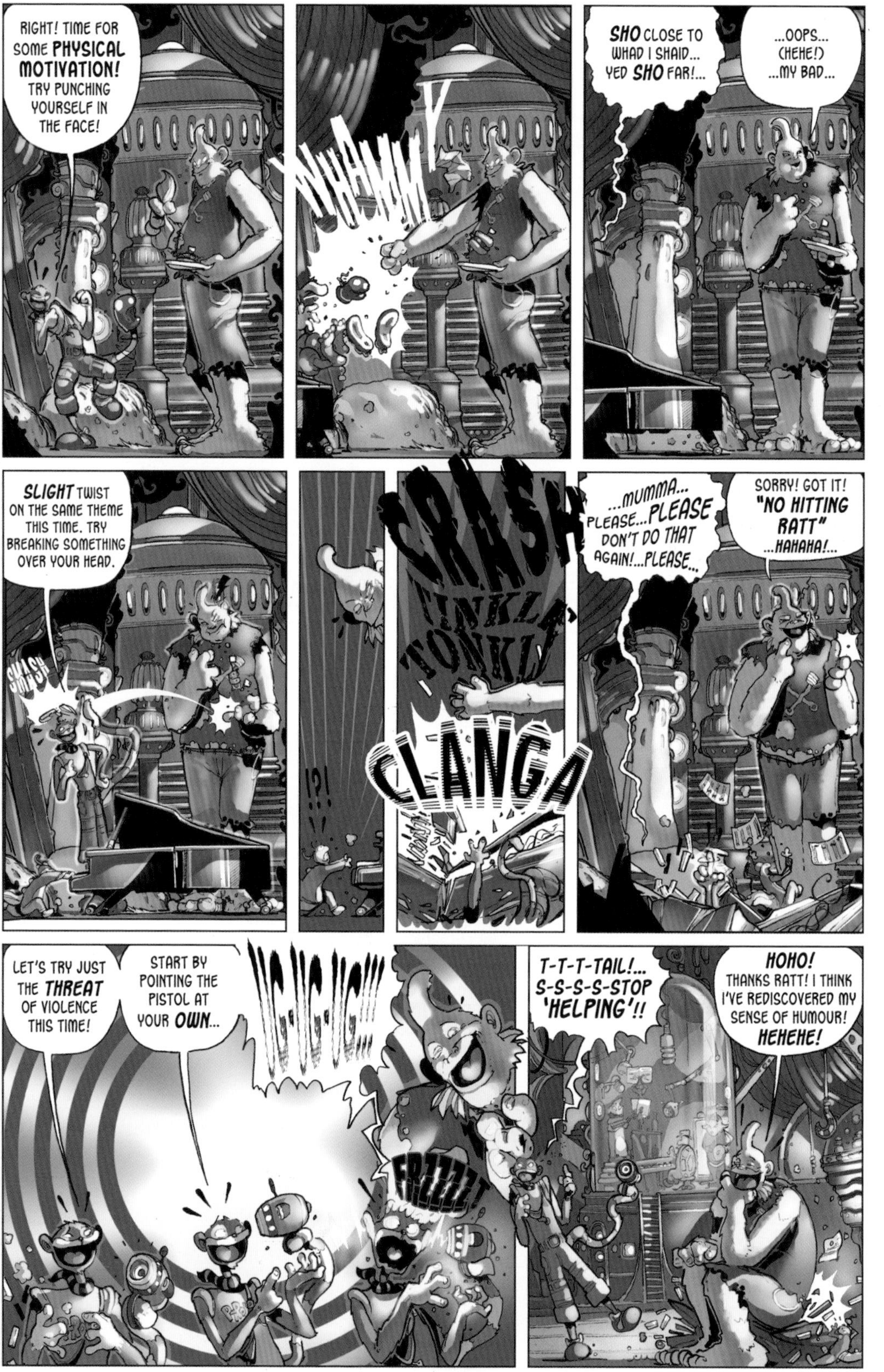
RIGHT! TIME FOR SOME PHYSICAL MOTIVATION! TRY PUNCHING YOURSELF IN THE FACE!
WHAMMY
SHO CLOSE TO WHAD I SHAID... YED SHO FAR!...
...OOPS... (HEHE!) ...MY BAD...
SLIGHT TWIST ON THE SAME THEME THIS TIME. TRY BREAKING SOMETHING OVER YOUR HEAD.
SMASH
CRASH
TINKLE
TONKLE
CLANGA
!?!
...MUMMA... PLEASE...PLEASE DON'T DO THAT AGAIN!...PLEASE...
SORRY! GOT IT! "NO HITTING RATT" ...HAHAHA!...
LET'S TRY JUST THE THREAT OF VIOLENCE THIS TIME!
START BY POINTING THE PISTOL AT YOUR OWN...
JIG-JIG-JIG!!!
FRZZZZT
T-T-T-TAIL!... S-S-S-S-STOP 'HELPING'!!
HOHO! THANKS RATT! I THINK I'VE REDISCOVERED MY SENSE OF HUMOUR! HEHEHE!

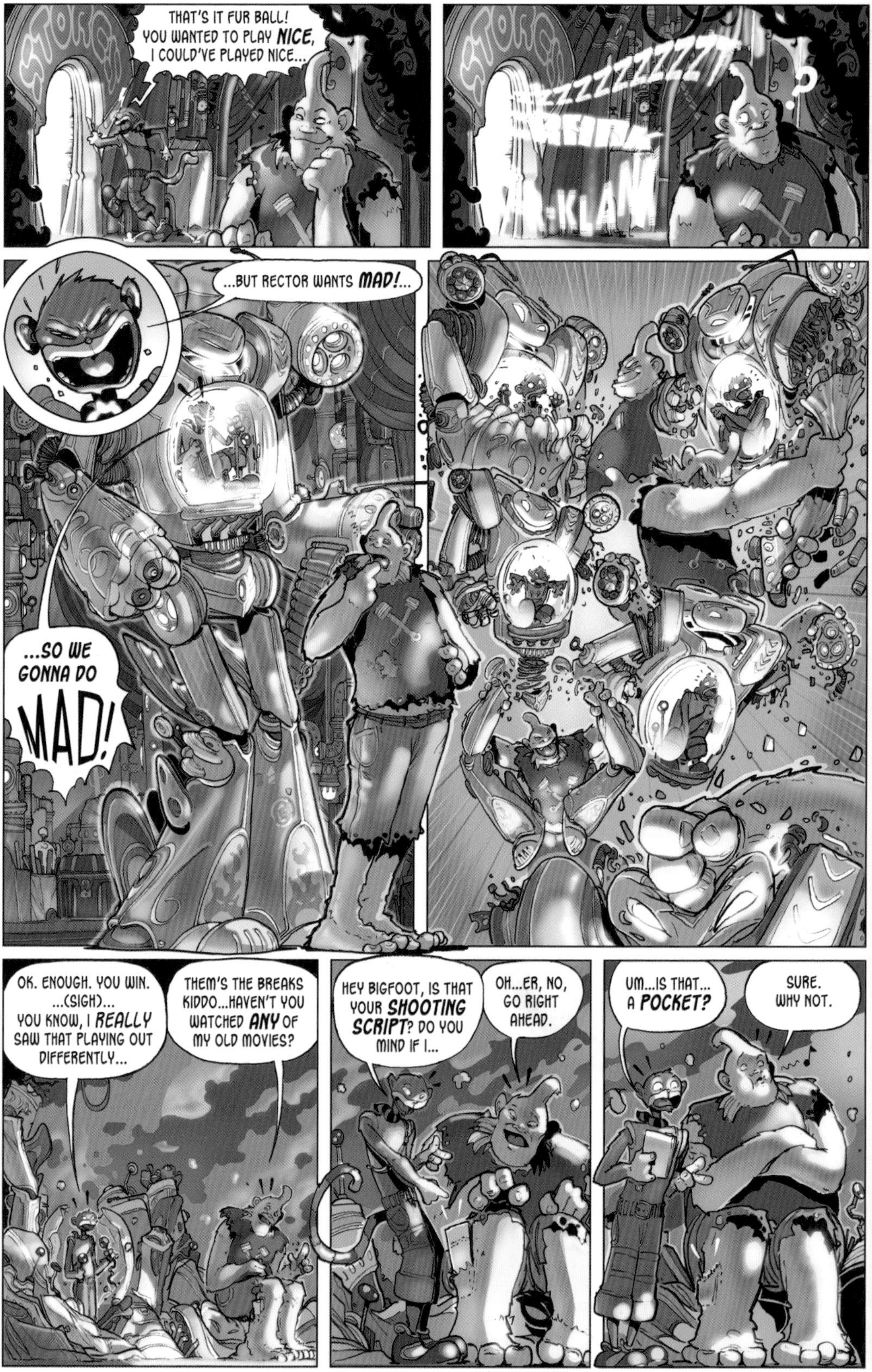
THAT'S IT FUR BALL! YOU WANTED TO PLAY NICE, I COULD'VE PLAYED NICE...
...BUT RECTOR WANTS MAD!...
...SO WE GONNA DO MAD!
OK. ENOUGH. YOU WIN. ...(SIGH)... YOU KNOW, I REALLY SAW THAT PLAYING OUT DIFFERENTLY...
THEM'S THE BREAKS KIDDO...HAVEN'T YOU WATCHED ANY OF MY OLD MOVIES?
HEY BIGFOOT, IS THAT YOUR SHOOTING SCRIPT? DO YOU MIND IF I...
OH...ER, NO, GO RIGHT AHEAD.
UM...IS THAT... A POCKET?
SURE. WHY NOT.

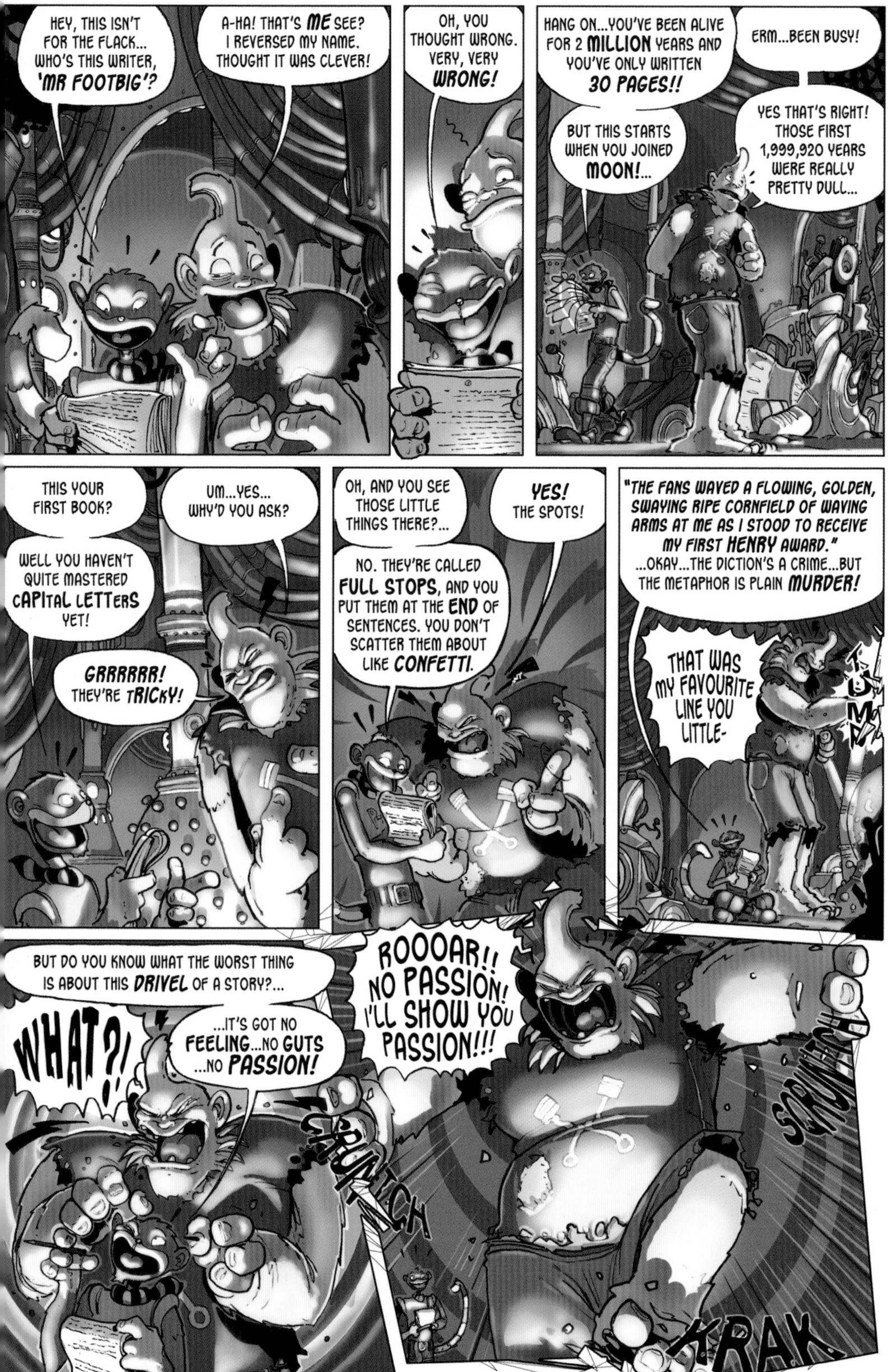
HEY, THIS ISN'T FOR THE FLACK... WHO'S THIS WRITER, 'MR FOOTBIG'?
A-HA! THAT'S ME SEE? I REVERSED MY NAME. THOUGHT IT WAS CLEVER!
OH, YOU THOUGHT WRONG. VERY, VERY WRONG!
HANG ON...YOU'VE BEEN ALIVE FOR 2 MILLION YEARS AND YOU'VE ONLY WRITTEN 30 PAGES!!
ERM...BEEN BUSY!
BUT THIS STARTS WHEN YOU JOINED MOON!...
YES THAT'S RIGHT! THOSE FIRST 1,999,920 YEARS WERE REALLY PRETTY DULL...
THIS YOUR FIRST BOOK?
UM...YES... WHY'D YOU ASK?
WELL YOU HAVEN'T QUITE MASTERED CAPItaL LETTErs YET!
GRRRRRR! THEY'RE tRICKY!
OH, AND YOU SEE THOSE LITTLE THINGS THERE?...
YES! THE SPOTS!
NO. THEY'RE CALLED FULL STOPS, AND YOU PUT THEM AT THE END OF SENTENCES. YOU DON'T SCATTER THEM ABOUT LIKE CONFETTI.
"THE FANS WAVED A FLOWING, GOLDEN, SWAYING RIPE CORNFIELD OF WAVING ARMS AT ME AS I STOOD TO RECEIVE MY FIRST HENRY AWARD." ...OKAY...THE DICTION'S A CRIME...BUT THE METAPHOR IS PLAIN MURDER!
THAT WAS MY FAVOURITE LINE YOU LITTLE-
BUT DO YOU KNOW WHAT THE WORST THING IS ABOUT THIS DRIVEL OF A STORY?...
WHAT?!
...IT'S GOT NO FEELING...NO GUTS ...NO PASSION!
ROOOAR!! NO PASSION! I'LL SHOW YOU PASSION!!!
KRAK

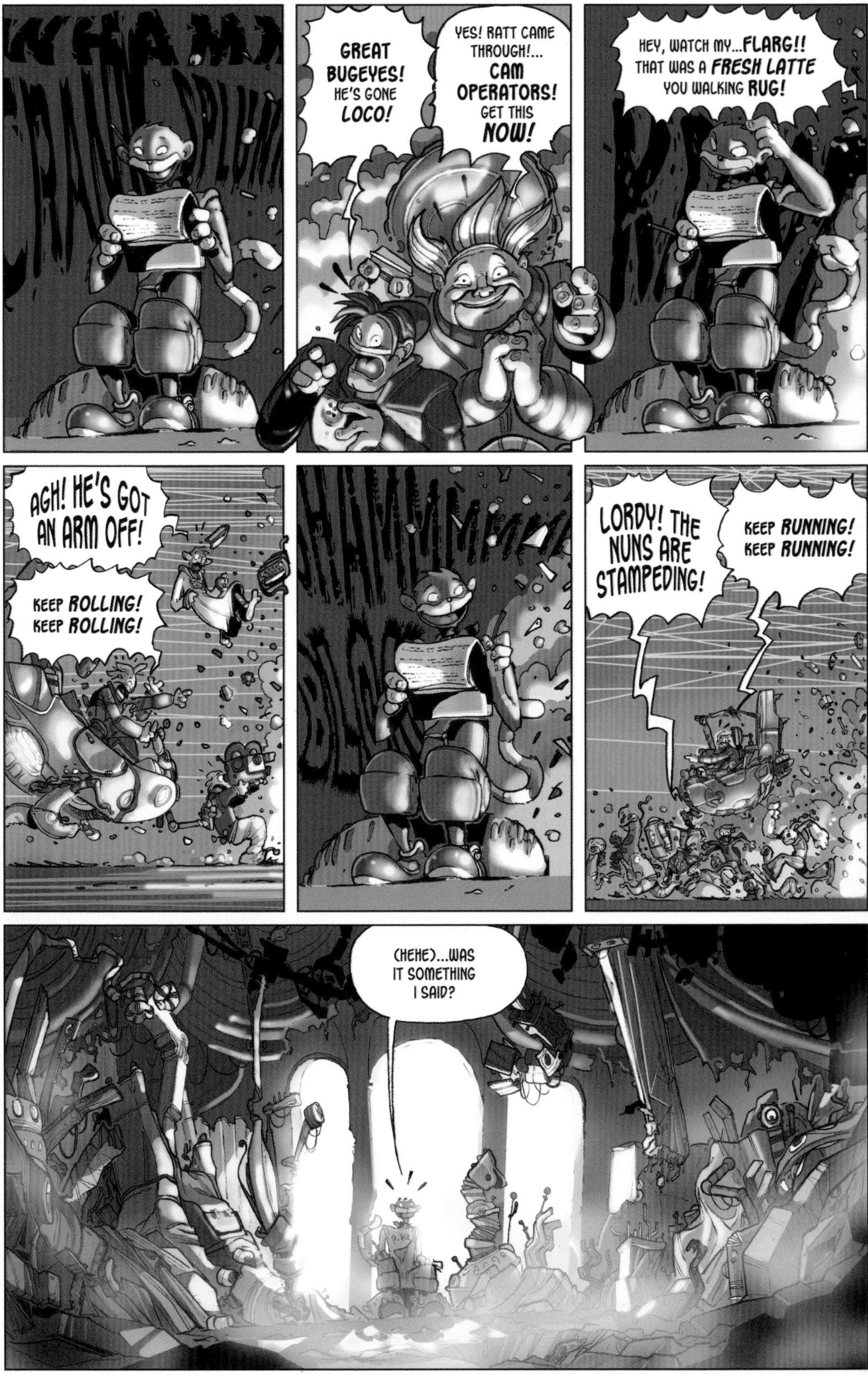
GREAT BUGEYES! HE'S GONE LOCO!
YES! RATT CAME THROUGH!... CAM OPERATORS! GET THIS NOW!
HEY, WATCH MY...FLARG!! THAT WAS A FRESH LATTE YOU WALKING RUG!
AGH! HE'S GOT AN ARM OFF!
KEEP ROLLING! KEEP ROLLING!
LORDY! THE NUNS ARE STAMPEDING!
KEEP RUNNING! KEEP RUNNING!
(HEHE)...WAS IT SOMETHING I SAID?

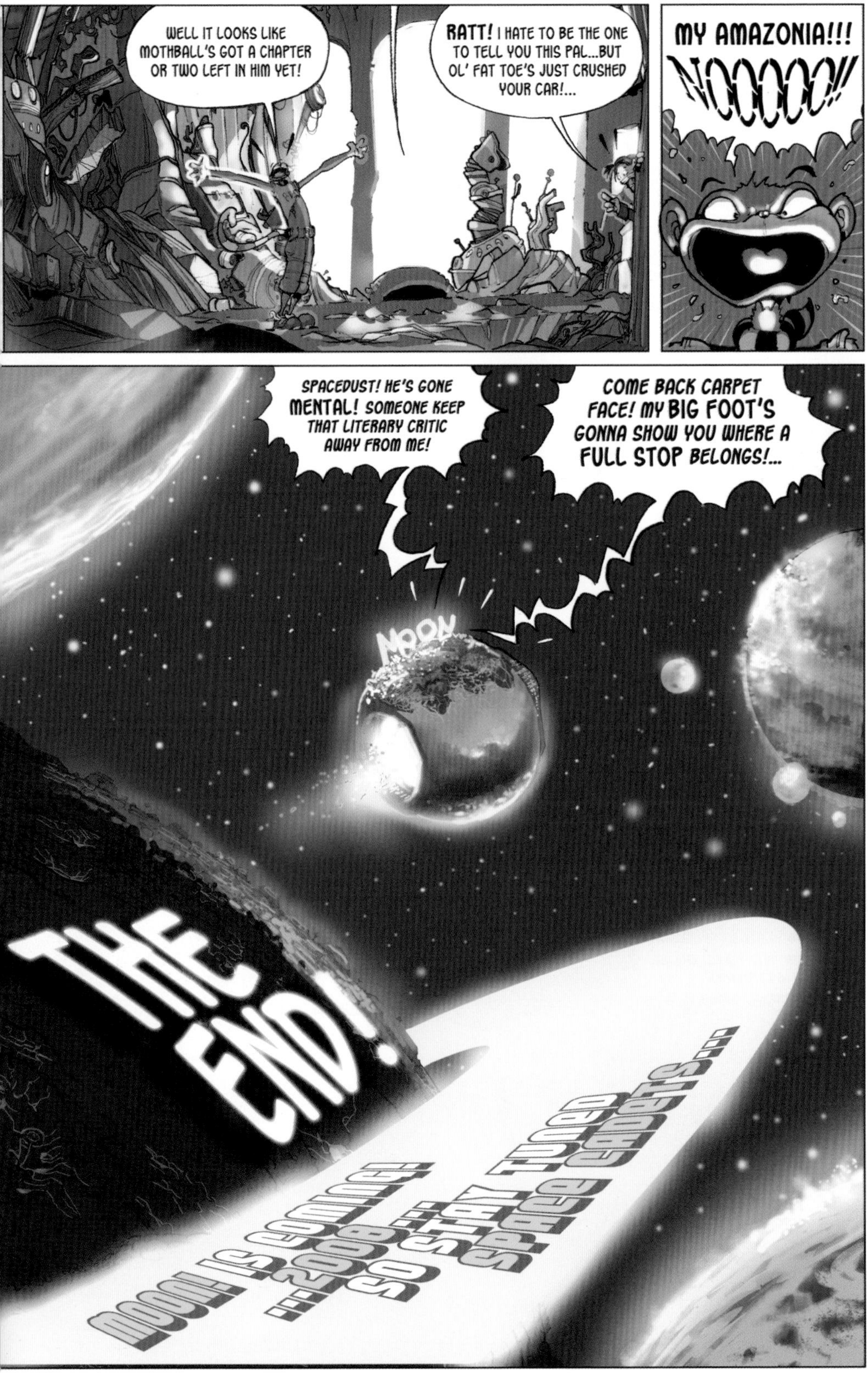

WELL IT LOOKS LIKE MOTHBALL'S GOT A CHAPTER OR TWO LEFT IN HIM YET!
RATT! I HATE TO BE THE ONE TO TELL YOU THIS PAL...BUT OL' FAT TOE'S JUST CRUSHED YOUR CAR!...
MY AMAZONIA!!!
NOOOOO!!
SPACEDUST! HE'S GONE MENTAL! SOMEONE KEEP THAT LITERARY CRITIC AWAY FROM ME!
COME BACK CARPET FACE! MY BIG FOOT'S GONNA SHOW YOU WHERE A FULL STOP BELONGS!...
NOON
THE END!
NOON! IS COMING!
...2008!...
SO STAY TUNED
SPACE CADETS...!

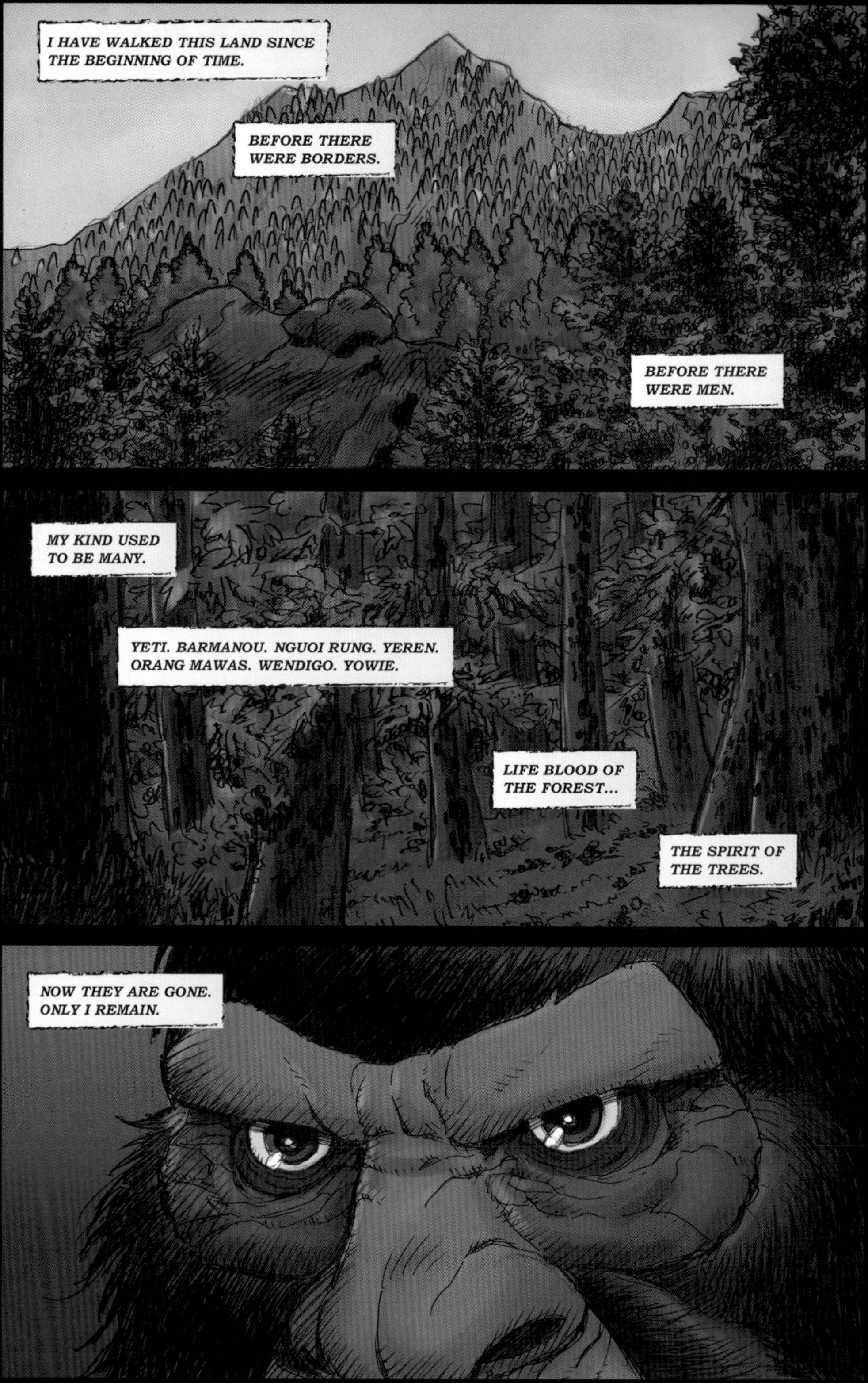
I HAVE WALKED THIS LAND SINCE THE BEGINNING OF TIME.
BEFORE THERE WERE BORDERS.
BEFORE THERE WERE MEN.
MY KIND USED TO BE MANY.
YETI. BARMANOU. NGUOI RUNG. YEREN. ORANG MAWAS. WENDIGO. YOWIE.
LIFE BLOOD OF THE FOREST...
THE SPIRIT OF THE TREES.
NOW THEY ARE GONE. ONLY I REMAIN.

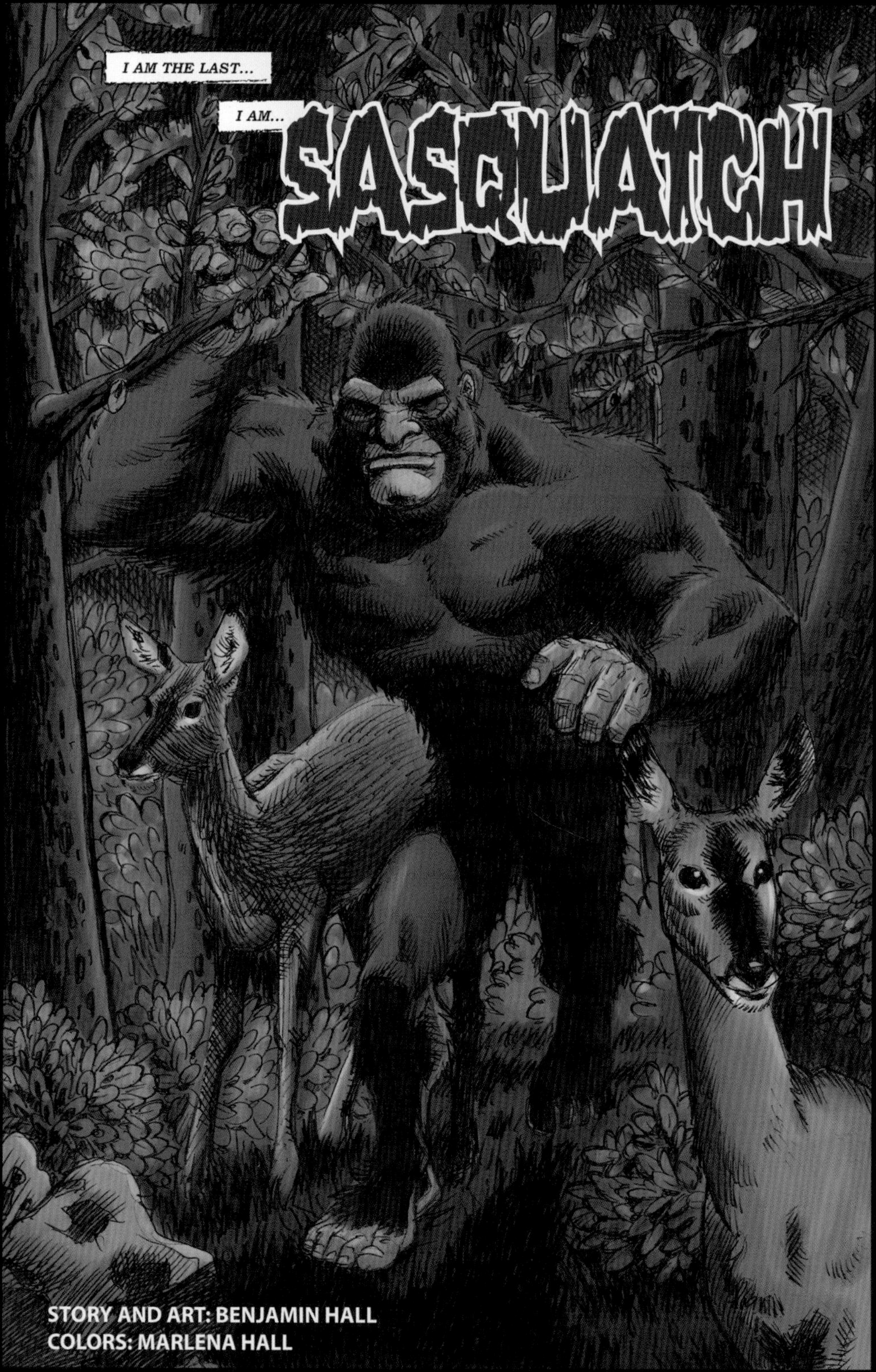
I AM THE LAST...
I AM...
SASQUATCH
STORY AND ART: BENJAMIN HALL
COLORS: MARLENA HALL

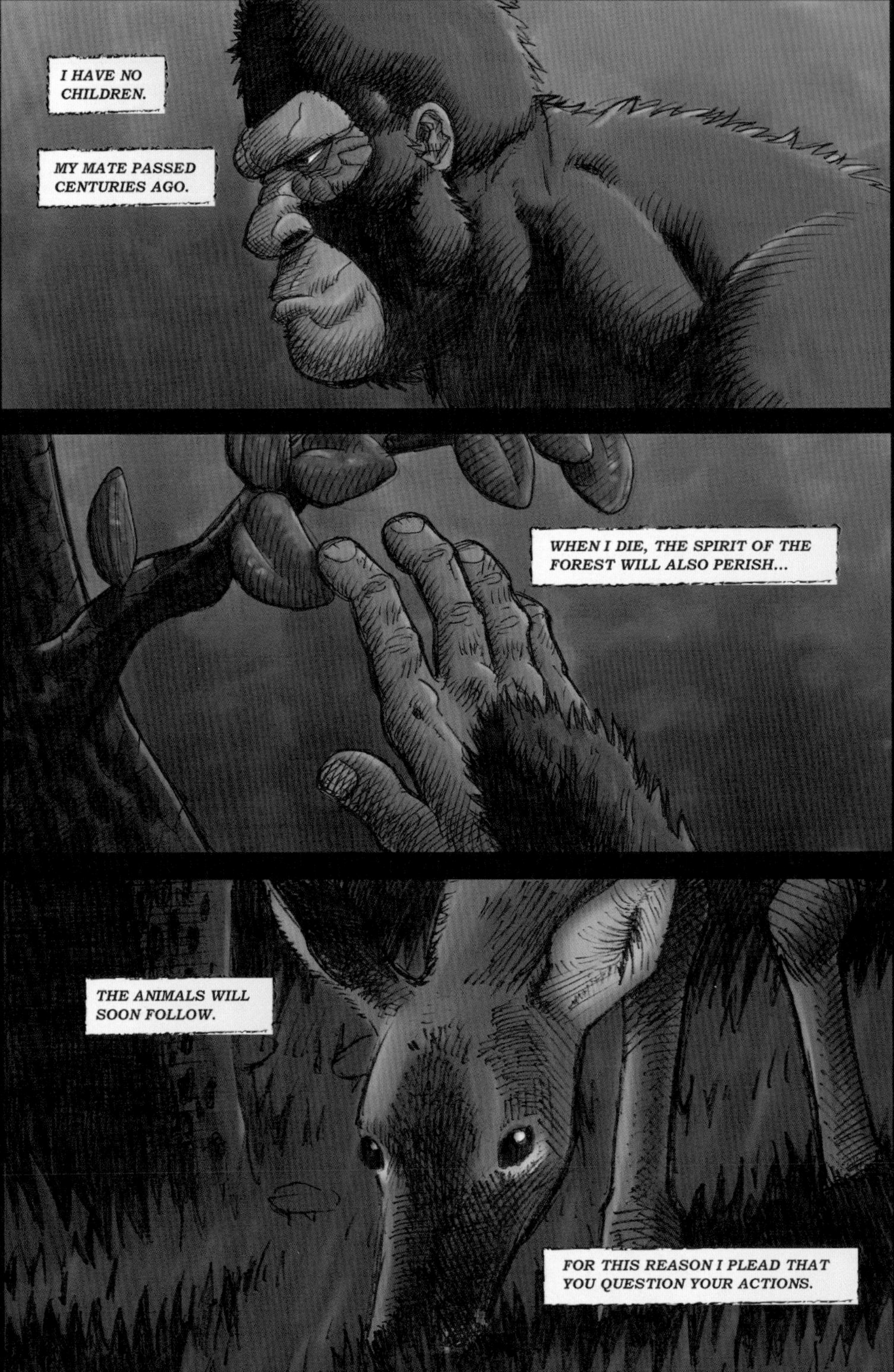
I HAVE NO CHILDREN.
MY MATE PASSED CENTURIES AGO.
WHEN I DIE, THE SPIRIT OF THE FOREST WILL ALSO PERISH...
THE ANIMALS WILL SOON FOLLOW.
FOR THIS REASON I PLEAD THAT YOU QUESTION YOUR ACTIONS.

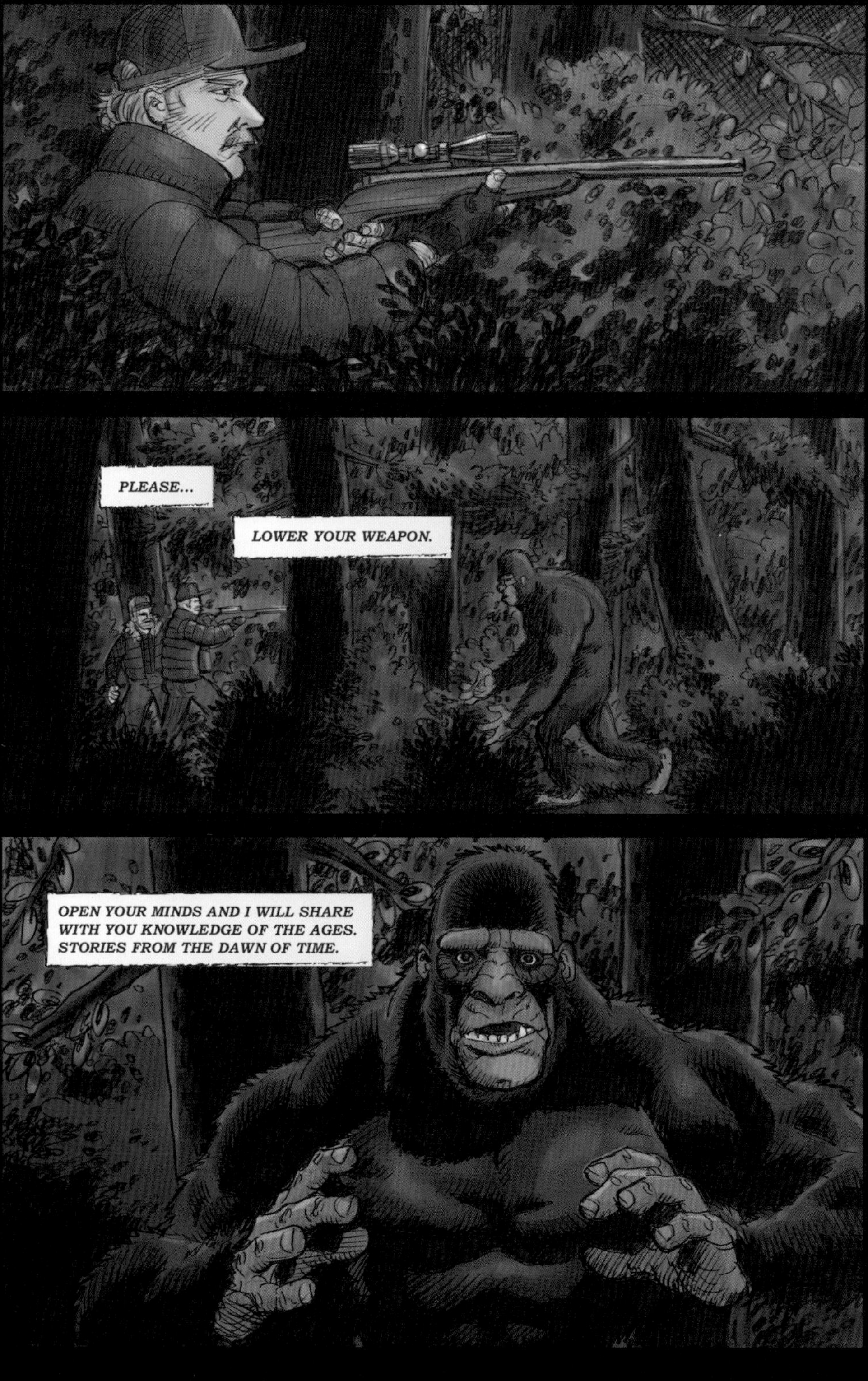
PLEASE...
LOWER YOUR WEAPON.
OPEN YOUR MINDS AND I WILL SHARE WITH YOU KNOWLEDGE OF THE AGES. STORIES FROM THE DAWN OF TIME.

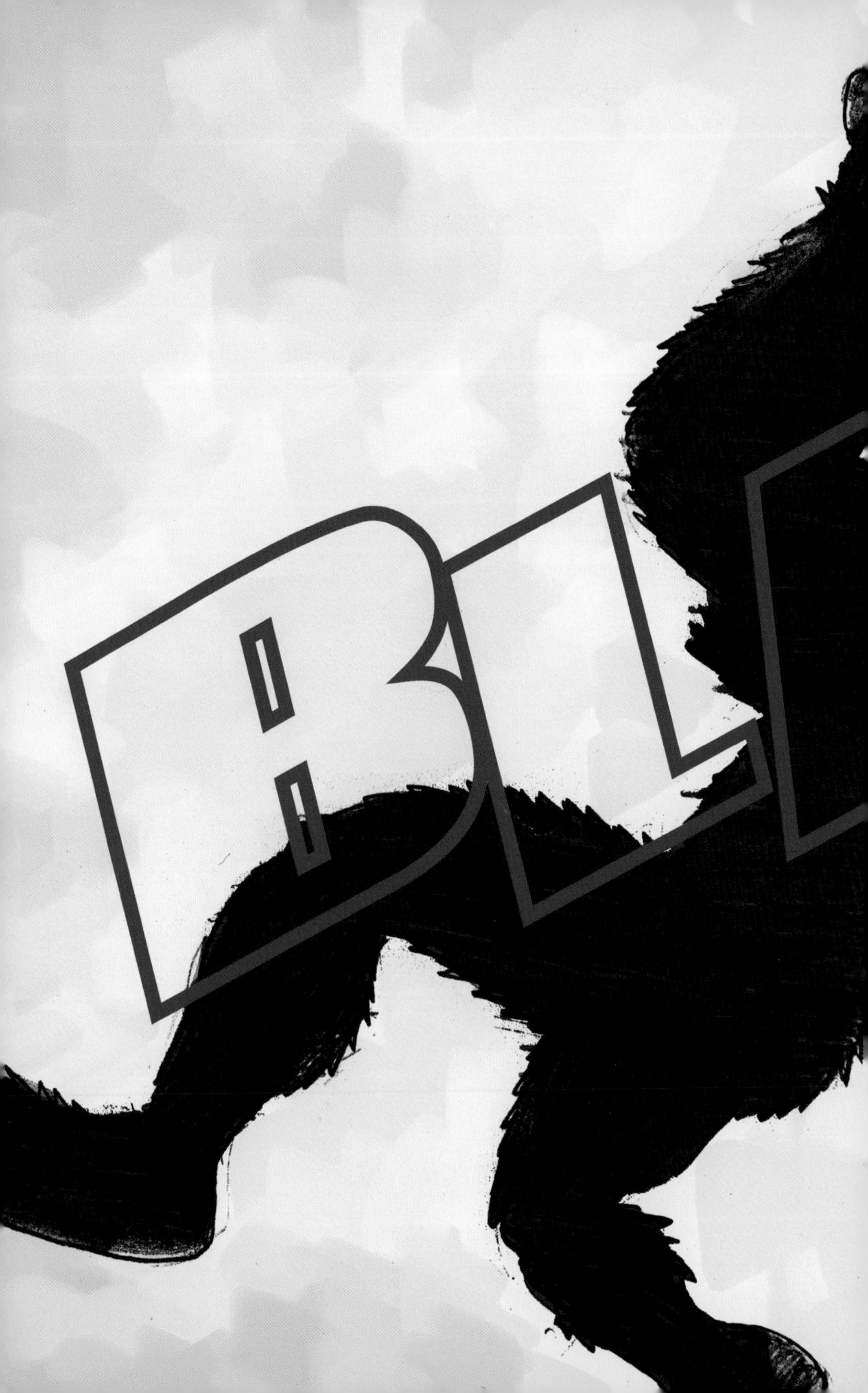

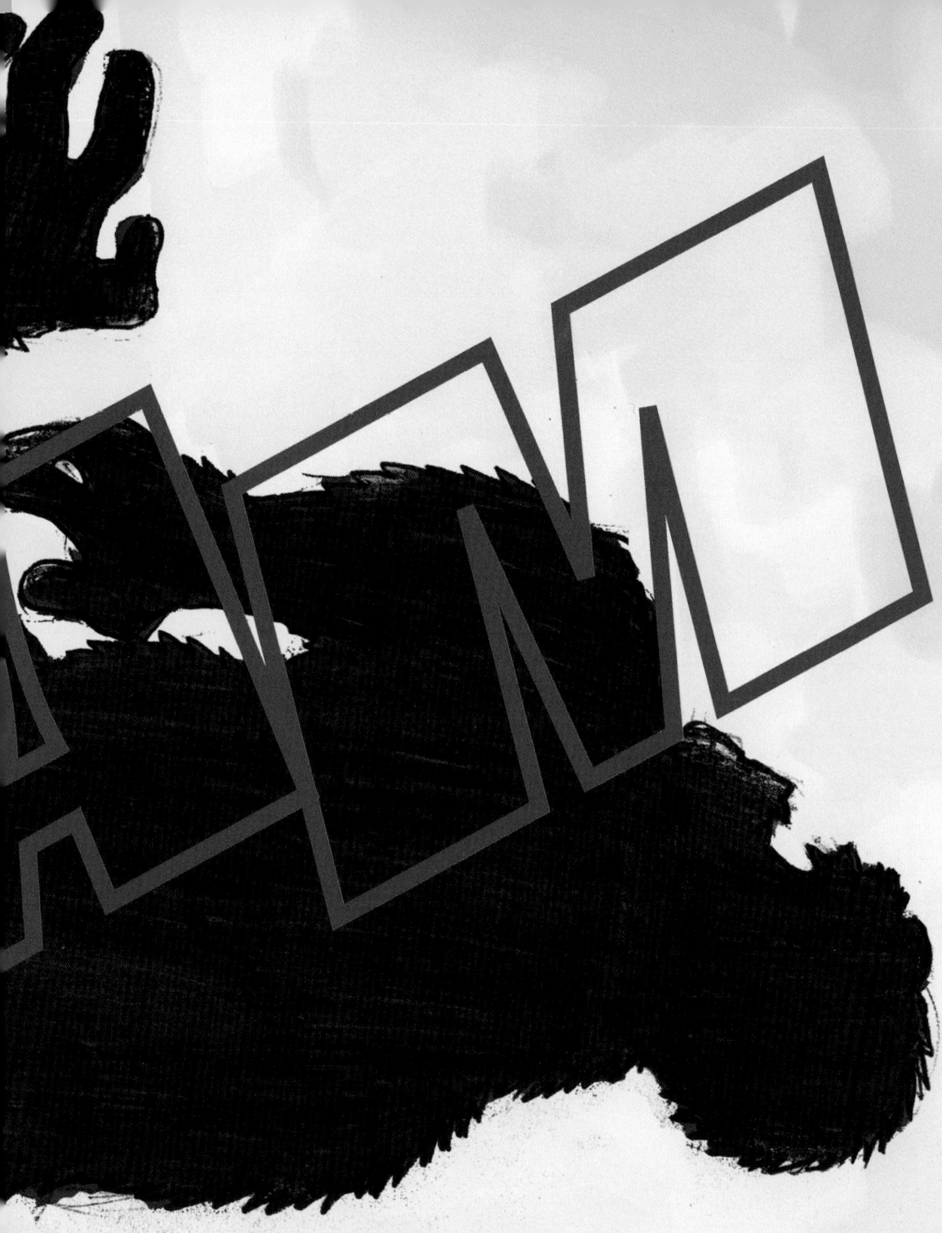

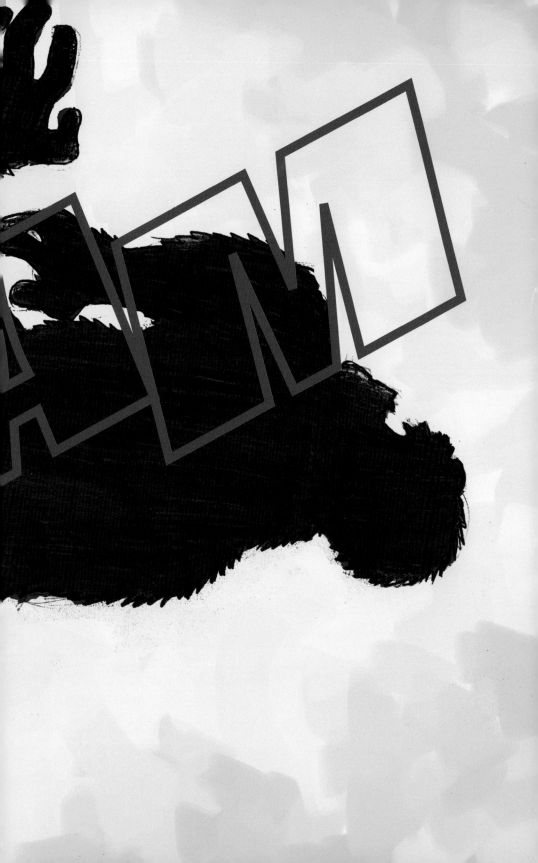

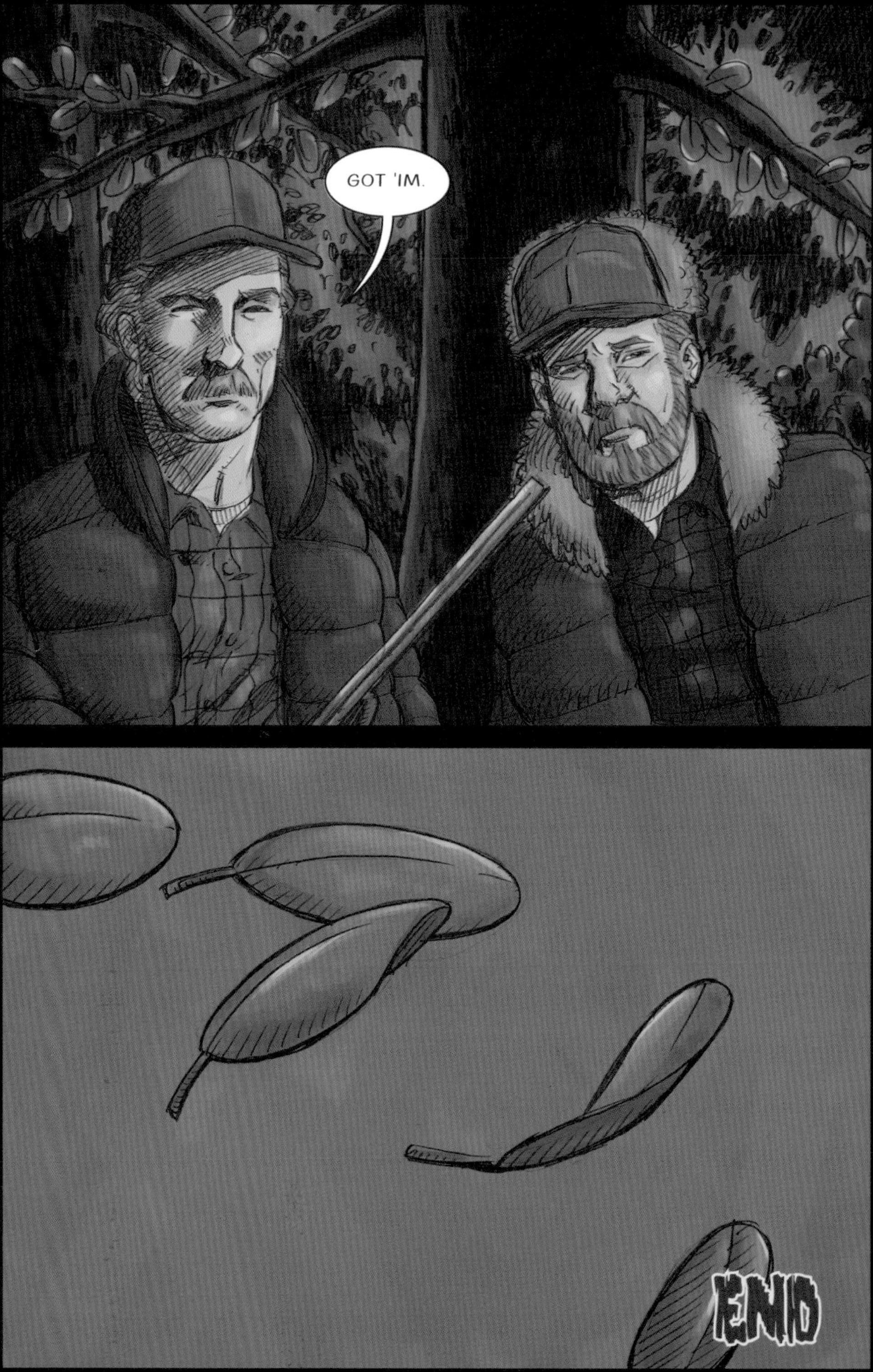
GOT 'IM.
END

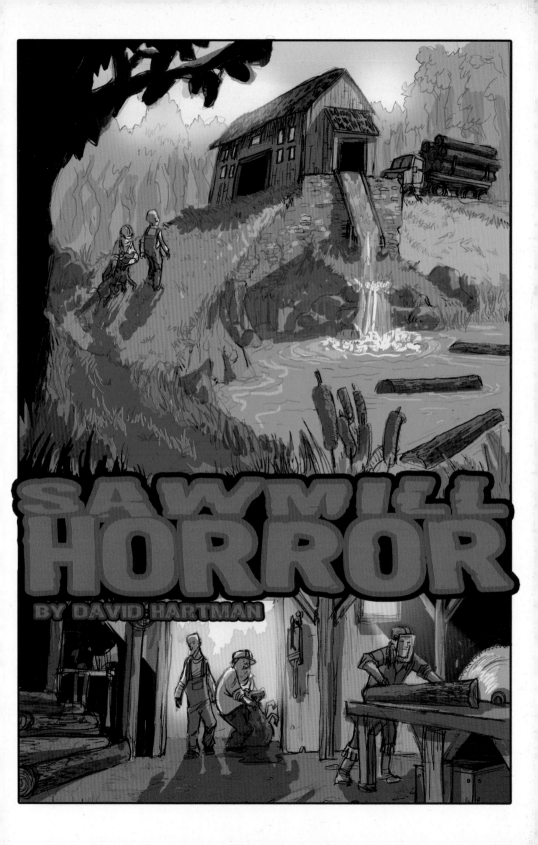

SAWMILL HORROR

BY DAVID HARTMAN

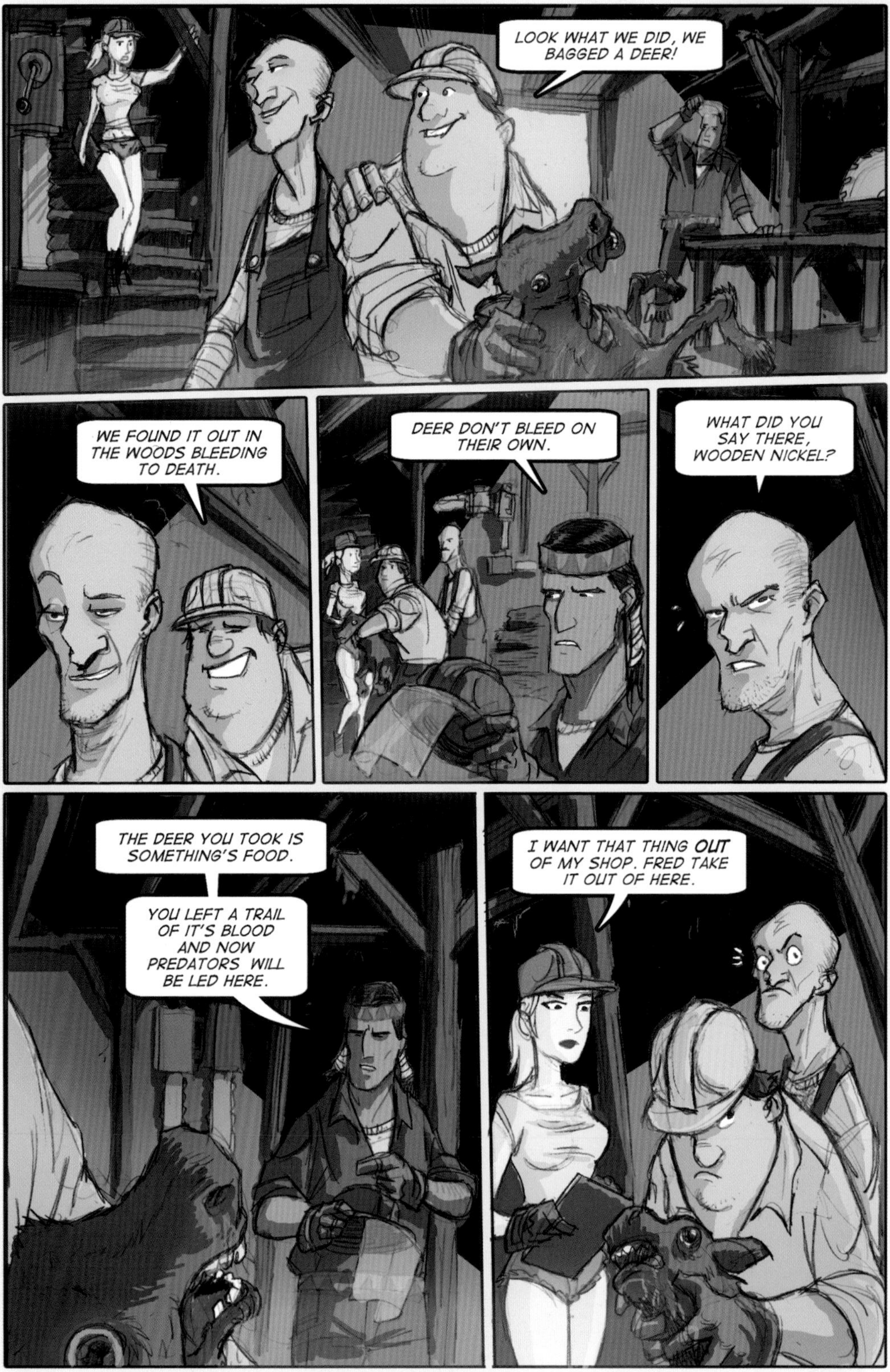
LOOK WHAT WE DID, WE BAGGED A DEER!
WE FOUND IT OUT IN THE WOODS BLEEDING TO DEATH.
DEER DON'T BLEED ON THEIR OWN.
WHAT DID YOU SAY THERE, WOODEN NICKEL?
THE DEER YOU TOOK IS SOMETHING'S FOOD.
YOU LEFT A TRAIL OF IT'S BLOOD AND NOW PREDATORS WILL BE LED HERE.
I WANT THAT THING **OUT** OF MY SHOP. FRED TAKE IT OUT OF HERE.

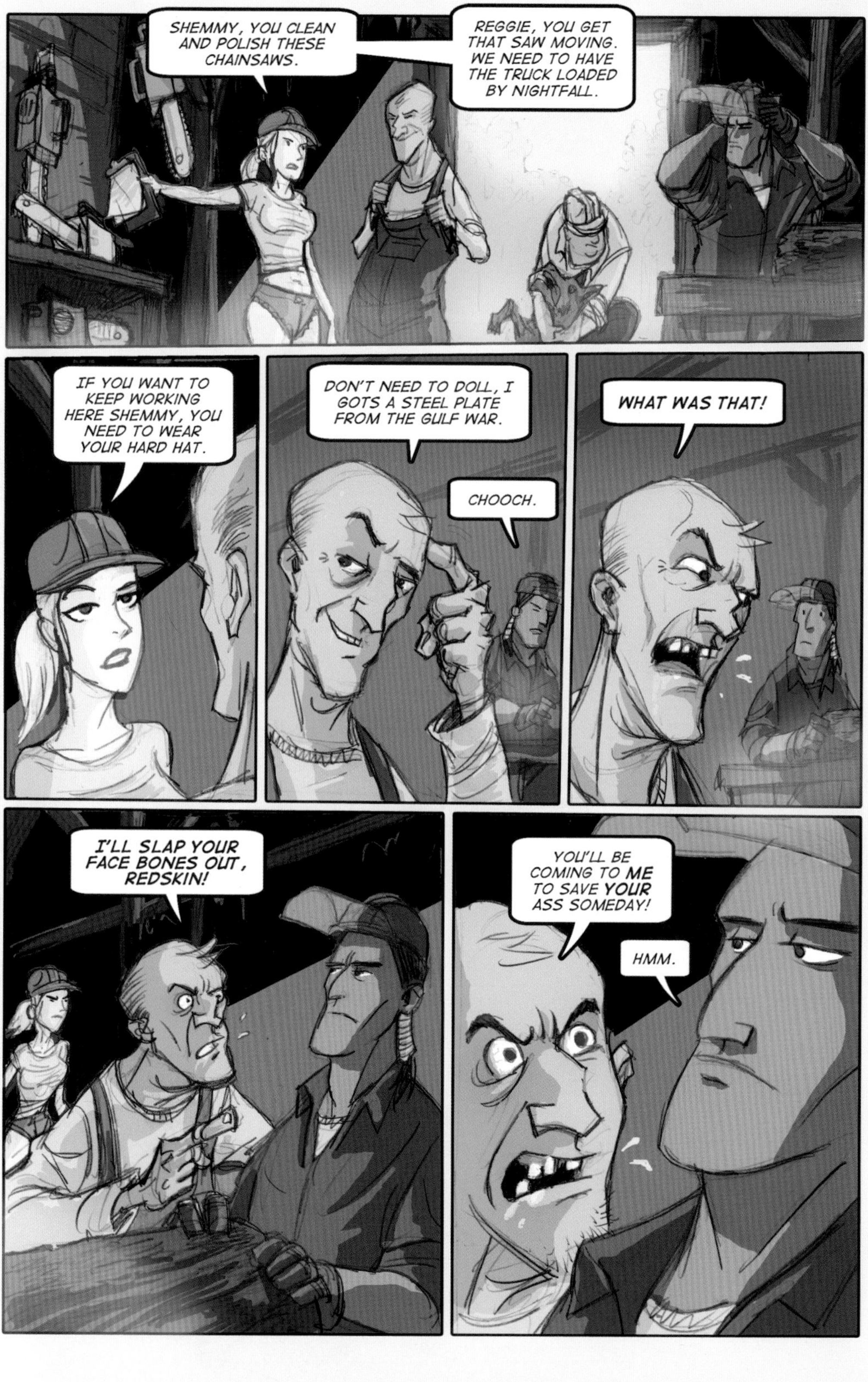
SHEMMY, YOU CLEAN AND POLISH THESE CHAINSAWS.
REGGIE, YOU GET THAT SAW MOVING. WE NEED TO HAVE THE TRUCK LOADED BY NIGHTFALL.
IF YOU WANT TO KEEP WORKING HERE SHEMMY, YOU NEED TO WEAR YOUR HARD HAT.
DON'T NEED TO DOLL, I GOTS A STEEL PLATE FROM THE GULF WAR.
CHOOCH.
WHAT WAS THAT!
I'LL SLAP YOUR FACE BONES OUT, REDSKIN!
YOU'LL BE COMING TO ME TO SAVE YOUR ASS SOMEDAY!
HMM.

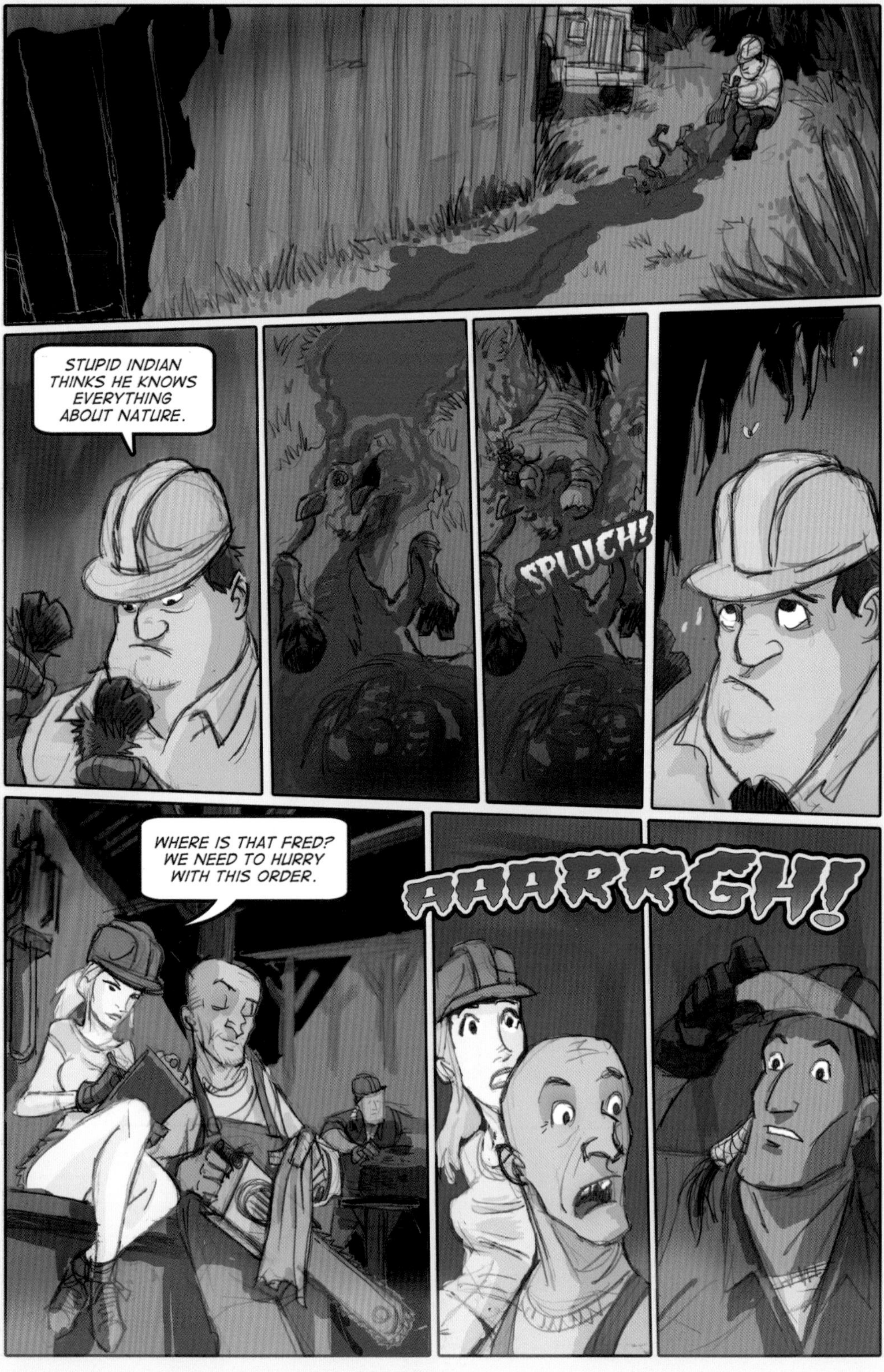
STUPID INDIAN THINKS HE KNOWS EVERYTHING ABOUT NATURE.
SPLUCH!
WHERE IS THAT FRED? WE NEED TO HURRY WITH THIS ORDER.
AAARRGH!

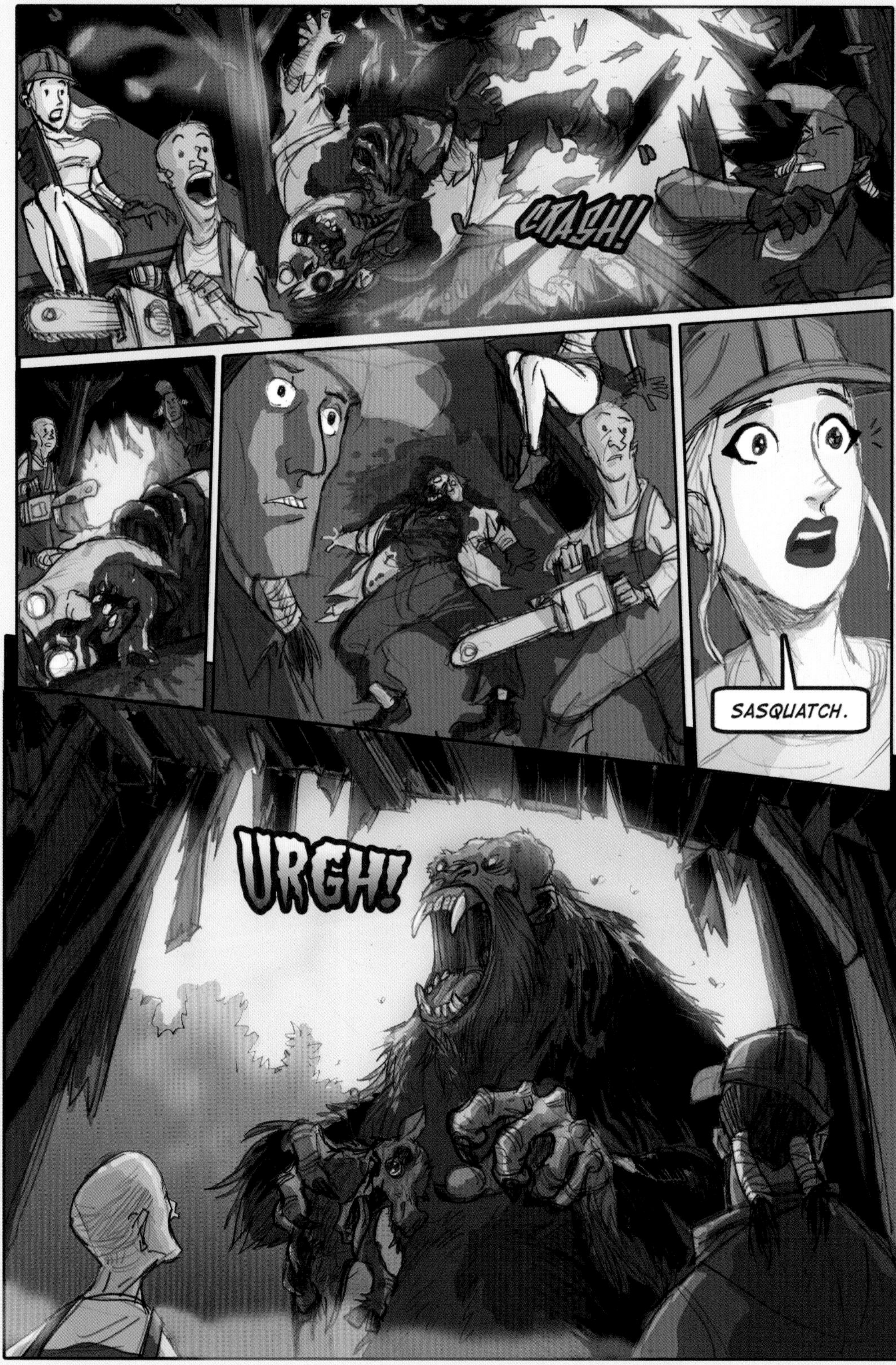
CRASH!
SASQUATCH.
URGH!

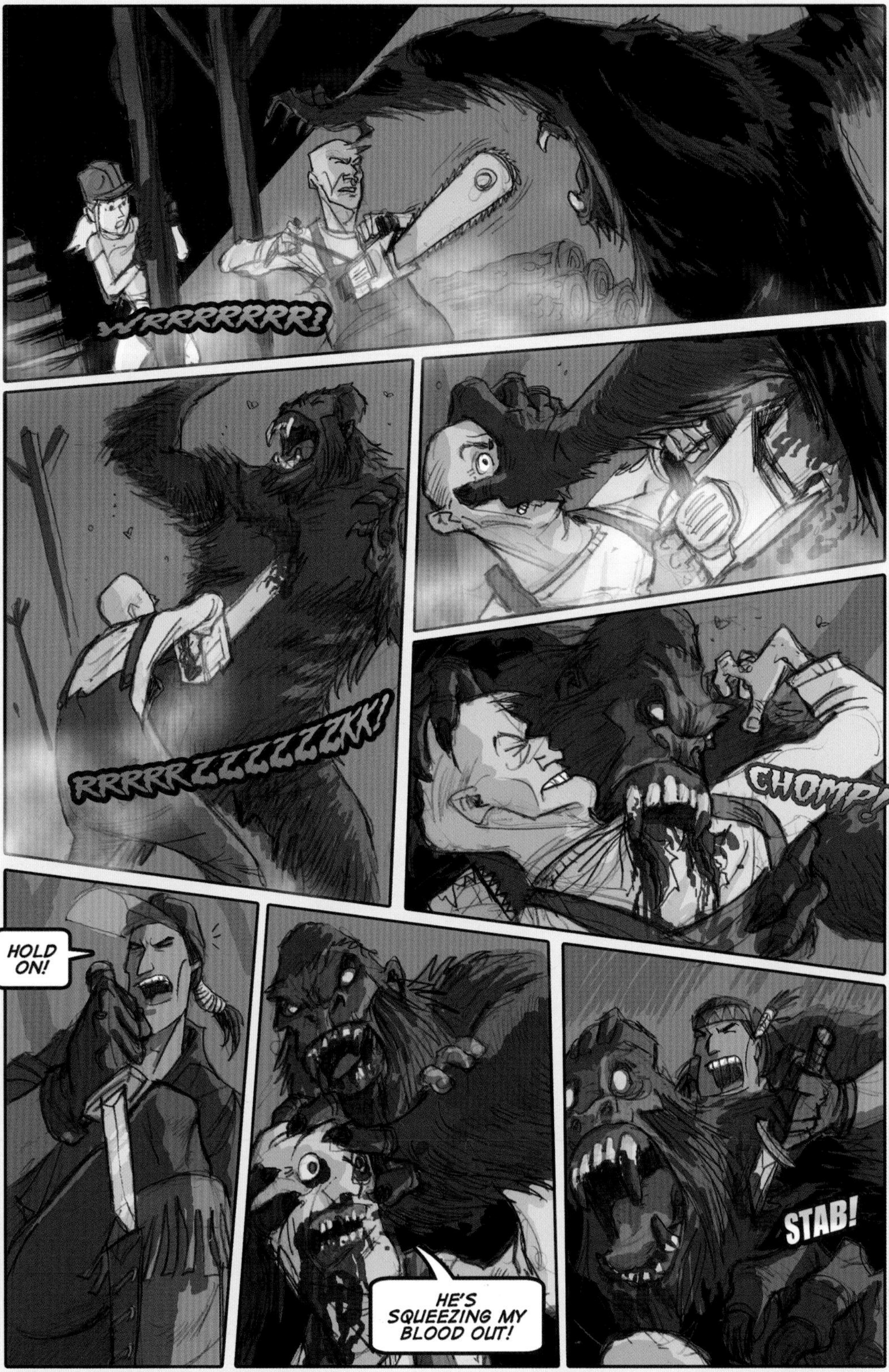
WRRRRRRRR!
RRRRRZZZZZZZKK!
CHOMP!
HOLD ON!
HE'S SQUEEZING MY BLOOD OUT!
STAB!

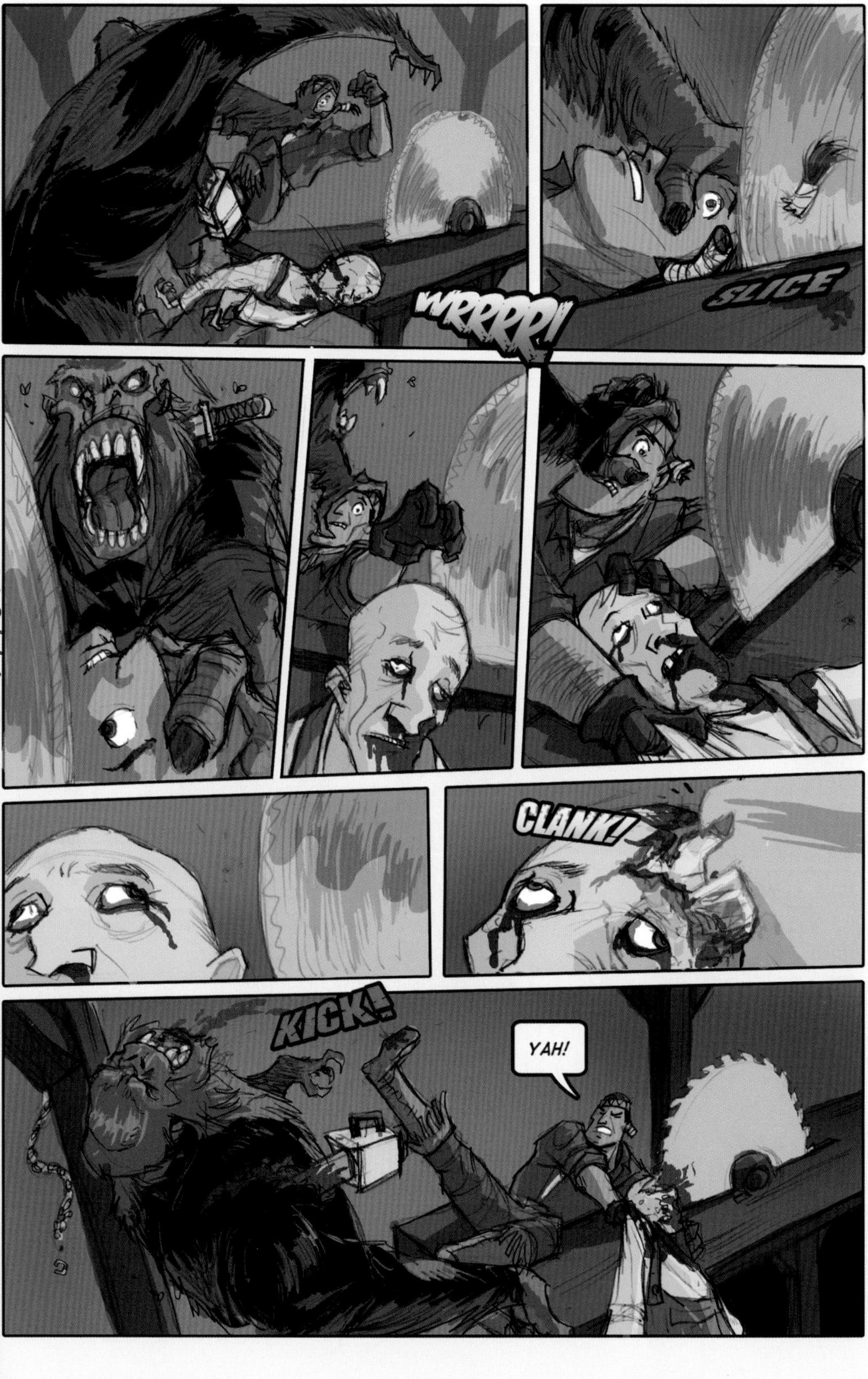
WRRRR!
SLICE
CLANK!
KICK!
YAH!

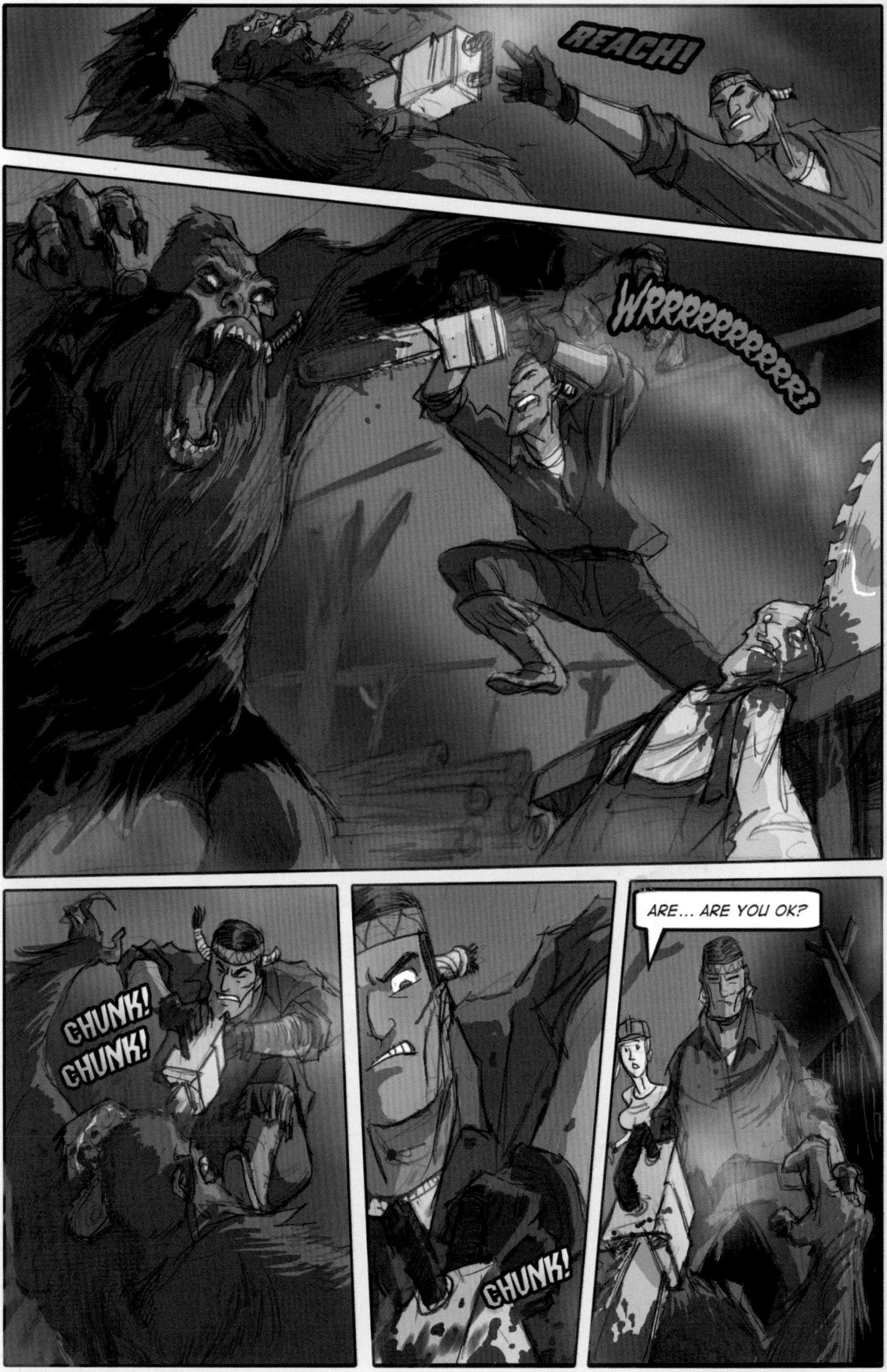
REACH!
WRRRRRRRRRRR!
CHUNK!
CHUNK!
CHUNK!
ARE... ARE YOU OK?

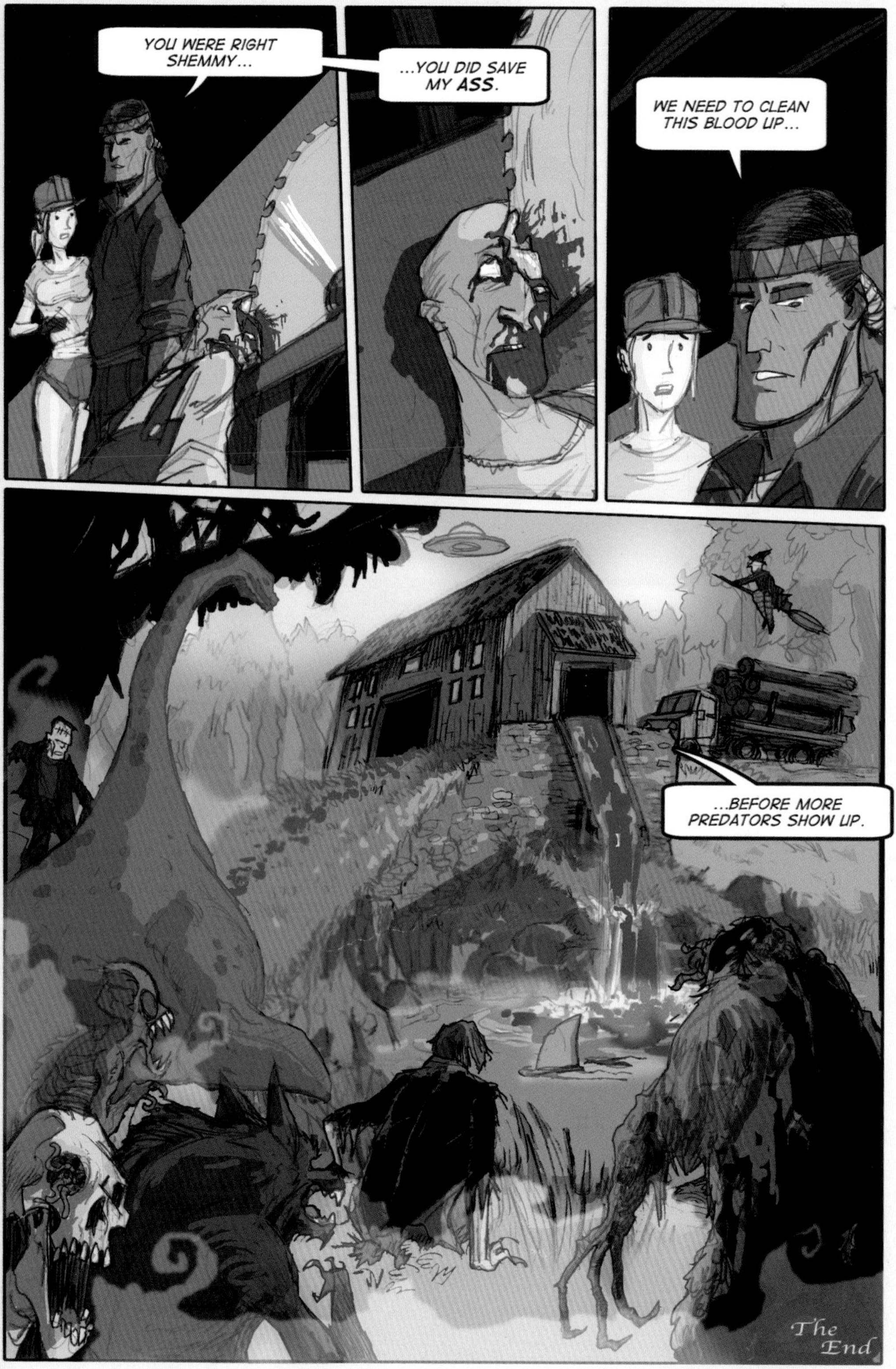
YOU WERE RIGHT SHEMMY...
...YOU DID SAVE MY ASS.
WE NEED TO CLEAN THIS BLOOD UP...
...BEFORE MORE PREDATORS SHOW UP.
The End

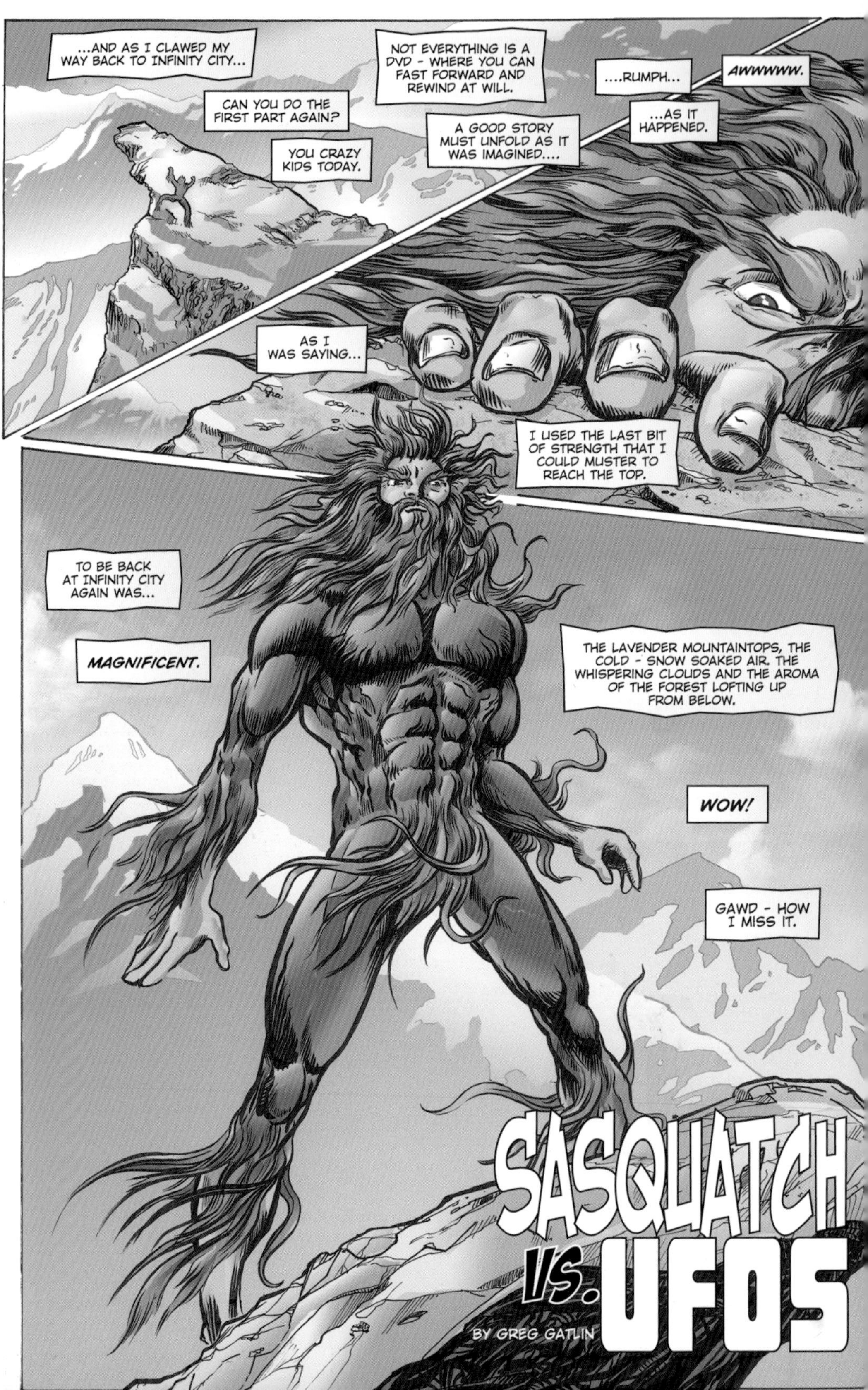
...AND AS I CLAWED MY WAY BACK TO INFINITY CITY...
CAN YOU DO THE FIRST PART AGAIN?
YOU CRAZY KIDS TODAY.
NOT EVERYTHING IS A DVD - WHERE YOU CAN FAST FORWARD AND REWIND AT WILL.
A GOOD STORY MUST UNFOLD AS IT WAS IMAGINED....
....RUMPH...
AWWWWW.
...AS IT HAPPENED.
AS I WAS SAYING...
I USED THE LAST BIT OF STRENGTH THAT I COULD MUSTER TO REACH THE TOP.
TO BE BACK AT INFINITY CITY AGAIN WAS...
MAGNIFICENT.
THE LAVENDER MOUNTAINTOPS, THE COLD - SNOW SOAKED AIR. THE WHISPERING CLOUDS AND THE AROMA OF THE FOREST LOFTING UP FROM BELOW.
WOW!
GAWD - HOW I MISS IT.
SASQUATCH VS. UFOS
BY GREG GATLIN

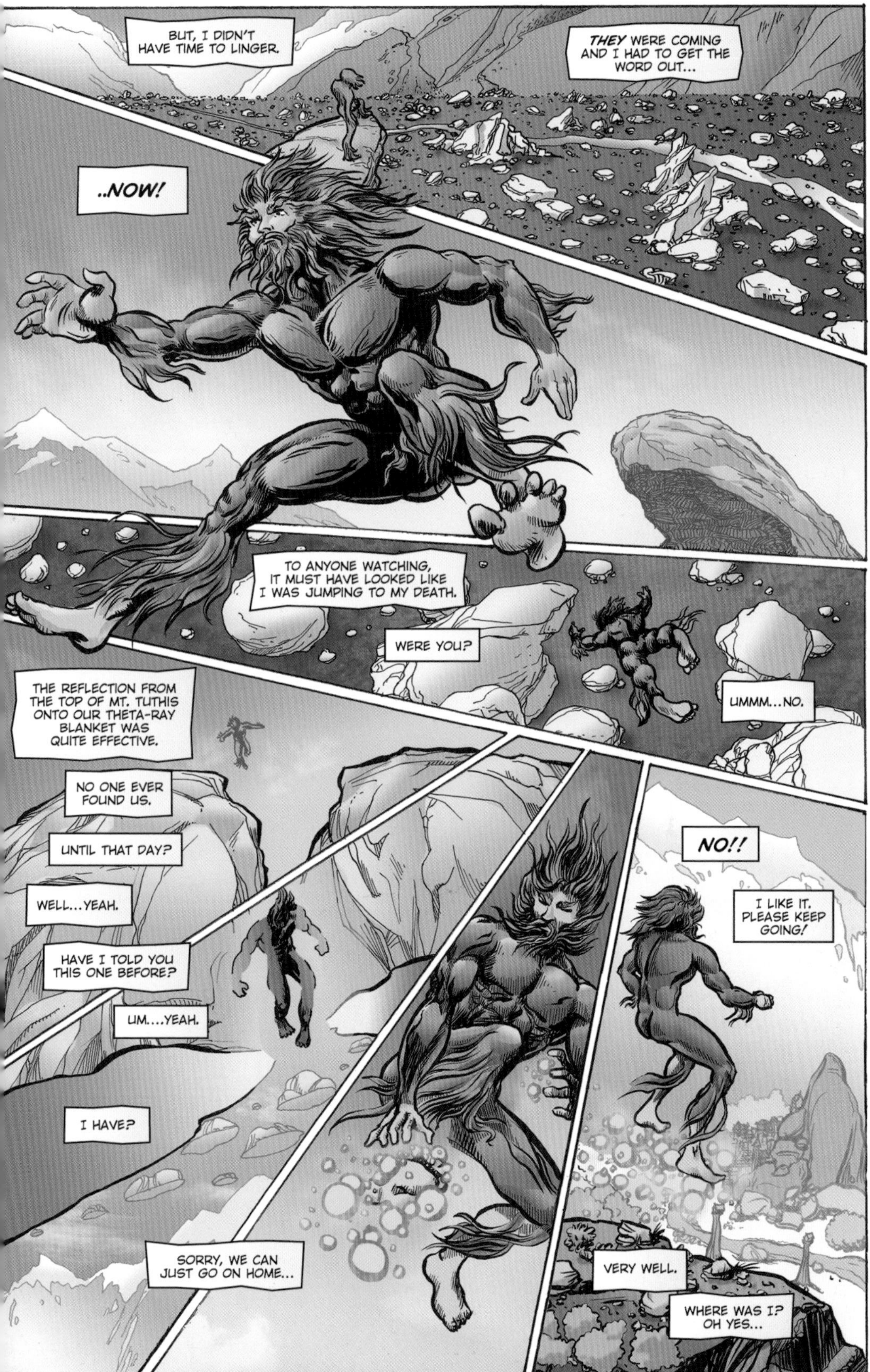
BUT, I DIDN'T HAVE TIME TO LINGER.
THEY WERE COMING AND I HAD TO GET THE WORD OUT...
..NOW!
TO ANYONE WATCHING, IT MUST HAVE LOOKED LIKE I WAS JUMPING TO MY DEATH.
WERE YOU?
UMMM...NO.
THE REFLECTION FROM THE TOP OF MT. TUTHIS ONTO OUR THETA-RAY BLANKET WAS QUITE EFFECTIVE.
NO ONE EVER FOUND US.
UNTIL THAT DAY?
WELL...YEAH.
HAVE I TOLD YOU THIS ONE BEFORE?
UM....YEAH.
I HAVE?
SORRY, WE CAN JUST GO ON HOME...
NO!!
I LIKE IT. PLEASE KEEP GOING!
VERY WELL.
WHERE WAS I? OH YES...

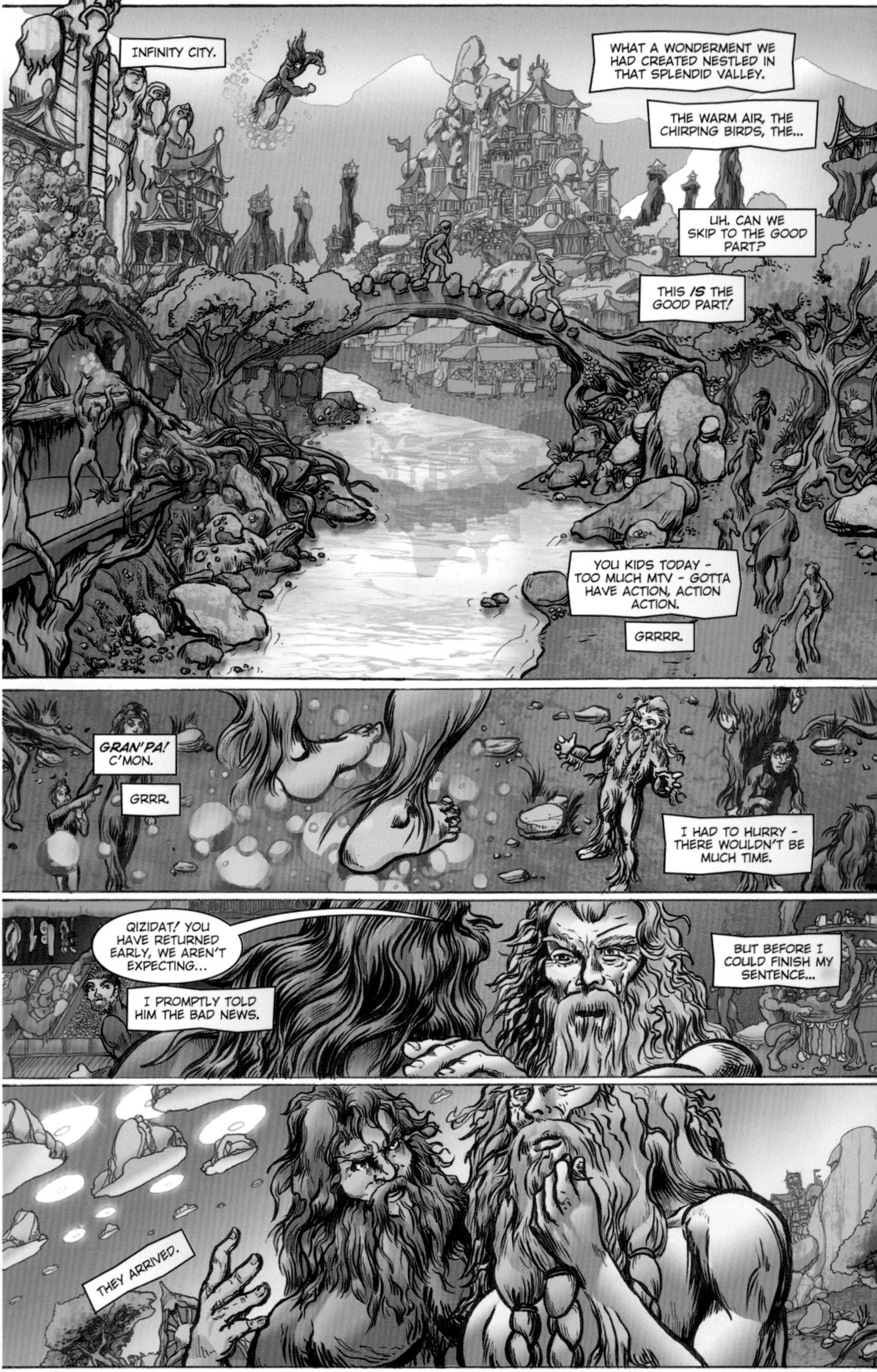
INFINITY CITY.
WHAT A WONDERMENT WE HAD CREATED NESTLED IN THAT SPLENDID VALLEY.
THE WARM AIR, THE CHIRPING BIRDS, THE...
UH. CAN WE SKIP TO THE GOOD PART?
THIS *IS* THE GOOD PART!
YOU KIDS TODAY - TOO MUCH MTV - GOTTA HAVE ACTION, ACTION ACTION.
GRRRR.
GRAN'PA! C'MON.
GRRR.
I HAD TO HURRY - THERE WOULDN'T BE MUCH TIME.
QIZIDAT! YOU HAVE RETURNED EARLY, WE AREN'T EXPECTING...
I PROMPTLY TOLD HIM THE BAD NEWS.
BUT BEFORE I COULD FINISH MY SENTENCE...
THEY ARRIVED.

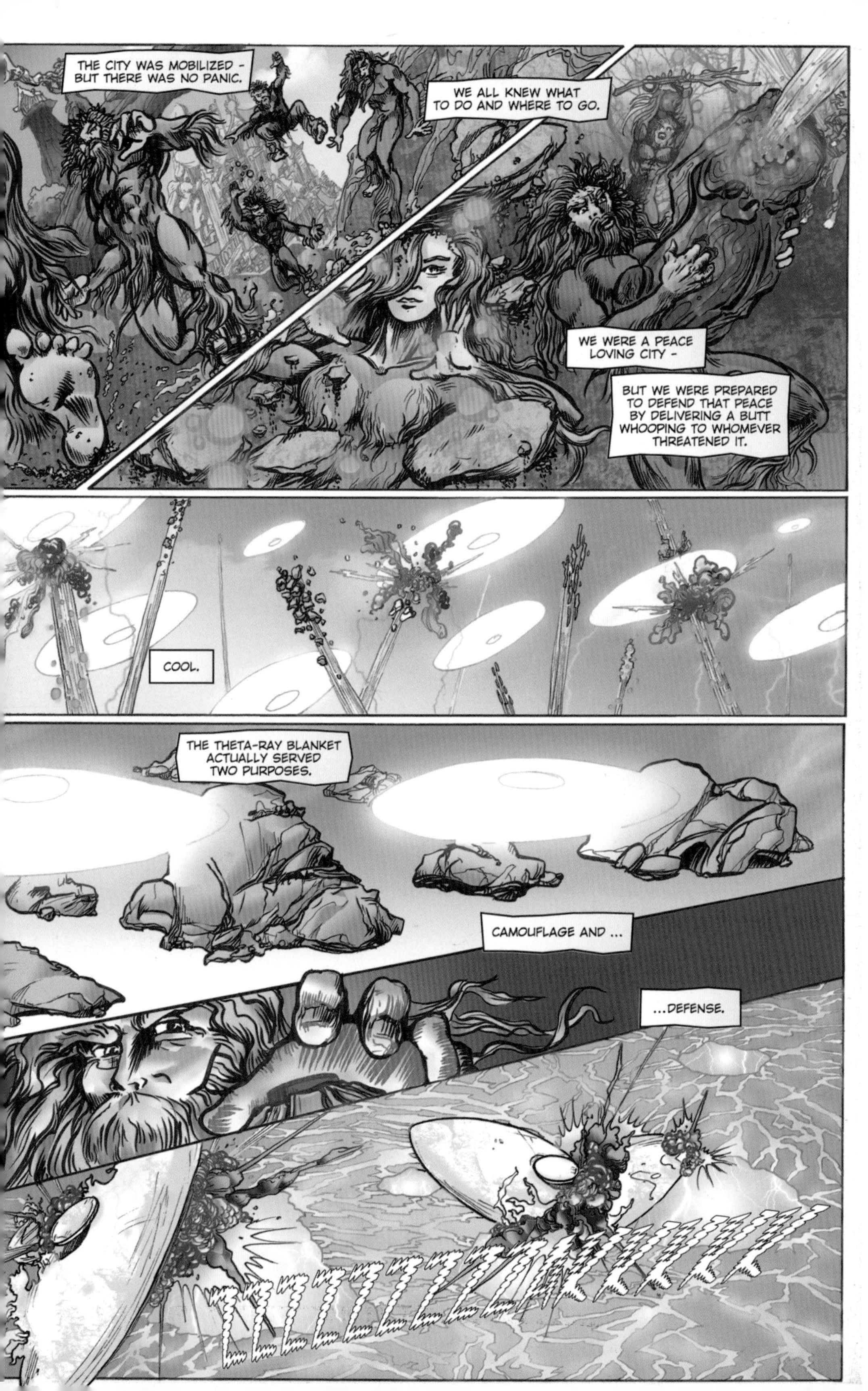
THE CITY WAS MOBILIZED - BUT THERE WAS NO PANIC.
WE ALL KNEW WHAT TO DO AND WHERE TO GO.
WE WERE A PEACE LOVING CITY -
BUT WE WERE PREPARED TO DEFEND THAT PEACE BY DELIVERING A BUTT WHOOPING TO WHOMEVER THREATENED IT.
COOL.
THE THETA-RAY BLANKET ACTUALLY SERVED TWO PURPOSES.
CAMOUFLAGE AND ...
...DEFENSE.

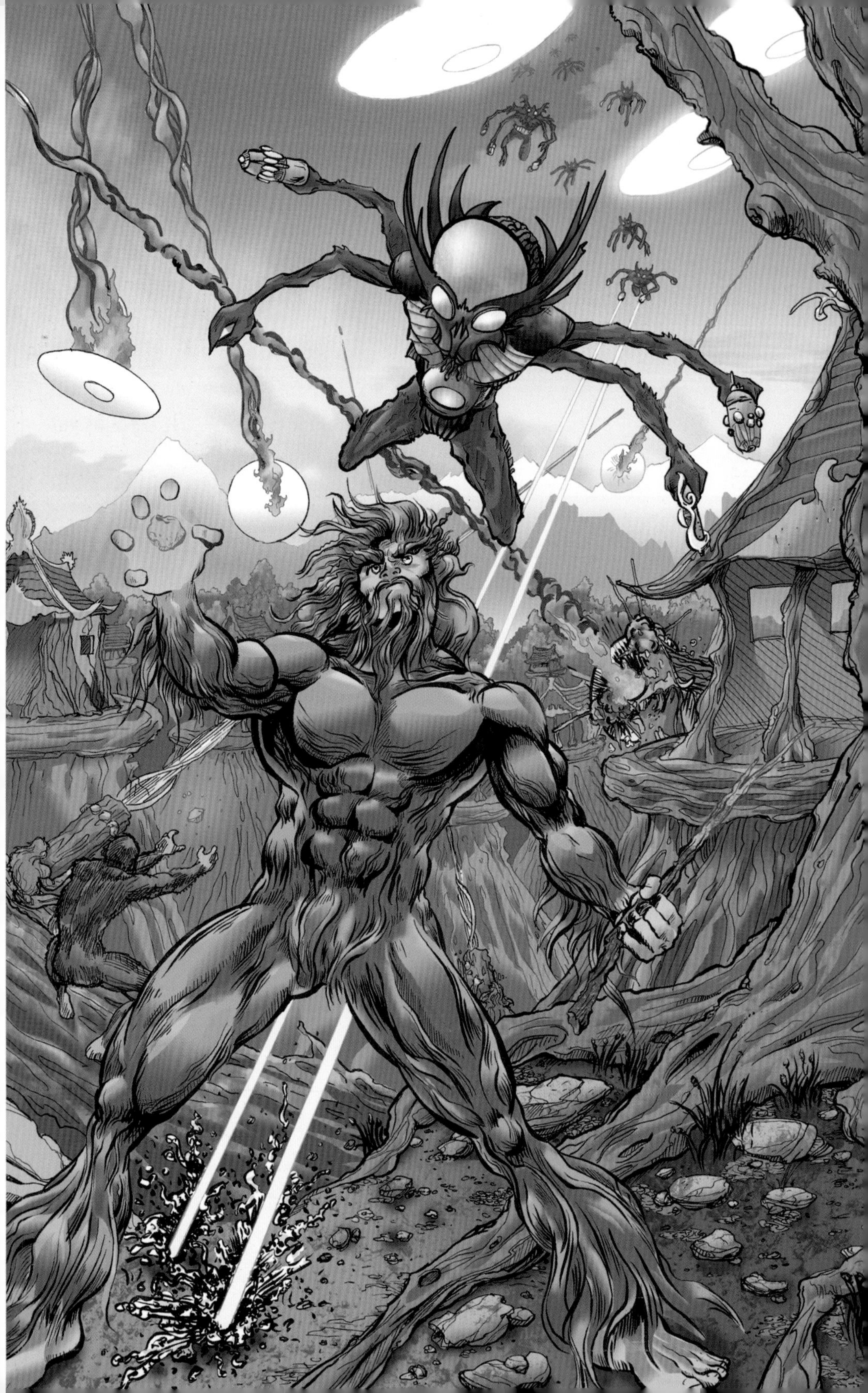

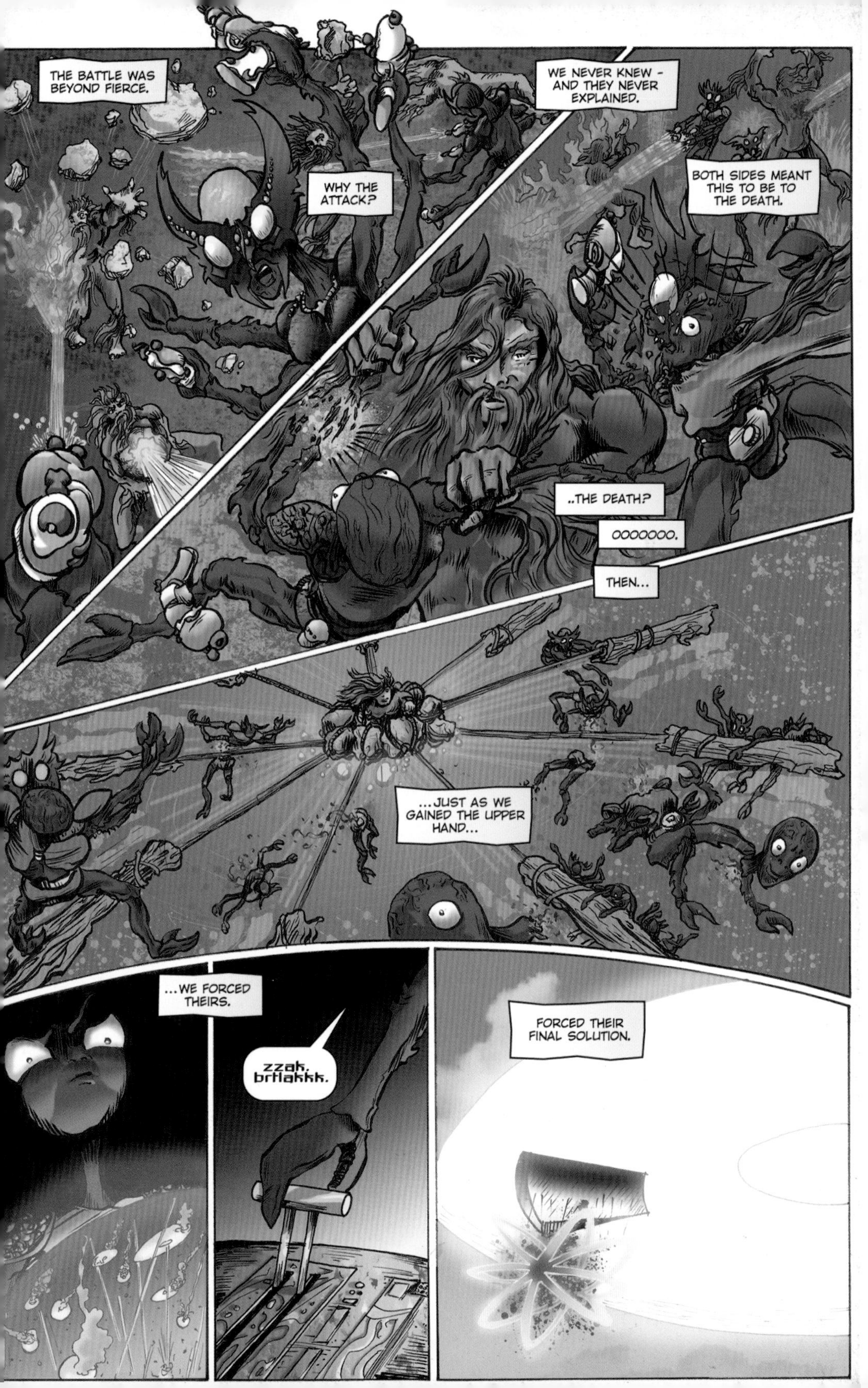
THE BATTLE WAS BEYOND FIERCE.
WHY THE ATTACK?
WE NEVER KNEW - AND THEY NEVER EXPLAINED.
BOTH SIDES MEANT THIS TO BE TO THE DEATH.
..THE DEATH?
OOOOOOO.
THEN...
...JUST AS WE GAINED THE UPPER HAND...
...WE FORCED THEIRS.
zzak. brtiakkk.
FORCED THEIR FINAL SOLUTION.

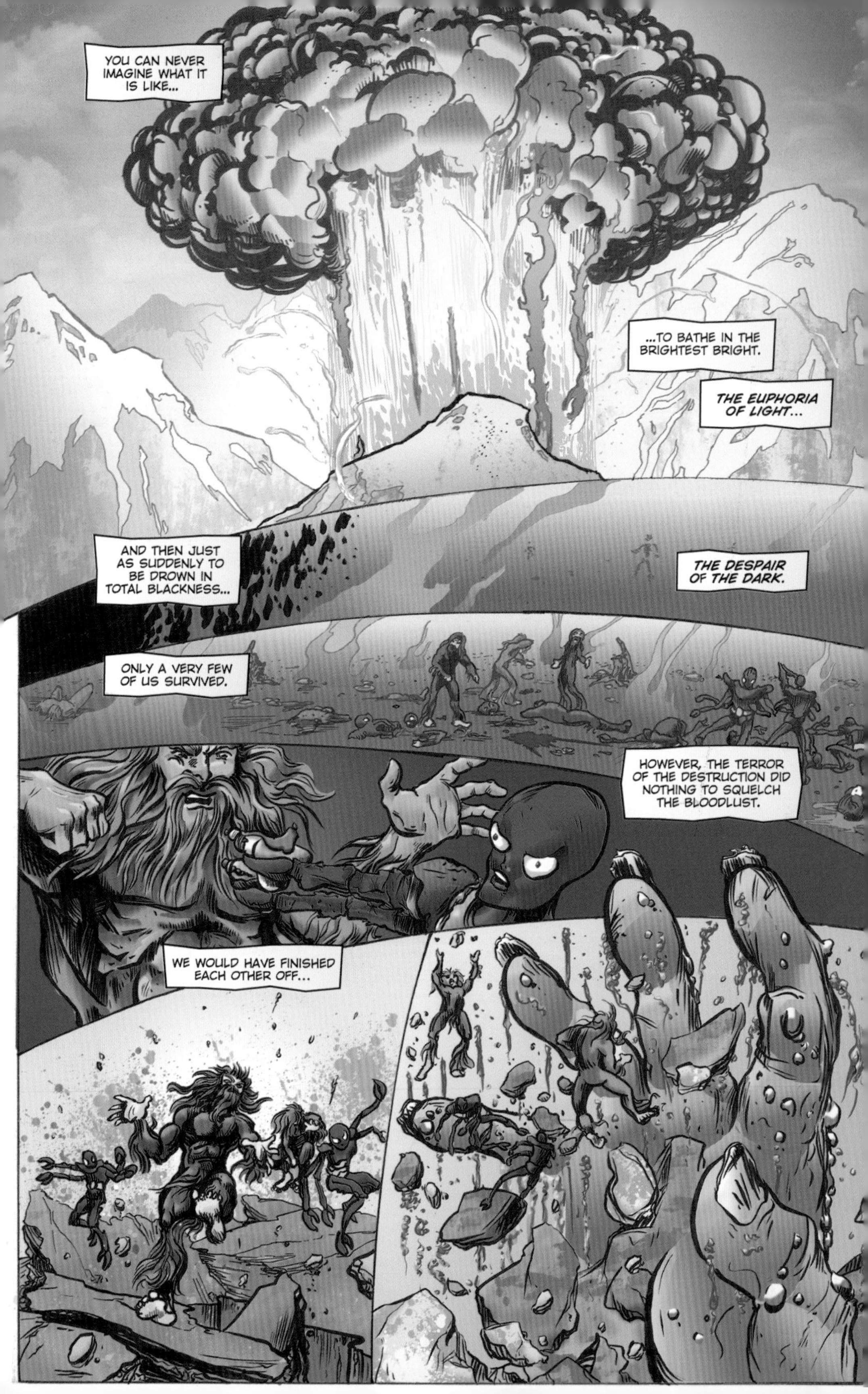

YOU CAN NEVER IMAGINE WHAT IT IS LIKE...
...TO BATHE IN THE BRIGHTEST BRIGHT.
THE EUPHORIA OF LIGHT...
AND THEN JUST AS SUDDENLY TO BE DROWN IN TOTAL BLACKNESS...
THE DESPAIR OF THE DARK.
ONLY A VERY FEW OF US SURVIVED.
HOWEVER, THE TERROR OF THE DESTRUCTION DID NOTHING TO SQUELCH THE BLOODLUST.
WE WOULD HAVE FINISHED EACH OTHER OFF...

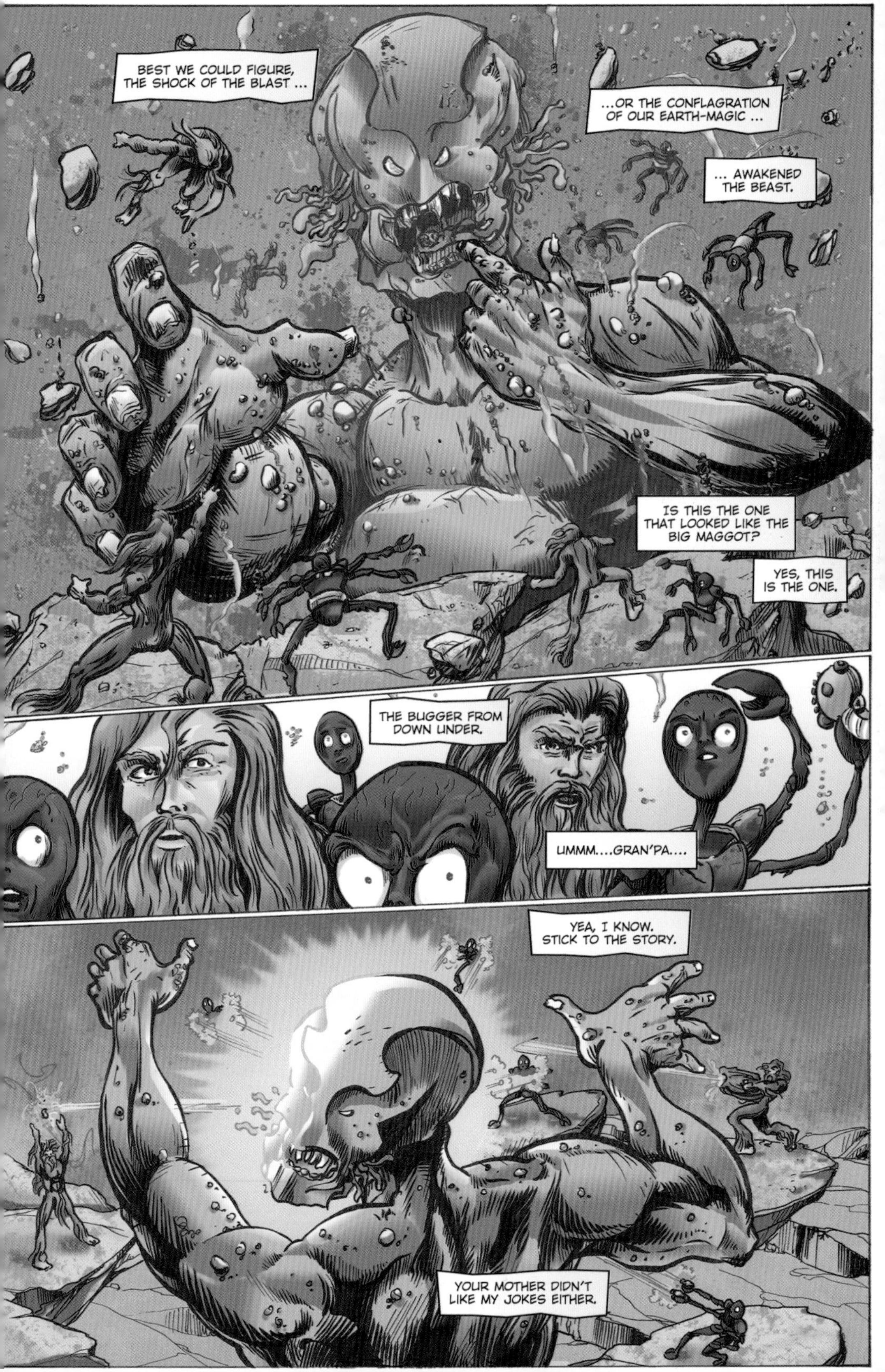
BEST WE COULD FIGURE, THE SHOCK OF THE BLAST ...
...OR THE CONFLAGRATION OF OUR EARTH-MAGIC ...
... AWAKENED THE BEAST.
IS THIS THE ONE THAT LOOKED LIKE THE BIG MAGGOT?
YES, THIS IS THE ONE.
THE BUGGER FROM DOWN UNDER.
UMMM....GRAN'PA....
YEA, I KNOW. STICK TO THE STORY.
YOUR MOTHER DIDN'T LIKE MY JOKES EITHER.

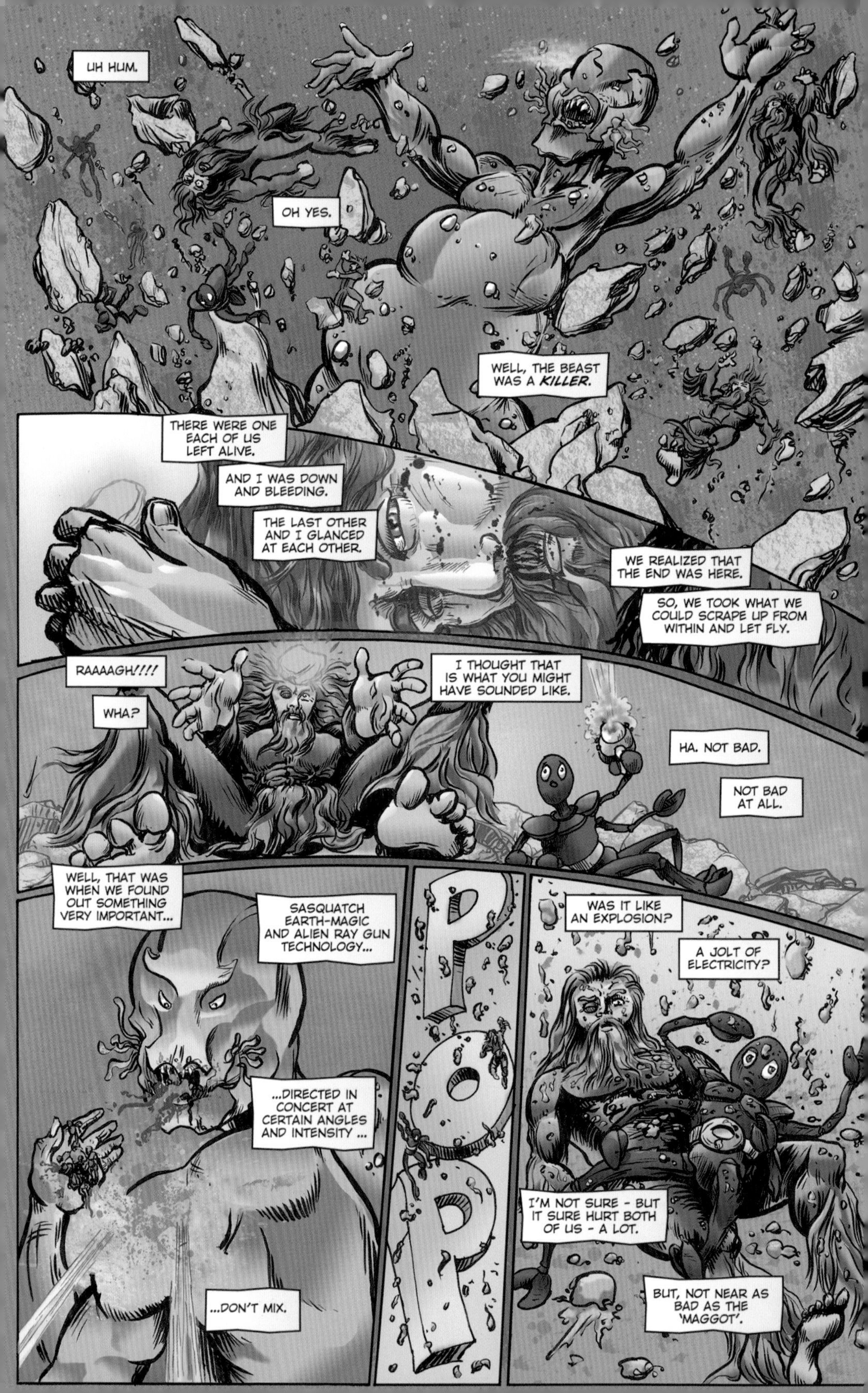
UH HUM.
OH YES.
WELL, THE BEAST WAS A *KILLER*.
THERE WERE ONE EACH OF US LEFT ALIVE.
AND I WAS DOWN AND BLEEDING.
THE LAST OTHER AND I GLANCED AT EACH OTHER.
WE REALIZED THAT THE END WAS HERE.
SO, WE TOOK WHAT WE COULD SCRAPE UP FROM WITHIN AND LET FLY.
RAAAAGH!!!!
WHA?
I THOUGHT THAT IS WHAT YOU MIGHT HAVE SOUNDED LIKE.
HA. NOT BAD.
NOT BAD AT ALL.
WELL, THAT WAS WHEN WE FOUND OUT SOMETHING VERY IMPORTANT...
SASQUATCH EARTH-MAGIC AND ALIEN RAY GUN TECHNOLOGY...
...DIRECTED IN CONCERT AT CERTAIN ANGLES AND INTENSITY ...
...DON'T MIX.
POP
WAS IT LIKE AN EXPLOSION?
A JOLT OF ELECTRICITY?
I'M NOT SURE - BUT IT SURE HURT BOTH OF US - A LOT.
BUT, NOT NEAR AS BAD AS THE 'MAGGOT'.

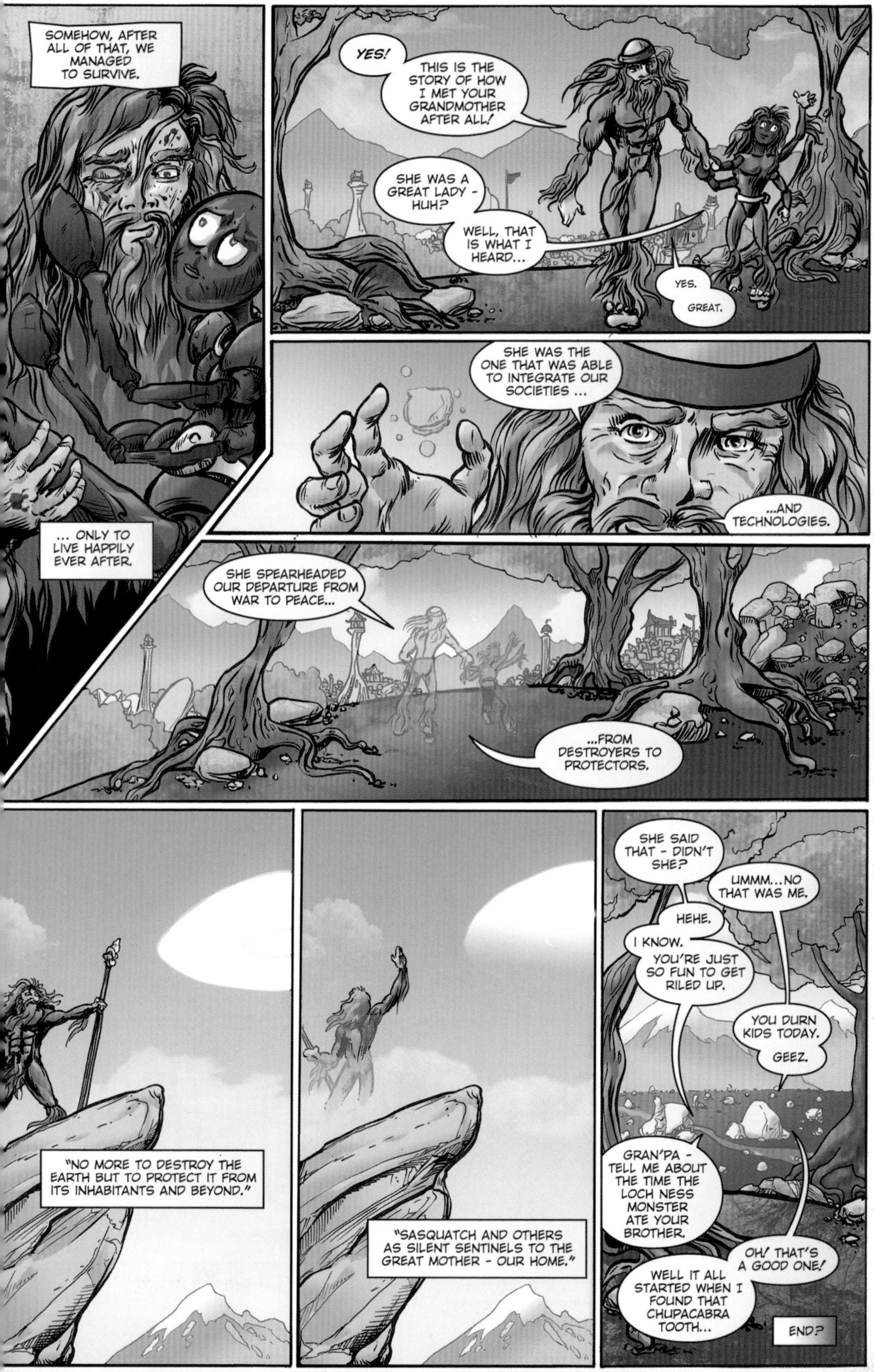
SOMEHOW, AFTER ALL OF THAT, WE MANAGED TO SURVIVE.
... ONLY TO LIVE HAPPILY EVER AFTER.
YES!
THIS IS THE STORY OF HOW I MET YOUR GRANDMOTHER AFTER ALL!
SHE WAS A GREAT LADY - HUH?
WELL, THAT IS WHAT I HEARD...
YES.
GREAT.
SHE WAS THE ONE THAT WAS ABLE TO INTEGRATE OUR SOCIETIES ...
...AND TECHNOLOGIES.
SHE SPEARHEADED OUR DEPARTURE FROM WAR TO PEACE...
...FROM DESTROYERS TO PROTECTORS.
"NO MORE TO DESTROY THE EARTH BUT TO PROTECT IT FROM ITS INHABITANTS AND BEYOND."
"SASQUATCH AND OTHERS AS SILENT SENTINELS TO THE GREAT MOTHER - OUR HOME."
SHE SAID THAT - DIDN'T SHE?
UMMM...NO THAT WAS ME.
HEHE.
I KNOW.
YOU'RE JUST SO FUN TO GET RILED UP.
YOU DURN KIDS TODAY.
GEEZ.
GRAN'PA - TELL ME ABOUT THE TIME THE LOCH NESS MONSTER ATE YOUR BROTHER.
OH! THAT'S A GOOD ONE!
WELL IT ALL STARTED WHEN I FOUND THAT CHUPACABRA TOOTH...
END?

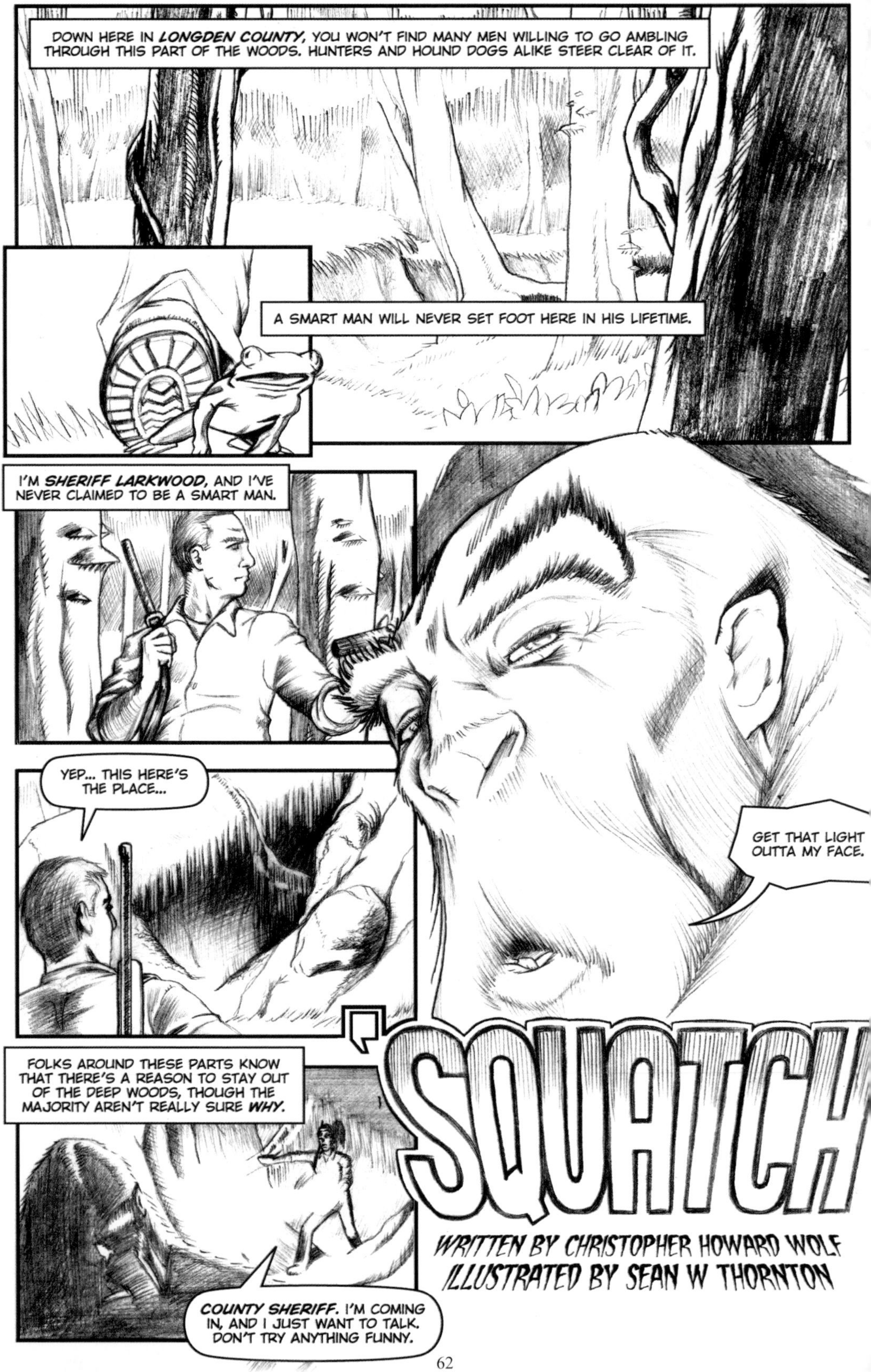
DOWN HERE IN LONGDEN COUNTY, YOU WON'T FIND MANY MEN WILLING TO GO AMBLING THROUGH THIS PART OF THE WOODS. HUNTERS AND HOUND DOGS ALIKE STEER CLEAR OF IT.
A SMART MAN WILL NEVER SET FOOT HERE IN HIS LIFETIME.
I'M SHERIFF LARKWOOD, AND I'VE NEVER CLAIMED TO BE A SMART MAN.
YEP... THIS HERE'S THE PLACE...
FOLKS AROUND THESE PARTS KNOW THAT THERE'S A REASON TO STAY OUT OF THE DEEP WOODS, THOUGH THE MAJORITY AREN'T REALLY SURE WHY.
COUNTY SHERIFF. I'M COMING IN, AND I JUST WANT TO TALK. DON'T TRY ANYTHING FUNNY.
GET THAT LIGHT OUTTA MY FACE.
'SQUATCH
WRITTEN BY CHRISTOPHER HOWARD WOLF
ILLUSTRATED BY SEAN W THORNTON

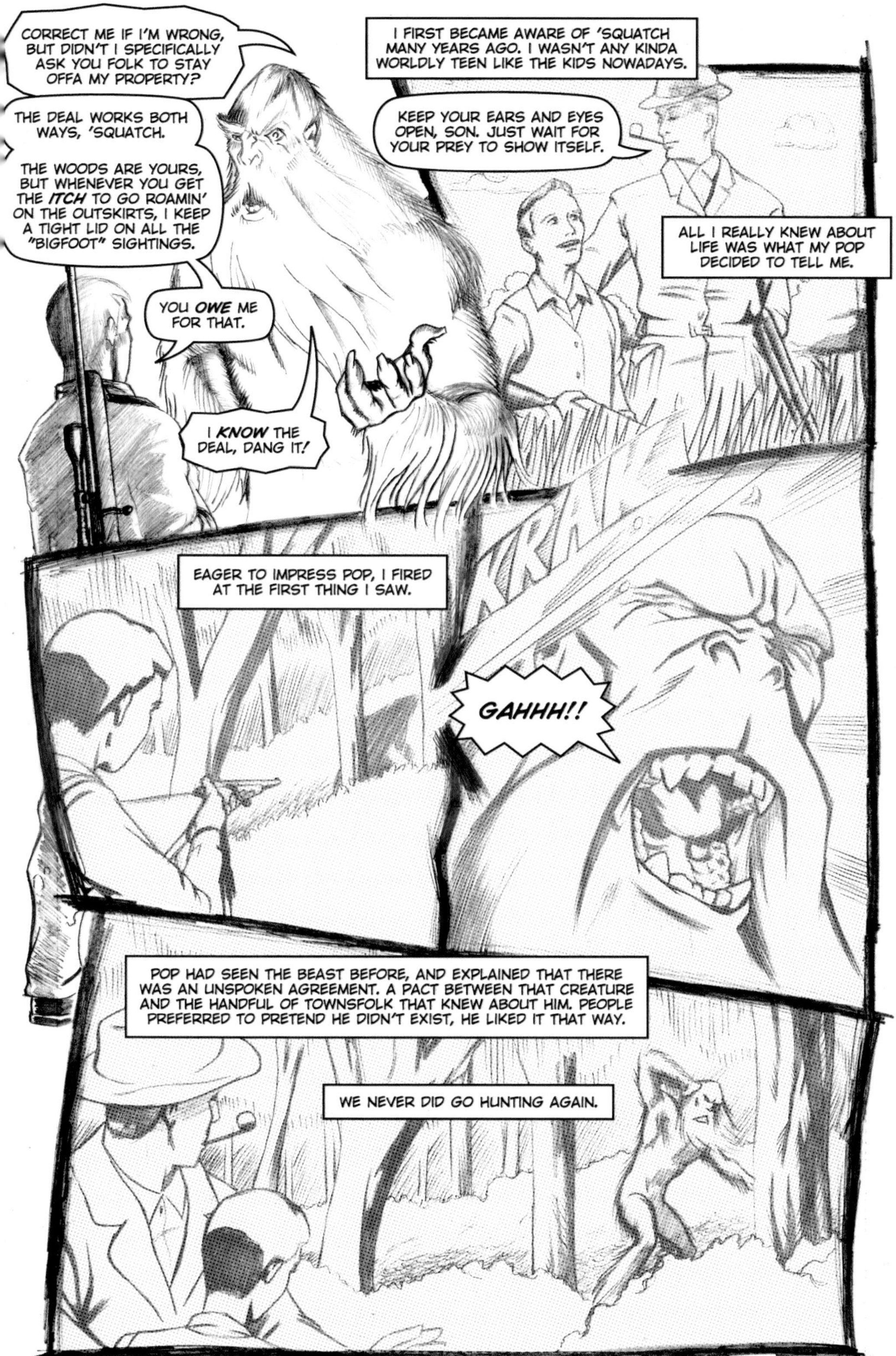
CORRECT ME IF I'M WRONG, BUT DIDN'T I SPECIFICALLY ASK YOU FOLK TO STAY OFFA MY PROPERTY?
THE DEAL WORKS BOTH WAYS, 'SQUATCH.
THE WOODS ARE YOURS, BUT WHENEVER YOU GET THE *ITCH* TO GO ROAMIN' ON THE OUTSKIRTS, I KEEP A TIGHT LID ON ALL THE "BIGFOOT" SIGHTINGS.
YOU *OWE* ME FOR THAT.
I *KNOW* THE DEAL, DANG IT!
I FIRST BECAME AWARE OF 'SQUATCH MANY YEARS AGO. I WASN'T ANY KINDA WORLDLY TEEN LIKE THE KIDS NOWADAYS.
KEEP YOUR EARS AND EYES OPEN, SON. JUST WAIT FOR YOUR PREY TO SHOW ITSELF.
ALL I REALLY KNEW ABOUT LIFE WAS WHAT MY POP DECIDED TO TELL ME.
EAGER TO IMPRESS POP, I FIRED AT THE FIRST THING I SAW.
GAHHH!!
POP HAD SEEN THE BEAST BEFORE, AND EXPLAINED THAT THERE WAS AN UNSPOKEN AGREEMENT. A PACT BETWEEN THAT CREATURE AND THE HANDFUL OF TOWNSFOLK THAT KNEW ABOUT HIM. PEOPLE PREFERRED TO PRETEND HE DIDN'T EXIST, HE LIKED IT THAT WAY.
WE NEVER DID GO HUNTING AGAIN.

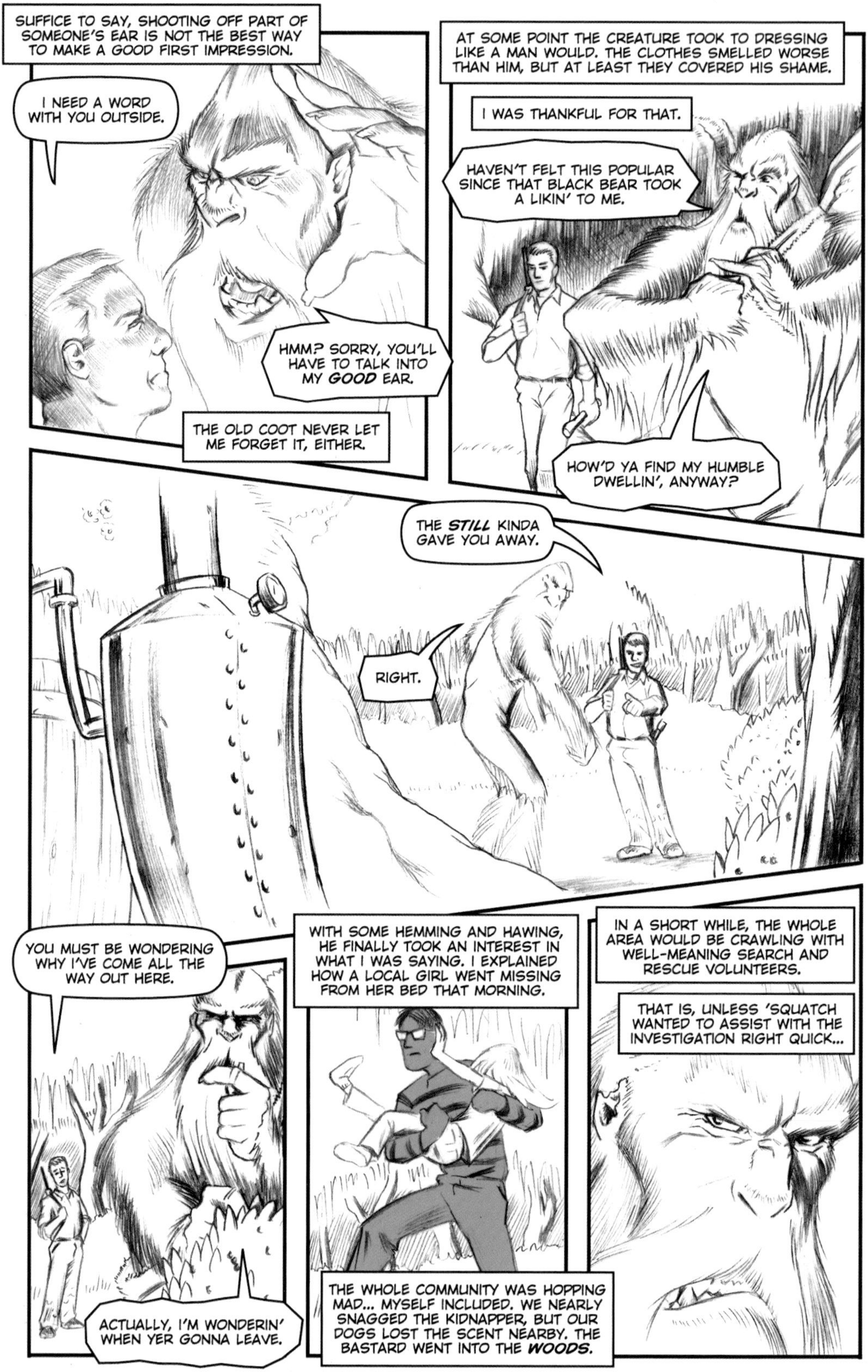
SUFFICE TO SAY, SHOOTING OFF PART OF SOMEONE'S EAR IS NOT THE BEST WAY TO MAKE A GOOD FIRST IMPRESSION.
I NEED A WORD WITH YOU OUTSIDE.
HMM? SORRY, YOU'LL HAVE TO TALK INTO MY GOOD EAR.
THE OLD COOT NEVER LET ME FORGET IT, EITHER.
AT SOME POINT THE CREATURE TOOK TO DRESSING LIKE A MAN WOULD. THE CLOTHES SMELLED WORSE THAN HIM, BUT AT LEAST THEY COVERED HIS SHAME.
I WAS THANKFUL FOR THAT.
HAVEN'T FELT THIS POPULAR SINCE THAT BLACK BEAR TOOK A LIKIN' TO ME.
HOW'D YA FIND MY HUMBLE DWELLIN', ANYWAY?
THE STILL KINDA GAVE YOU AWAY.
RIGHT.
YOU MUST BE WONDERING WHY I'VE COME ALL THE WAY OUT HERE.
ACTUALLY, I'M WONDERIN' WHEN YER GONNA LEAVE.
WITH SOME HEMMING AND HAWING, HE FINALLY TOOK AN INTEREST IN WHAT I WAS SAYING. I EXPLAINED HOW A LOCAL GIRL WENT MISSING FROM HER BED THAT MORNING.
THE WHOLE COMMUNITY WAS HOPPING MAD... MYSELF INCLUDED. WE NEARLY SNAGGED THE KIDNAPPER, BUT OUR DOGS LOST THE SCENT NEARBY. THE BASTARD WENT INTO THE WOODS.
IN A SHORT WHILE, THE WHOLE AREA WOULD BE CRAWLING WITH WELL-MEANING SEARCH AND RESCUE VOLUNTEERS.
THAT IS, UNLESS 'SQUATCH WANTED TO ASSIST WITH THE INVESTIGATION RIGHT QUICK...

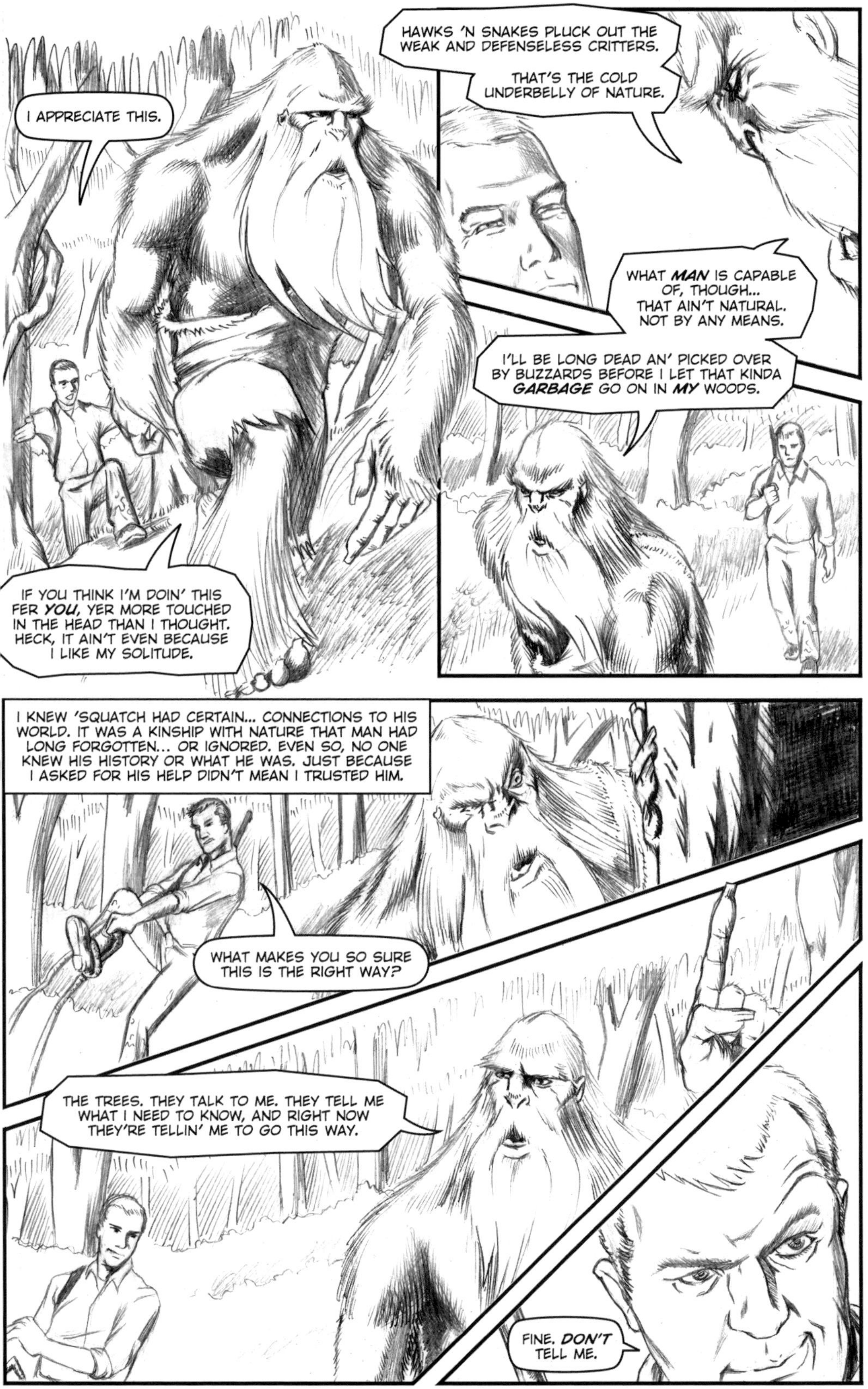
I APPRECIATE THIS.
IF YOU THINK I'M DOIN' THIS FER *YOU*, YER MORE TOUCHED IN THE HEAD THAN I THOUGHT. HECK, IT AIN'T EVEN BECAUSE I LIKE MY SOLITUDE.
HAWKS 'N SNAKES PLUCK OUT THE WEAK AND DEFENSELESS CRITTERS.
THAT'S THE COLD UNDERBELLY OF NATURE.
WHAT *MAN* IS CAPABLE OF, THOUGH... THAT AIN'T NATURAL. NOT BY ANY MEANS.
I'LL BE LONG DEAD AN' PICKED OVER BY BUZZARDS BEFORE I LET THAT KINDA *GARBAGE* GO ON IN *MY* WOODS.
I KNEW 'SQUATCH HAD CERTAIN... CONNECTIONS TO HIS WORLD. IT WAS A KINSHIP WITH NATURE THAT MAN HAD LONG FORGOTTEN... OR IGNORED. EVEN SO, NO ONE KNEW HIS HISTORY OR WHAT HE WAS. JUST BECAUSE I ASKED FOR HIS HELP DIDN'T MEAN I TRUSTED HIM.
WHAT MAKES YOU SO SURE THIS IS THE RIGHT WAY?
THE TREES. THEY TALK TO ME. THEY TELL ME WHAT I NEED TO KNOW, AND RIGHT NOW THEY'RE TELLIN' ME TO GO THIS WAY.
FINE. *DON'T* TELL ME.

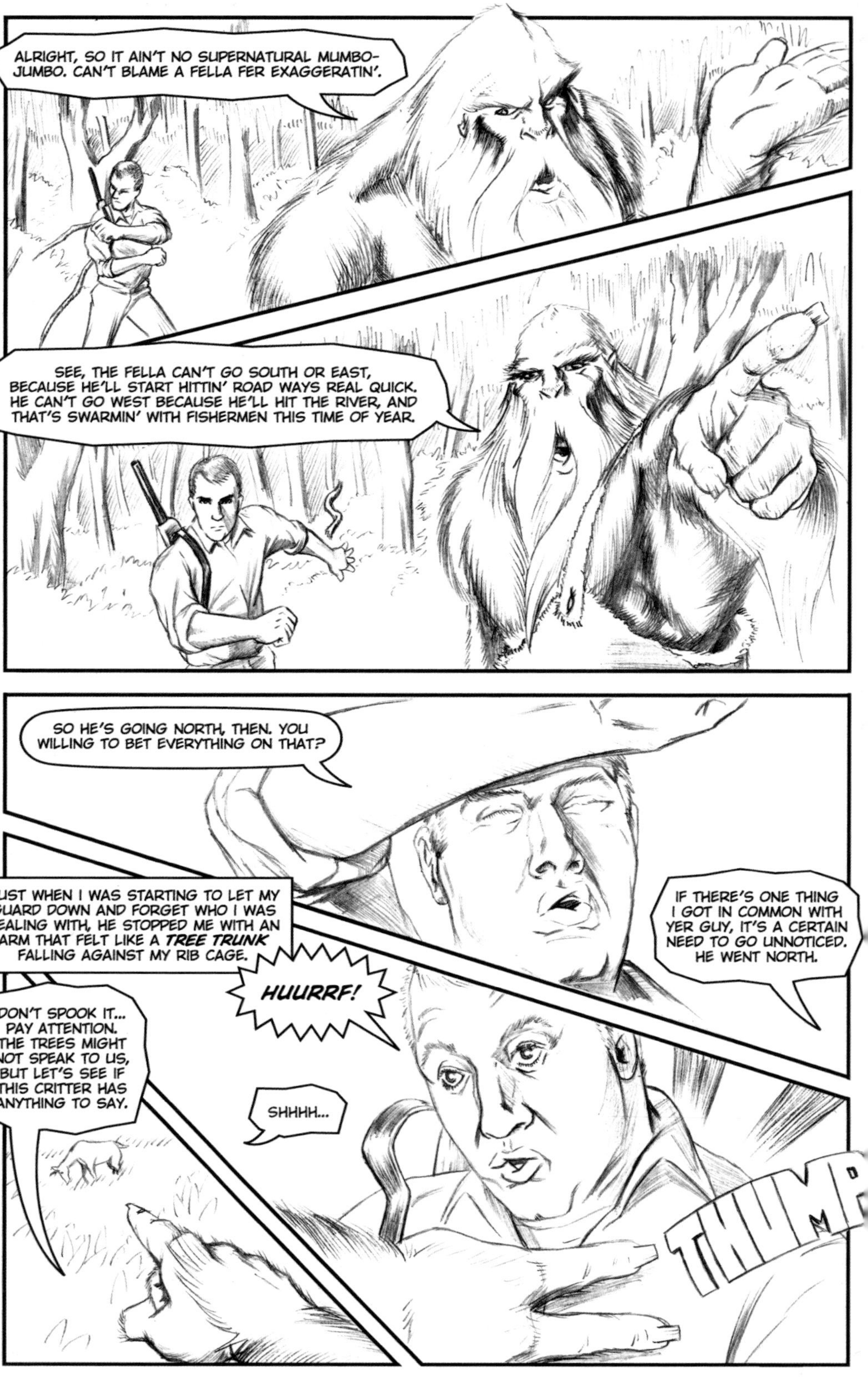
ALRIGHT, SO IT AIN'T NO SUPERNATURAL MUMBO-JUMBO. CAN'T BLAME A FELLA FER EXAGGERATIN'.
SEE, THE FELLA CAN'T GO SOUTH OR EAST, BECAUSE HE'LL START HITTIN' ROAD WAYS REAL QUICK. HE CAN'T GO WEST BECAUSE HE'LL HIT THE RIVER, AND THAT'S SWARMIN' WITH FISHERMEN THIS TIME OF YEAR.
SO HE'S GOING NORTH, THEN. YOU WILLING TO BET EVERYTHING ON THAT?
IF THERE'S ONE THING I GOT IN COMMON WITH YER GUY, IT'S A CERTAIN NEED TO GO UNNOTICED. HE WENT NORTH.
JUST WHEN I WAS STARTING TO LET MY GUARD DOWN AND FORGET WHO I WAS DEALING WITH, HE STOPPED ME WITH AN ARM THAT FELT LIKE A *TREE TRUNK* FALLING AGAINST MY RIB CAGE.
HUURRF!
THUMP
SHHHH...
DON'T SPOOK IT... PAY ATTENTION. THE TREES MIGHT NOT SPEAK TO US, BUT LET'S SEE IF THIS CRITTER HAS ANYTHING TO SAY.

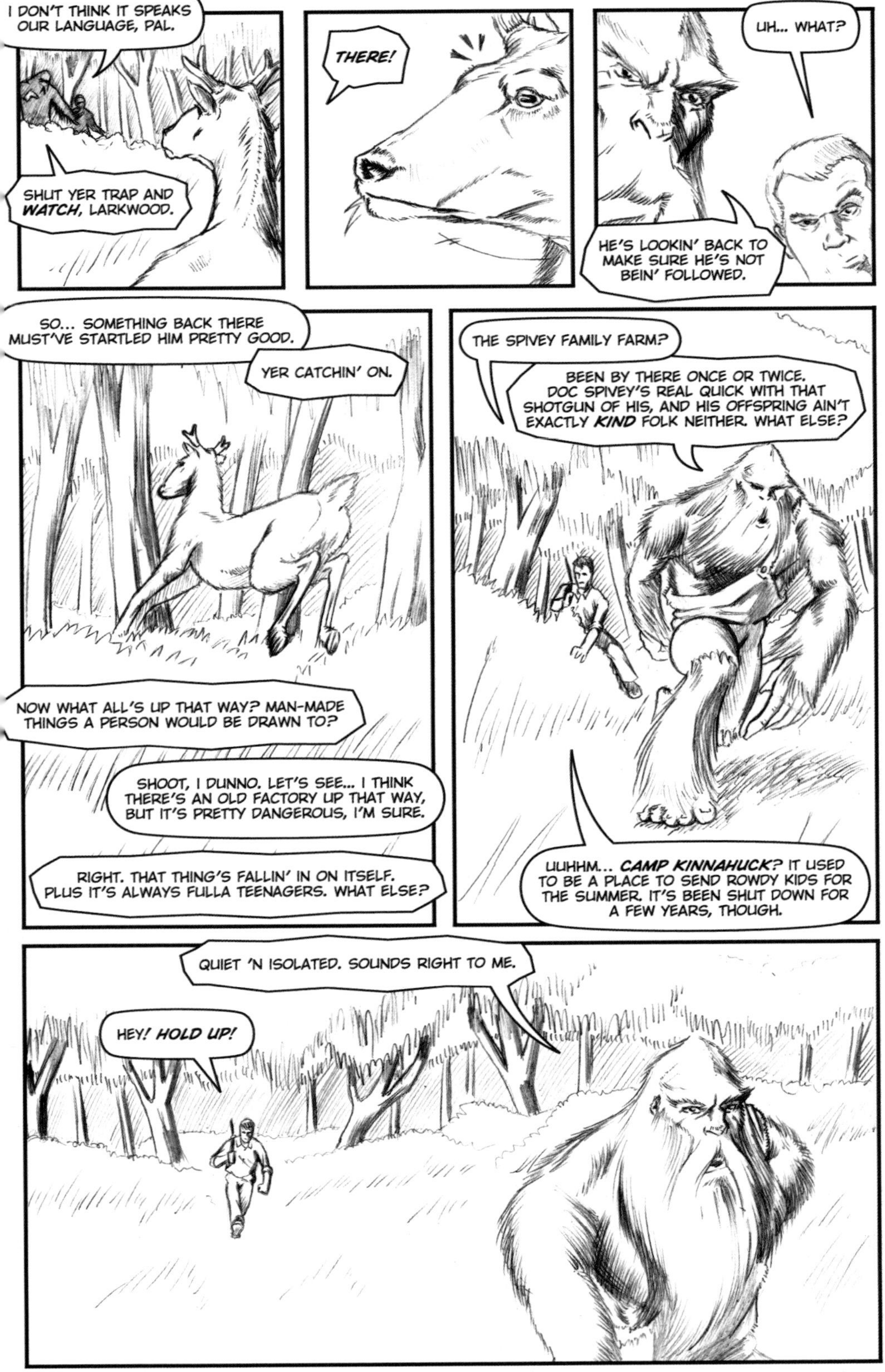
I DON'T THINK IT SPEAKS OUR LANGUAGE, PAL.
SHUT YER TRAP AND **WATCH**, LARKWOOD.
THERE!
UH... WHAT?
HE'S LOOKIN' BACK TO MAKE SURE HE'S NOT BEIN' FOLLOWED.
SO... SOMETHING BACK THERE MUST'VE STARTLED HIM PRETTY GOOD.
YER CATCHIN' ON.
NOW WHAT ALL'S UP THAT WAY? MAN-MADE THINGS A PERSON WOULD BE DRAWN TO?
SHOOT, I DUNNO. LET'S SEE... I THINK THERE'S AN OLD FACTORY UP THAT WAY, BUT IT'S PRETTY DANGEROUS, I'M SURE.
RIGHT. THAT THING'S FALLIN' IN ON ITSELF. PLUS IT'S ALWAYS FULLA TEENAGERS. WHAT ELSE?
THE SPIVEY FAMILY FARM?
BEEN BY THERE ONCE OR TWICE. DOC SPIVEY'S REAL QUICK WITH THAT SHOTGUN OF HIS, AND HIS OFFSPRING AIN'T EXACTLY **KIND** FOLK NEITHER. WHAT ELSE?
UUHHM... **CAMP KINNAHUCK?** IT USED TO BE A PLACE TO SEND ROWDY KIDS FOR THE SUMMER. IT'S BEEN SHUT DOWN FOR A FEW YEARS, THOUGH.
QUIET 'N ISOLATED. SOUNDS RIGHT TO ME.
HEY! **HOLD UP!**

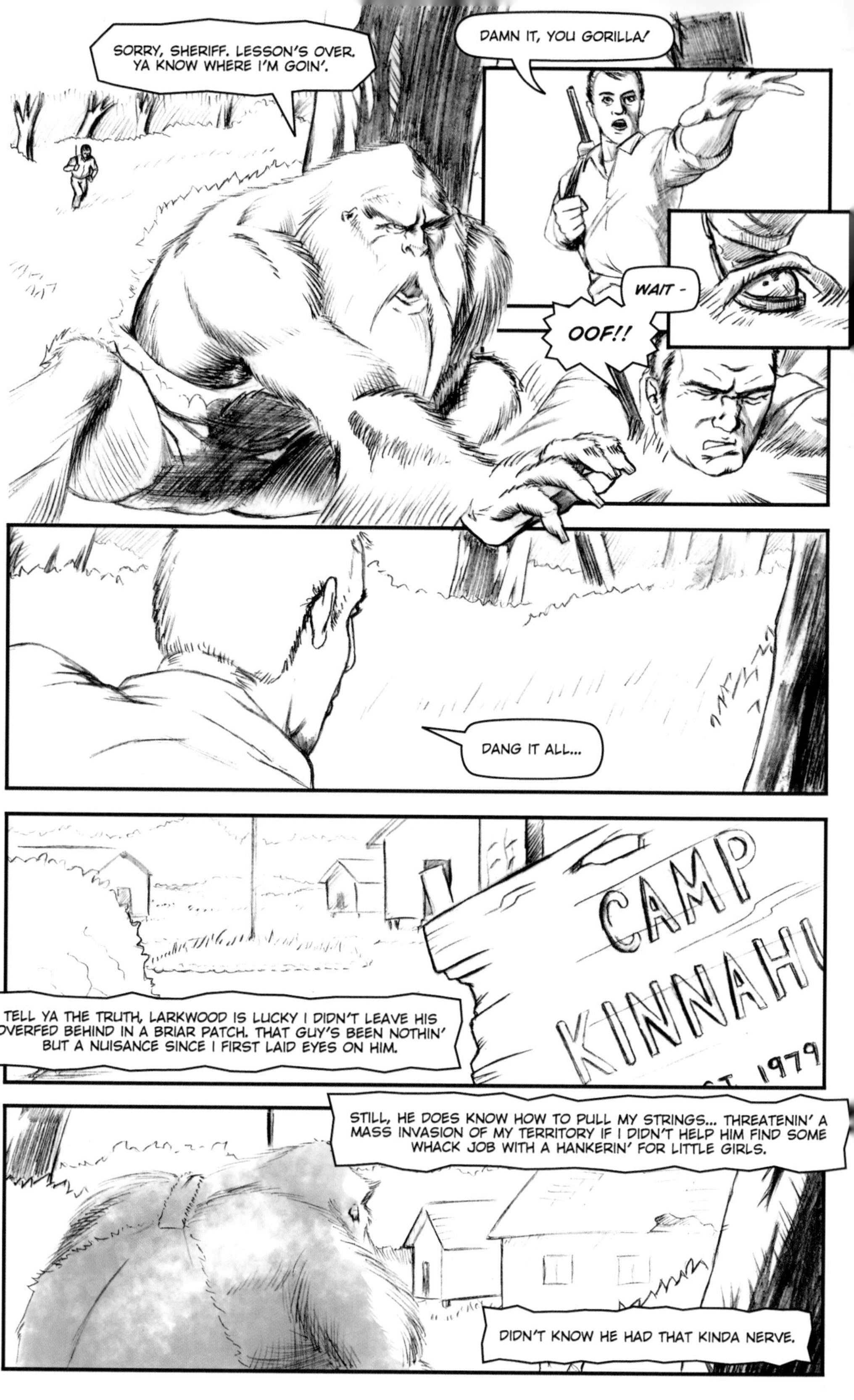
SORRY, SHERIFF. LESSON'S OVER. YA KNOW WHERE I'M GOIN'.
DAMN IT, YOU GORILLA!
WAIT -
OOF!!
DANG IT ALL...
CAMP KINNAHU
1979
TELL YA THE TRUTH, LARKWOOD IS LUCKY I DIDN'T LEAVE HIS OVERFED BEHIND IN A BRIAR PATCH. THAT GUY'S BEEN NOTHIN' BUT A NUISANCE SINCE I FIRST LAID EYES ON HIM.
STILL, HE DOES KNOW HOW TO PULL MY STRINGS... THREATENIN' A MASS INVASION OF MY TERRITORY IF I DIDN'T HELP HIM FIND SOME WHACK JOB WITH A HANKERIN' FOR LITTLE GIRLS.
DIDN'T KNOW HE HAD THAT KINDA NERVE.

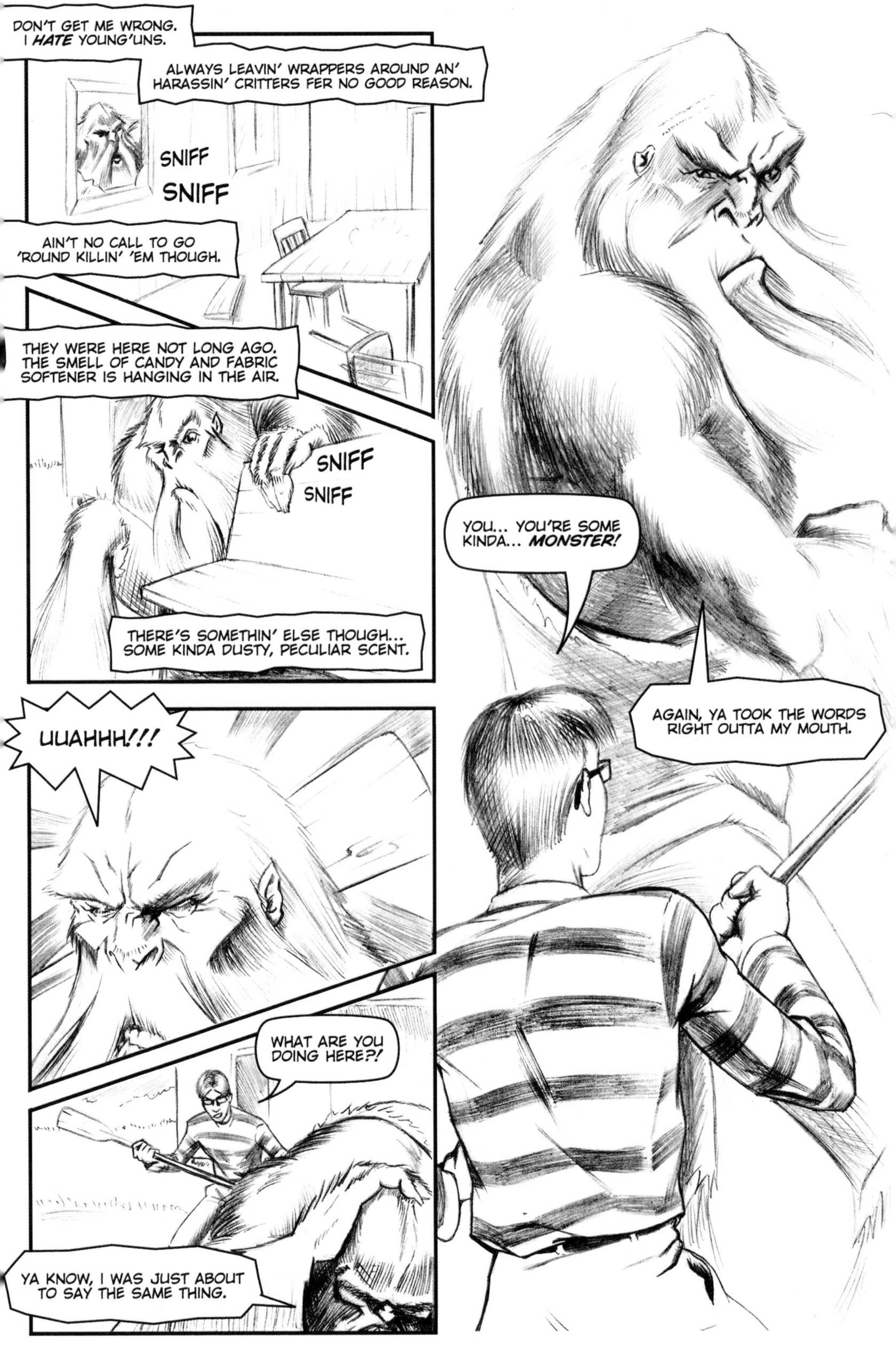
DON'T GET ME WRONG. I HATE YOUNG'UNS.
ALWAYS LEAVIN' WRAPPERS AROUND AN' HARASSIN' CRITTERS FER NO GOOD REASON.
SNIFF
SNIFF
AIN'T NO CALL TO GO 'ROUND KILLIN' 'EM THOUGH.
THEY WERE HERE NOT LONG AGO. THE SMELL OF CANDY AND FABRIC SOFTENER IS HANGING IN THE AIR.
SNIFF
SNIFF
THERE'S SOMETHIN' ELSE THOUGH... SOME KINDA DUSTY, PECULIAR SCENT.
UUAHHH!!!
WHAT ARE YOU DOING HERE?!
YA KNOW, I WAS JUST ABOUT TO SAY THE SAME THING.
YOU... YOU'RE SOME KINDA... MONSTER!
AGAIN, YA TOOK THE WORDS RIGHT OUTTA MY MOUTH.

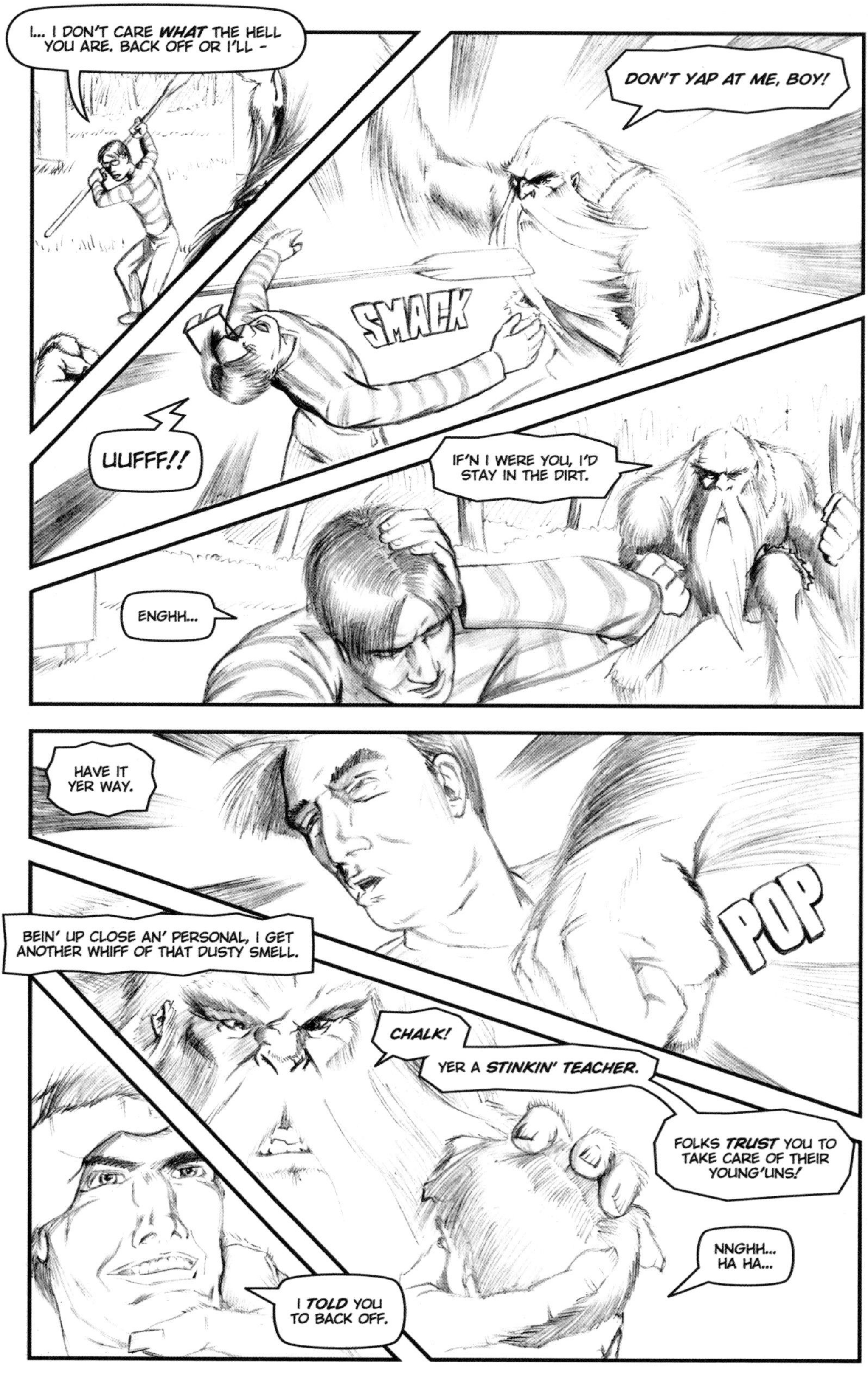
I... I DON'T CARE *WHAT* THE HELL YOU ARE. BACK OFF OR I'LL -
DON'T YAP AT ME, BOY!
SMACK
UUFFF!!
IF'N I WERE YOU, I'D STAY IN THE DIRT.
ENGHH...
HAVE IT YER WAY.
POP
BEIN' UP CLOSE AN' PERSONAL, I GET ANOTHER WHIFF OF THAT DUSTY SMELL.
CHALK!
YER A *STINKIN' TEACHER.*
FOLKS *TRUST* YOU TO TAKE CARE OF THEIR YOUNG'UNS!
NNGHH... HA HA...
I *TOLD* YOU TO BACK OFF.

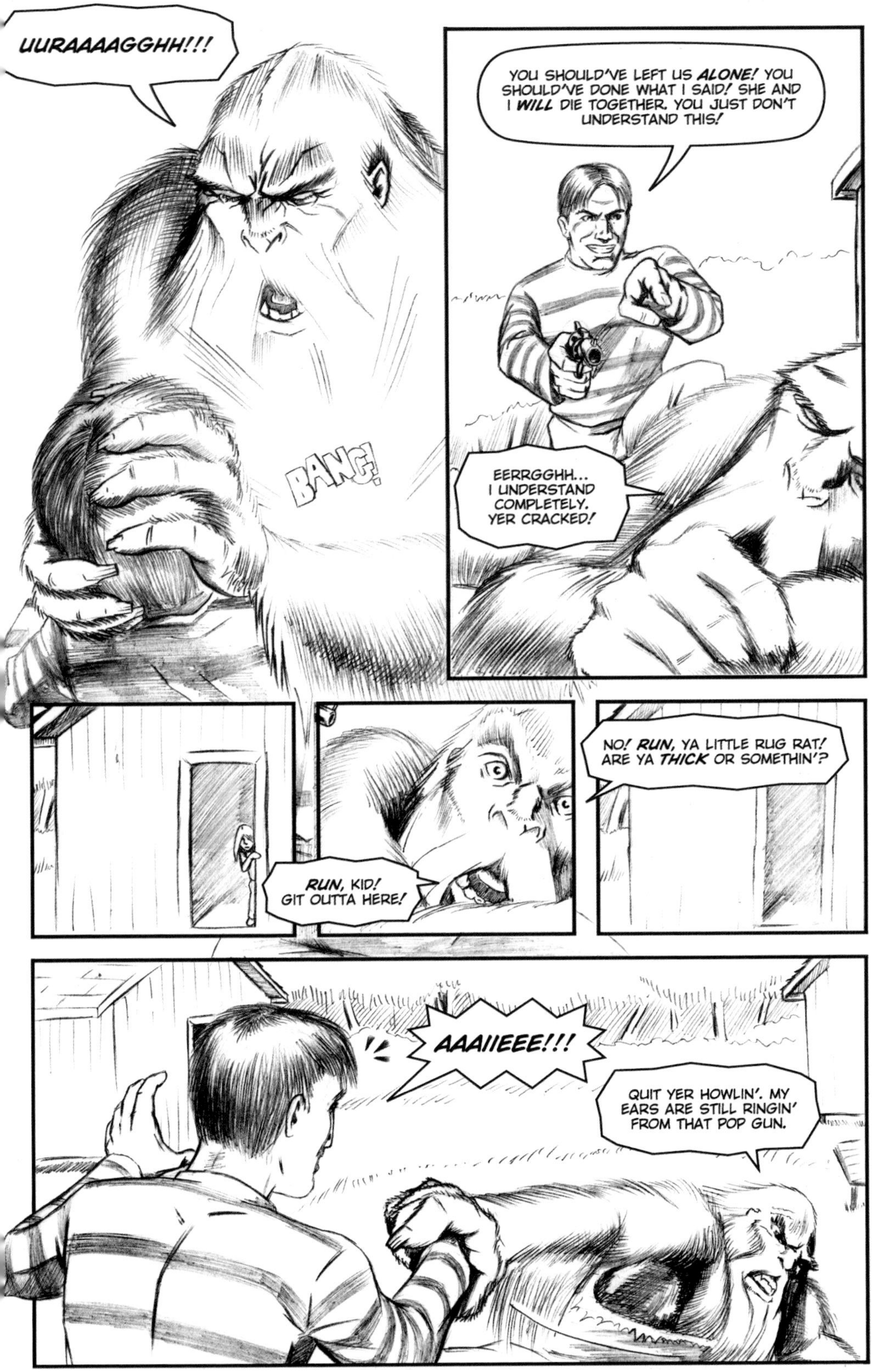
UURAAAAGGHH!!!
BANG!
YOU SHOULD'VE LEFT US ALONE! YOU SHOULD'VE DONE WHAT I SAID! SHE AND I WILL DIE TOGETHER. YOU JUST DON'T UNDERSTAND THIS!
EERRGGHH... I UNDERSTAND COMPLETELY. YER CRACKED!
RUN, KID! GIT OUTTA HERE!
NO! RUN, YA LITTLE RUG RAT! ARE YA THICK OR SOMETHIN'?
AAAIIEEE!!!
QUIT YER HOWLIN'. MY EARS ARE STILL RINGIN' FROM THAT POP GUN.

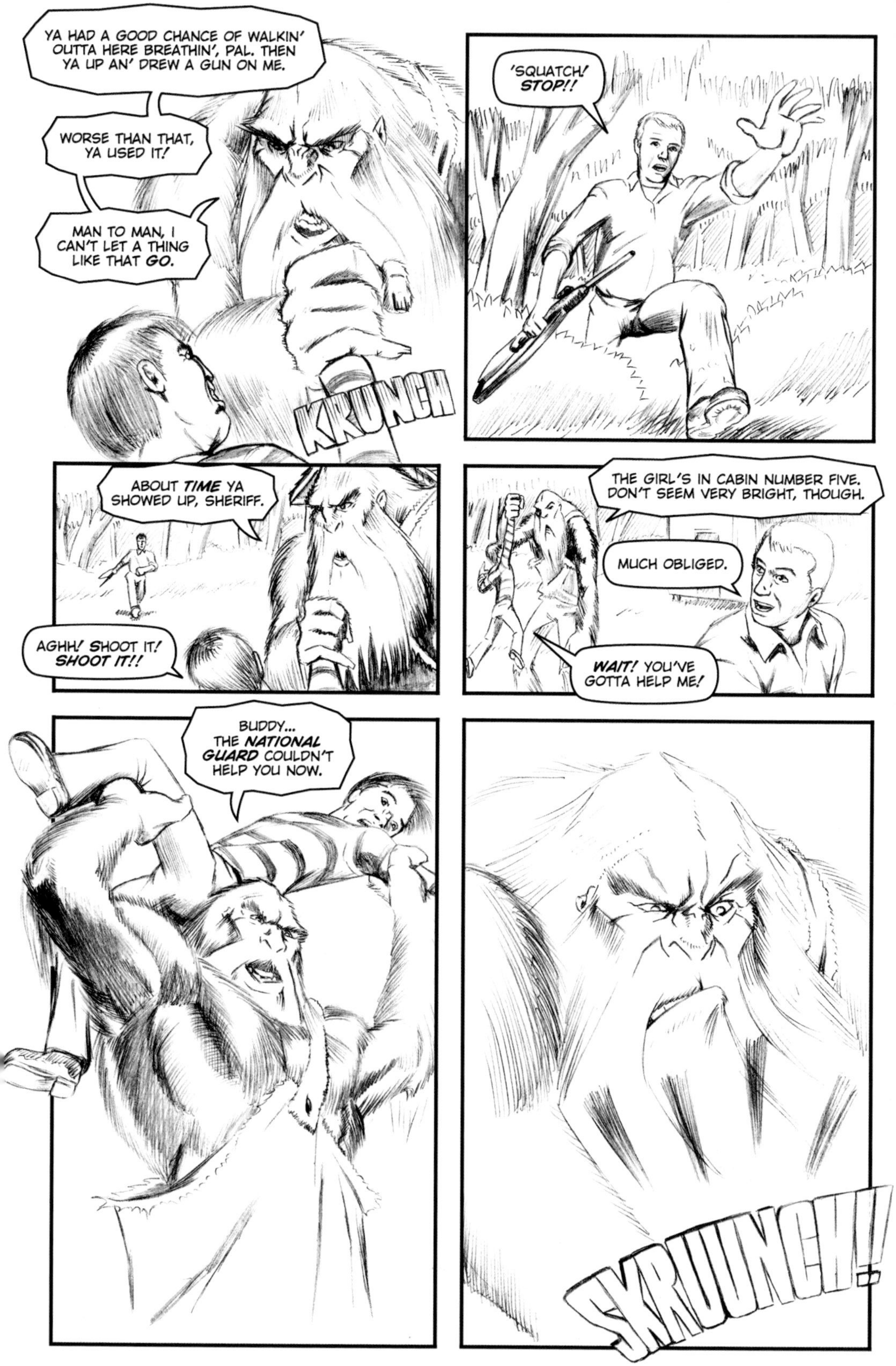
YA HAD A GOOD CHANCE OF WALKIN' OUTTA HERE BREATHIN', PAL. THEN YA UP AN' DREW A GUN ON ME.
WORSE THAN THAT, YA USED IT!
MAN TO MAN, I CAN'T LET A THING LIKE THAT GO.
KRUNCH
'SQUATCH! STOP!!
ABOUT TIME YA SHOWED UP, SHERIFF.
AGHH! SHOOT IT! SHOOT IT!!
THE GIRL'S IN CABIN NUMBER FIVE. DON'T SEEM VERY BRIGHT, THOUGH.
MUCH OBLIGED.
WAIT! YOU'VE GOTTA HELP ME!
BUDDY... THE NATIONAL GUARD COULDN'T HELP YOU NOW.
SKRUUNCH!!

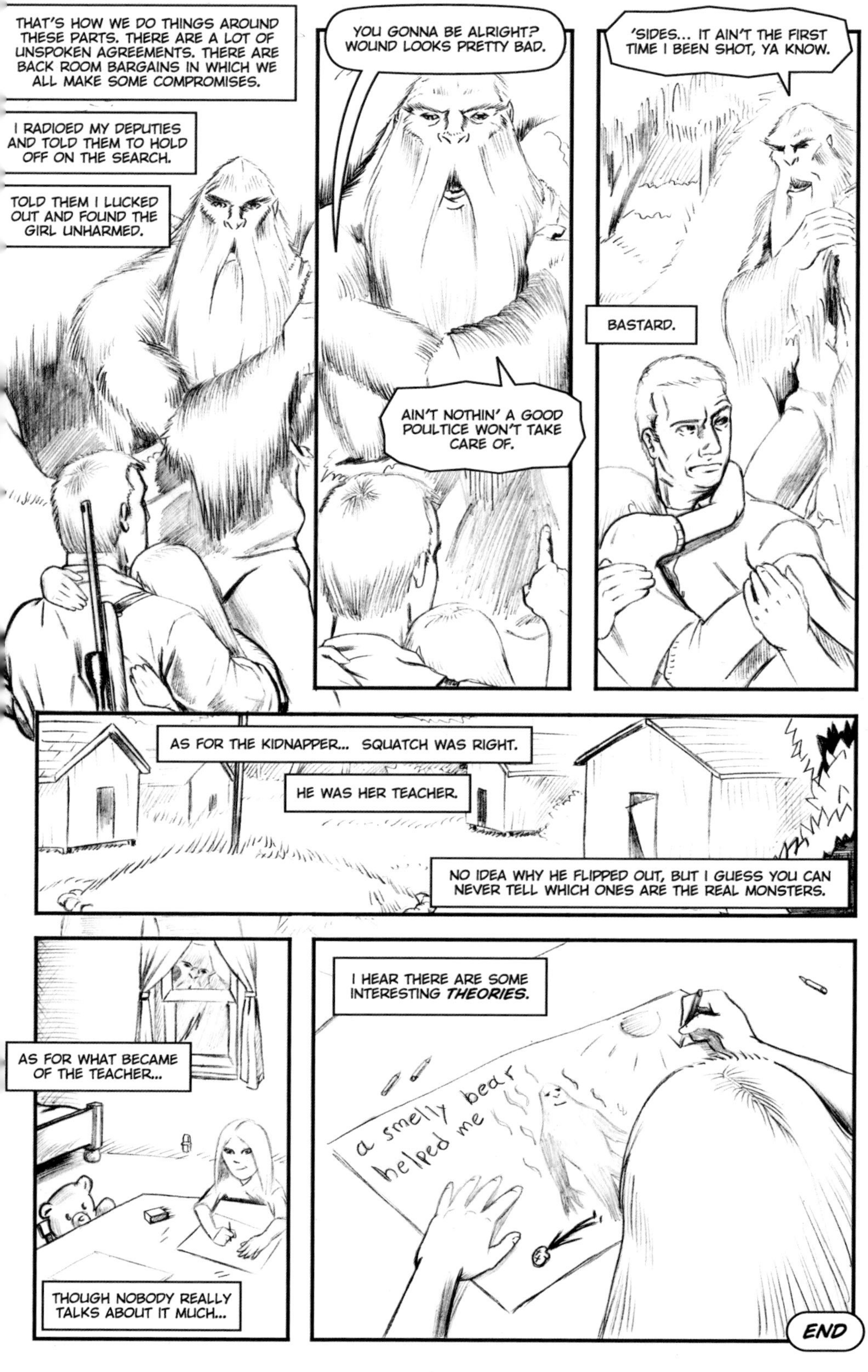
THAT'S HOW WE DO THINGS AROUND THESE PARTS. THERE ARE A LOT OF UNSPOKEN AGREEMENTS. THERE ARE BACK ROOM BARGAINS IN WHICH WE ALL MAKE SOME COMPROMISES.
I RADIOED MY DEPUTIES AND TOLD THEM TO HOLD OFF ON THE SEARCH.
TOLD THEM I LUCKED OUT AND FOUND THE GIRL UNHARMED.
YOU GONNA BE ALRIGHT? WOUND LOOKS PRETTY BAD.
AIN'T NOTHIN' A GOOD POULTICE WON'T TAKE CARE OF.
'SIDES... IT AIN'T THE FIRST TIME I BEEN SHOT, YA KNOW.
BASTARD.
AS FOR THE KIDNAPPER... SQUATCH WAS RIGHT.
HE WAS HER TEACHER.
NO IDEA WHY HE FLIPPED OUT, BUT I GUESS YOU CAN NEVER TELL WHICH ONES ARE THE REAL MONSTERS.
AS FOR WHAT BECAME OF THE TEACHER...
THOUGH NOBODY REALLY TALKS ABOUT IT MUCH...
I HEAR THERE ARE SOME INTERESTING THEORIES.
a smelly bear helped me
END

SMALLFOOT

WRITTEN & ILLUSTRATED BY OTIS FRAMPTON

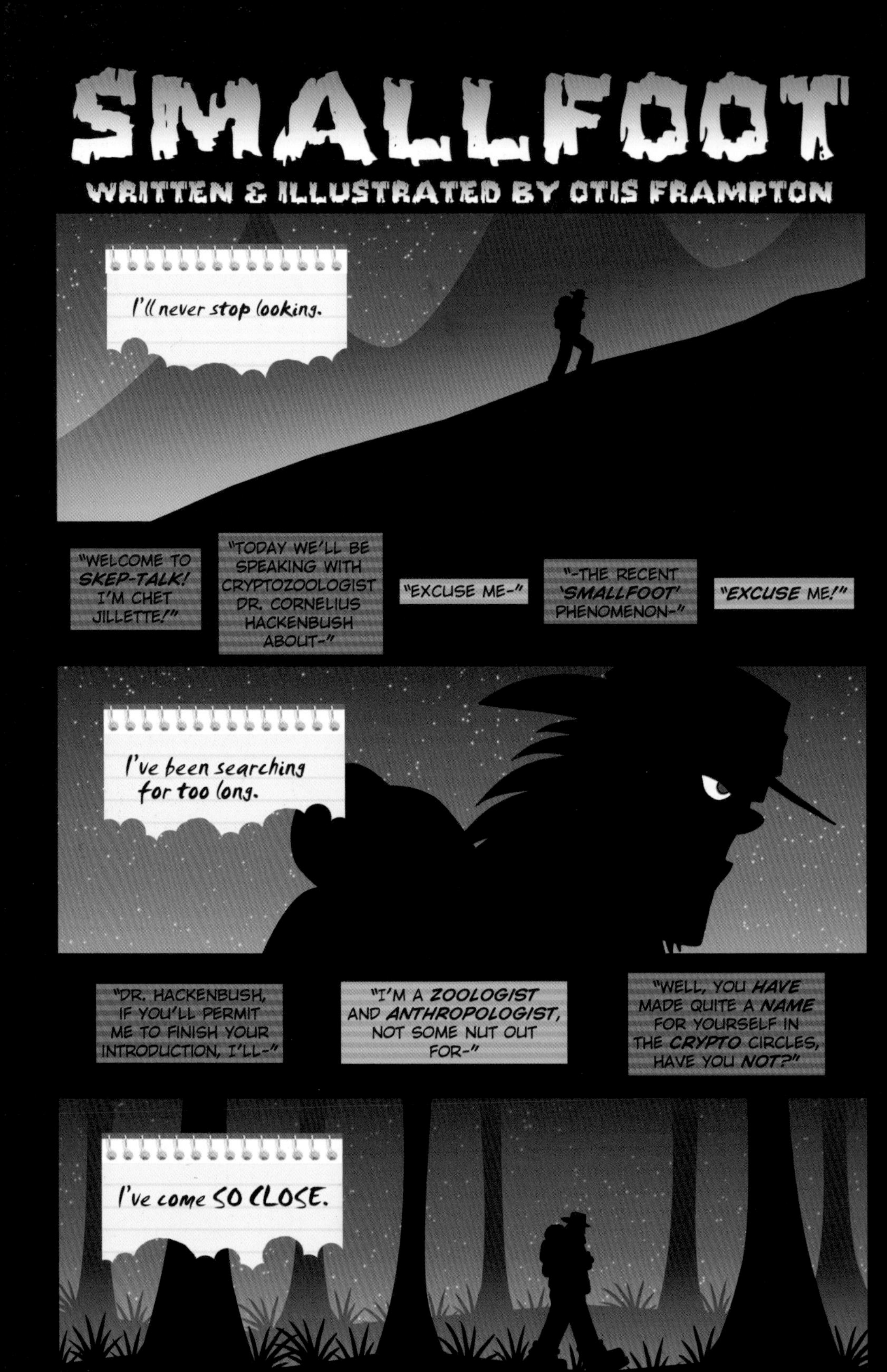

I'll never stop looking.
"WELCOME TO SKEP-TALK! I'M CHET JILLETTE!"
"TODAY WE'LL BE SPEAKING WITH CRYPTOZOOLOGIST DR. CORNELIUS HACKENBUSH ABOUT-"
"EXCUSE ME-"
"-THE RECENT 'SMALLFOOT' PHENOMENON-"
"EXCUSE ME!"
I've been searching for too long.
"DR. HACKENBUSH, IF YOU'LL PERMIT ME TO FINISH YOUR INTRODUCTION, I'LL-"
"I'M A ZOOLOGIST AND ANTHROPOLOGIST, NOT SOME NUT OUT FOR-"
"WELL, YOU HAVE MADE QUITE A NAME FOR YOURSELF IN THE CRYPTO CIRCLES, HAVE YOU NOT?"
I've come SO CLOSE.

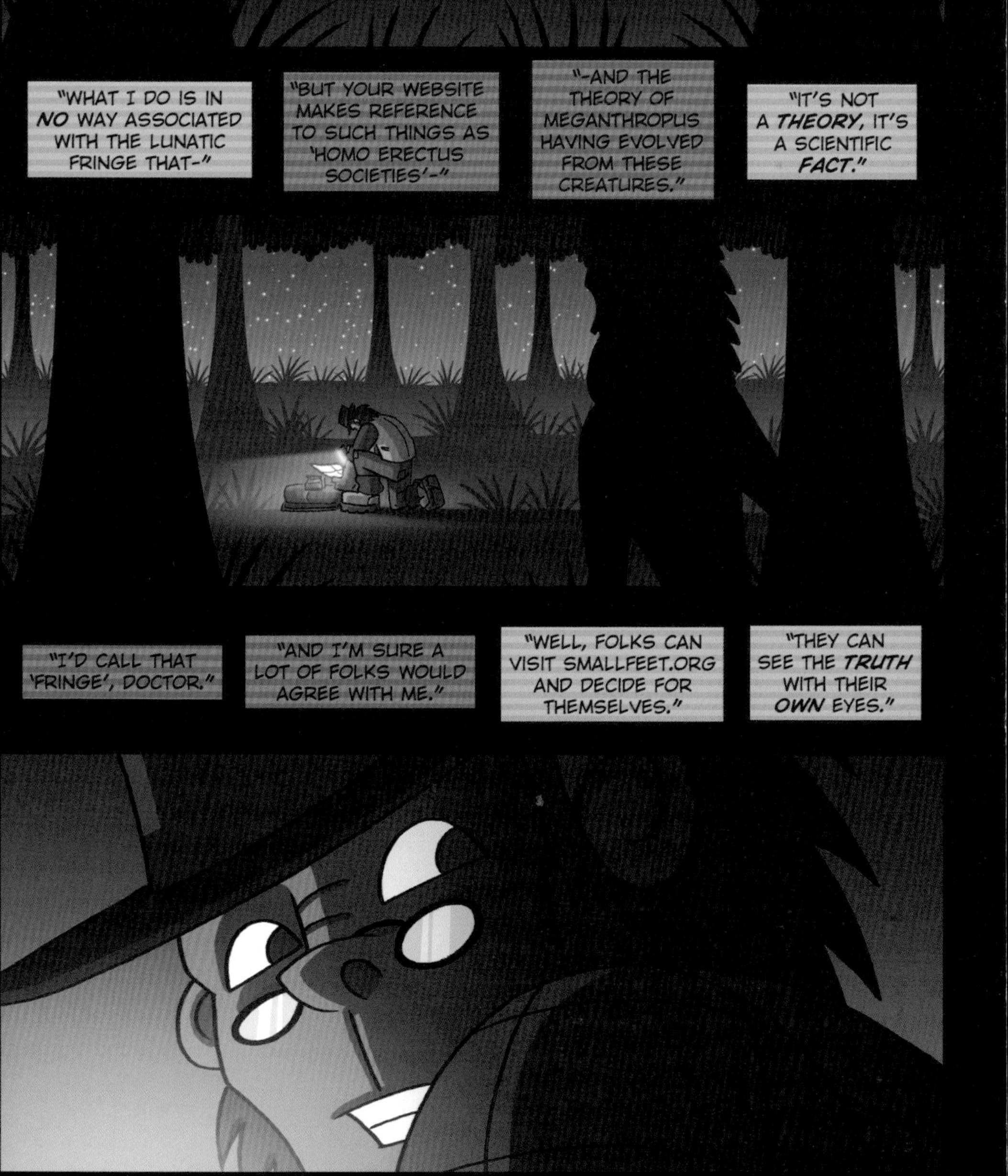
"WHAT I DO IS IN **NO** WAY ASSOCIATED WITH THE LUNATIC FRINGE THAT-"
"BUT YOUR WEBSITE MAKES REFERENCE TO SUCH THINGS AS 'HOMO ERECTUS SOCIETIES'-"
"-AND THE THEORY OF MEGANTHROPUS HAVING EVOLVED FROM THESE CREATURES."
"IT'S NOT A **THEORY**, IT'S A SCIENTIFIC **FACT**."
"I'D CALL THAT 'FRINGE', DOCTOR."
"AND I'M SURE A LOT OF FOLKS WOULD AGREE WITH ME."
"WELL, FOLKS CAN VISIT SMALLFEET.ORG AND DECIDE FOR THEMSELVES."
"THEY CAN SEE THE **TRUTH** WITH THEIR **OWN** EYES."

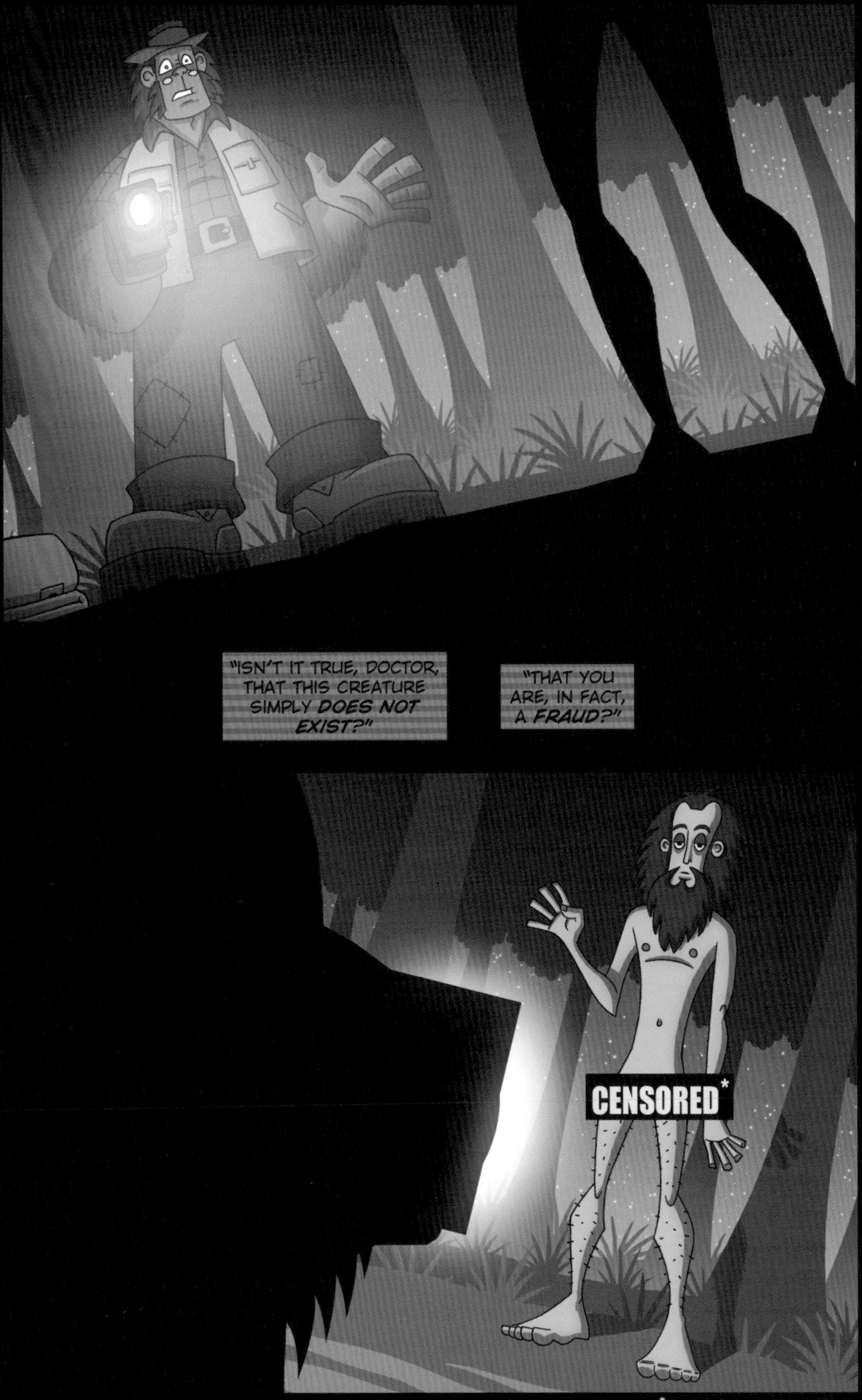
"ISN'T IT TRUE, DOCTOR, THAT THIS CREATURE SIMPLY DOES NOT EXIST?"
"THAT YOU ARE, IN FACT, A FRAUD?"
CENSORED*

* By order of the editor.

"FRAUD?"

"HOW *DARE* YOU, SIR!"

"WHERE IS THE EVIDENCE, DOCTOR?"

*"HOW **DARE**-"*

"WHERE IS THE *PROOF?!*"

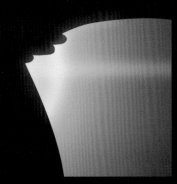

"I HAVE REAMS OF EMPIRICAL-"
"A BLURRY PHOTO?"
"-AND PRACTICAL EVIDENCE, AND-"
"A MOLD OF WHAT APPEARS TO BE A CHILD'S FOOT?"
"THEY EXIST, I TELL YOU!"
"THANK YOU, DOCTOR."
"THEY EXIST!"
"AND WE'LL BE RIGHT BACK AFTER THESE MESSAGES!"
I'll never stop looking.
Never.

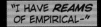

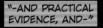

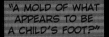

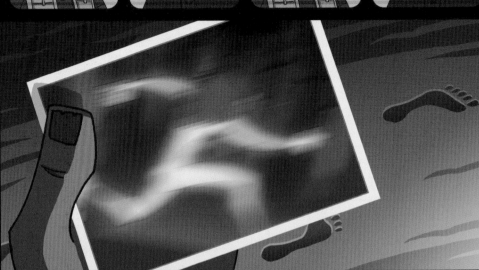

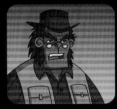

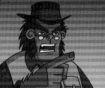

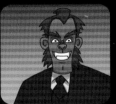

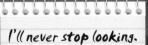

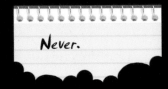

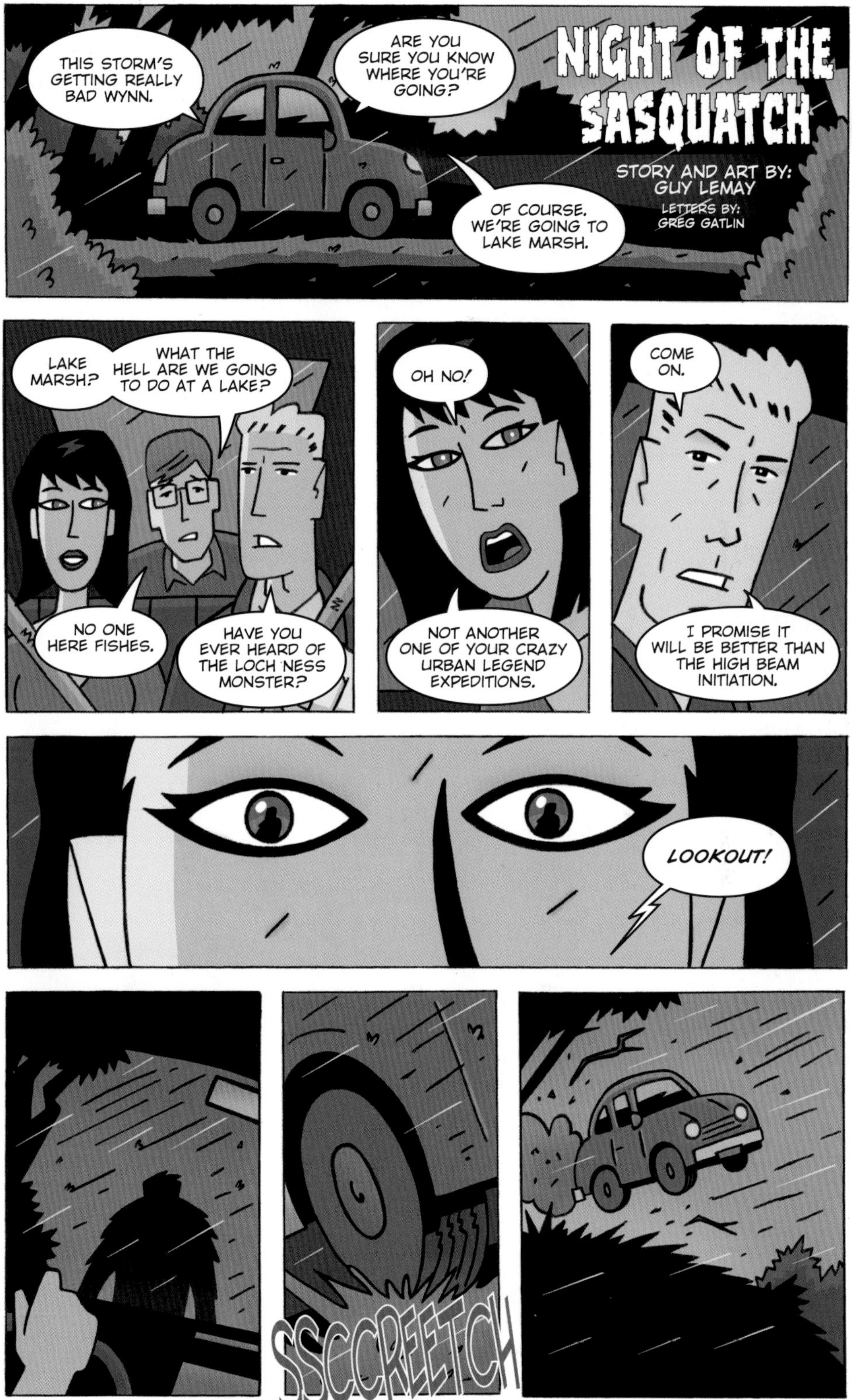
NIGHT OF THE SASQUATCH
STORY AND ART BY: GUY LEMAY
LETTERS BY: GREG GATLIN
THIS STORM'S GETTING REALLY BAD WYNN.
ARE YOU SURE YOU KNOW WHERE YOU'RE GOING?
OF COURSE. WE'RE GOING TO LAKE MARSH.
LAKE MARSH?
WHAT THE HELL ARE WE GOING TO DO AT A LAKE?
NO ONE HERE FISHES.
HAVE YOU EVER HEARD OF THE LOCH NESS MONSTER?
OH NO!
NOT ANOTHER ONE OF YOUR CRAZY URBAN LEGEND EXPEDITIONS.
COME ON.
I PROMISE IT WILL BE BETTER THAN THE HIGH BEAM INITIATION.
LOOKOUT!
SSCCREETCH

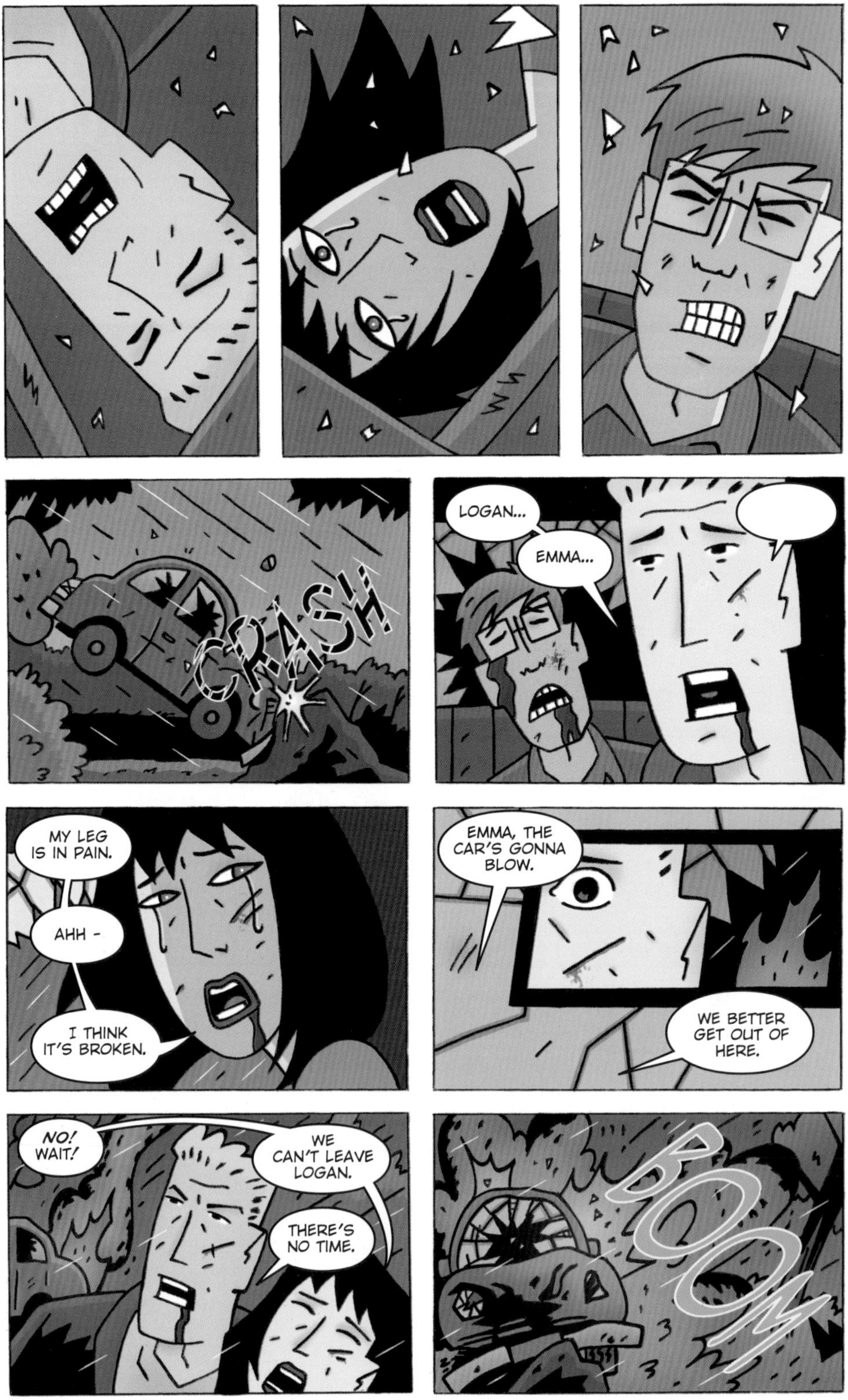
CRASH
LOGAN...
EMMA...
MY LEG IS IN PAIN.
AHH -
I THINK IT'S BROKEN.
EMMA, THE CAR'S GONNA BLOW.
WE BETTER GET OUT OF HERE.
NO! WAIT!
WE CAN'T LEAVE LOGAN.
THERE'S NO TIME.
BOOM

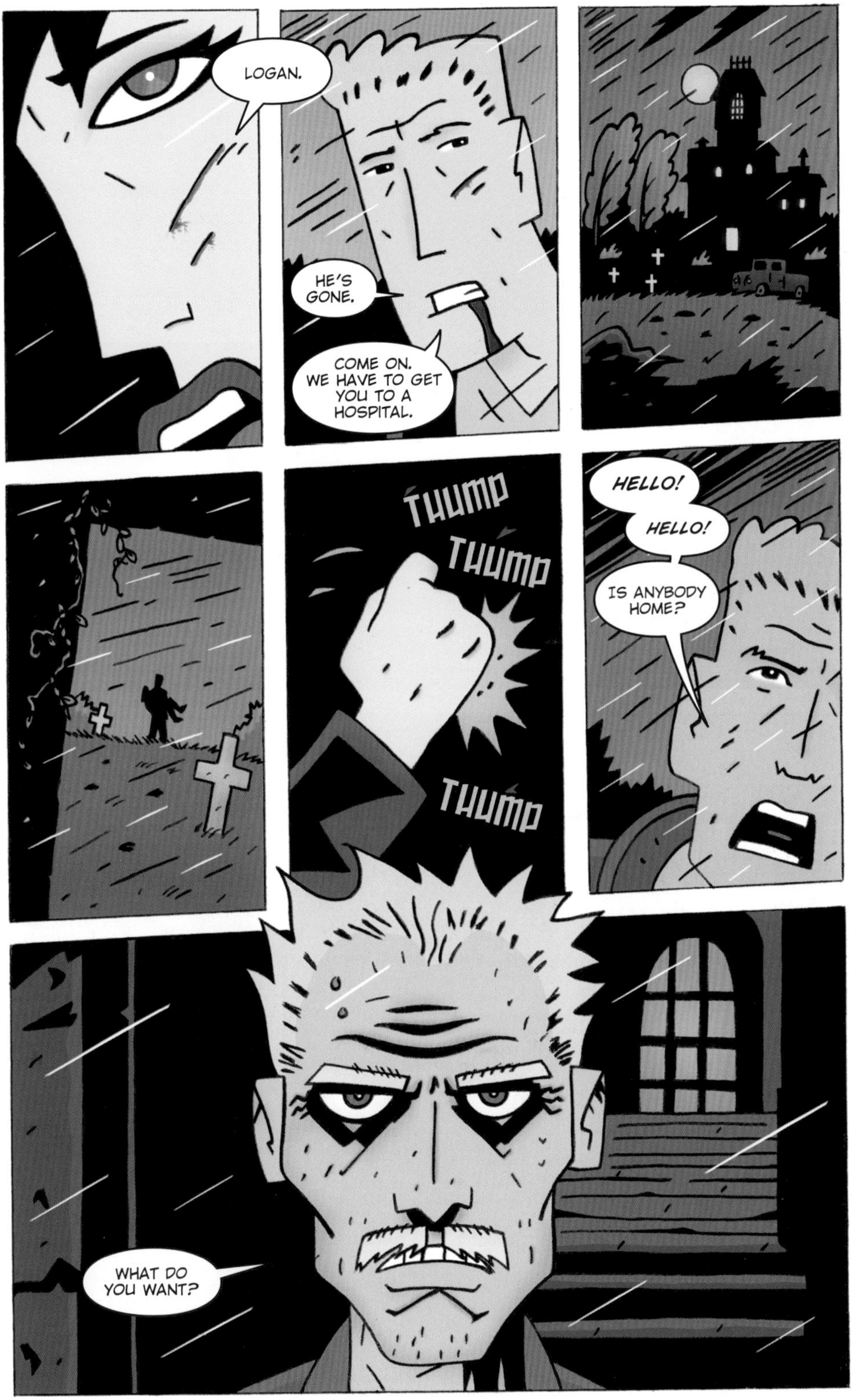
LOGAN.
HE'S GONE.
COME ON. WE HAVE TO GET YOU TO A HOSPITAL.
THUMP
THUMP
THUMP
HELLO!
HELLO!
IS ANYBODY HOME?
WHAT DO YOU WANT?

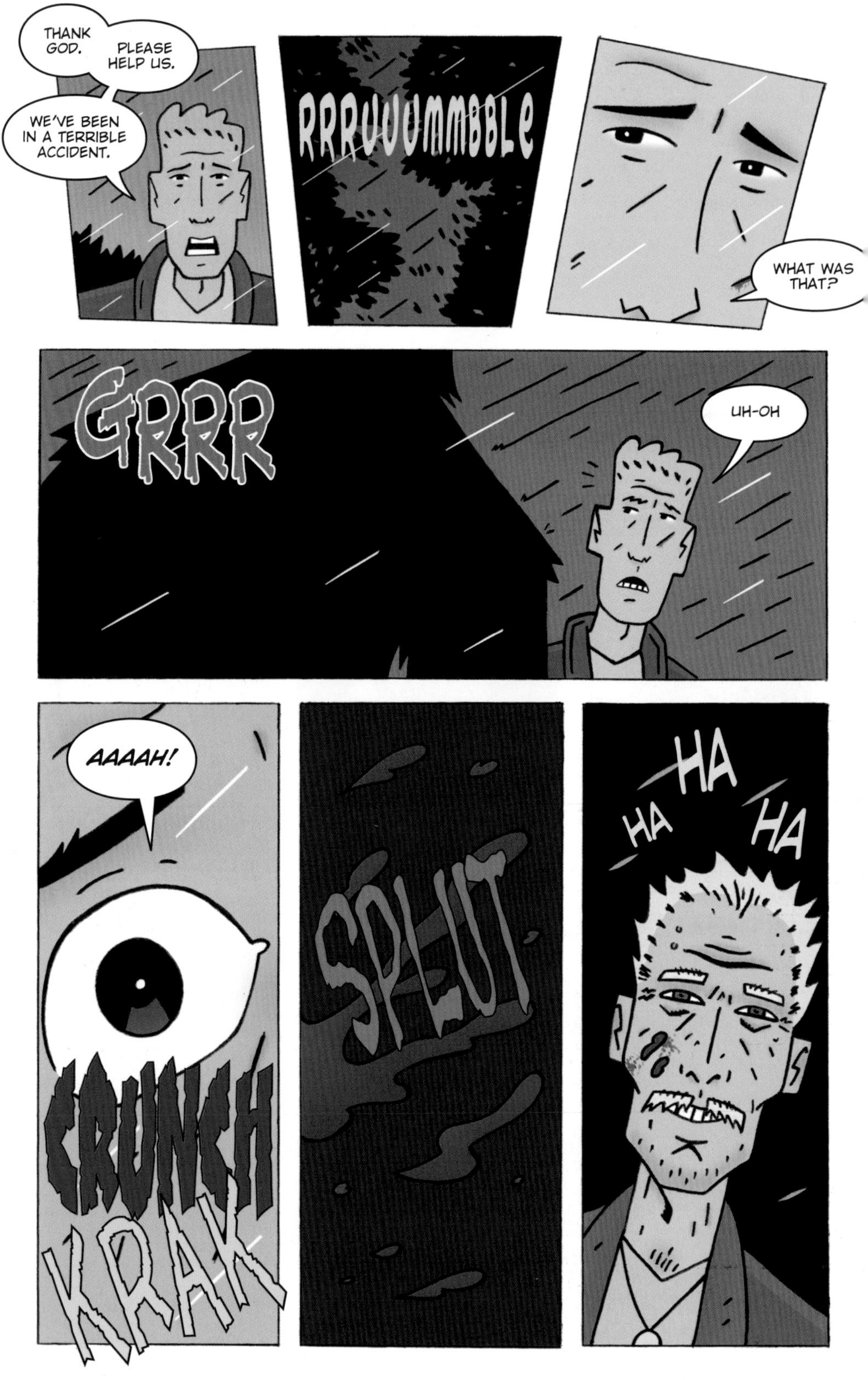
THANK GOD.
PLEASE HELP US.
WE'VE BEEN IN A TERRIBLE ACCIDENT.
RRRUUUMMBBLE
WHAT WAS THAT?
GRRR
UH-OH
AAAAH!
CRUNCH
KRAK
SPLUT
HA
HA
HA

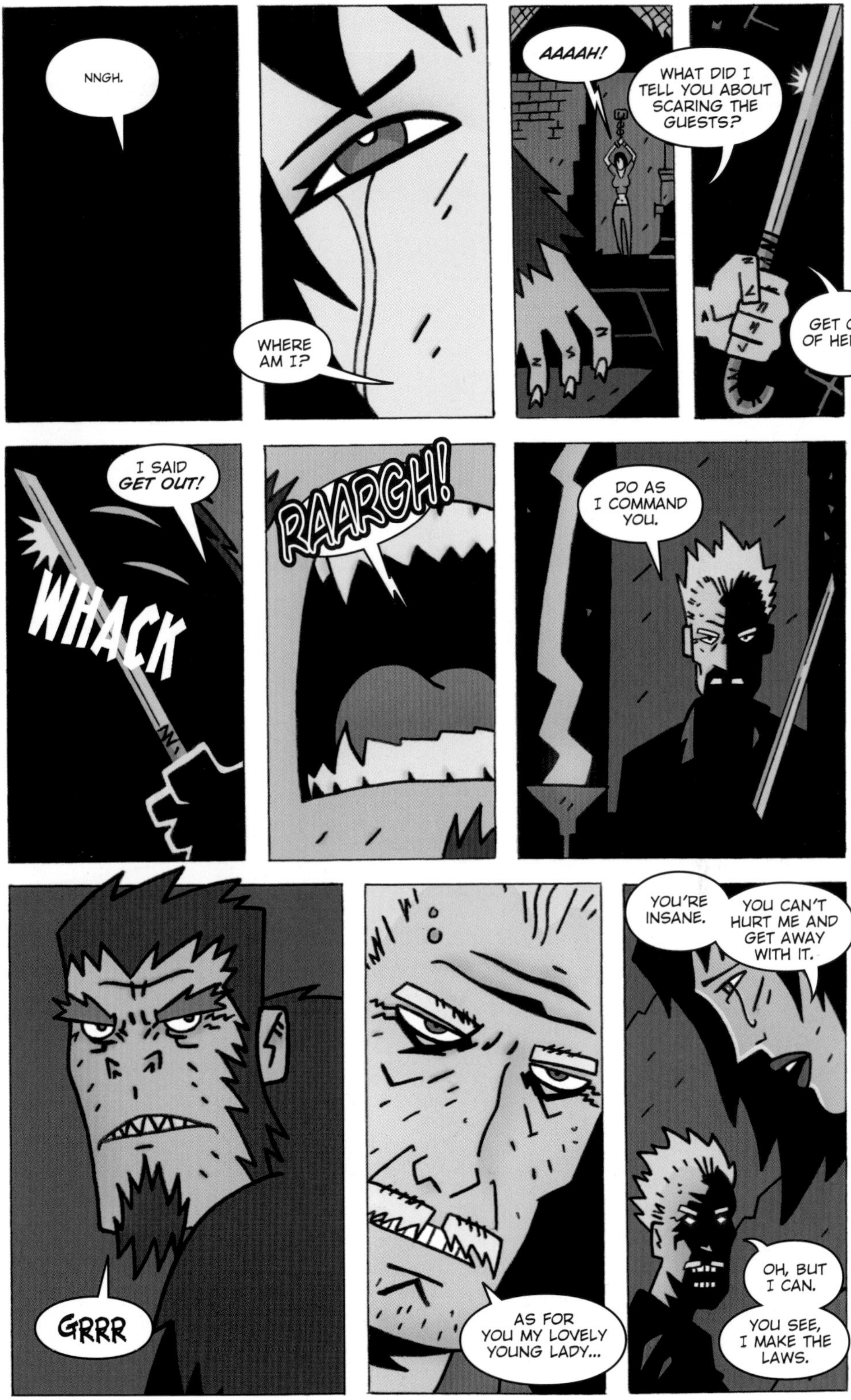
NNGH.
WHERE AM I?
AAAAH!
WHAT DID I TELL YOU ABOUT SCARING THE GUESTS?
GET OUT OF HERE!
I SAID GET OUT!
WHACK
RAARGH!
DO AS I COMMAND YOU.
GRRR
AS FOR YOU MY LOVELY YOUNG LADY...
YOU'RE INSANE.
YOU CAN'T HURT ME AND GET AWAY WITH IT.
OH, BUT I CAN.
YOU SEE, I MAKE THE LAWS.

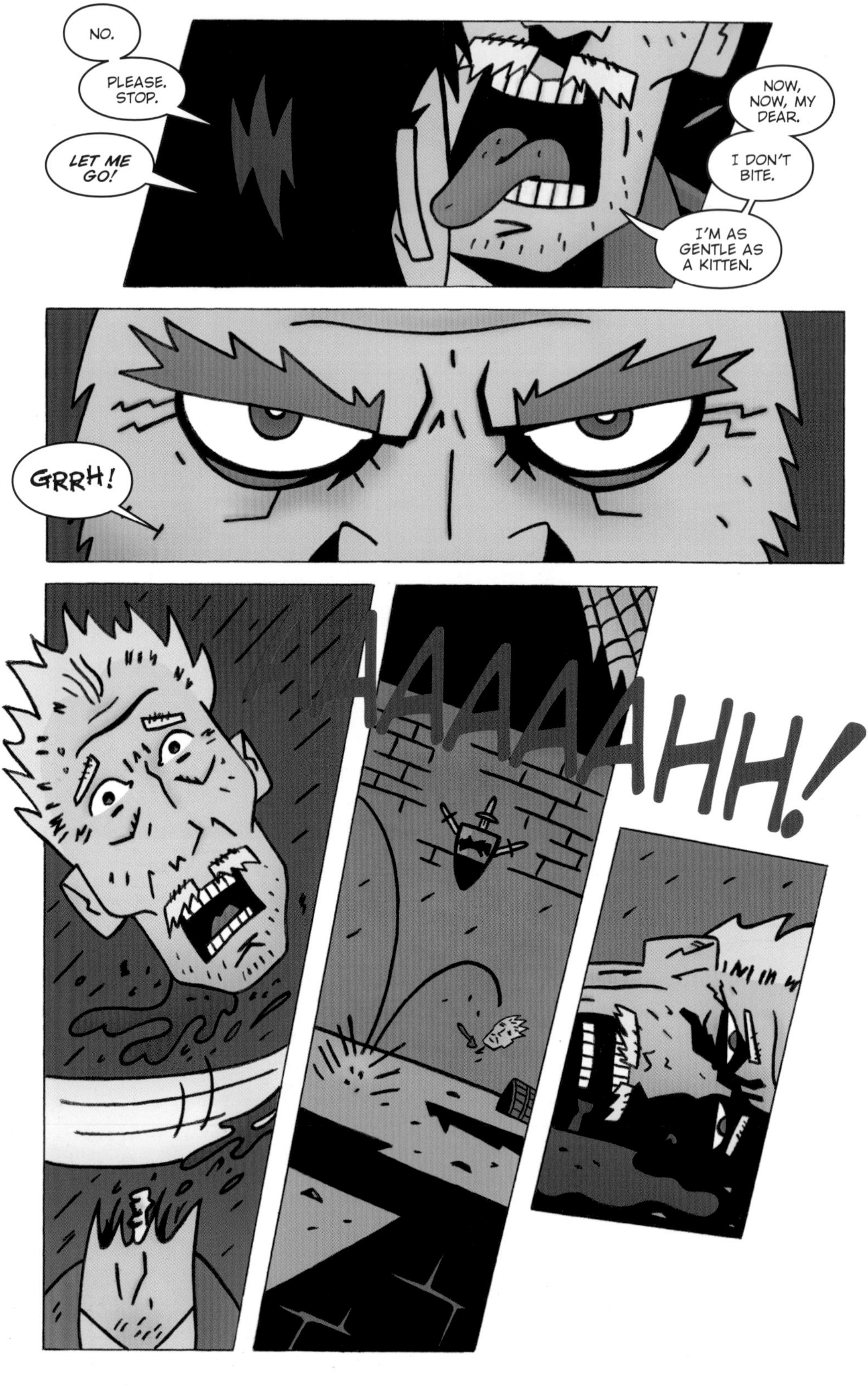
NO.
PLEASE. STOP.
LET ME GO!
NOW, NOW, MY DEAR.
I DON'T BITE.
I'M AS GENTLE AS A KITTEN.
GRRH!
AAAAAAAHH!

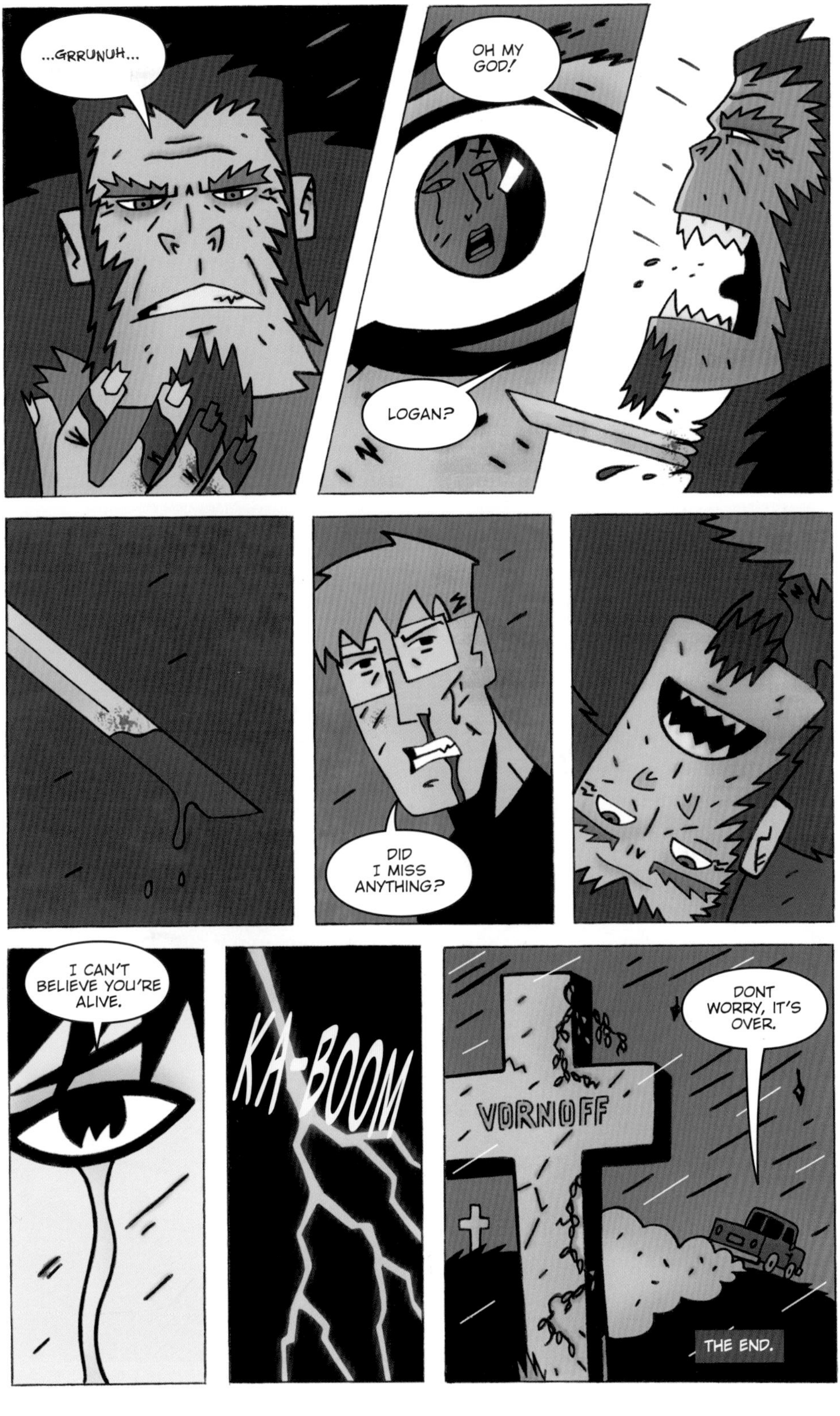
...GRRUNUH...
OH MY GOD!
LOGAN?
DID I MISS ANYTHING?
I CAN'T BELIEVE YOU'RE ALIVE.
KA-BOOM
VORNOFF
DONT WORRY, IT'S OVER.
THE END.

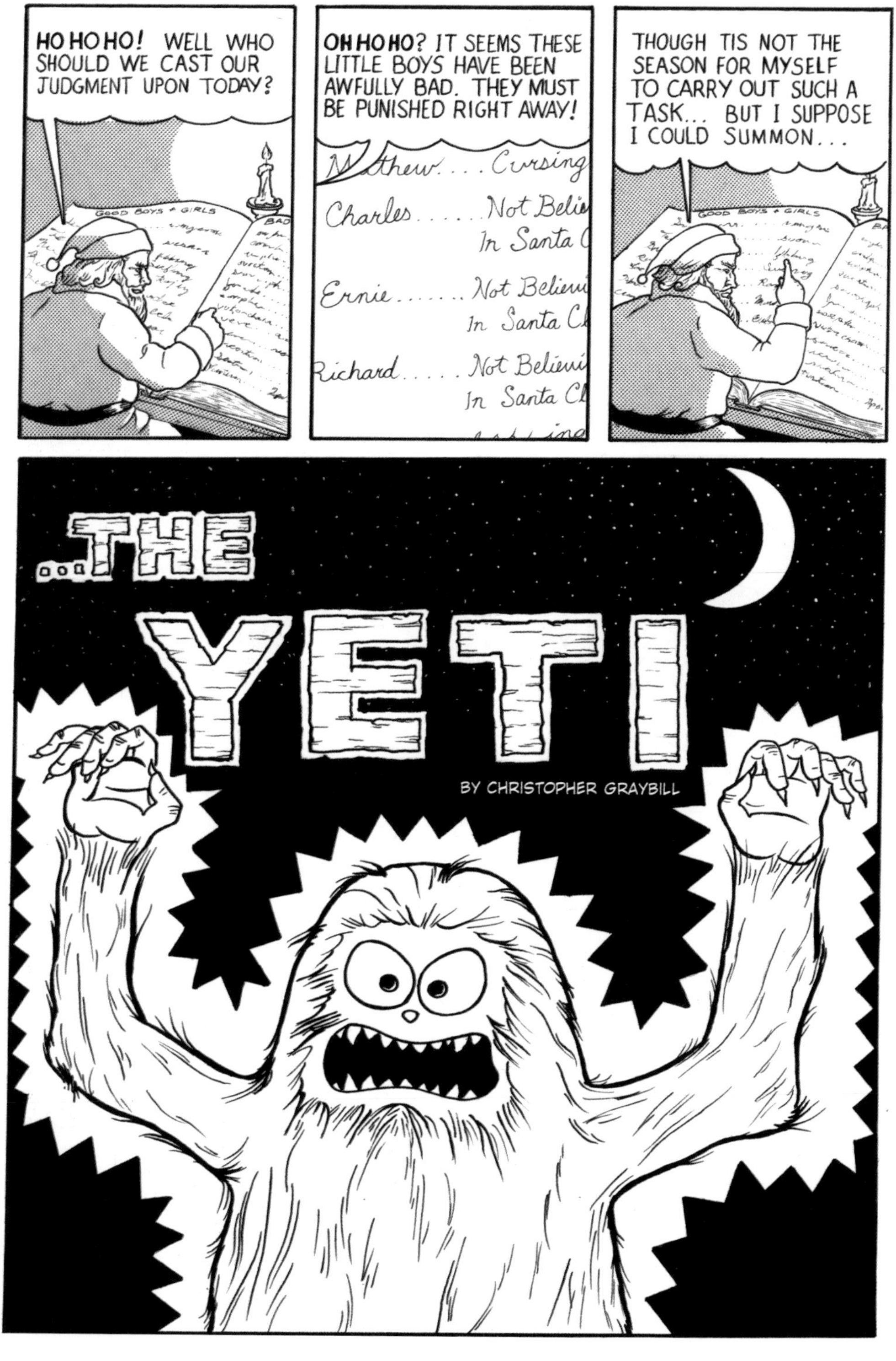
HO HO HO! WELL WHO SHOULD WE CAST OUR JUDGMENT UPON TODAY?
GOOD BOYS + GIRLS
BAD
OH HO HO? IT SEEMS THESE LITTLE BOYS HAVE BEEN AWFULLY BAD. THEY MUST BE PUNISHED RIGHT AWAY!
Charles
Ernie
Richard
THOUGH TIS NOT THE SEASON FOR MYSELF TO CARRY OUT SUCH A TASK... BUT I SUPPOSE I COULD SUMMON...
...THE
YETI
BY CHRISTOPHER GRAYBILL

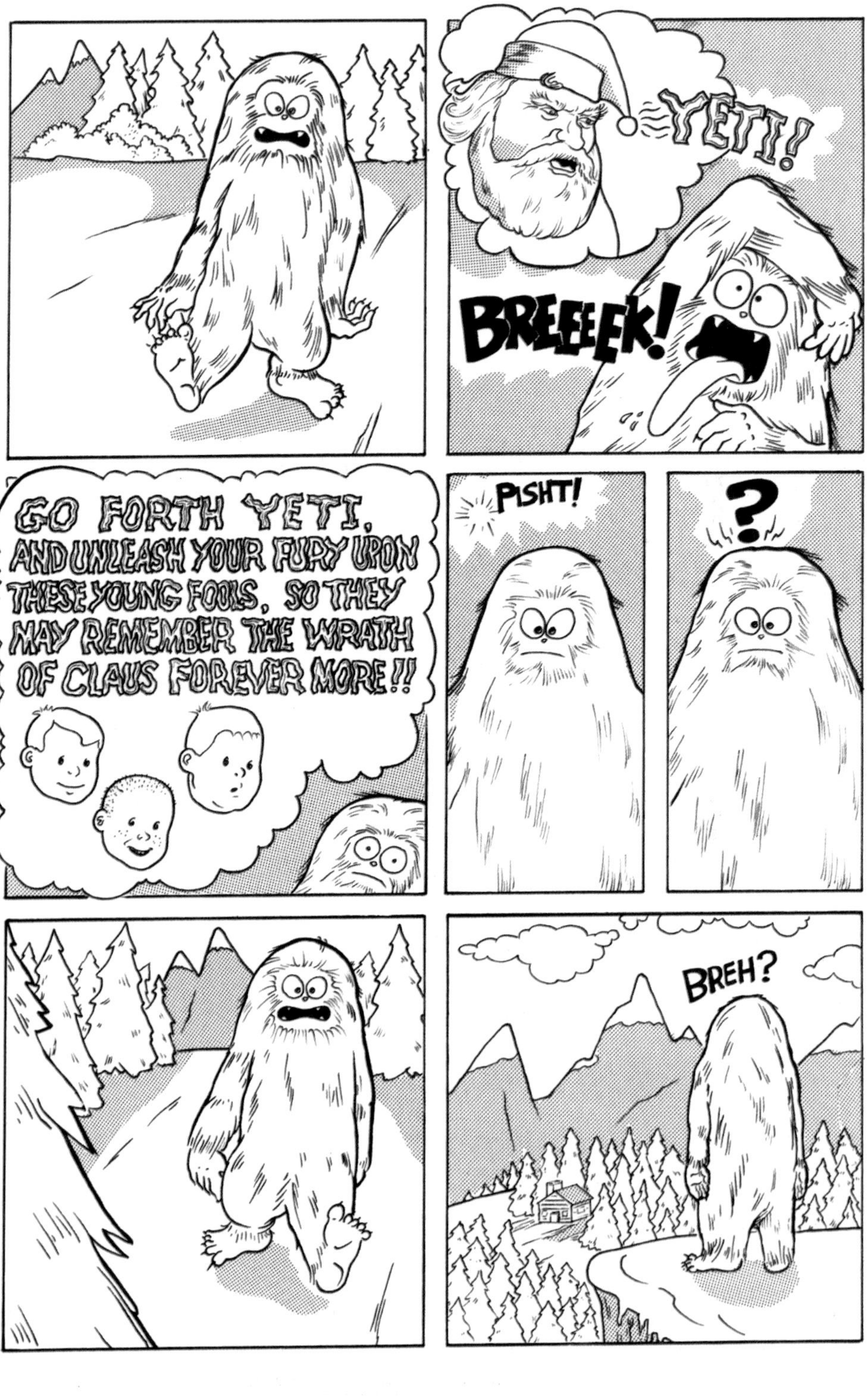
YETI!
BREEEEK!
GO FORTH YETI,
AND UNLEASH YOUR FURY UPON THESE YOUNG FOOLS, SO THEY MAY REMEMBER THE WRATH OF CLAUS FOREVER MORE!!
PISHT!
?
BREH?

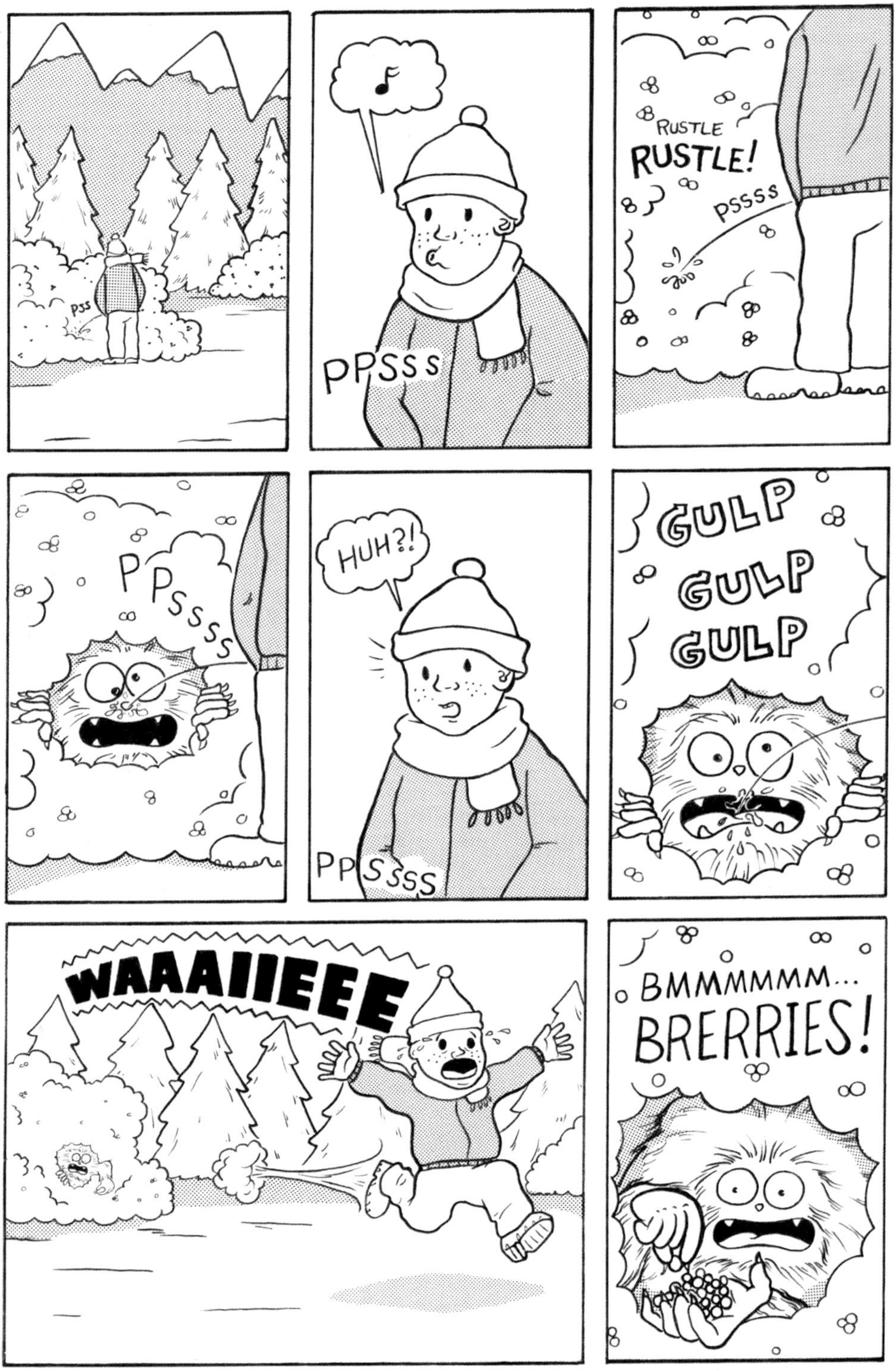
PSS
PPSSS
RUSTLE
RUSTLE!
PSSSS
PPSSSSS
HUH?!
PPSSSS
GULP
GULP
GULP
WAAAIIEEE
BMMMMMM...
BRERRIES!

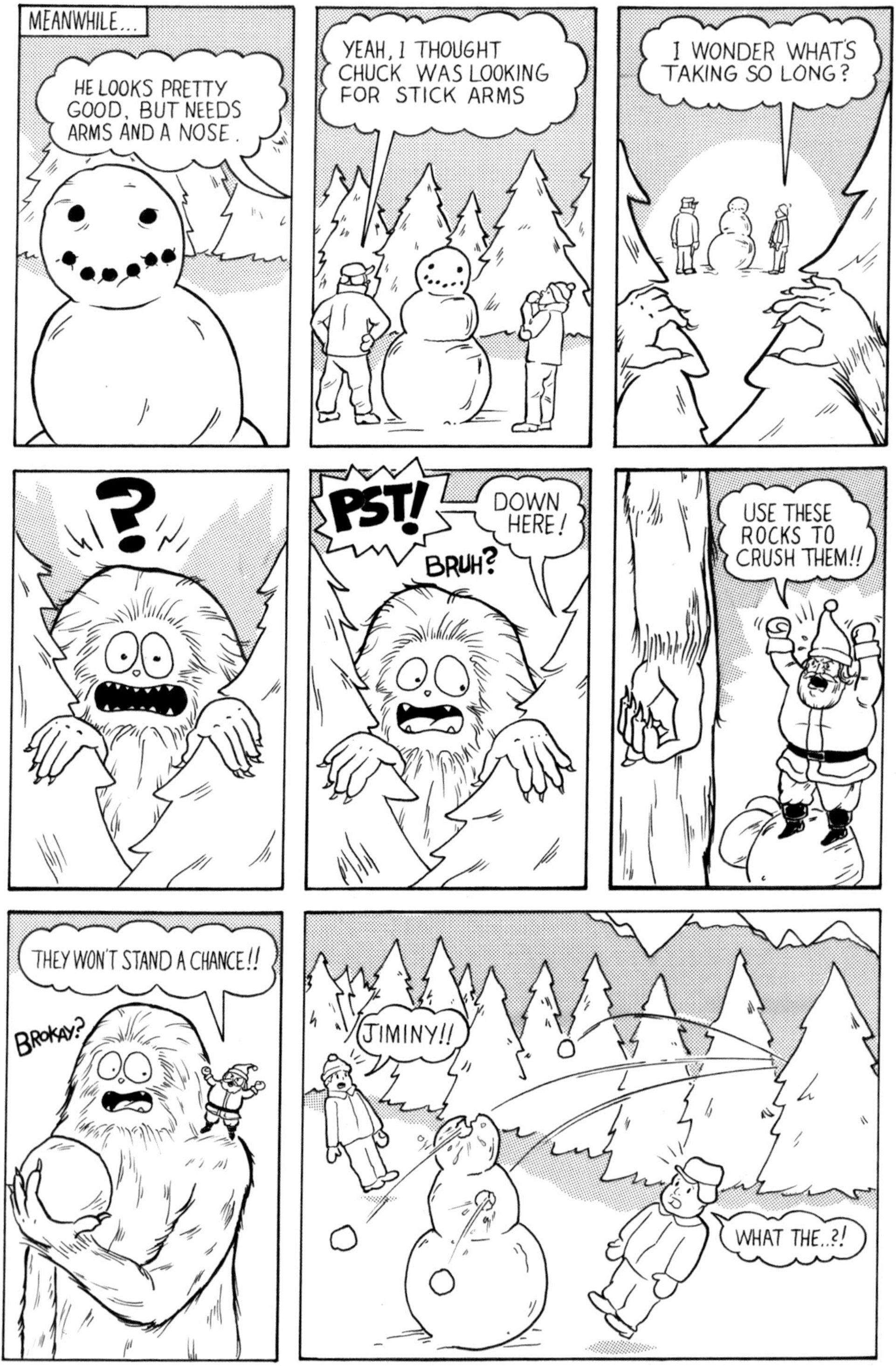

MEANWHILE...
HE LOOKS PRETTY GOOD, BUT NEEDS ARMS AND A NOSE.
YEAH, I THOUGHT CHUCK WAS LOOKING FOR STICK ARMS
I WONDER WHAT'S TAKING SO LONG?
?
PST!
DOWN HERE!
BRUH?
USE THESE ROCKS TO CRUSH THEM!!
THEY WON'T STAND A CHANCE!!
BROKAY?
JIMINY!!
WHAT THE..?!

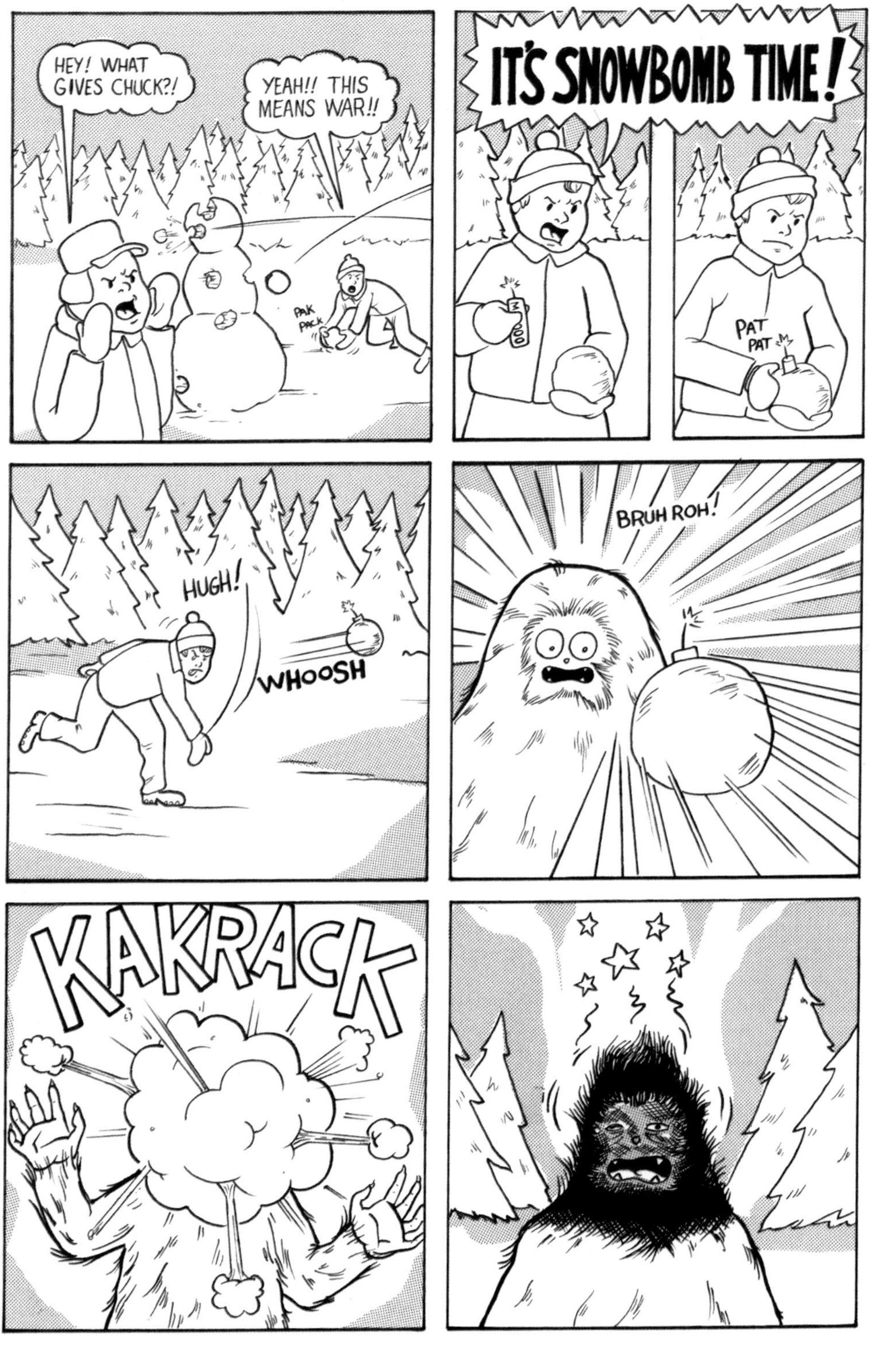
HEY! WHAT GIVES CHUCK?!
YEAH!! THIS MEANS WAR!!
PAK PACK
IT'S SNOWBOMB TIME!
PAT PAT
HUGH!
WHOOSH
BRUH ROH!
KAKRACK

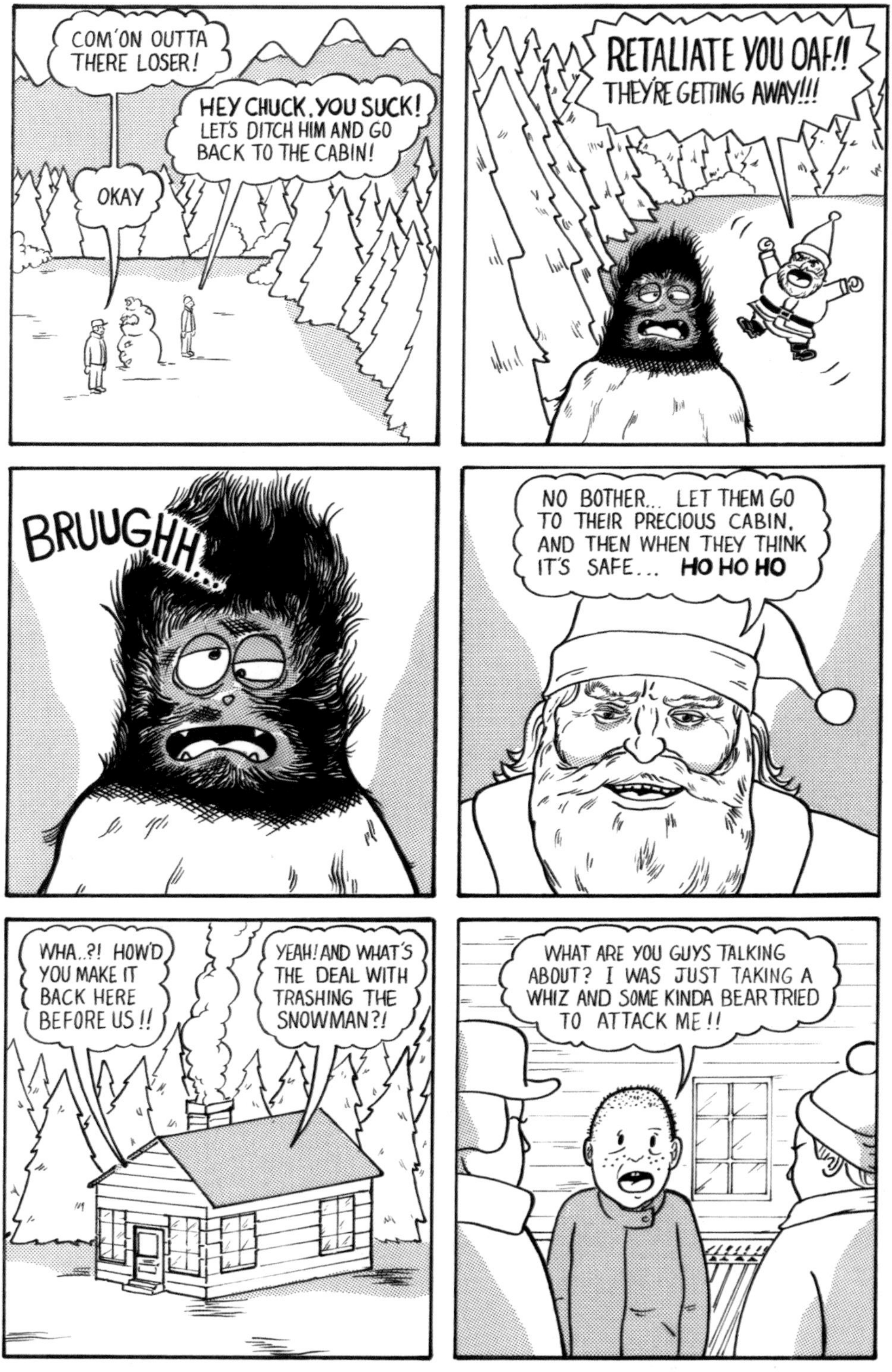
COM'ON OUTTA THERE LOSER!
HEY CHUCK, YOU SUCK! LET'S DITCH HIM AND GO BACK TO THE CABIN!
OKAY
RETALIATE YOU OAF!! THEY'RE GETTING AWAY!!!
BRUUGHH...
NO BOTHER... LET THEM GO TO THEIR PRECIOUS CABIN, AND THEN WHEN THEY THINK IT'S SAFE... HO HO HO
WHA..?! HOW'D YOU MAKE IT BACK HERE BEFORE US!!
YEAH! AND WHAT'S THE DEAL WITH TRASHING THE SNOWMAN?!
WHAT ARE YOU GUYS TALKING ABOUT? I WAS JUST TAKING A WHIZ AND SOME KINDA BEAR TRIED TO ATTACK ME!!

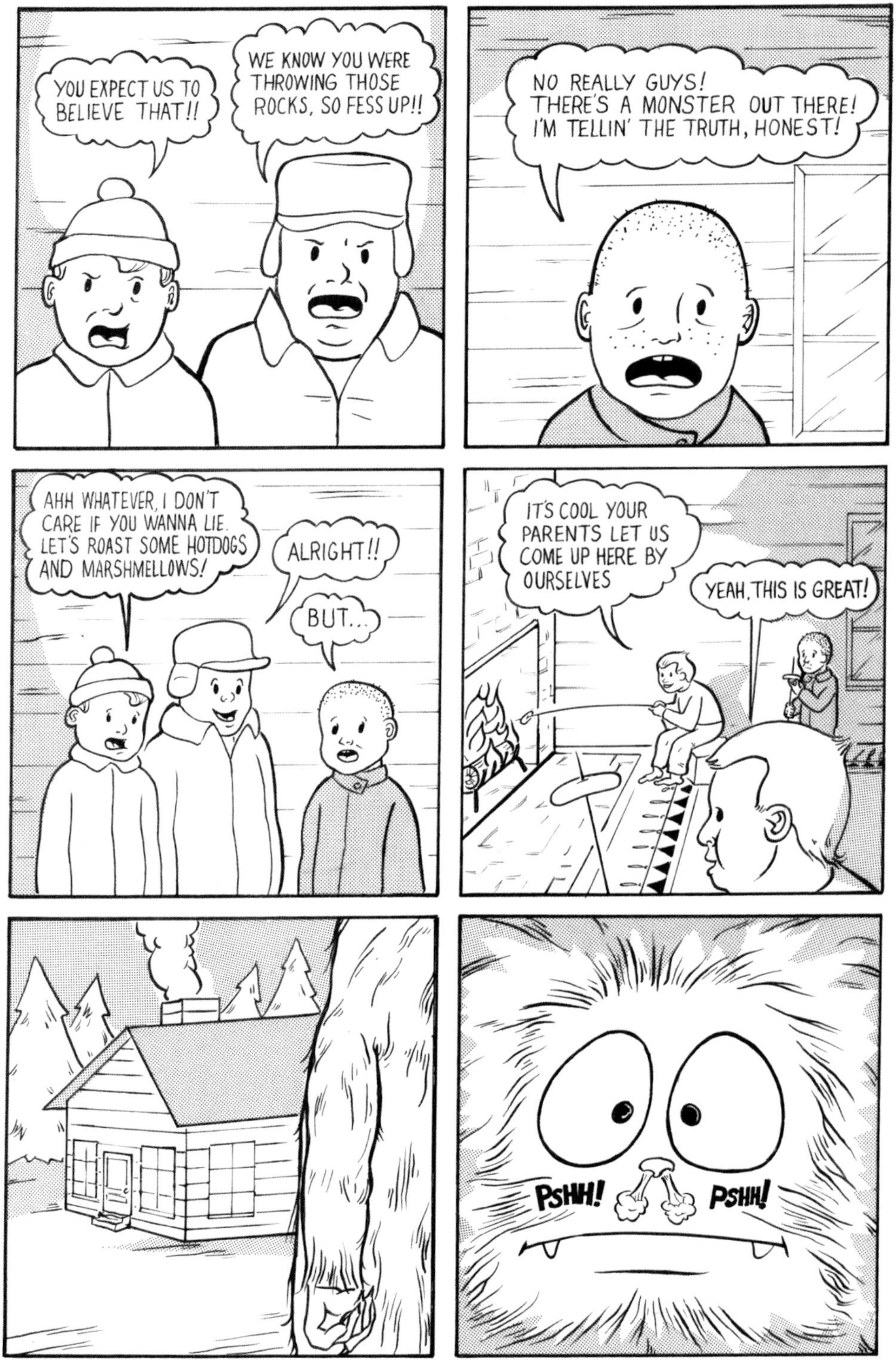
YOU EXPECT US TO BELIEVE THAT!!
WE KNOW YOU WERE THROWING THOSE ROCKS, SO FESS UP!!
NO REALLY GUYS! THERE'S A MONSTER OUT THERE! I'M TELLIN' THE TRUTH, HONEST!
AHH WHATEVER, I DON'T CARE IF YOU WANNA LIE. LET'S ROAST SOME HOTDOGS AND MARSHMELLOWS!
ALRIGHT!!
BUT...
IT'S COOL YOUR PARENTS LET US COME UP HERE BY OURSELVES
YEAH, THIS IS GREAT!
PSHH!
PSHH!

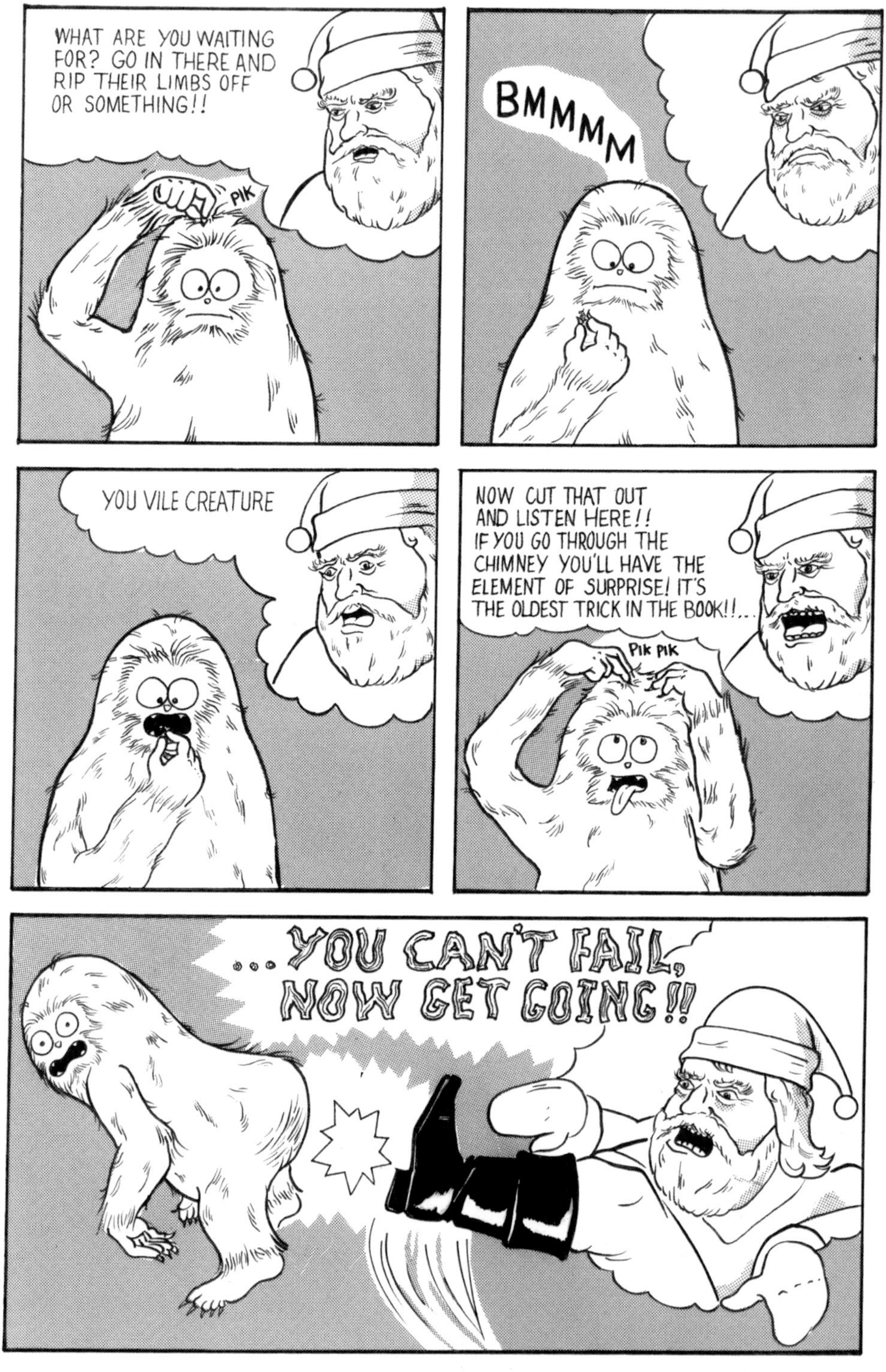
WHAT ARE YOU WAITING FOR? GO IN THERE AND RIP THEIR LIMBS OFF OR SOMETHING!!
PIK
BMMMM
YOU VILE CREATURE
NOW CUT THAT OUT AND LISTEN HERE!! IF YOU GO THROUGH THE CHIMNEY YOU'LL HAVE THE ELEMENT OF SURPRISE! IT'S THE OLDEST TRICK IN THE BOOK!!...
PIK PIK
...YOU CAN'T FAIL, NOW GET GOING!!

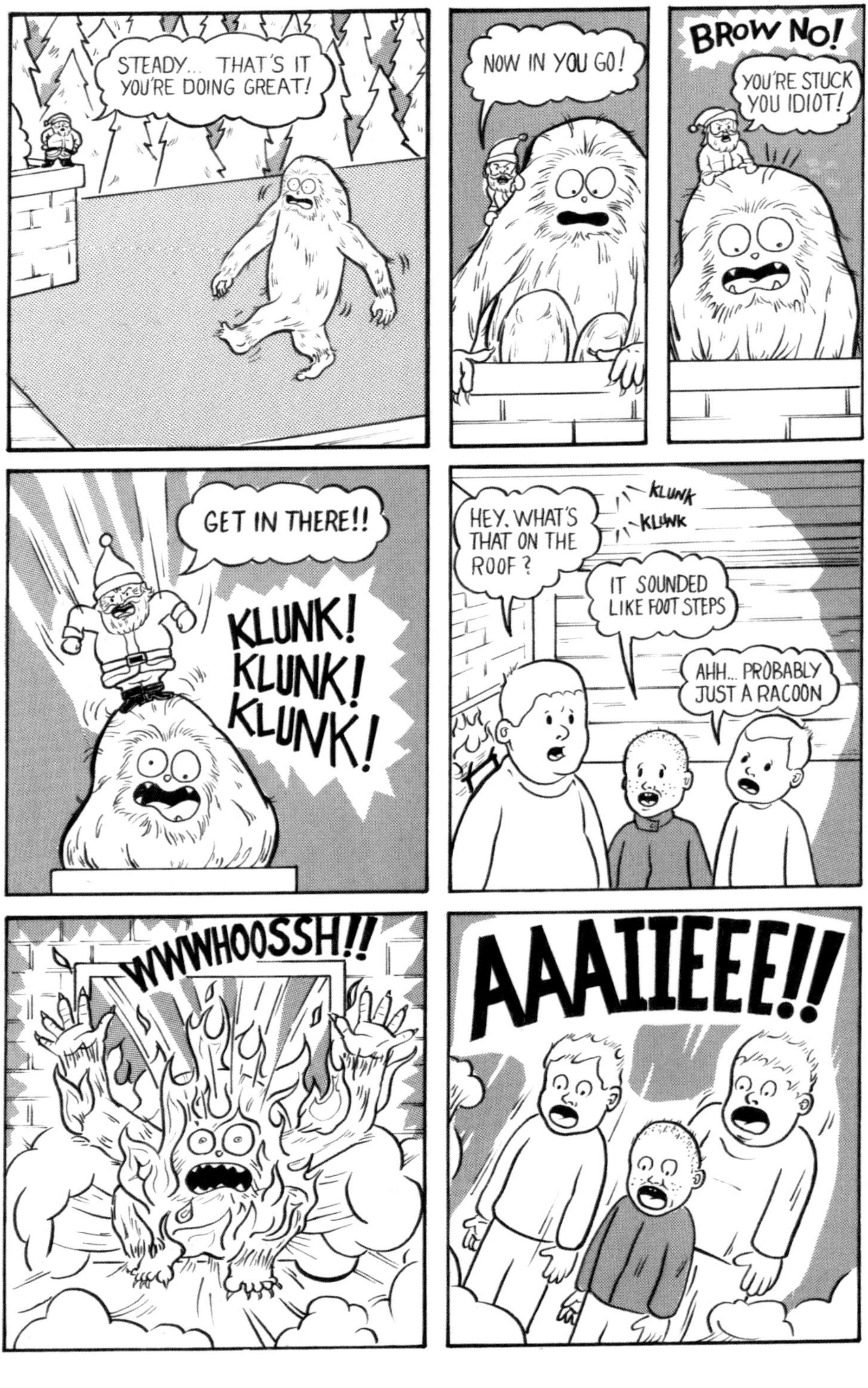
STEADY... THAT'S IT YOU'RE DOING GREAT!
NOW IN YOU GO!
BROW NO!
YOU'RE STUCK YOU IDIOT!
GET IN THERE!!
KLUNK! KLUNK! KLUNK!
KLUNK
KLUNK
HEY, WHAT'S THAT ON THE ROOF?
IT SOUNDED LIKE FOOT STEPS
AHH... PROBABLY JUST A RACOON
WWWHOOSSH!!
AAAIEEE!!

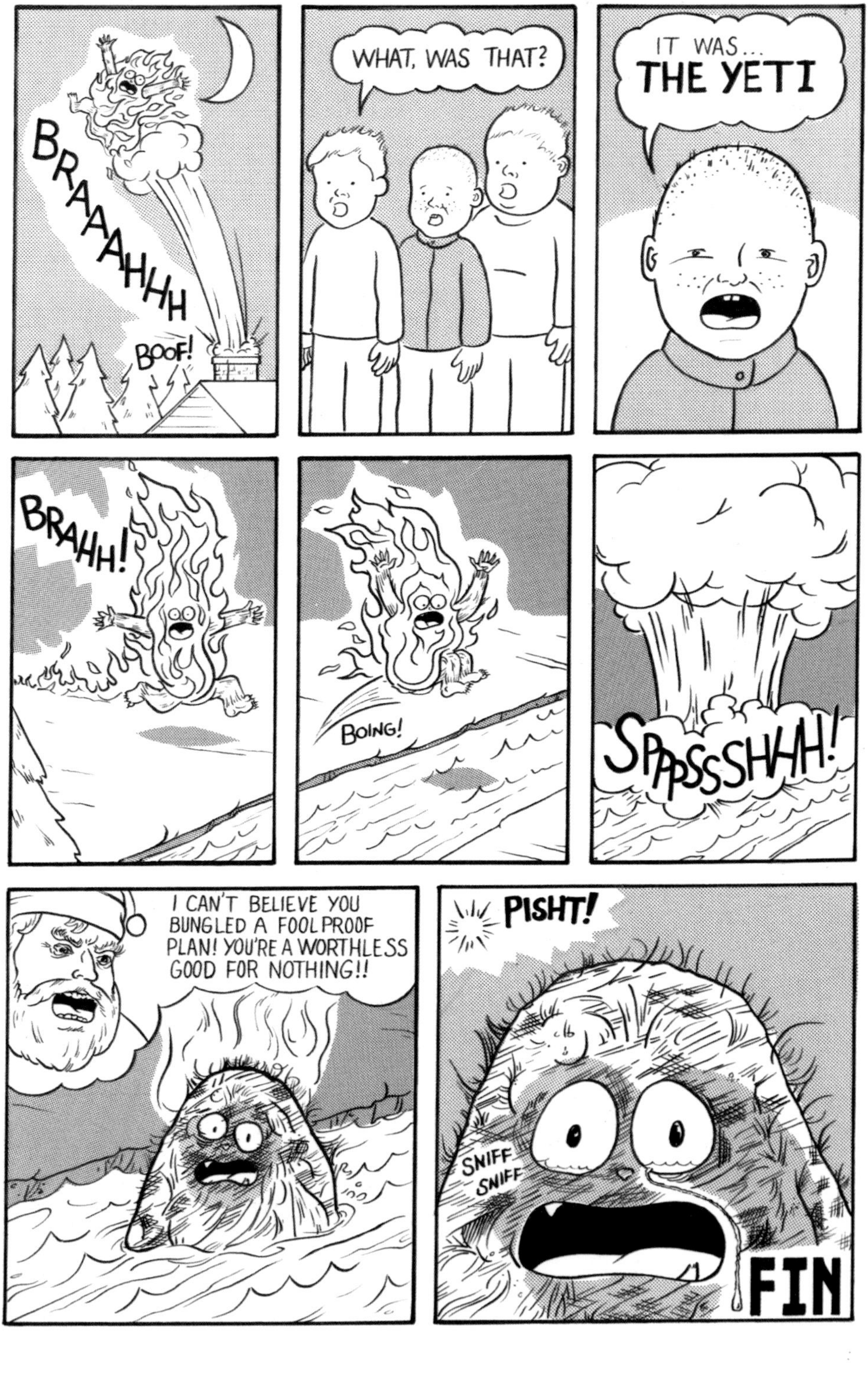
BRAAAAHHHH
BOOF!
WHAT, WAS THAT?
IT WAS...
THE YETI
BRAHH!
BOING!
SPPPSSSHHH!
I CAN'T BELIEVE YOU BUNGLED A FOOLPROOF PLAN! YOU'RE A WORTHLESS GOOD FOR NOTHING!!
PISHT!
SNIFF SNIFF
FIN

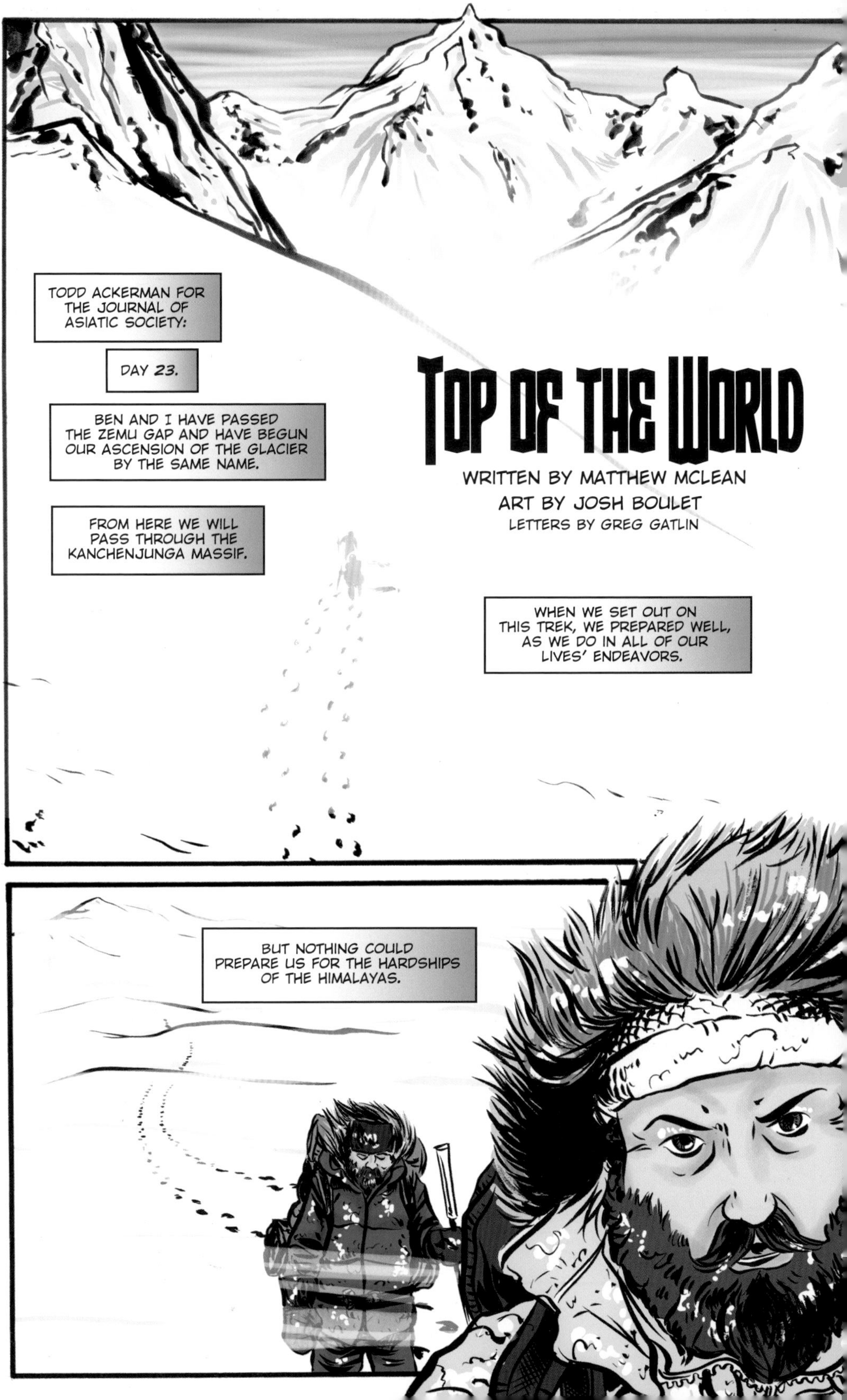
TODD ACKERMAN FOR THE JOURNAL OF ASIATIC SOCIETY:
DAY 23.
BEN AND I HAVE PASSED THE ZEMU GAP AND HAVE BEGUN OUR ASCENSION OF THE GLACIER BY THE SAME NAME.
FROM HERE WE WILL PASS THROUGH THE KANCHENJUNGA MASSIF.
TOP OF THE WORLD
WRITTEN BY MATTHEW MCLEAN
ART BY JOSH BOULET
LETTERS BY GREG GATLIN
WHEN WE SET OUT ON THIS TREK, WE PREPARED WELL, AS WE DO IN ALL OF OUR LIVES' ENDEAVORS.
BUT NOTHING COULD PREPARE US FOR THE HARDSHIPS OF THE HIMALAYAS.

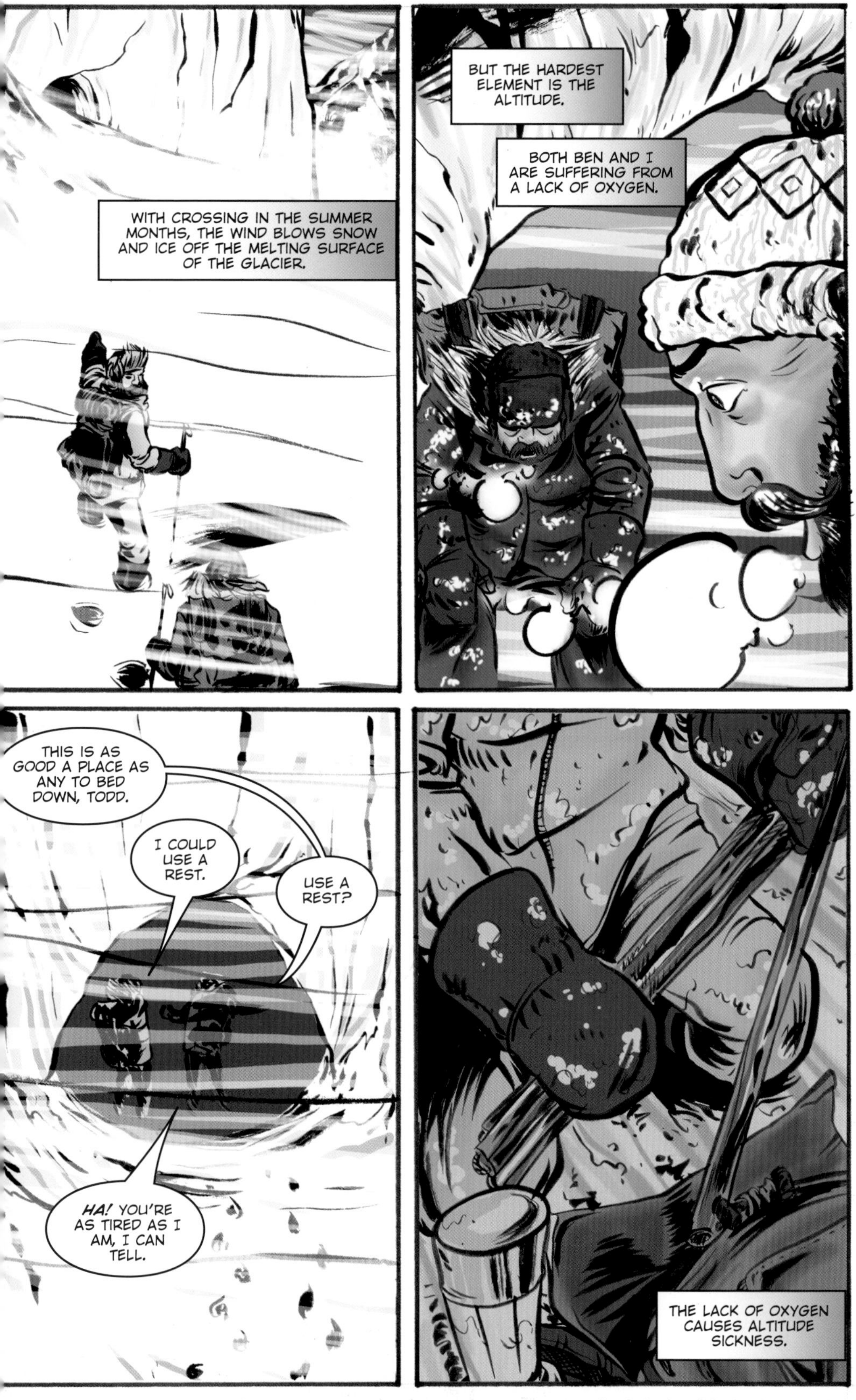
WITH CROSSING IN THE SUMMER MONTHS, THE WIND BLOWS SNOW AND ICE OFF THE MELTING SURFACE OF THE GLACIER.
BUT THE HARDEST ELEMENT IS THE ALTITUDE.
BOTH BEN AND I ARE SUFFERING FROM A LACK OF OXYGEN.
THIS IS AS GOOD A PLACE AS ANY TO BED DOWN, TODD.
I COULD USE A REST.
USE A REST?
HA! YOU'RE AS TIRED AS I AM, I CAN TELL.
THE LACK OF OXYGEN CAUSES ALTITUDE SICKNESS.

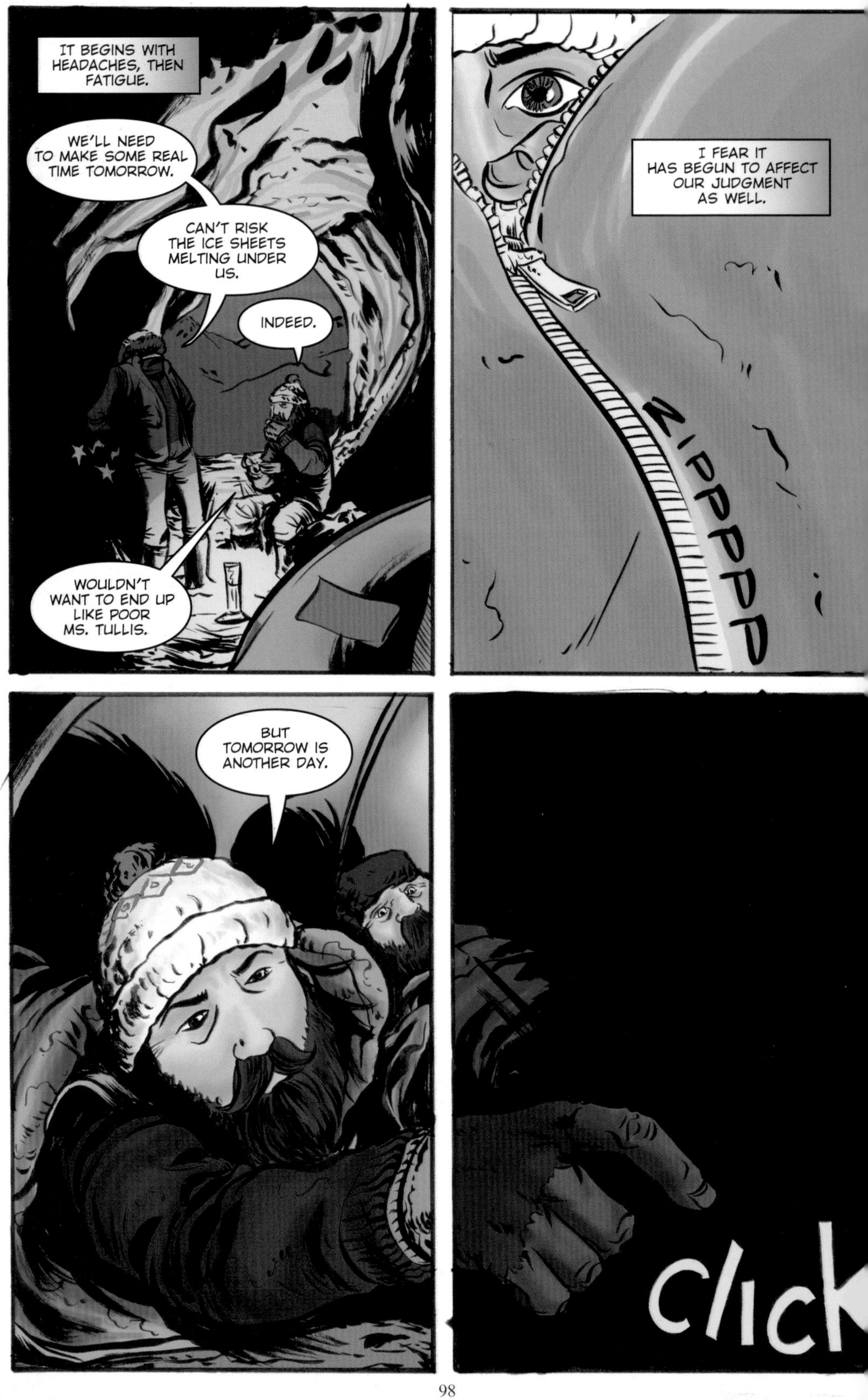
IT BEGINS WITH HEADACHES, THEN FATIGUE.
WE'LL NEED TO MAKE SOME REAL TIME TOMORROW.
CAN'T RISK THE ICE SHEETS MELTING UNDER US.
INDEED.
WOULDN'T WANT TO END UP LIKE POOR MS. TULLIS.
I FEAR IT HAS BEGUN TO AFFECT OUR JUDGMENT AS WELL.
ZIPPPPPP
BUT TOMORROW IS ANOTHER DAY.
CLICK

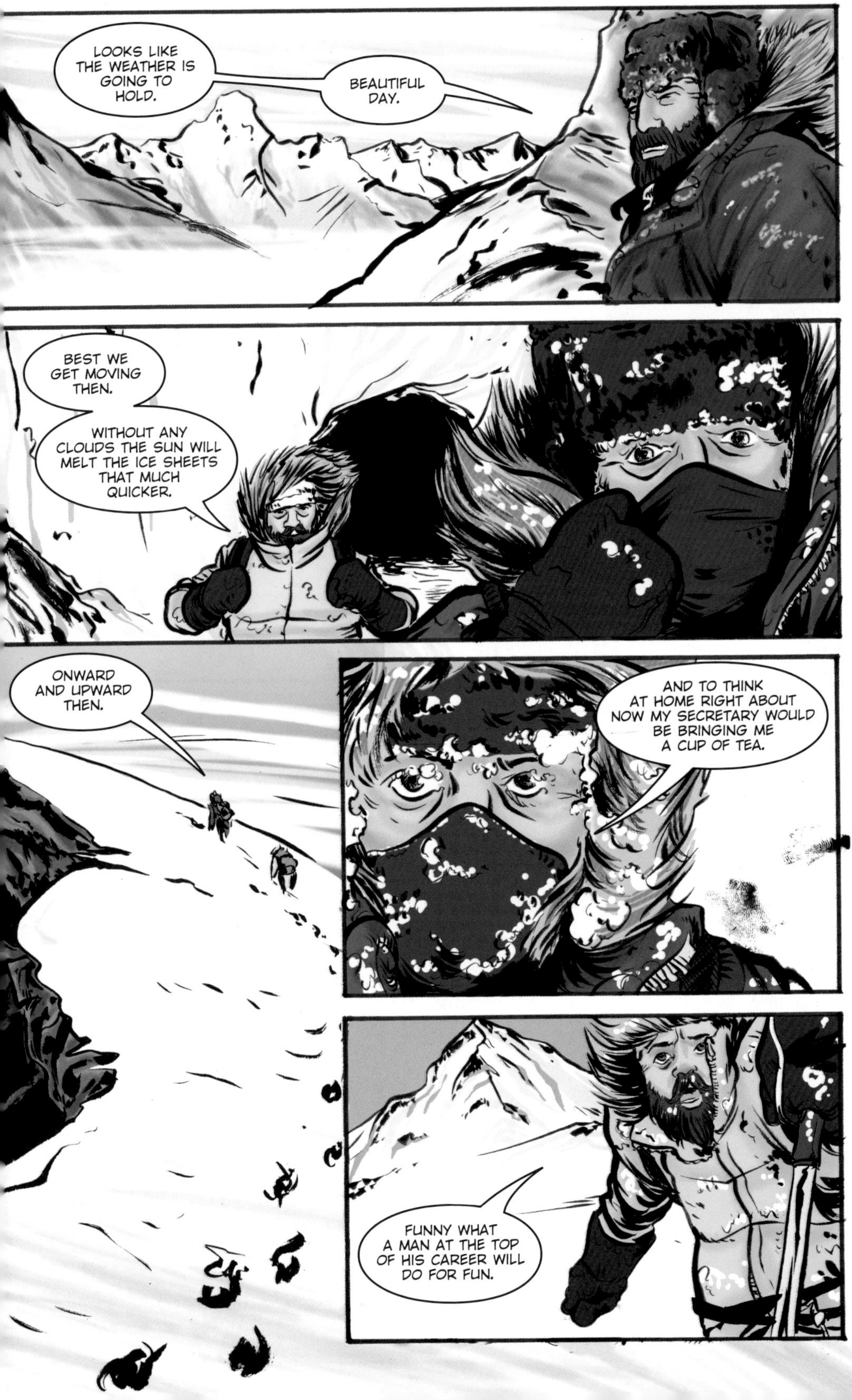

LOOKS LIKE THE WEATHER IS GOING TO HOLD.
BEAUTIFUL DAY.
BEST WE GET MOVING THEN.
WITHOUT ANY CLOUDS THE SUN WILL MELT THE ICE SHEETS THAT MUCH QUICKER.
ONWARD AND UPWARD THEN.
AND TO THINK AT HOME RIGHT ABOUT NOW MY SECRETARY WOULD BE BRINGING ME A CUP OF TEA.
FUNNY WHAT A MAN AT THE TOP OF HIS CAREER WILL DO FOR FUN.

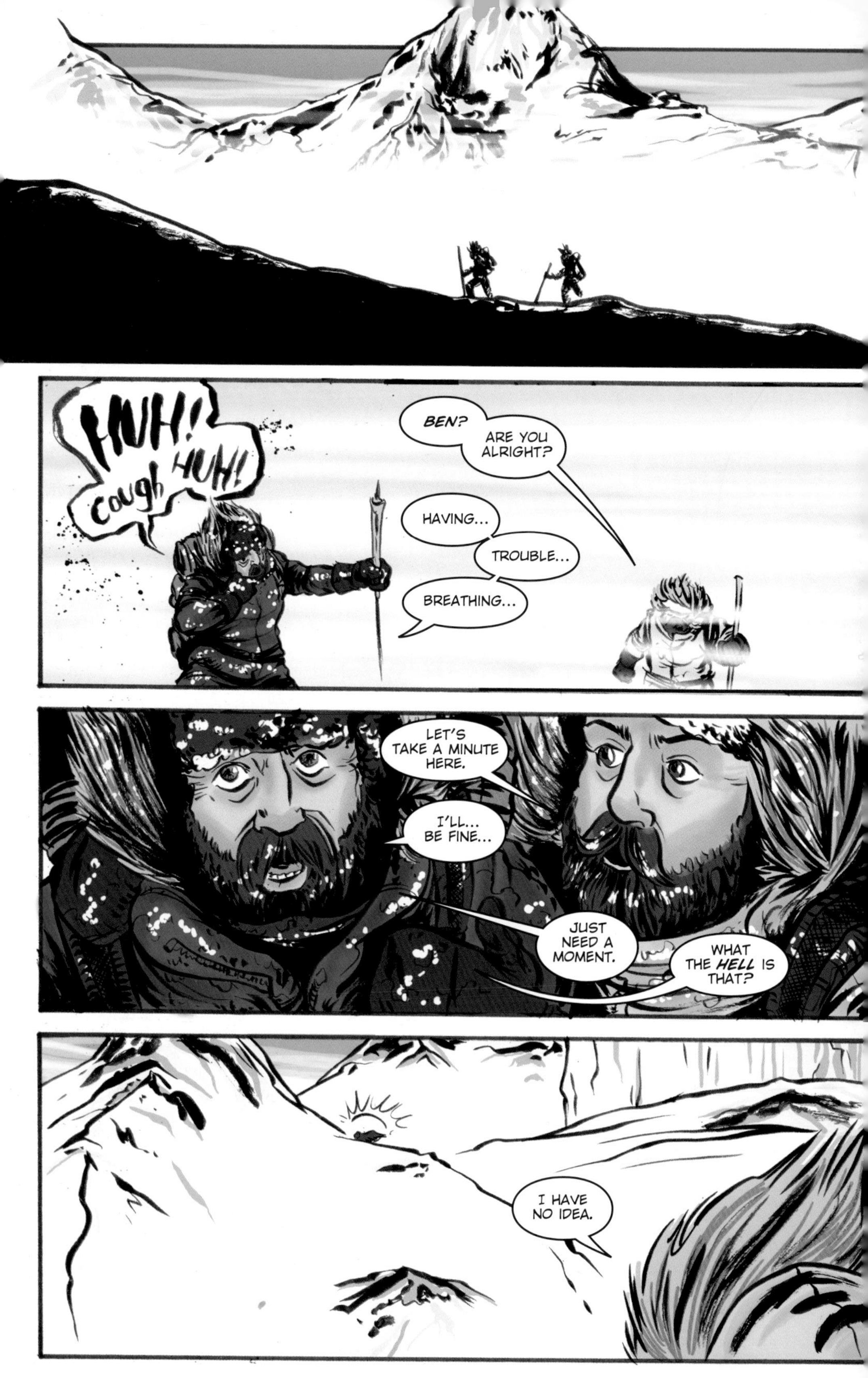
HUH! Cough HUH!
BEN? ARE YOU ALRIGHT?
HAVING...
TROUBLE...
BREATHING...
LET'S TAKE A MINUTE HERE.
I'LL... BE FINE...
JUST NEED A MOMENT.
WHAT THE HELL IS THAT?
I HAVE NO IDEA.

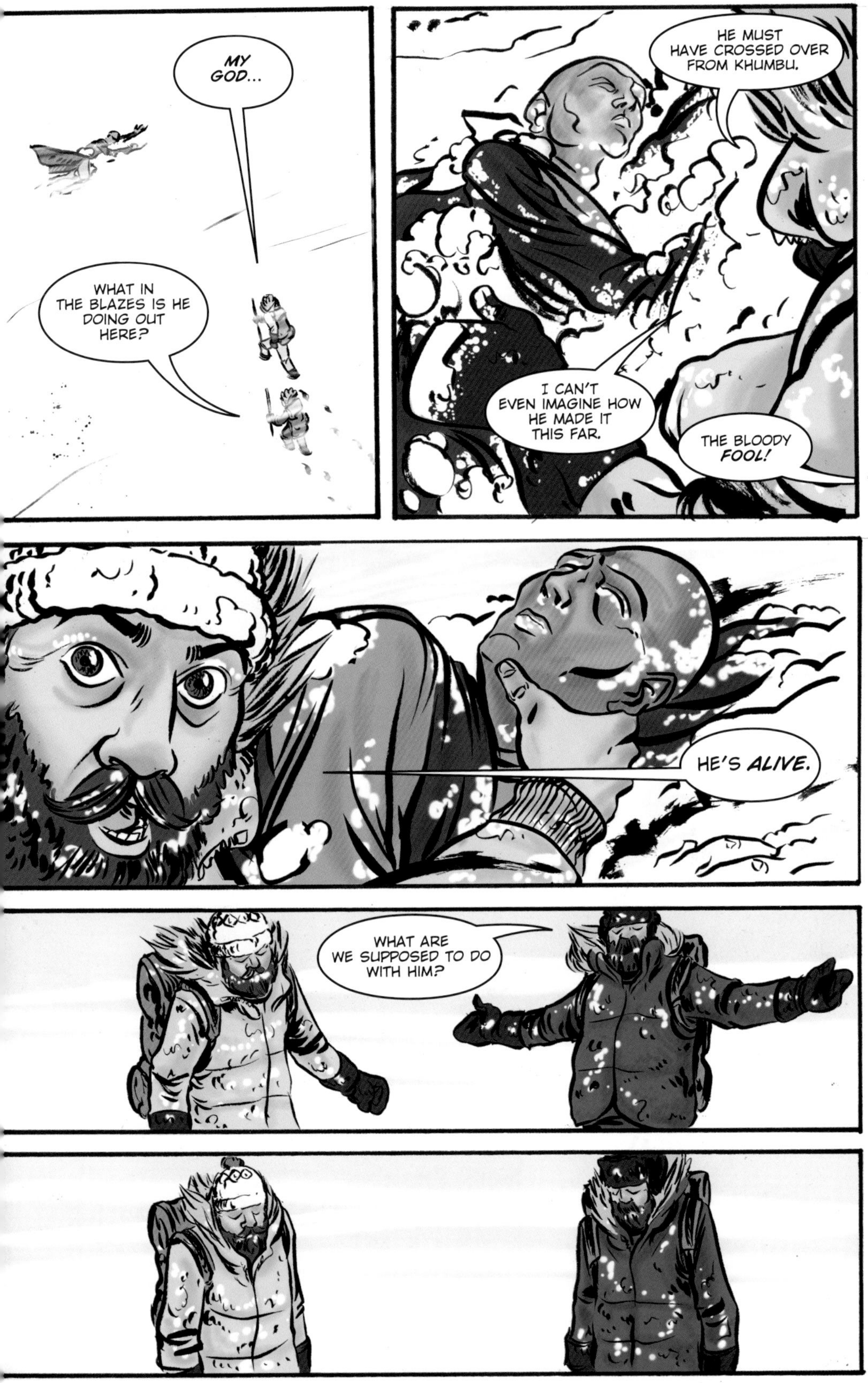
MY GOD...
WHAT IN THE BLAZES IS HE DOING OUT HERE?
HE MUST HAVE CROSSED OVER FROM KHUMBU.
I CAN'T EVEN IMAGINE HOW HE MADE IT THIS FAR.
THE BLOODY *FOOL!*
HE'S *ALIVE.*
WHAT ARE WE SUPPOSED TO DO WITH HIM?

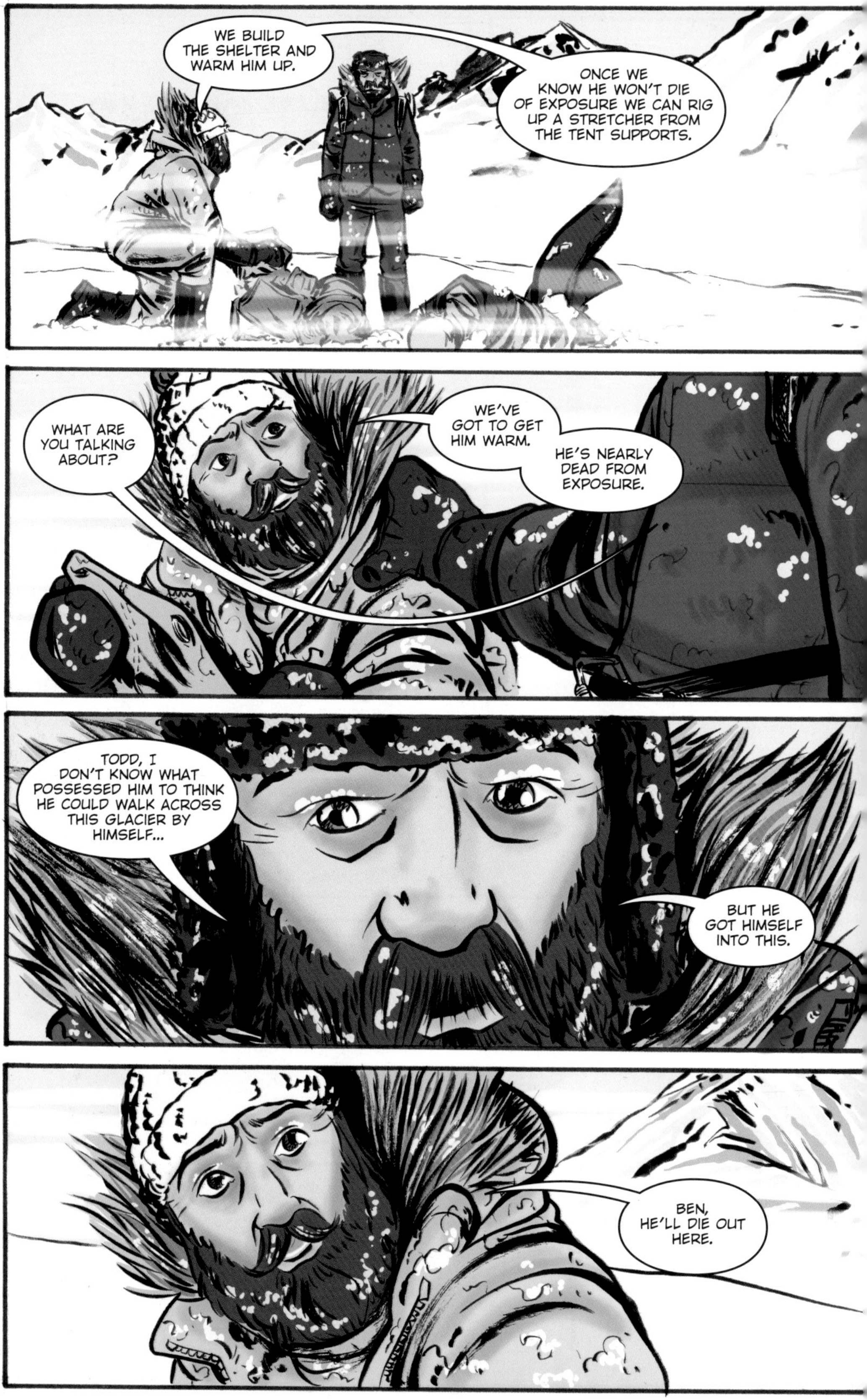
WE BUILD THE SHELTER AND WARM HIM UP.
ONCE WE KNOW HE WON'T DIE OF EXPOSURE WE CAN RIG UP A STRETCHER FROM THE TENT SUPPORTS.
WHAT ARE YOU TALKING ABOUT?
WE'VE GOT TO GET HIM WARM.
HE'S NEARLY DEAD FROM EXPOSURE.
TODD, I DON'T KNOW WHAT POSSESSED HIM TO THINK HE COULD WALK ACROSS THIS GLACIER BY HIMSELF...
BUT HE GOT HIMSELF INTO THIS.
BEN, HE'LL DIE OUT HERE.

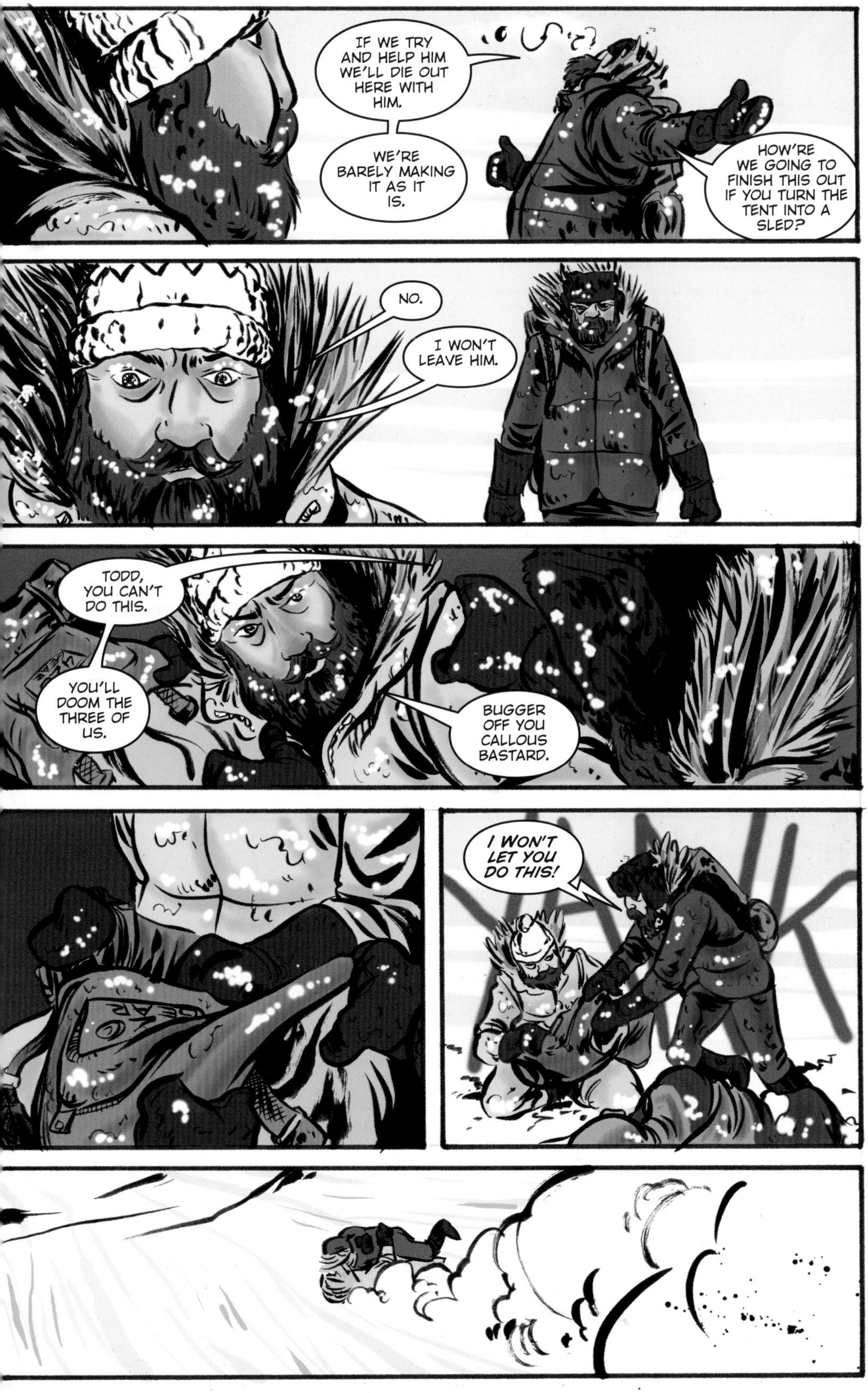
IF WE TRY AND HELP HIM WE'LL DIE OUT HERE WITH HIM.
WE'RE BARELY MAKING IT AS IT IS.
HOW'RE WE GOING TO FINISH THIS OUT IF YOU TURN THE TENT INTO A SLED?
NO.
I WON'T LEAVE HIM.
TODD, YOU CAN'T DO THIS.
YOU'LL DOOM THE THREE OF US.
BUGGER OFF YOU CALLOUS BASTARD.
I WON'T LET YOU DO THIS!
YANK

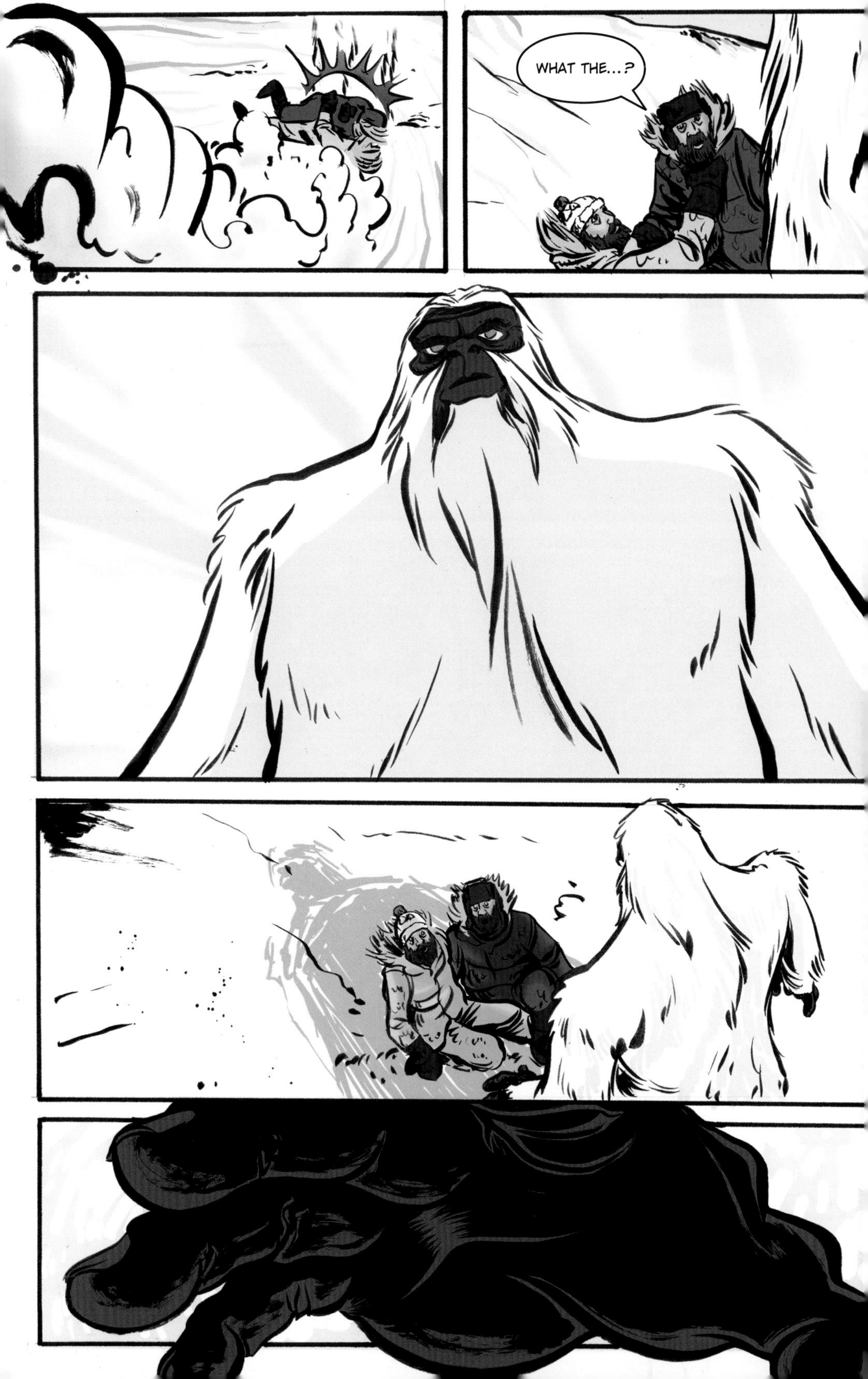
WHAT THE...?

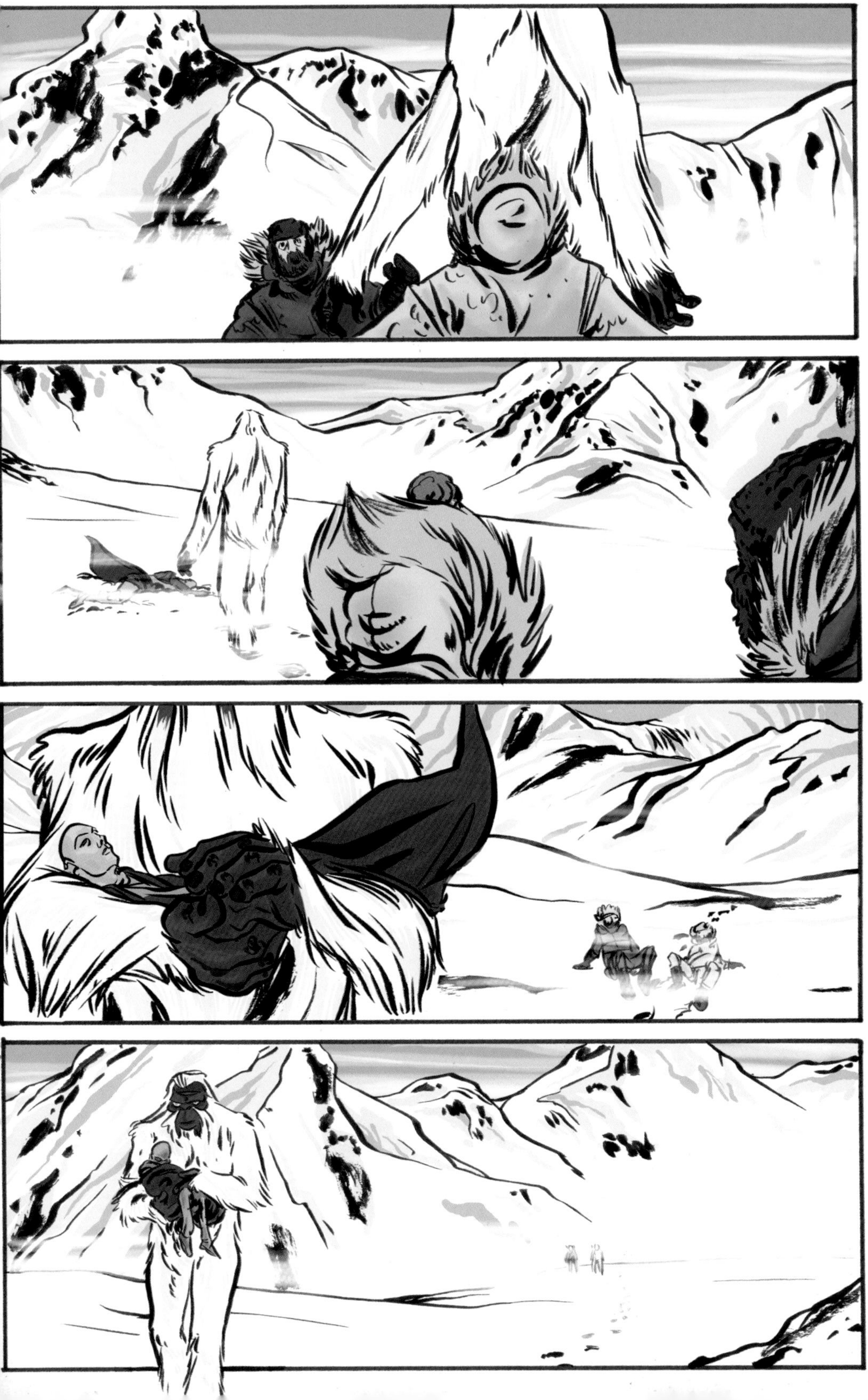

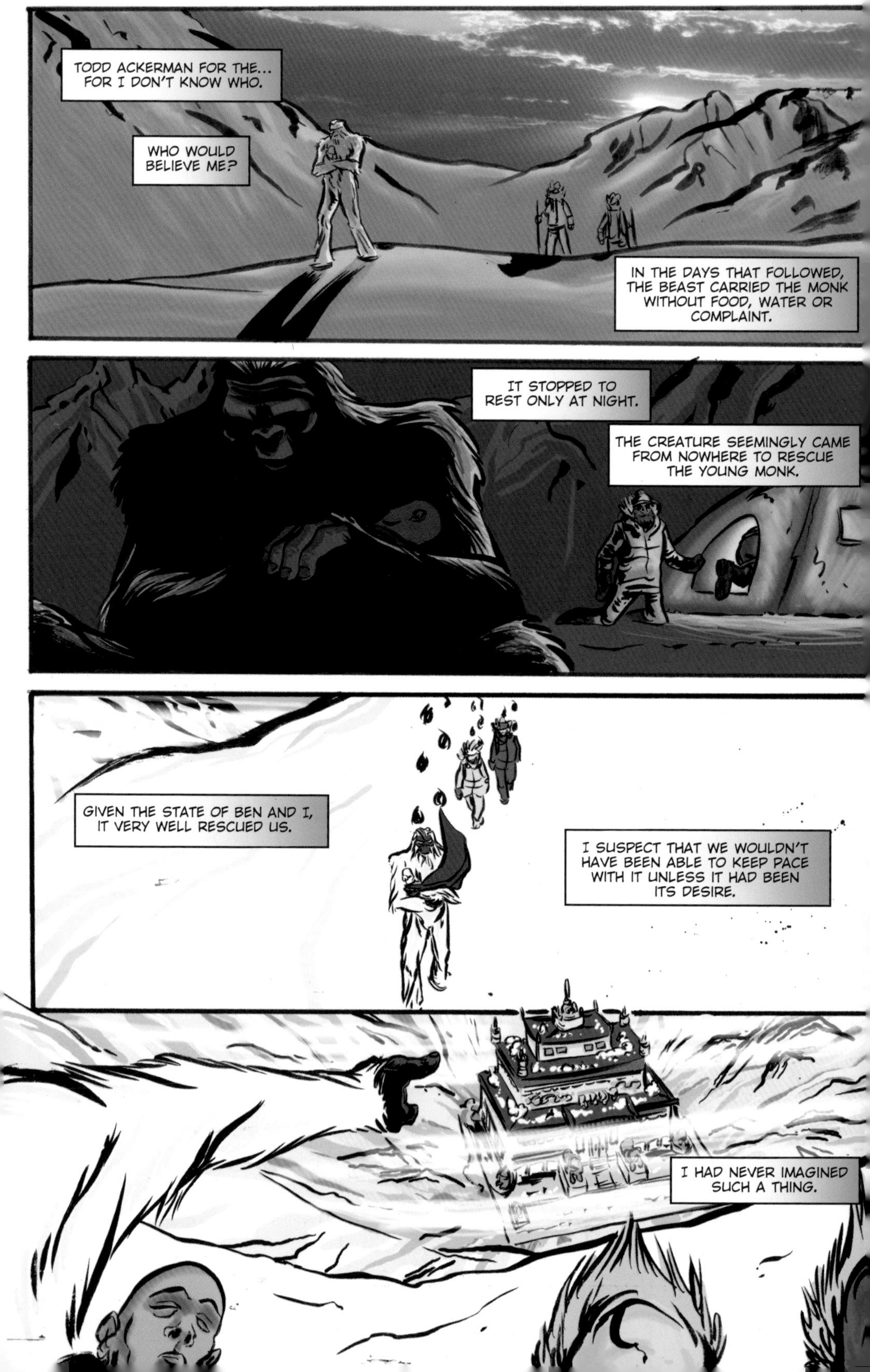
TODD ACKERMAN FOR THE... FOR I DON'T KNOW WHO.
WHO WOULD BELIEVE ME?
IN THE DAYS THAT FOLLOWED, THE BEAST CARRIED THE MONK WITHOUT FOOD, WATER OR COMPLAINT.
IT STOPPED TO REST ONLY AT NIGHT.
THE CREATURE SEEMINGLY CAME FROM NOWHERE TO RESCUE THE YOUNG MONK.
GIVEN THE STATE OF BEN AND I, IT VERY WELL RESCUED US.
I SUSPECT THAT WE WOULDN'T HAVE BEEN ABLE TO KEEP PACE WITH IT UNLESS IT HAD BEEN ITS DESIRE.
I HAD NEVER IMAGINED SUCH A THING.

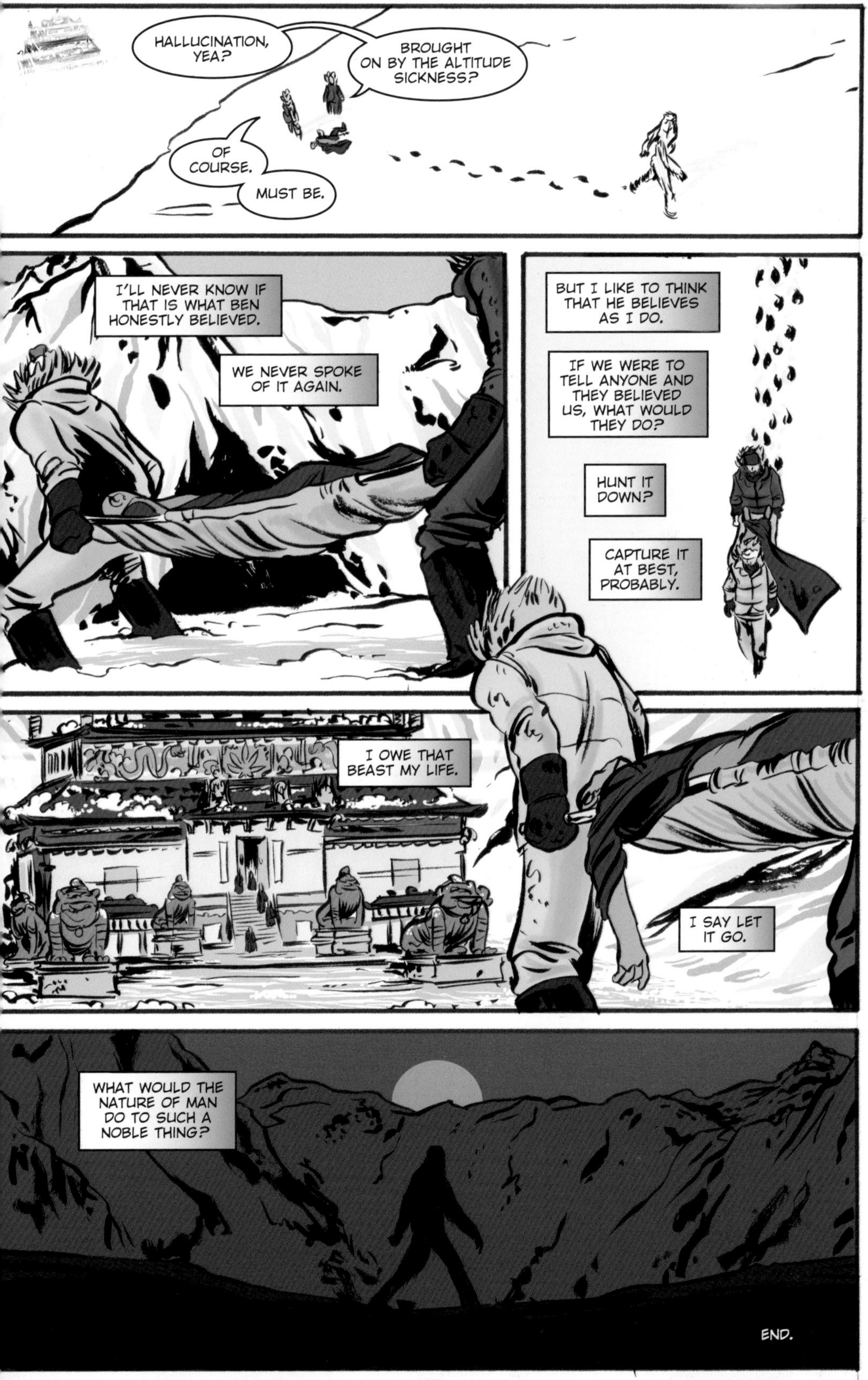

HALLUCINATION, YEA?
BROUGHT ON BY THE ALTITUDE SICKNESS?
OF COURSE.
MUST BE.
I'LL NEVER KNOW IF THAT IS WHAT BEN HONESTLY BELIEVED.
WE NEVER SPOKE OF IT AGAIN.
BUT I LIKE TO THINK THAT HE BELIEVES AS I DO.
IF WE WERE TO TELL ANYONE AND THEY BELIEVED US, WHAT WOULD THEY DO?
HUNT IT DOWN?
CAPTURE IT AT BEST, PROBABLY.
I OWE THAT BEAST MY LIFE.
I SAY LET IT GO.
WHAT WOULD THE NATURE OF MAN DO TO SUCH A NOBLE THING?
END.

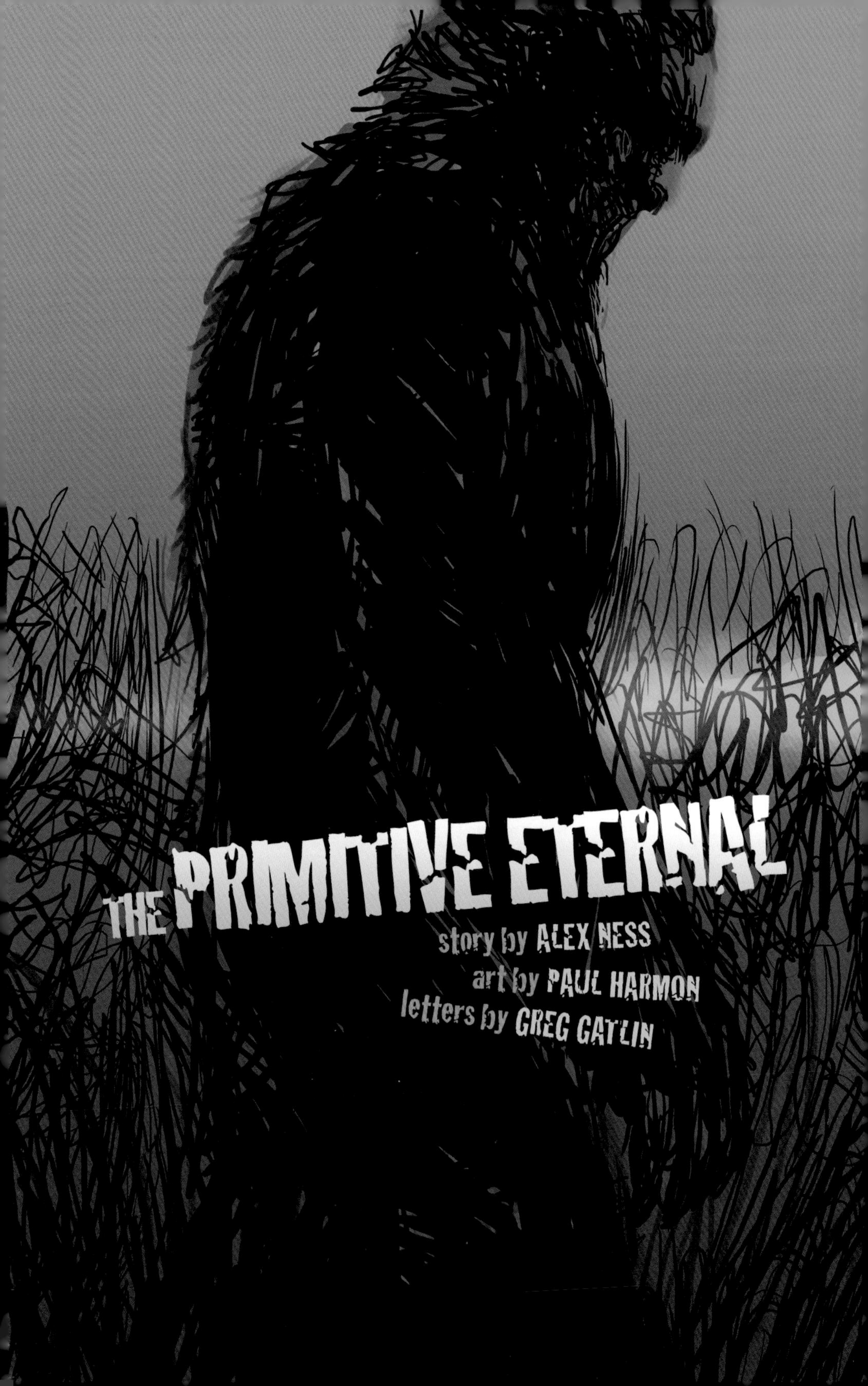
THE PRIMITIVE ETERNAL
story by ALEX NESS
art by PAUL HARMON
letters by GREG GATLIN

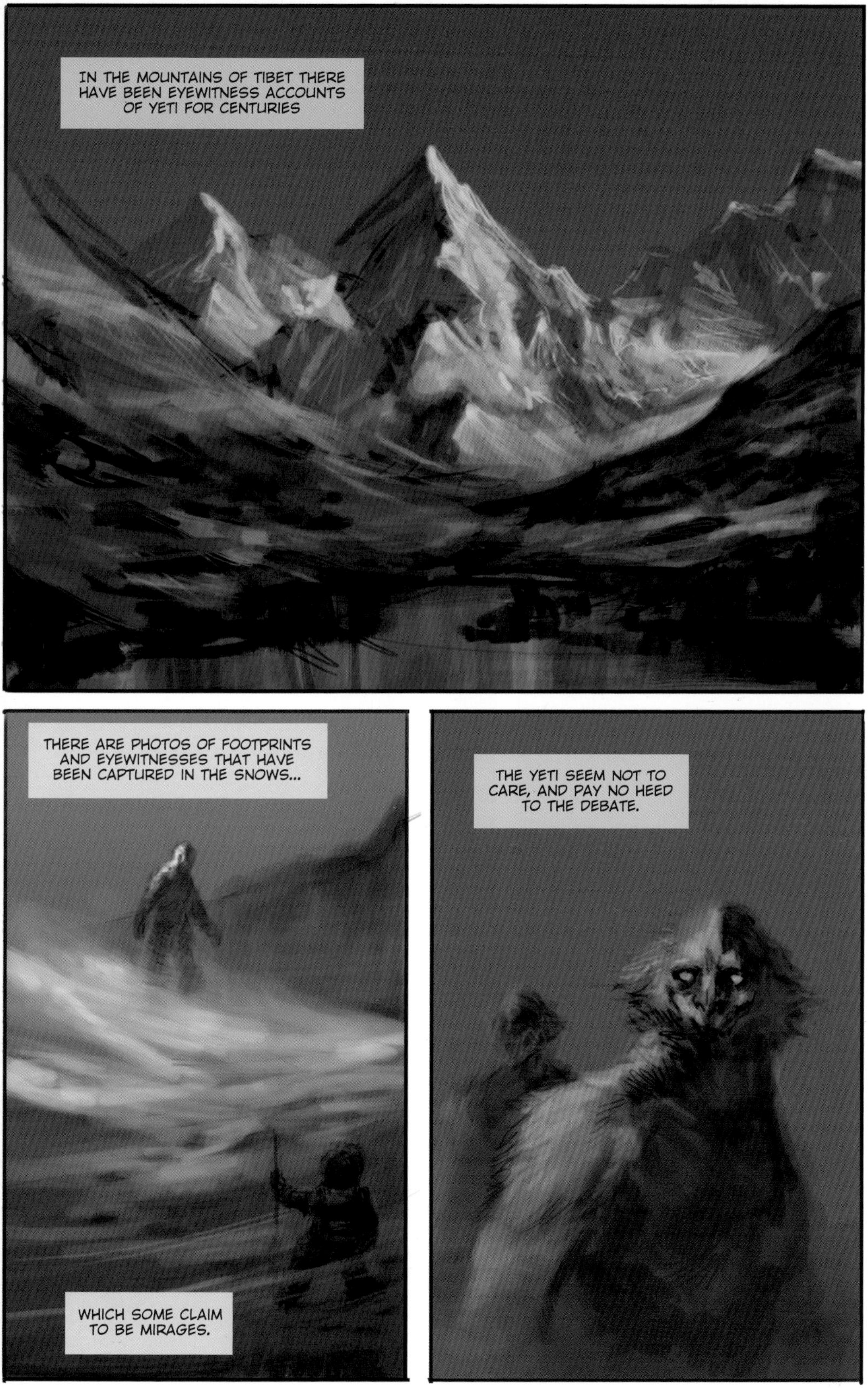
IN THE MOUNTAINS OF TIBET THERE HAVE BEEN EYEWITNESS ACCOUNTS OF YETI FOR CENTURIES
THERE ARE PHOTOS OF FOOTPRINTS AND EYEWITNESSES THAT HAVE BEEN CAPTURED IN THE SNOWS...
WHICH SOME CLAIM TO BE MIRAGES.
THE YETI SEEM NOT TO CARE, AND PAY NO HEED TO THE DEBATE.

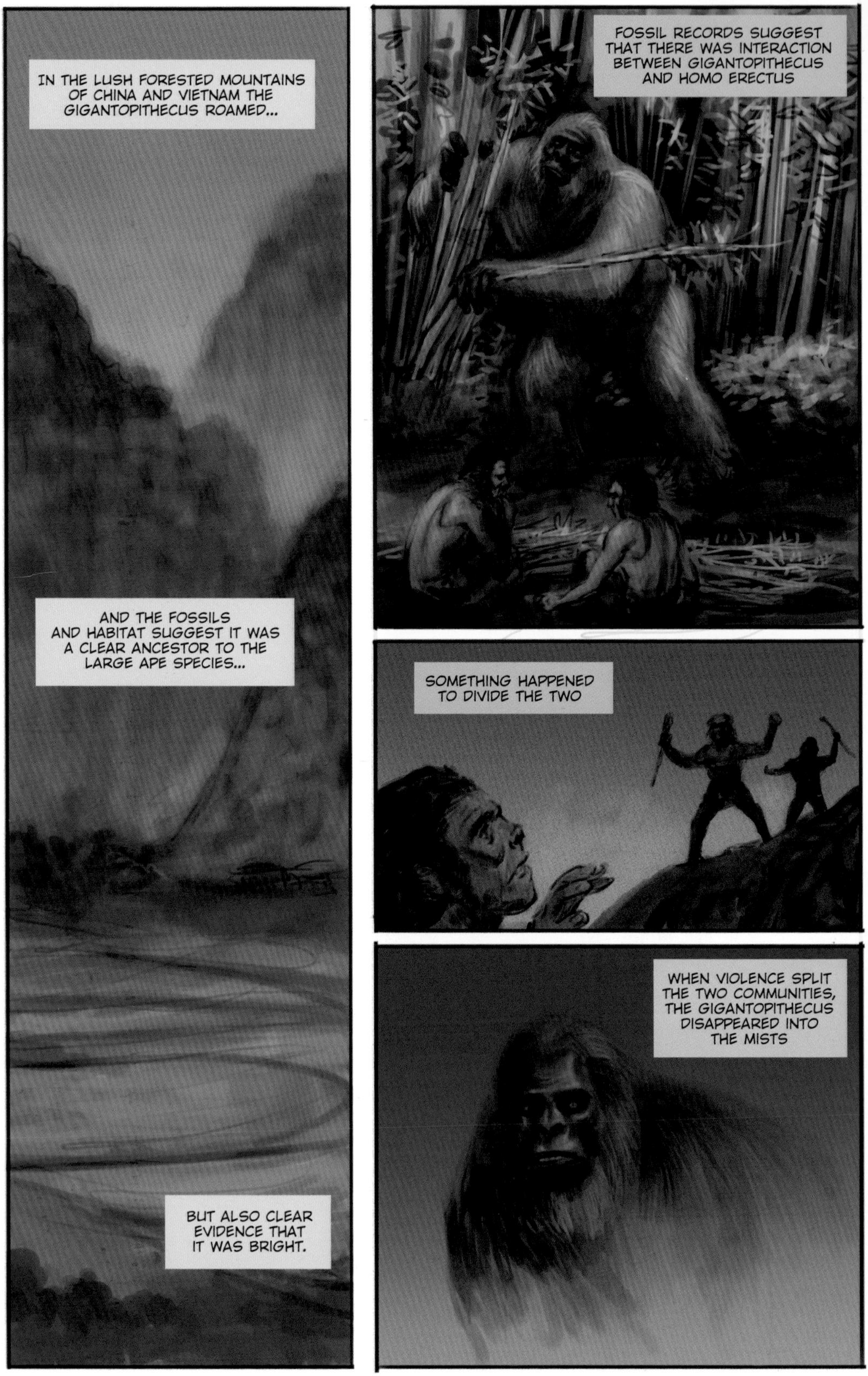
IN THE LUSH FORESTED MOUNTAINS OF CHINA AND VIETNAM THE GIGANTOPITHECUS ROAMED...
AND THE FOSSILS AND HABITAT SUGGEST IT WAS A CLEAR ANCESTOR TO THE LARGE APE SPECIES...
BUT ALSO CLEAR EVIDENCE THAT IT WAS BRIGHT.
FOSSIL RECORDS SUGGEST THAT THERE WAS INTERACTION BETWEEN GIGANTOPITHECUS AND HOMO ERECTUS
SOMETHING HAPPENED TO DIVIDE THE TWO
WHEN VIOLENCE SPLIT THE TWO COMMUNITIES, THE GIGANTOPITHECUS DISAPPEARED INTO THE MISTS

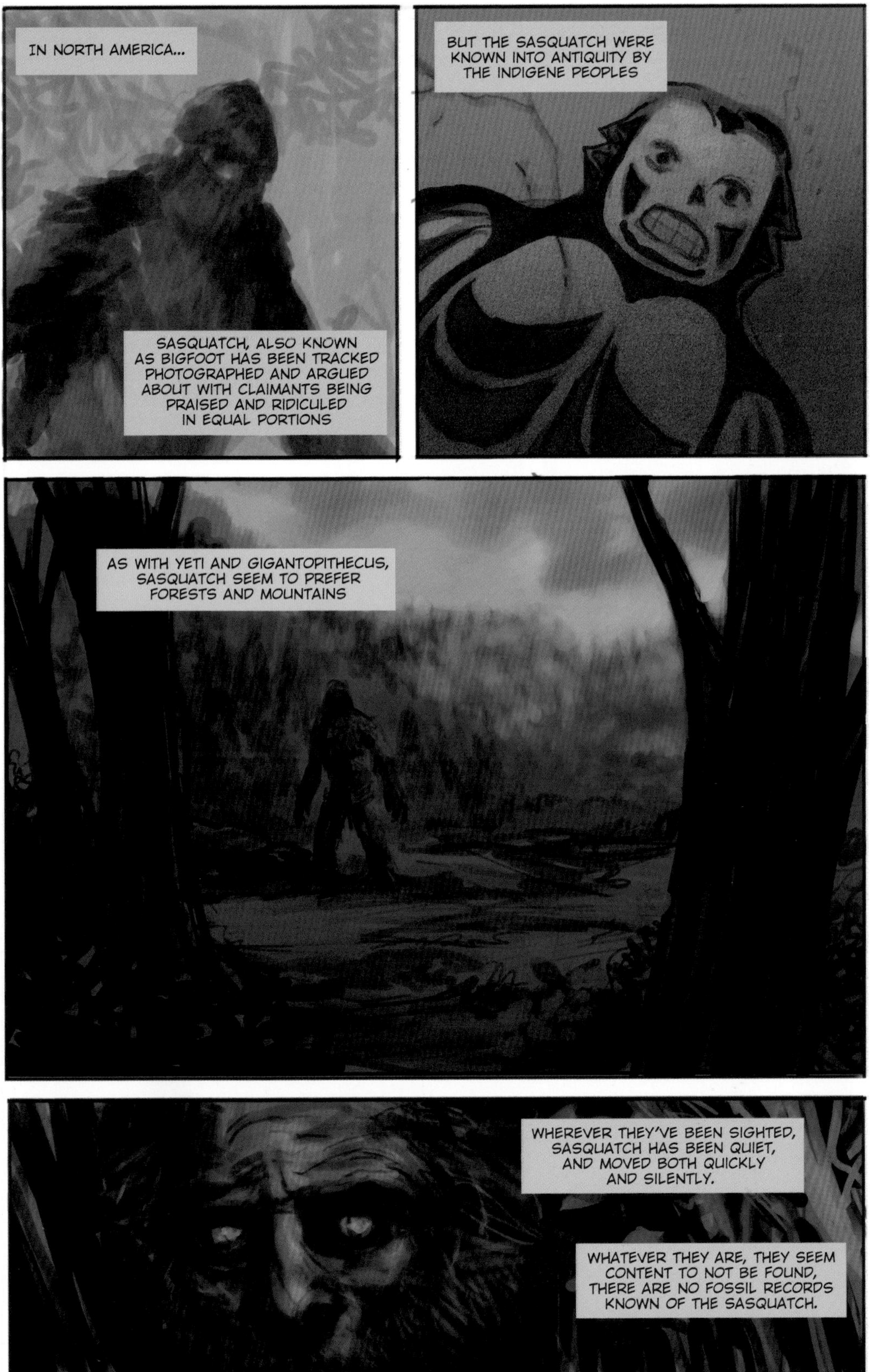
IN NORTH AMERICA...
SASQUATCH, ALSO KNOWN AS BIGFOOT HAS BEEN TRACKED PHOTOGRAPHED AND ARGUED ABOUT WITH CLAIMANTS BEING PRAISED AND RIDICULED IN EQUAL PORTIONS
BUT THE SASQUATCH WERE KNOWN INTO ANTIQUITY BY THE INDIGENE PEOPLES
AS WITH YETI AND GIGANTOPITHECUS, SASQUATCH SEEM TO PREFER FORESTS AND MOUNTAINS
WHEREVER THEY'VE BEEN SIGHTED, SASQUATCH HAS BEEN QUIET, AND MOVED BOTH QUICKLY AND SILENTLY.
WHATEVER THEY ARE, THEY SEEM CONTENT TO NOT BE FOUND, THERE ARE NO FOSSIL RECORDS KNOWN OF THE SASQUATCH.

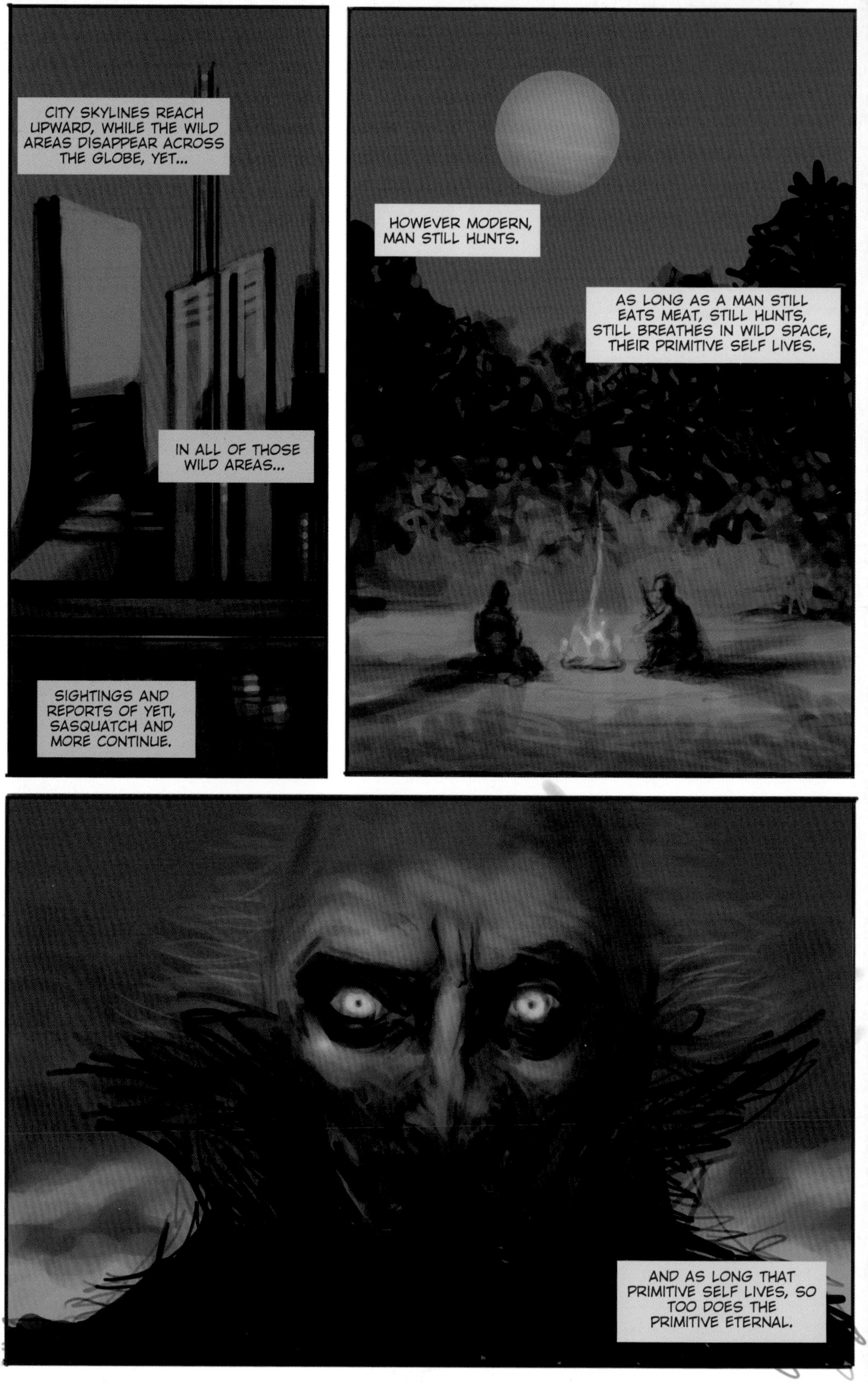
CITY SKYLINES REACH UPWARD, WHILE THE WILD AREAS DISAPPEAR ACROSS THE GLOBE, YET...
IN ALL OF THOSE WILD AREAS...
SIGHTINGS AND REPORTS OF YETI, SASQUATCH AND MORE CONTINUE.
HOWEVER MODERN, MAN STILL HUNTS.
AS LONG AS A MAN STILL EATS MEAT, STILL HUNTS, STILL BREATHES IN WILD SPACE, THEIR PRIMITIVE SELF LIVES.
AND AS LONG THAT PRIMITIVE SELF LIVES, SO TOO DOES THE PRIMITIVE ETERNAL.

HEART MOUNTAIN, WY: 1942

written & illustrated by
Tom Kurzanski

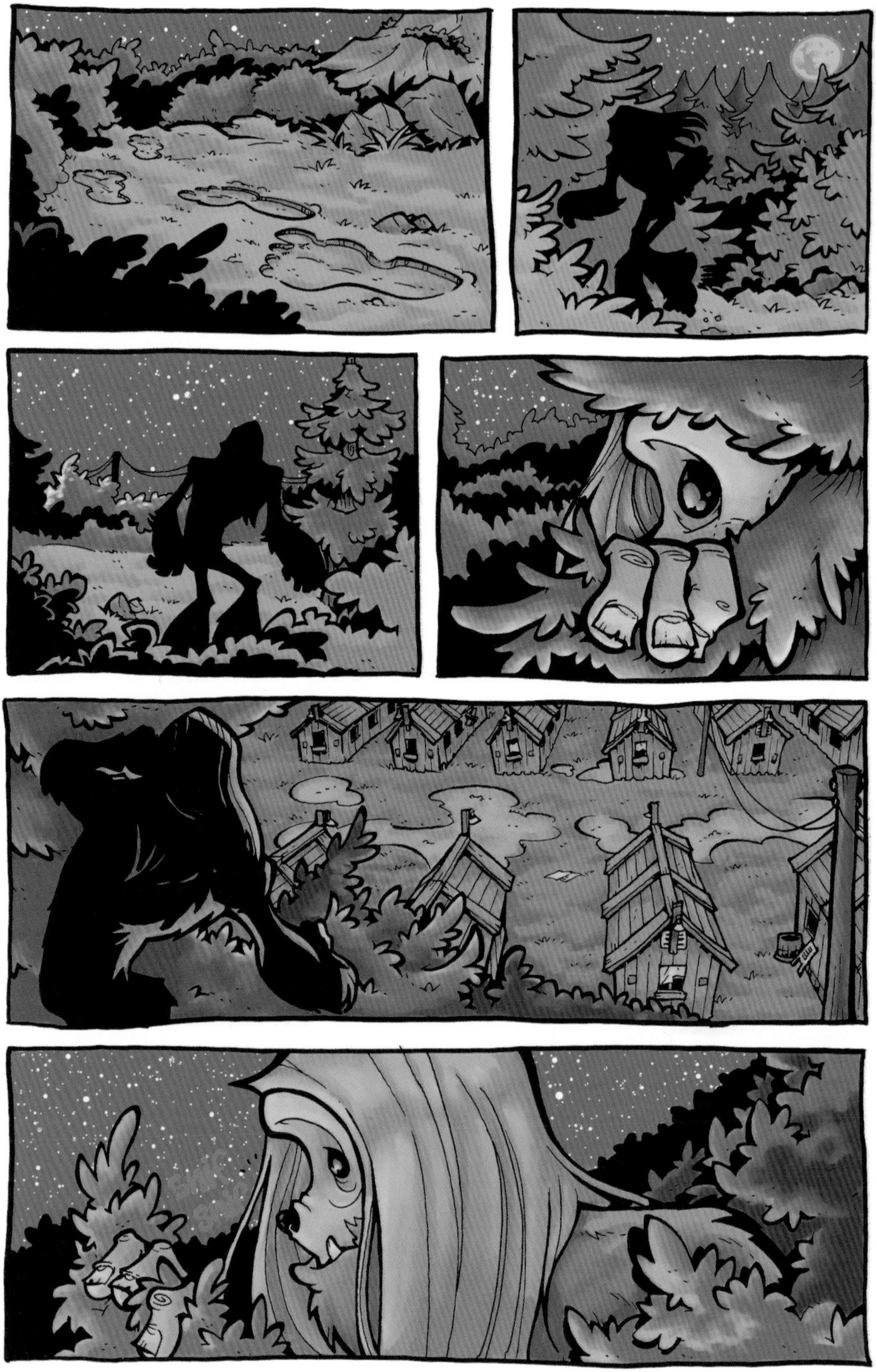

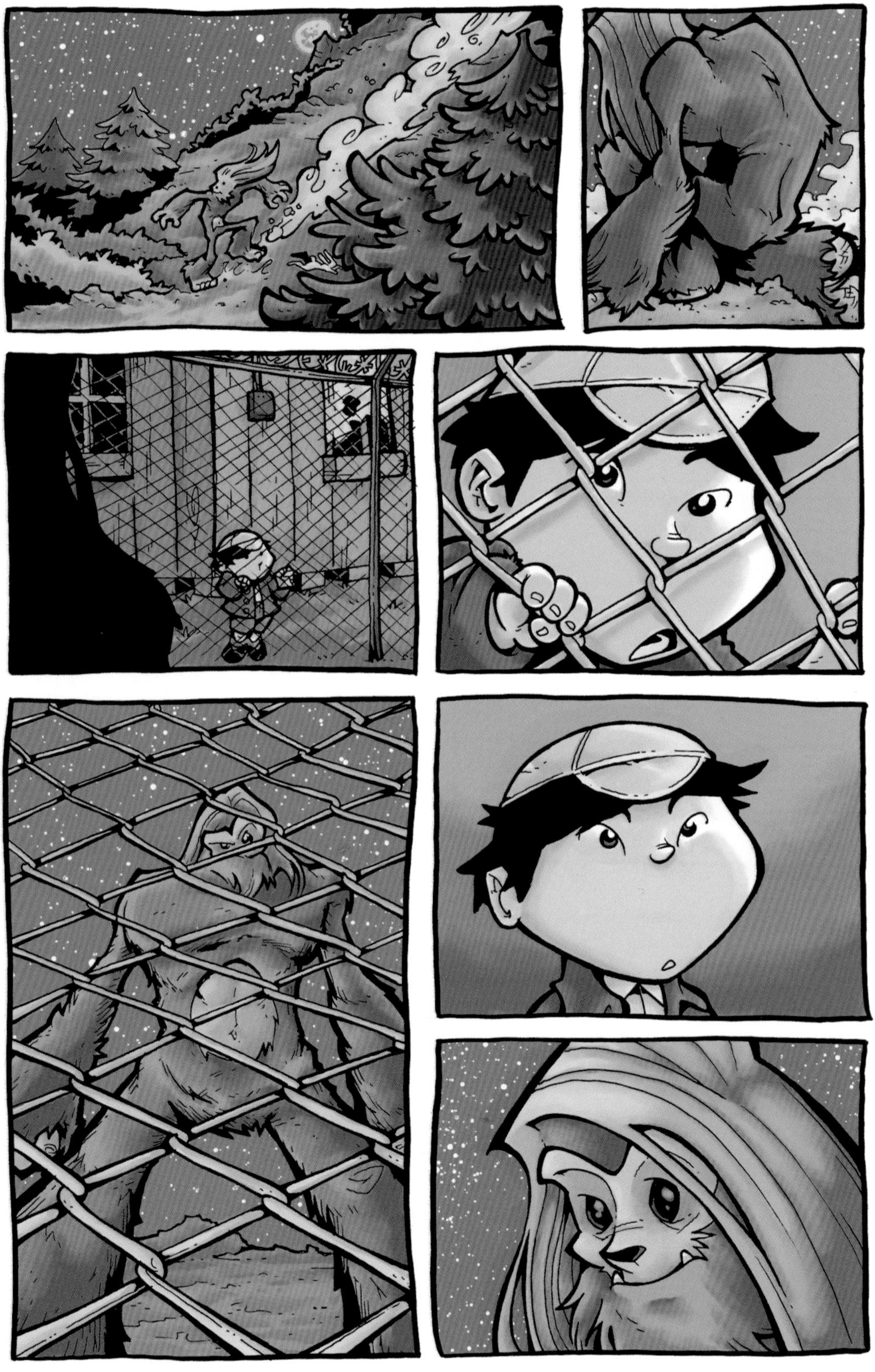

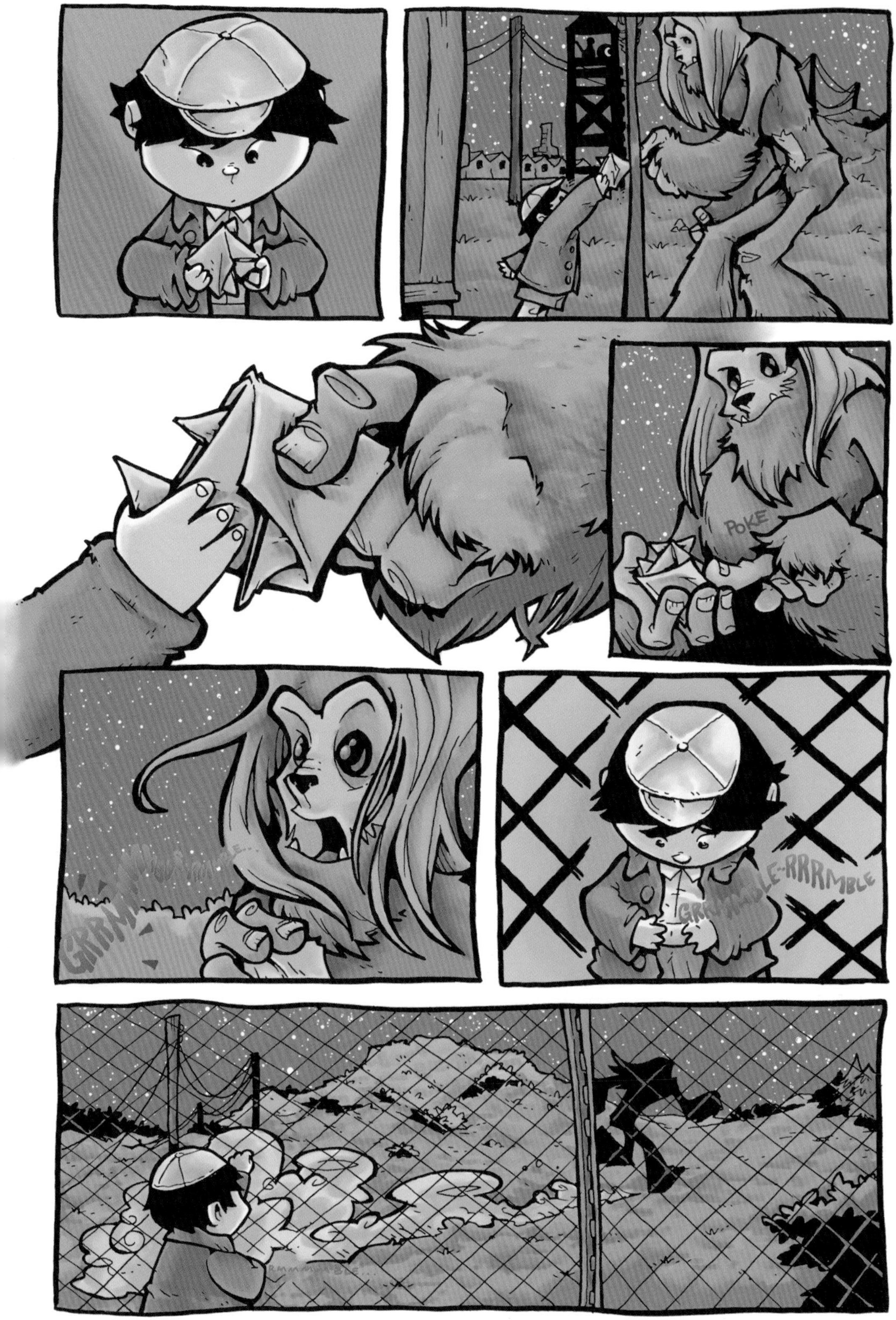
POKE
-RRRMBLE

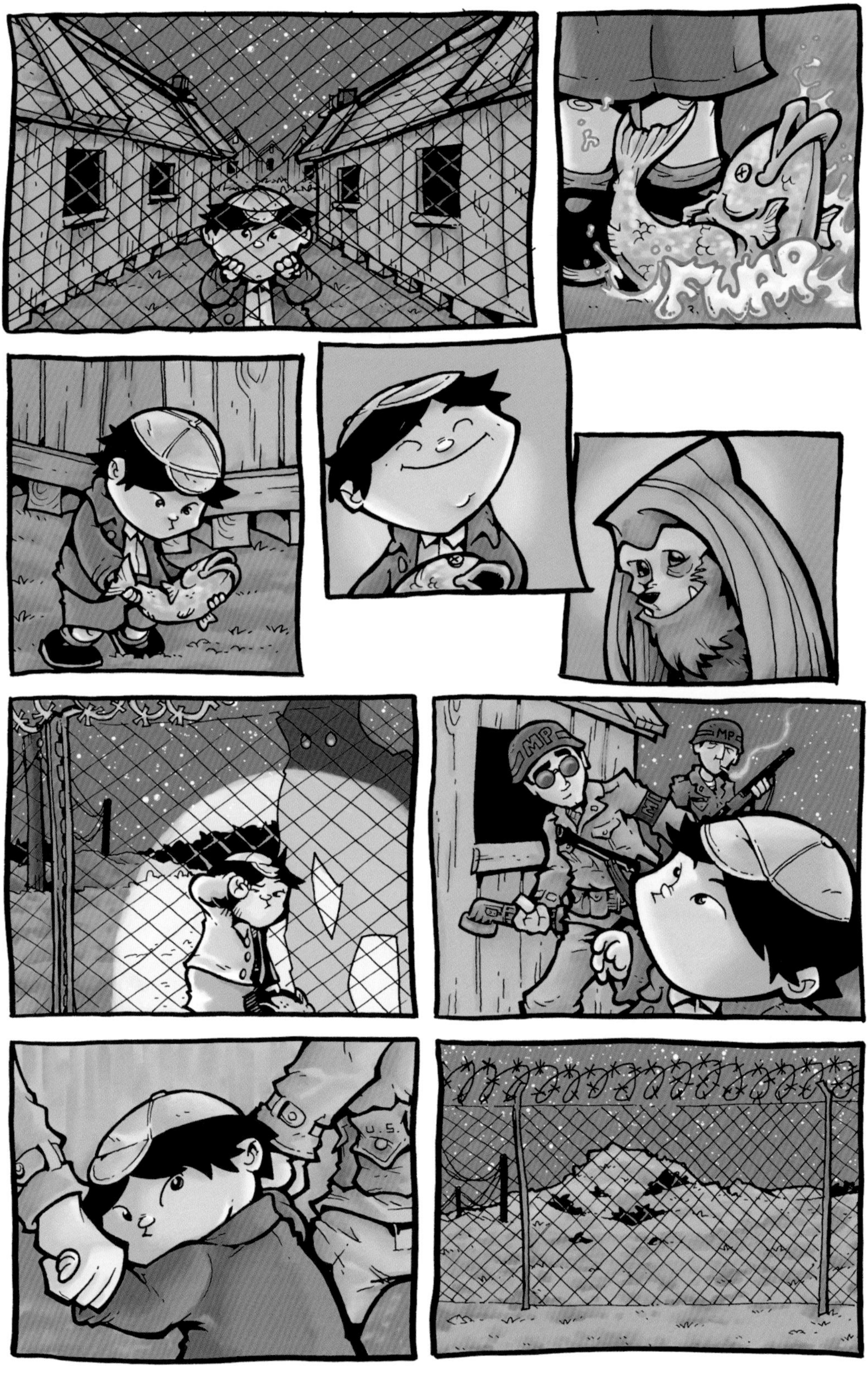
FWAP
MP
MP
U.S.

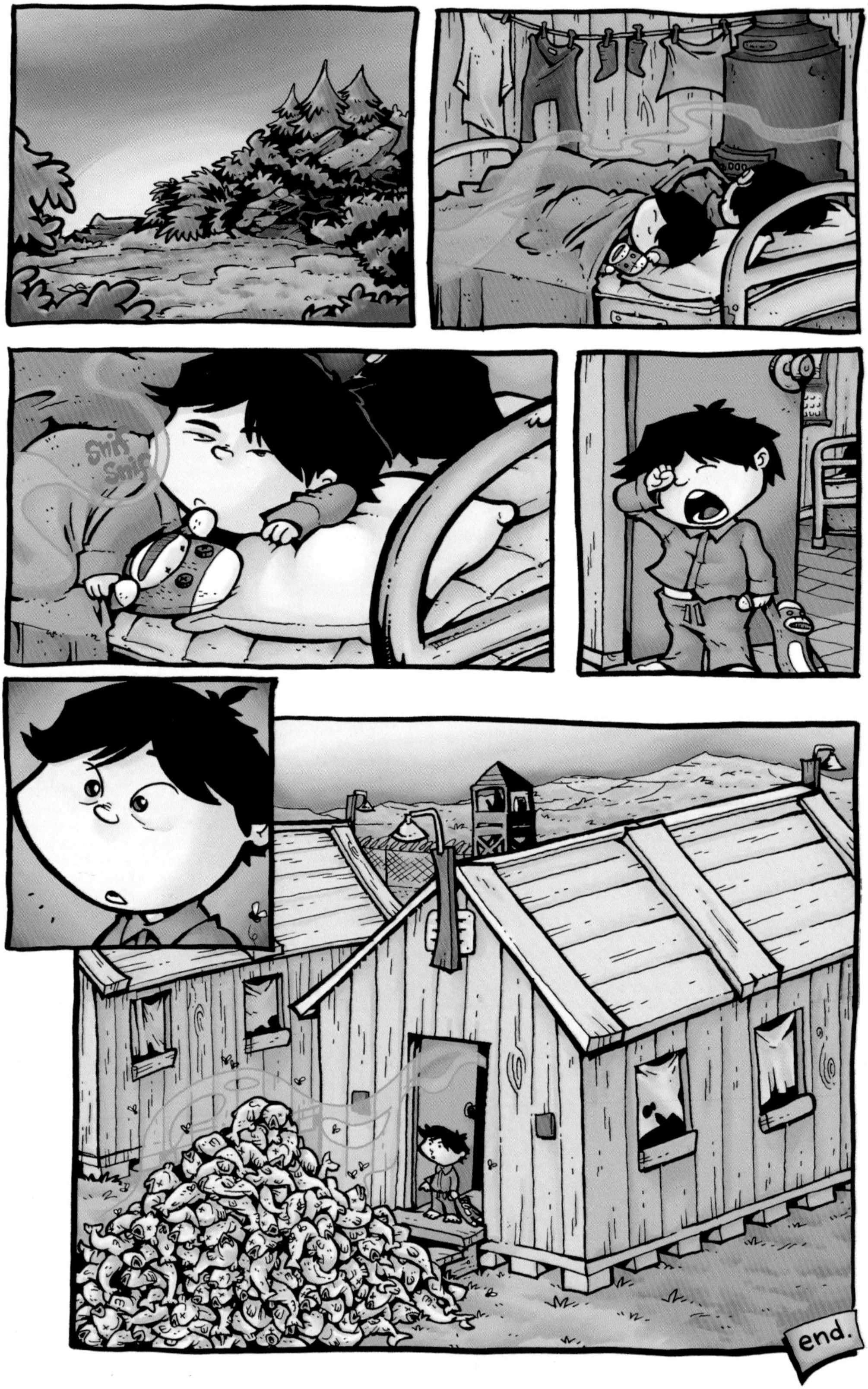
Snif
Snif
end.

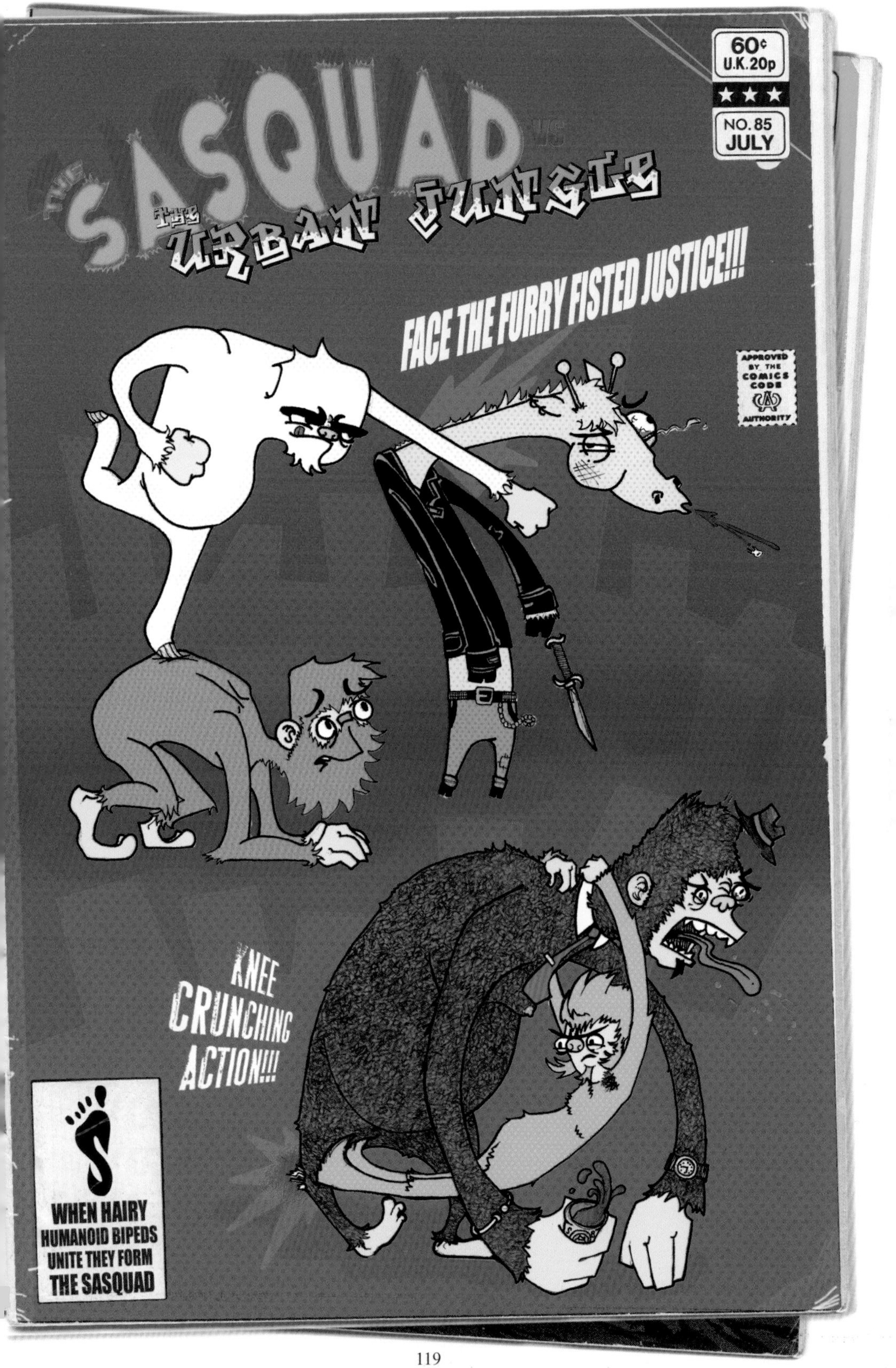
60¢
U.K.20p
NO.85
JULY
THE SASQUAD VS THE URBAN JUNGLE
FACE THE FURRY FISTED JUSTICE!!!
APPROVED BY THE COMICS CODE AUTHORITY
KNEE CRUNCHING ACTION!!!
WHEN HAIRY HUMANOID BIPEDS UNITE THEY FORM THE SASQUAD

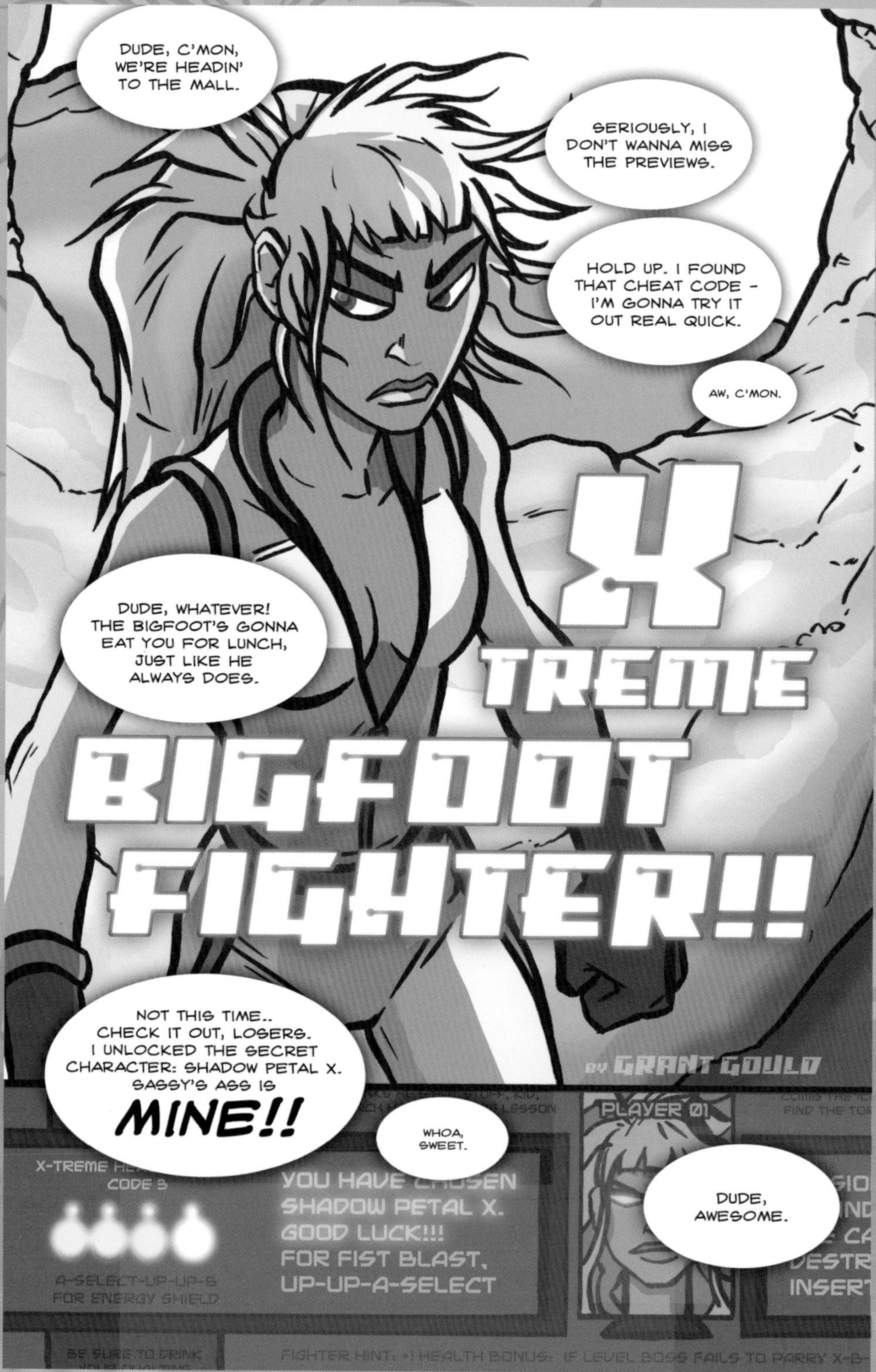
DUDE, C'MON, WE'RE HEADIN' TO THE MALL.
SERIOUSLY, I DON'T WANNA MISS THE PREVIEWS.
HOLD UP. I FOUND THAT CHEAT CODE - I'M GONNA TRY IT OUT REAL QUICK.
AW, C'MON.
X TREME BIGFOOT FIGHTER!!
DUDE, WHATEVER! THE BIGFOOT'S GONNA EAT YOU FOR LUNCH, JUST LIKE HE ALWAYS DOES.
NOT THIS TIME.. CHECK IT OUT, LOSERS. I UNLOCKED THE SECRET CHARACTER: SHADOW PETAL X. SASSY'S ASS IS MINE!!
BY GRANT GOULD
PLAYER 01
CODE 3
SHADOW PETAL X.
GOOD LUCK!!!
FOR FIST BLAST,
UP-UP-A-SELECT
A-SELECT-UP-UP-B
FOR ENERGY SHIELD
WHOA, SWEET.
DUDE, AWESOME.

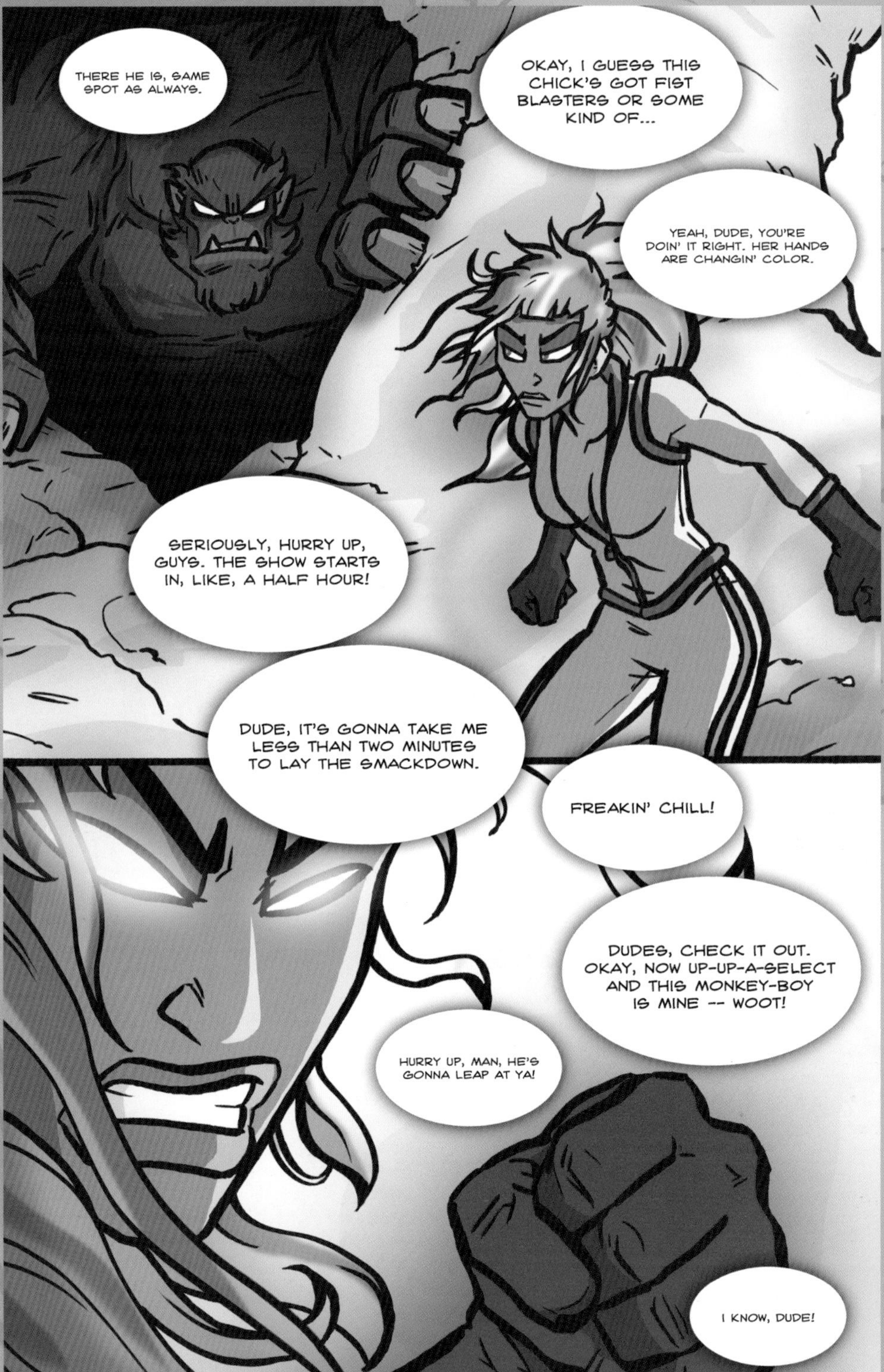
THERE HE IS, SAME SPOT AS ALWAYS.
OKAY, I GUESS THIS CHICK'S GOT FIST BLASTERS OR SOME KIND OF...
YEAH, DUDE, YOU'RE DOIN' IT RIGHT. HER HANDS ARE CHANGIN' COLOR.
SERIOUSLY, HURRY UP, GUYS. THE SHOW STARTS IN, LIKE, A HALF HOUR!
DUDE, IT'S GONNA TAKE ME LESS THAN TWO MINUTES TO LAY THE SMACKDOWN.
FREAKIN' CHILL!
DUDES, CHECK IT OUT. OKAY, NOW UP-UP-A-SELECT AND THIS MONKEY-BOY IS MINE -- WOOT!
HURRY UP, MAN, HE'S GONNA LEAP AT YA!
I KNOW, DUDE!

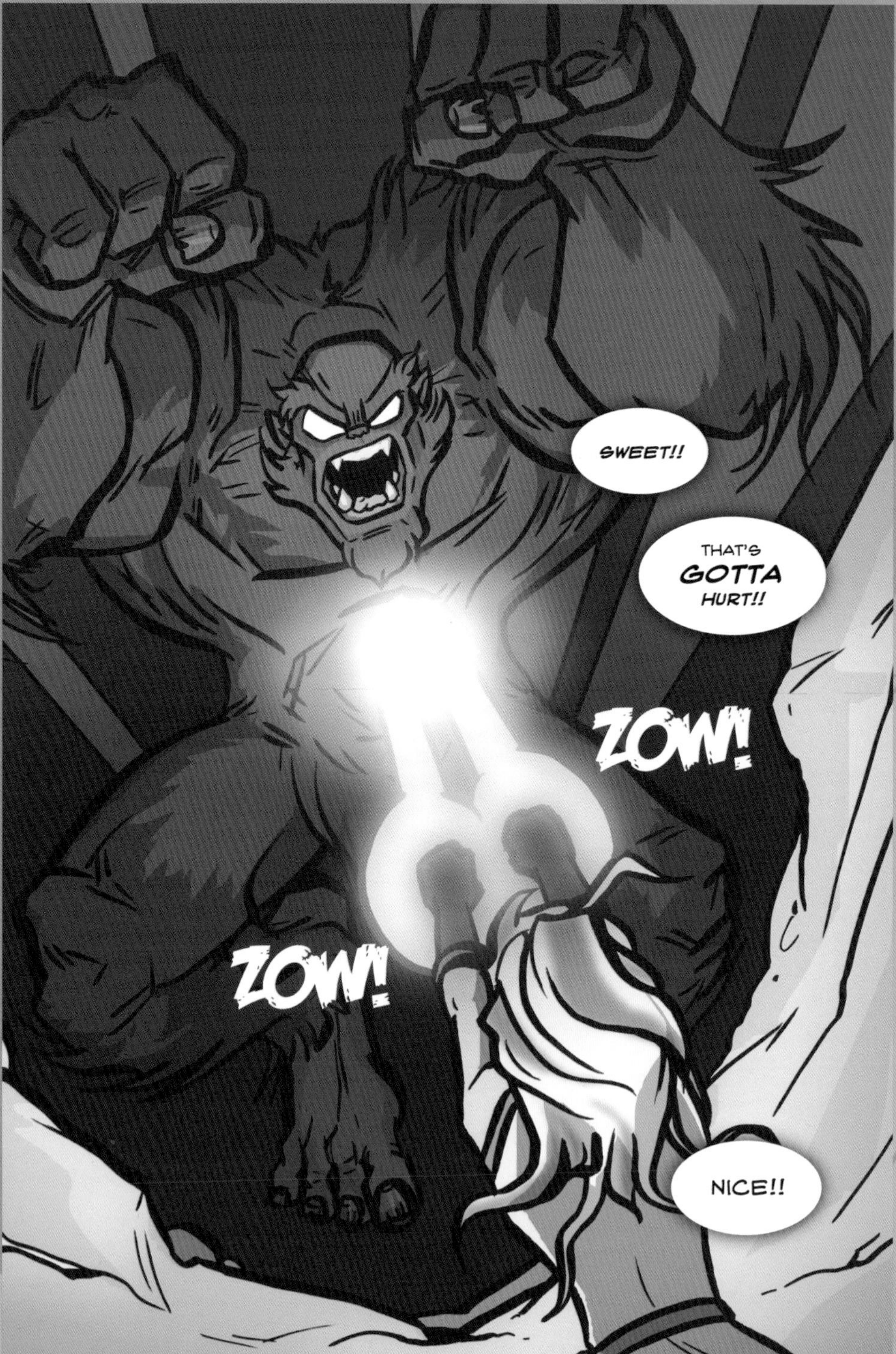
SWEET!!
THAT'S GOTTA HURT!!
ZOW!
ZOW!
NICE!!

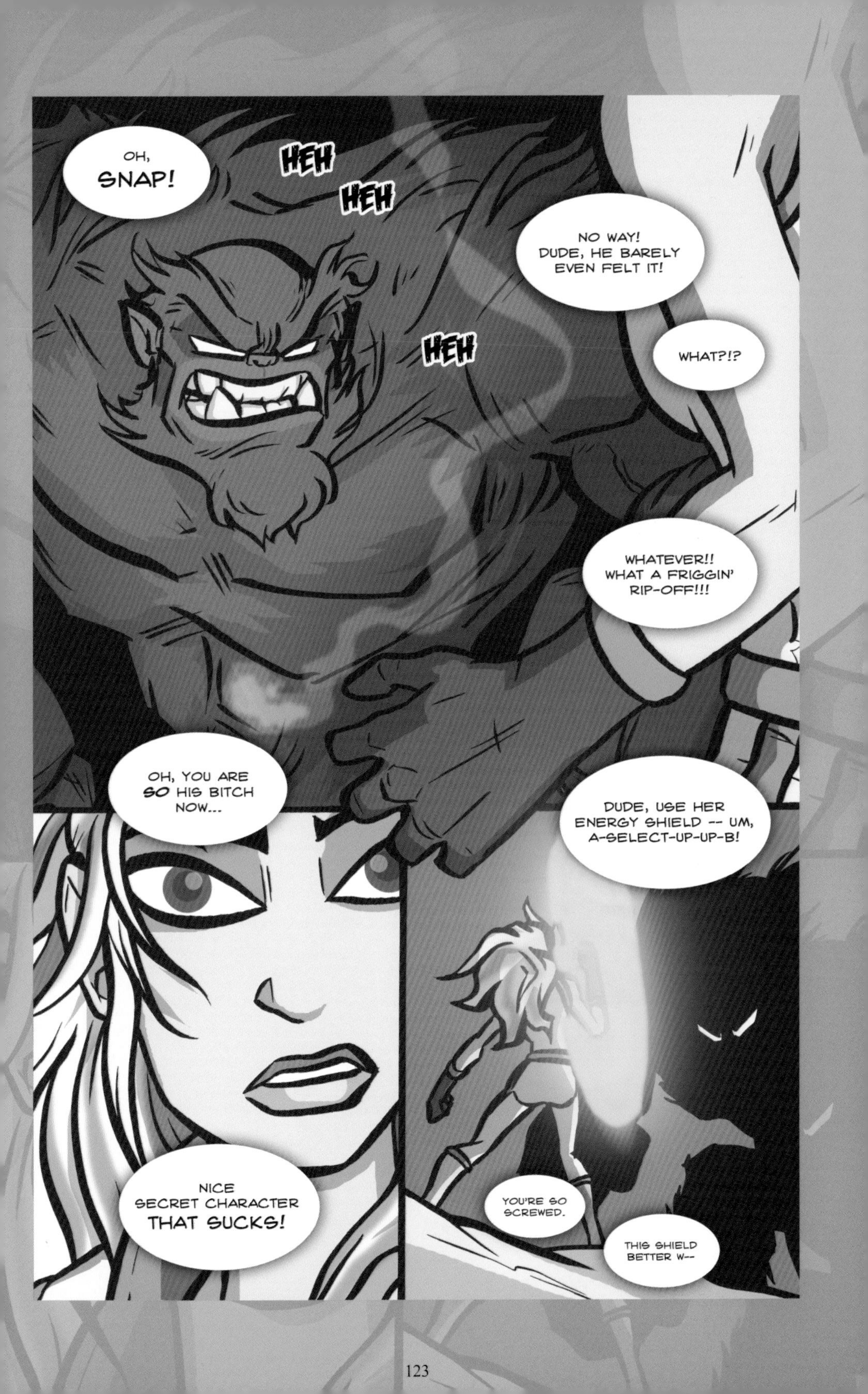
OH,
SNAP!
HEH
HEH
NO WAY!
DUDE, HE BARELY
EVEN FELT IT!
HEH
WHAT?!?
WHATEVER!!
WHAT A FRIGGIN'
RIP-OFF!!!
OH, YOU ARE
SO HIS BITCH
NOW...
NICE
SECRET CHARACTER
THAT SUCKS!
DUDE, USE HER
ENERGY SHIELD -- UM,
A-SELECT-UP-UP-B!
YOU'RE SO
SCREWED.
THIS SHIELD
BETTER W--

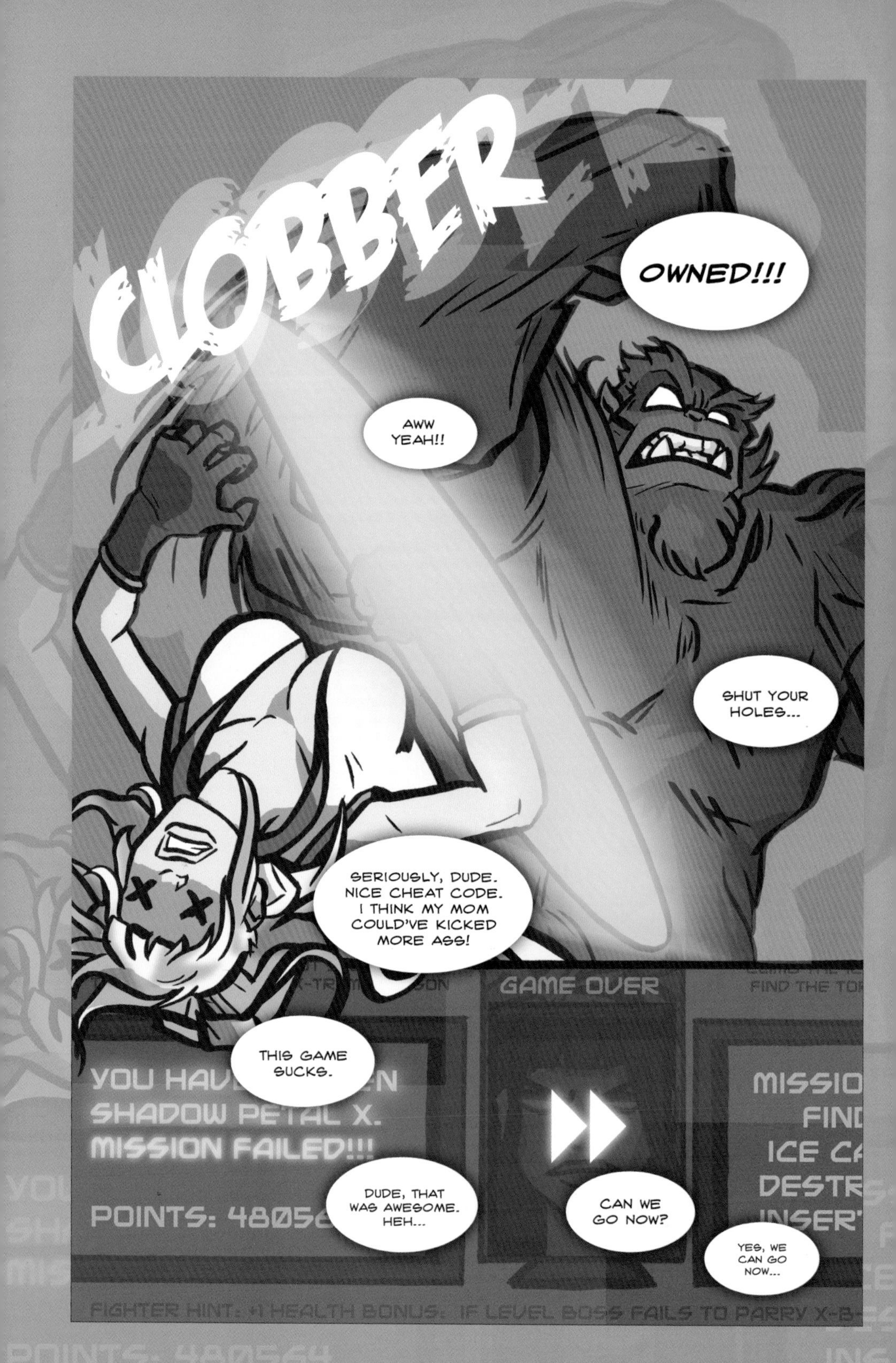
CLOBBER
OWNED!!!
AWW YEAH!!
SHUT YOUR HOLES...
SERIOUSLY, DUDE. NICE CHEAT CODE. I THINK MY MOM COULD'VE KICKED MORE ASS!
GAME OVER
FIND THE TO
THIS GAME SUCKS.
YOU HAV EN
SHADOW PETAL X.
MISSION FAILED!!!
POINTS: 48056
DUDE, THAT WAS AWESOME. HEH...
CAN WE GO NOW?
YES, WE CAN GO NOW...
MISSIO
FIND
ICE CA
DESTR
INSERT
FIGHTER HINT: +1 HEALTH BONUS: IF LEVEL BOSS FAILS TO PARRY X-B-
POINTS: 480564

WHEN A FOOL LOVES A WOMAN

BY MARIO WYTCH
& MYKAL ADAMS

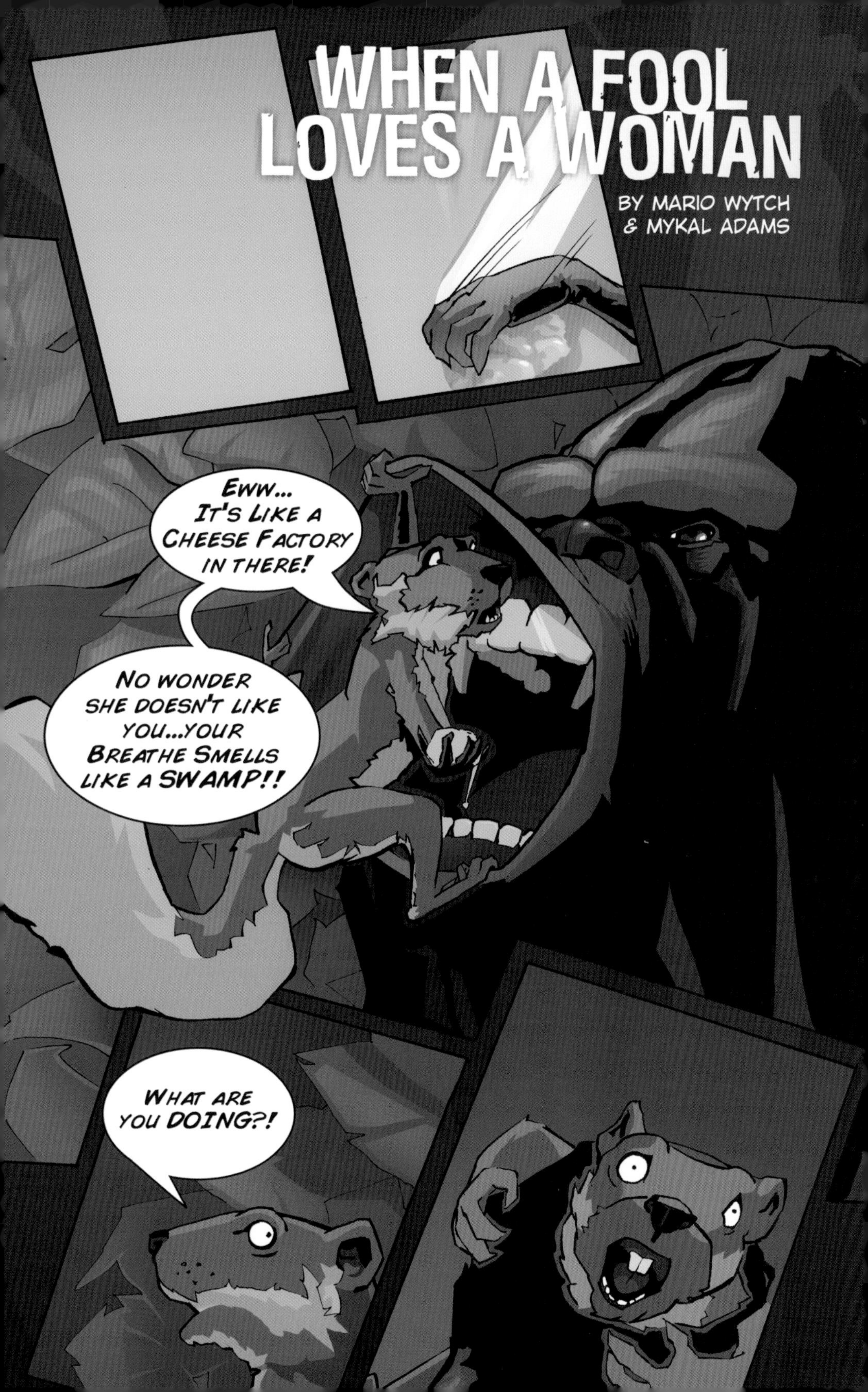
EWW... IT'S LIKE A CHEESE FACTORY IN THERE!
NO WONDER SHE DOESN'T LIKE YOU...YOUR BREATHE SMELLS LIKE A SWAMP!!
WHAT ARE YOU DOING?!

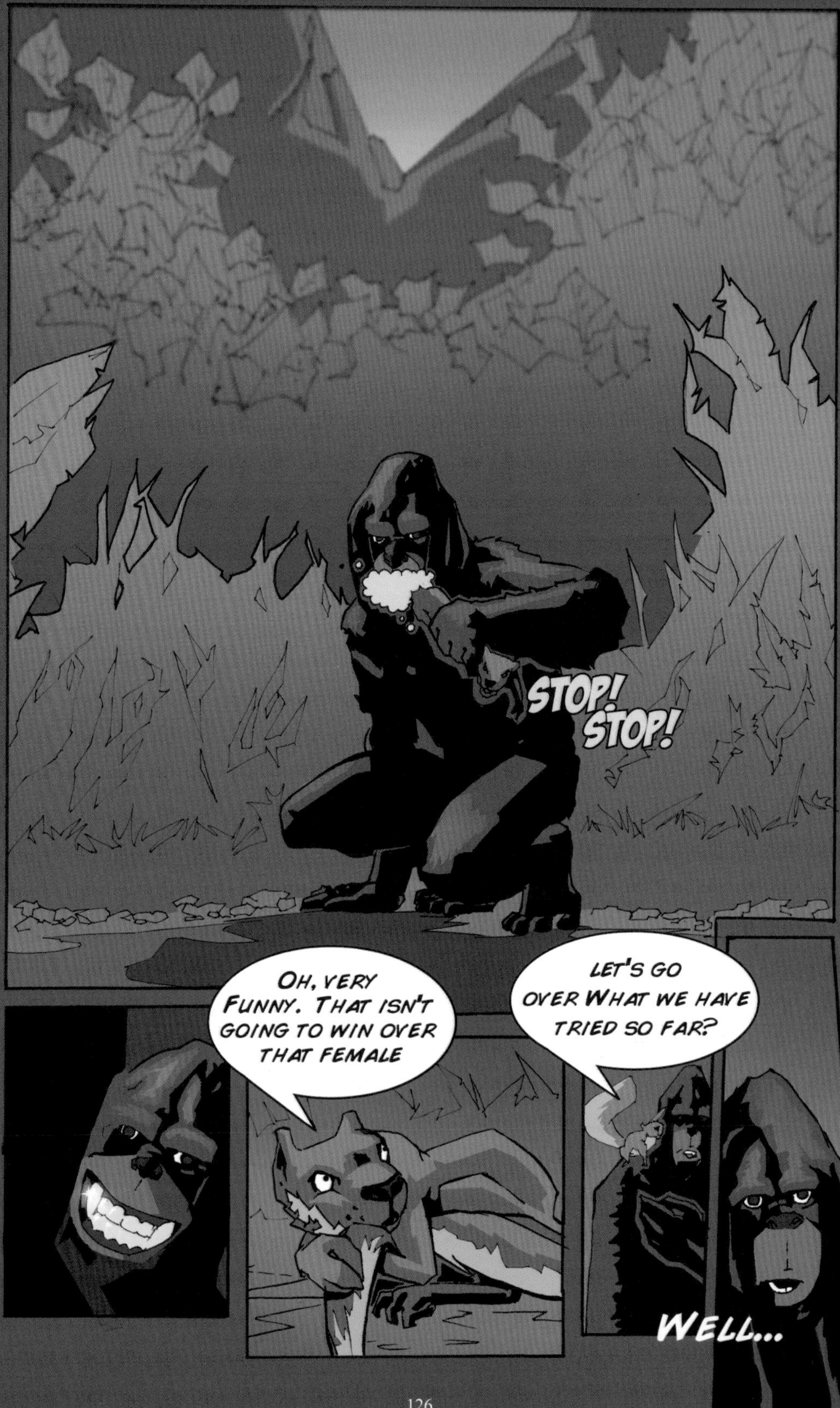
STOP! STOP!
OH, VERY FUNNY. THAT ISN'T GOING TO WIN OVER THAT FEMALE
LET'S GO OVER WHAT WE HAVE TRIED SO FAR?
WELL...

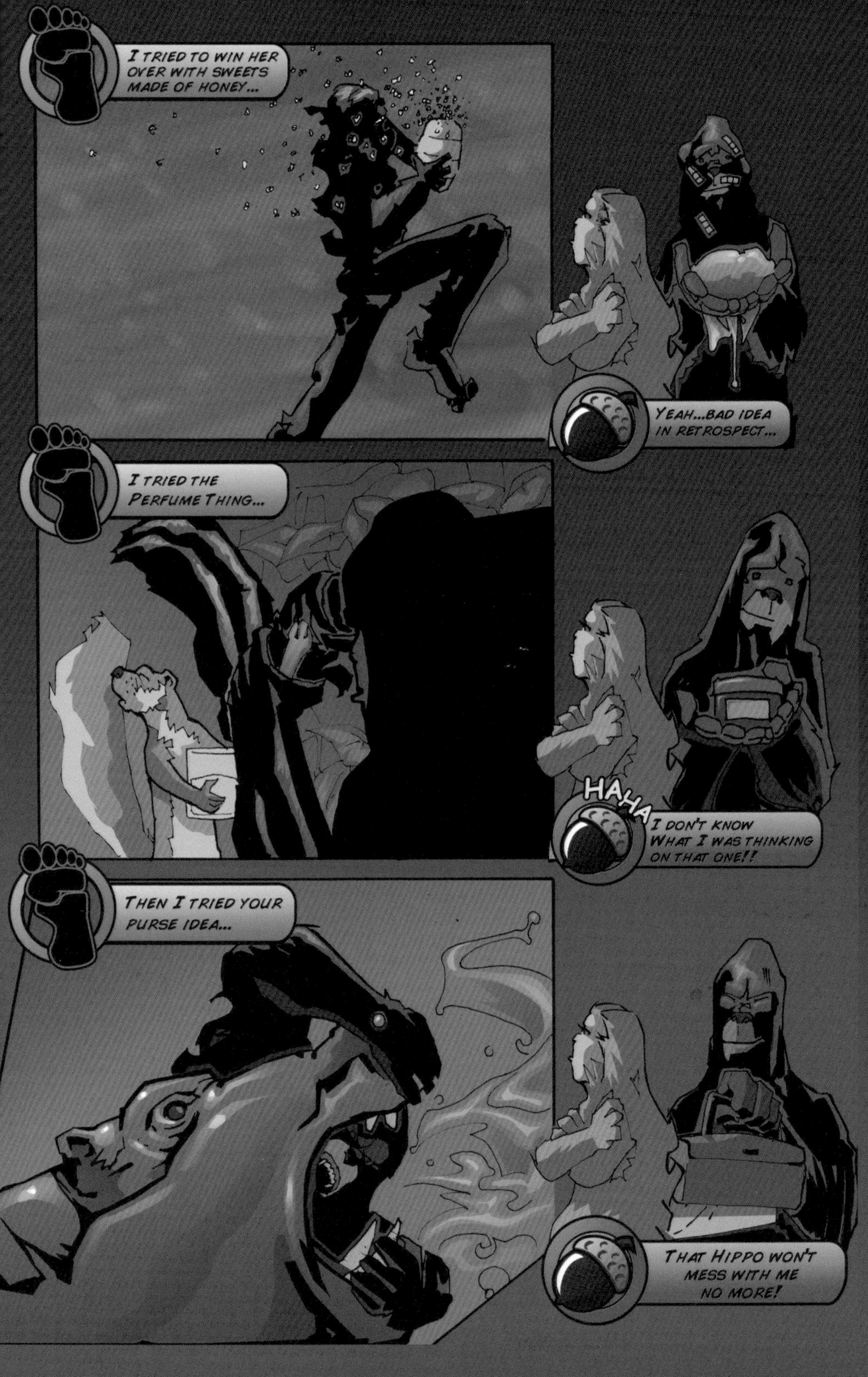

I TRIED TO WIN HER OVER WITH SWEETS MADE OF HONEY...
YEAH...BAD IDEA IN RETROSPECT...
I TRIED THE PERFUME THING...
HAHA
I DON'T KNOW WHAT I WAS THINKING ON THAT ONE!!
THEN I TRIED YOUR PURSE IDEA...
THAT HIPPO WON'T MESS WITH ME NO MORE!

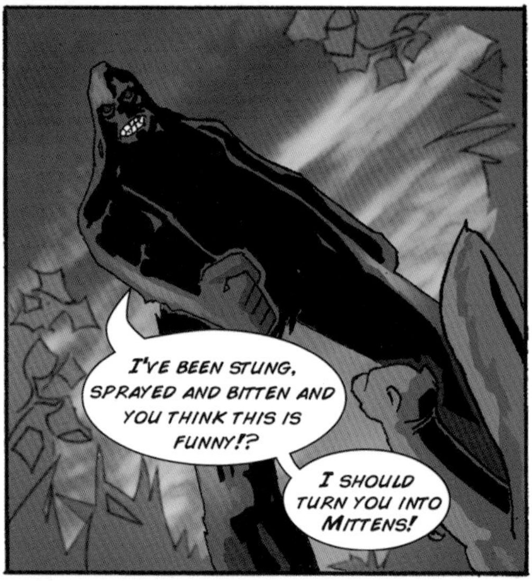
I'VE BEEN STUNG, SPRAYED AND BITTEN AND YOU THINK THIS IS FUNNY!?
I SHOULD TURN YOU INTO MITTENS!

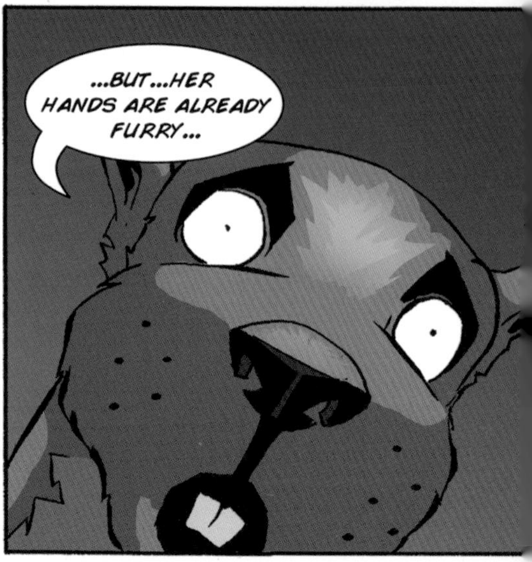
...BUT...HER HANDS ARE ALREADY FURRY...

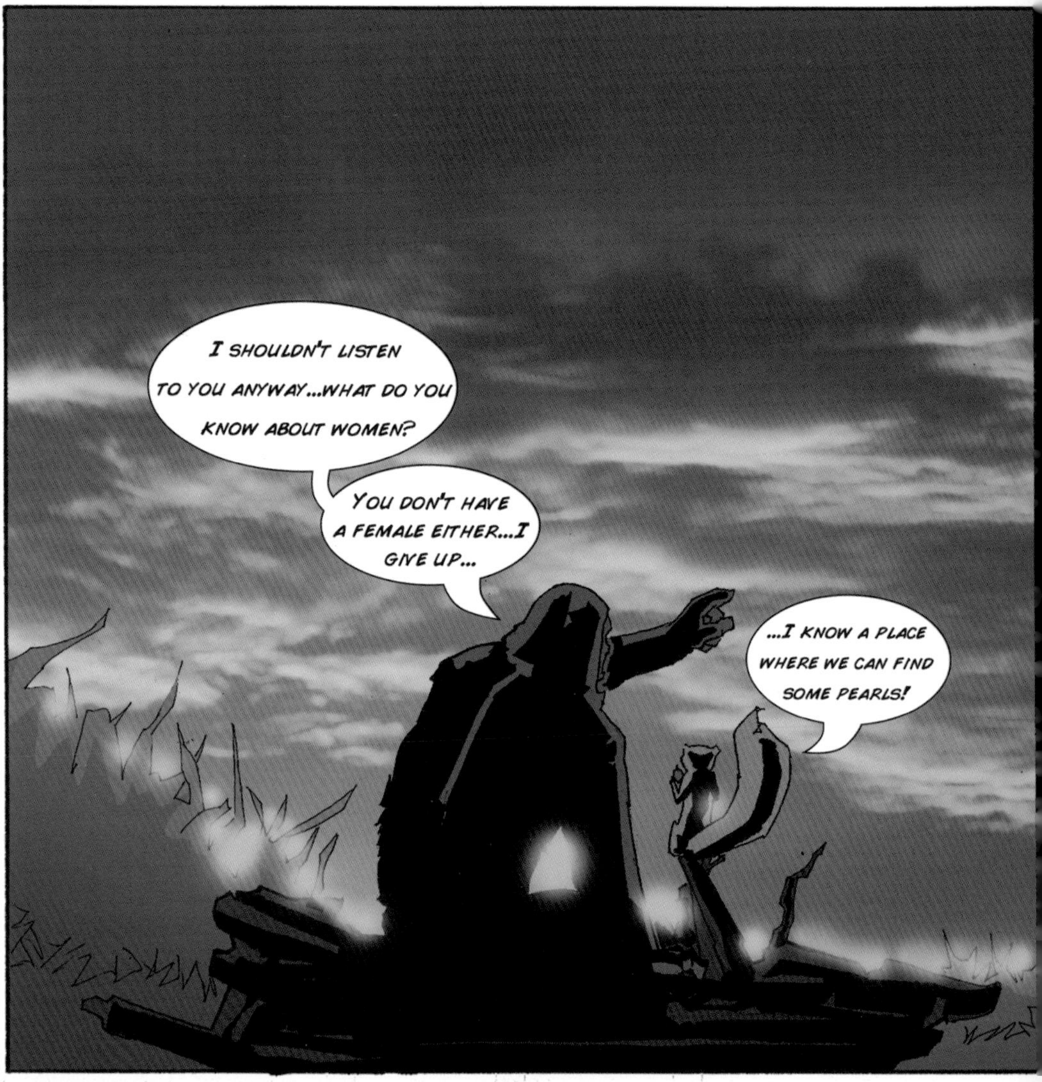
I SHOULDN'T LISTEN TO YOU ANYWAY...WHAT DO YOU KNOW ABOUT WOMEN?
YOU DON'T HAVE A FEMALE EITHER...I GIVE UP...
...I KNOW A PLACE WHERE WE CAN FIND SOME PEARLS!

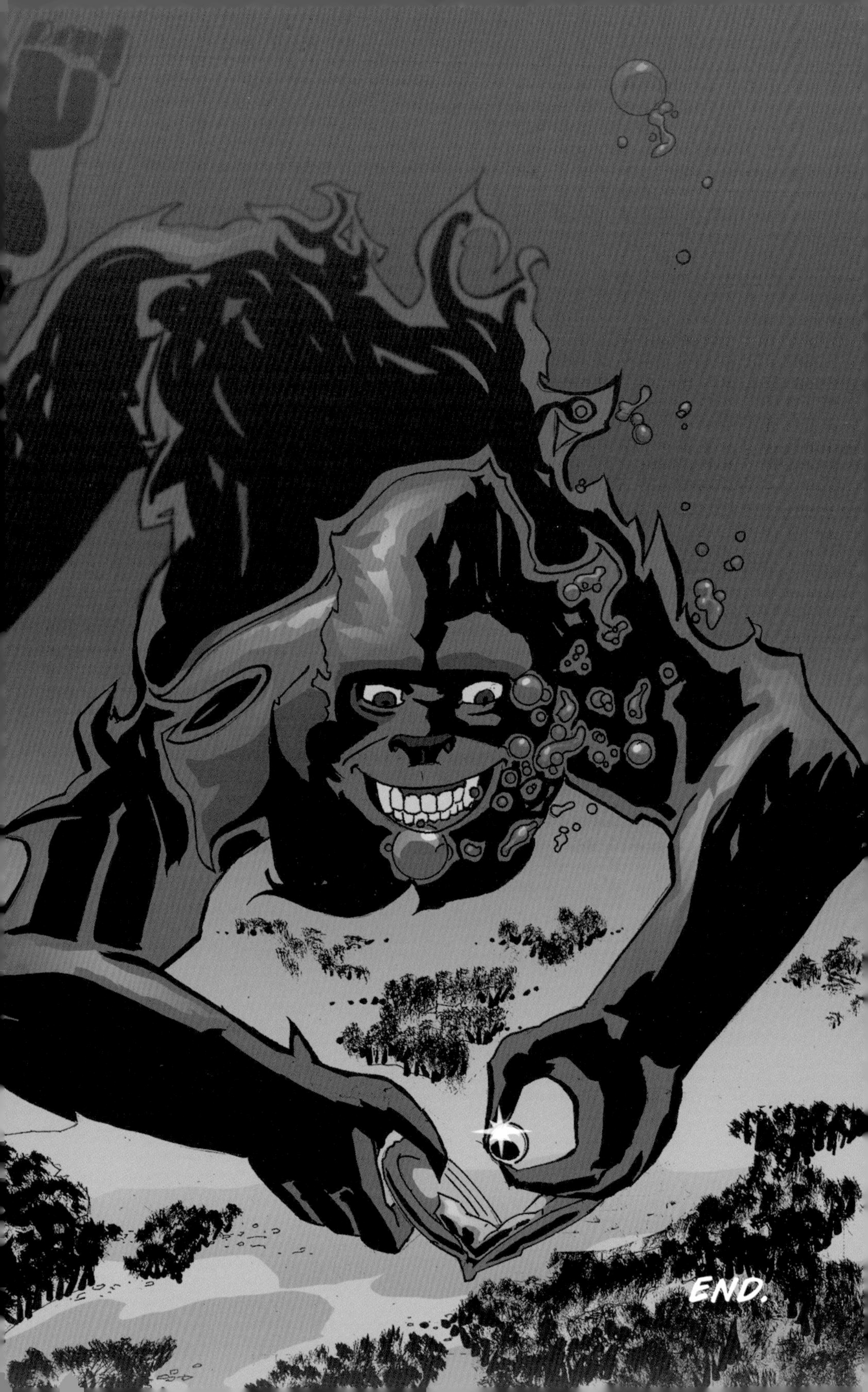
END.

A YETI TALE!

CONCEPT BY WES MOLEBASH
AND THEN STOLEN AND
BUTCHERED BY PAT BUSSEY.

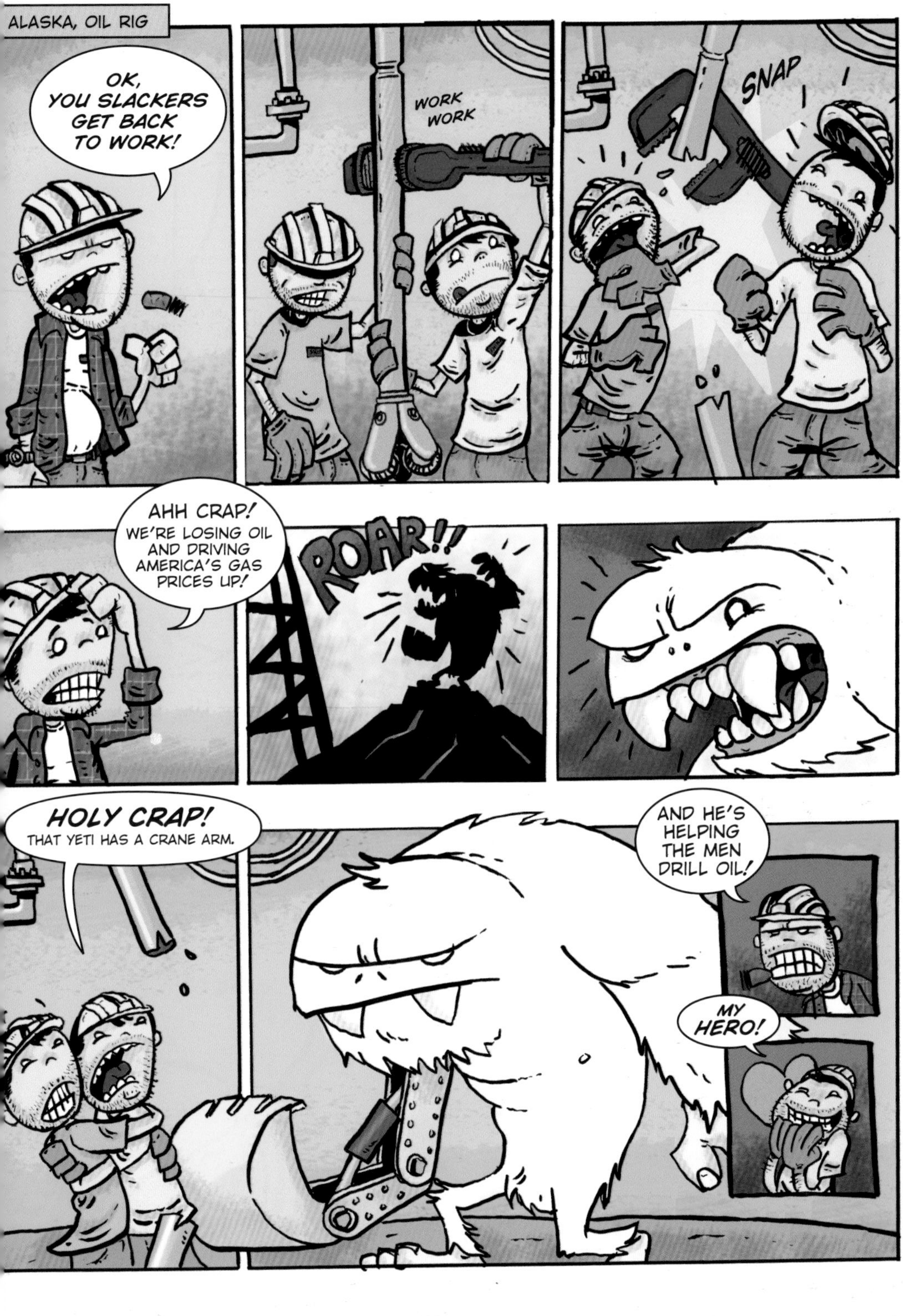
ALASKA, OIL RIG
OK, YOU SLACKERS GET BACK TO WORK!
WORK WORK
SNAP
AHH CRAP! WE'RE LOSING OIL AND DRIVING AMERICA'S GAS PRICES UP!
ROAR!!
HOLY CRAP! THAT YETI HAS A CRANE ARM.
AND HE'S HELPING THE MEN DRILL OIL!
MY HERO!

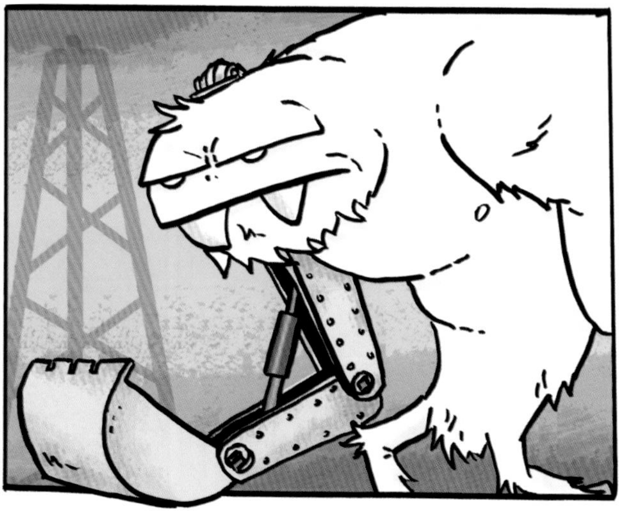

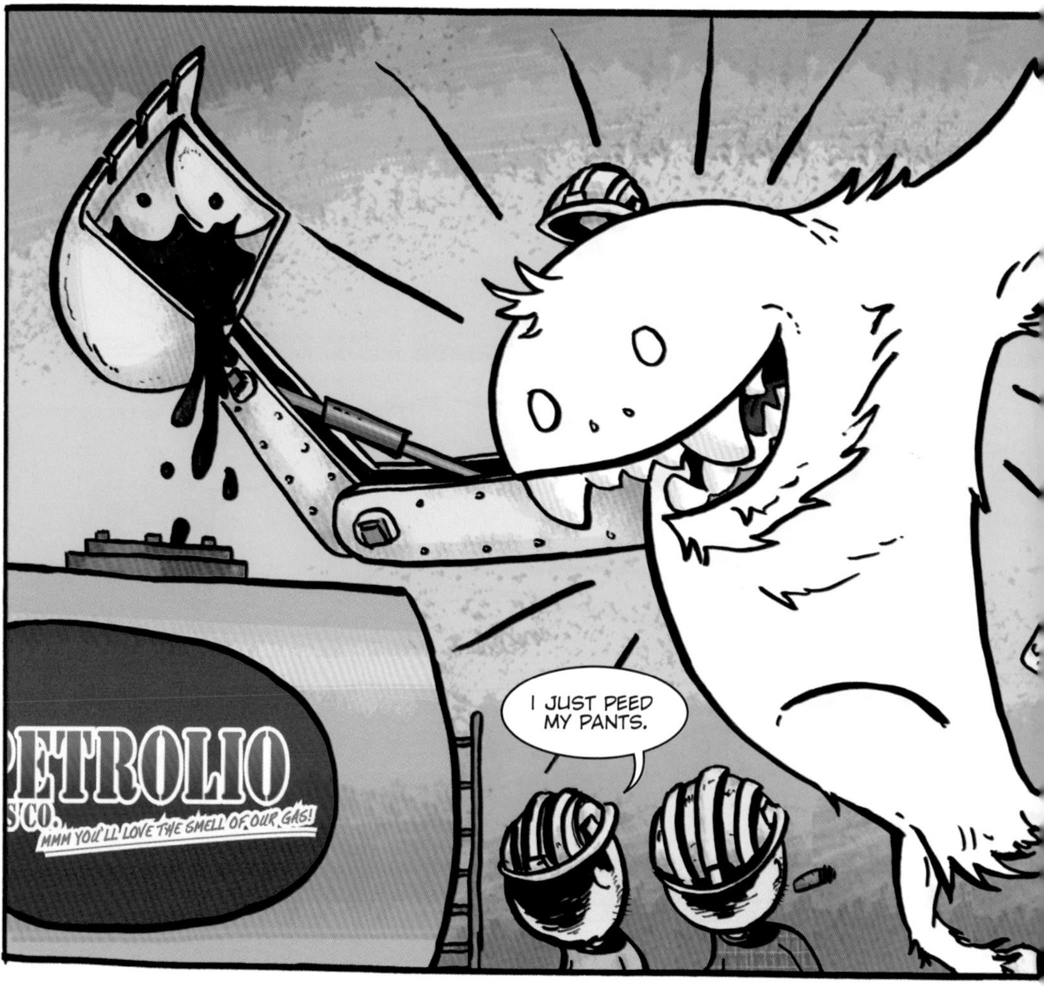
I JUST PEED MY PANTS.
PETROLIO
S CO.
MMM YOU'LL LOVE THE SMELL OF OUR GAS!

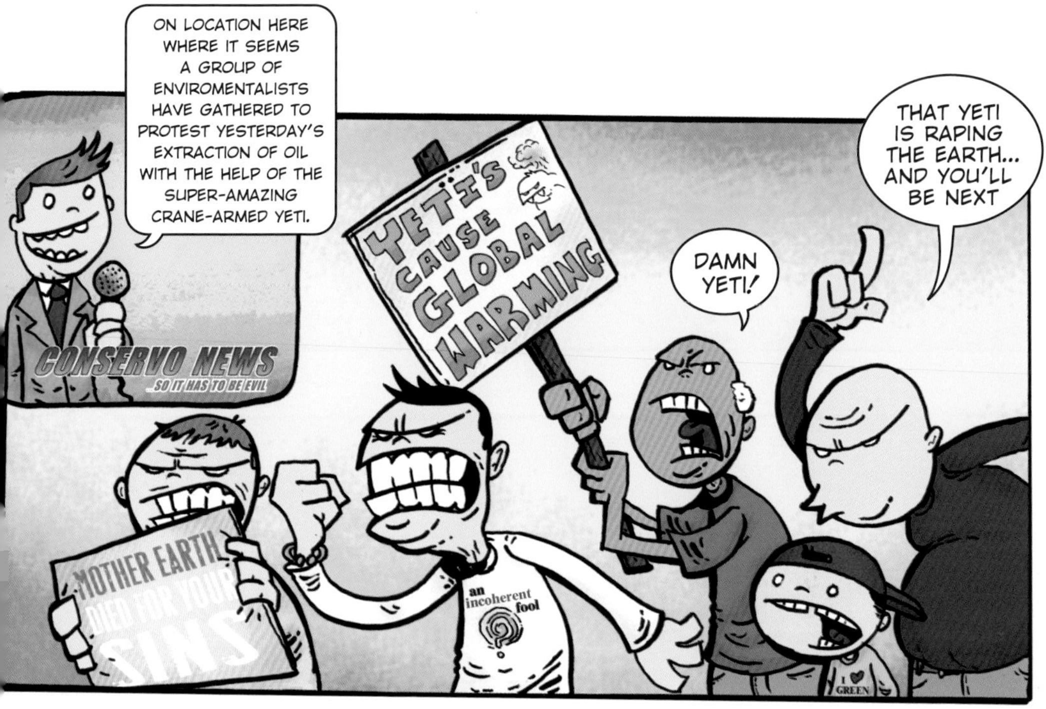
ON LOCATION HERE WHERE IT SEEMS A GROUP OF ENVIROMENTALISTS HAVE GATHERED TO PROTEST YESTERDAY'S EXTRACTION OF OIL WITH THE HELP OF THE SUPER-AMAZING CRANE-ARMED YETI.
CONSERVO NEWS
...SO IT HAS TO BE EVIL
YETI'S CAUSE GLOBAL WARMING
DAMN YETI!
THAT YETI IS RAPING THE EARTH... AND YOU'LL BE NEXT
MOTHER EARTH DIED FOR YOUR SINS
an incoherent fool
GREEN

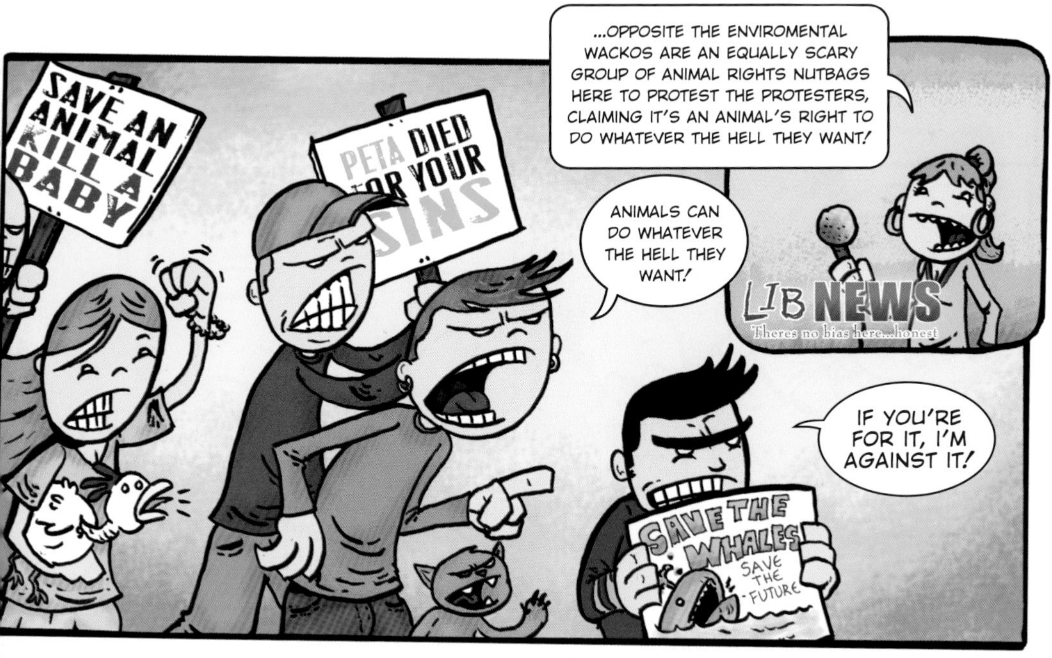
...OPPOSITE THE ENVIROMENTAL WACKOS ARE AN EQUALLY SCARY GROUP OF ANIMAL RIGHTS NUTBAGS HERE TO PROTEST THE PROTESTERS, CLAIMING IT'S AN ANIMAL'S RIGHT TO DO WHATEVER THE HELL THEY WANT!
SAVE AN ANIMAL KILL A BABY
PETA DIED FOR YOUR SINS
ANIMALS CAN DO WHATEVER THE HELL THEY WANT!
LIB NEWS
Theres no bias here...honest
IF YOU'RE FOR IT, I'M AGAINST IT!
SAVE THE WHALES
SAVE THE FUTURE

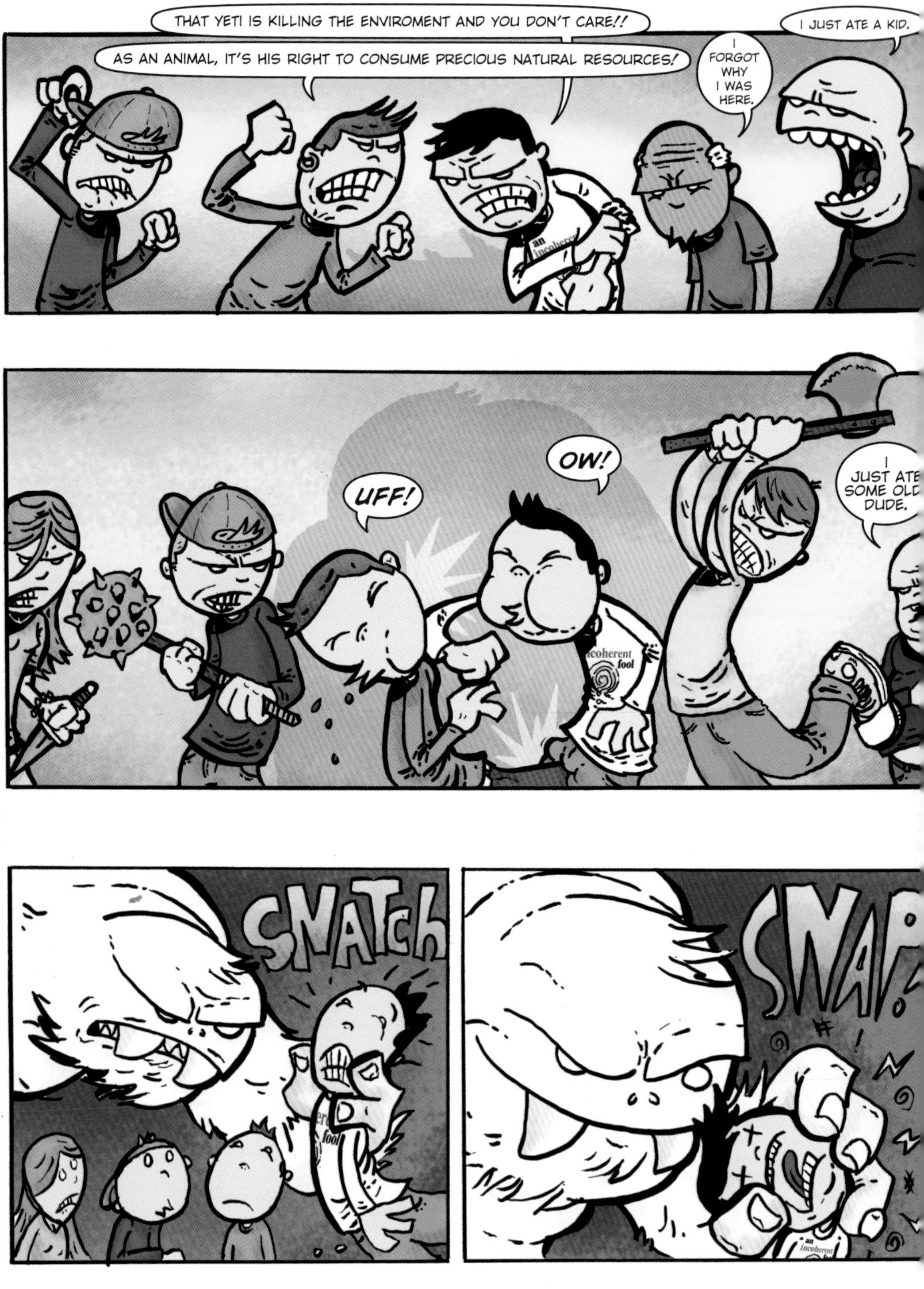
THAT YETI IS KILLING THE ENVIROMENT AND YOU DON'T CARE!!
AS AN ANIMAL, IT'S HIS RIGHT TO CONSUME PRECIOUS NATURAL RESOURCES!
I FORGOT WHY I WAS HERE.
I JUST ATE A KID.
an incoherent
UFF!
OW!
I JUST ATE SOME OLD DUDE.
incoherent fool
SNATCH
fool
SNAP
an incoherent

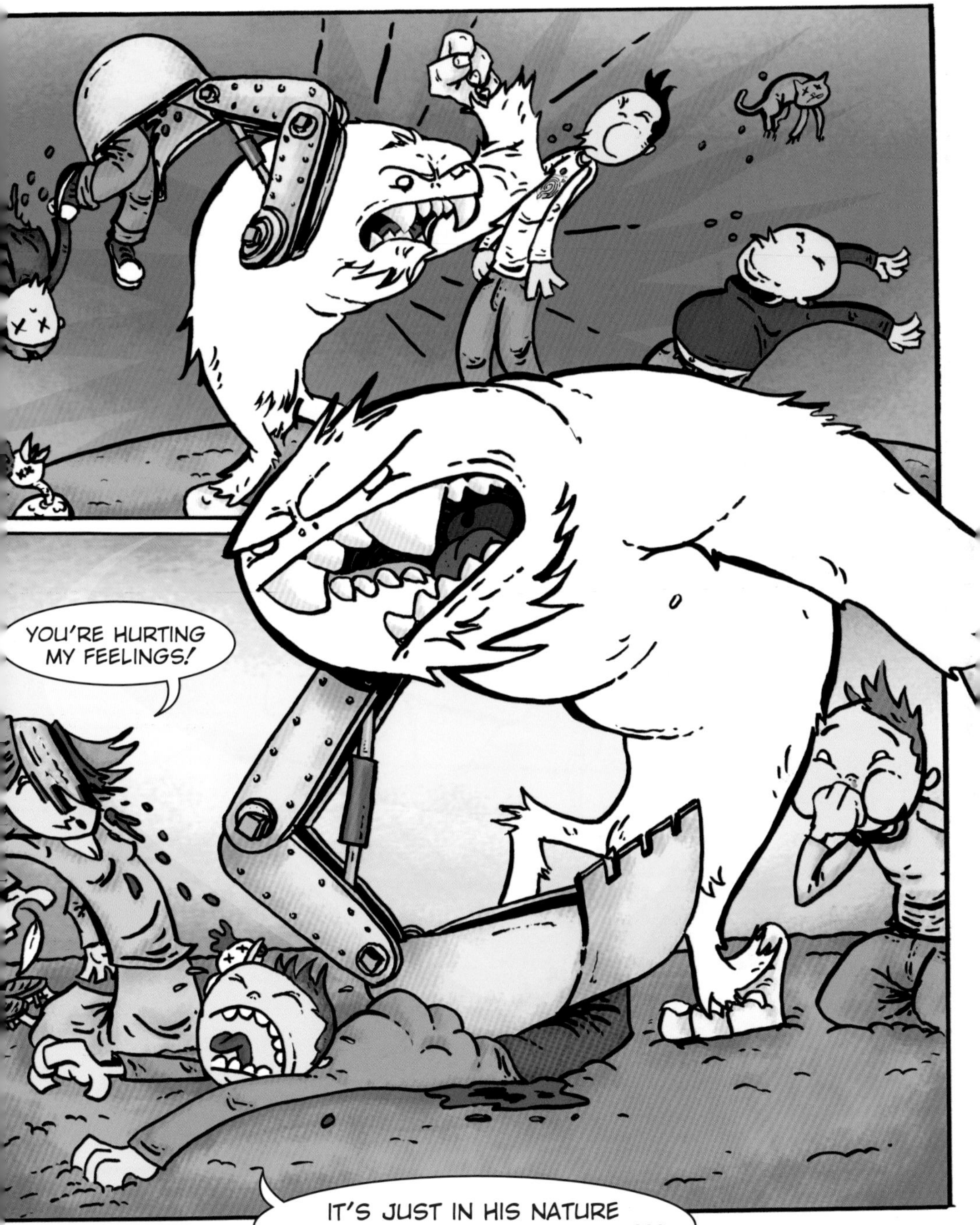
YOU'RE HURTING MY FEELINGS!
IT'S JUST IN HIS NATURE TO FIGHT AND DRILL FOR OIL!!!

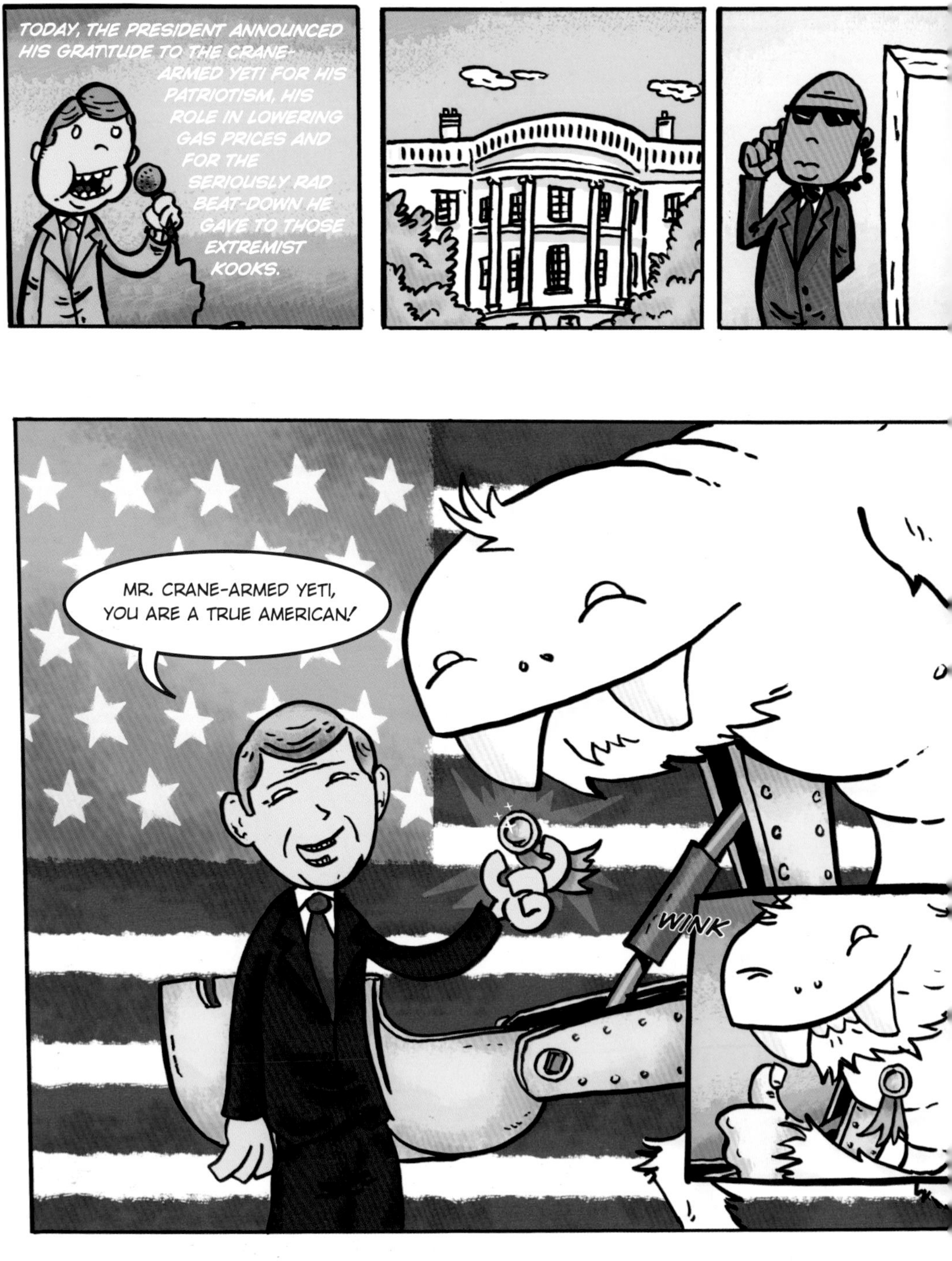
TODAY, THE PRESIDENT ANNOUNCED HIS GRATITUDE TO THE CRANE-ARMED YETI FOR HIS PATRIOTISM, HIS ROLE IN LOWERING GAS PRICES AND FOR THE SERIOUSLY RAD BEAT-DOWN HE GAVE TO THOSE EXTREMIST KOOKS.
MR. CRANE-ARMED YETI, YOU ARE A TRUE AMERICAN!
WINK

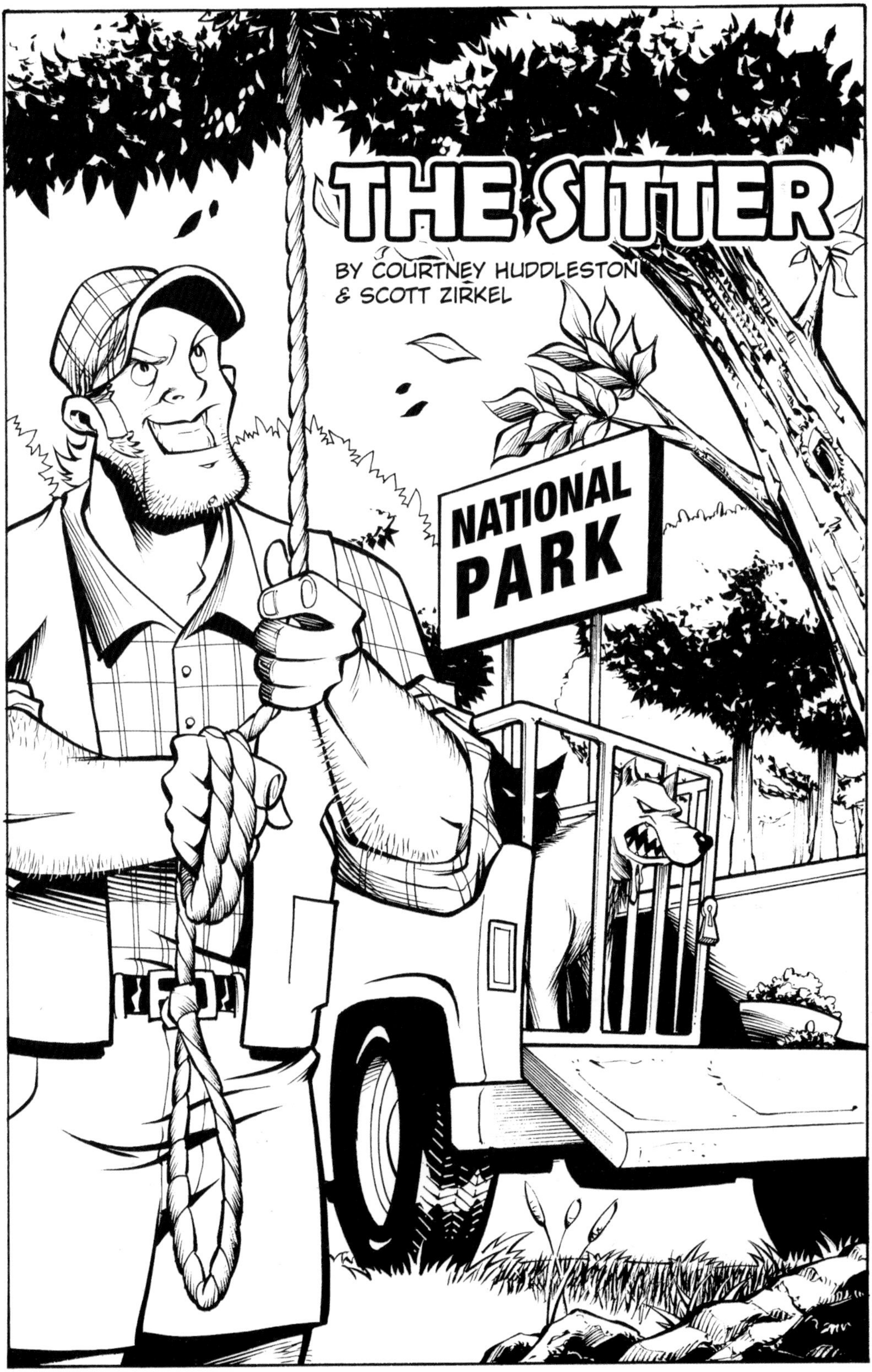
THE SITTER
BY COURTNEY HUDDLESTON
& SCOTT ZIRKEL
NATIONAL
PARK

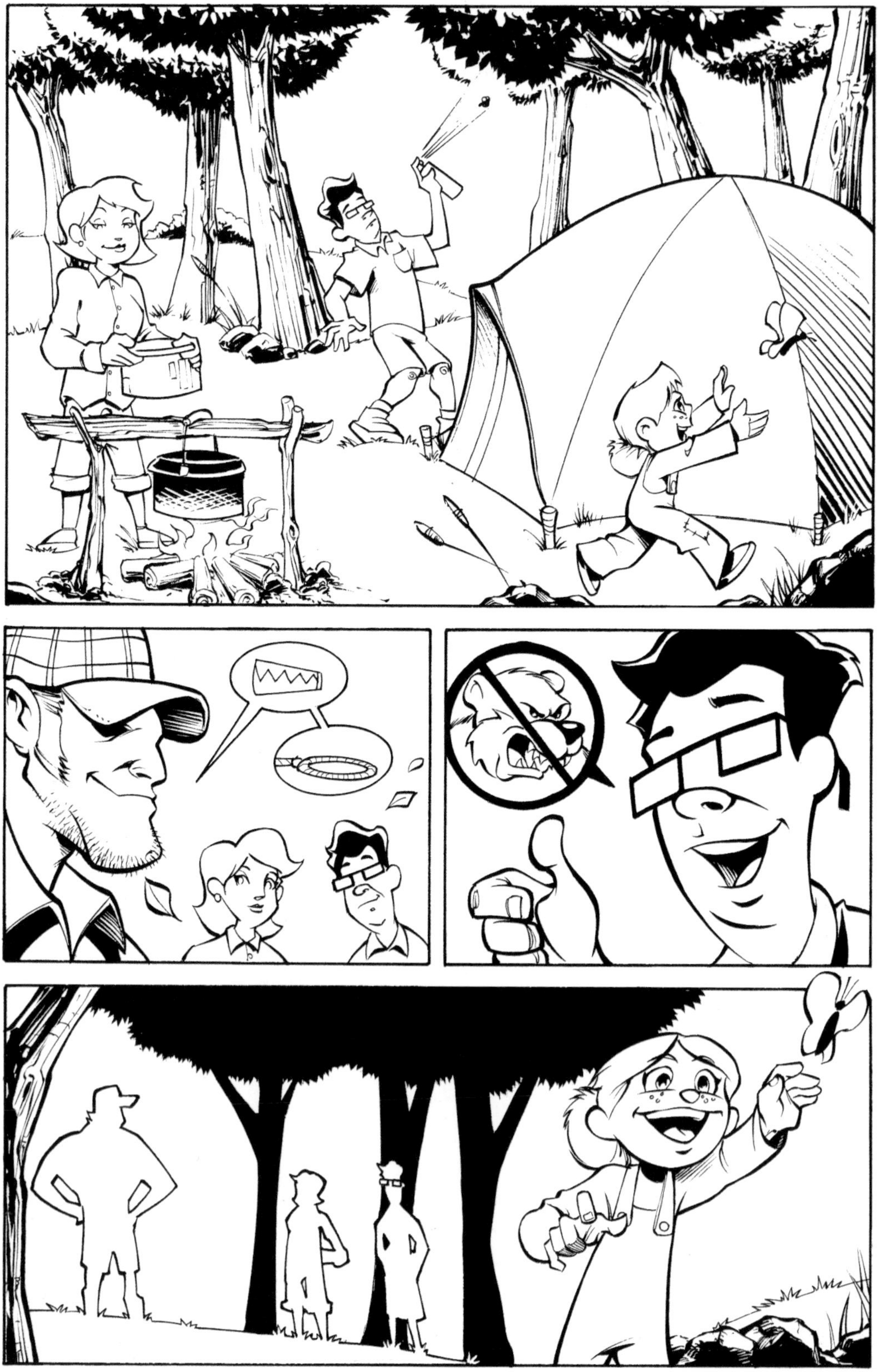

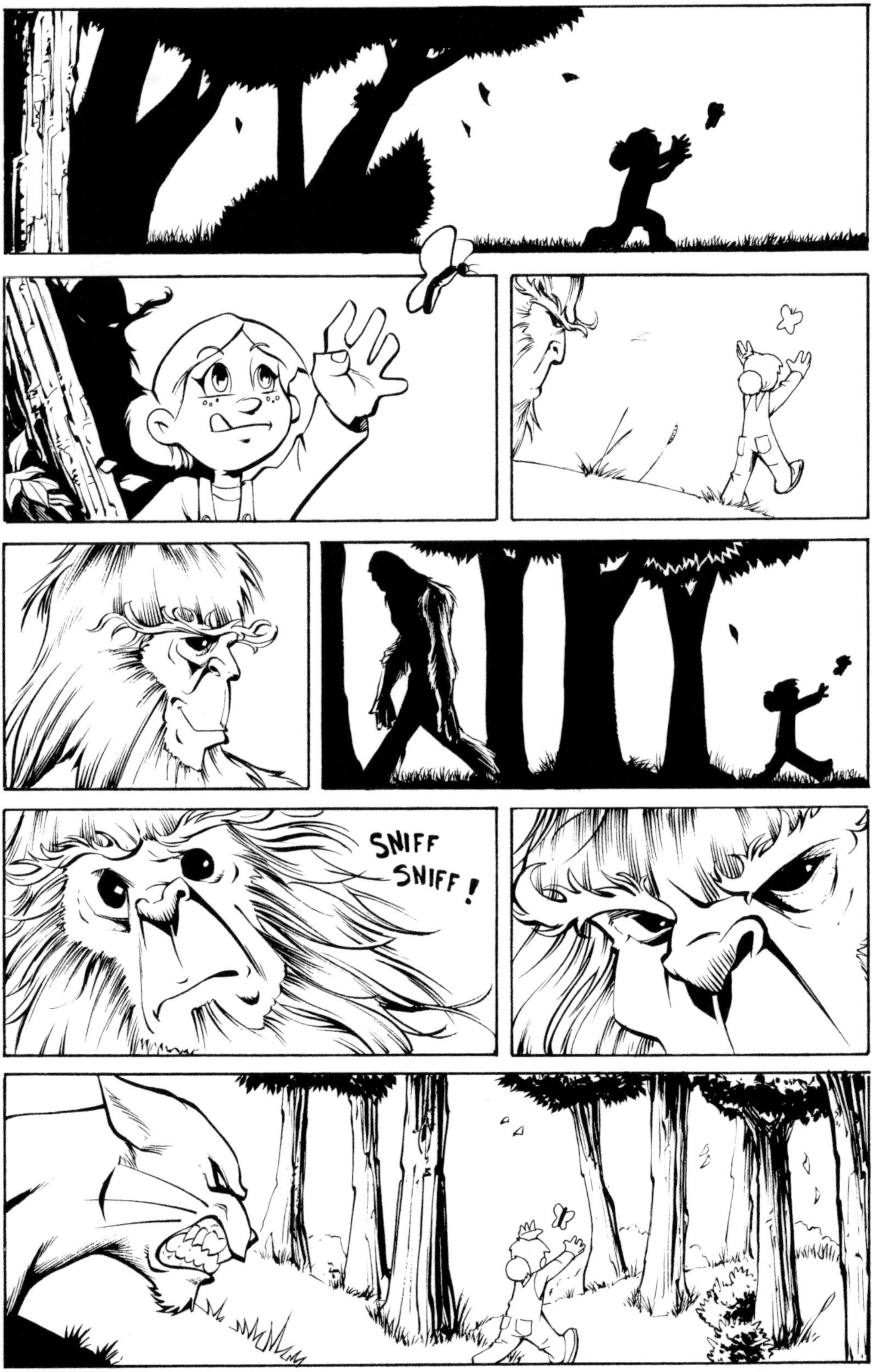
SNIFF
SNIFF!

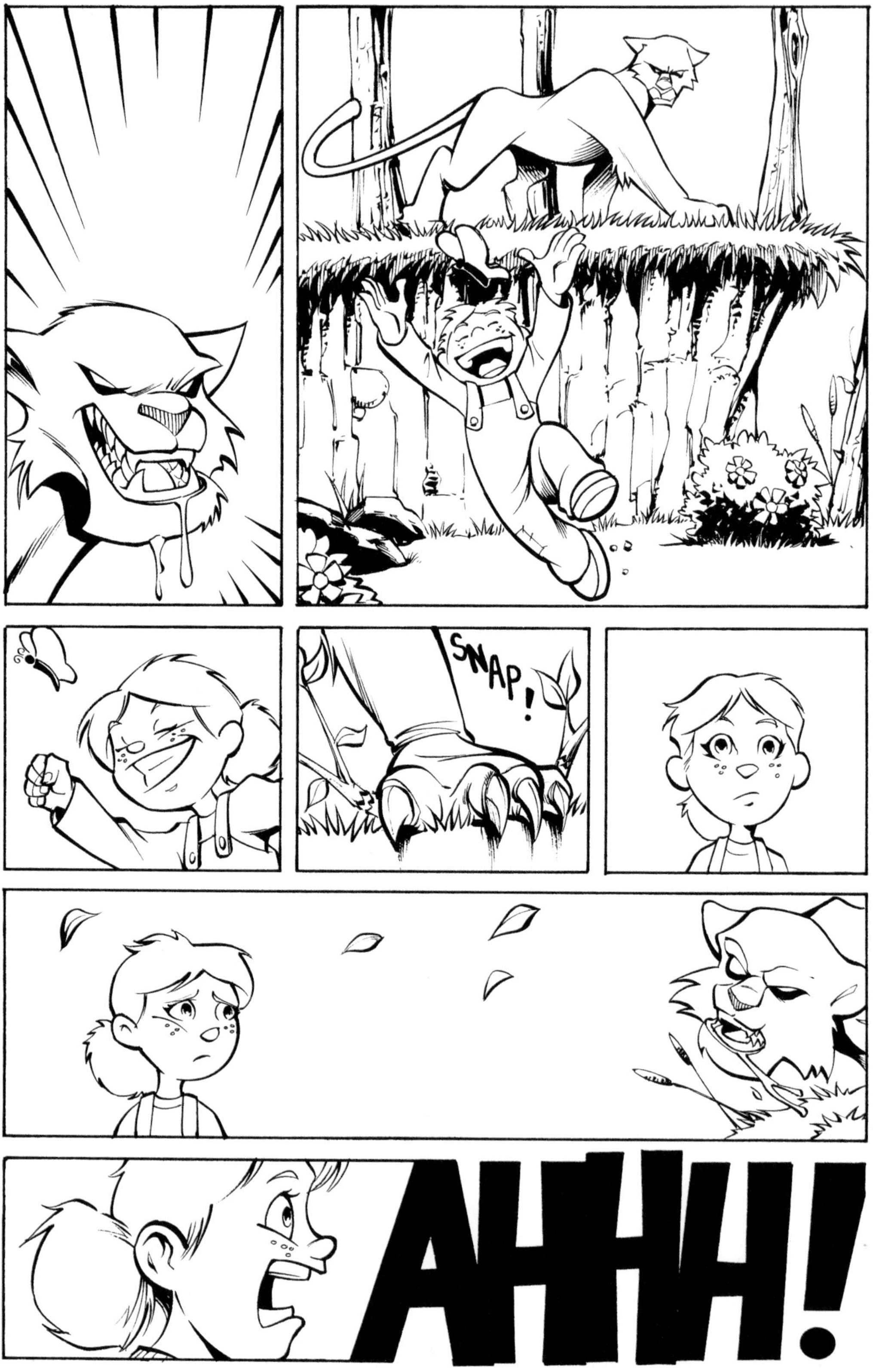
SNAP!
AHHH!

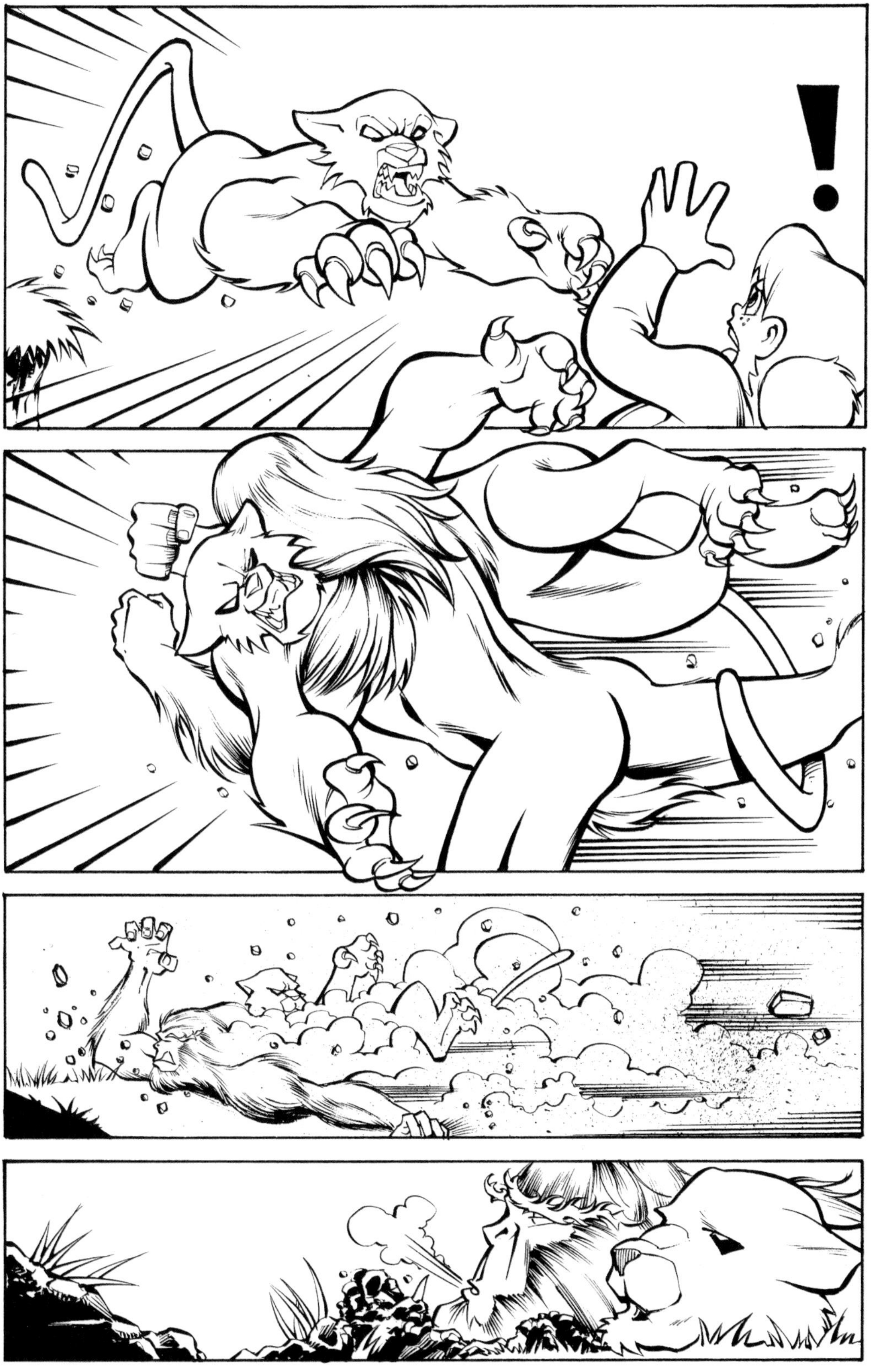
!

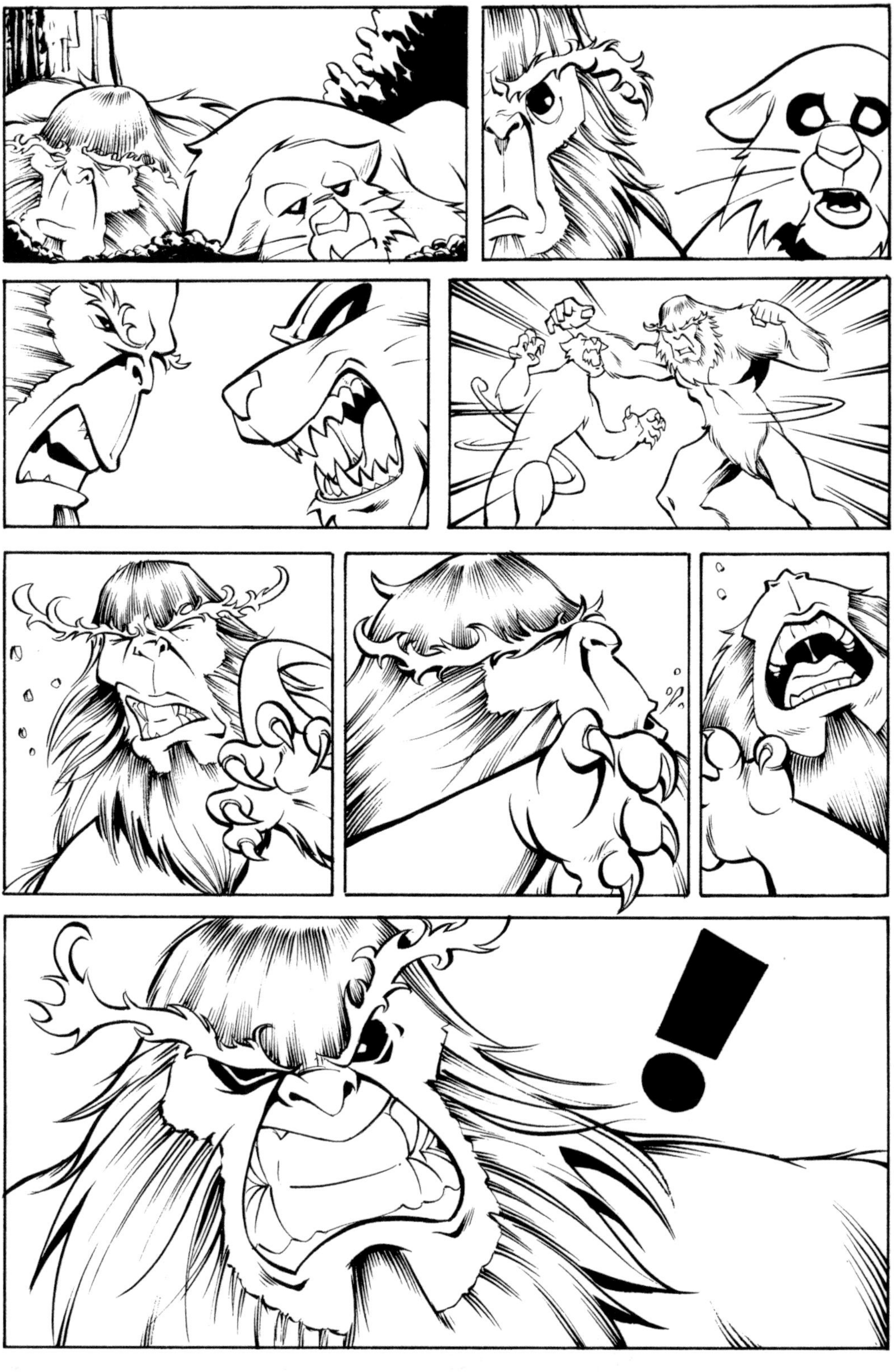
!

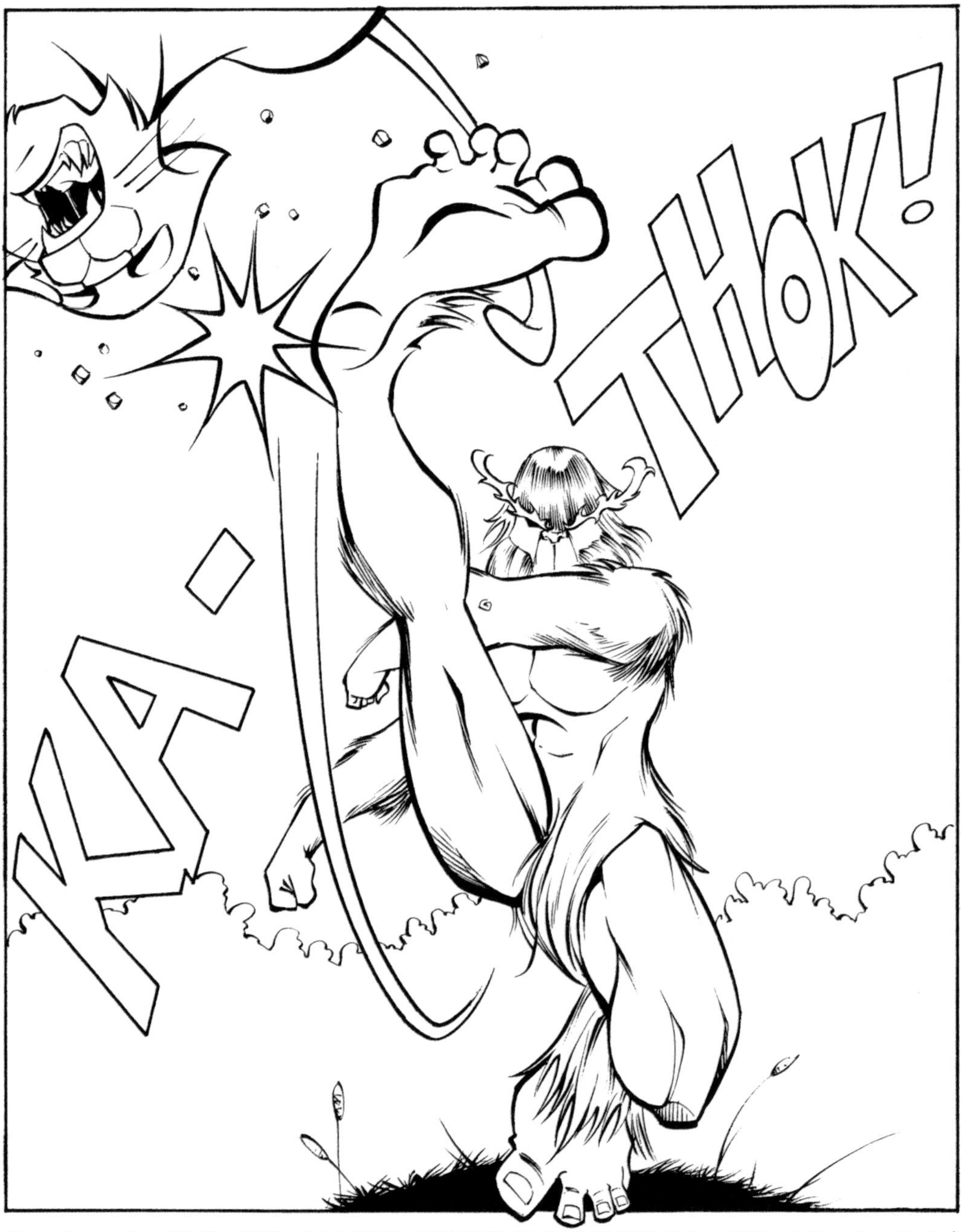
KA-THOK!

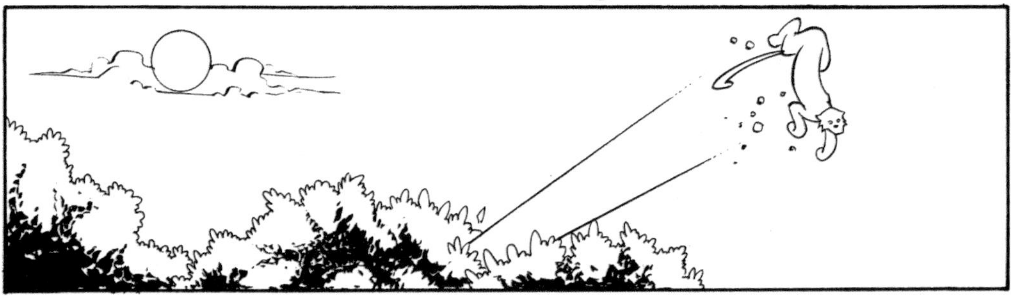

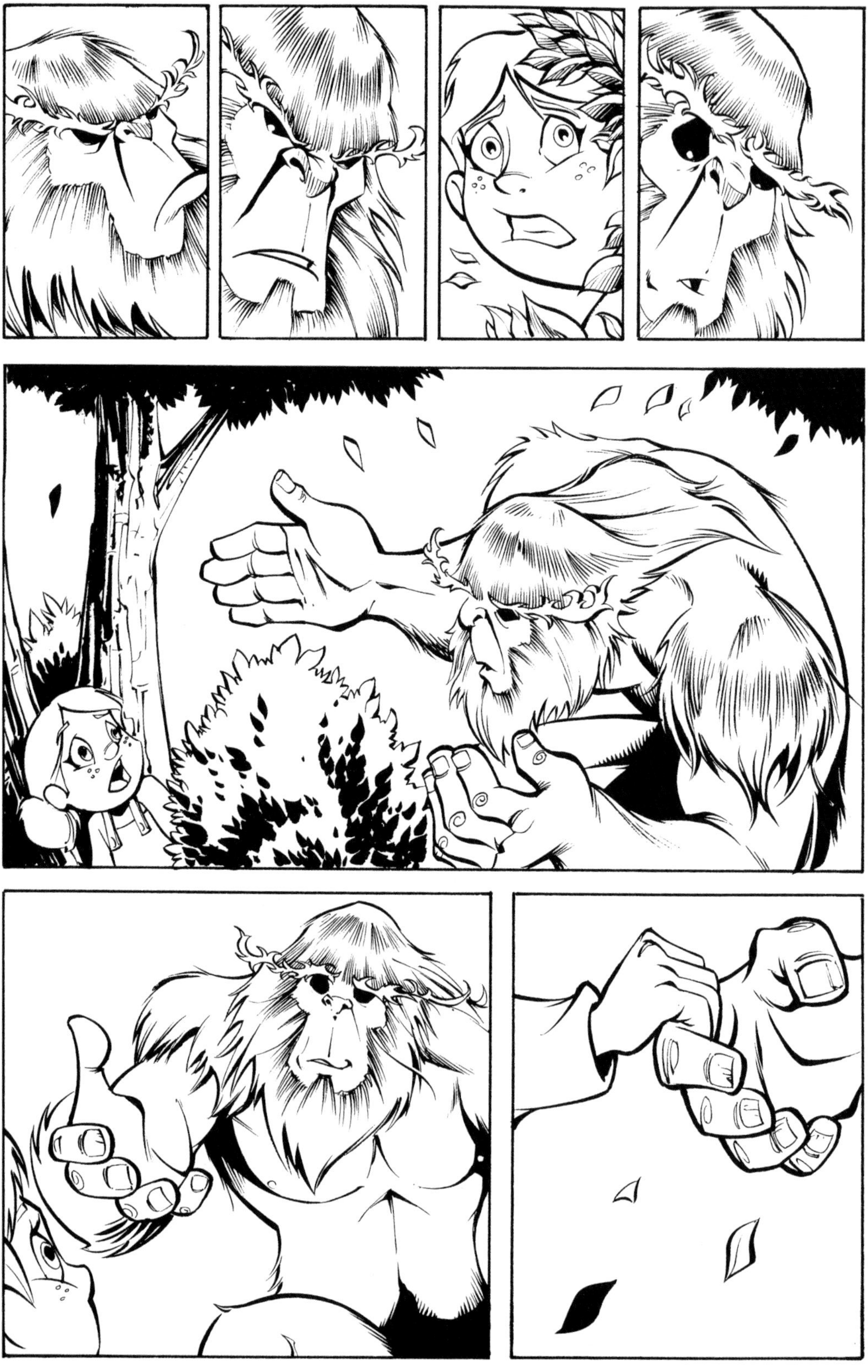

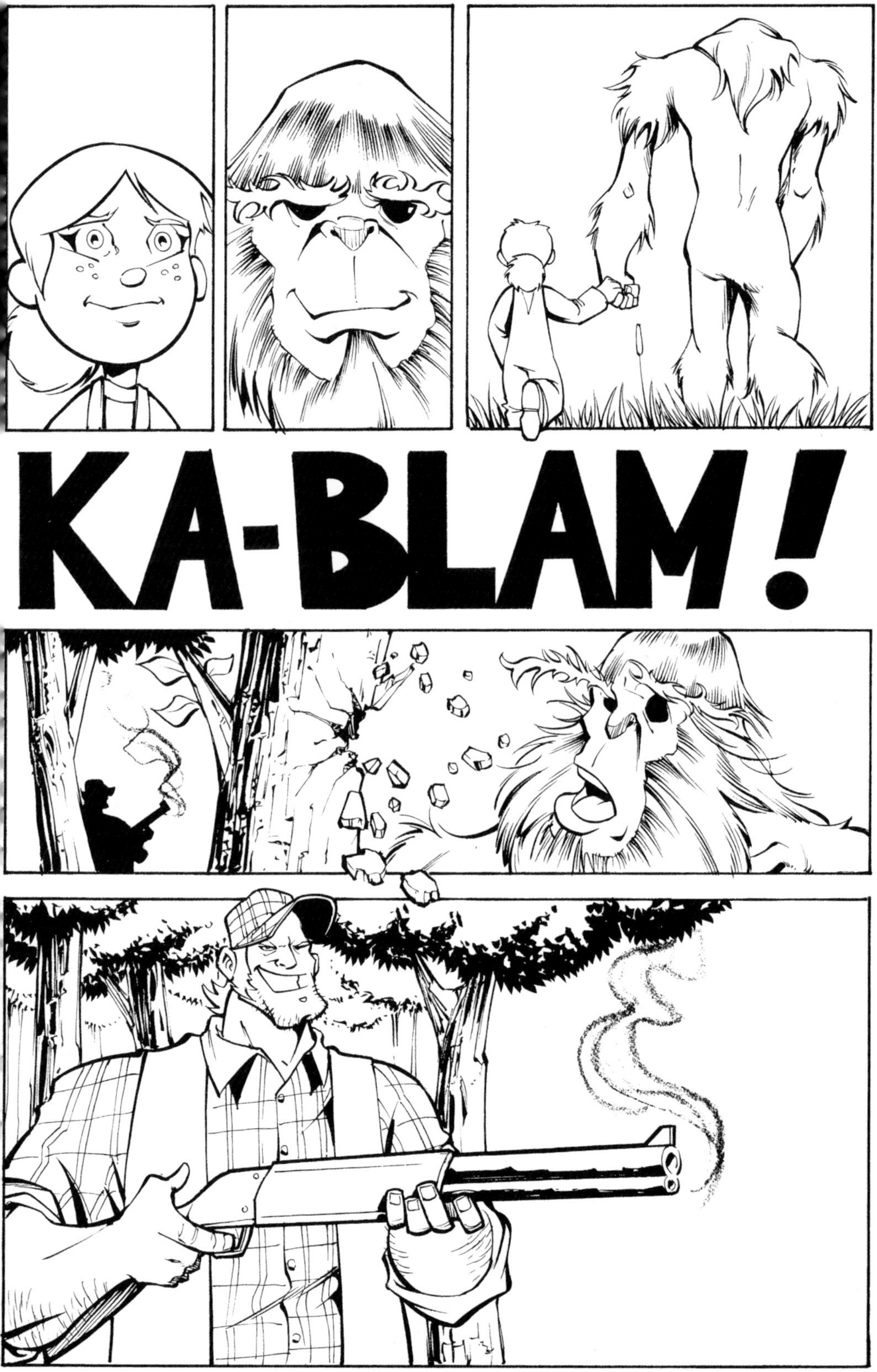
KA-BLAM!

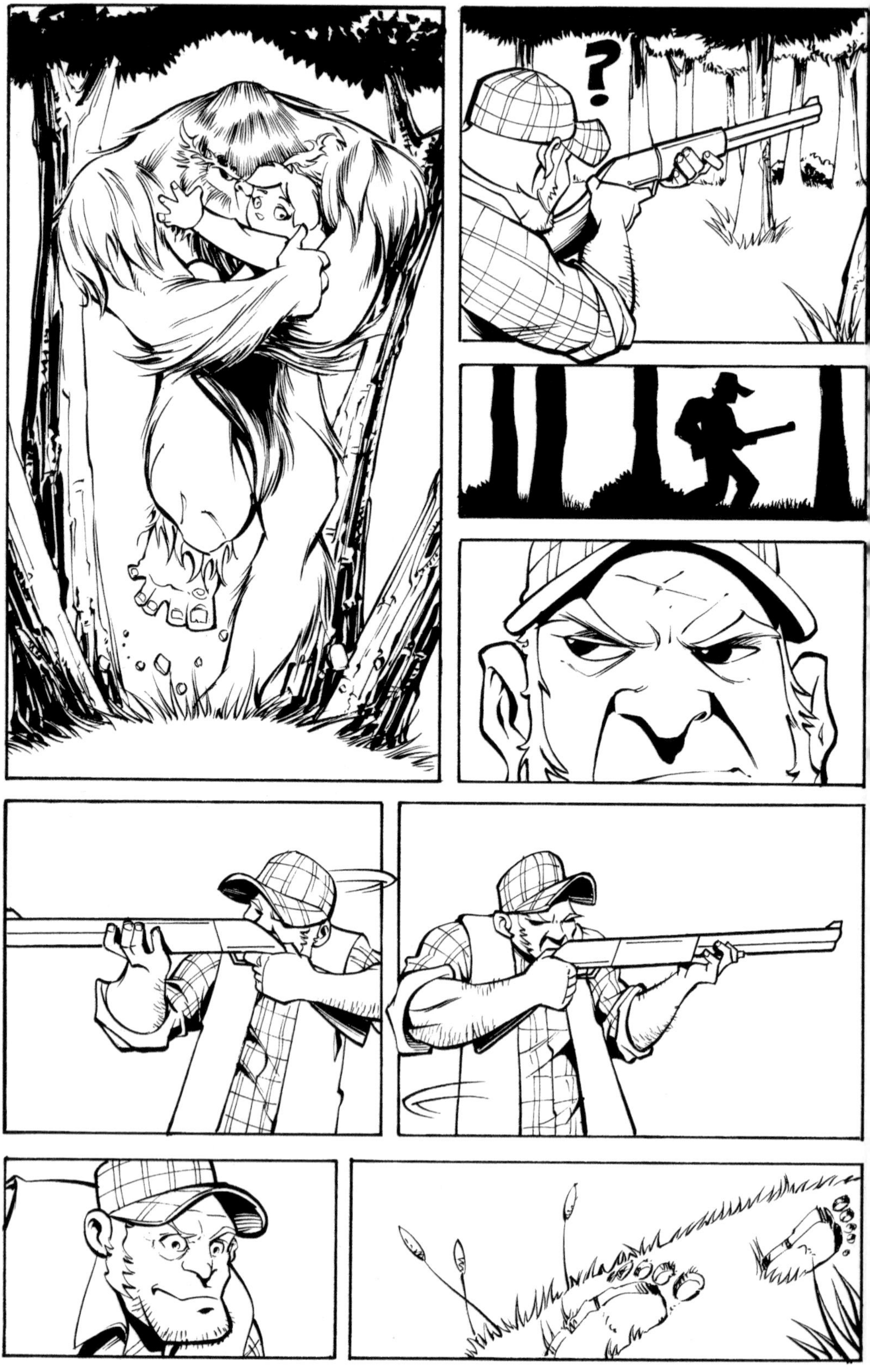
?

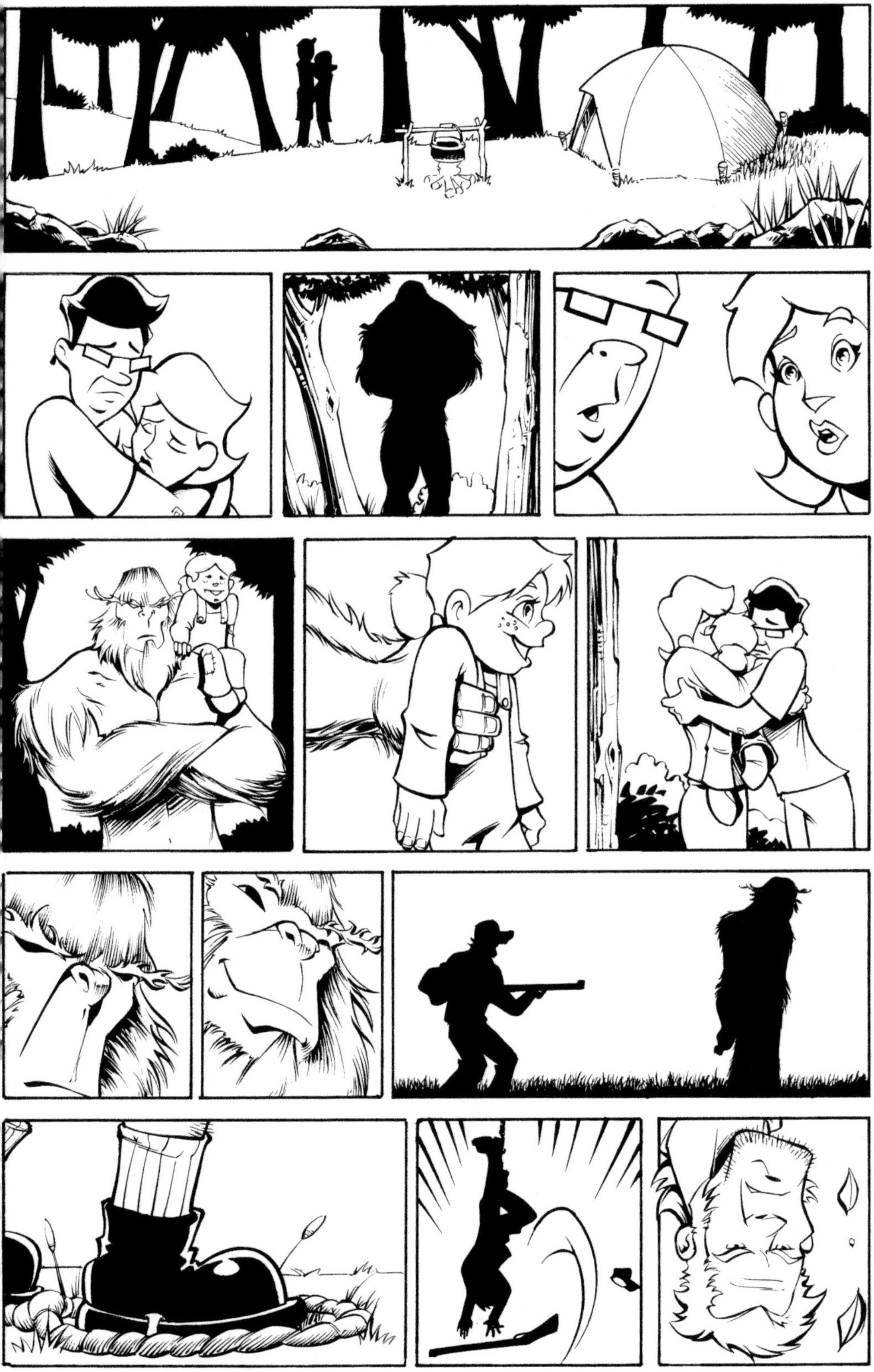

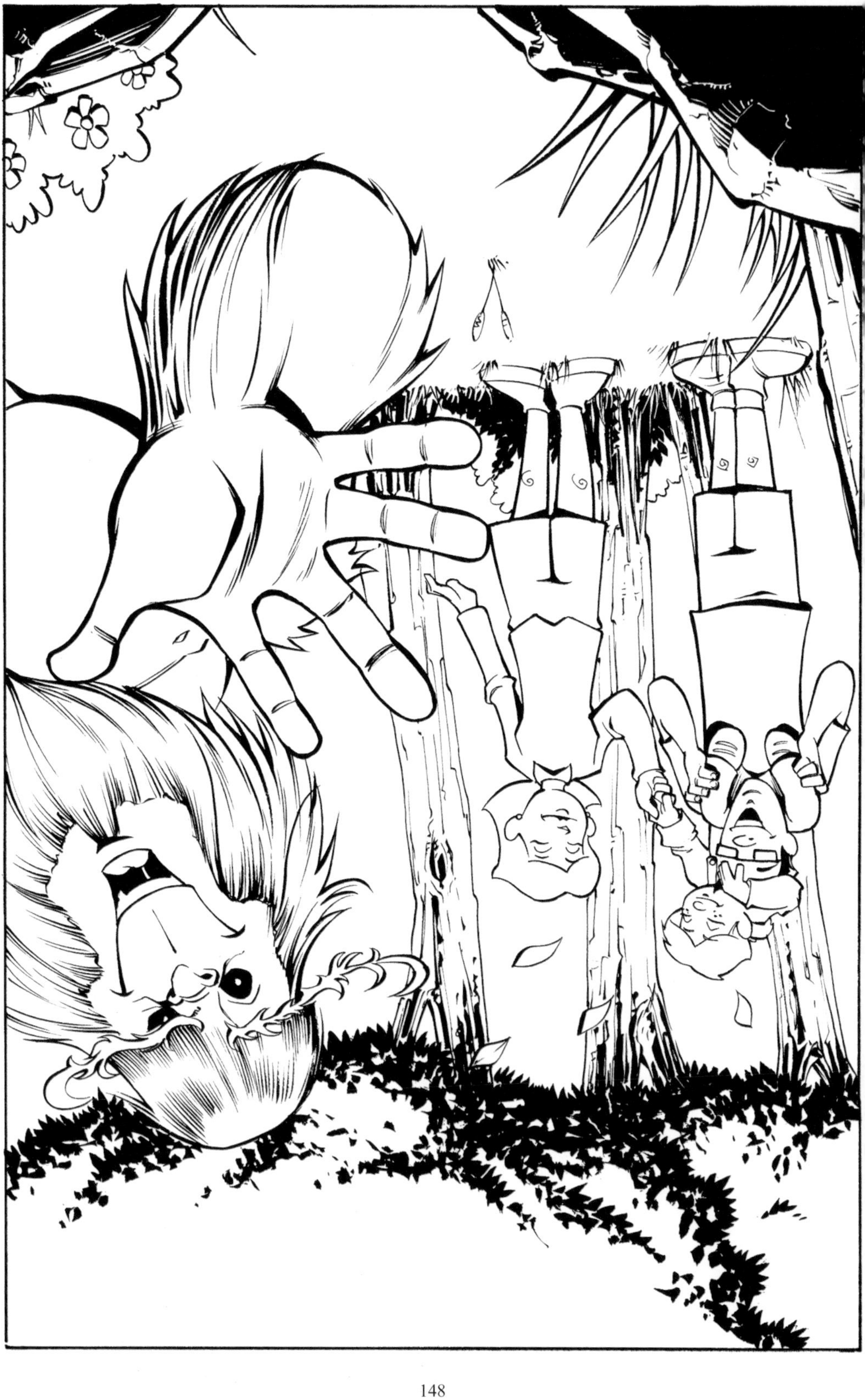

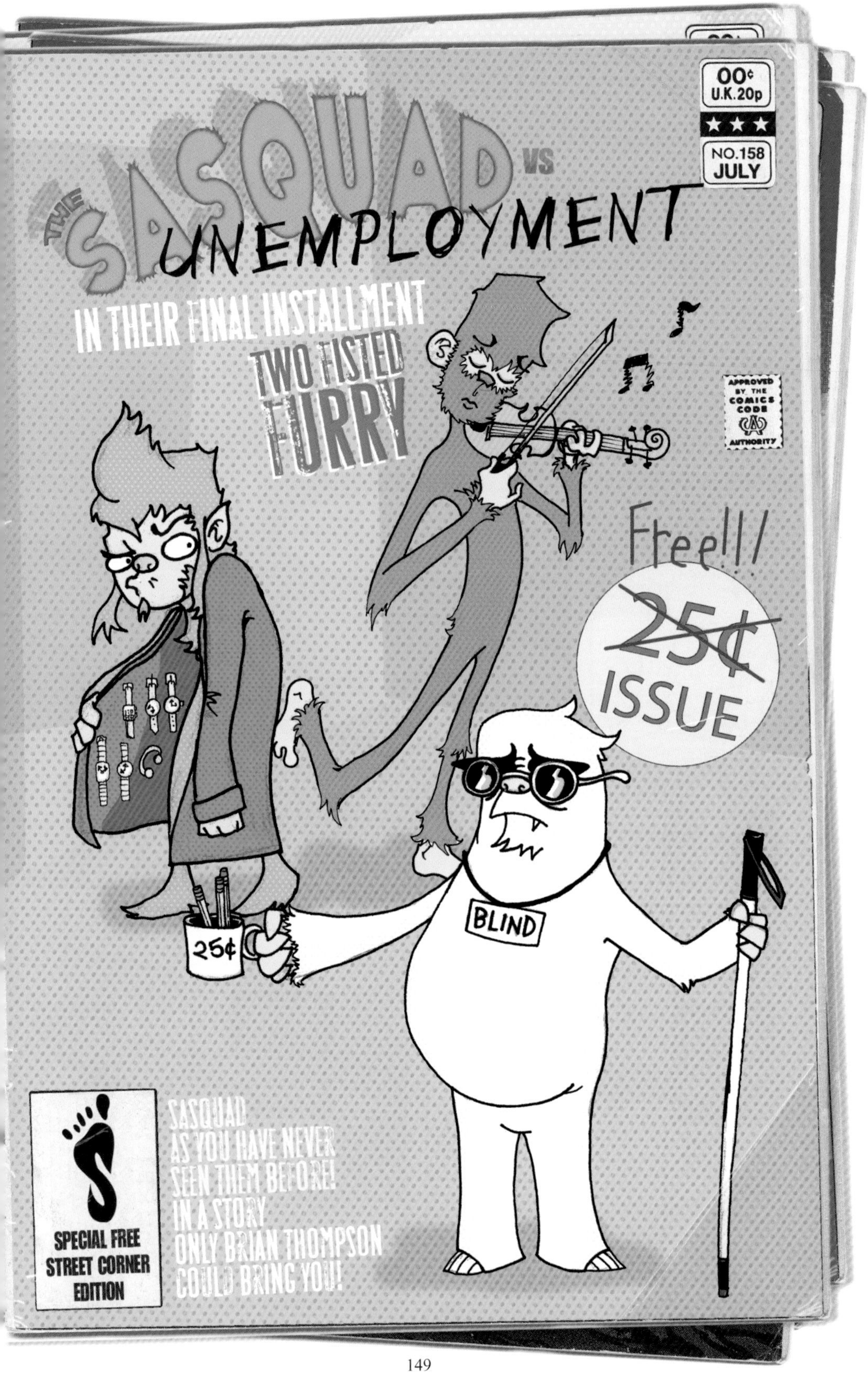
00¢
U.K.20p
NO.158
JULY
THE SASQUAD VS
UNEMPLOYMENT
IN THEIR FINAL INSTALLMENT
TWO FISTED FURRY
APPROVED BY THE COMICS CODE AUTHORITY
Free!!!
25¢
ISSUE
BLIND
25¢
SPECIAL FREE
STREET CORNER
EDITION
SASQUAD
AS YOU HAVE NEVER
SEEN THEM BEFORE!
IN A STORY
ONLY BRIAN THOMPSON
COULD BRING YOU!

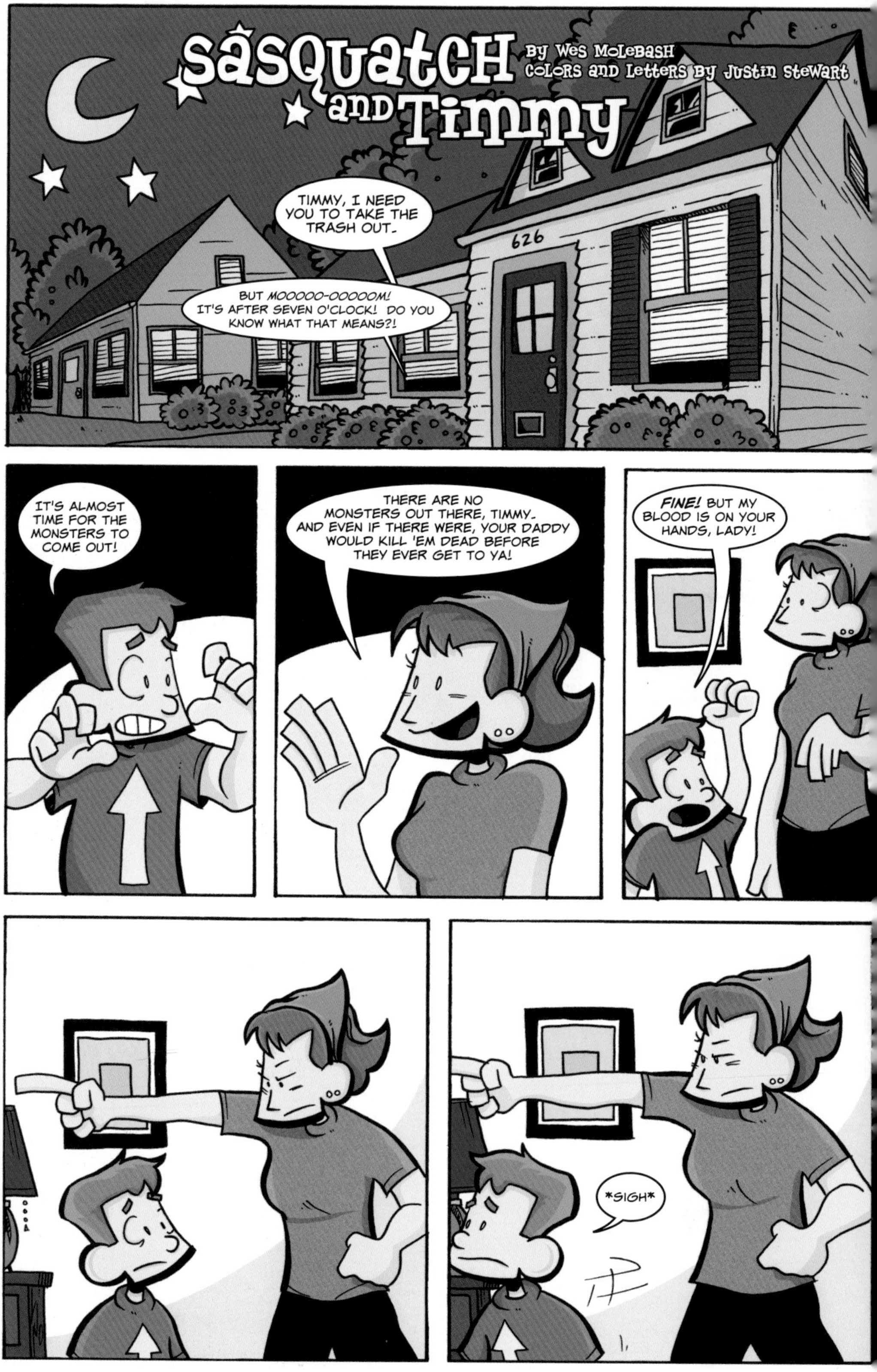
Sasquatch and Timmy
By Wes Molebash
Colors and Letters by Justin Stewart
TIMMY, I NEED YOU TO TAKE THE TRASH OUT.
BUT MOOOOO-OOOOOM! IT'S AFTER SEVEN O'CLOCK! DO YOU KNOW WHAT THAT MEANS?!
626
IT'S ALMOST TIME FOR THE MONSTERS TO COME OUT!
THERE ARE NO MONSTERS OUT THERE, TIMMY. AND EVEN IF THERE WERE, YOUR DADDY WOULD KILL 'EM DEAD BEFORE THEY EVER GET TO YA!
FINE! BUT MY BLOOD IS ON YOUR HANDS, LADY!
SIGH

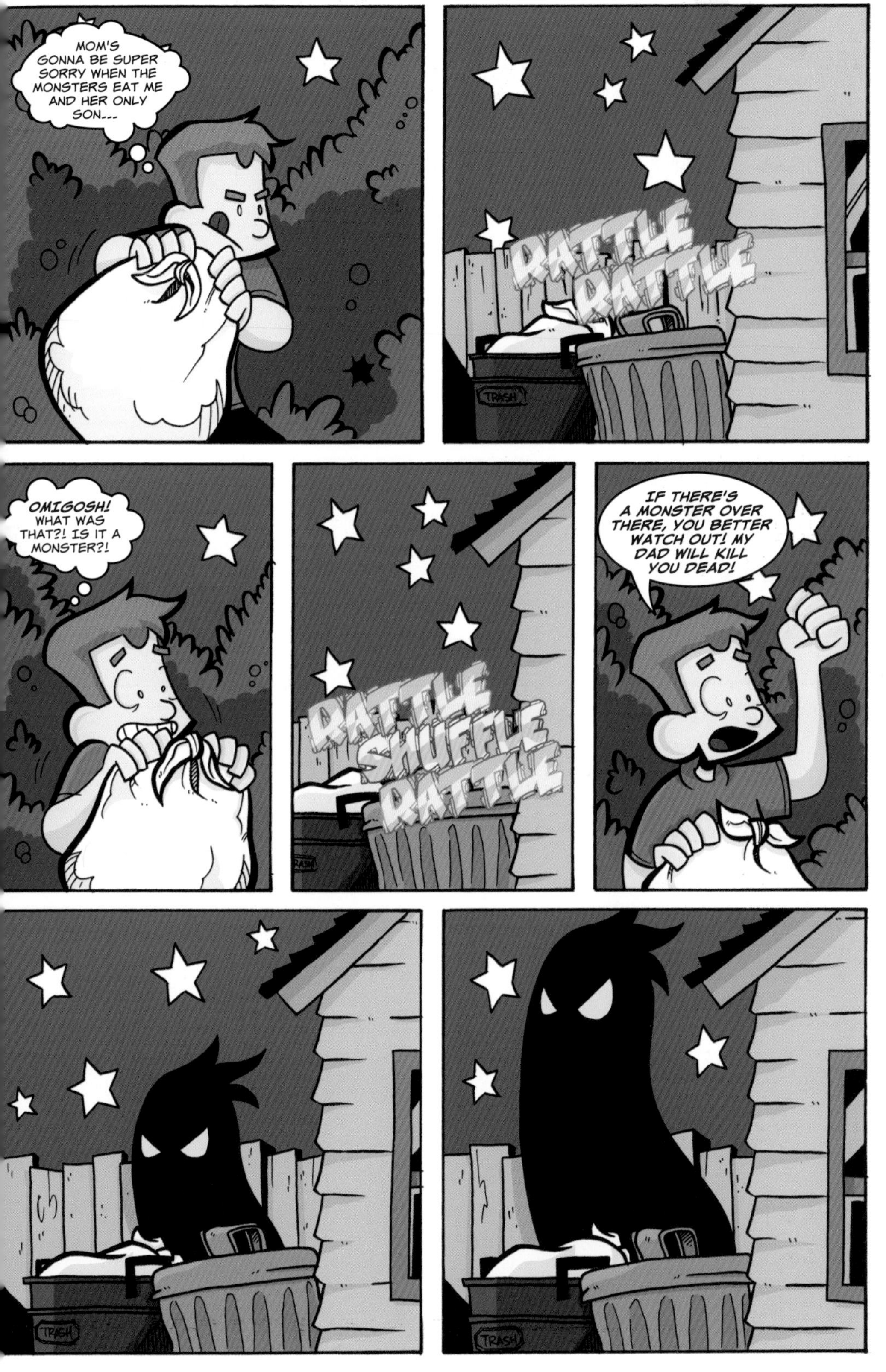
MOM'S GONNA BE SUPER SORRY WHEN THE MONSTERS EAT ME AND HER ONLY SON...
RATTLE RATTLE
TRASH
OMIGOSH! WHAT WAS THAT?! IS IT A MONSTER?!
RATTLE SHUFFLE RATTLE
IF THERE'S A MONSTER OVER THERE, YOU BETTER WATCH OUT! MY DAD WILL KILL YOU DEAD!
TRASH
TRASH

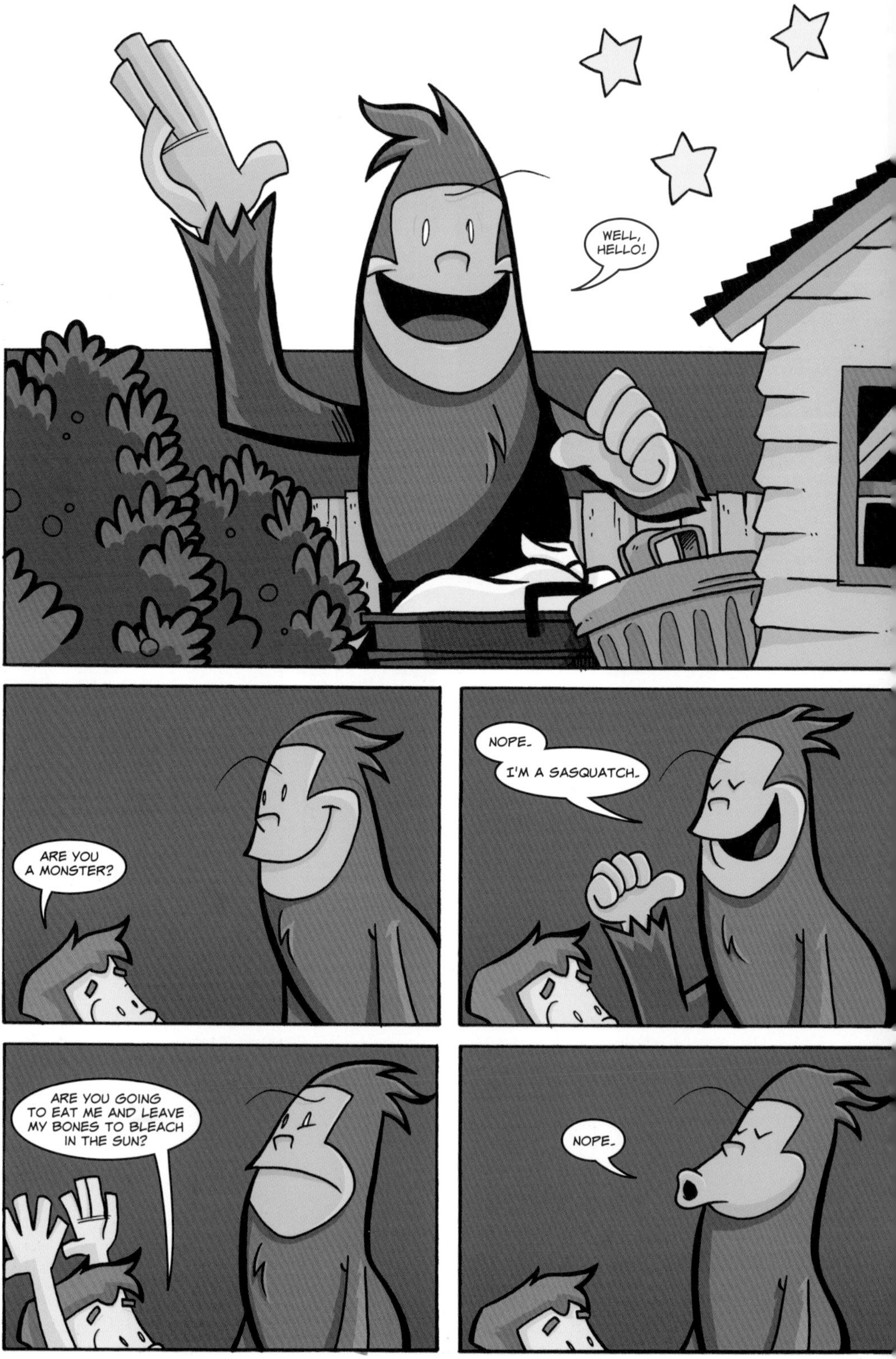
WELL, HELLO!
ARE YOU A MONSTER?
NOPE.
I'M A SASQUATCH.
ARE YOU GOING TO EAT ME AND LEAVE MY BONES TO BLEACH IN THE SUN?
NOPE.

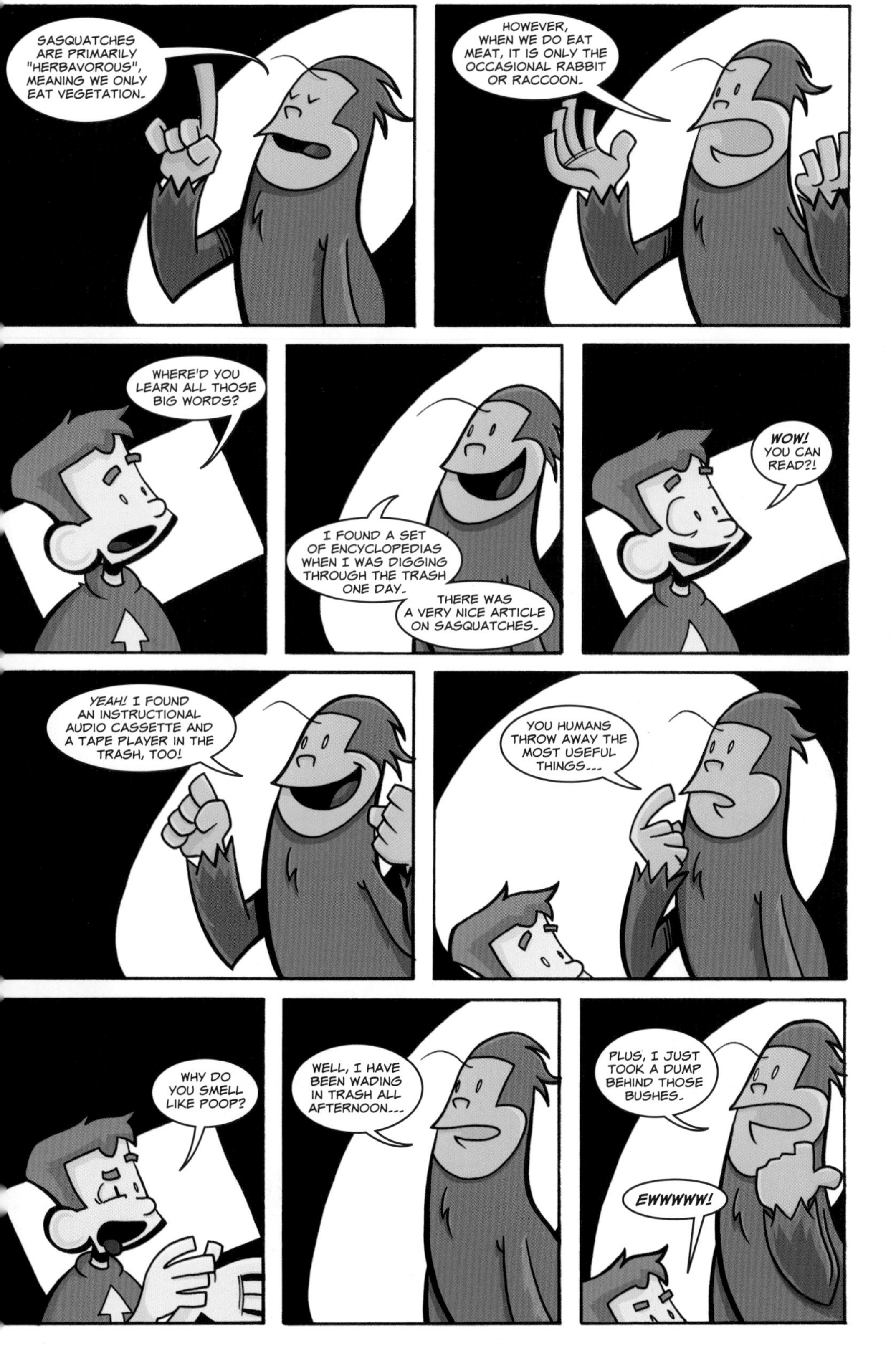
SASQUATCHES ARE PRIMARILY "HERBAVOROUS", MEANING WE ONLY EAT VEGETATION.
HOWEVER, WHEN WE DO EAT MEAT, IT IS ONLY THE OCCASIONAL RABBIT OR RACCOON.
WHERE'D YOU LEARN ALL THOSE BIG WORDS?
I FOUND A SET OF ENCYCLOPEDIAS WHEN I WAS DIGGING THROUGH THE TRASH ONE DAY.
THERE WAS A VERY NICE ARTICLE ON SASQUATCHES.
WOW! YOU CAN READ?!
YEAH! I FOUND AN INSTRUCTIONAL AUDIO CASSETTE AND A TAPE PLAYER IN THE TRASH, TOO!
YOU HUMANS THROW AWAY THE MOST USEFUL THINGS...
WHY DO YOU SMELL LIKE POOP?
WELL, I HAVE BEEN WADING IN TRASH ALL AFTERNOON...
PLUS, I JUST TOOK A DUMP BEHIND THOSE BUSHES.
EWWWWW!

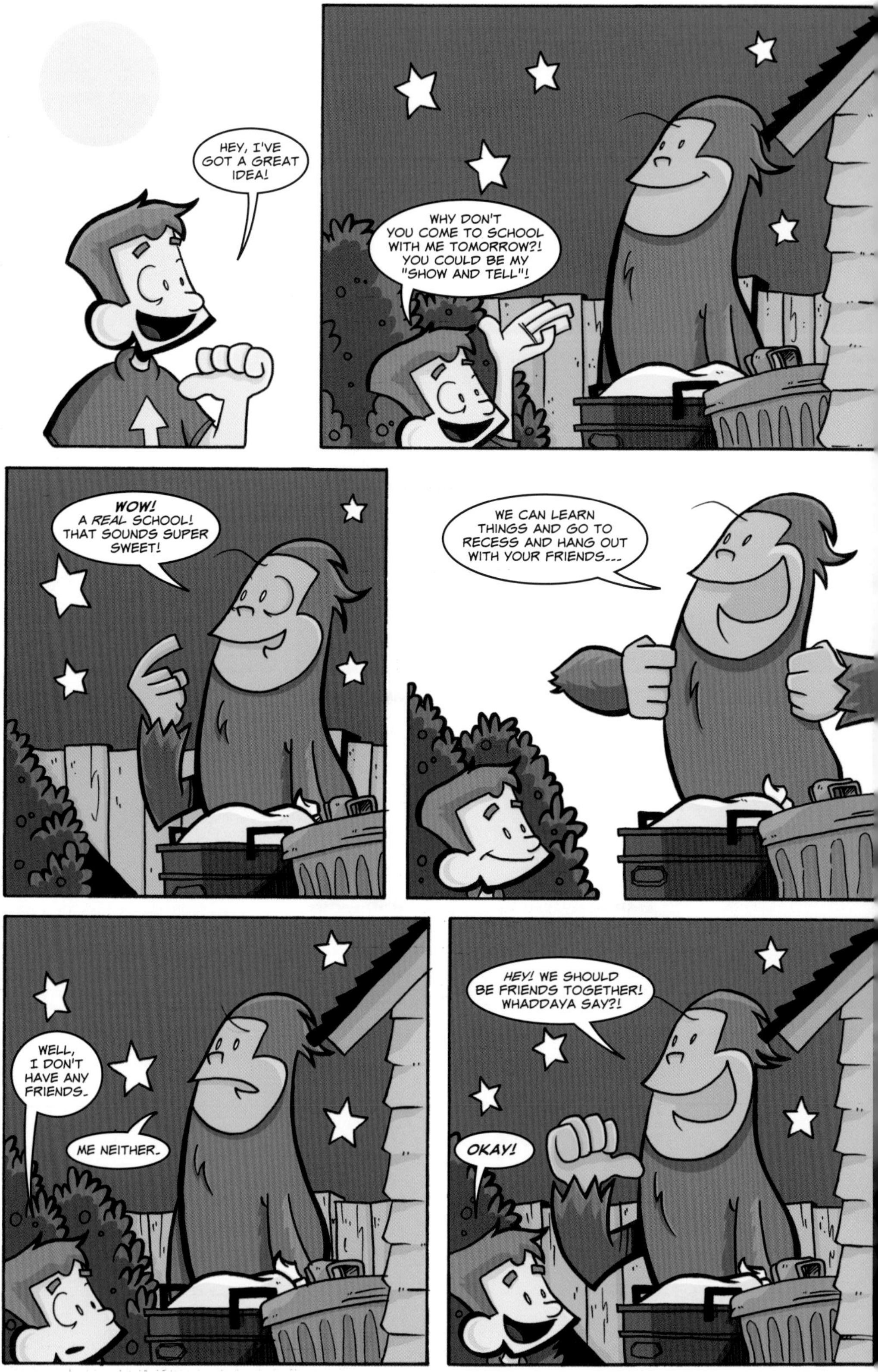
HEY, I'VE GOT A GREAT IDEA!
WHY DON'T YOU COME TO SCHOOL WITH ME TOMORROW?! YOU COULD BE MY "SHOW AND TELL"!
WOW! A REAL SCHOOL! THAT SOUNDS SUPER SWEET!
WE CAN LEARN THINGS AND GO TO RECESS AND HANG OUT WITH YOUR FRIENDS...
WELL, I DON'T HAVE ANY FRIENDS.
ME NEITHER.
HEY! WE SHOULD BE FRIENDS TOGETHER! WHADDAYA SAY?!
OKAY!

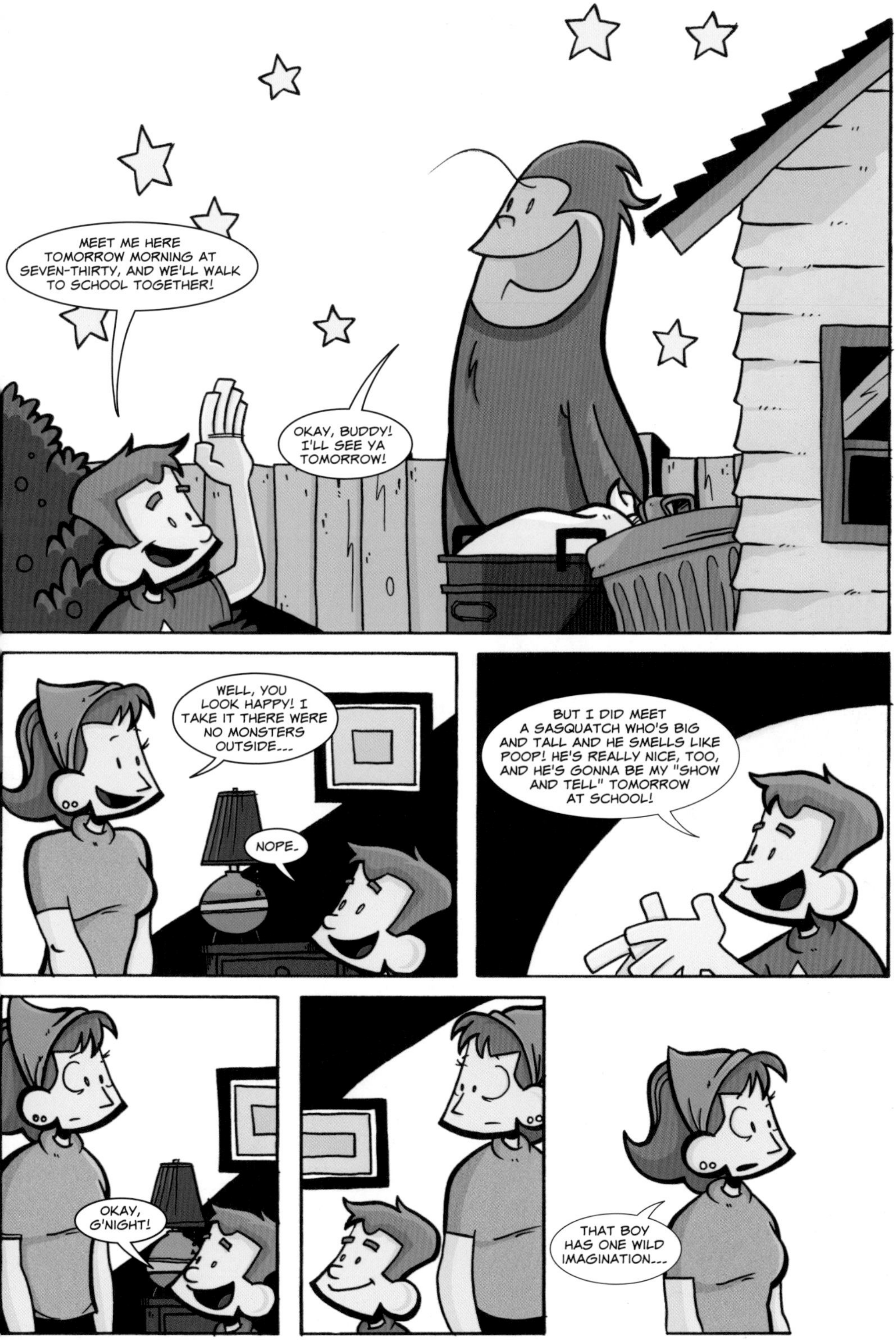
MEET ME HERE TOMORROW MORNING AT SEVEN-THIRTY, AND WE'LL WALK TO SCHOOL TOGETHER!
OKAY, BUDDY! I'LL SEE YA TOMORROW!
WELL, YOU LOOK HAPPY! I TAKE IT THERE WERE NO MONSTERS OUTSIDE...
NOPE.
BUT I DID MEET A SASQUATCH WHO'S BIG AND TALL AND HE SMELLS LIKE POOP! HE'S REALLY NICE, TOO, AND HE'S GONNA BE MY "SHOW AND TELL" TOMORROW AT SCHOOL!
OKAY, G'NIGHT!
THAT BOY HAS ONE WILD IMAGINATION...

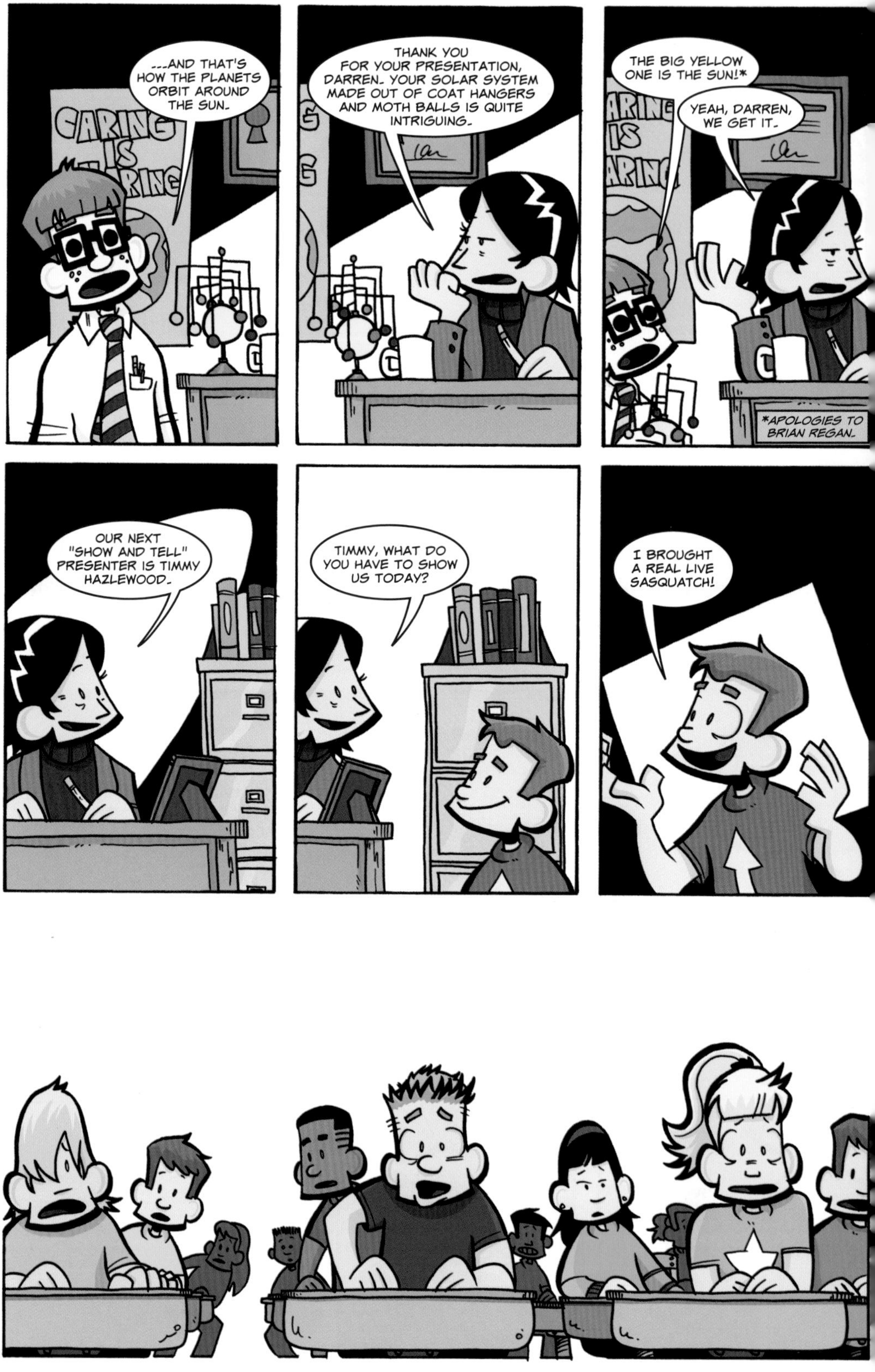
...AND THAT'S HOW THE PLANETS ORBIT AROUND THE SUN.
CARING IS CARING
THANK YOU FOR YOUR PRESENTATION, DARREN. YOUR SOLAR SYSTEM MADE OUT OF COAT HANGERS AND MOTH BALLS IS QUITE INTRIGUING.
THE BIG YELLOW ONE IS THE SUN!*
YEAH, DARREN, WE GET IT.
*APOLOGIES TO BRIAN REGAN.
OUR NEXT "SHOW AND TELL" PRESENTER IS TIMMY HAZLEWOOD.
TIMMY, WHAT DO YOU HAVE TO SHOW US TODAY?
I BROUGHT A REAL LIVE SASQUATCH!

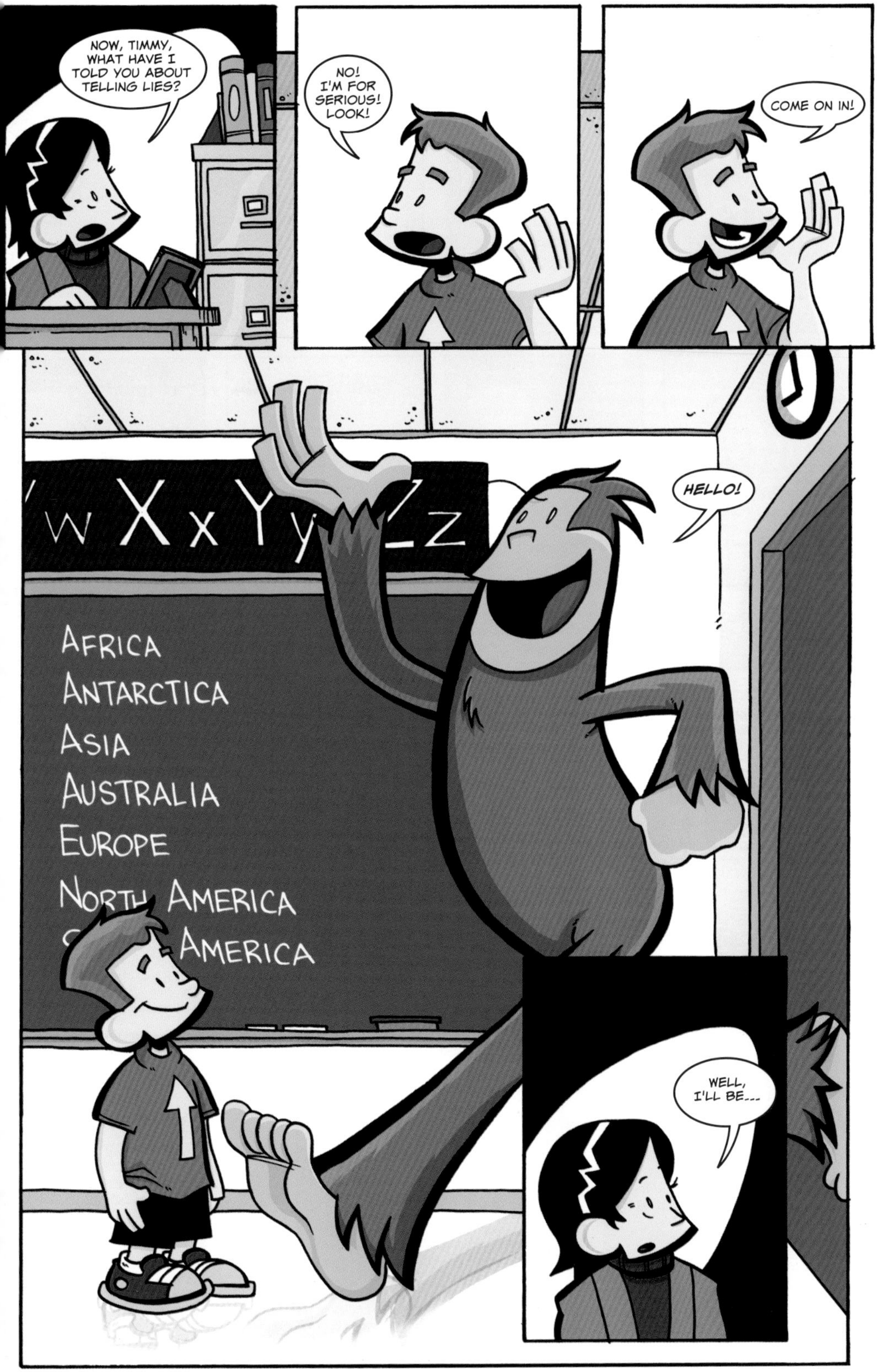
NOW, TIMMY, WHAT HAVE I TOLD YOU ABOUT TELLING LIES?
NO! I'M FOR SERIOUS! LOOK!
COME ON IN!
HELLO!
AFRICA
ANTARCTICA
ASIA
AUSTRALIA
EUROPE
NORTH AMERICA
AMERICA
WELL, I'LL BE...

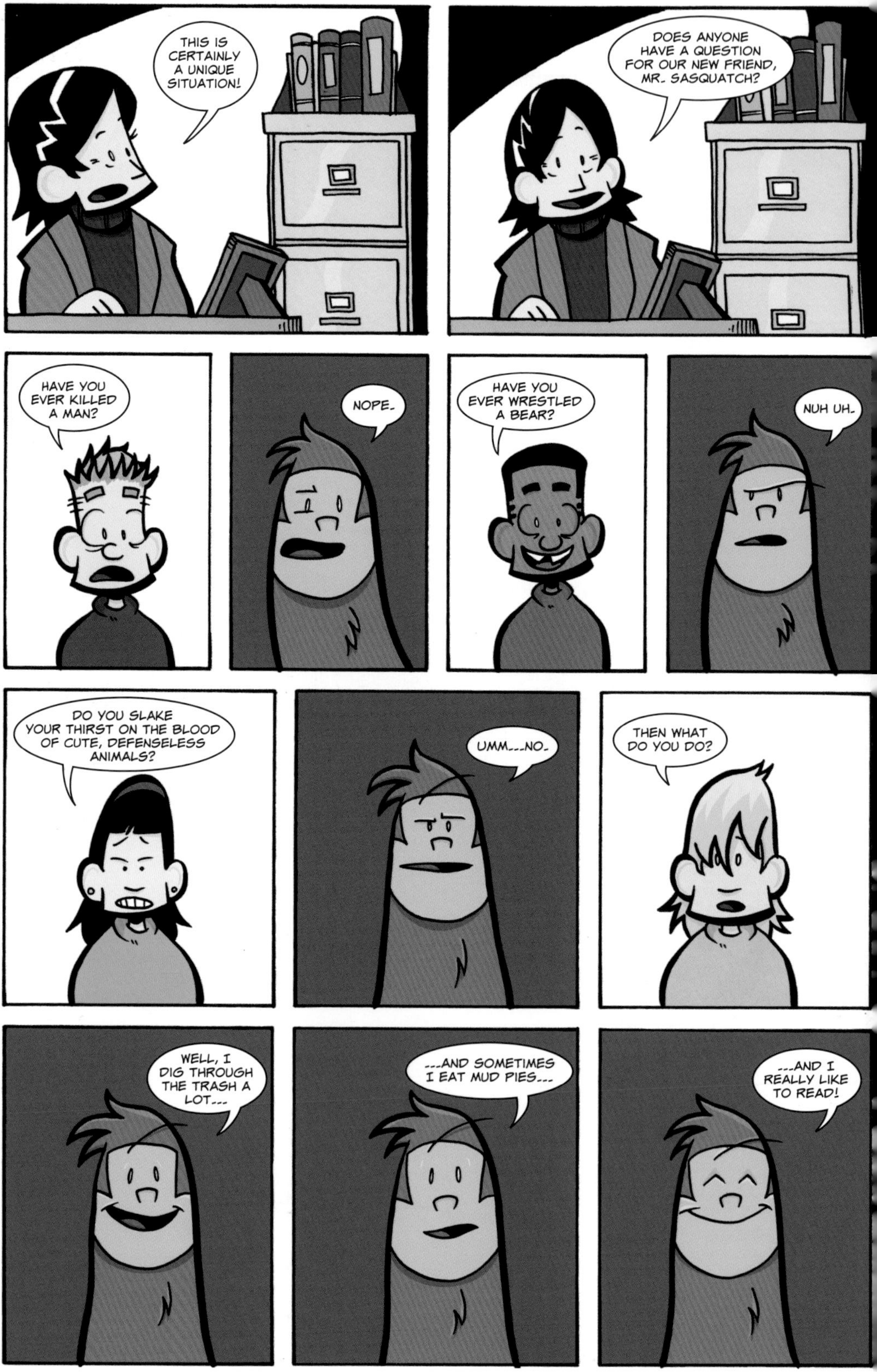
THIS IS CERTAINLY A UNIQUE SITUATION!
DOES ANYONE HAVE A QUESTION FOR OUR NEW FRIEND, MR. SASQUATCH?
HAVE YOU EVER KILLED A MAN?
NOPE.
HAVE YOU EVER WRESTLED A BEAR?
NUH UH.
DO YOU SLAKE YOUR THIRST ON THE BLOOD OF CUTE, DEFENSELESS ANIMALS?
UMM...NO.
THEN WHAT DO YOU DO?
WELL, I DIG THROUGH THE TRASH A LOT...
...AND SOMETIMES I EAT MUD PIES...
...AND I REALLY LIKE TO READ!

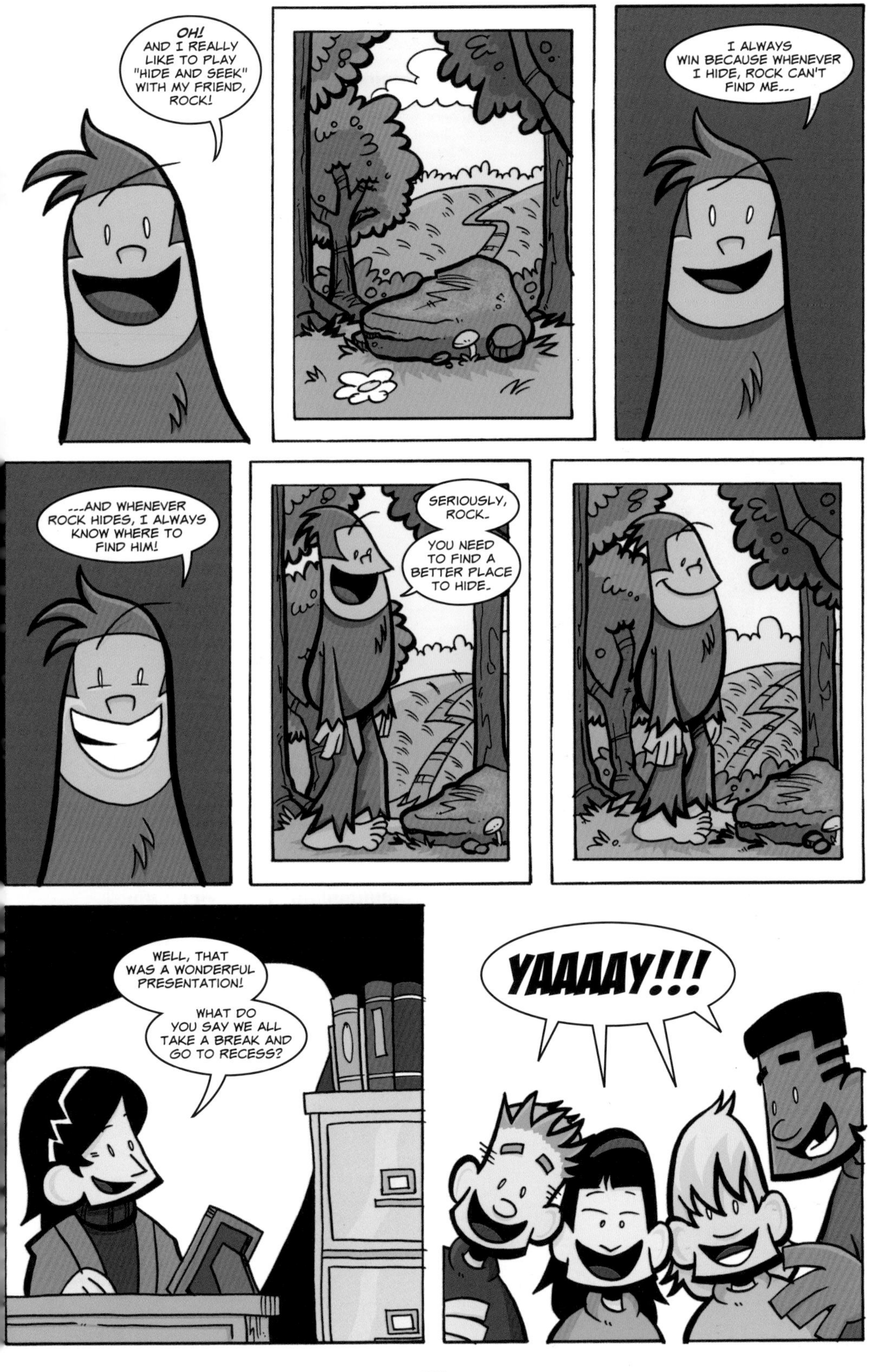
OH! AND I REALLY LIKE TO PLAY "HIDE AND SEEK" WITH MY FRIEND, ROCK!
I ALWAYS WIN BECAUSE WHENEVER I HIDE, ROCK CAN'T FIND ME...
...AND WHENEVER ROCK HIDES, I ALWAYS KNOW WHERE TO FIND HIM!
SERIOUSLY, ROCK.
YOU NEED TO FIND A BETTER PLACE TO HIDE.
WELL, THAT WAS A WONDERFUL PRESENTATION!
WHAT DO YOU SAY WE ALL TAKE A BREAK AND GO TO RECESS?
YAAAAY!!!

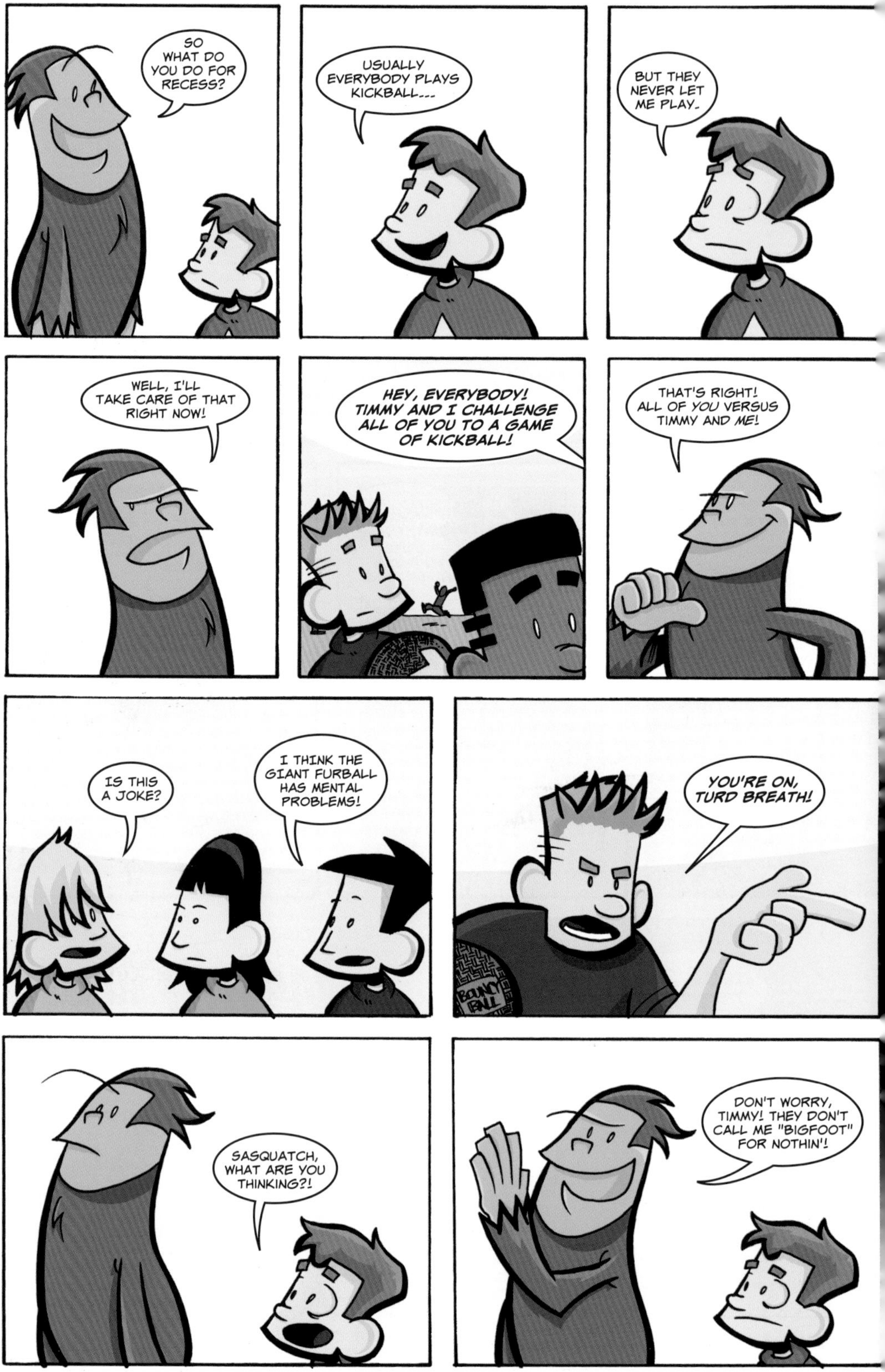
SO WHAT DO YOU DO FOR RECESS?
USUALLY EVERYBODY PLAYS KICKBALL...
BUT THEY NEVER LET ME PLAY.
WELL, I'LL TAKE CARE OF THAT RIGHT NOW!
HEY, EVERYBODY! TIMMY AND I CHALLENGE ALL OF YOU TO A GAME OF KICKBALL!
THAT'S RIGHT! ALL OF YOU VERSUS TIMMY AND ME!
IS THIS A JOKE?
I THINK THE GIANT FURBALL HAS MENTAL PROBLEMS!
YOU'RE ON, TURD BREATH!
BOUNCY BALL
SASQUATCH, WHAT ARE YOU THINKING?!
DON'T WORRY, TIMMY! THEY DON'T CALL ME "BIGFOOT" FOR NOTHIN'!

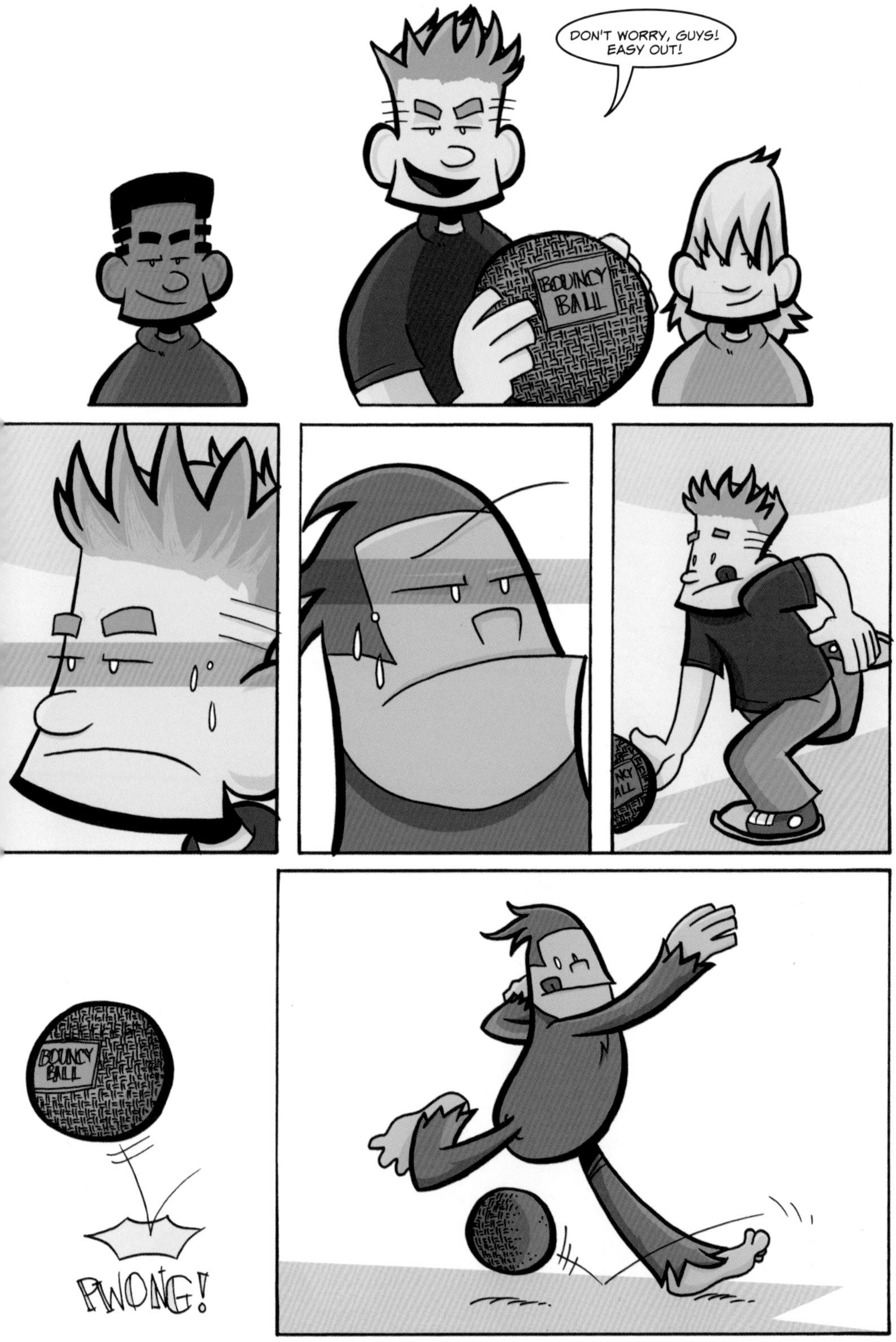
DON'T WORRY, GUYS! EASY OUT!
BOUNCY BALL
BOUNCY BALL
PWONG!

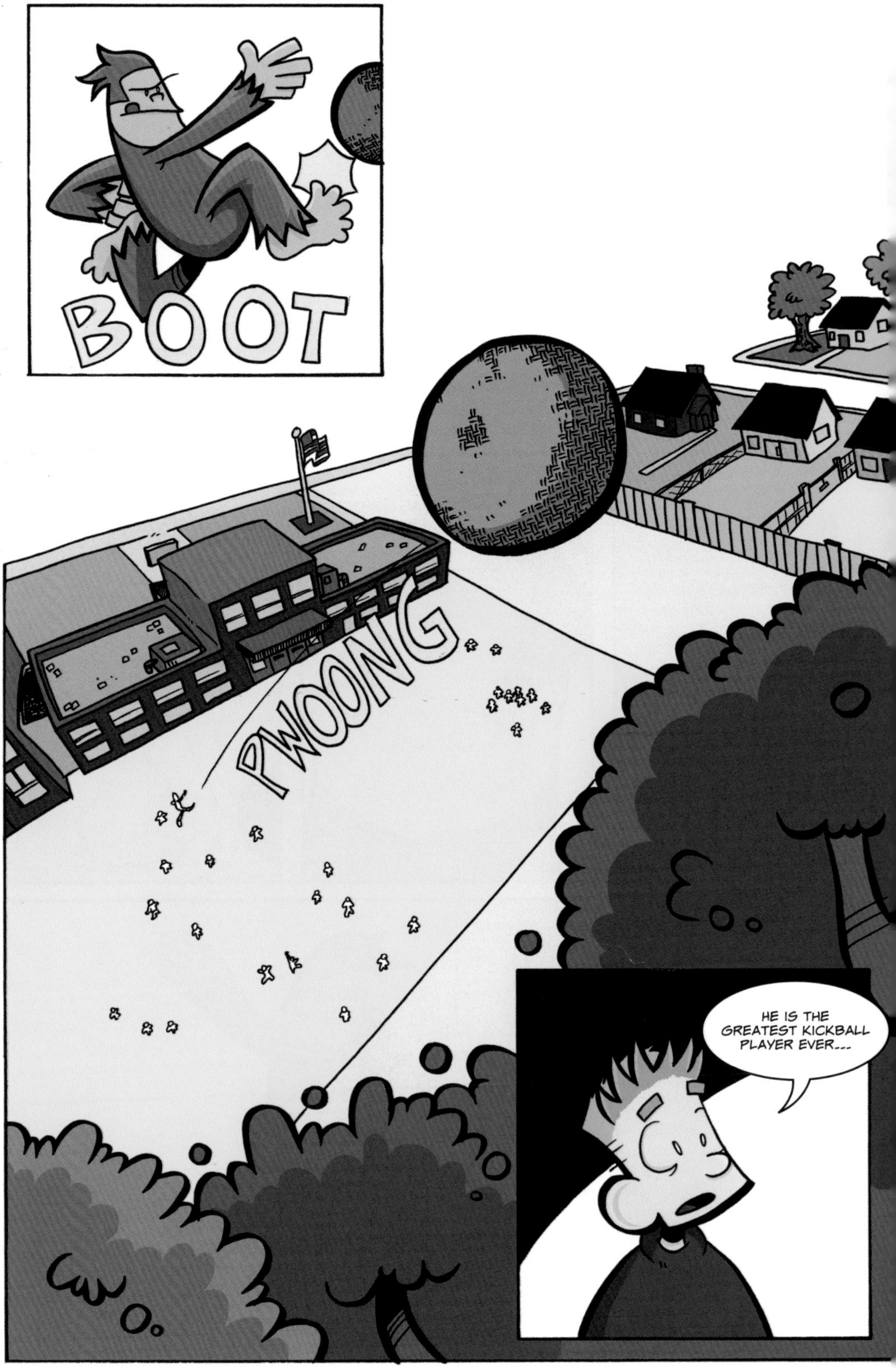
BOOT
PWOONG
HE IS THE GREATEST KICKBALL PLAYER EVER...

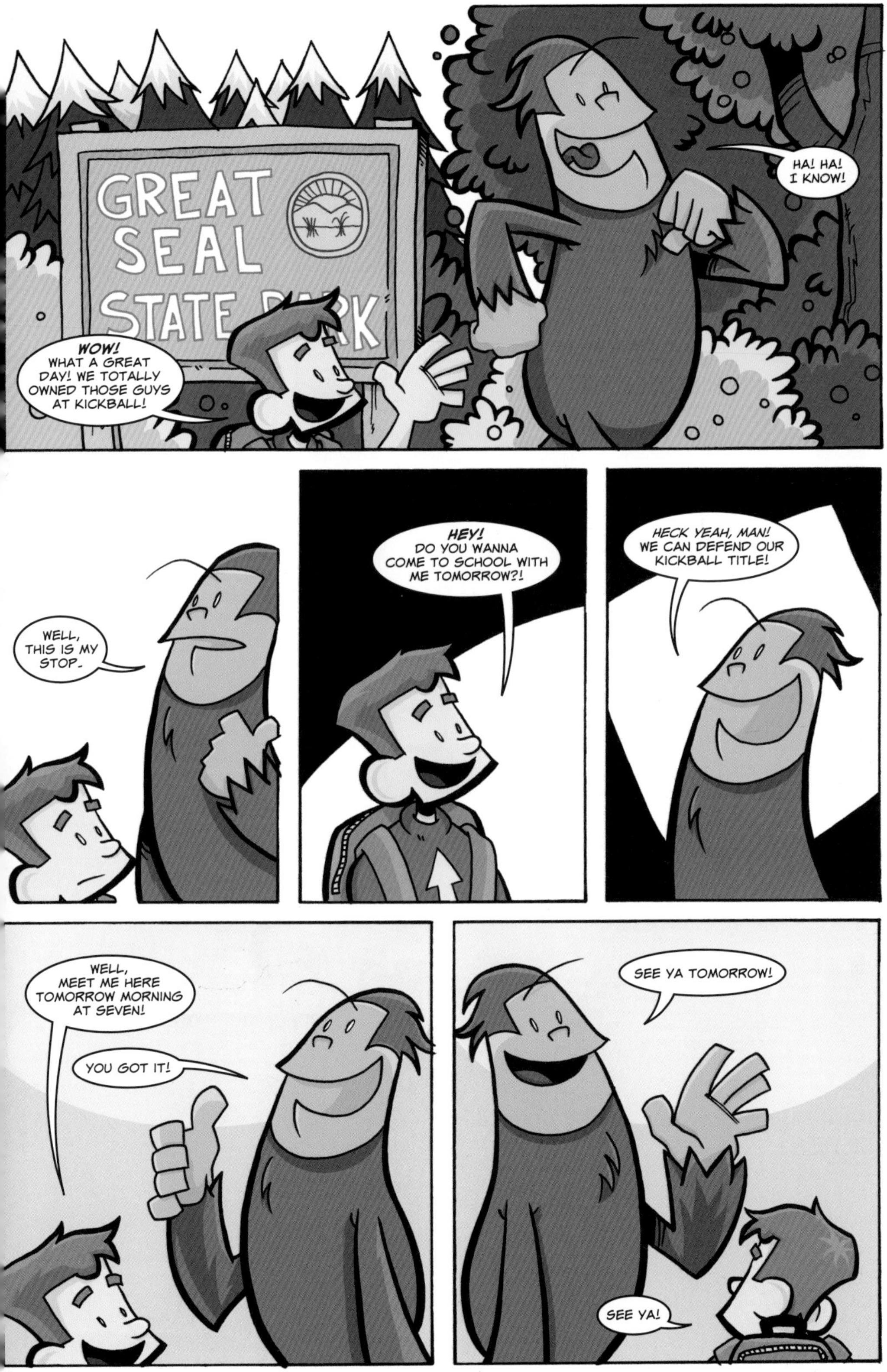
GREAT SEAL STATE PARK
WOW! WHAT A GREAT DAY! WE TOTALLY OWNED THOSE GUYS AT KICKBALL!
HA! HA! I KNOW!
WELL, THIS IS MY STOP.
HEY! DO YOU WANNA COME TO SCHOOL WITH ME TOMORROW?!
HECK YEAH, MAN! WE CAN DEFEND OUR KICKBALL TITLE!
WELL, MEET ME HERE TOMORROW MORNING AT SEVEN!
YOU GOT IT!
SEE YA TOMORROW!
SEE YA!

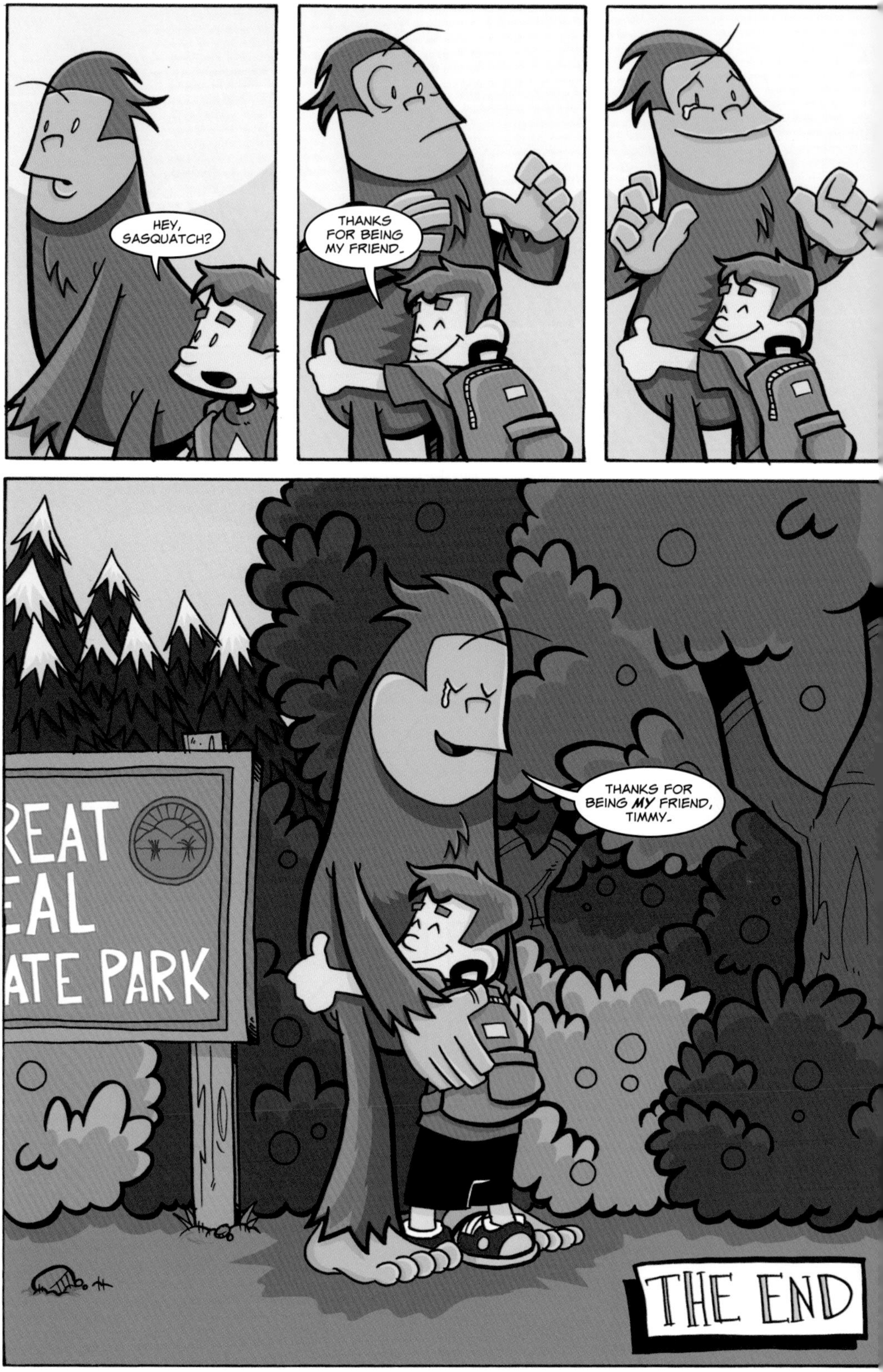
HEY, SASQUATCH?
THANKS FOR BEING MY FRIEND.
REAT
EAL
ATE PARK
THANKS FOR BEING *MY* FRIEND, TIMMY.
THE END

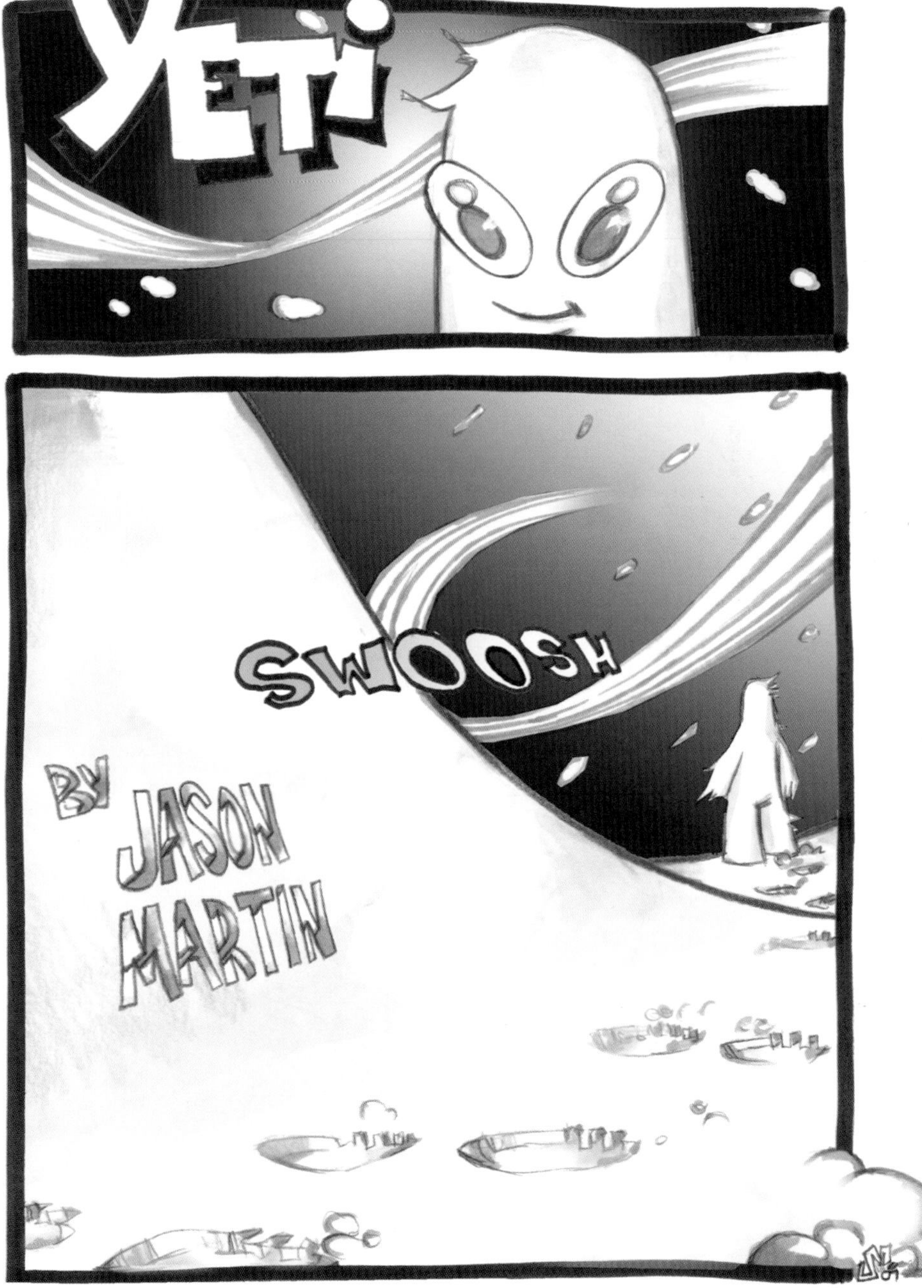
YETI
SWOOSH
BY JASON MARTIN

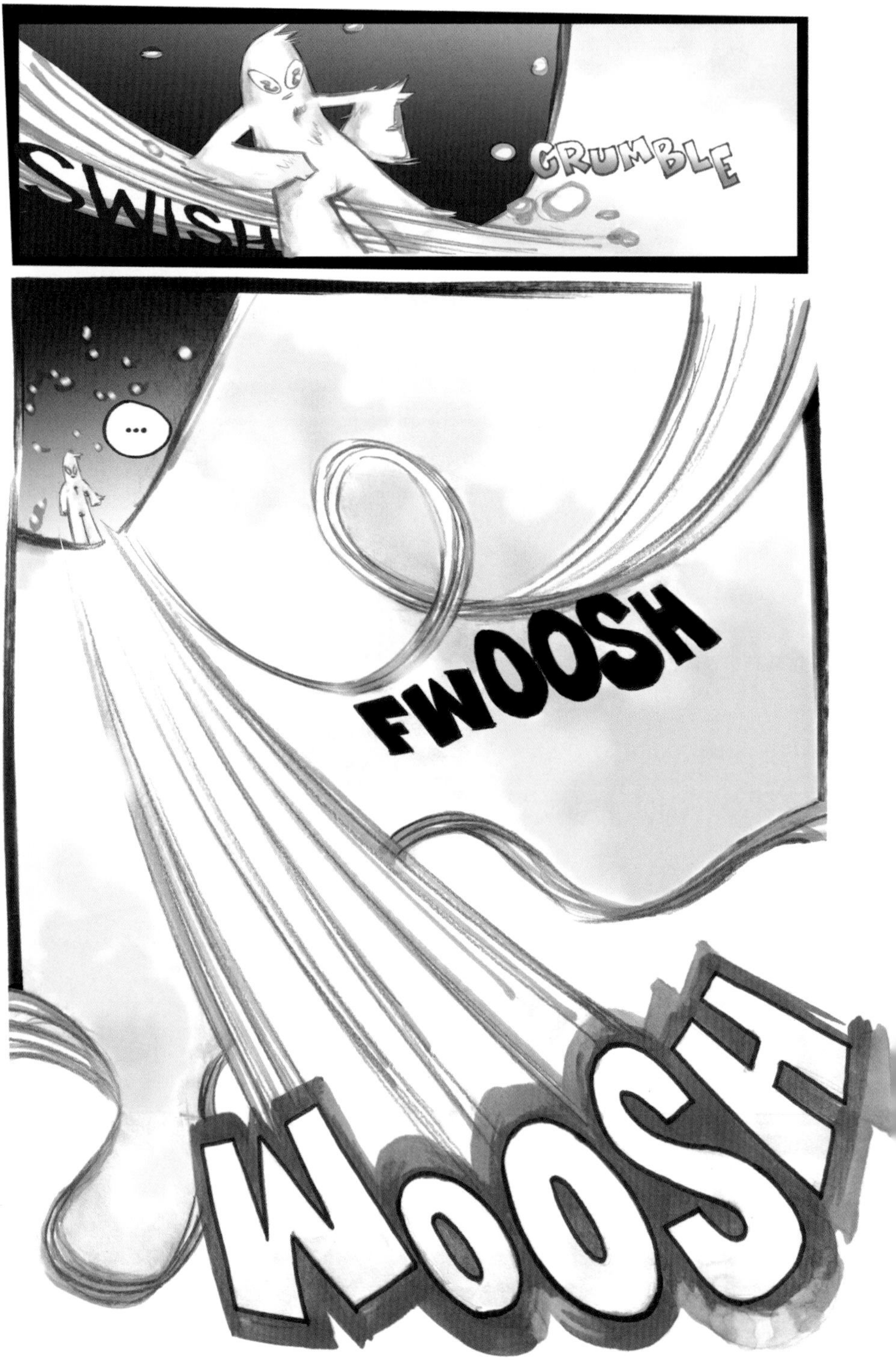
SWISH
CRUMBLE
...
FWOOSH
WOOSH

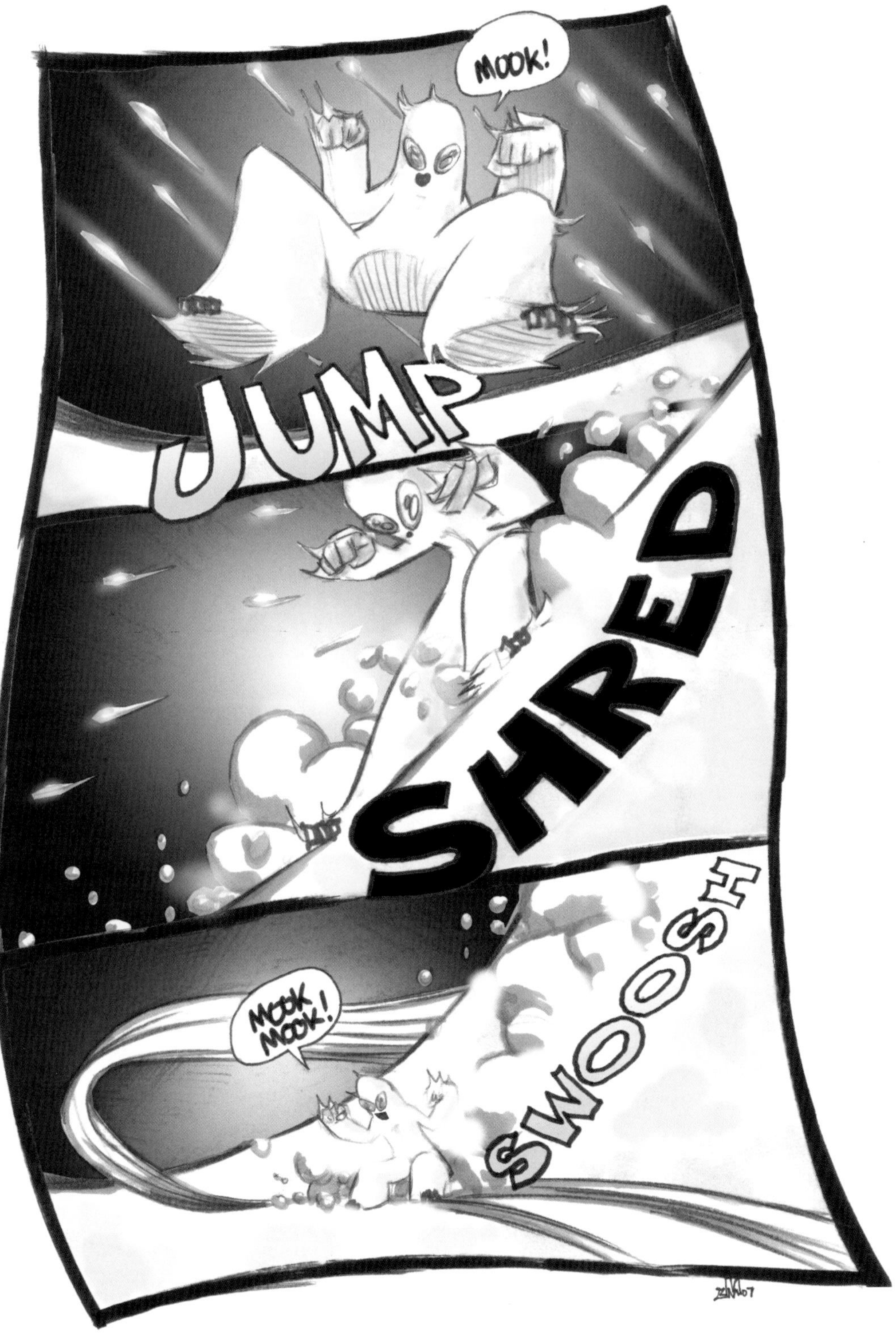
MOOK!
JUMP
SHRED
SWOOSH
MOOK MOOK!

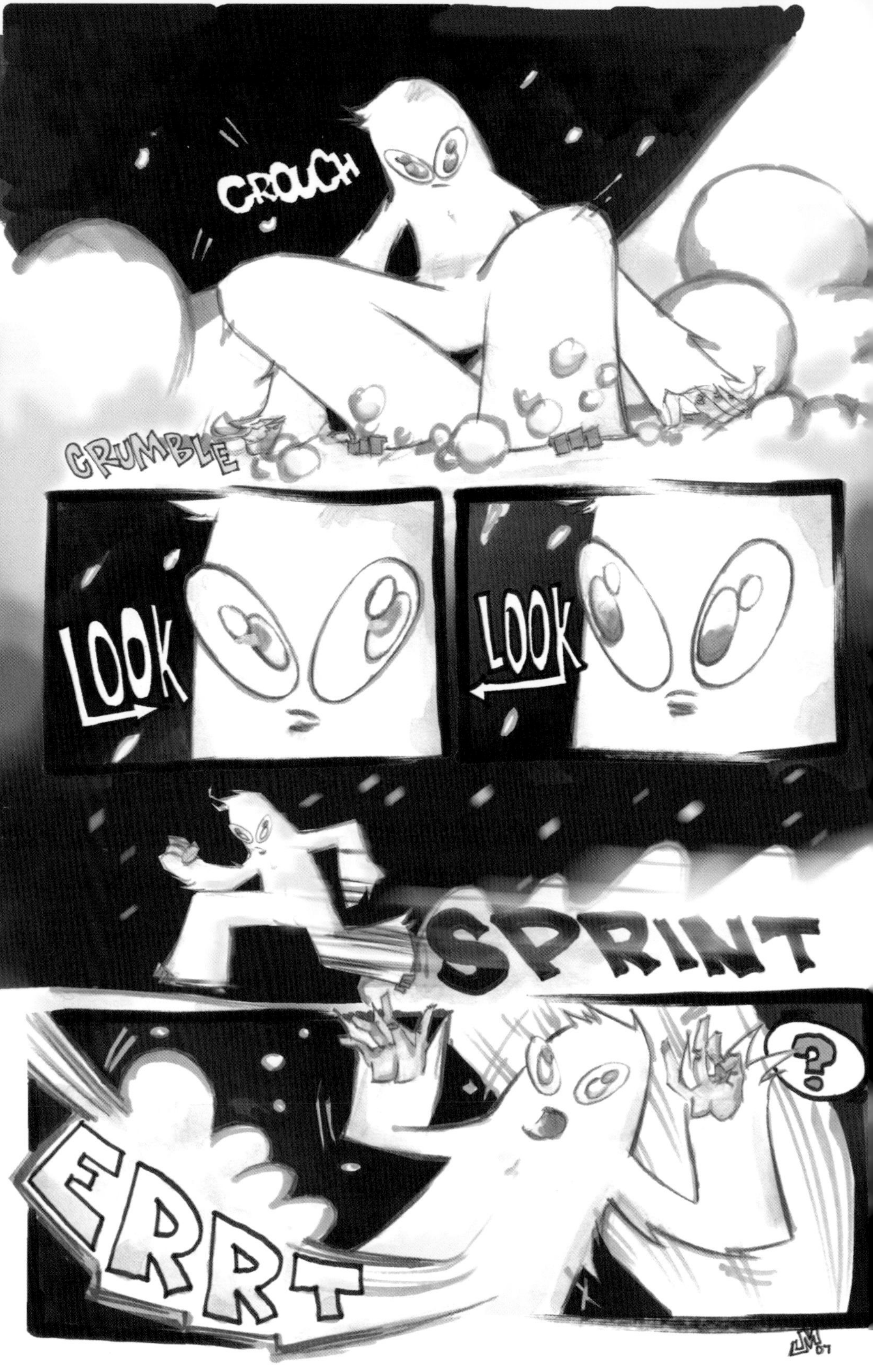
CROUCH
CRUMBLE
LOOK
LOOK
SPRINT
ERRT
?

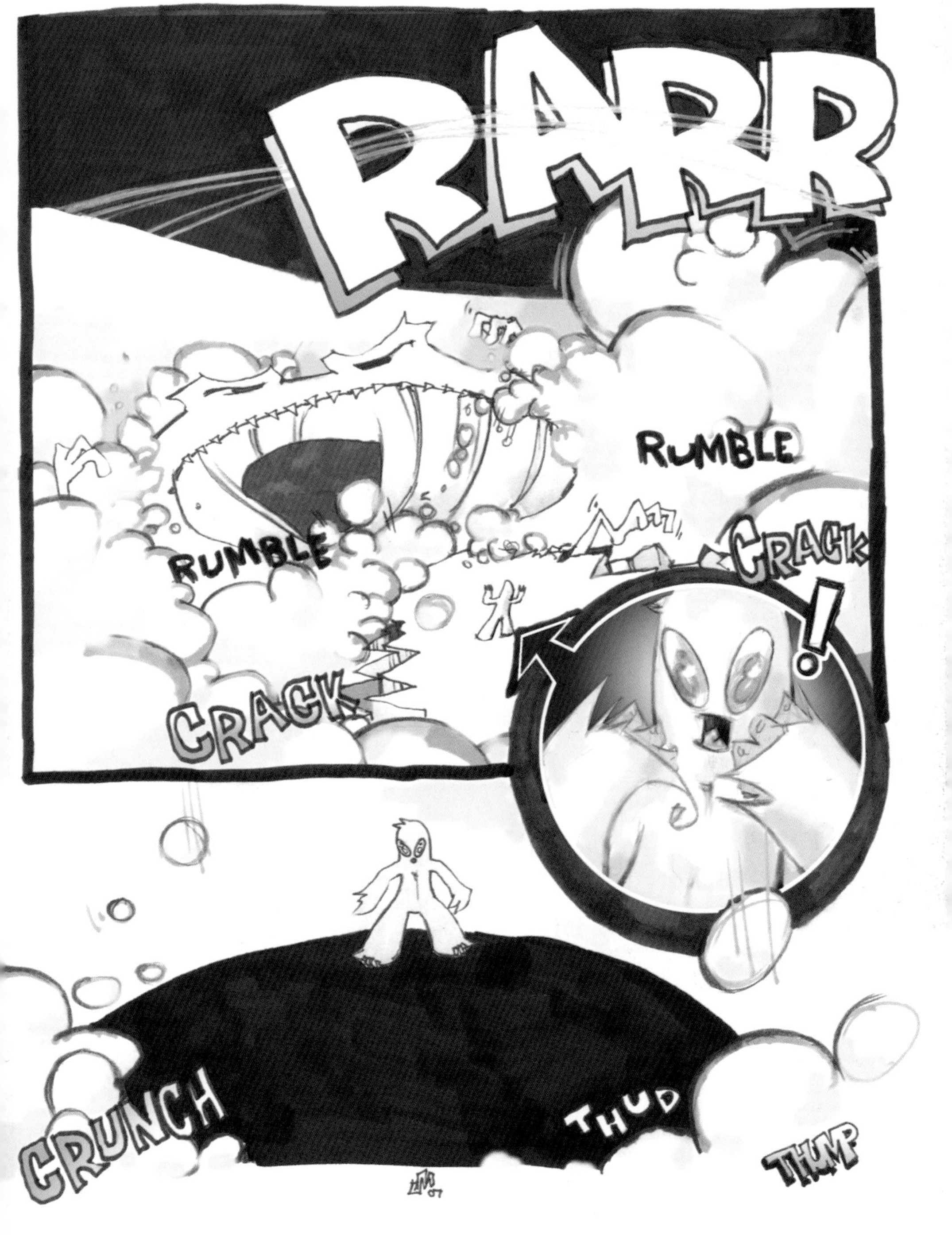
RARR
RUMBLE
RUMBLE
CRACK
CRACK
!
CRUNCH
THUD
THUMP

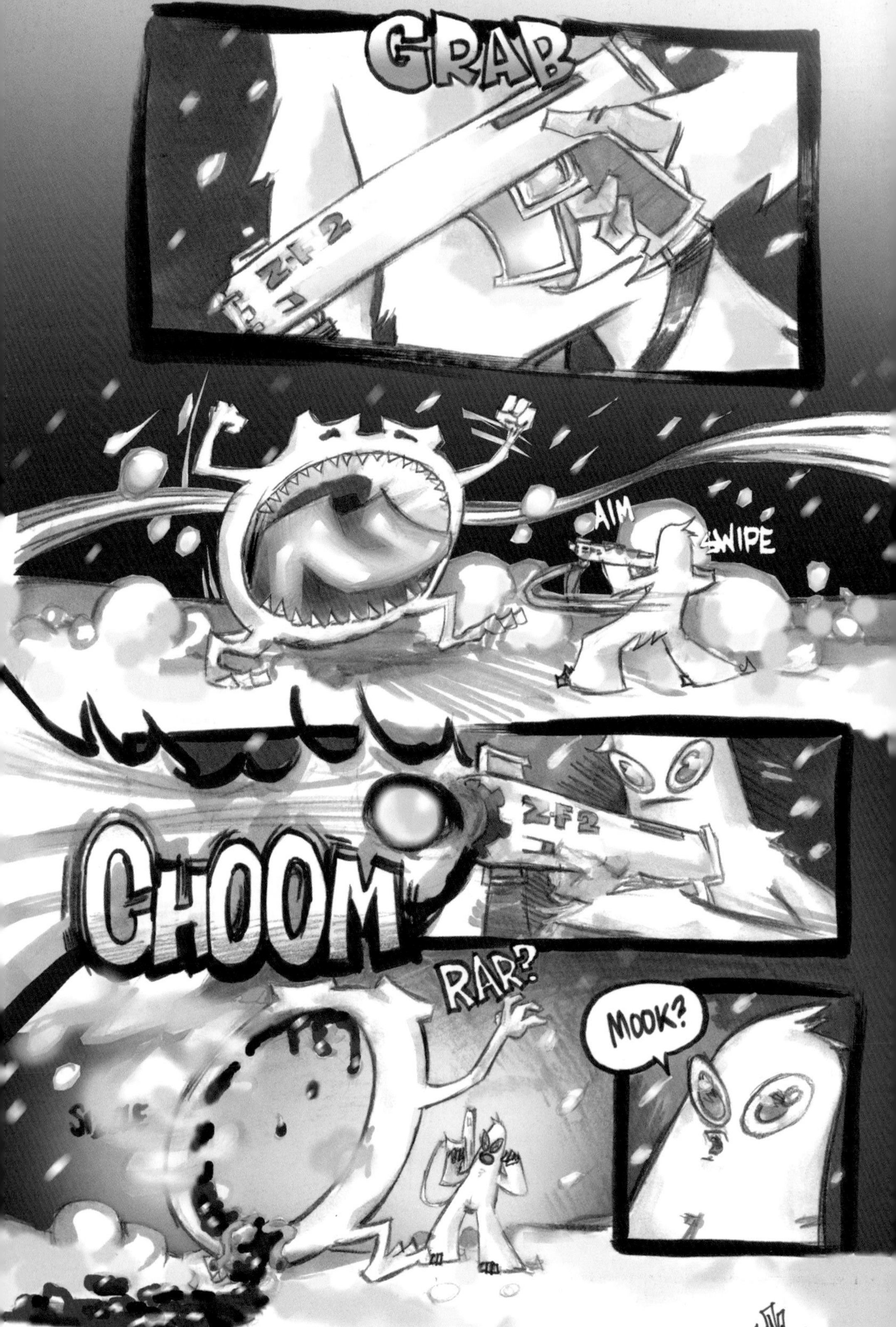
GRAB
AIM
SWIPE
CHOOM
RAR?
MOOK?

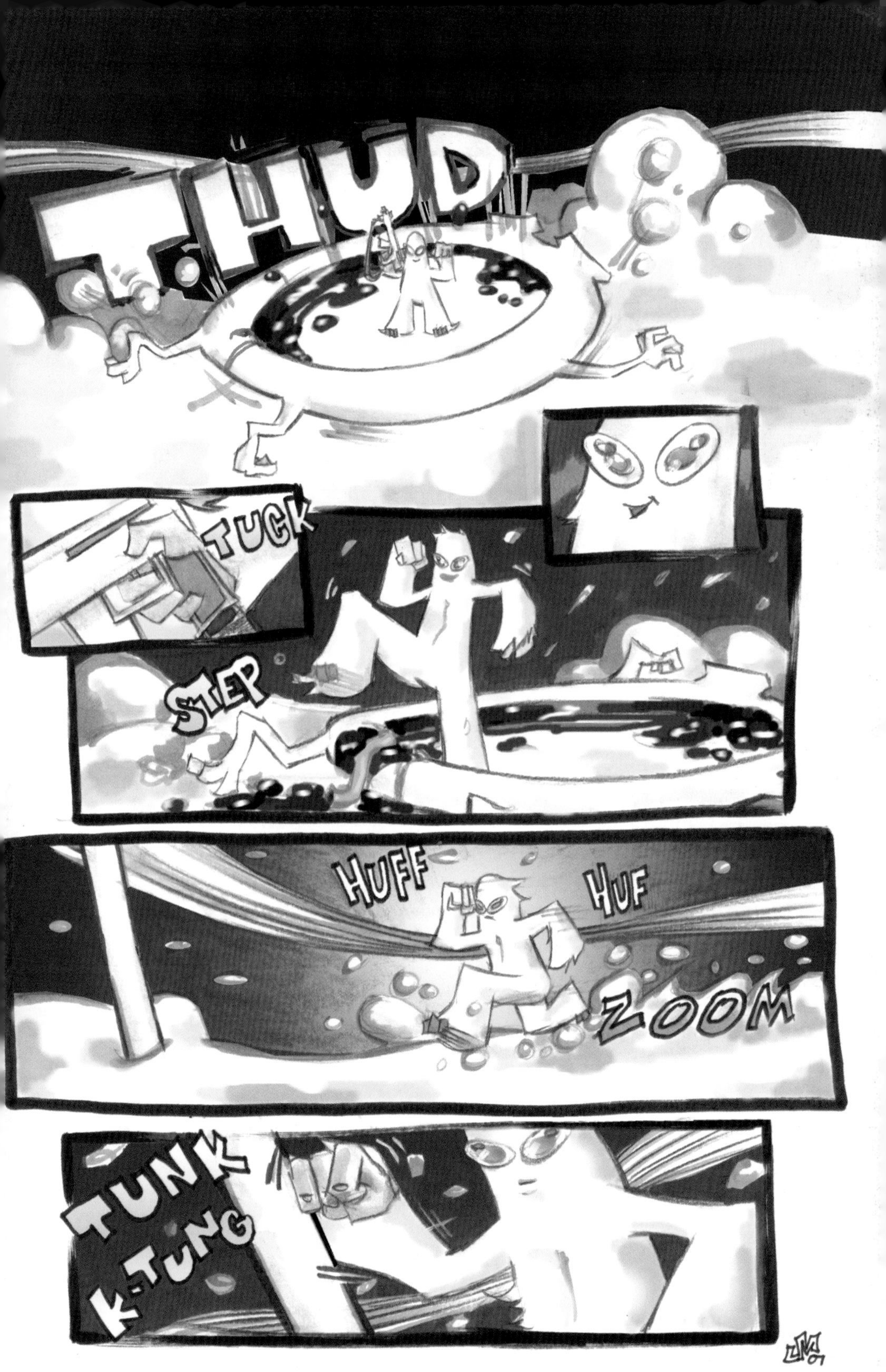

THUD
TUCK
STEP
HUFF
HUF
ZOOM
TUNK
K-TUNG

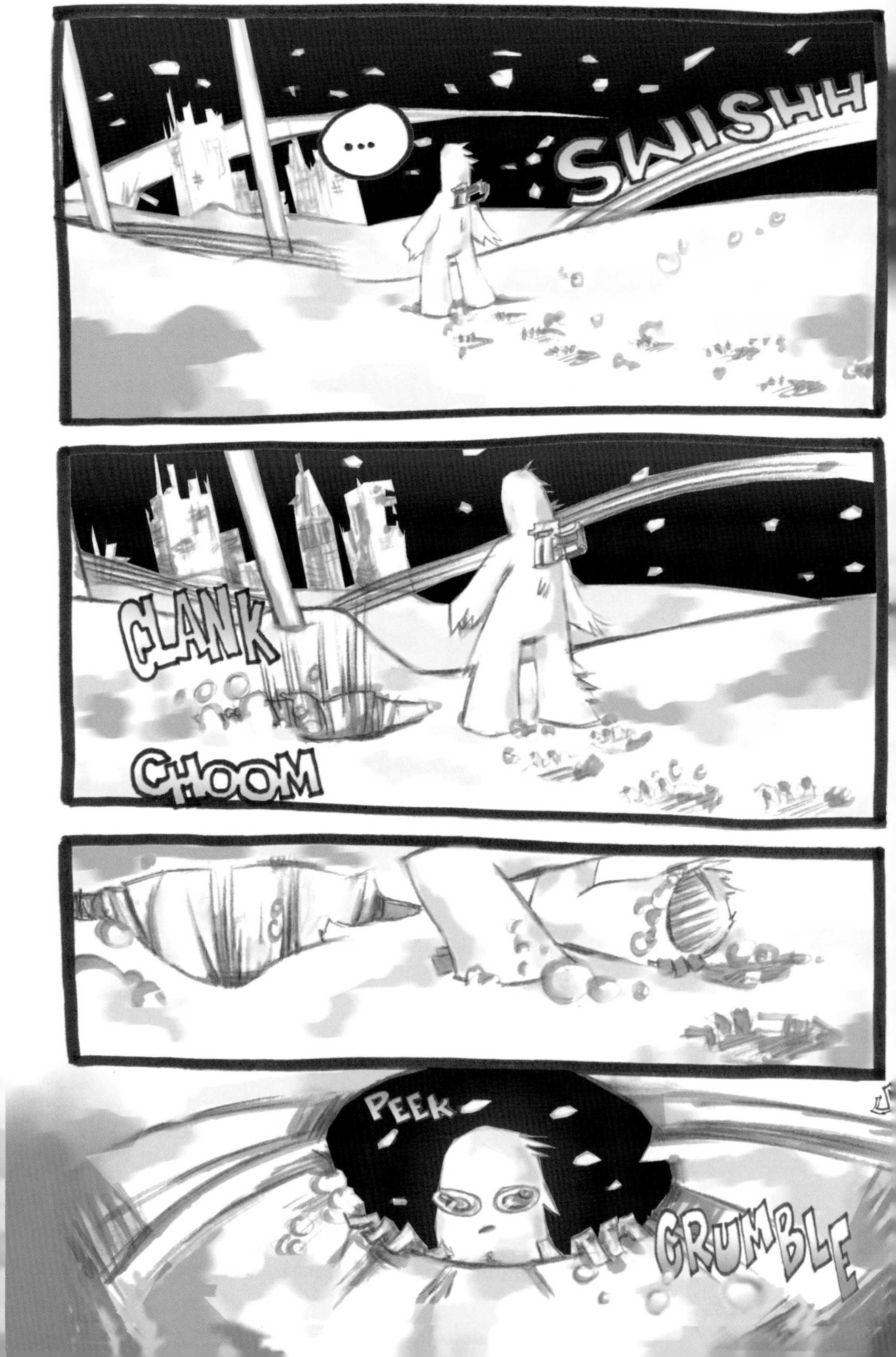
...
SWISHH
CLANK
CHOOM
PEEK
CRUMBLE

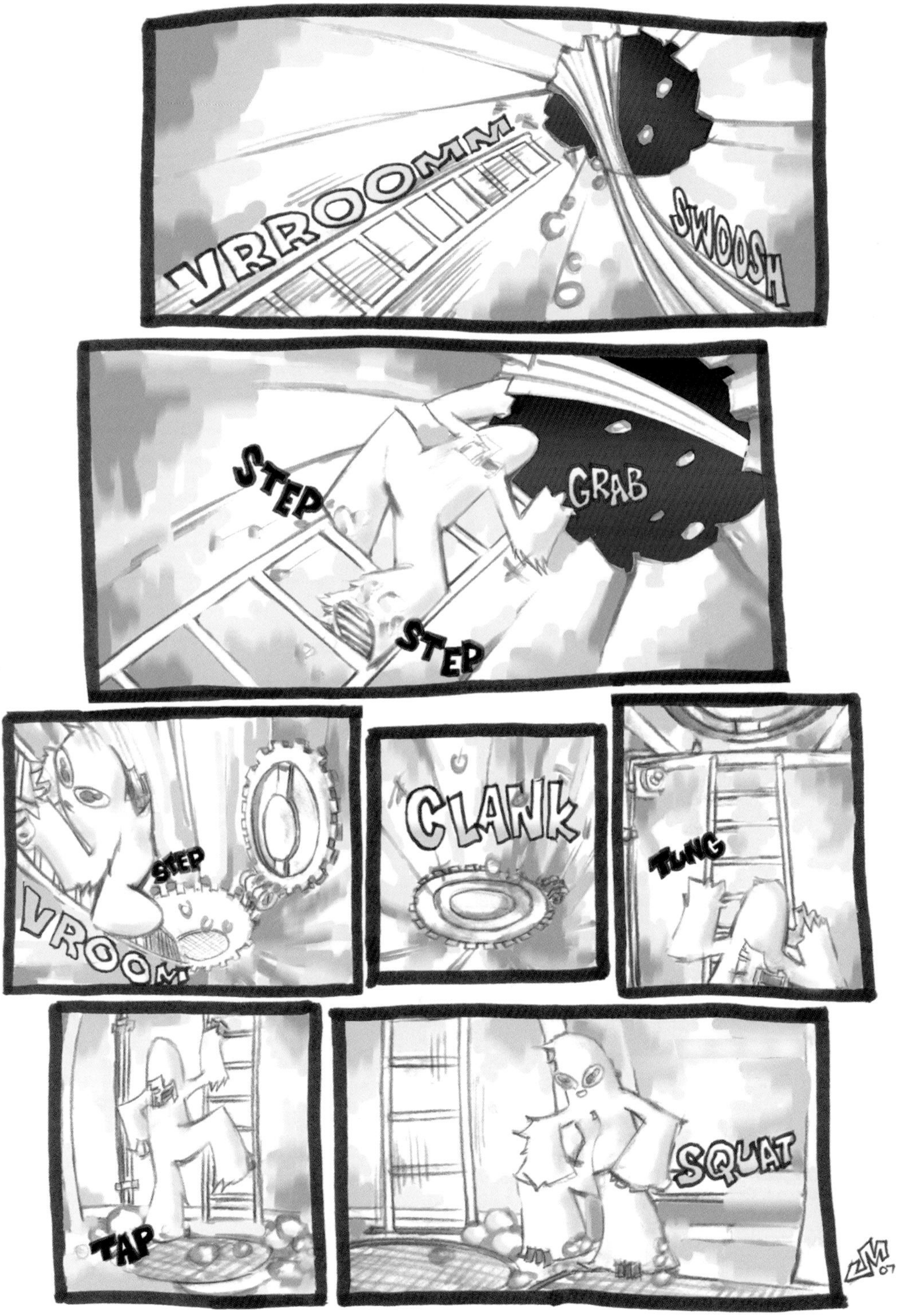
VRROOMM
SWOOSH
STEP
GRAB
STEP
STEP
VROOM
CLANK
TUNG
TAP
SQUAT
JM 07

GRAB
TINK
ZIP
UNFURL
LE SIGH.

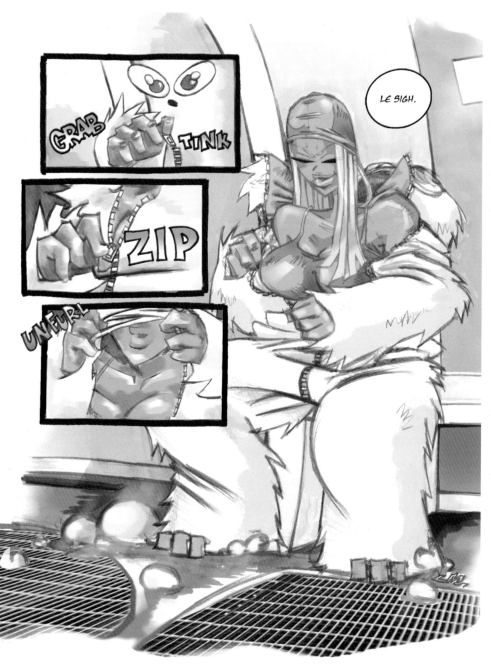

IN THE YEARS, DECADES, AND GENERATIONS FOLLOWING THE BURNT EARTH, WE SURVIVORS HAVE TAKEN TO WEARING PROTECTIVE COATS AS WE VENTURE BACK OUT INTO THE WORLD. COVERED IN LONG FUR TO PROTECT US FROM THE HARSH ELEMENTS, AND DESIGNED TO FIT IN AMONGST THE MONSTERS THAT NOW WALK FREELY ON THE ASH COVERED LANDS ABOVE US, THEY ARE NAMED AFTER THE FABLED BEASTS OF TIMES GONE BY THAT THEY RESEMBLE... THEY ARE OUR PROTECTORS.

YETI

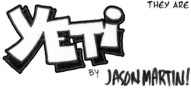

BY JASON MARTIN!

BLOODY FOREST OF SASQUATCH

STORY AND ART BY BRYAN BAUGH

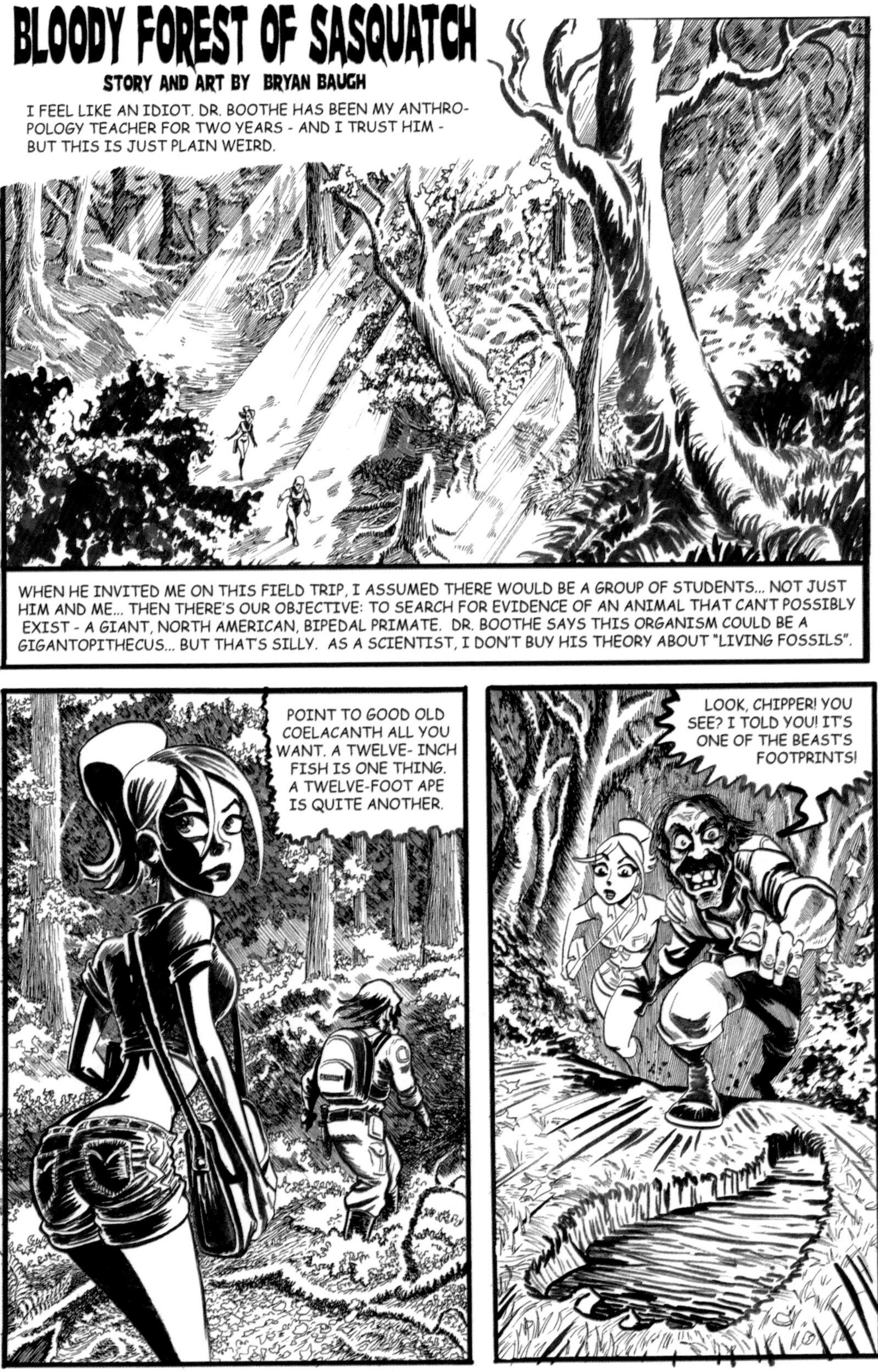
I FEEL LIKE AN IDIOT. DR. BOOTHE HAS BEEN MY ANTHROPOLOGY TEACHER FOR TWO YEARS - AND I TRUST HIM - BUT THIS IS JUST PLAIN WEIRD.
WHEN HE INVITED ME ON THIS FIELD TRIP, I ASSUMED THERE WOULD BE A GROUP OF STUDENTS... NOT JUST HIM AND ME... THEN THERE'S OUR OBJECTIVE: TO SEARCH FOR EVIDENCE OF AN ANIMAL THAT CAN'T POSSIBLY EXIST - A GIANT, NORTH AMERICAN, BIPEDAL PRIMATE. DR. BOOTHE SAYS THIS ORGANISM COULD BE A GIGANTOPITHECUS... BUT THAT'S SILLY. AS A SCIENTIST, I DON'T BUY HIS THEORY ABOUT "LIVING FOSSILS".
POINT TO GOOD OLD COELACANTH ALL YOU WANT. A TWELVE- INCH FISH IS ONE THING. A TWELVE-FOOT APE IS QUITE ANOTHER.
LOOK, CHIPPER! YOU SEE? I TOLD YOU! IT'S ONE OF THE BEAST'S FOOTPRINTS!

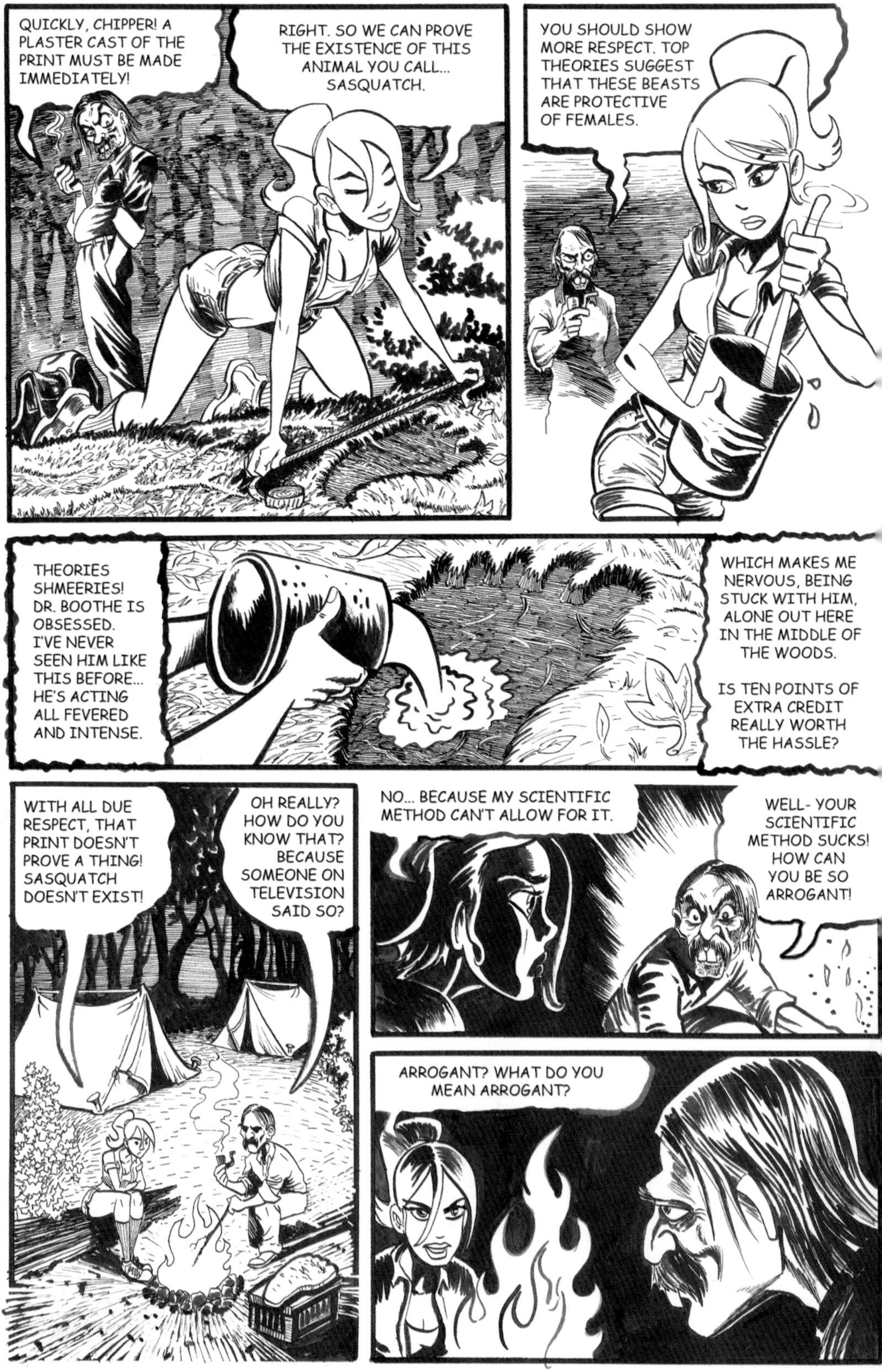
QUICKLY, CHIPPER! A PLASTER CAST OF THE PRINT MUST BE MADE IMMEDIATELY!
RIGHT. SO WE CAN PROVE THE EXISTENCE OF THIS ANIMAL YOU CALL... SASQUATCH.
YOU SHOULD SHOW MORE RESPECT. TOP THEORIES SUGGEST THAT THESE BEASTS ARE PROTECTIVE OF FEMALES.
THEORIES SHMEERIES! DR. BOOTHE IS OBSESSED. I'VE NEVER SEEN HIM LIKE THIS BEFORE... HE'S ACTING ALL FEVERED AND INTENSE.
WHICH MAKES ME NERVOUS, BEING STUCK WITH HIM, ALONE OUT HERE IN THE MIDDLE OF THE WOODS.
IS TEN POINTS OF EXTRA CREDIT REALLY WORTH THE HASSLE?
WITH ALL DUE RESPECT, THAT PRINT DOESN'T PROVE A THING! SASQUATCH DOESN'T EXIST!
OH REALLY? HOW DO YOU KNOW THAT? BECAUSE SOMEONE ON TELEVISION SAID SO?
NO... BECAUSE MY SCIENTIFIC METHOD CAN'T ALLOW FOR IT.
WELL- YOUR SCIENTIFIC METHOD SUCKS! HOW CAN YOU BE SO ARROGANT!
ARROGANT? WHAT DO YOU MEAN ARROGANT?

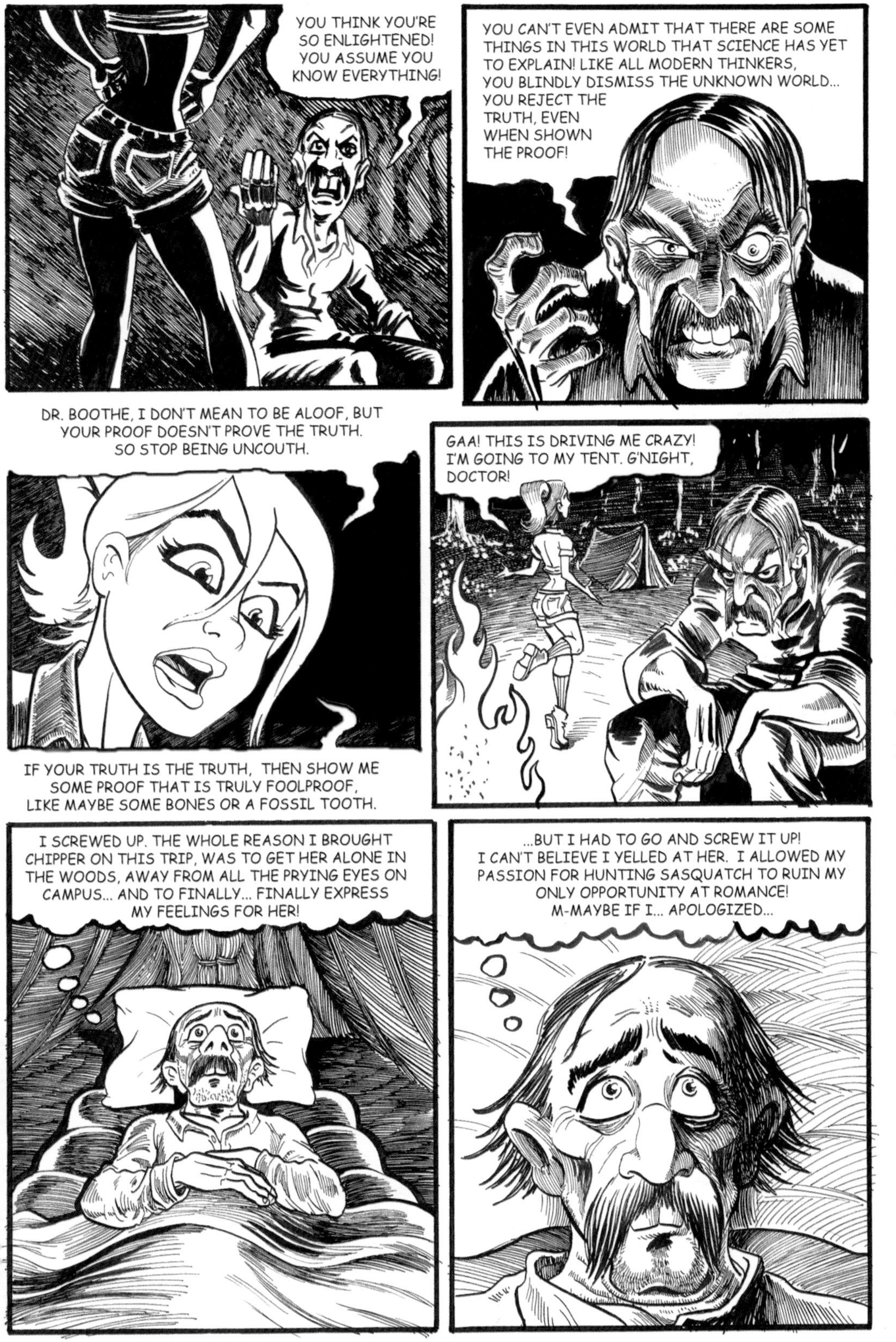
YOU THINK YOU'RE SO ENLIGHTENED! YOU ASSUME YOU KNOW EVERYTHING!
YOU CAN'T EVEN ADMIT THAT THERE ARE SOME THINGS IN THIS WORLD THAT SCIENCE HAS YET TO EXPLAIN! LIKE ALL MODERN THINKERS, YOU BLINDLY DISMISS THE UNKNOWN WORLD... YOU REJECT THE TRUTH, EVEN WHEN SHOWN THE PROOF!
DR. BOOTHE, I DON'T MEAN TO BE ALOOF, BUT YOUR PROOF DOESN'T PROVE THE TRUTH. SO STOP BEING UNCOUTH.
IF YOUR TRUTH IS THE TRUTH, THEN SHOW ME SOME PROOF THAT IS TRULY FOOLPROOF, LIKE MAYBE SOME BONES OR A FOSSIL TOOTH.
GAA! THIS IS DRIVING ME CRAZY! I'M GOING TO MY TENT. G'NIGHT, DOCTOR!
I SCREWED UP. THE WHOLE REASON I BROUGHT CHIPPER ON THIS TRIP, WAS TO GET HER ALONE IN THE WOODS, AWAY FROM ALL THE PRYING EYES ON CAMPUS... AND TO FINALLY... FINALLY EXPRESS MY FEELINGS FOR HER!
...BUT I HAD TO GO AND SCREW IT UP! I CAN'T BELIEVE I YELLED AT HER. I ALLOWED MY PASSION FOR HUNTING SASQUATCH TO RUIN MY ONLY OPPORTUNITY AT ROMANCE! M-MAYBE IF I... APOLOGIZED...

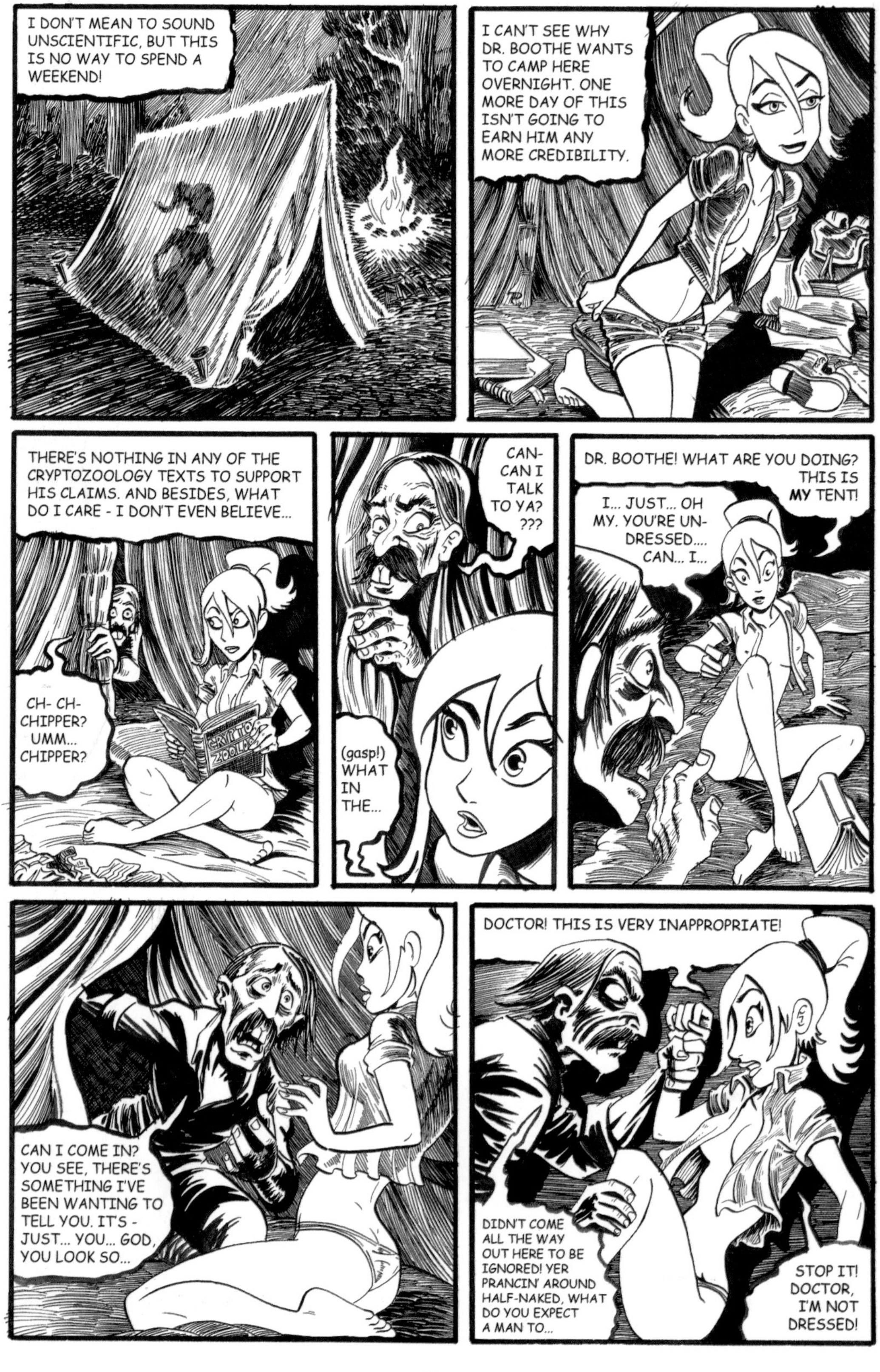
I DON'T MEAN TO SOUND UNSCIENTIFIC, BUT THIS IS NO WAY TO SPEND A WEEKEND!
I CAN'T SEE WHY DR. BOOTHE WANTS TO CAMP HERE OVERNIGHT. ONE MORE DAY OF THIS ISN'T GOING TO EARN HIM ANY MORE CREDIBILITY.
THERE'S NOTHING IN ANY OF THE CRYPTOZOOLOGY TEXTS TO SUPPORT HIS CLAIMS. AND BESIDES, WHAT DO I CARE - I DON'T EVEN BELIEVE...
CH- CH- CHIPPER? UMM... CHIPPER?
CAN- CAN I TALK TO YA? ???
(gasp!) WHAT IN THE...
DR. BOOTHE! WHAT ARE YOU DOING? THIS IS **MY** TENT!
I... JUST... OH MY. YOU'RE UN-DRESSED.... CAN... I...
CAN I COME IN? YOU SEE, THERE'S SOMETHING I'VE BEEN WANTING TO TELL YOU. IT'S - JUST... YOU... GOD, YOU LOOK SO...
DOCTOR! THIS IS VERY INAPPROPRIATE!
DIDN'T COME ALL THE WAY OUT HERE TO BE IGNORED! YER PRANCIN' AROUND HALF-NAKED, WHAT DO YOU EXPECT A MAN TO...
STOP IT! DOCTOR, I'M NOT DRESSED!

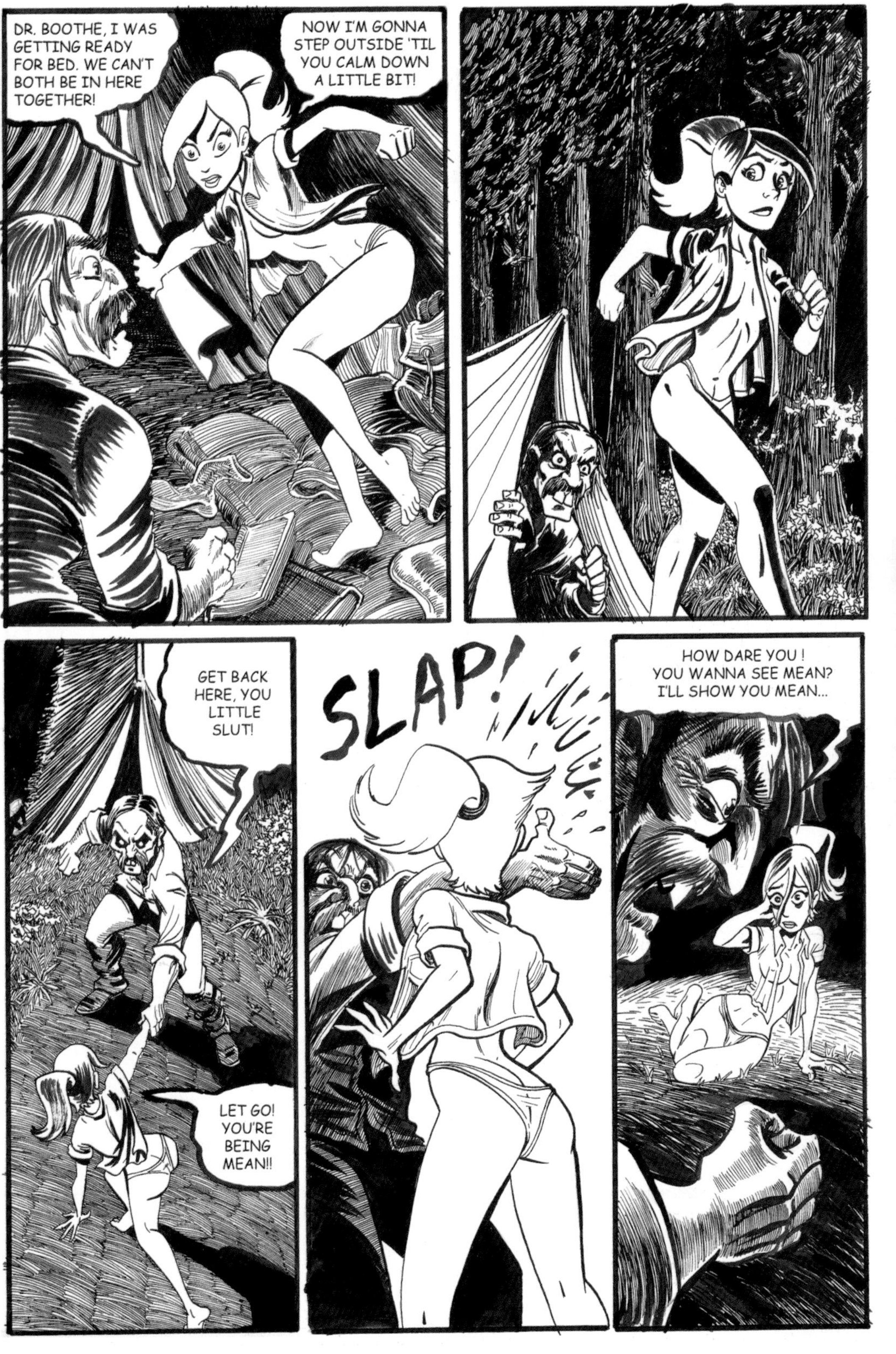

DR. BOOTHE, I WAS GETTING READY FOR BED. WE CAN'T BOTH BE IN HERE TOGETHER!
NOW I'M GONNA STEP OUTSIDE 'TIL YOU CALM DOWN A LITTLE BIT!
GET BACK HERE, YOU LITTLE SLUT!
LET GO! YOU'RE BEING MEAN!!
SLAP!
HOW DARE YOU ! YOU WANNA SEE MEAN? I'LL SHOW YOU MEAN...

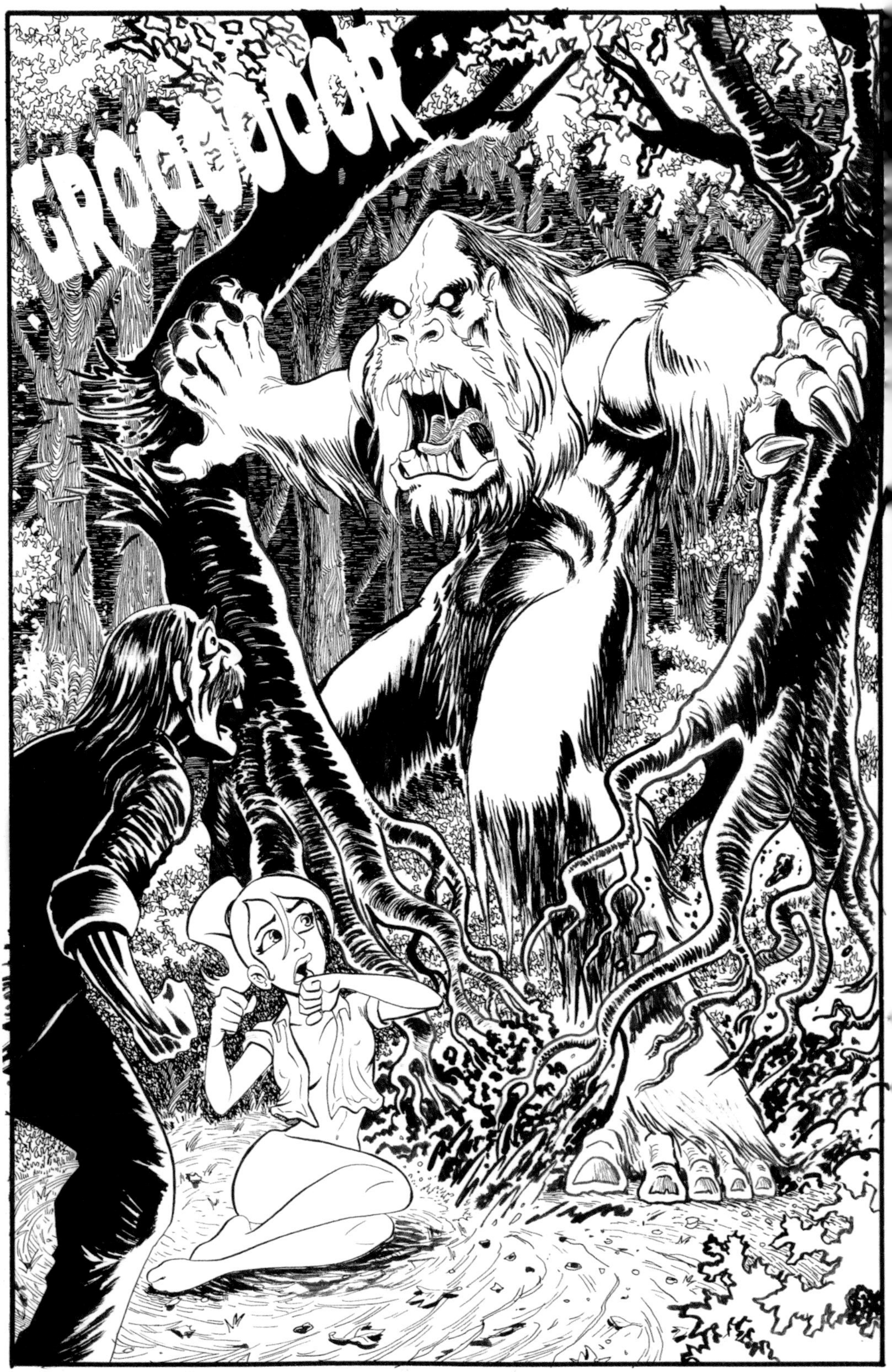
GROOOOOOR!

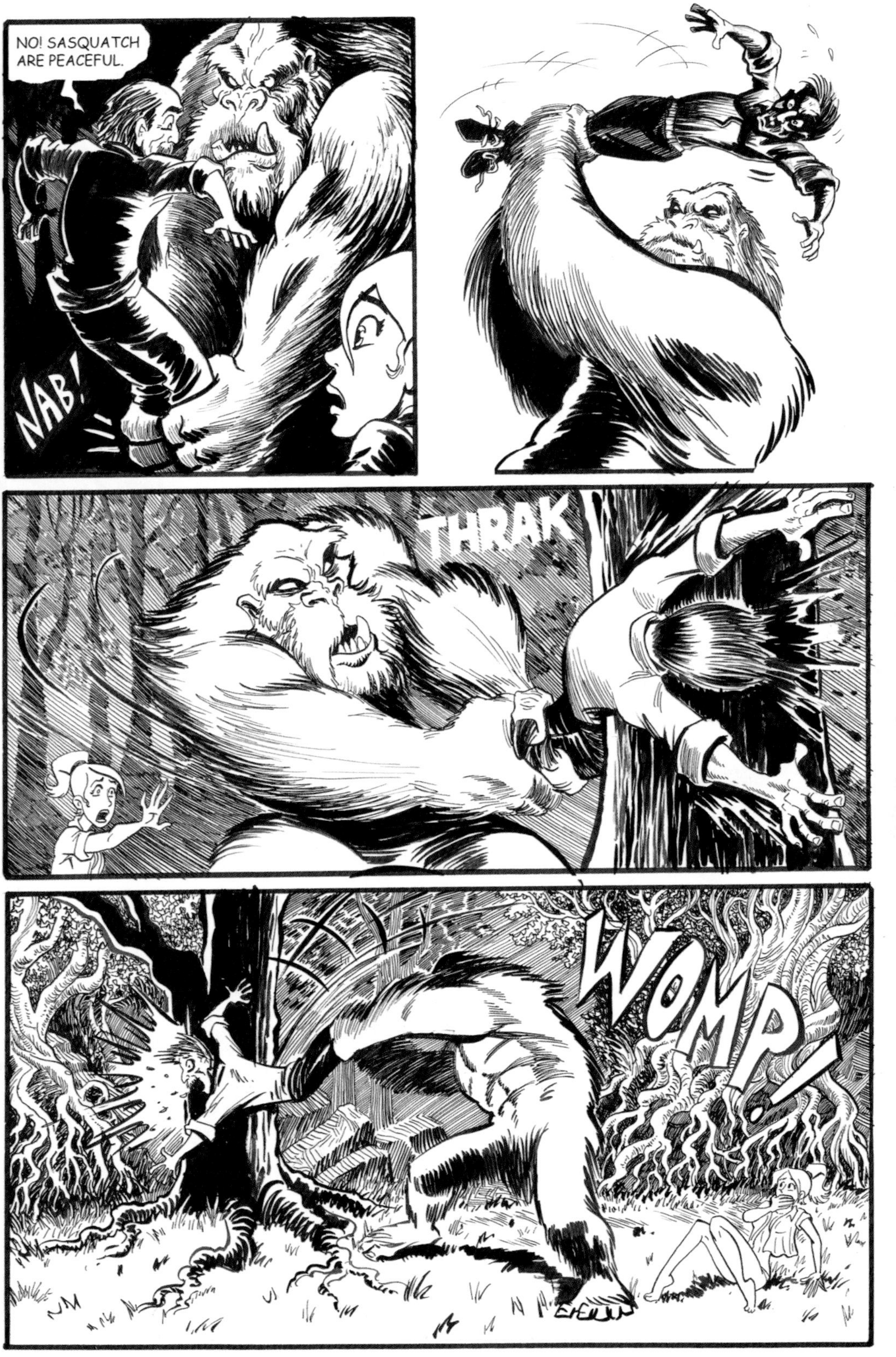
NO! SASQUATCH ARE PEACEFUL.
NAB!
THRAK
WOMP!

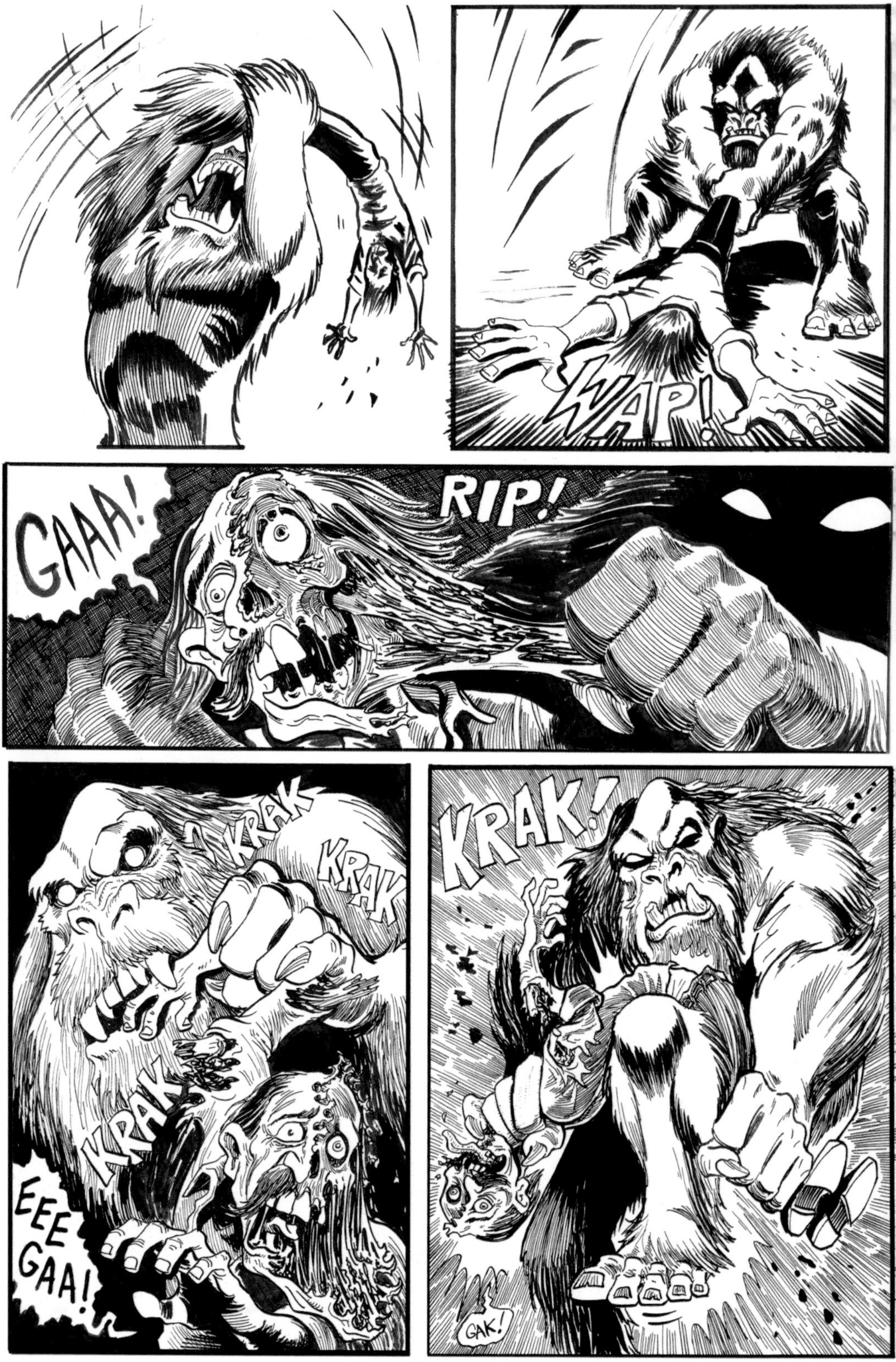
WAP!
GAAA!
RIP!
KRAK
KRAK
KRAK
EEE GAA!
KRAK!
GAK!

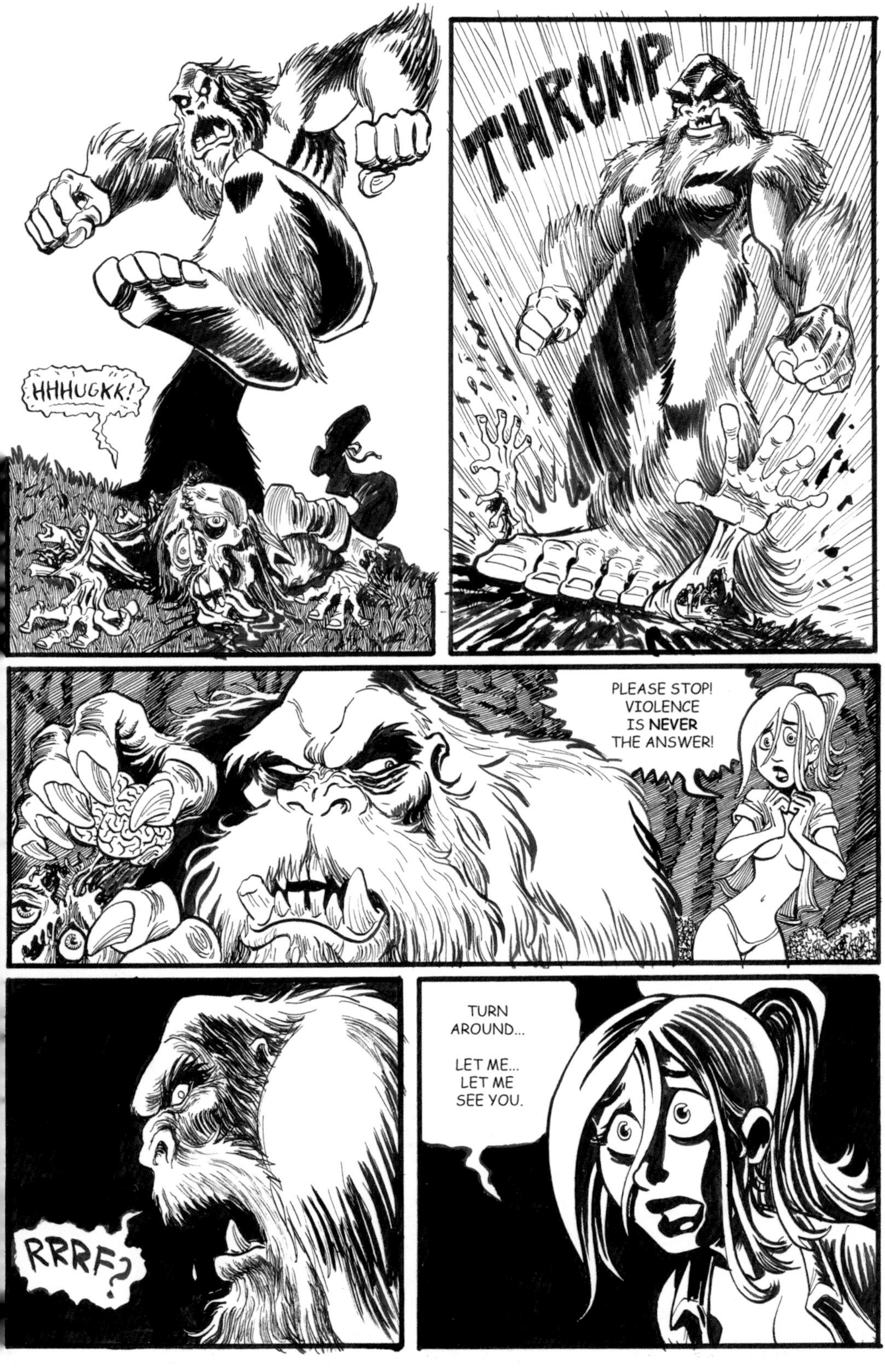
HHHUGKK!
THROMP
PLEASE STOP! VIOLENCE IS **NEVER** THE ANSWER!
RRRF?
TURN AROUND...
LET ME... LET ME SEE YOU.

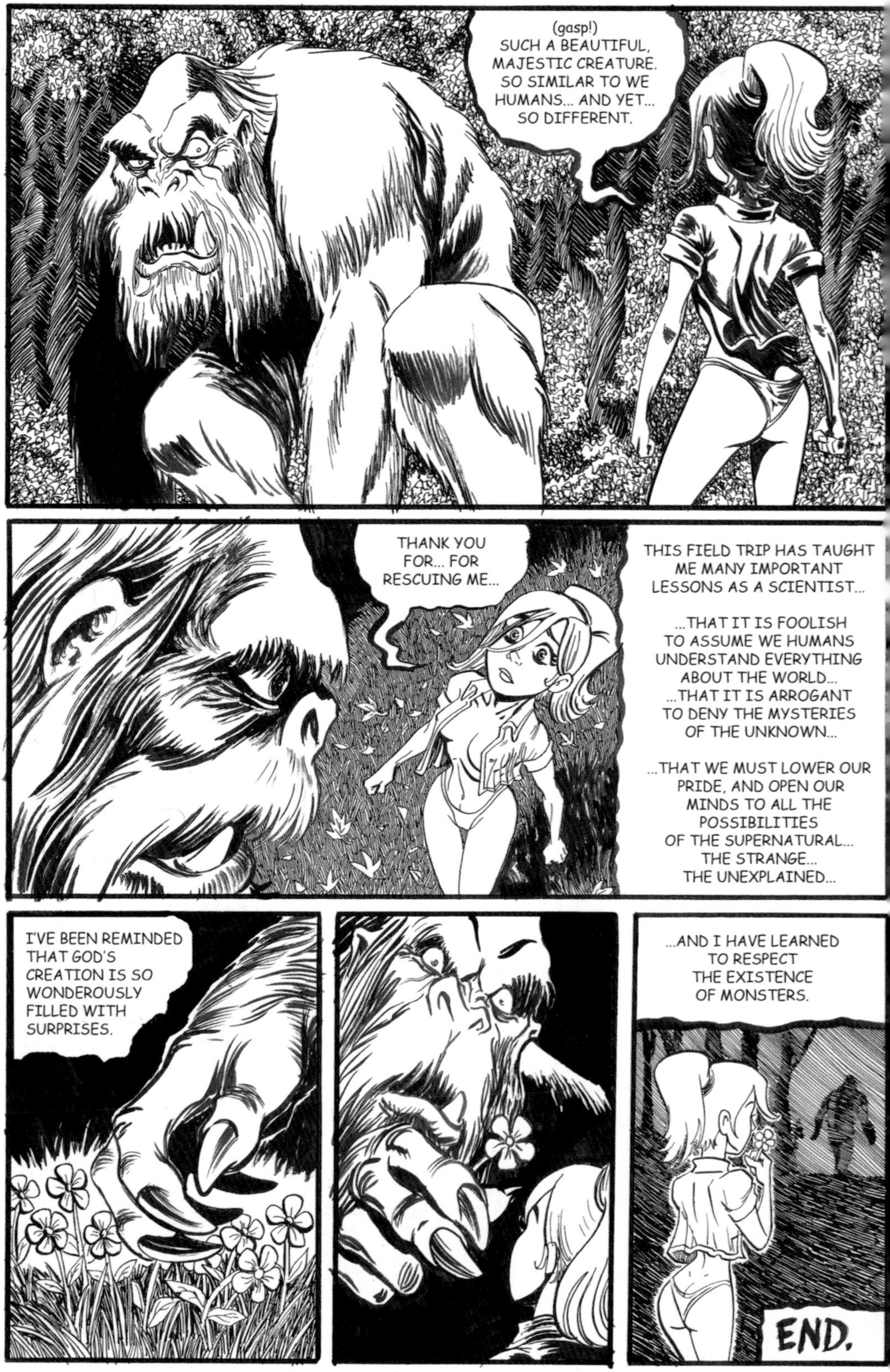
(gasp!) SUCH A BEAUTIFUL, MAJESTIC CREATURE. SO SIMILAR TO WE HUMANS... AND YET... SO DIFFERENT.
THANK YOU FOR... FOR RESCUING ME...
THIS FIELD TRIP HAS TAUGHT ME MANY IMPORTANT LESSONS AS A SCIENTIST...
...THAT IT IS FOOLISH TO ASSUME WE HUMANS UNDERSTAND EVERYTHING ABOUT THE WORLD... ...THAT IT IS ARROGANT TO DENY THE MYSTERIES OF THE UNKNOWN...
...THAT WE MUST LOWER OUR PRIDE, AND OPEN OUR MINDS TO ALL THE POSSIBILITIES OF THE SUPERNATURAL... THE STRANGE... THE UNEXPLAINED...
I'VE BEEN REMINDED THAT GOD'S CREATION IS SO WONDEROUSLY FILLED WITH SURPRISES.
...AND I HAVE LEARNED TO RESPECT THE EXISTENCE OF MONSTERS.
END.

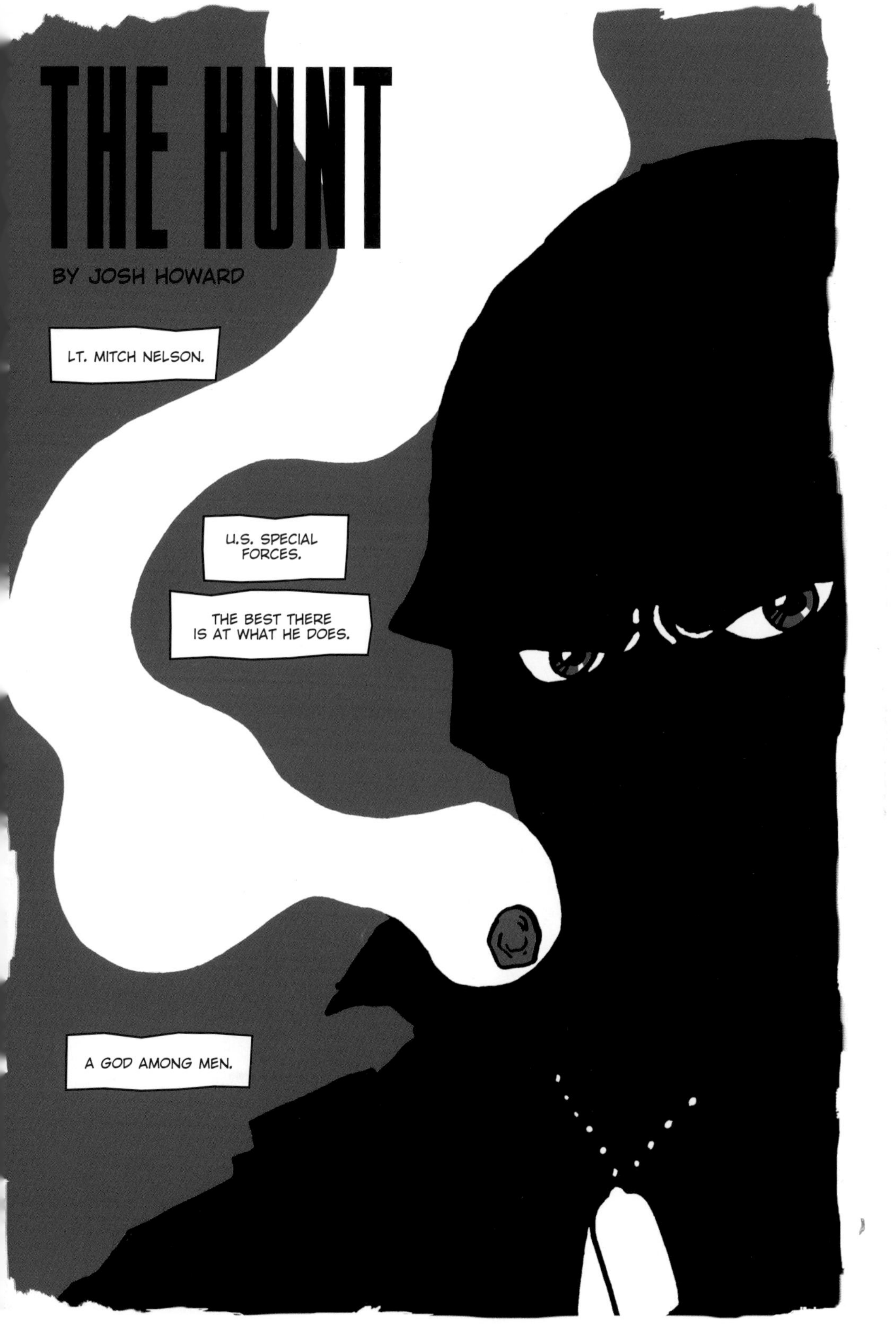
THE HUNT
BY JOSH HOWARD
LT. MITCH NELSON.
U.S. SPECIAL FORCES.
THE BEST THERE IS AT WHAT HE DOES.
A GOD AMONG MEN.

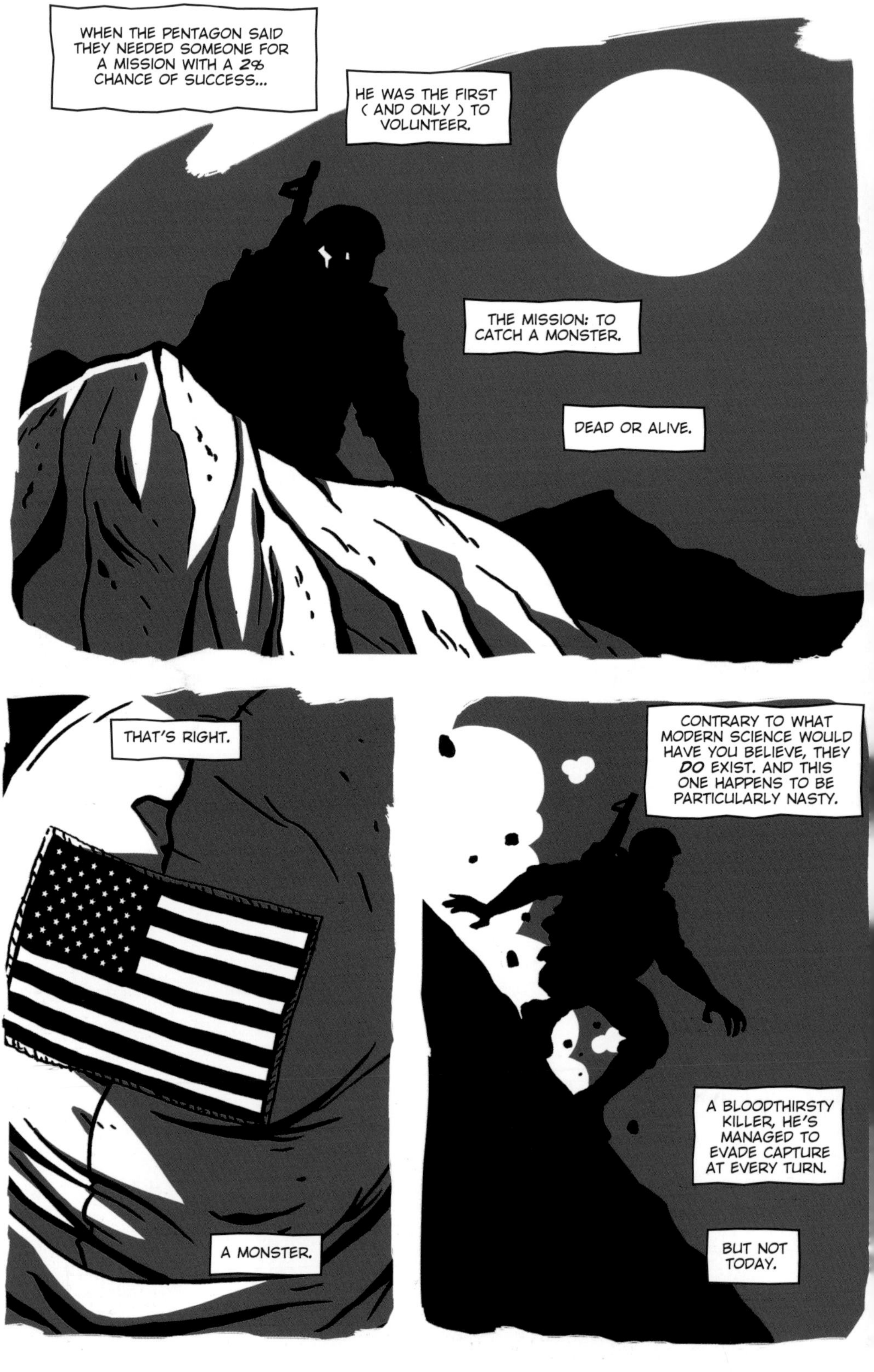
WHEN THE PENTAGON SAID THEY NEEDED SOMEONE FOR A MISSION WITH A 2% CHANCE OF SUCCESS...
HE WAS THE FIRST (AND ONLY) TO VOLUNTEER.
THE MISSION: TO CATCH A MONSTER.
DEAD OR ALIVE.
THAT'S RIGHT.
A MONSTER.
CONTRARY TO WHAT MODERN SCIENCE WOULD HAVE YOU BELIEVE, THEY *DO* EXIST. AND THIS ONE HAPPENS TO BE PARTICULARLY NASTY.
A BLOODTHIRSTY KILLER, HE'S MANAGED TO EVADE CAPTURE AT EVERY TURN.
BUT NOT TODAY.

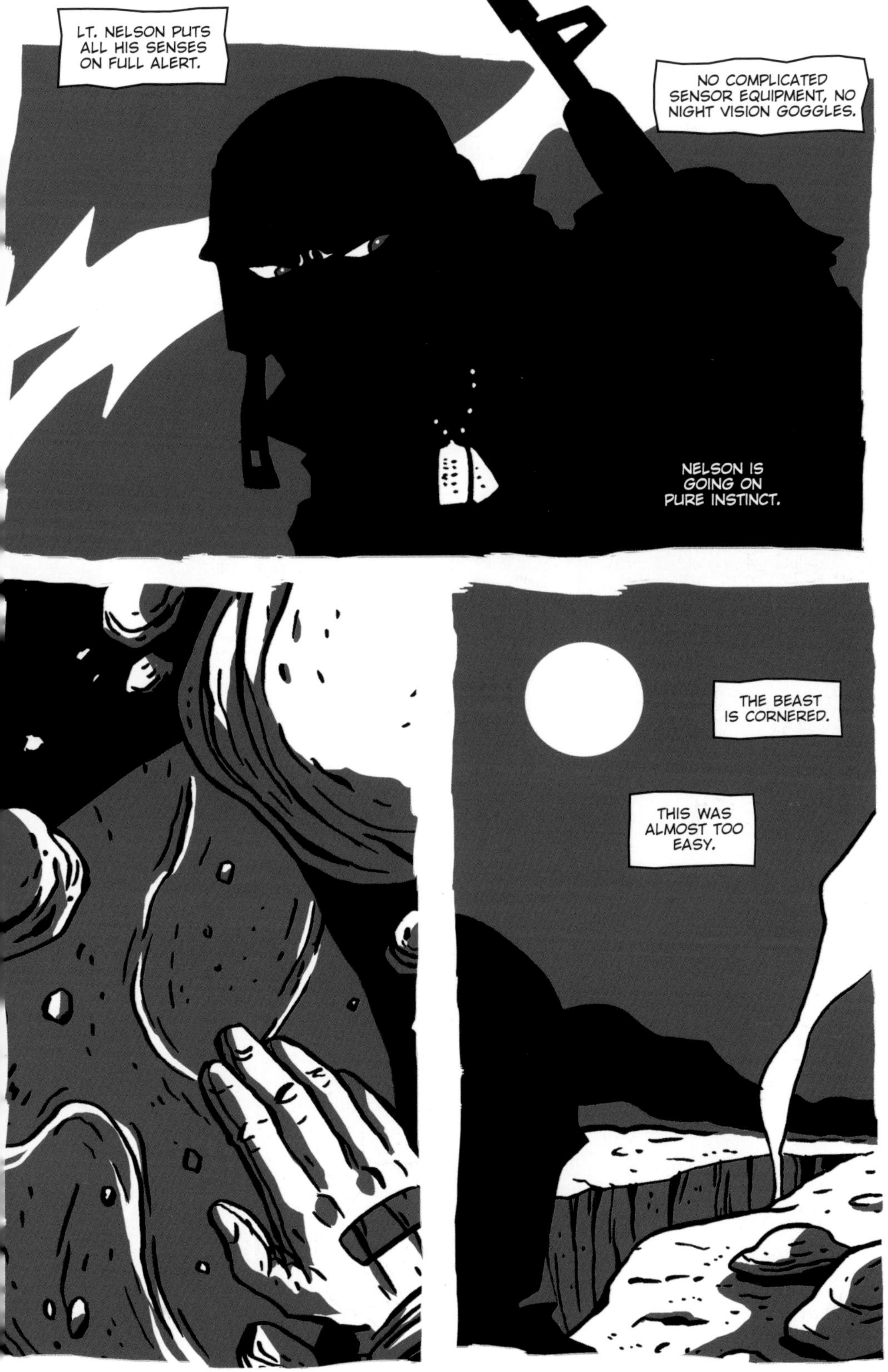
LT. NELSON PUTS ALL HIS SENSES ON FULL ALERT.
NO COMPLICATED SENSOR EQUIPMENT, NO NIGHT VISION GOGGLES.
NELSON IS GOING ON PURE INSTINCT.
THE BEAST IS CORNERED.
THIS WAS ALMOST TOO EASY.

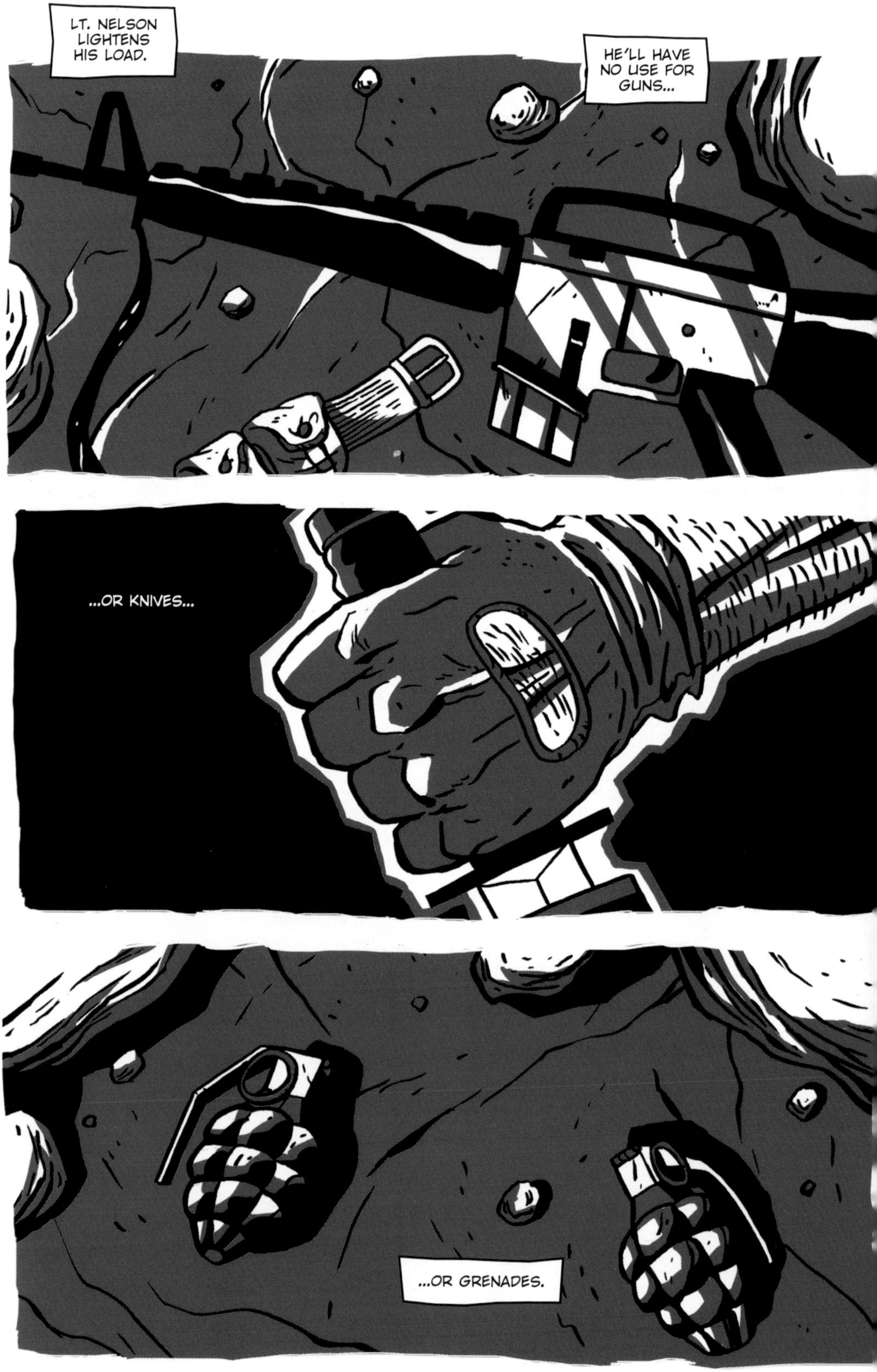
LT. NELSON LIGHTENS HIS LOAD.
HE'LL HAVE NO USE FOR GUNS...
...OR KNIVES...
...OR GRENADES.

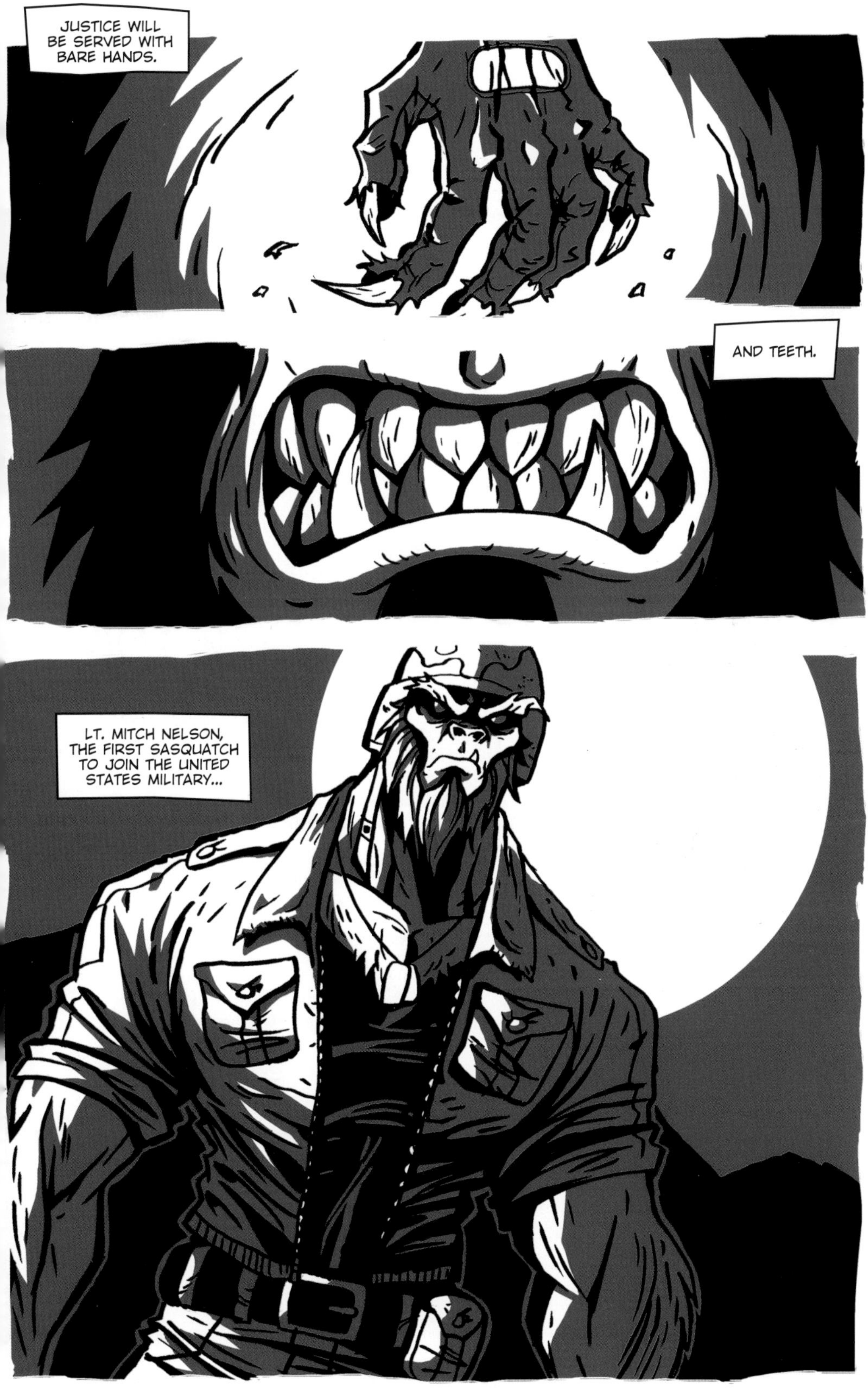
JUSTICE WILL BE SERVED WITH BARE HANDS.
AND TEETH.
LT. MITCH NELSON, THE FIRST SASQUATCH TO JOIN THE UNITED STATES MILITARY...

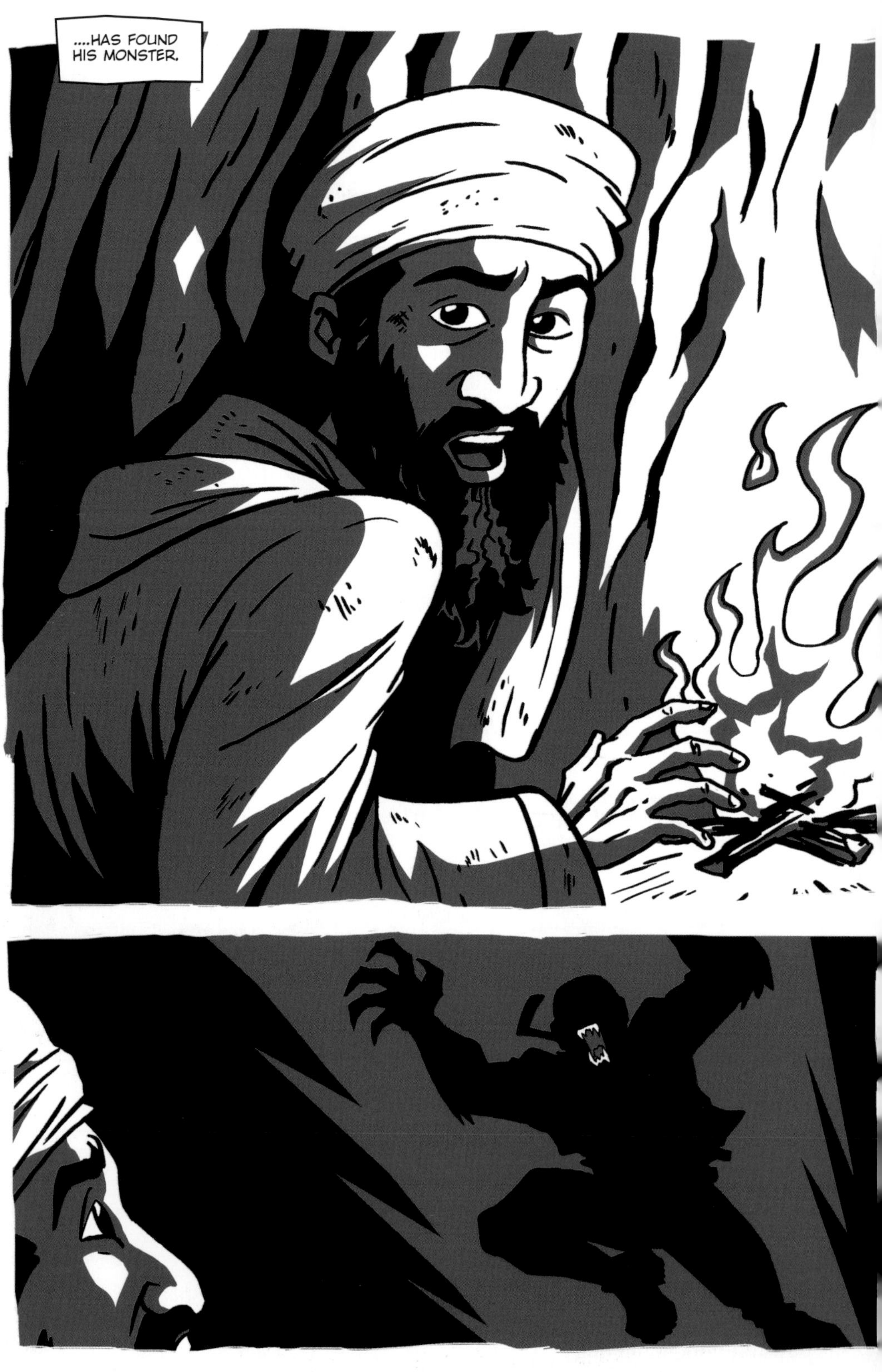
....HAS FOUND HIS MONSTER.

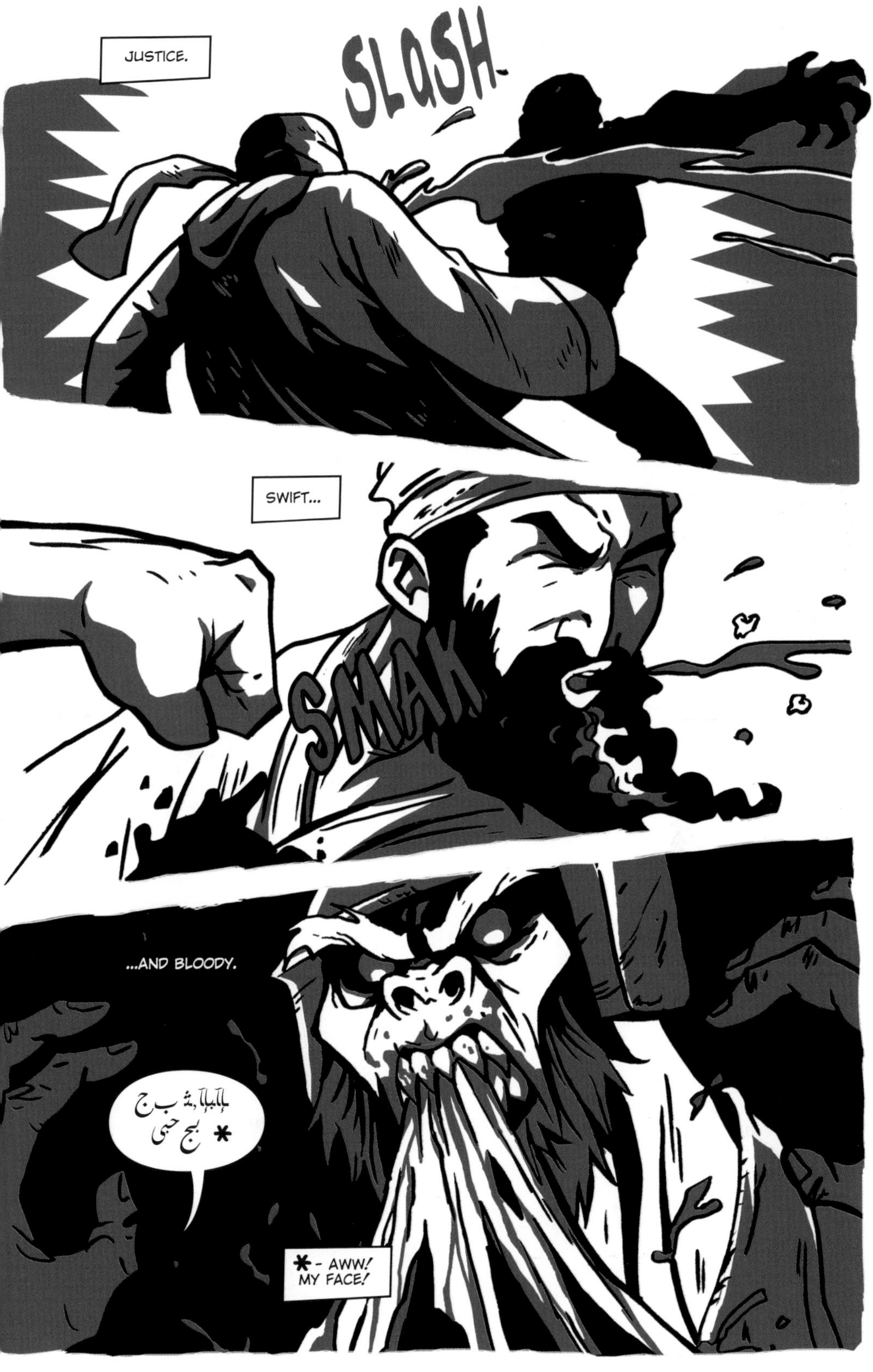
JUSTICE.
SLASH
SWIFT...
SMAK
...AND BLOODY.
*- AWW! MY FACE!

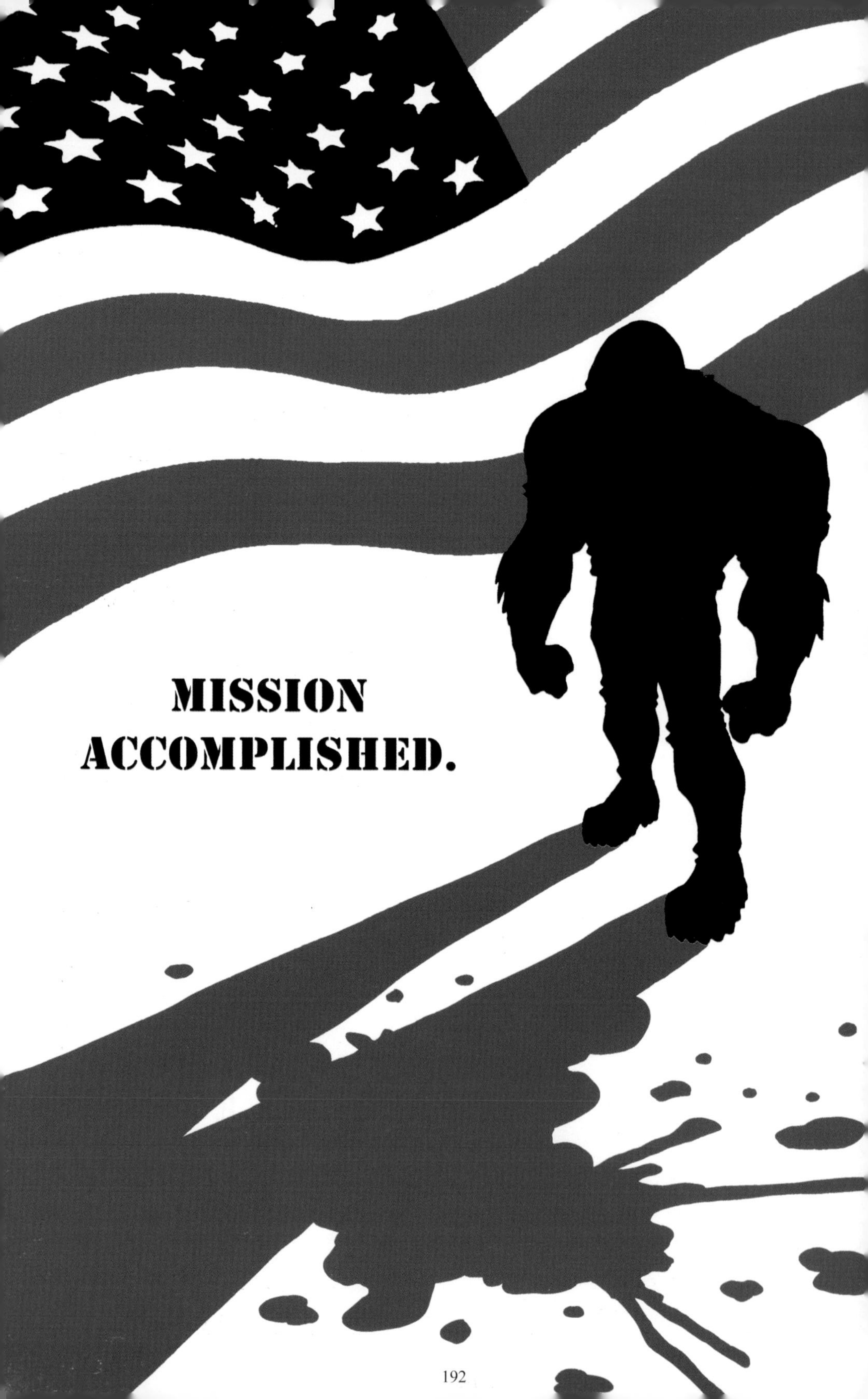
MISSION
ACCOMPLISHED.

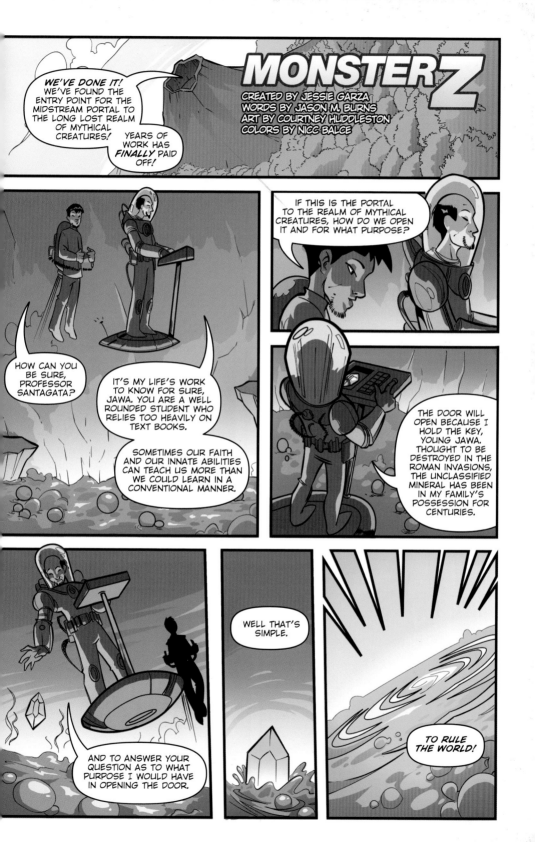

MONSTER Z

CREATED BY JESSIE GARZA
WORDS BY JASON M. BURNS
ART BY COURTNEY HUDDLESTON
COLORS BY NICC BALCE

WE'VE DONE IT! WE'VE FOUND THE ENTRY POINT FOR THE MIDSTREAM PORTAL TO THE LONG LOST REALM OF MYTHICAL CREATURES! YEARS OF WORK HAS *FINALLY* PAID OFF!

IF THIS IS THE PORTAL TO THE REALM OF MYTHICAL CREATURES, HOW DO WE OPEN IT AND FOR WHAT PURPOSE?

HOW CAN YOU BE SURE, PROFESSOR SANTAGATA?

IT'S MY LIFE'S WORK TO KNOW FOR SURE, JAWA. YOU ARE A WELL ROUNDED STUDENT WHO RELIES TOO HEAVILY ON TEXT BOOKS.

SOMETIMES OUR FAITH AND OUR INNATE ABILITIES CAN TEACH US MORE THAN WE COULD LEARN IN A CONVENTIONAL MANNER.

THE DOOR WILL OPEN BECAUSE I HOLD THE KEY, YOUNG JAWA. THOUGHT TO BE DESTROYED IN THE ROMAN INVASIONS, THE UNCLASSIFIED MINERAL HAS BEEN IN MY FAMILY'S POSSESSION FOR CENTURIES.

WELL THAT'S SIMPLE.

AND TO ANSWER YOUR QUESTION AS TO WHAT PURPOSE I WOULD HAVE IN OPENING THE DOOR.

TO RULE THE WORLD!

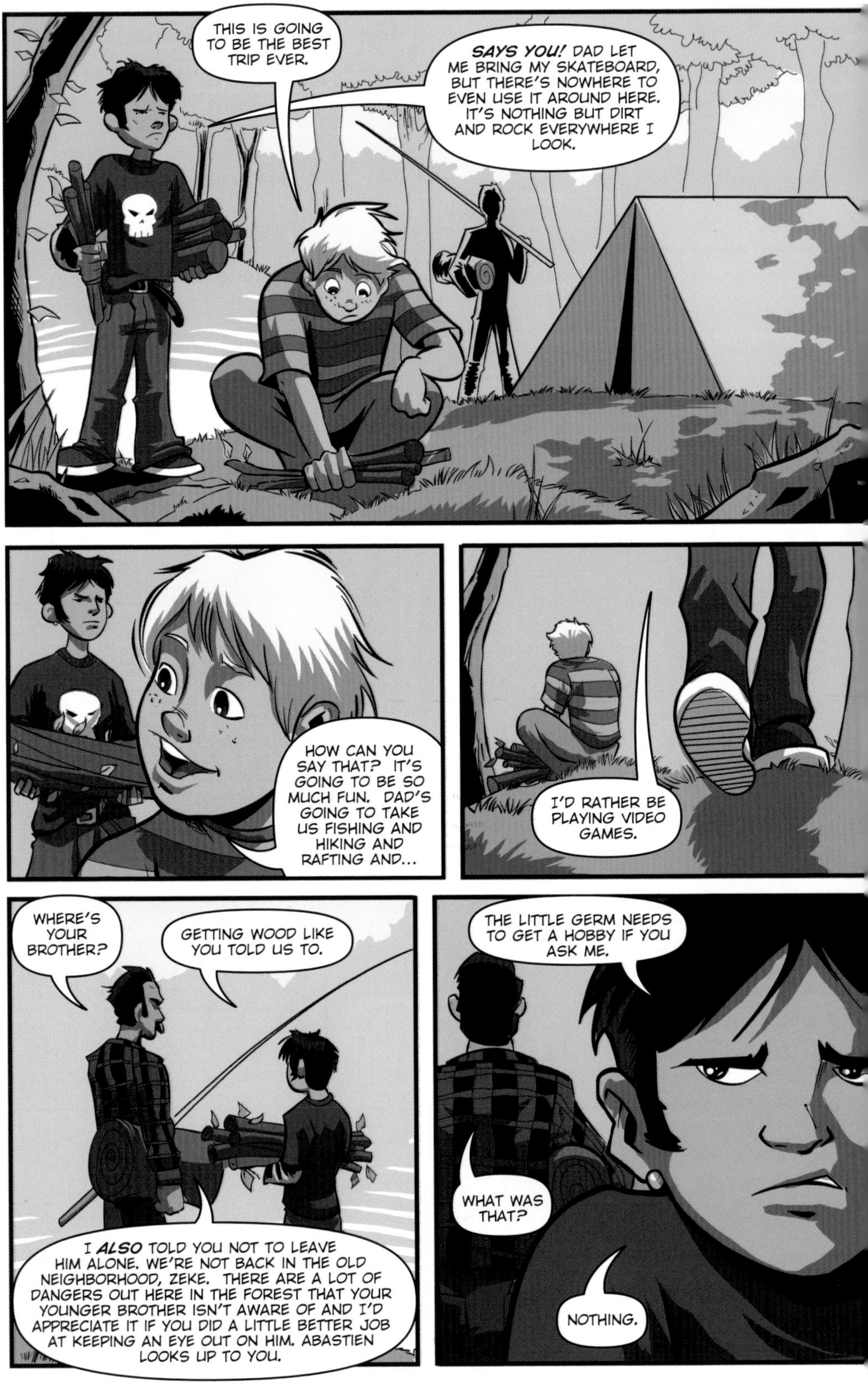
THIS IS GOING TO BE THE BEST TRIP EVER.
SAYS YOU! DAD LET ME BRING MY SKATEBOARD, BUT THERE'S NOWHERE TO EVEN USE IT AROUND HERE. IT'S NOTHING BUT DIRT AND ROCK EVERYWHERE I LOOK.
HOW CAN YOU SAY THAT? IT'S GOING TO BE SO MUCH FUN. DAD'S GOING TO TAKE US FISHING AND HIKING AND RAFTING AND...
I'D RATHER BE PLAYING VIDEO GAMES.
WHERE'S YOUR BROTHER?
GETTING WOOD LIKE YOU TOLD US TO.
I ALSO TOLD YOU NOT TO LEAVE HIM ALONE. WE'RE NOT BACK IN THE OLD NEIGHBORHOOD, ZEKE. THERE ARE A LOT OF DANGERS OUT HERE IN THE FOREST THAT YOUR YOUNGER BROTHER ISN'T AWARE OF AND I'D APPRECIATE IT IF YOU DID A LITTLE BETTER JOB AT KEEPING AN EYE OUT ON HIM. ABASTIEN LOOKS UP TO YOU.
THE LITTLE GERM NEEDS TO GET A HOBBY IF YOU ASK ME.
WHAT WAS THAT?
NOTHING.

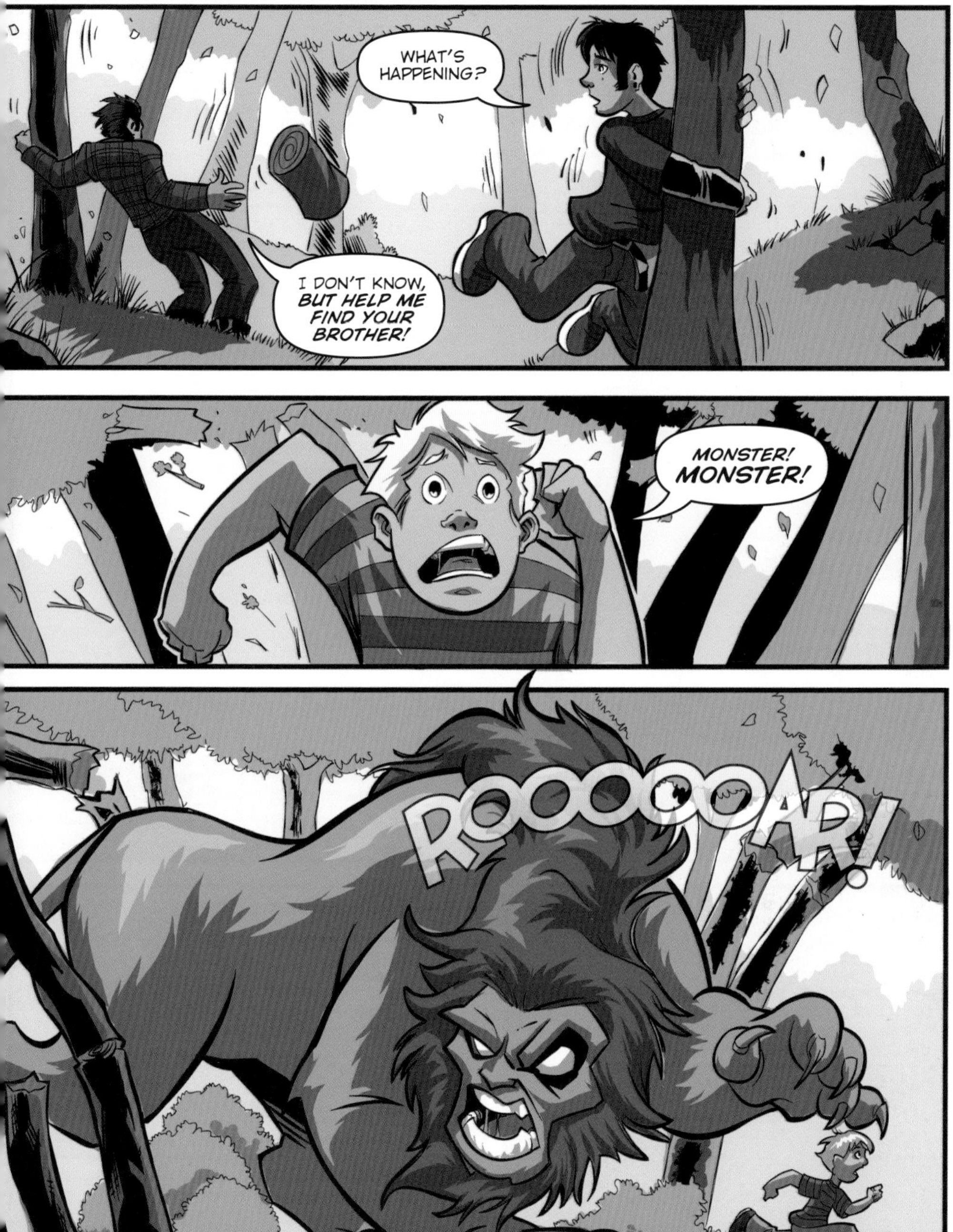
WHAT'S HAPPENING?
I DON'T KNOW, BUT HELP ME FIND YOUR BROTHER!
MONSTER! MONSTER!
ROOOOOAR!

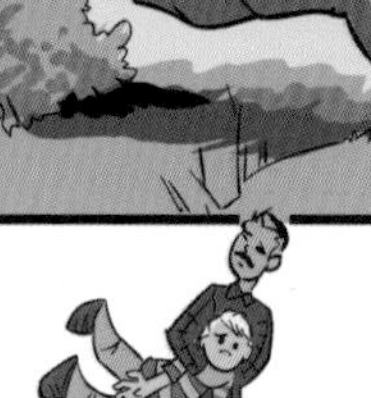

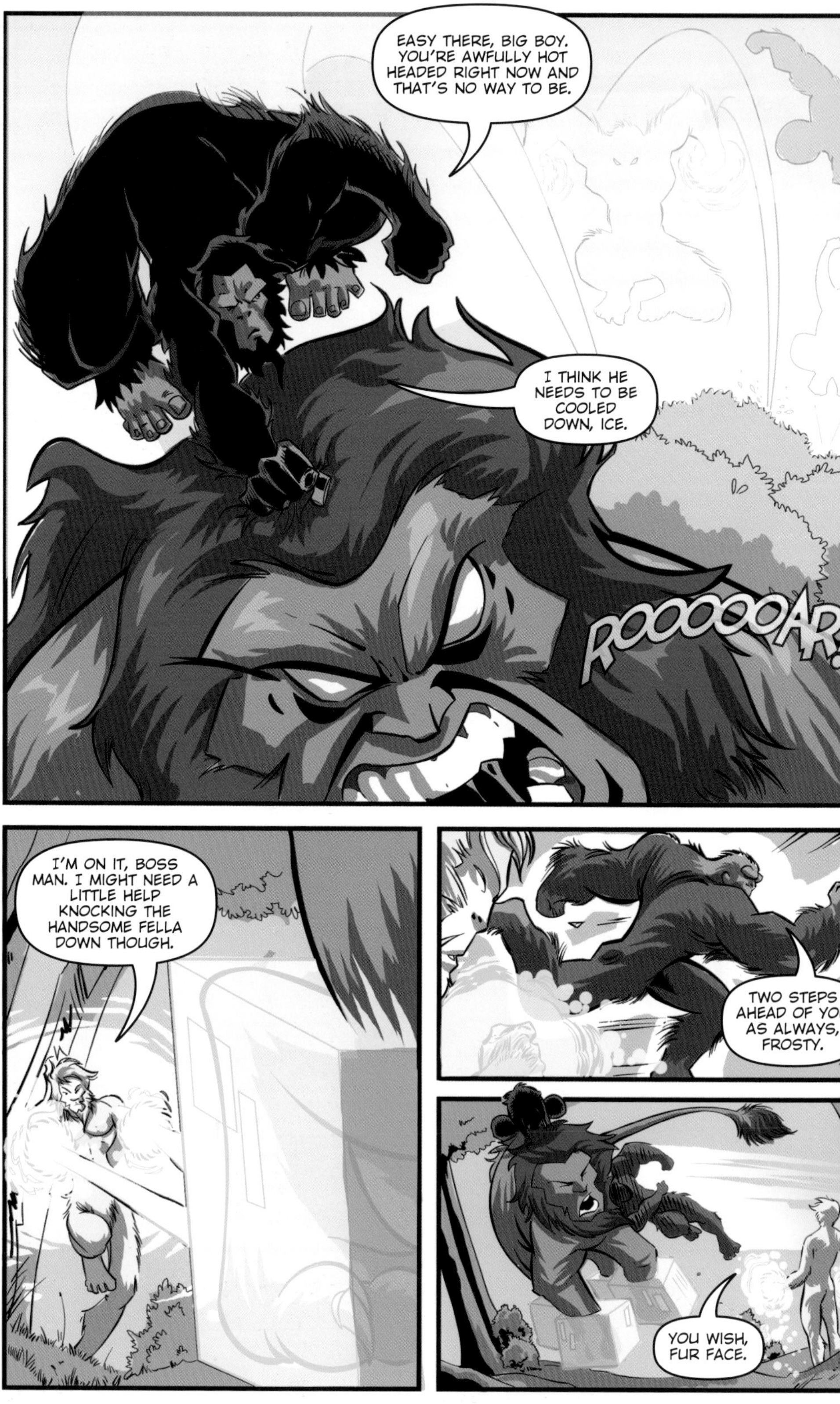
EASY THERE, BIG BOY. YOU'RE AWFULLY HOT HEADED RIGHT NOW AND THAT'S NO WAY TO BE.
I THINK HE NEEDS TO BE COOLED DOWN, ICE.
ROOOOOAR!
I'M ON IT, BOSS MAN. I MIGHT NEED A LITTLE HELP KNOCKING THE HANDSOME FELLA DOWN THOUGH.
TWO STEPS AHEAD OF YOU AS ALWAYS, FROSTY.
YOU WISH, FUR FACE.

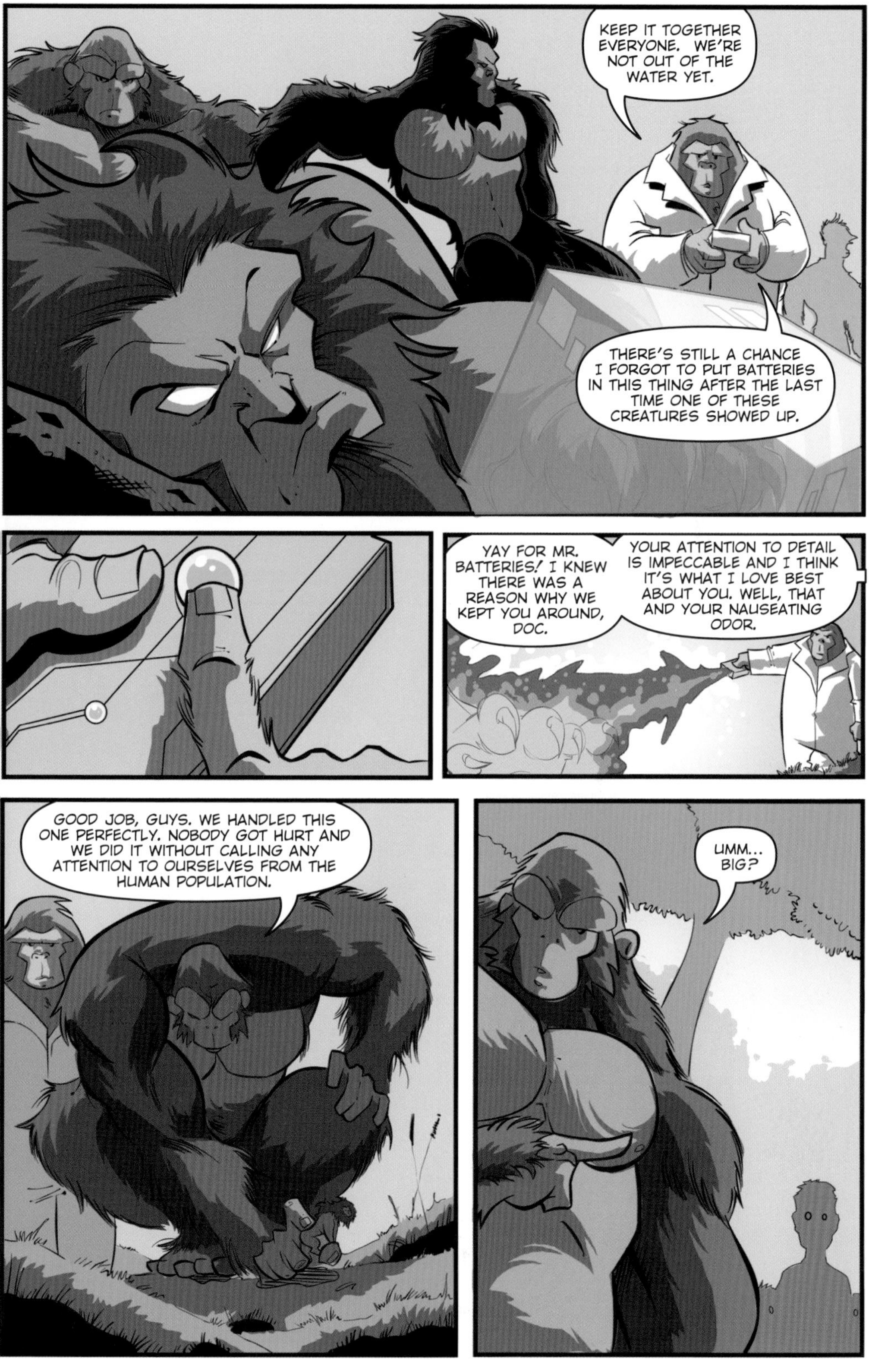
KEEP IT TOGETHER EVERYONE. WE'RE NOT OUT OF THE WATER YET.
THERE'S STILL A CHANCE I FORGOT TO PUT BATTERIES IN THIS THING AFTER THE LAST TIME ONE OF THESE CREATURES SHOWED UP.
YAY FOR MR. BATTERIES! I KNEW THERE WAS A REASON WHY WE KEPT YOU AROUND, DOC.
YOUR ATTENTION TO DETAIL IS IMPECCABLE AND I THINK IT'S WHAT I LOVE BEST ABOUT YOU. WELL, THAT AND YOUR NAUSEATING ODOR.
GOOD JOB, GUYS. WE HANDLED THIS ONE PERFECTLY. NOBODY GOT HURT AND WE DID IT WITHOUT CALLING ANY ATTENTION TO OURSELVES FROM THE HUMAN POPULATION.
UMM... BIG?

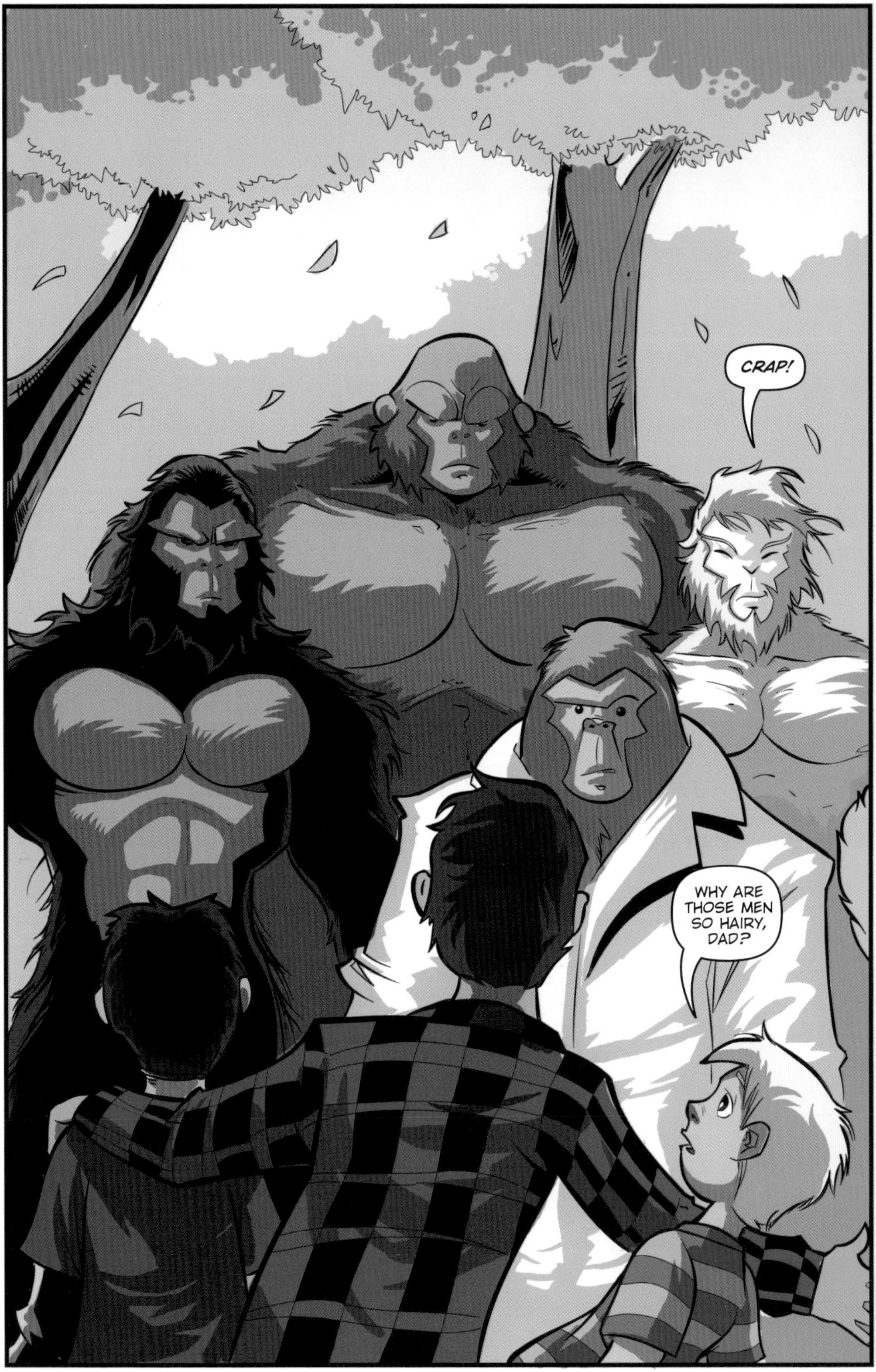
CRAP!
WHY ARE THOSE MEN SO HAIRY, DAD?

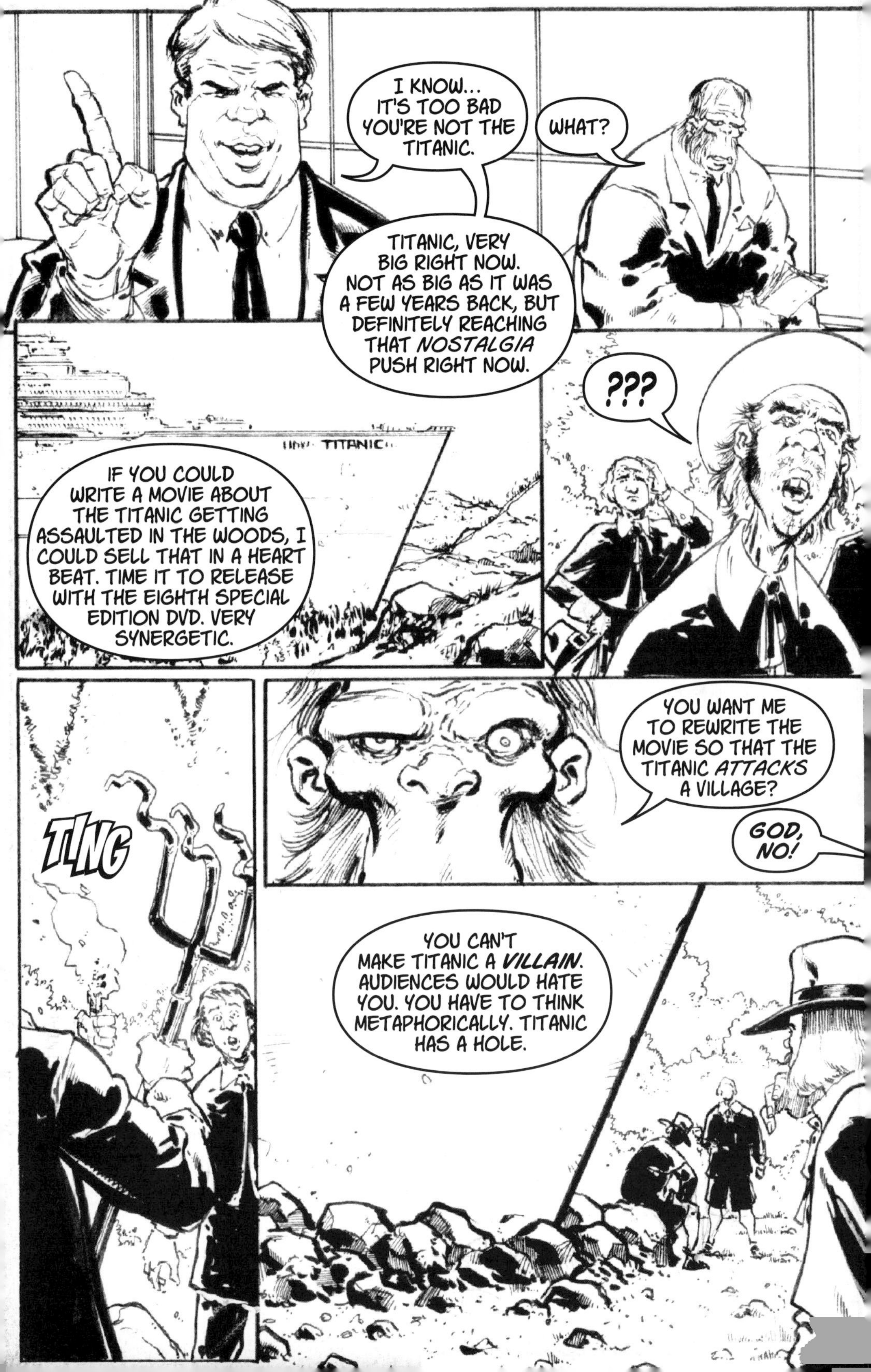
I KNOW... IT'S TOO BAD YOU'RE NOT THE TITANIC.
WHAT?
TITANIC, VERY BIG RIGHT NOW. NOT AS BIG AS IT WAS A FEW YEARS BACK, BUT DEFINITELY REACHING THAT *NOSTALGIA* PUSH RIGHT NOW.
TITANIC
IF YOU COULD WRITE A MOVIE ABOUT THE TITANIC GETTING ASSAULTED IN THE WOODS, I COULD SELL THAT IN A HEART BEAT. TIME IT TO RELEASE WITH THE EIGHTH SPECIAL EDITION DVD. VERY SYNERGETIC.
???
TING
YOU WANT ME TO REWRITE THE MOVIE SO THAT THE TITANIC *ATTACKS* A VILLAGE?
GOD, NO!
YOU CAN'T MAKE TITANIC A *VILLAIN*. AUDIENCES WOULD HATE YOU. YOU HAVE TO THINK METAPHORICALLY. TITANIC HAS A HOLE.

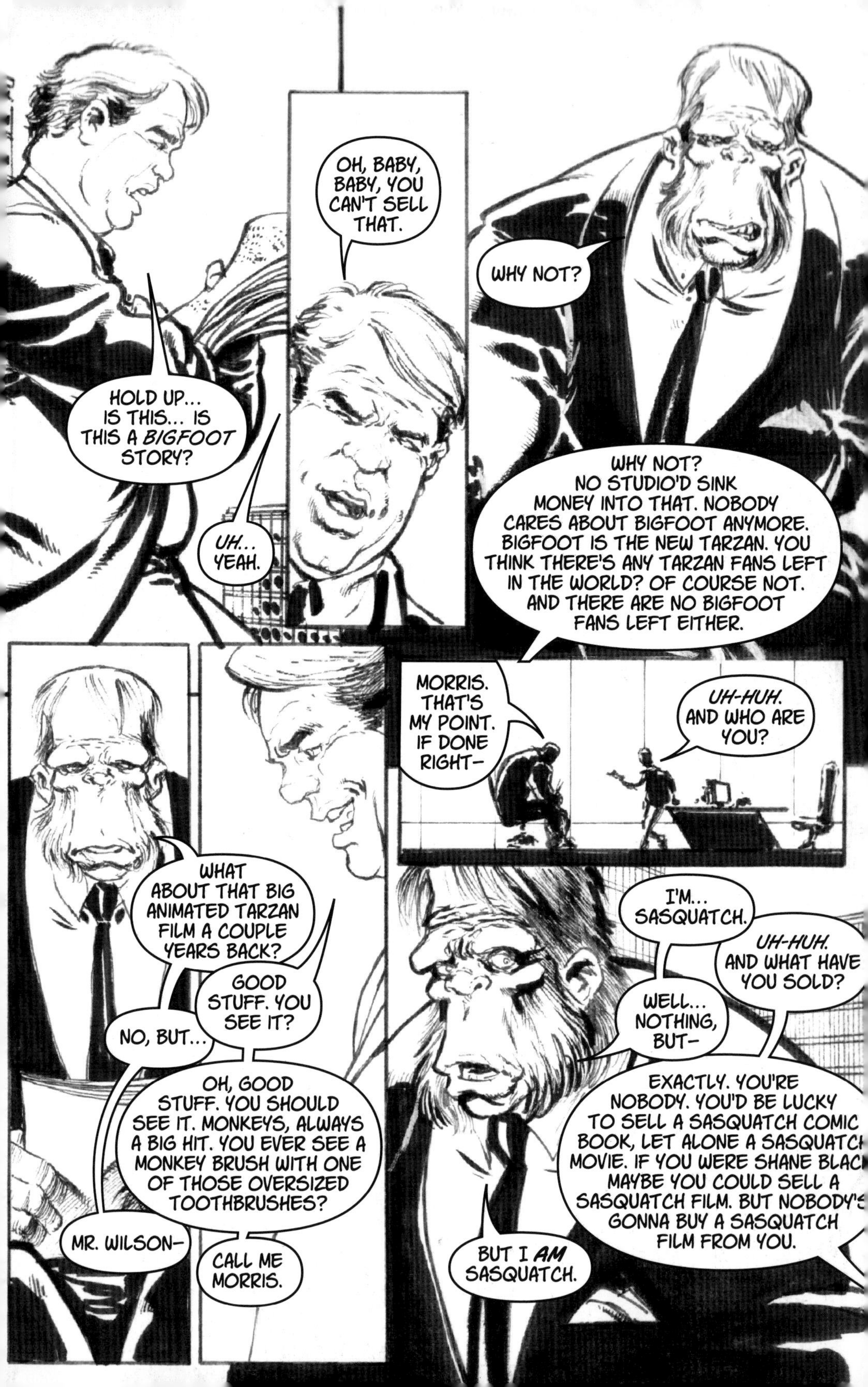
HOLD UP... IS THIS... IS THIS A *BIGFOOT* STORY?
UH... YEAH.
OH, BABY, BABY, YOU CAN'T SELL THAT.
WHY NOT?
WHY NOT? NO STUDIO'D SINK MONEY INTO THAT. NOBODY CARES ABOUT BIGFOOT ANYMORE. BIGFOOT IS THE NEW TARZAN. YOU THINK THERE'S ANY TARZAN FANS LEFT IN THE WORLD? OF COURSE NOT. AND THERE ARE NO BIGFOOT FANS LEFT EITHER.
WHAT ABOUT THAT BIG ANIMATED TARZAN FILM A COUPLE YEARS BACK?
GOOD STUFF. YOU SEE IT?
NO, BUT...
OH, GOOD STUFF. YOU SHOULD SEE IT. MONKEYS, ALWAYS A BIG HIT. YOU EVER SEE A MONKEY BRUSH WITH ONE OF THOSE OVERSIZED TOOTHBRUSHES?
MR. WILSON–
CALL ME MORRIS.
MORRIS. THAT'S MY POINT. IF DONE RIGHT–
UH-HUH. AND WHO ARE YOU?
I'M... SASQUATCH.
UH-HUH. AND WHAT HAVE YOU SOLD?
WELL... NOTHING, BUT–
EXACTLY. YOU'RE NOBODY. YOU'D BE LUCKY TO SELL A SASQUATCH COMIC BOOK, LET ALONE A SASQUATCH MOVIE. IF YOU WERE SHANE BLACK MAYBE YOU COULD SELL A SASQUATCH FILM. BUT NOBODY'S GONNA BUY A SASQUATCH FILM FROM YOU.
BUT I ***AM*** SASQUATCH.

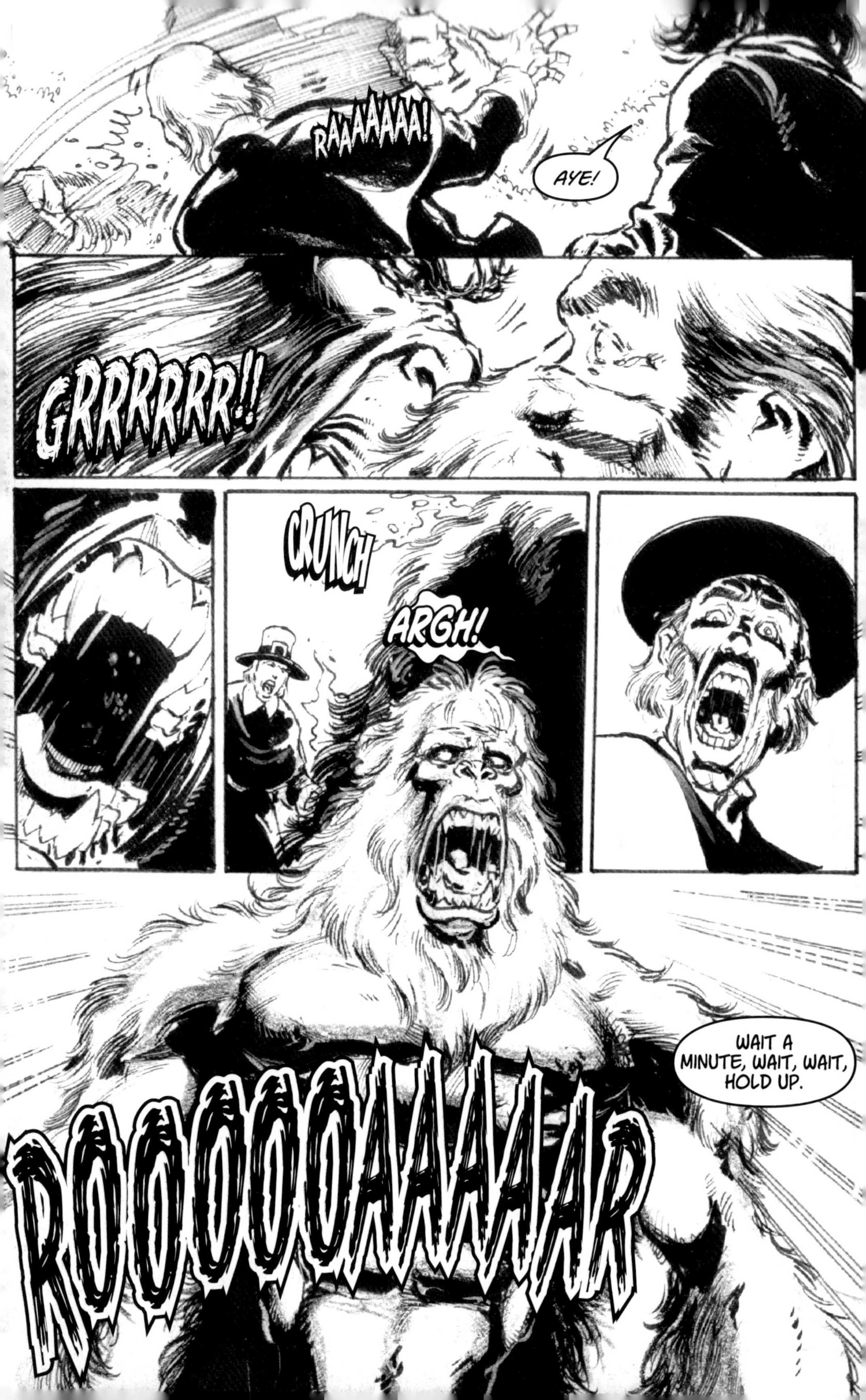
RAAAAAAA!
AYE!
GRRRRRR!!
CRUNCH
ARGH!
WAIT A MINUTE, WAIT, WAIT, HOLD UP.
ROOOOOAAAAAR

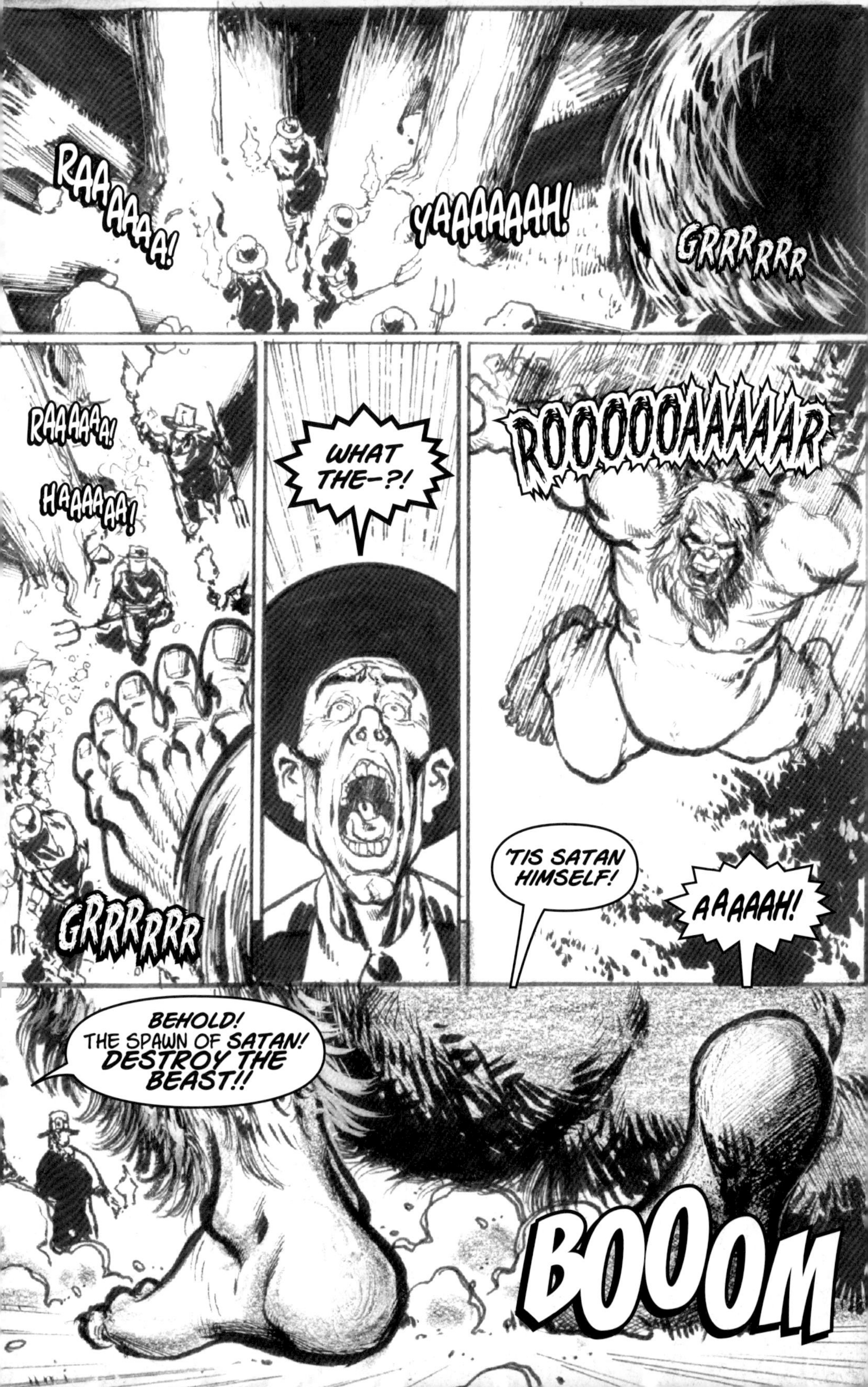
RAAAAAAA!
YAAAAAAAH!
GRRRRRR
RAAAAAA!
HAAAAAA!
GRRRRRR
WHAT THE-?!
ROOOOOOAAAAAR
'TIS SATAN HIMSELF!
AAAAAH!
BEHOLD! THE SPAWN OF SATAN! DESTROY THE BEAST!!
BOOOOM

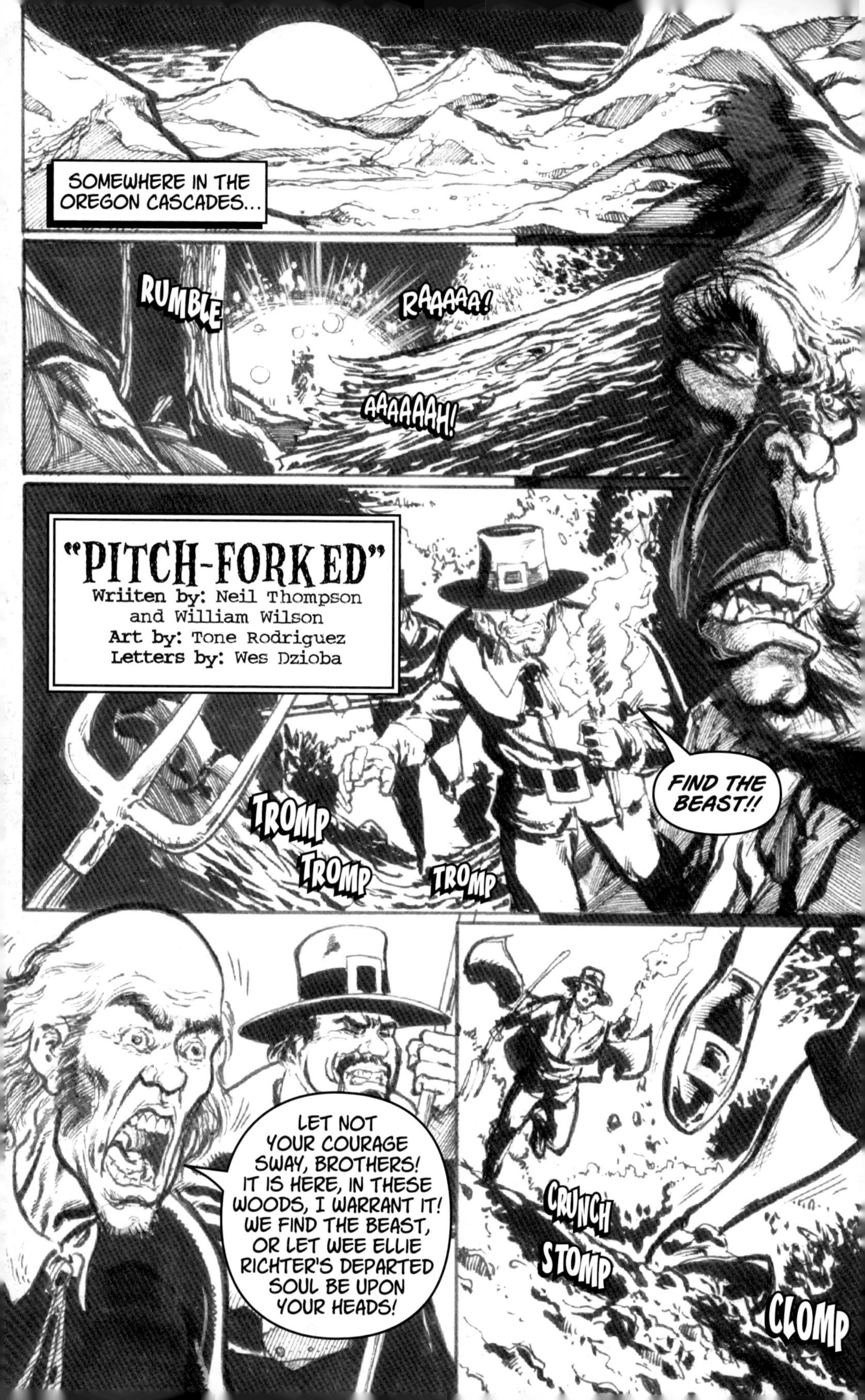
SOMEWHERE IN THE OREGON CASCADES...
RUMBLE
RAAAAA!
AAAAAAH!
"PITCH-FORKED"
Wriiten by: Neil Thompson and William Wilson
Art by: Tone Rodriguez
Letters by: Wes Dzioba
FIND THE BEAST!!
TROMP
TROMP
TROMP
LET NOT YOUR COURAGE SWAY, BROTHERS! IT IS HERE, IN THESE WOODS, I WARRANT IT! WE FIND THE BEAST, OR LET WEE ELLIE RICHTER'S DEPARTED SOUL BE UPON YOUR HEADS!
CRUNCH
STOMP
CLOMP

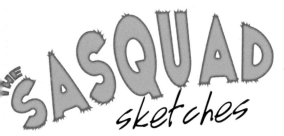

THE SASQUAD sketches

Sasquad vs. the North Pole

After careful review this issue was tabled as several children in the focus groups started to cry. And one child was heard saying "Hell yeah, now i can kick Santa in the groin, too!"

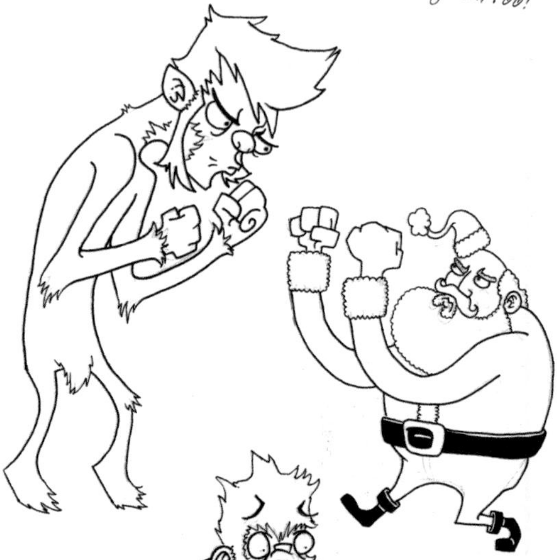

Sasquad vs. the Imaginary Friends

In the original designs, the artist and creator, Brian Thompson, was going for a more dignified comic approach, trying to tackle real world problems... but he later gave up.

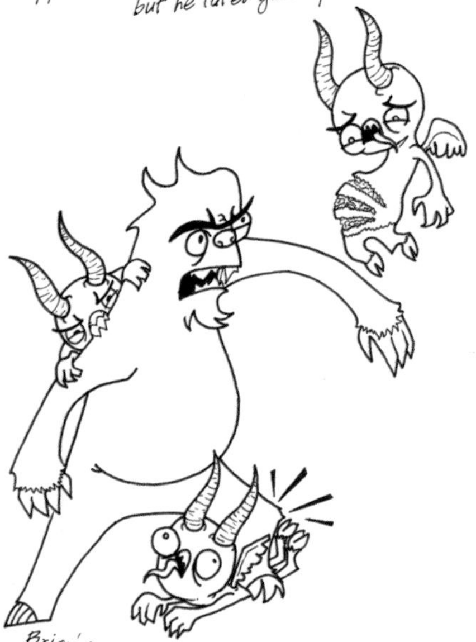

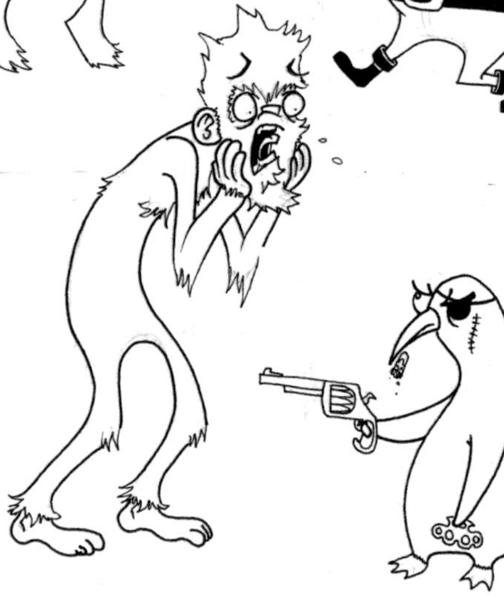

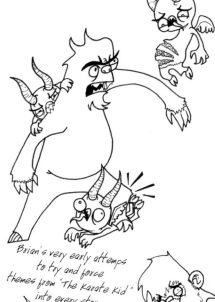

Brian's very early attemps to try and force themes from "The Karate Kid" into every story

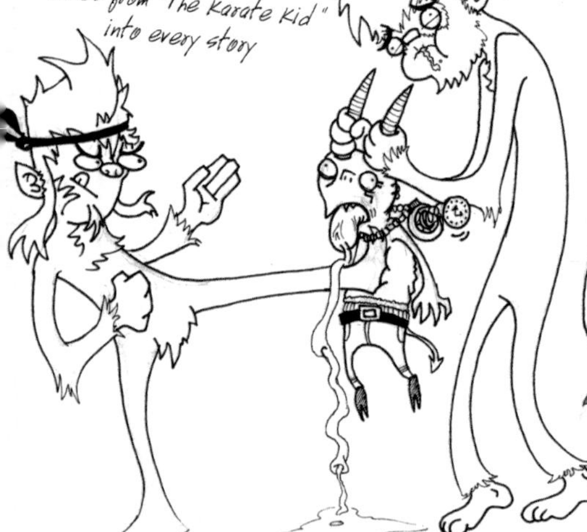

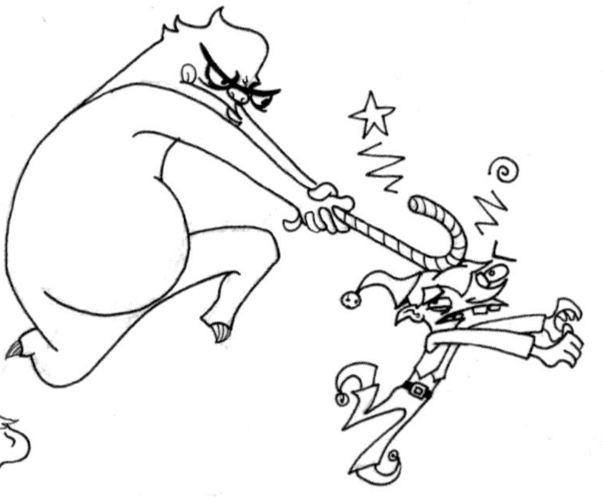

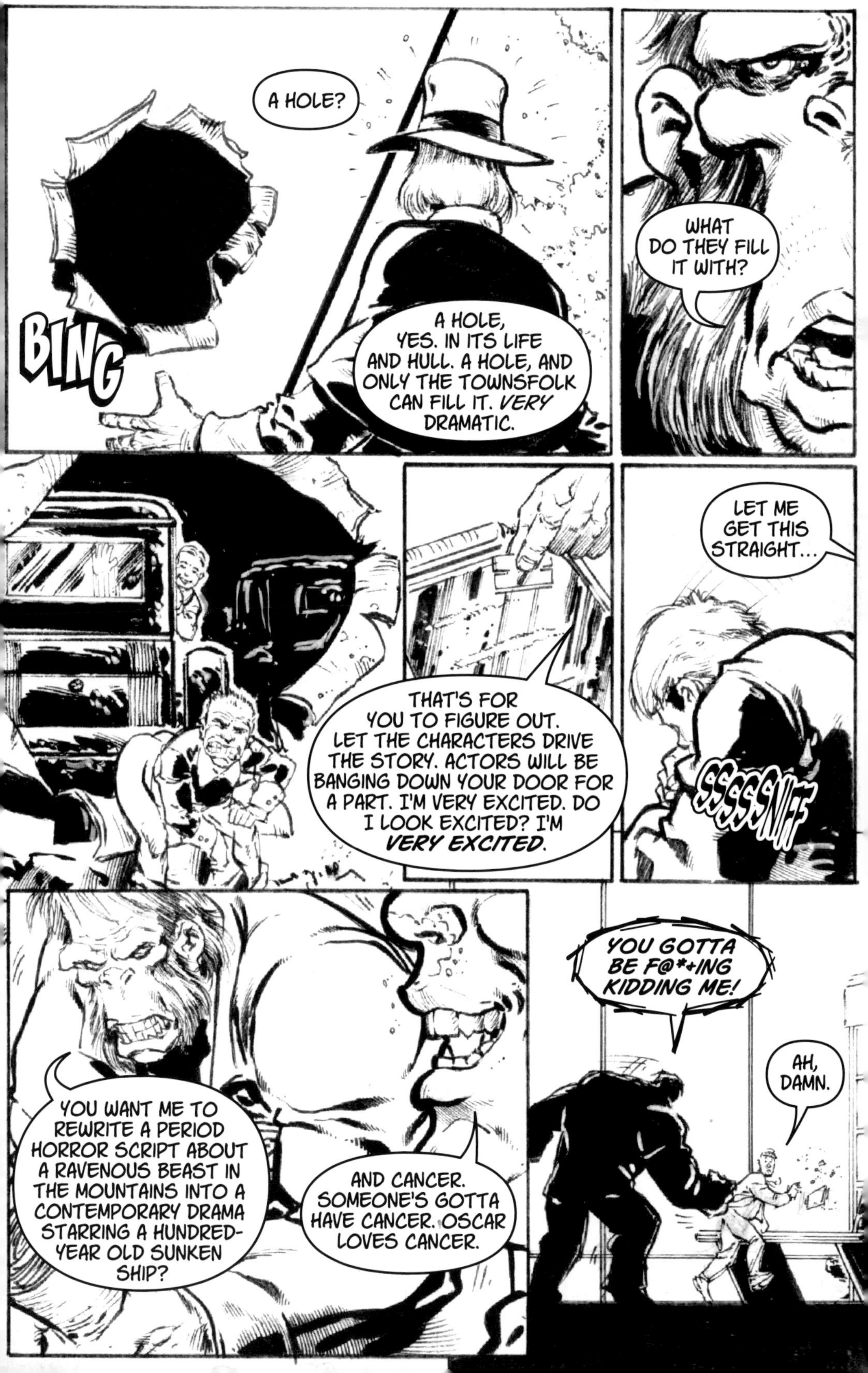
A HOLE?
BING
A HOLE, YES. IN ITS LIFE AND HULL. A HOLE, AND ONLY THE TOWNSFOLK CAN FILL IT. *VERY* DRAMATIC.
WHAT DO THEY FILL IT WITH?
THAT'S FOR YOU TO FIGURE OUT. LET THE CHARACTERS DRIVE THE STORY. ACTORS WILL BE BANGING DOWN YOUR DOOR FOR A PART. I'M VERY EXCITED. DO I LOOK EXCITED? I'M ***VERY EXCITED***.
LET ME GET THIS STRAIGHT...
SSSSSNIFF
YOU WANT ME TO REWRITE A PERIOD HORROR SCRIPT ABOUT A RAVENOUS BEAST IN THE MOUNTAINS INTO A CONTEMPORARY DRAMA STARRING A HUNDRED-YEAR OLD SUNKEN SHIP?
AND CANCER. SOMEONE'S GOTTA HAVE CANCER. OSCAR LOVES CANCER.
YOU GOTTA BE F@+ING KIDDING ME!*
AH, DAMN.

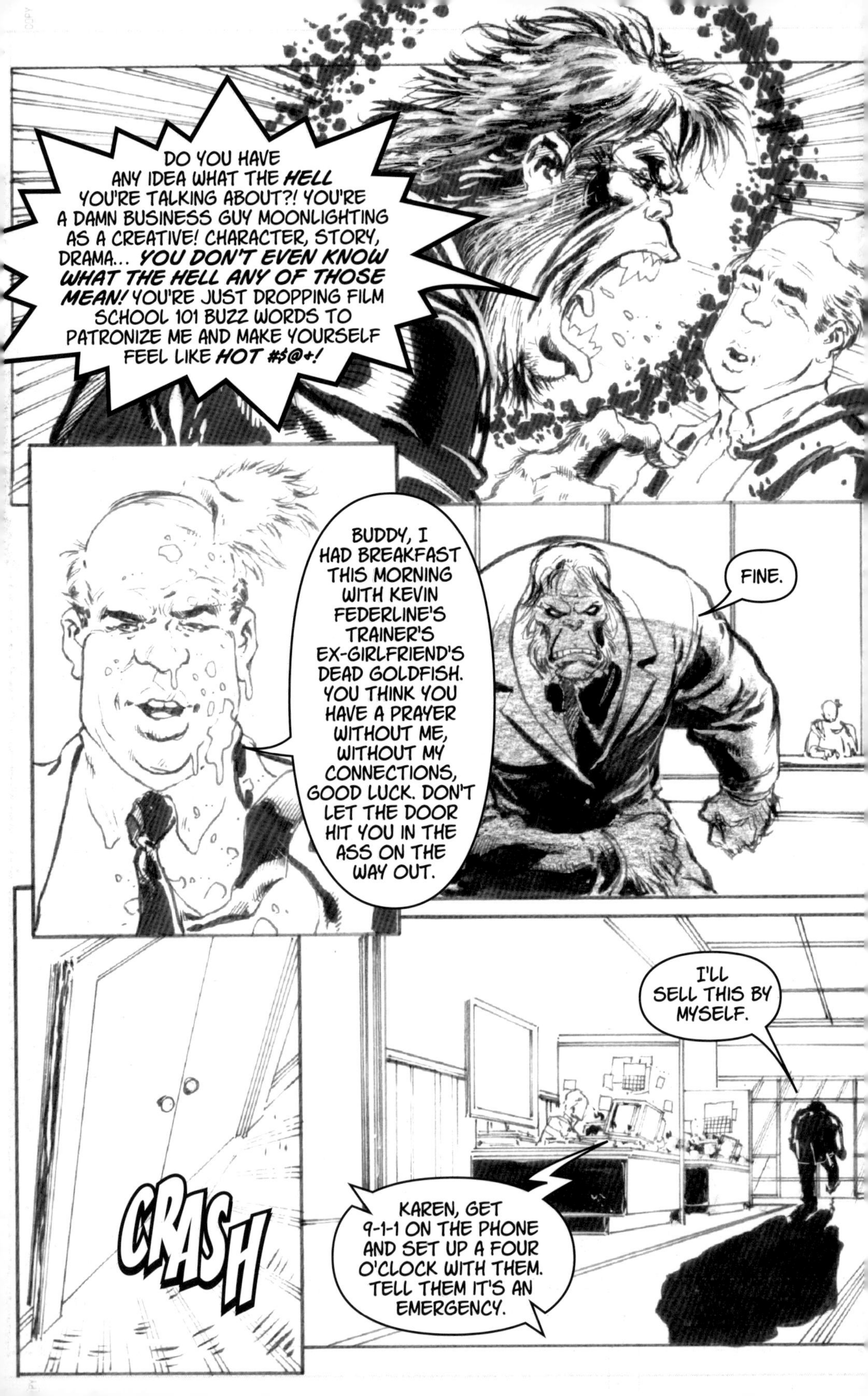
DO YOU HAVE ANY IDEA WHAT THE ***HELL*** YOU'RE TALKING ABOUT?! YOU'RE A DAMN BUSINESS GUY MOONLIGHTING AS A CREATIVE! CHARACTER, STORY, DRAMA... ***YOU DON'T EVEN KNOW WHAT THE HELL ANY OF THOSE MEAN!*** YOU'RE JUST DROPPING FILM SCHOOL 101 BUZZ WORDS TO PATRONIZE ME AND MAKE YOURSELF FEEL LIKE ***HOT #$@+!***
BUDDY, I HAD BREAKFAST THIS MORNING WITH KEVIN FEDERLINE'S TRAINER'S EX-GIRLFRIEND'S DEAD GOLDFISH. YOU THINK YOU HAVE A PRAYER WITHOUT ME, WITHOUT MY CONNECTIONS, GOOD LUCK. DON'T LET THE DOOR HIT YOU IN THE ASS ON THE WAY OUT.
FINE.
CRASH
I'LL SELL THIS BY MYSELF.
KAREN, GET 9-1-1 ON THE PHONE AND SET UP A FOUR O'CLOCK WITH THEM. TELL THEM IT'S AN EMERGENCY.

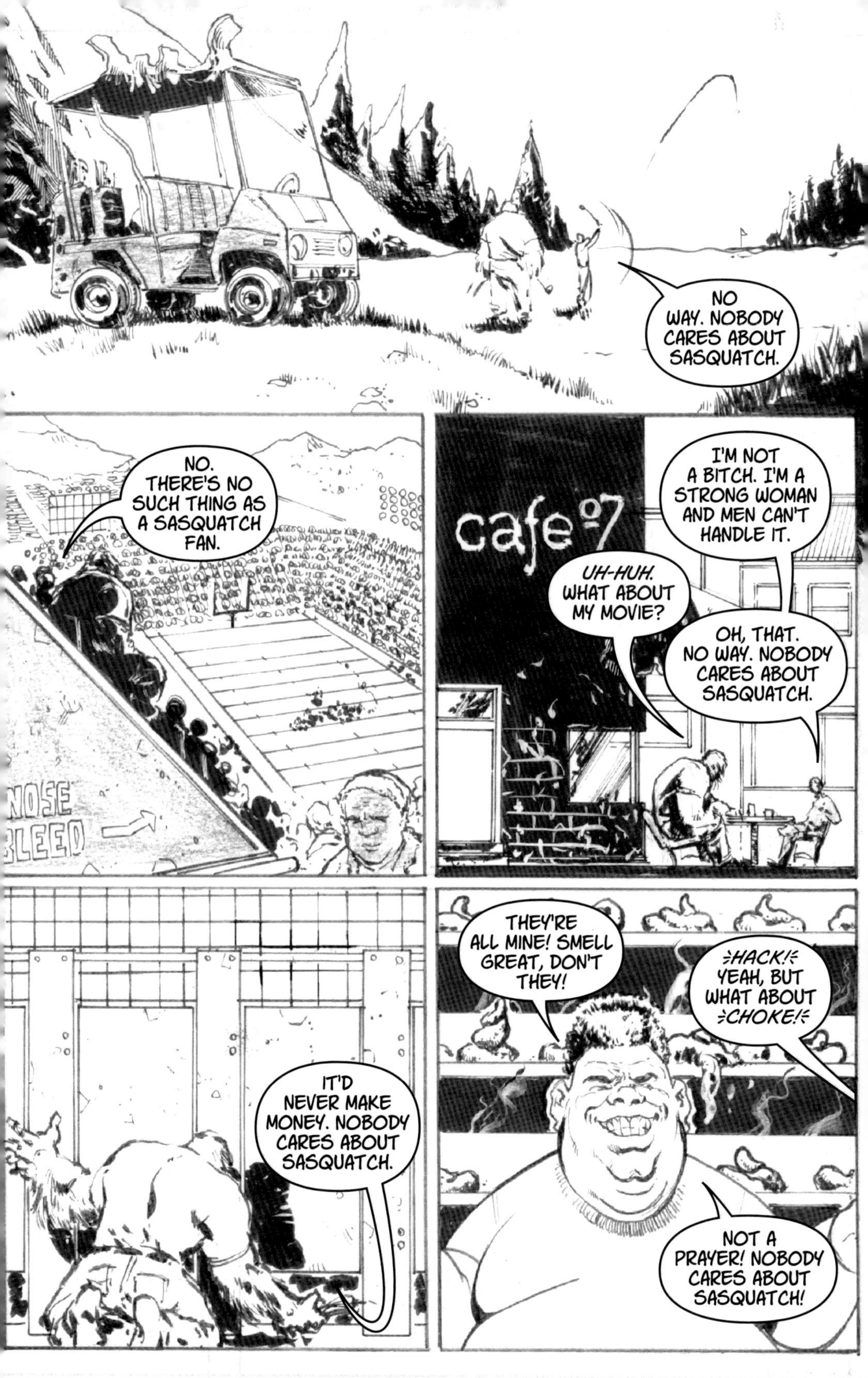

NO WAY. NOBODY CARES ABOUT SASQUATCH.
NO. THERE'S NO SUCH THING AS A SASQUATCH FAN.
NOSE BLEED
cafe o7
I'M NOT A BITCH. I'M A STRONG WOMAN AND MEN CAN'T HANDLE IT.
UH-HUH. WHAT ABOUT MY MOVIE?
OH, THAT. NO WAY. NOBODY CARES ABOUT SASQUATCH.
IT'D NEVER MAKE MONEY. NOBODY CARES ABOUT SASQUATCH.
THEY'RE ALL MINE! SMELL GREAT, DON'T THEY!
HACK! YEAH, BUT WHAT ABOUT *CHOKE!*
NOT A PRAYER! NOBODY CARES ABOUT SASQUATCH!

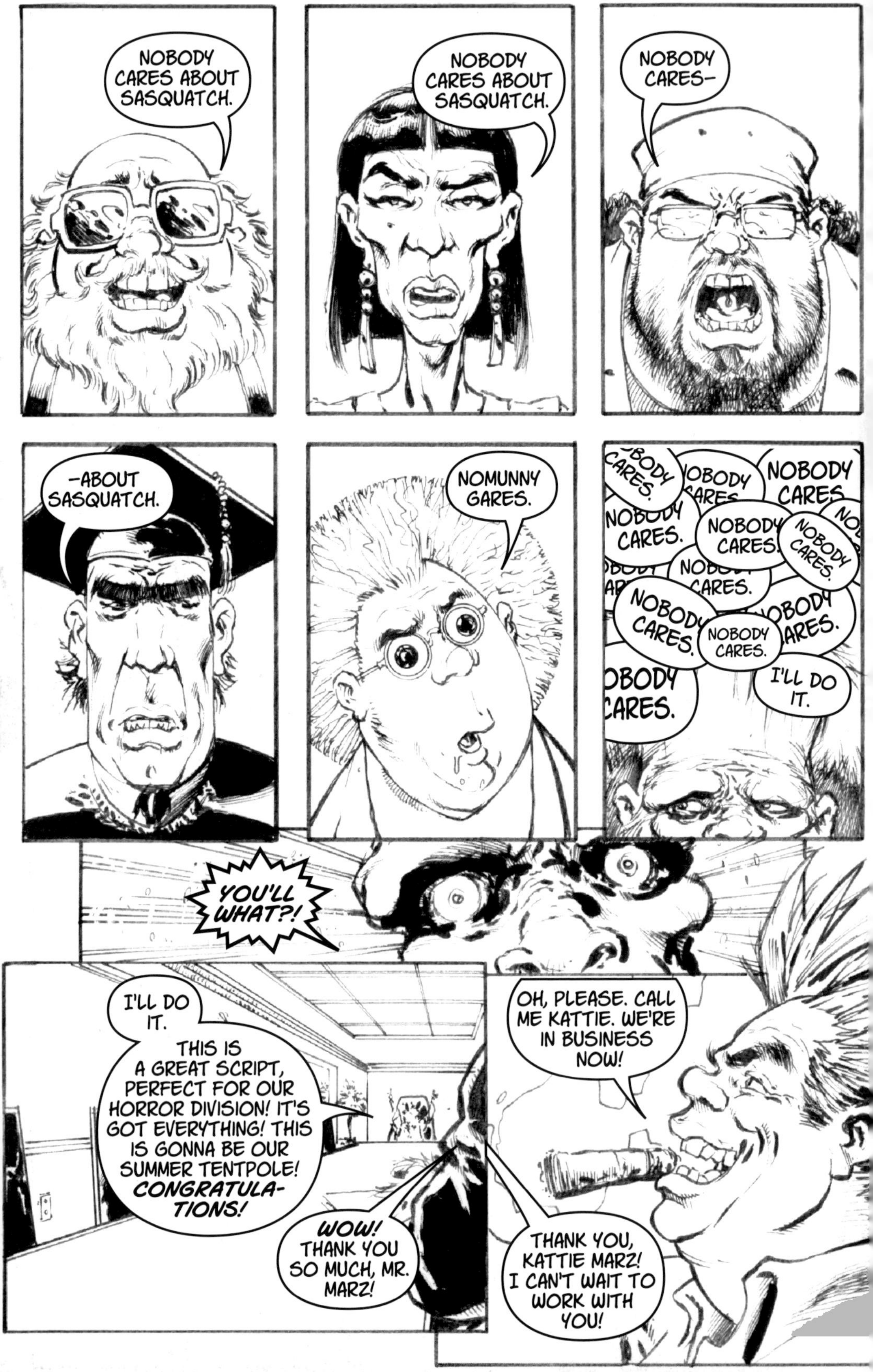
NOBODY CARES ABOUT SASQUATCH.
NOBODY CARES ABOUT SASQUATCH.
NOBODY CARES–
–ABOUT SASQUATCH.
NOMUNNY GARES.
NOBODY CARES.
NOBODY CARES.
NOBODY CARES.
NOBODY CARES.
NOBODY CARES.
NOBODY CARES.
NOBODY CARES.
I'LL DO IT.
YOU'LL WHAT?!
I'LL DO IT.
THIS IS A GREAT SCRIPT, PERFECT FOR OUR HORROR DIVISION! IT'S GOT EVERYTHING! THIS IS GONNA BE OUR SUMMER TENTPOLE! CONGRATULATIONS!
WOW! THANK YOU SO MUCH, MR. MARZ!
OH, PLEASE. CALL ME KATTIE. WE'RE IN BUSINESS NOW!
THANK YOU, KATTIE MARZ! I CAN'T WAIT TO WORK WITH YOU!

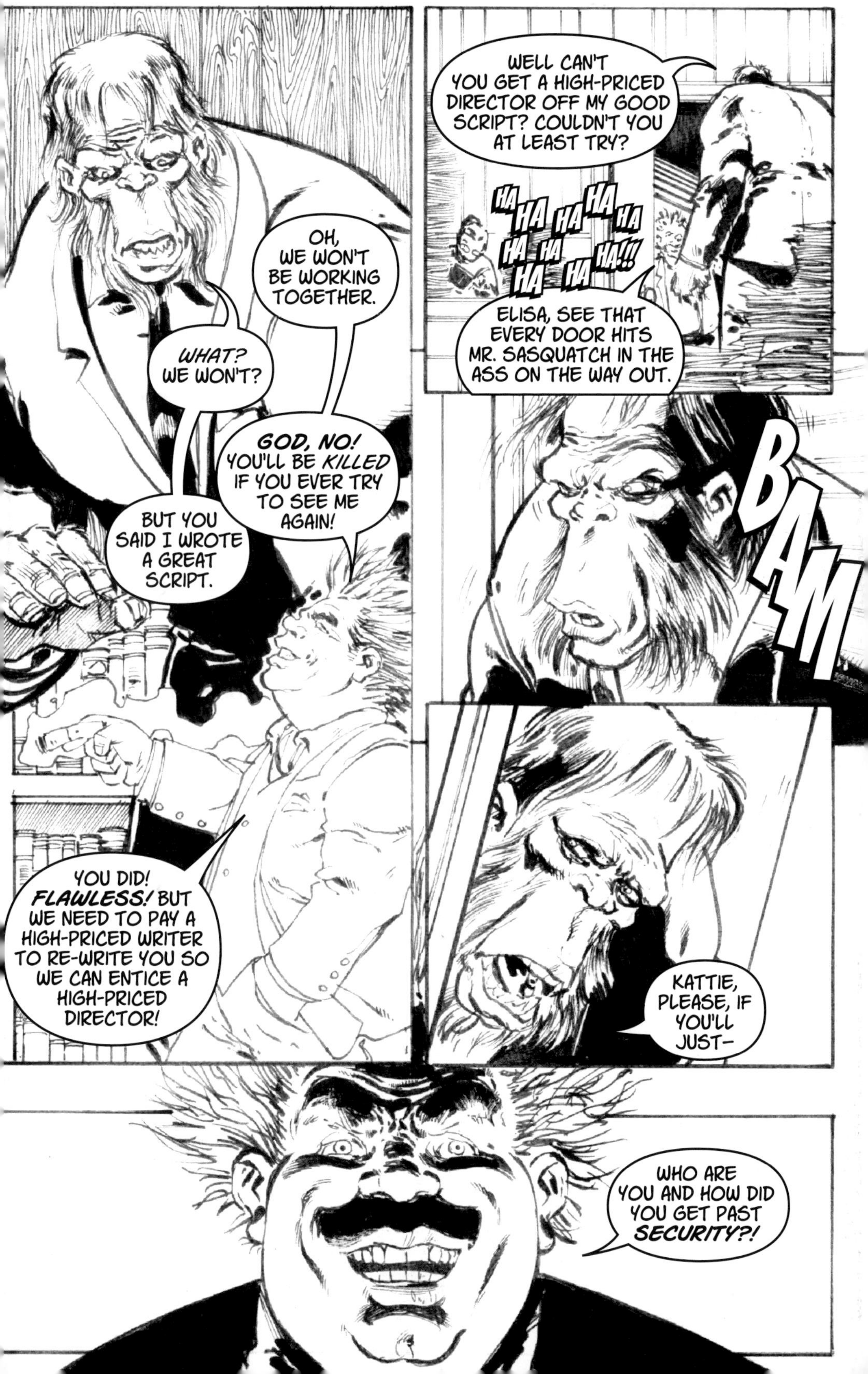
WHAT? WE WON'T?
OH, WE WON'T BE WORKING TOGETHER.
BUT YOU SAID I WROTE A GREAT SCRIPT.
GOD, NO! YOU'LL BE KILLED IF YOU EVER TRY TO SEE ME AGAIN!
YOU DID! FLAWLESS! BUT WE NEED TO PAY A HIGH-PRICED WRITER TO RE-WRITE YOU SO WE CAN ENTICE A HIGH-PRICED DIRECTOR!
WELL CAN'T YOU GET A HIGH-PRICED DIRECTOR OFF MY GOOD SCRIPT? COULDN'T YOU AT LEAST TRY?
HA HA HA HA HA HA HA HA HA HA HA!!!
ELISA, SEE THAT EVERY DOOR HITS MR. SASQUATCH IN THE ASS ON THE WAY OUT.
BAM
KATTIE, PLEASE, IF YOU'LL JUST–
WHO ARE YOU AND HOW DID YOU GET PAST SECURITY?!

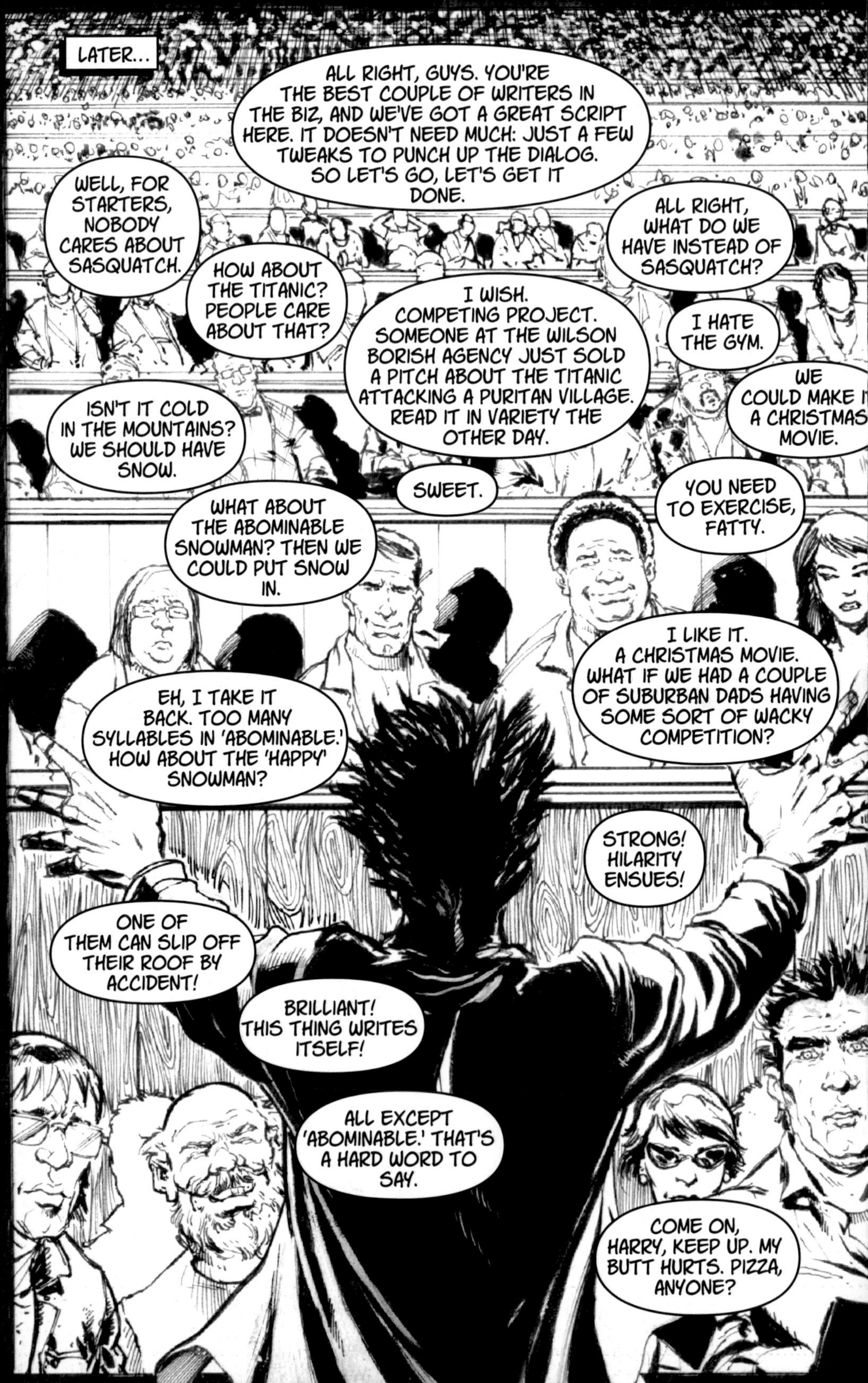
LATER...
ALL RIGHT, GUYS. YOU'RE THE BEST COUPLE OF WRITERS IN THE BIZ, AND WE'VE GOT A GREAT SCRIPT HERE. IT DOESN'T NEED MUCH: JUST A FEW TWEAKS TO PUNCH UP THE DIALOG. SO LET'S GO, LET'S GET IT DONE.
WELL, FOR STARTERS, NOBODY CARES ABOUT SASQUATCH.
ALL RIGHT, WHAT DO WE HAVE INSTEAD OF SASQUATCH?
HOW ABOUT THE TITANIC? PEOPLE CARE ABOUT THAT?
I WISH. COMPETING PROJECT. SOMEONE AT THE WILSON BORISH AGENCY JUST SOLD A PITCH ABOUT THE TITANIC ATTACKING A PURITAN VILLAGE. READ IT IN VARIETY THE OTHER DAY.
I HATE THE GYM.
ISN'T IT COLD IN THE MOUNTAINS? WE SHOULD HAVE SNOW.
WE COULD MAKE IT A CHRISTMAS MOVIE.
SWEET.
YOU NEED TO EXERCISE, FATTY.
WHAT ABOUT THE ABOMINABLE SNOWMAN? THEN WE COULD PUT SNOW IN.
I LIKE IT. A CHRISTMAS MOVIE. WHAT IF WE HAD A COUPLE OF SUBURBAN DADS HAVING SOME SORT OF WACKY COMPETITION?
EH, I TAKE IT BACK. TOO MANY SYLLABLES IN 'ABOMINABLE.' HOW ABOUT THE 'HAPPY' SNOWMAN?
STRONG! HILARITY ENSUES!
ONE OF THEM CAN SLIP OFF THEIR ROOF BY ACCIDENT!
BRILLIANT! THIS THING WRITES ITSELF!
ALL EXCEPT 'ABOMINABLE.' THAT'S A HARD WORD TO SAY.
COME ON, HARRY, KEEP UP. MY BUTT HURTS. PIZZA, ANYONE?

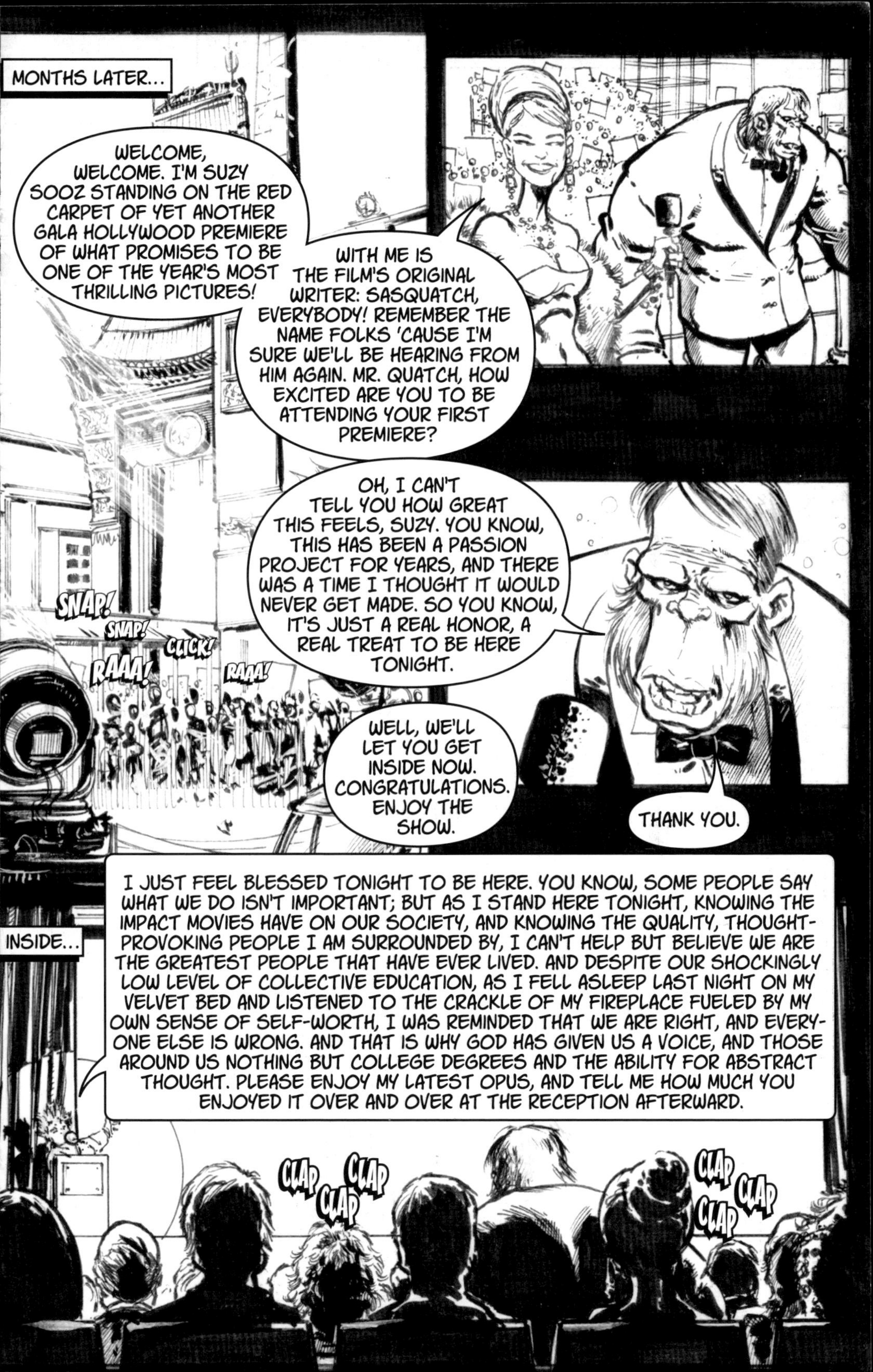
MONTHS LATER...
WELCOME, WELCOME. I'M SUZY SOOZ STANDING ON THE RED CARPET OF YET ANOTHER GALA HOLLYWOOD PREMIERE OF WHAT PROMISES TO BE ONE OF THE YEAR'S MOST THRILLING PICTURES!
WITH ME IS THE FILM'S ORIGINAL WRITER: SASQUATCH, EVERYBODY! REMEMBER THE NAME FOLKS 'CAUSE I'M SURE WE'LL BE HEARING FROM HIM AGAIN. MR. QUATCH, HOW EXCITED ARE YOU TO BE ATTENDING YOUR FIRST PREMIERE?
OH, I CAN'T TELL YOU HOW GREAT THIS FEELS, SUZY. YOU KNOW, THIS HAS BEEN A PASSION PROJECT FOR YEARS, AND THERE WAS A TIME I THOUGHT IT WOULD NEVER GET MADE. SO YOU KNOW, IT'S JUST A REAL HONOR, A REAL TREAT TO BE HERE TONIGHT.
SNAP!
SNAP!
CLICK!
RAAA!
RAAA!
WELL, WE'LL LET YOU GET INSIDE NOW. CONGRATULATIONS. ENJOY THE SHOW.
THANK YOU.
INSIDE...
I JUST FEEL BLESSED TONIGHT TO BE HERE. YOU KNOW, SOME PEOPLE SAY WHAT WE DO ISN'T IMPORTANT; BUT AS I STAND HERE TONIGHT, KNOWING THE IMPACT MOVIES HAVE ON OUR SOCIETY, AND KNOWING THE QUALITY, THOUGHT-PROVOKING PEOPLE I AM SURROUNDED BY, I CAN'T HELP BUT BELIEVE WE ARE THE GREATEST PEOPLE THAT HAVE EVER LIVED. AND DESPITE OUR SHOCKINGLY LOW LEVEL OF COLLECTIVE EDUCATION, AS I FELL ASLEEP LAST NIGHT ON MY VELVET BED AND LISTENED TO THE CRACKLE OF MY FIREPLACE FUELED BY MY OWN SENSE OF SELF-WORTH, I WAS REMINDED THAT WE ARE RIGHT, AND EVERY-ONE ELSE IS WRONG. AND THAT IS WHY GOD HAS GIVEN US A VOICE, AND THOSE AROUND US NOTHING BUT COLLEGE DEGREES AND THE ABILITY FOR ABSTRACT THOUGHT. PLEASE ENJOY MY LATEST OPUS, AND TELL ME HOW MUCH YOU ENJOYED IT OVER AND OVER AT THE RECEPTION AFTERWARD.
CLAP
CLAP
CLAP
CLAP
CLAP
CLAP

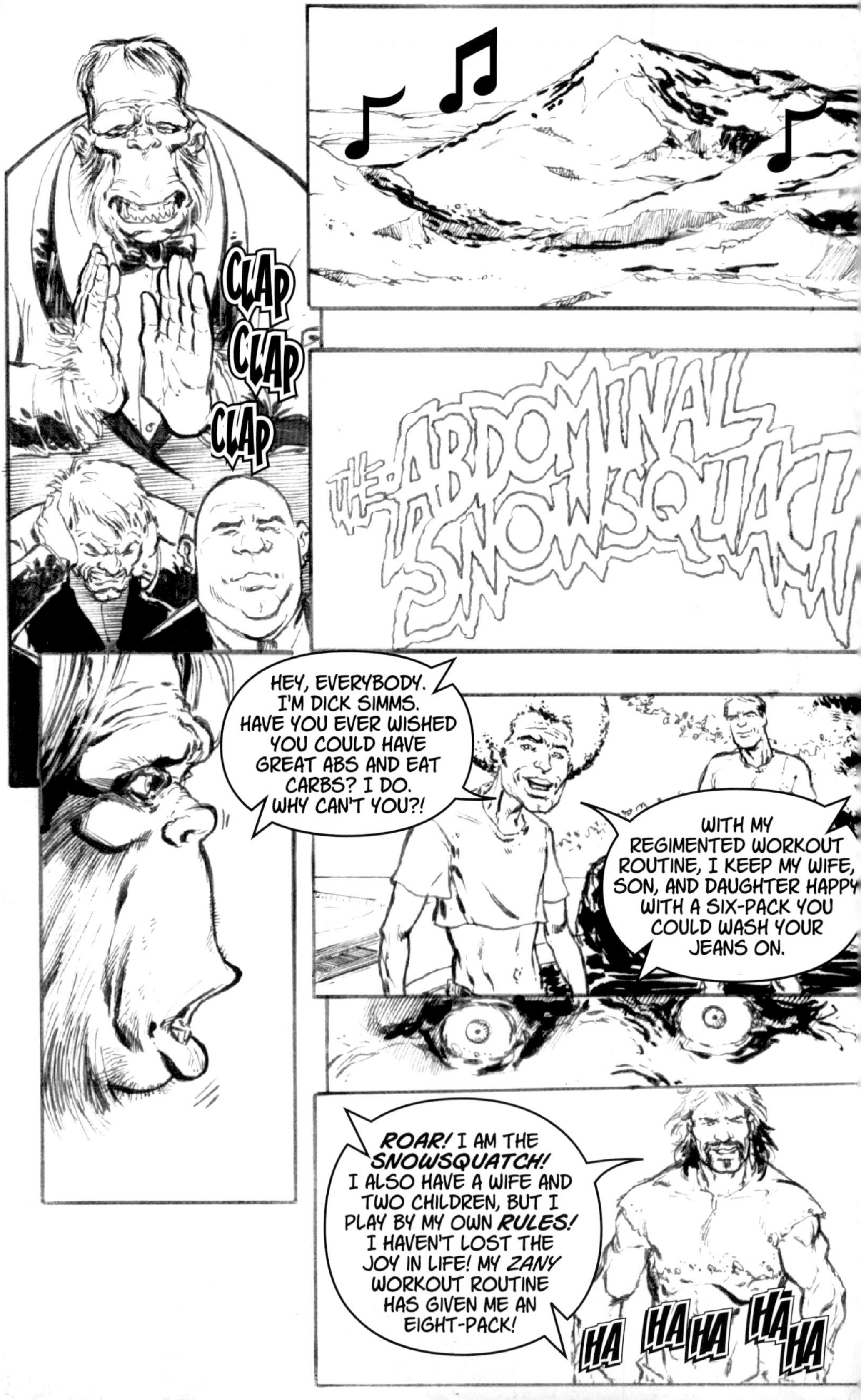
CLAP
CLAP
CLAP
THE ABDOMINAL SNOWSQUATCH
HEY, EVERYBODY. I'M DICK SIMMS. HAVE YOU EVER WISHED YOU COULD HAVE GREAT ABS AND EAT CARBS? I DO. WHY CAN'T YOU?!
WITH MY REGIMENTED WORKOUT ROUTINE, I KEEP MY WIFE, SON, AND DAUGHTER HAPPY WITH A SIX-PACK YOU COULD WASH YOUR JEANS ON.
ROAR! I AM THE *SNOWSQUATCH!* I ALSO HAVE A WIFE AND TWO CHILDREN, BUT I PLAY BY MY OWN *RULES!* I HAVEN'T LOST THE JOY IN LIFE! MY *ZANY* WORKOUT ROUTINE HAS GIVEN ME AN EIGHT-PACK!
HA HA HA HA HA HA

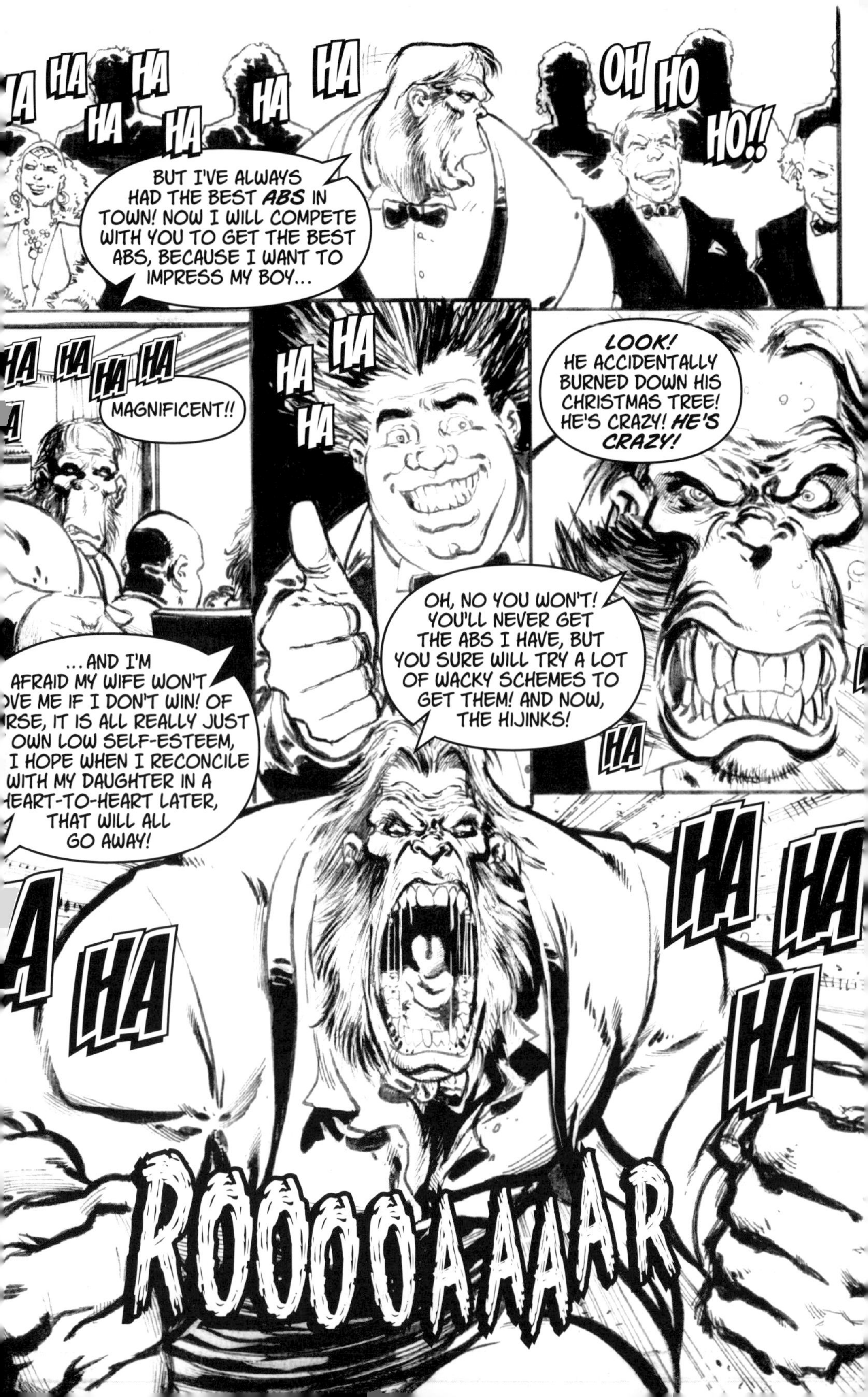
HA HA HA HA HA HA HA HA
BUT I'VE ALWAYS HAD THE BEST ABS IN TOWN! NOW I WILL COMPETE WITH YOU TO GET THE BEST ABS, BECAUSE I WANT TO IMPRESS MY BOY...
OH HO HO!!
HA HA HA HA
MAGNIFICENT!!
HA HA HA
LOOK! HE ACCIDENTALLY BURNED DOWN HIS CHRISTMAS TREE! HE'S CRAZY! HE'S CRAZY!
...AND I'M AFRAID MY WIFE WON'T OVE ME IF I DON'T WIN! OF RSE, IT IS ALL REALLY JUST OWN LOW SELF-ESTEEM, I HOPE WHEN I RECONCILE WITH MY DAUGHTER IN A HEART-TO-HEART LATER, THAT WILL ALL GO AWAY!
OH, NO YOU WON'T! YOU'LL NEVER GET THE ABS I HAVE, BUT YOU SURE WILL TRY A LOT OF WACKY SCHEMES TO GET THEM! AND NOW, THE HIJINKS!
HA
HA HA HA HA HA
ROOOOAAAAR

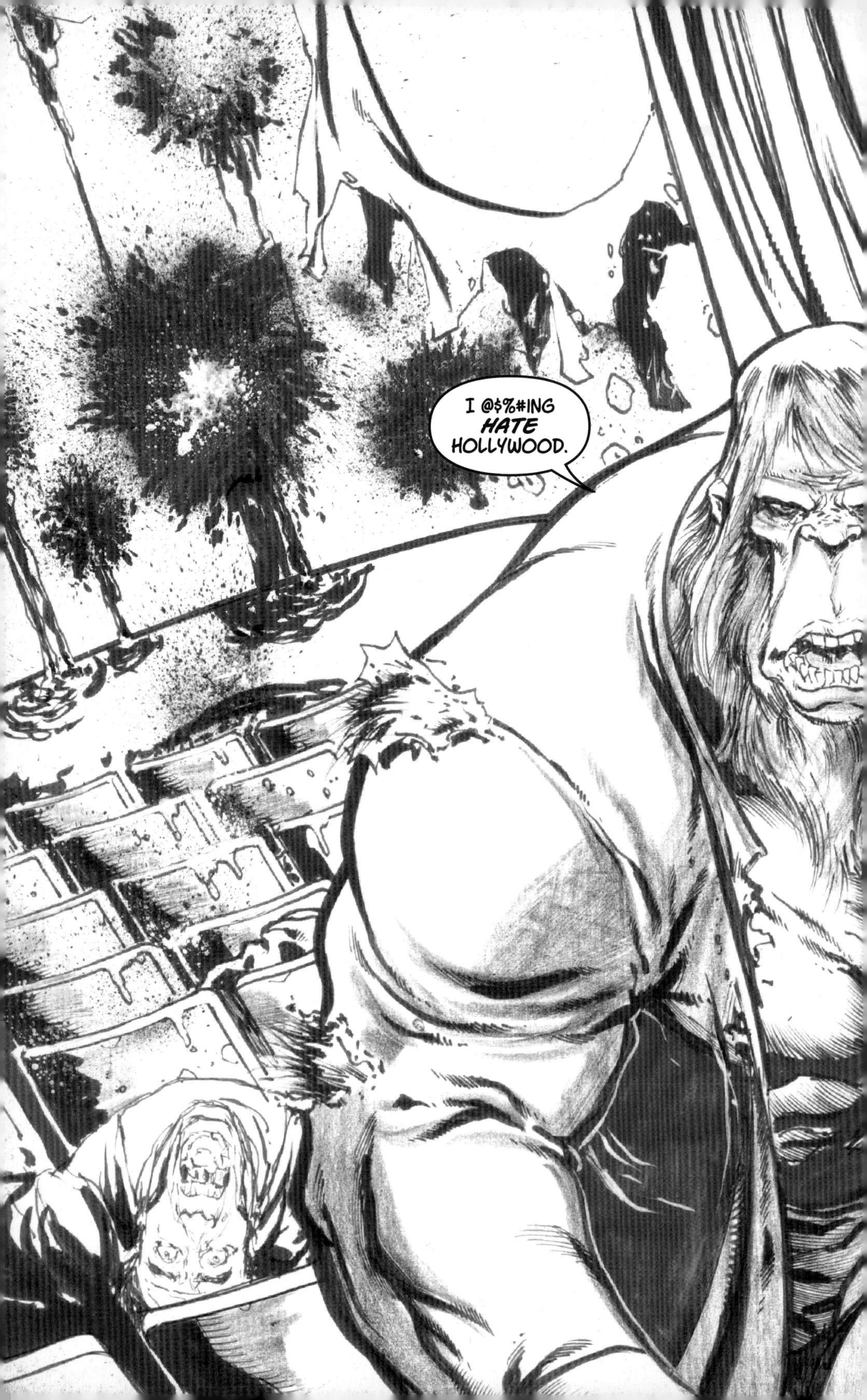
I @$%#ING *HATE* HOLLYWOOD.

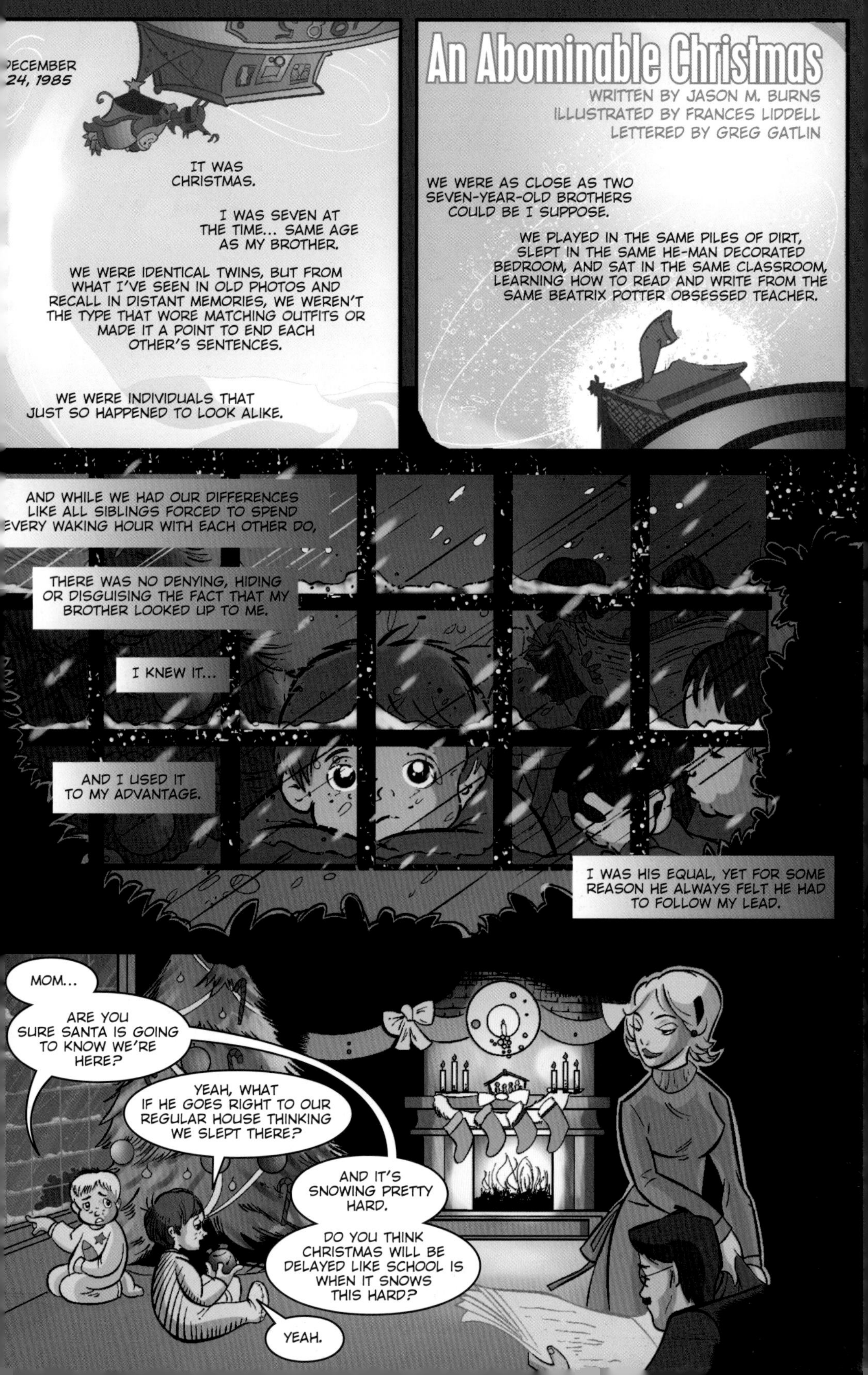

DECEMBER 24, 1985
IT WAS CHRISTMAS.
I WAS SEVEN AT THE TIME... SAME AGE AS MY BROTHER.
WE WERE IDENTICAL TWINS, BUT FROM WHAT I'VE SEEN IN OLD PHOTOS AND RECALL IN DISTANT MEMORIES, WE WEREN'T THE TYPE THAT WORE MATCHING OUTFITS OR MADE IT A POINT TO END EACH OTHER'S SENTENCES.
WE WERE INDIVIDUALS THAT JUST SO HAPPENED TO LOOK ALIKE.
An Abominable Christmas
WRITTEN BY JASON M. BURNS
ILLUSTRATED BY FRANCES LIDDELL
LETTERED BY GREG GATLIN
WE WERE AS CLOSE AS TWO SEVEN-YEAR-OLD BROTHERS COULD BE I SUPPOSE.
WE PLAYED IN THE SAME PILES OF DIRT, SLEPT IN THE SAME HE-MAN DECORATED BEDROOM, AND SAT IN THE SAME CLASSROOM, LEARNING HOW TO READ AND WRITE FROM THE SAME BEATRIX POTTER OBSESSED TEACHER.
AND WHILE WE HAD OUR DIFFERENCES LIKE ALL SIBLINGS FORCED TO SPEND EVERY WAKING HOUR WITH EACH OTHER DO,
THERE WAS NO DENYING, HIDING OR DISGUISING THE FACT THAT MY BROTHER LOOKED UP TO ME.
I KNEW IT...
AND I USED IT TO MY ADVANTAGE.
I WAS HIS EQUAL, YET FOR SOME REASON HE ALWAYS FELT HE HAD TO FOLLOW MY LEAD.
MOM...
ARE YOU SURE SANTA IS GOING TO KNOW WE'RE HERE?
YEAH, WHAT IF HE GOES RIGHT TO OUR REGULAR HOUSE THINKING WE SLEPT THERE?
AND IT'S SNOWING PRETTY HARD.
DO YOU THINK CHRISTMAS WILL BE DELAYED LIKE SCHOOL IS WHEN IT SNOWS THIS HARD?
YEAH.

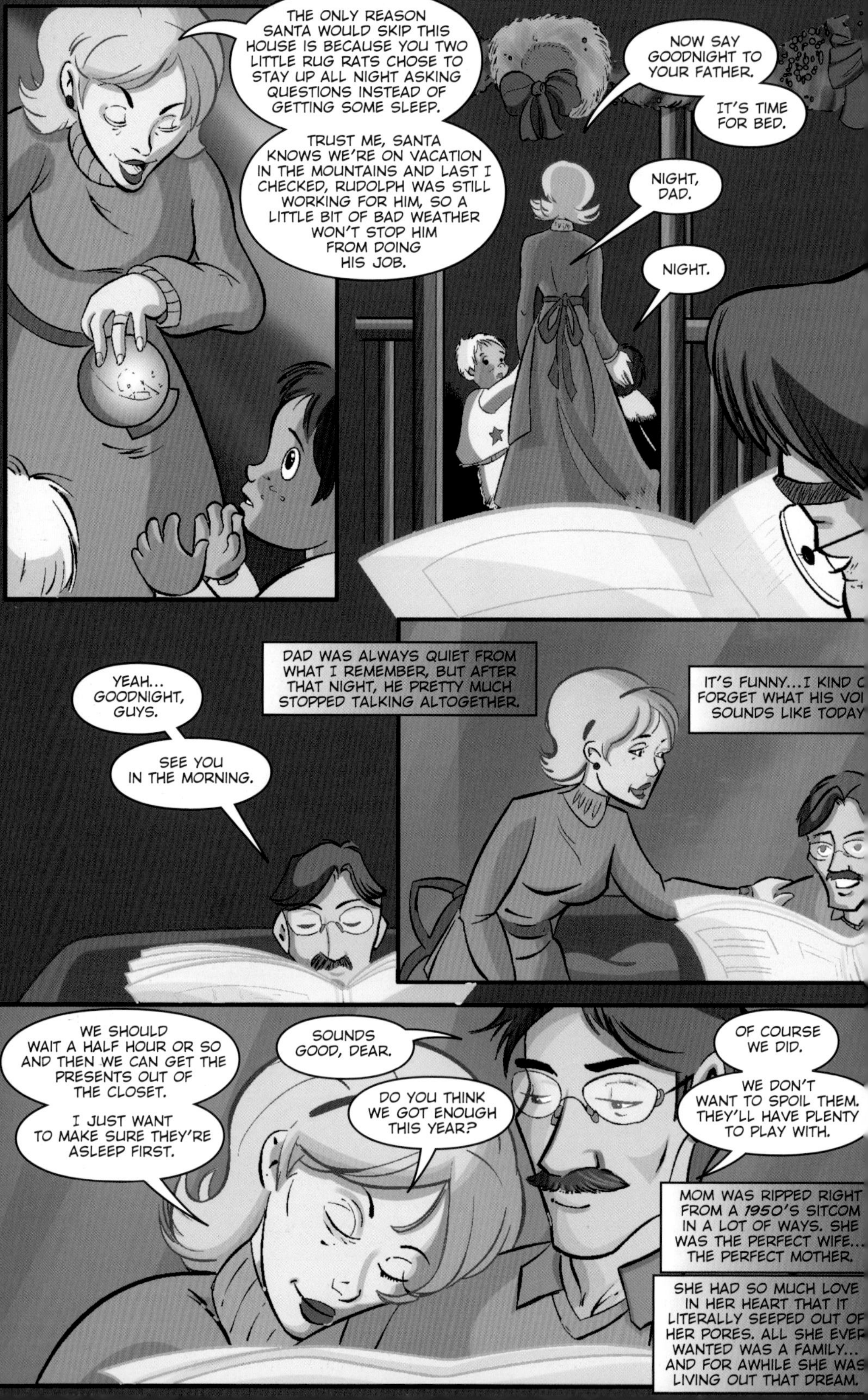
THE ONLY REASON SANTA WOULD SKIP THIS HOUSE IS BECAUSE YOU TWO LITTLE RUG RATS CHOSE TO STAY UP ALL NIGHT ASKING QUESTIONS INSTEAD OF GETTING SOME SLEEP.
TRUST ME, SANTA KNOWS WE'RE ON VACATION IN THE MOUNTAINS AND LAST I CHECKED, RUDOLPH WAS STILL WORKING FOR HIM, SO A LITTLE BIT OF BAD WEATHER WON'T STOP HIM FROM DOING HIS JOB.
NOW SAY GOODNIGHT TO YOUR FATHER.
IT'S TIME FOR BED.
NIGHT, DAD.
NIGHT.
YEAH... GOODNIGHT, GUYS.
SEE YOU IN THE MORNING.
DAD WAS ALWAYS QUIET FROM WHAT I REMEMBER, BUT AFTER THAT NIGHT, HE PRETTY MUCH STOPPED TALKING ALTOGETHER.
IT'S FUNNY...I KIND
FORGET WHAT HIS VOI
SOUNDS LIKE TODAY
WE SHOULD WAIT A HALF HOUR OR SO AND THEN WE CAN GET THE PRESENTS OUT OF THE CLOSET.
I JUST WANT TO MAKE SURE THEY'RE ASLEEP FIRST.
SOUNDS GOOD, DEAR.
DO YOU THINK WE GOT ENOUGH THIS YEAR?
OF COURSE WE DID.
WE DON'T WANT TO SPOIL THEM. THEY'LL HAVE PLENTY TO PLAY WITH.
MOM WAS RIPPED RIGHT FROM A *1950'S* SITCOM IN A LOT OF WAYS. SHE WAS THE PERFECT WIFE... THE PERFECT MOTHER.
SHE HAD SO MUCH LOVE IN HER HEART THAT IT LITERALLY SEEPED OUT OF HER PORES. ALL SHE EVER WANTED WAS A FAMILY... AND FOR AWHILE SHE WAS LIVING OUT THAT DREAM.

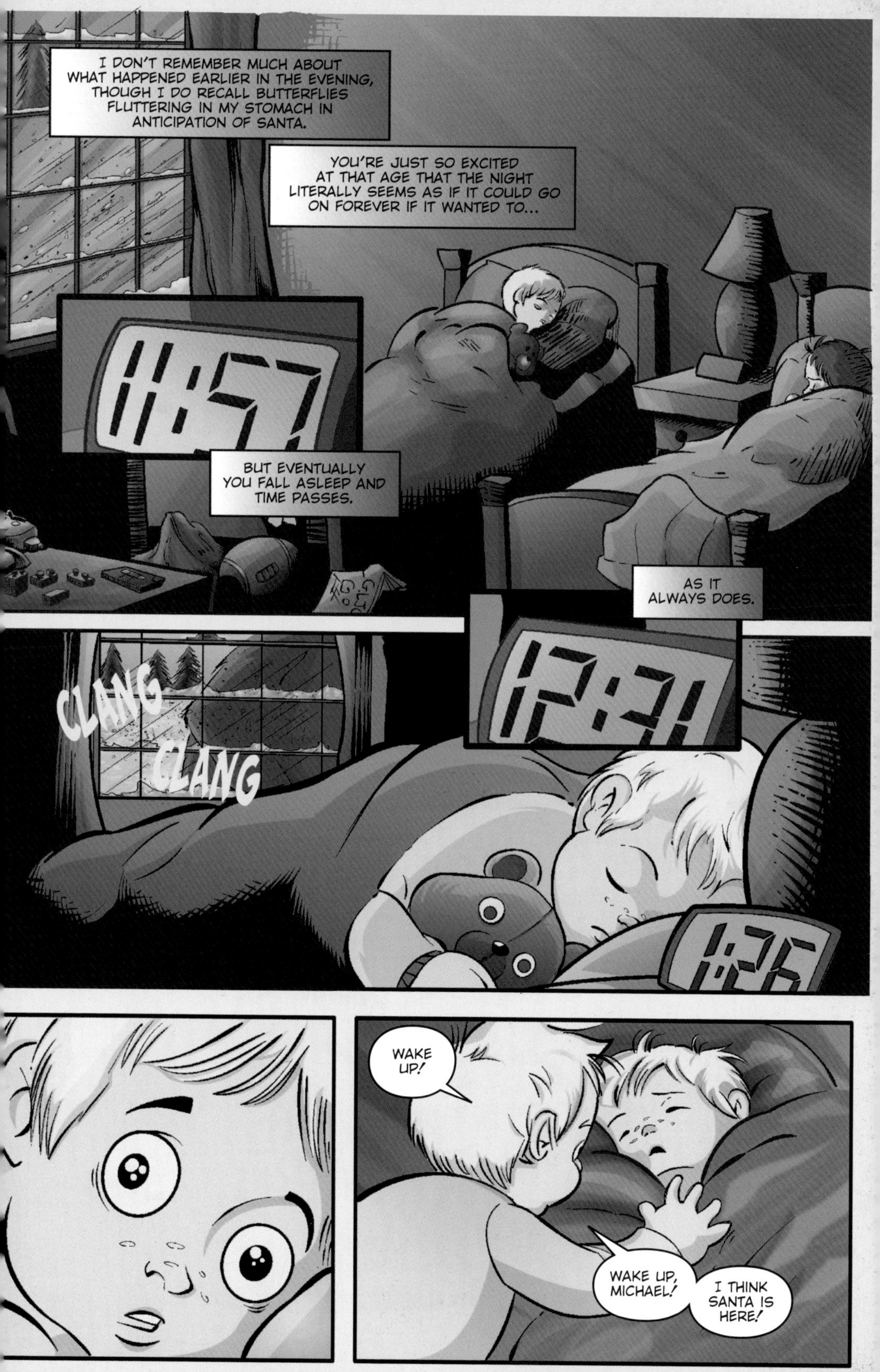
I DON'T REMEMBER MUCH ABOUT WHAT HAPPENED EARLIER IN THE EVENING, THOUGH I DO RECALL BUTTERFLIES FLUTTERING IN MY STOMACH IN ANTICIPATION OF SANTA.
YOU'RE JUST SO EXCITED AT THAT AGE THAT THE NIGHT LITERALLY SEEMS AS IF IT COULD GO ON FOREVER IF IT WANTED TO...
11:57
BUT EVENTUALLY YOU FALL ASLEEP AND TIME PASSES.
AS IT ALWAYS DOES.
12:21
CLANG
CLANG
1:26
WAKE UP!
WAKE UP, MICHAEL!
I THINK SANTA IS HERE!

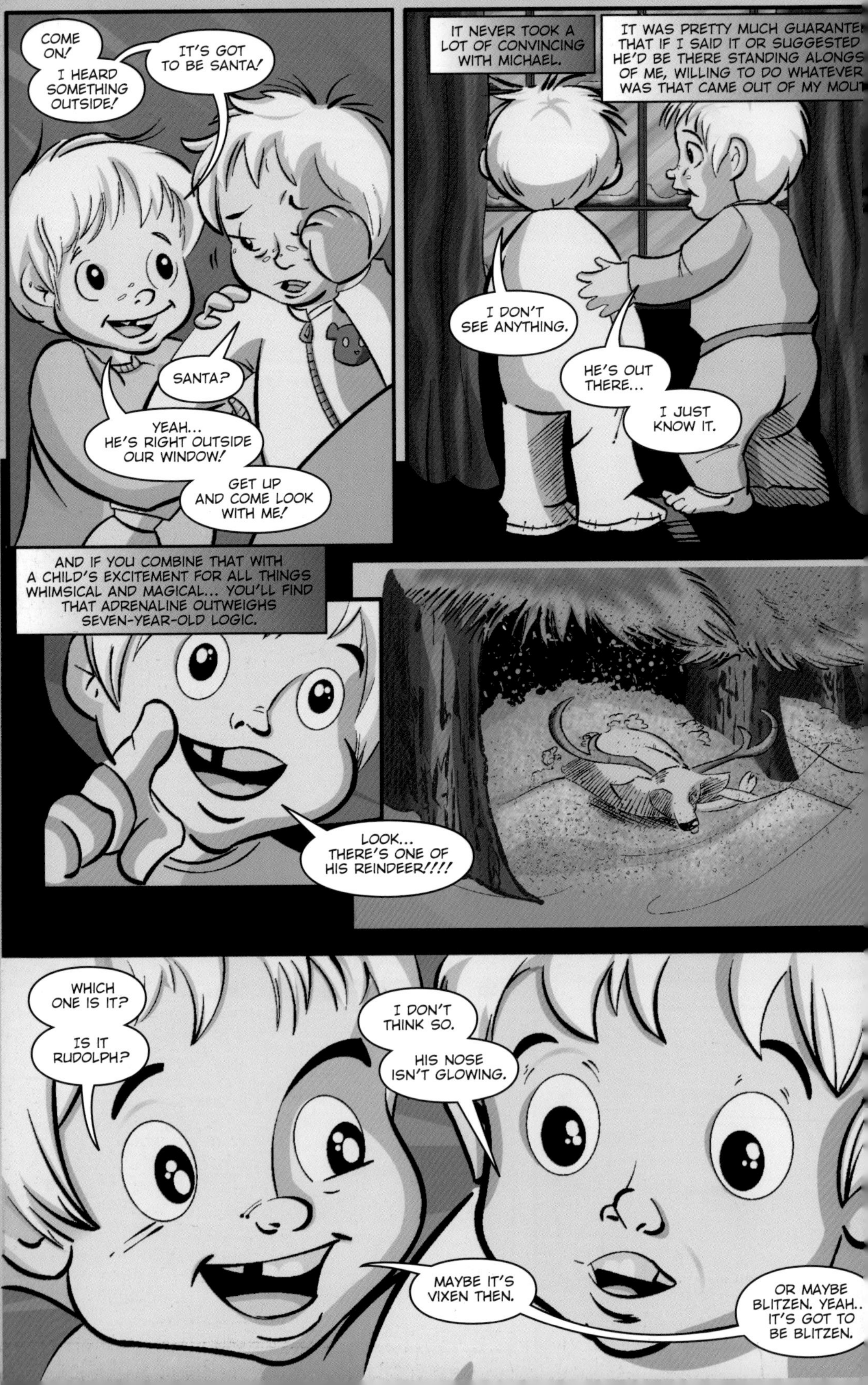
COME ON!
I HEARD SOMETHING OUTSIDE!
IT'S GOT TO BE SANTA!
SANTA?
YEAH... HE'S RIGHT OUTSIDE OUR WINDOW!
GET UP AND COME LOOK WITH ME!
IT NEVER TOOK A LOT OF CONVINCING WITH MICHAEL.
IT WAS PRETTY MUCH GUARANTE THAT IF I SAID IT OR SUGGESTED HE'D BE THERE STANDING ALONGS OF ME, WILLING TO DO WHATEVER WAS THAT CAME OUT OF MY MOUT
I DON'T SEE ANYTHING.
HE'S OUT THERE...
I JUST KNOW IT.
AND IF YOU COMBINE THAT WITH A CHILD'S EXCITEMENT FOR ALL THINGS WHIMSICAL AND MAGICAL... YOU'LL FIND THAT ADRENALINE OUTWEIGHS SEVEN-YEAR-OLD LOGIC.
LOOK... THERE'S ONE OF HIS REINDEER!!!!
WHICH ONE IS IT?
IS IT RUDOLPH?
I DON'T THINK SO.
HIS NOSE ISN'T GLOWING.
MAYBE IT'S VIXEN THEN.
OR MAYBE BLITZEN. YEAH... IT'S GOT TO BE BLITZEN.

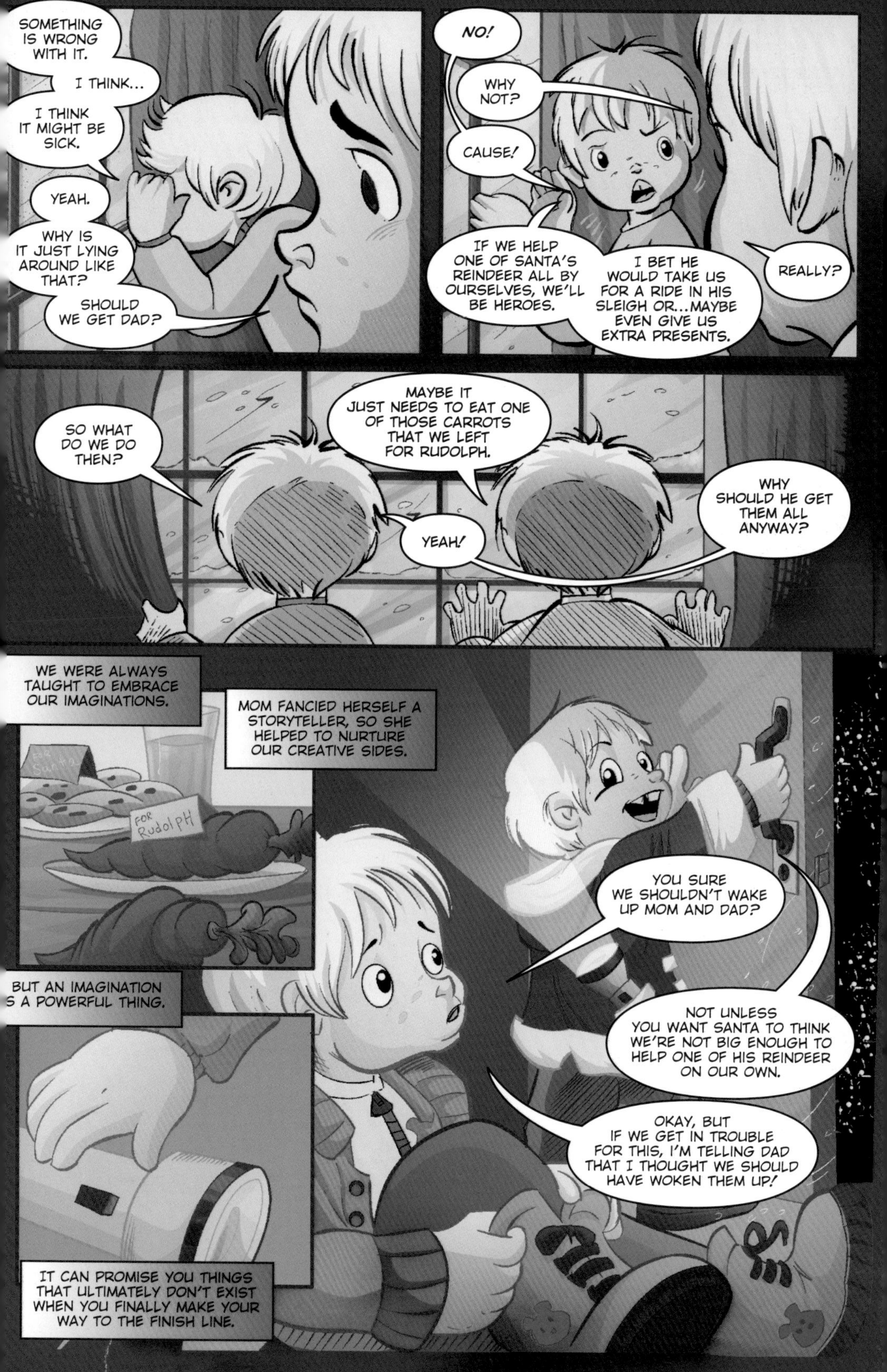
SOMETHING IS WRONG WITH IT.
I THINK...
I THINK IT MIGHT BE SICK.
YEAH.
WHY IS IT JUST LYING AROUND LIKE THAT?
SHOULD WE GET DAD?
NO!
WHY NOT?
CAUSE!
IF WE HELP ONE OF SANTA'S REINDEER ALL BY OURSELVES, WE'LL BE HEROES.
I BET HE WOULD TAKE US FOR A RIDE IN HIS SLEIGH OR...MAYBE EVEN GIVE US EXTRA PRESENTS.
REALLY?
SO WHAT DO WE DO THEN?
MAYBE IT JUST NEEDS TO EAT ONE OF THOSE CARROTS THAT WE LEFT FOR RUDOLPH.
YEAH!
WHY SHOULD HE GET THEM ALL ANYWAY?
WE WERE ALWAYS TAUGHT TO EMBRACE OUR IMAGINATIONS.
MOM FANCIED HERSELF A STORYTELLER, SO SHE HELPED TO NURTURE OUR CREATIVE SIDES.
FOR Rudolph
BUT AN IMAGINATION S A POWERFUL THING.
YOU SURE WE SHOULDN'T WAKE UP MOM AND DAD?
NOT UNLESS YOU WANT SANTA TO THINK WE'RE NOT BIG ENOUGH TO HELP ONE OF HIS REINDEER ON OUR OWN.
OKAY, BUT IF WE GET IN TROUBLE FOR THIS, I'M TELLING DAD THAT I THOUGHT WE SHOULD HAVE WOKEN THEM UP!
IT CAN PROMISE YOU THINGS THAT ULTIMATELY DON'T EXIST WHEN YOU FINALLY MAKE YOUR WAY TO THE FINISH LINE.

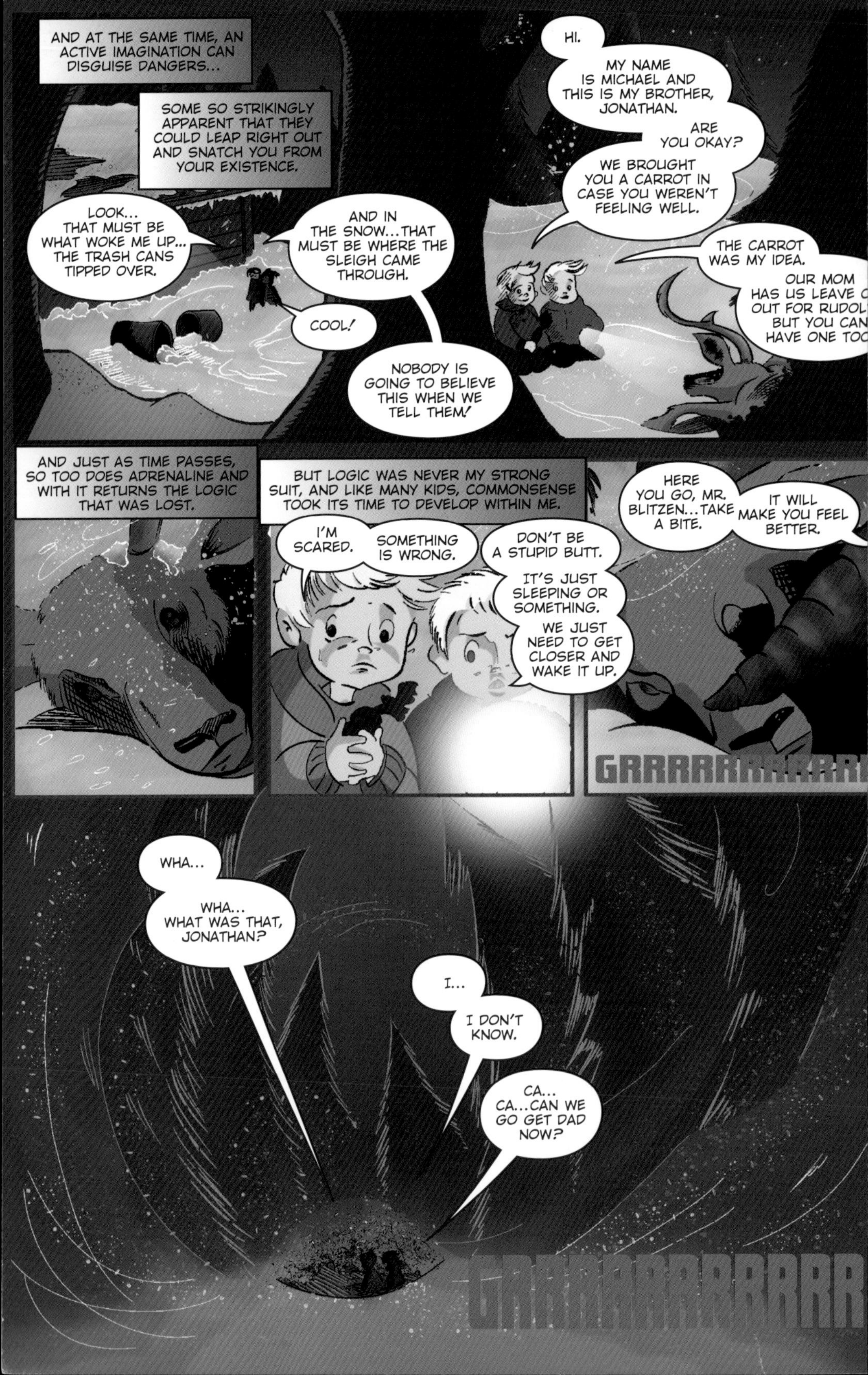
AND AT THE SAME TIME, AN ACTIVE IMAGINATION CAN DISGUISE DANGERS...
SOME SO STRIKINGLY APPARENT THAT THEY COULD LEAP RIGHT OUT AND SNATCH YOU FROM YOUR EXISTENCE.
LOOK... THAT MUST BE WHAT WOKE ME UP... THE TRASH CANS TIPPED OVER.
AND IN THE SNOW...THAT MUST BE WHERE THE SLEIGH CAME THROUGH.
COOL!
NOBODY IS GOING TO BELIEVE THIS WHEN WE TELL THEM!
HI.
MY NAME IS MICHAEL AND THIS IS MY BROTHER, JONATHAN.
ARE YOU OKAY?
WE BROUGHT YOU A CARROT IN CASE YOU WEREN'T FEELING WELL.
THE CARROT WAS MY IDEA.
AND JUST AS TIME PASSES, SO TOO DOES ADRENALINE AND WITH IT RETURNS THE LOGIC THAT WAS LOST.
BUT LOGIC WAS NEVER MY STRONG SUIT, AND LIKE MANY KIDS, COMMONSENSE TOOK ITS TIME TO DEVELOP WITHIN ME.
I'M SCARED.
SOMETHING IS WRONG.
DON'T BE A STUPID BUTT.
IT'S JUST SLEEPING OR SOMETHING.
WE JUST NEED TO GET CLOSER AND WAKE IT UP.
HERE YOU GO, MR. BLITZEN...TAKE A BITE.
IT WILL MAKE YOU FEEL BETTER.
GRRRRRRRRRRR
WHA...
WHA... WHAT WAS THAT, JONATHAN?
I...
I DON'T KNOW.
CA... CA...CAN WE GO GET DAD NOW?
GRRRRRRRRRRR

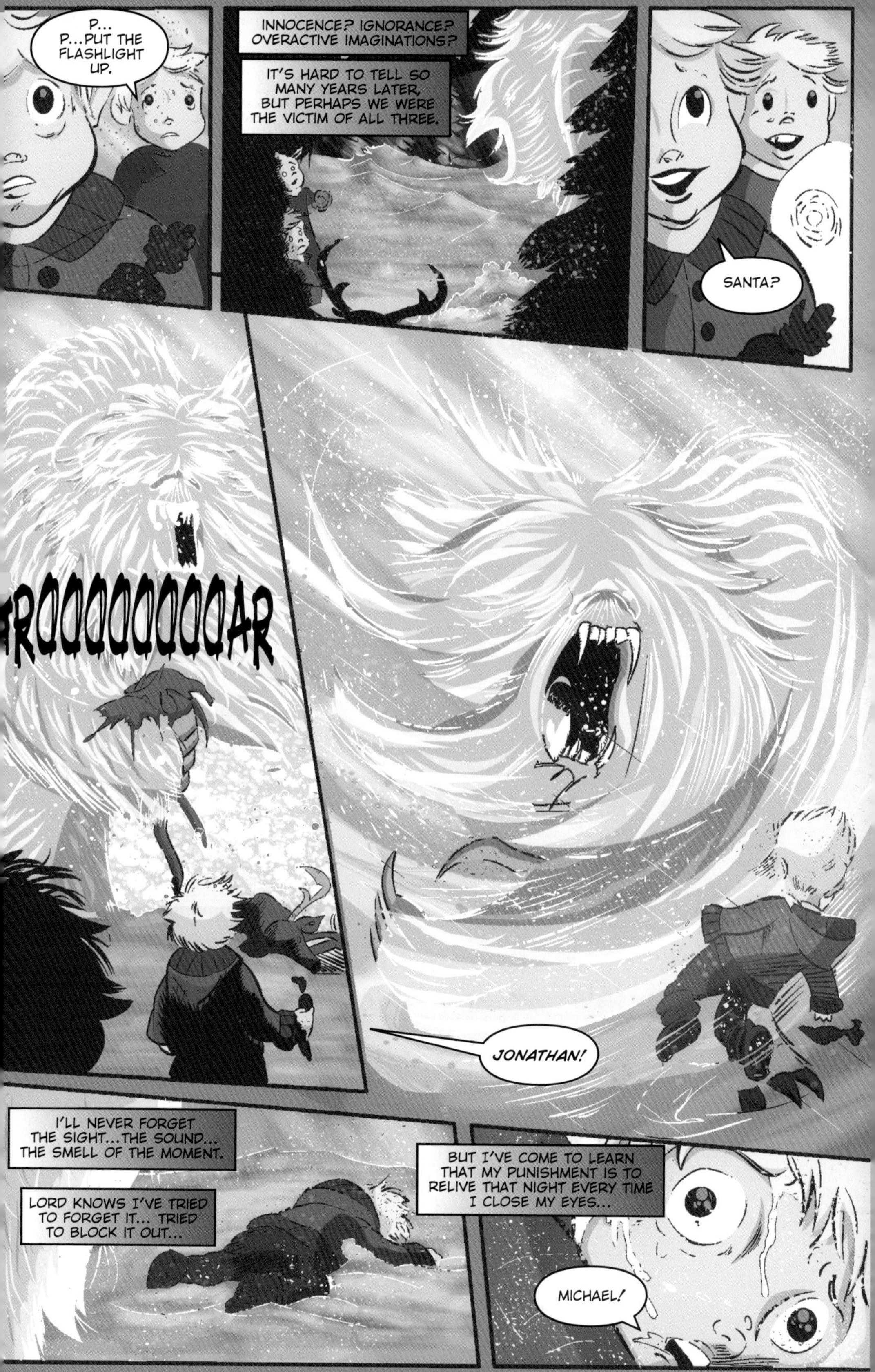
P...
P...PUT THE FLASHLIGHT UP.
INNOCENCE? IGNORANCE? OVERACTIVE IMAGINATIONS?
IT'S HARD TO TELL SO MANY YEARS LATER, BUT PERHAPS WE WERE THE VICTIM OF ALL THREE.
SANTA?
ROOOOOOOOAR
JONATHAN!
I'LL NEVER FORGET THE SIGHT...THE SOUND... THE SMELL OF THE MOMENT.
LORD KNOWS I'VE TRIED TO FORGET IT... TRIED TO BLOCK IT OUT...
BUT I'VE COME TO LEARN THAT MY PUNISHMENT IS TO RELIVE THAT NIGHT EVERY TIME I CLOSE MY EYES...
MICHAEL!

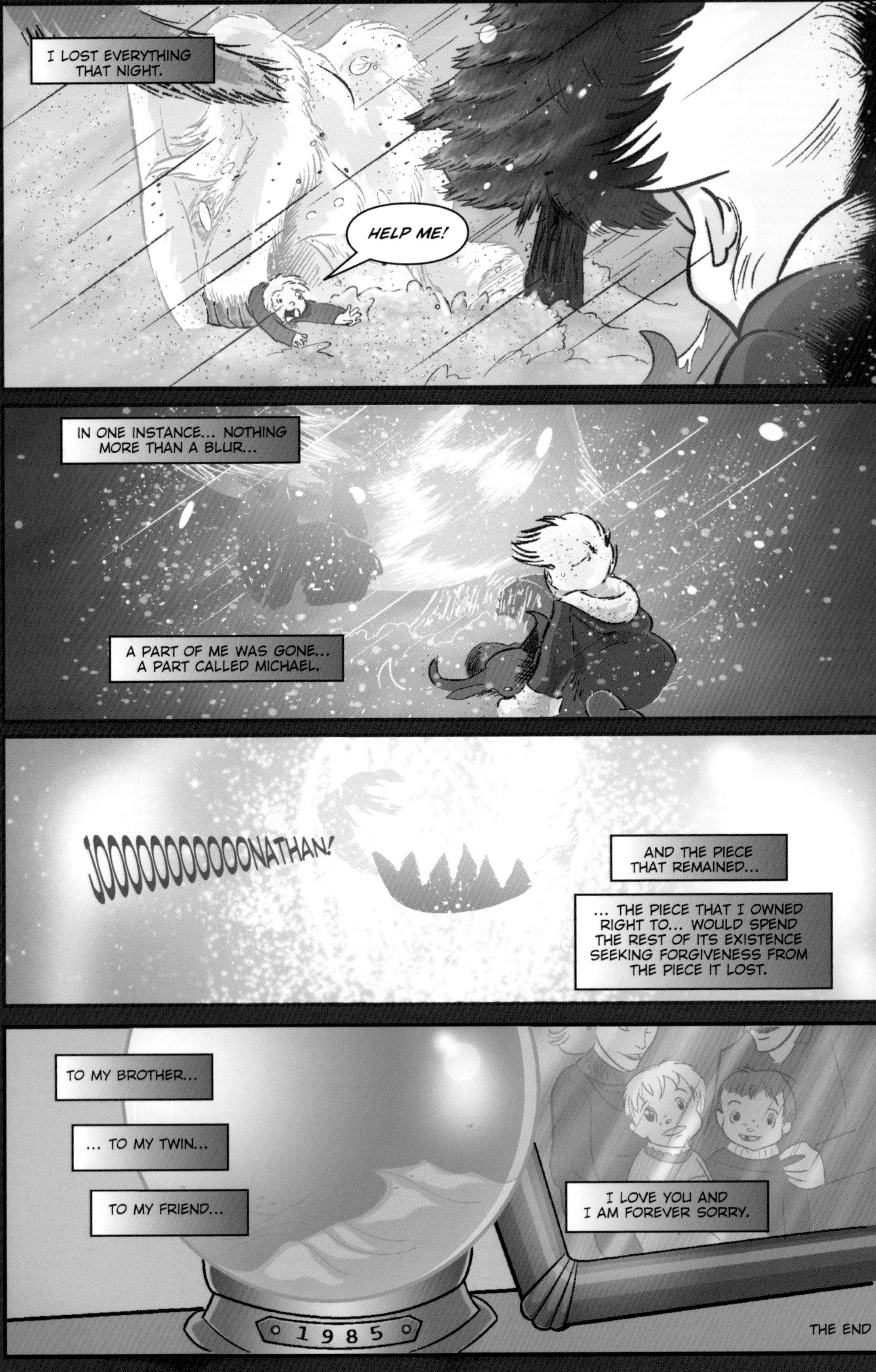
I LOST EVERYTHING THAT NIGHT.
HELP ME!
IN ONE INSTANCE... NOTHING MORE THAN A BLUR...
A PART OF ME WAS GONE... A PART CALLED MICHAEL.
JOOOOOOOOOOONATHAN!
AND THE PIECE THAT REMAINED...
... THE PIECE THAT I OWNED RIGHT TO... WOULD SPEND THE REST OF ITS EXISTENCE SEEKING FORGIVENESS FROM THE PIECE IT LOST.
TO MY BROTHER...
... TO MY TWIN...
TO MY FRIEND...
I LOVE YOU AND I AM FOREVER SORRY.
1985
THE END

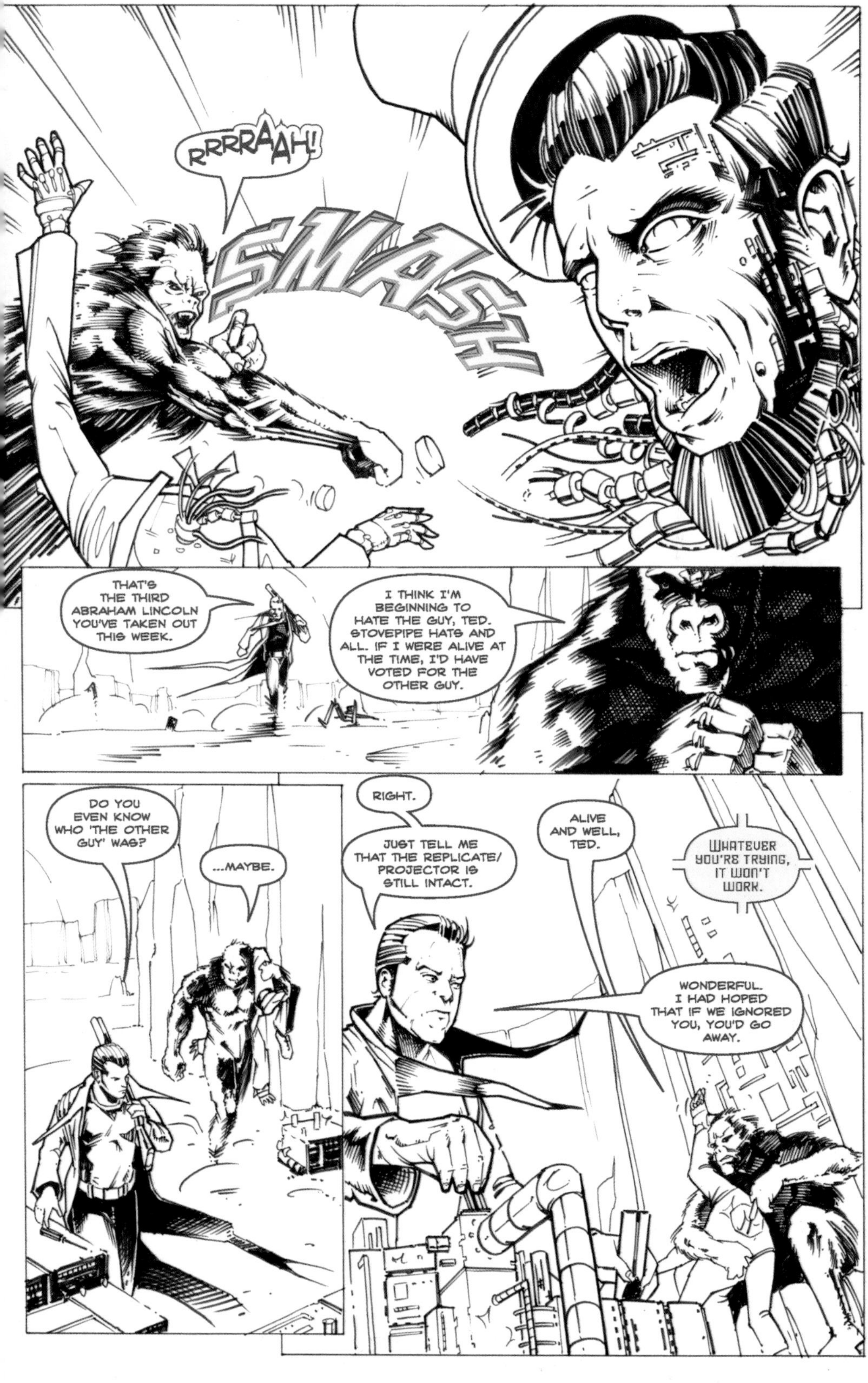
RRRRAAH!!
SMASH
THAT'S THE THIRD ABRAHAM LINCOLN YOU'VE TAKEN OUT THIS WEEK.
I THINK I'M BEGINNING TO HATE THE GUY, TED. STOVEPIPE HATS AND ALL. IF I WERE ALIVE AT THE TIME, I'D HAVE VOTED FOR THE OTHER GUY.
DO YOU EVEN KNOW WHO 'THE OTHER GUY' WAS?
...MAYBE.
RIGHT.
JUST TELL ME THAT THE REPLICATE/ PROJECTOR IS STILL INTACT.
ALIVE AND WELL, TED.
WHATEVER YOU'RE TRYING, IT WON'T WORK.
WONDERFUL. I HAD HOPED THAT IF WE IGNORED YOU, YOU'D GO AWAY.

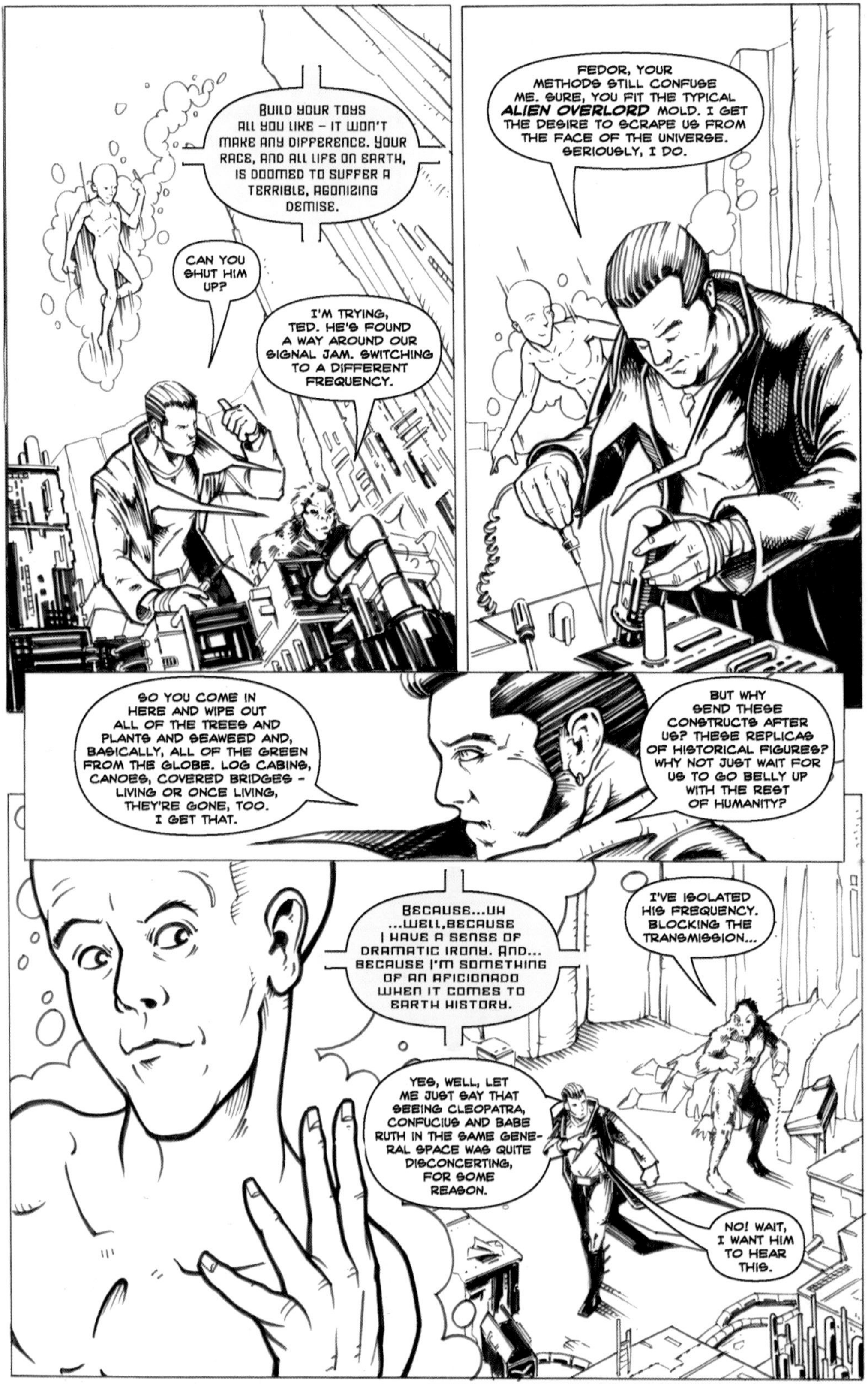

BUILD YOUR TOYS ALL YOU LIKE – IT WON'T MAKE ANY DIFFERENCE. YOUR RACE, AND ALL LIFE ON EARTH, IS DOOMED TO SUFFER A TERRIBLE, AGONIZING DEMISE.
CAN YOU SHUT HIM UP?
I'M TRYING, TED. HE'S FOUND A WAY AROUND OUR SIGNAL JAM. SWITCHING TO A DIFFERENT FREQUENCY.
FEDOR, YOUR METHODS STILL CONFUSE ME. SURE, YOU FIT THE TYPICAL ALIEN OVERLORD MOLD. I GET THE DESIRE TO SCRAPE US FROM THE FACE OF THE UNIVERSE. SERIOUSLY, I DO.
SO YOU COME IN HERE AND WIPE OUT ALL OF THE TREES AND PLANTS AND SEAWEED AND, BASICALLY, ALL OF THE GREEN FROM THE GLOBE. LOG CABINS, CANOES, COVERED BRIDGES – LIVING OR ONCE LIVING, THEY'RE GONE, TOO. I GET THAT.
BUT WHY SEND THESE CONSTRUCTS AFTER US? THESE REPLICAS OF HISTORICAL FIGURES? WHY NOT JUST WAIT FOR US TO GO BELLY UP WITH THE REST OF HUMANITY?
BECAUSE...UH ...WELL, BECAUSE I HAVE A SENSE OF DRAMATIC IRONY. AND... BECAUSE I'M SOMETHING OF AN AFICIONADO WHEN IT COMES TO EARTH HISTORY.
I'VE ISOLATED HIS FREQUENCY. BLOCKING THE TRANSMISSION...
YES, WELL, LET ME JUST SAY THAT SEEING CLEOPATRA, CONFUCIUS AND BABE RUTH IN THE SAME GENERAL SPACE WAS QUITE DISCONCERTING, FOR SOME REASON.
NO! WAIT, I WANT HIM TO HEAR THIS.

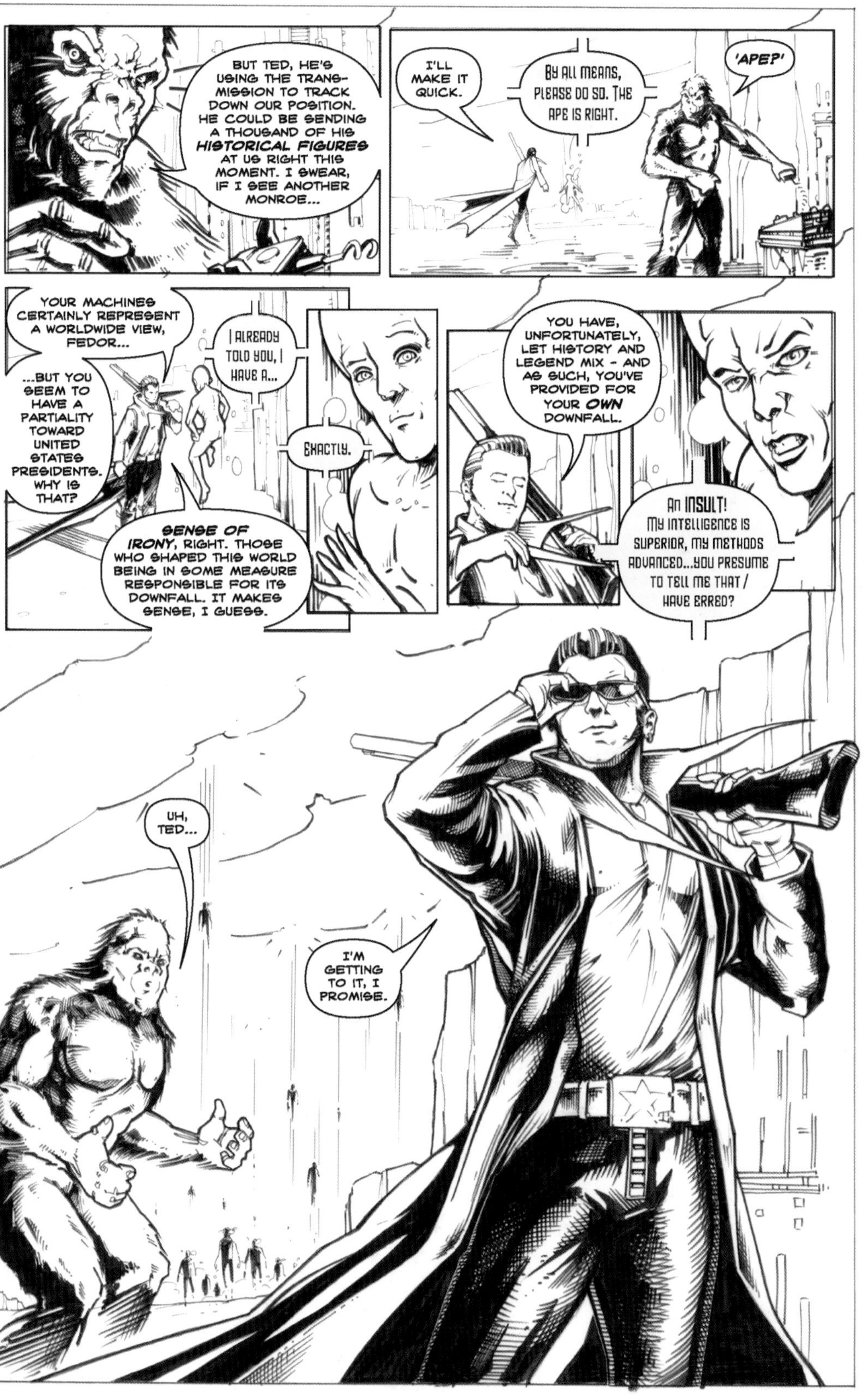
BUT TED, HE'S USING THE TRANSMISSION TO TRACK DOWN OUR POSITION. HE COULD BE SENDING A THOUSAND OF HIS HISTORICAL FIGURES AT US RIGHT THIS MOMENT. I SWEAR, IF I SEE ANOTHER MONROE...
I'LL MAKE IT QUICK.
BY ALL MEANS, PLEASE DO SO. THE APE IS RIGHT.
'APE?'
YOUR MACHINES CERTAINLY REPRESENT A WORLDWIDE VIEW, FEDOR...
...BUT YOU SEEM TO HAVE A PARTIALITY TOWARD UNITED STATES PRESIDENTS. WHY IS THAT?
I ALREADY TOLD YOU, I HAVE A...
SENSE OF IRONY, RIGHT. THOSE WHO SHAPED THIS WORLD BEING IN SOME MEASURE RESPONSIBLE FOR ITS DOWNFALL. IT MAKES SENSE, I GUESS.
EXACTLY.
YOU HAVE, UNFORTUNATELY, LET HISTORY AND LEGEND MIX - AND AS SUCH, YOU'VE PROVIDED FOR YOUR OWN DOWNFALL.
AN INSULT! MY INTELLIGENCE IS SUPERIOR, MY METHODS ADVANCED...YOU PRESUME TO TELL ME THAT I HAVE ERRED?
UH, TED...
I'M GETTING TO IT, I PROMISE.

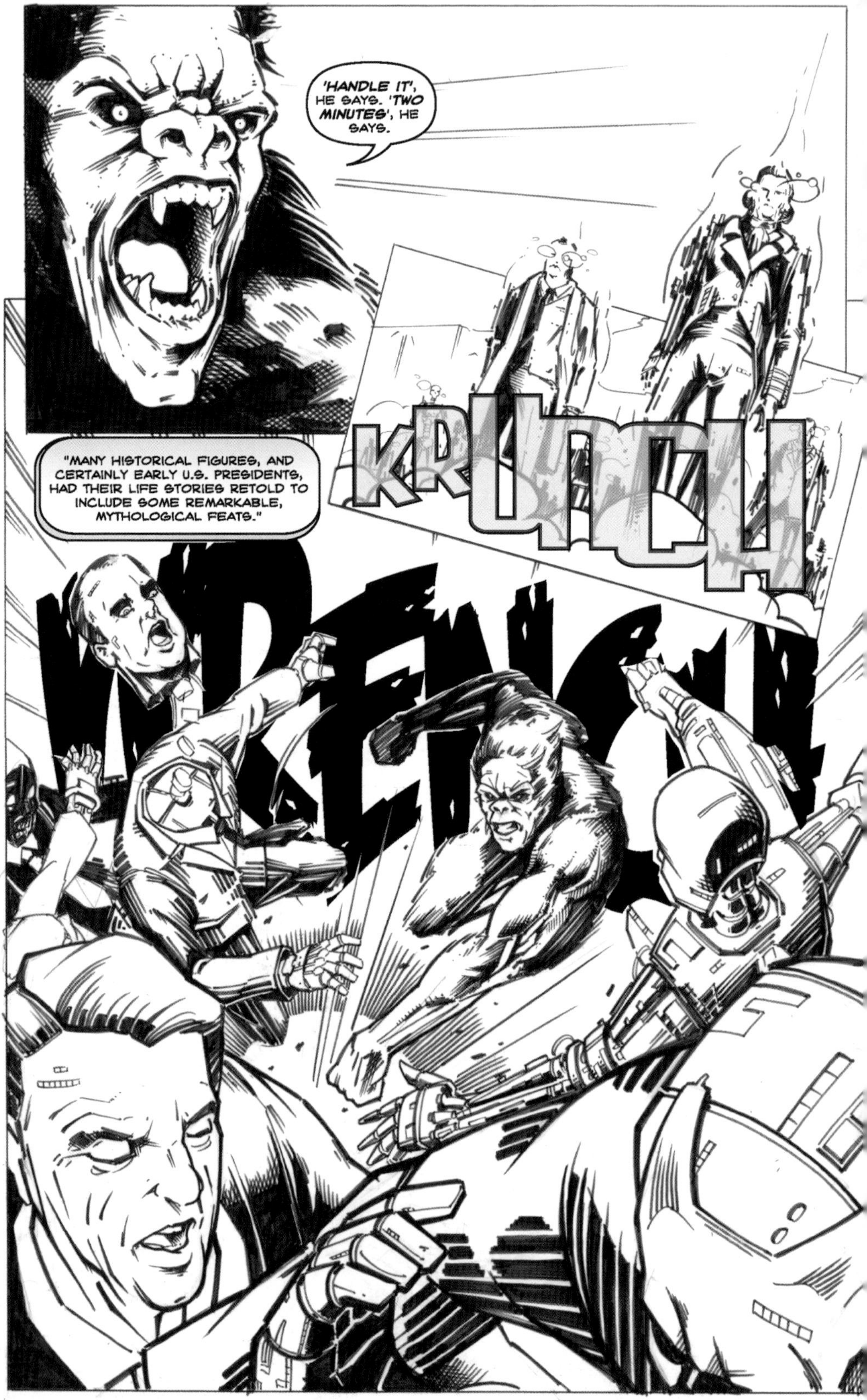
'HANDLE IT', HE SAYS. 'TWO MINUTES', HE SAYS.
"MANY HISTORICAL FIGURES, AND CERTAINLY EARLY U.S. PRESIDENTS, HAD THEIR LIFE STORIES RETOLD TO INCLUDE SOME REMARKABLE, MYTHOLOGICAL FEATS."
KRUNCH

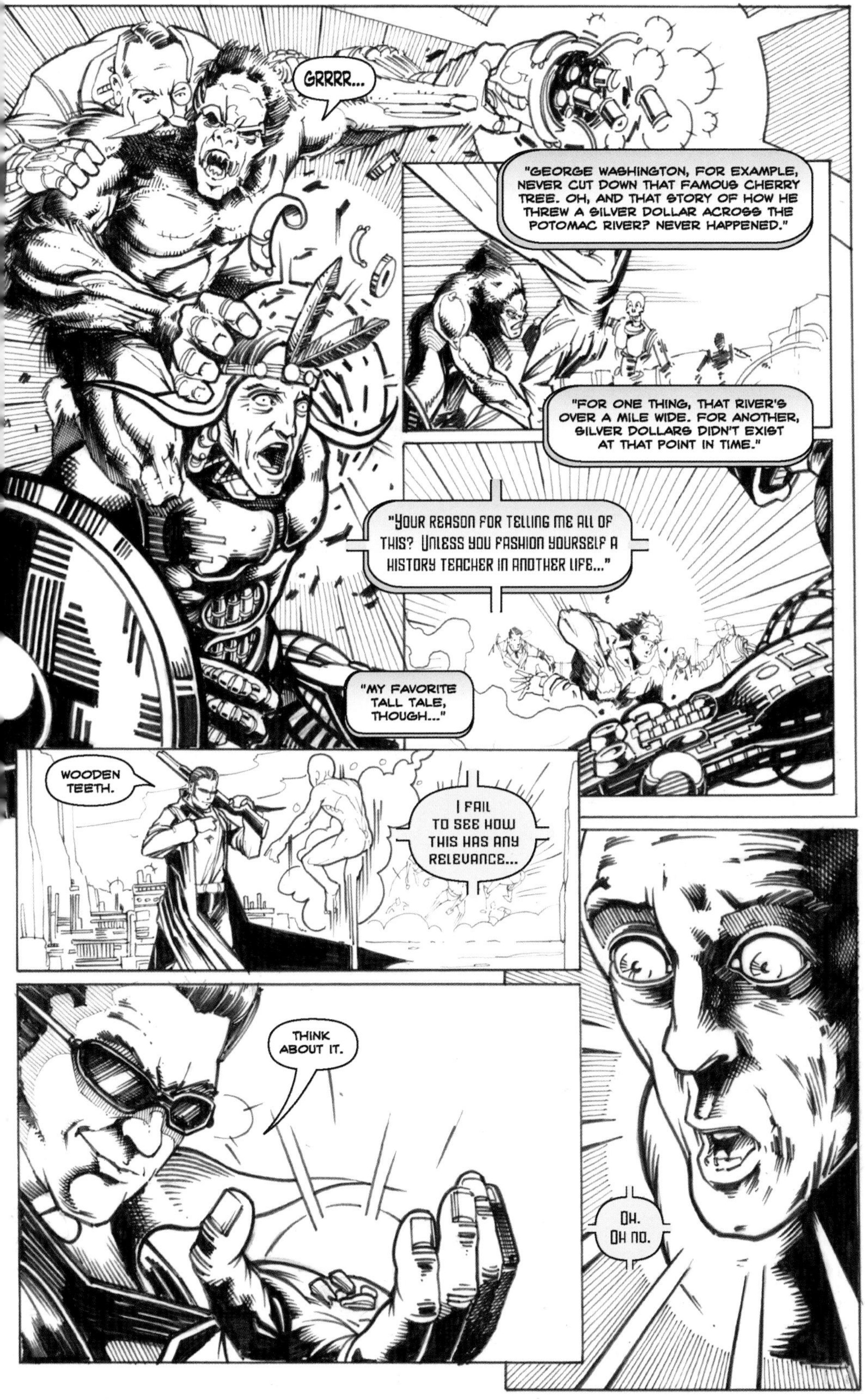
GRRRR...
"GEORGE WASHINGTON, FOR EXAMPLE, NEVER CUT DOWN THAT FAMOUS CHERRY TREE. OH, AND THAT STORY OF HOW HE THREW A SILVER DOLLAR ACROSS THE POTOMAC RIVER? NEVER HAPPENED."
"FOR ONE THING, THAT RIVER'S OVER A MILE WIDE. FOR ANOTHER, SILVER DOLLARS DIDN'T EXIST AT THAT POINT IN TIME."
"YOUR REASON FOR TELLING ME ALL OF THIS? UNLESS YOU FASHION YOURSELF A HISTORY TEACHER IN ANOTHER LIFE..."
"MY FAVORITE TALL TALE, THOUGH..."
WOODEN TEETH.
I FAIL TO SEE HOW THIS HAS ANY RELEVANCE...
THINK ABOUT IT.
OH. OH NO.

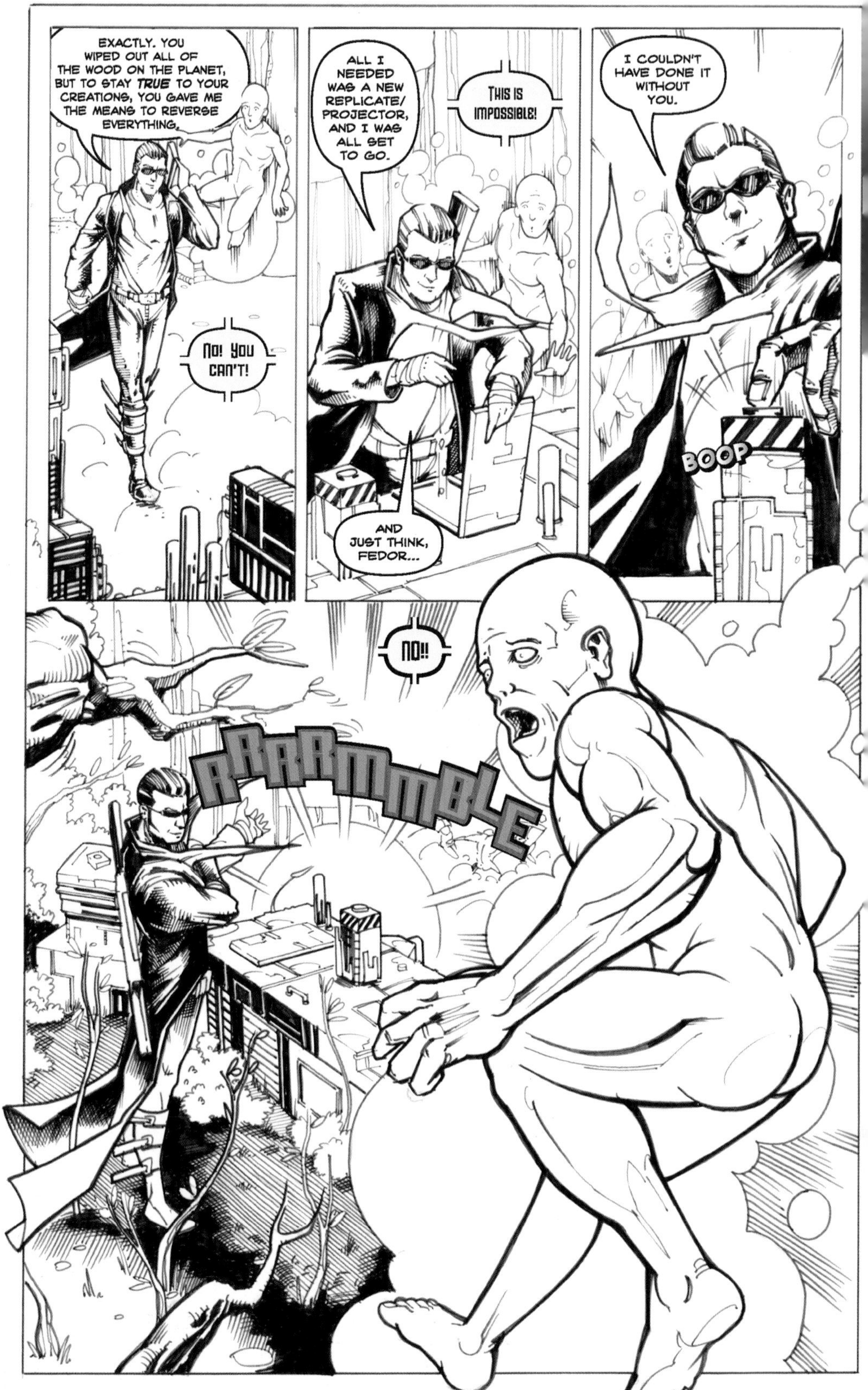
EXACTLY. YOU WIPED OUT ALL OF THE WOOD ON THE PLANET, BUT TO STAY TRUE TO YOUR CREATIONS, YOU GAVE ME THE MEANS TO REVERSE EVERYTHING.
NO! YOU CAN'T!
ALL I NEEDED WAS A NEW REPLICATE/ PROJECTOR, AND I WAS ALL SET TO GO.
THIS IS IMPOSSIBLE!
AND JUST THINK, FEDOR...
I COULDN'T HAVE DONE IT WITHOUT YOU.
BOOP
NO!!
RRRRMMMBLE

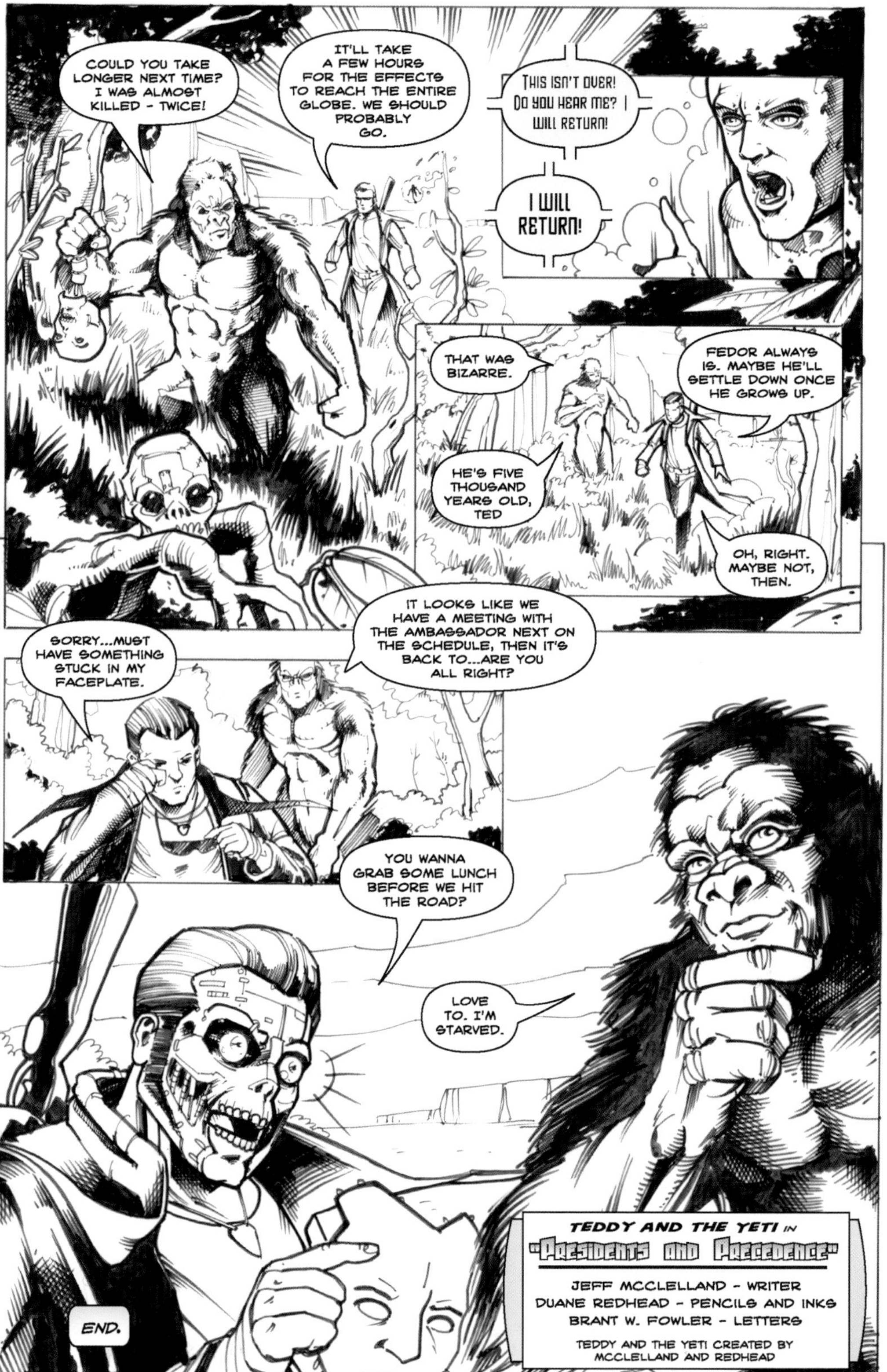
COULD YOU TAKE LONGER NEXT TIME? I WAS ALMOST KILLED - TWICE!
IT'LL TAKE A FEW HOURS FOR THE EFFECTS TO REACH THE ENTIRE GLOBE. WE SHOULD PROBABLY GO.
THIS ISN'T OVER! DO YOU HEAR ME? I WILL RETURN!
I WILL RETURN!
THAT WAS BIZARRE.
FEDOR ALWAYS IS. MAYBE HE'LL SETTLE DOWN ONCE HE GROWS UP.
HE'S FIVE THOUSAND YEARS OLD, TED
OH, RIGHT. MAYBE NOT, THEN.
IT LOOKS LIKE WE HAVE A MEETING WITH THE AMBASSADOR NEXT ON THE SCHEDULE, THEN IT'S BACK TO...ARE YOU ALL RIGHT?
SORRY...MUST HAVE SOMETHING STUCK IN MY FACEPLATE.
YOU WANNA GRAB SOME LUNCH BEFORE WE HIT THE ROAD?
LOVE TO. I'M STARVED.
END.
TEDDY AND THE YETI IN
"PRESIDENTS AND PRECEDENCE"
JEFF MCCLELLAND - WRITER
DUANE REDHEAD - PENCILS AND INKS
BRANT W. FOWLER - LETTERS
TEDDY AND THE YETI CREATED BY MCCLELLAND AND REDHEAD

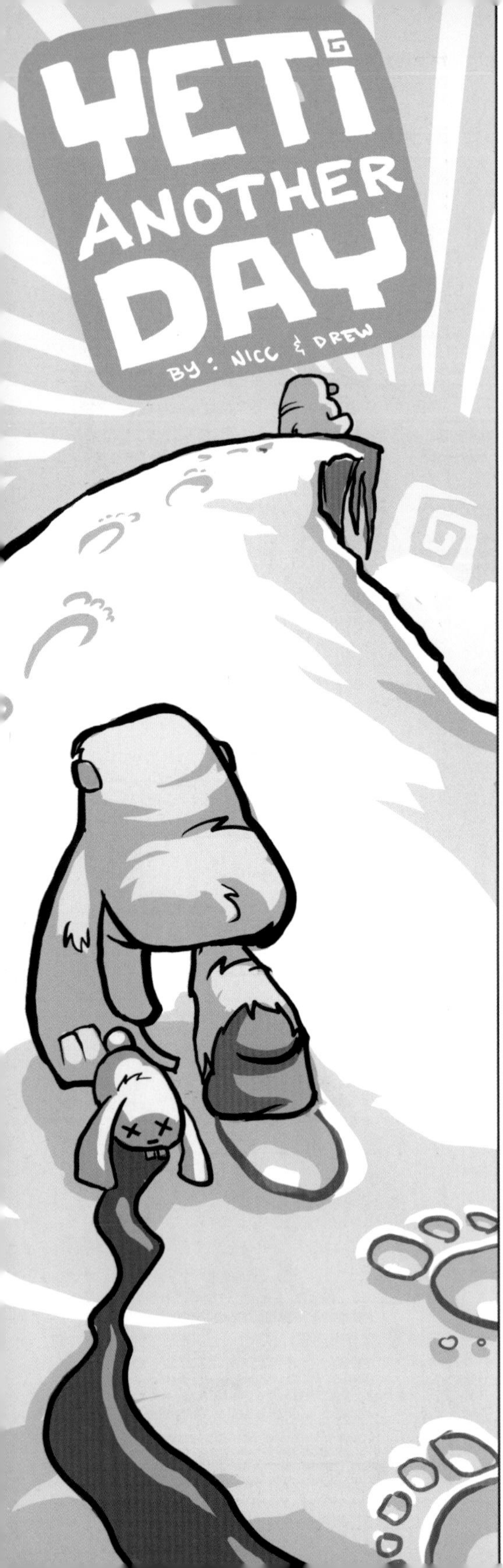
YETI ANOTHER DAY
BY: NICC & DREW

BUNNY FOR BREKKIE

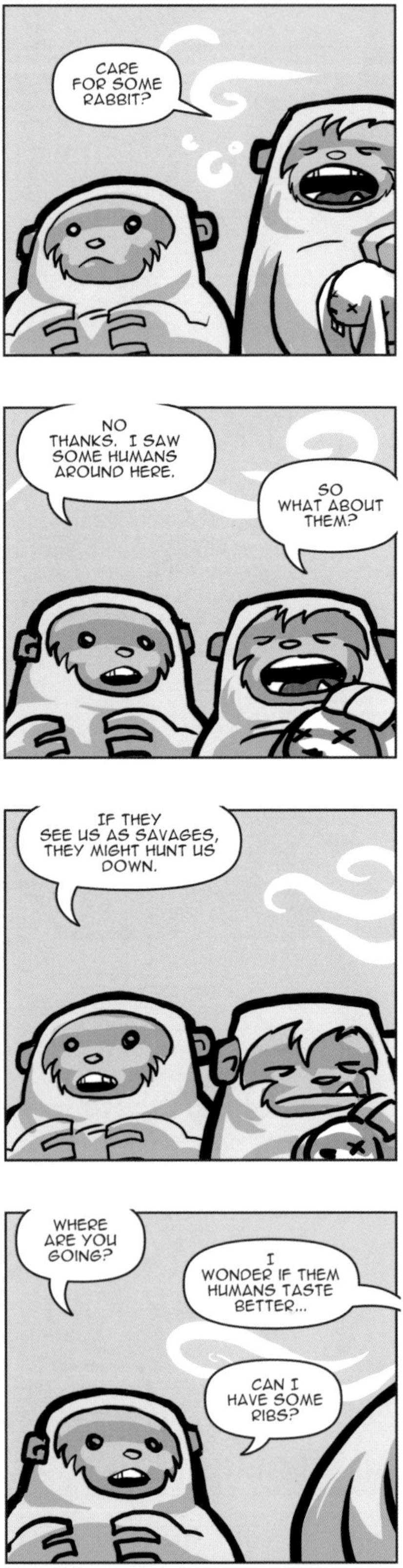
CARE FOR SOME RABBIT?
NO THANKS. I SAW SOME HUMANS AROUND HERE.
SO WHAT ABOUT THEM?
IF THEY SEE US AS SAVAGES, THEY MIGHT HUNT US DOWN.
WHERE ARE YOU GOING?
I WONDER IF THEM HUMANS TASTE BETTER...
CAN I HAVE SOME RIBS?

WHAT'S IN A NAME?

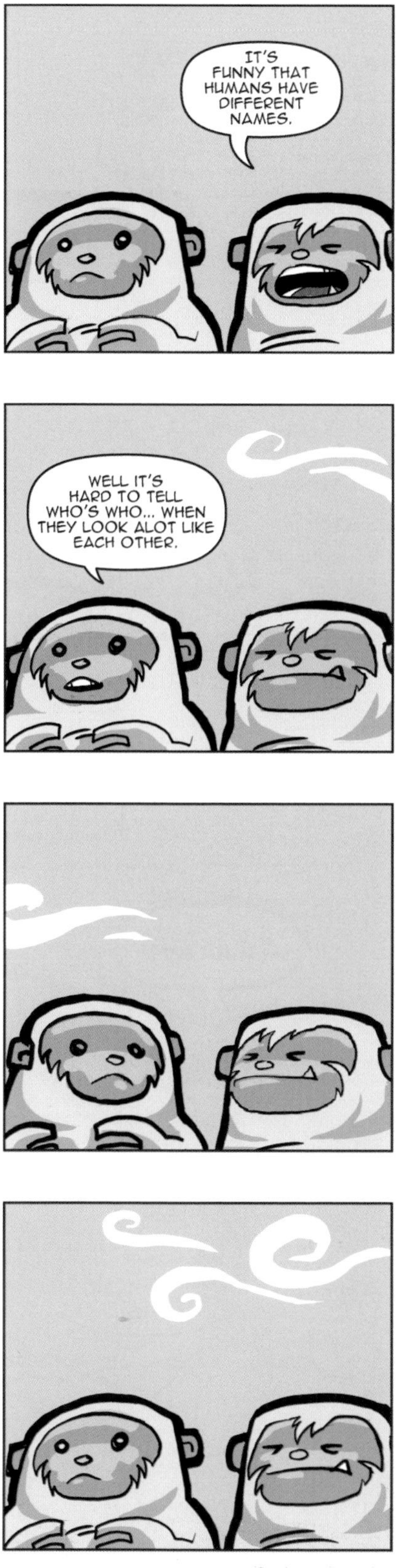
IT'S FUNNY THAT HUMANS HAVE DIFFERENT NAMES.
WELL IT'S HARD TO TELL WHO'S WHO... WHEN THEY LOOK ALOT LIKE EACH OTHER.

HUMAN NUMBERS

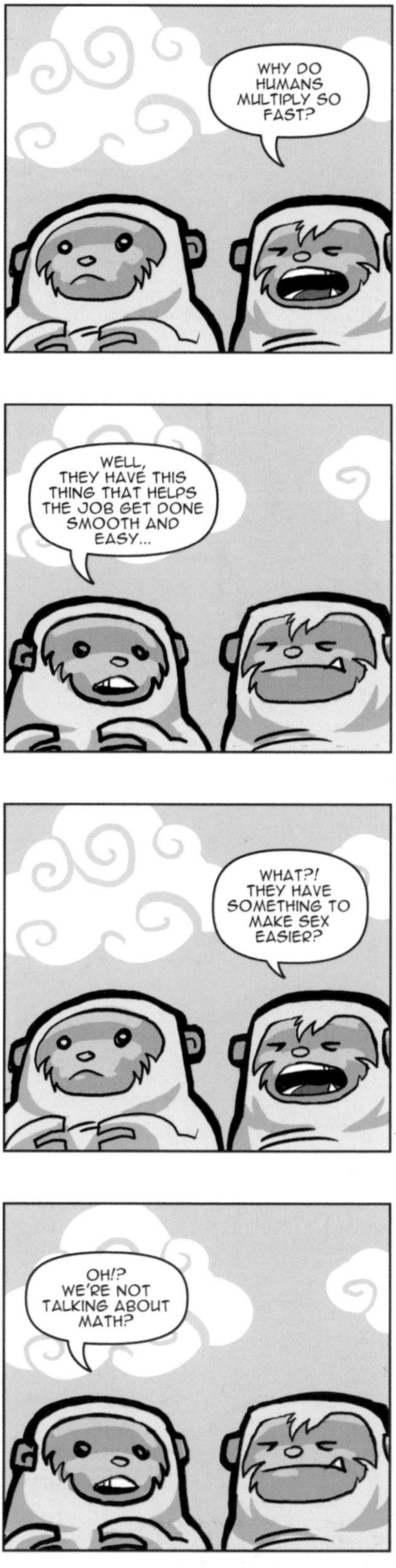
WHY DO HUMANS MULTIPLY SO FAST?
WELL, THEY HAVE THIS THING THAT HELPS THE JOB GET DONE SMOOTH AND EASY...
WHAT?! THEY HAVE SOMETHING TO MAKE SEX EASIER?
OH!? WE'RE NOT TALKING ABOUT MATH?

I DUB THEE...

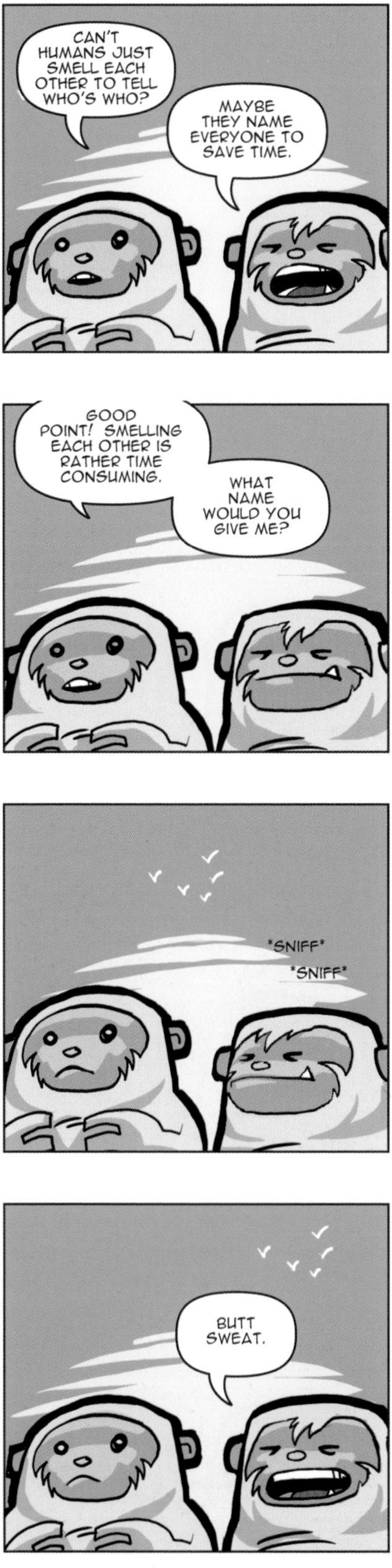
CAN'T HUMANS JUST SMELL EACH OTHER TO TELL WHO'S WHO?
MAYBE THEY NAME EVERYONE TO SAVE TIME.
GOOD POINT! SMELLING EACH OTHER IS RATHER TIME CONSUMING.
WHAT NAME WOULD YOU GIVE ME?
SNIFF
SNIFF
BUTT SWEAT.

HUGE BIRD

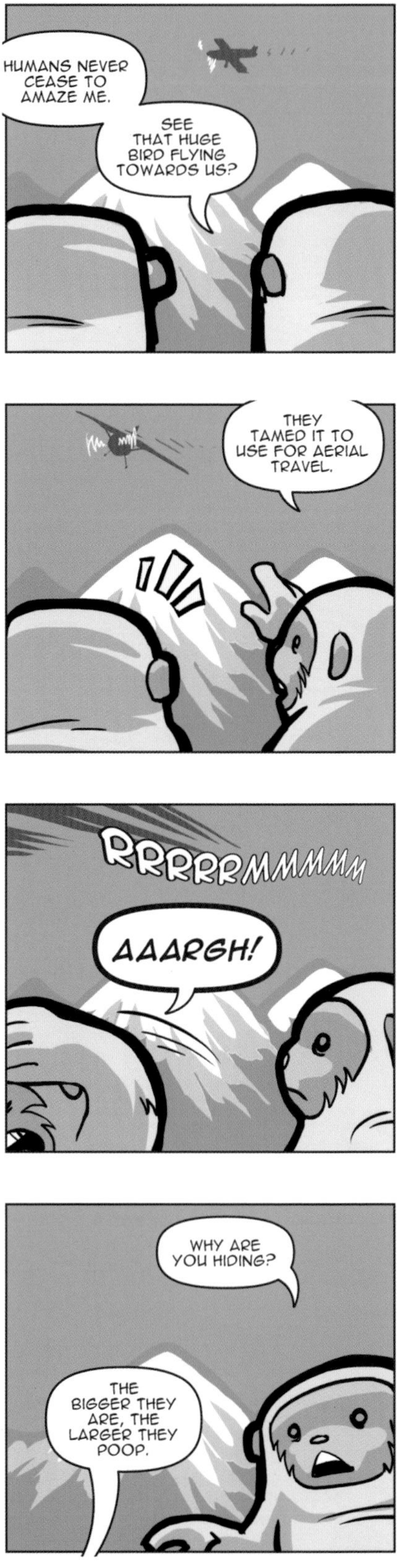
HUMANS NEVER CEASE TO AMAZE ME.
SEE THAT HUGE BIRD FLYING TOWARDS US?
THEY TAMED IT TO USE FOR AERIAL TRAVEL.
RRRRRMMMMM
AAARGH!
WHY ARE YOU HIDING?
THE BIGGER THEY ARE, THE LARGER THEY POOP.

BIRD DROPPINGS

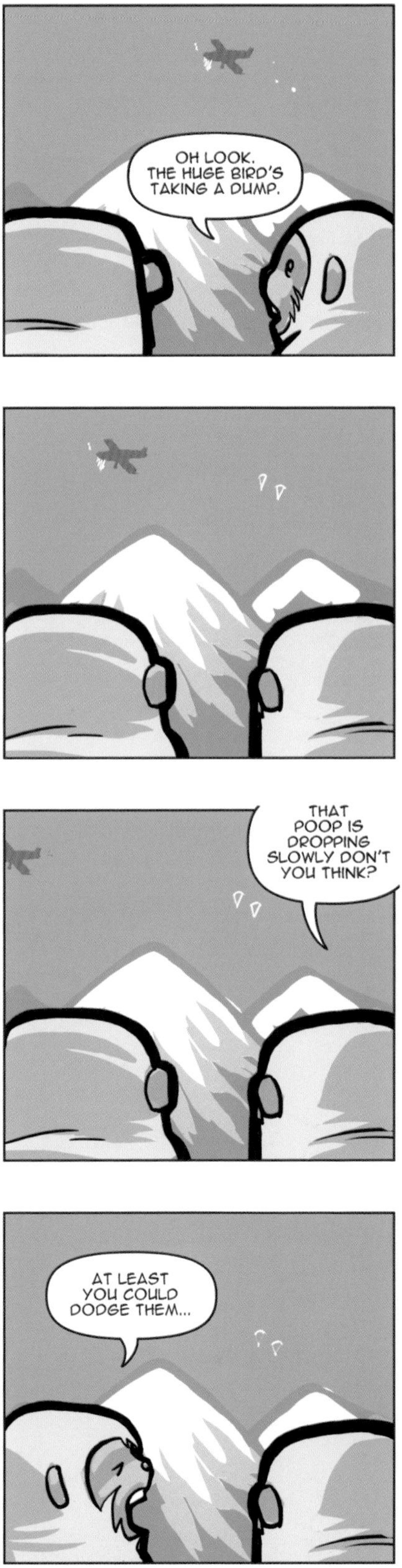
OH LOOK. THE HUGE BIRD'S TAKING A DUMP.
THAT POOP IS DROPPING SLOWLY DON'T YOU THINK?
AT LEAST YOU COULD DODGE THEM...

SNOWBALL

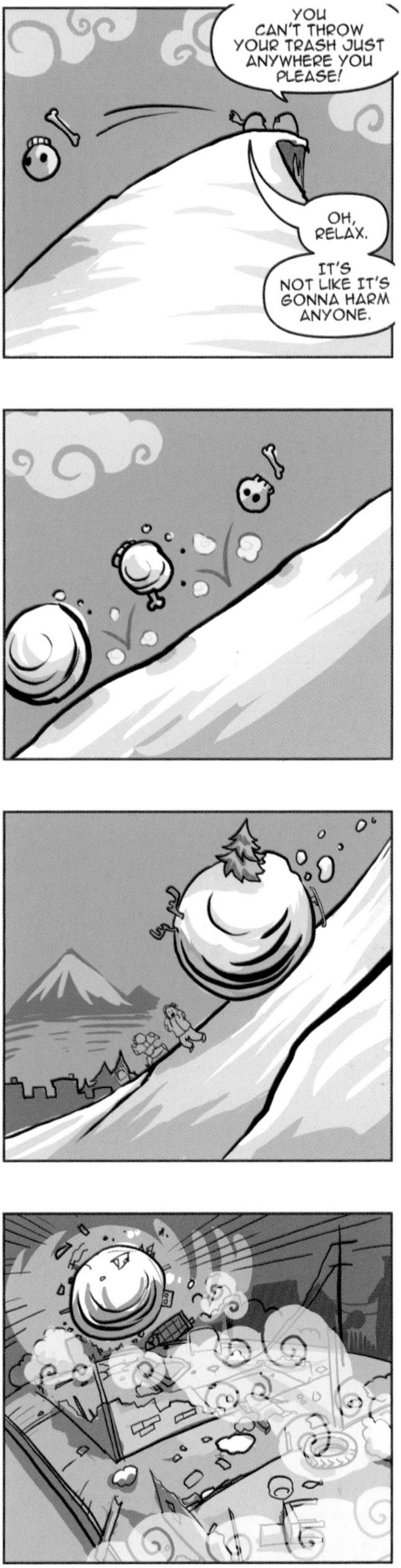
YOU CAN'T THROW YOUR TRASH JUST ANYWHERE YOU PLEASE!
OH, RELAX.
IT'S NOT LIKE IT'S GONNA HARM ANYONE.

SAVAGES

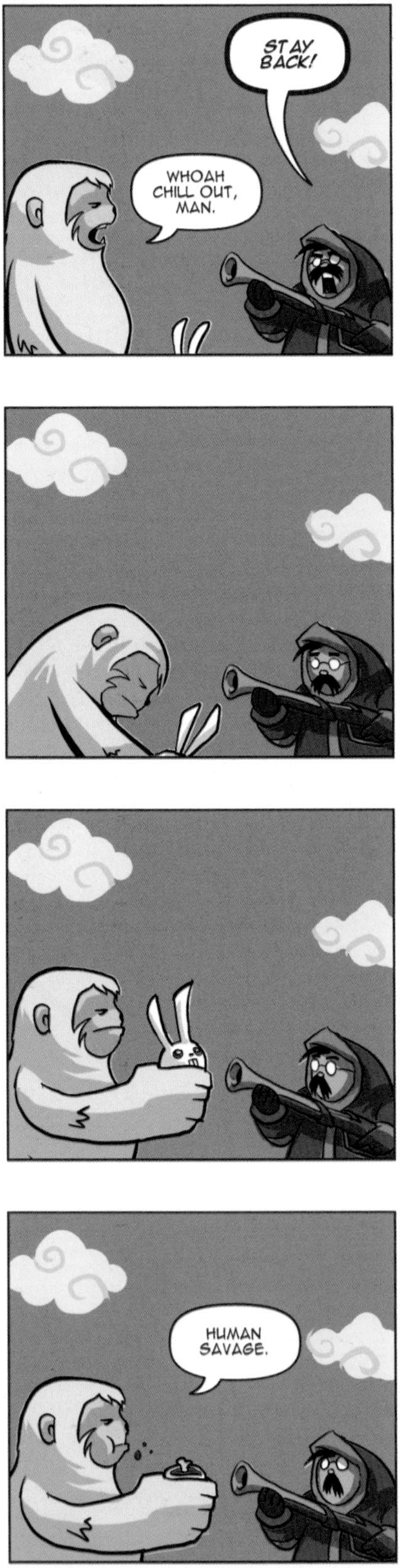
STAY BACK!
WHOAH CHILL OUT, MAN.
HUMAN SAVAGE.

COMMUNICATION

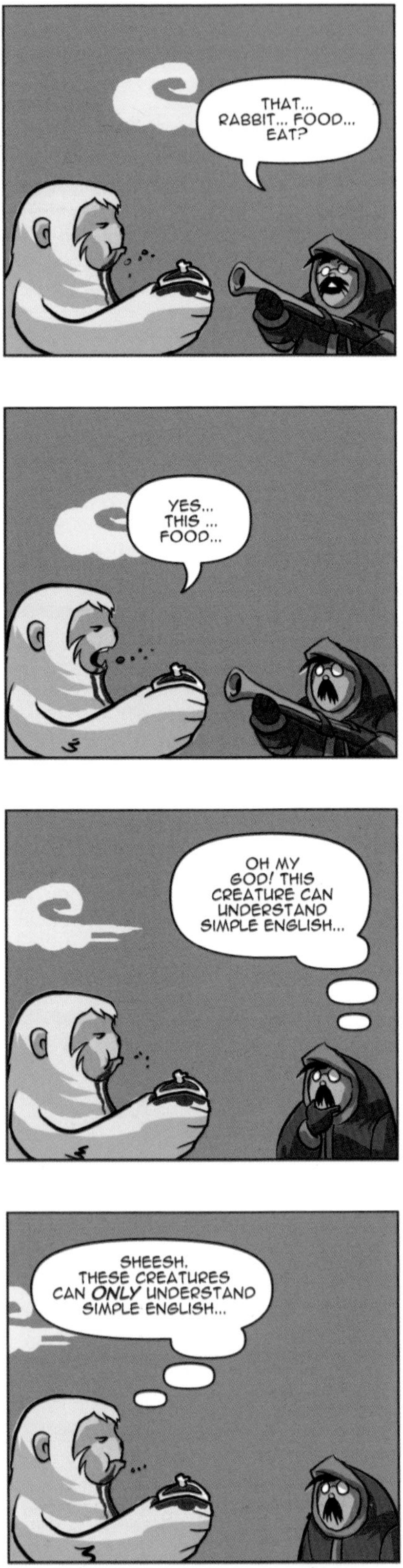
THAT... RABBIT... FOOD... EAT?
YES... THIS ... FOOD...
OH MY GOD! THIS CREATURE CAN UNDERSTAND SIMPLE ENGLISH...
SHEESH. THESE CREATURES CAN ONLY UNDERSTAND SIMPLE ENGLISH...

HUNTER FOR DINNER

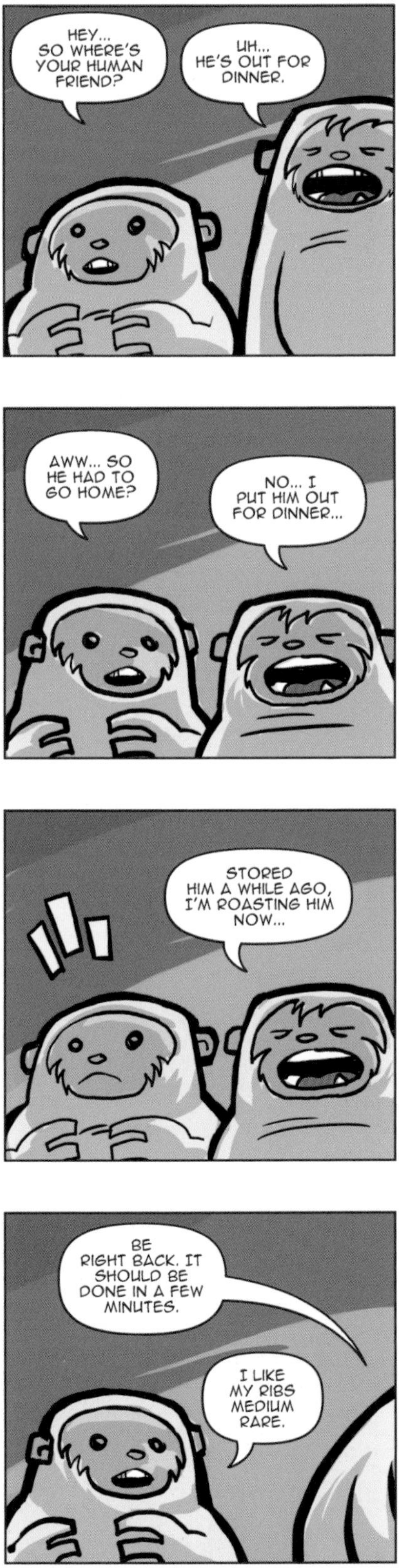
HEY... SO WHERE'S YOUR HUMAN FRIEND?
UH... HE'S OUT FOR DINNER.
AWW... SO HE HAD TO GO HOME?
NO... I PUT HIM OUT FOR DINNER...
STORED HIM A WHILE AGO, I'M ROASTING HIM NOW...
BE RIGHT BACK. IT SHOULD BE DONE IN A FEW MINUTES.
I LIKE MY RIBS MEDIUM RARE.

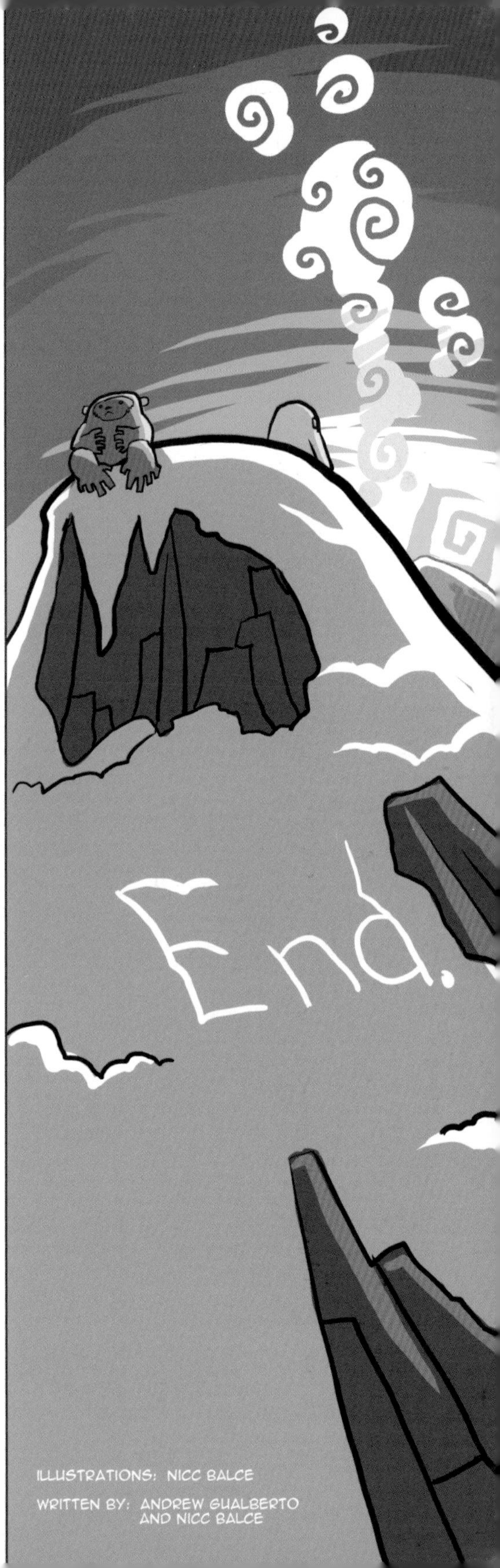
End.
ILLUSTRATIONS: NICC BALCE
WRITTEN BY: ANDREW GUALBERTO AND NICC BALCE

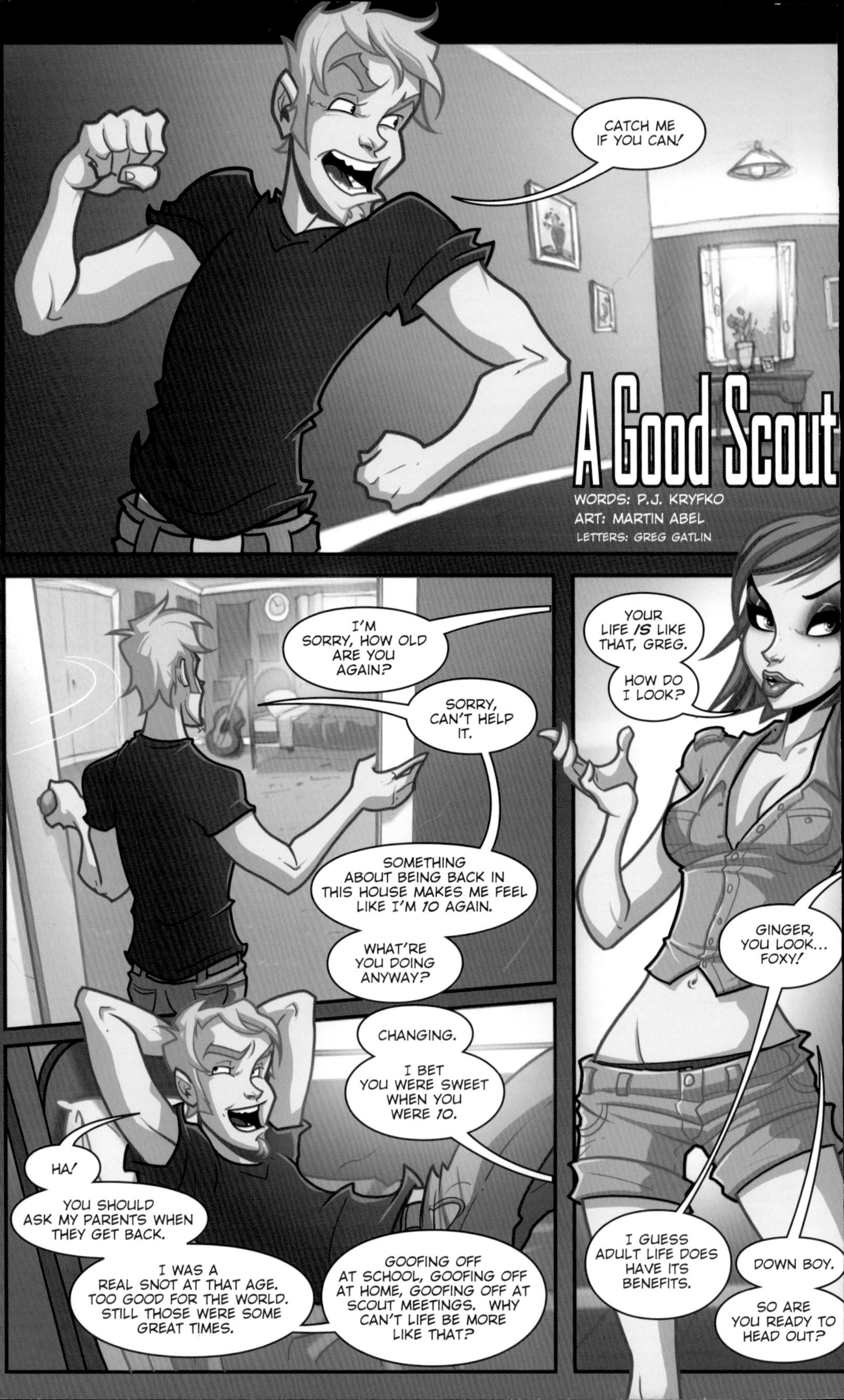
CATCH ME IF YOU CAN!
A Good Scout
WORDS: P.J. KRYFKO
ART: MARTIN ABEL
LETTERS: GREG GATLIN
I'M SORRY, HOW OLD ARE YOU AGAIN?
SORRY, CAN'T HELP IT.
SOMETHING ABOUT BEING BACK IN THIS HOUSE MAKES ME FEEL LIKE I'M 10 AGAIN.
WHAT'RE YOU DOING ANYWAY?
CHANGING.
I BET YOU WERE SWEET WHEN YOU WERE 10.
HA!
YOU SHOULD ASK MY PARENTS WHEN THEY GET BACK.
I WAS A REAL SNOT AT THAT AGE. TOO GOOD FOR THE WORLD. STILL THOSE WERE SOME GREAT TIMES.
GOOFING OFF AT SCHOOL, GOOFING OFF AT HOME, GOOFING OFF AT SCOUT MEETINGS. WHY CAN'T LIFE BE MORE LIKE THAT?
YOUR LIFE IS LIKE THAT, GREG.
HOW DO I LOOK?
GINGER, YOU LOOK... FOXY!
I GUESS ADULT LIFE DOES HAVE ITS BENEFITS.
DOWN BOY.
SO ARE YOU READY TO HEAD OUT?

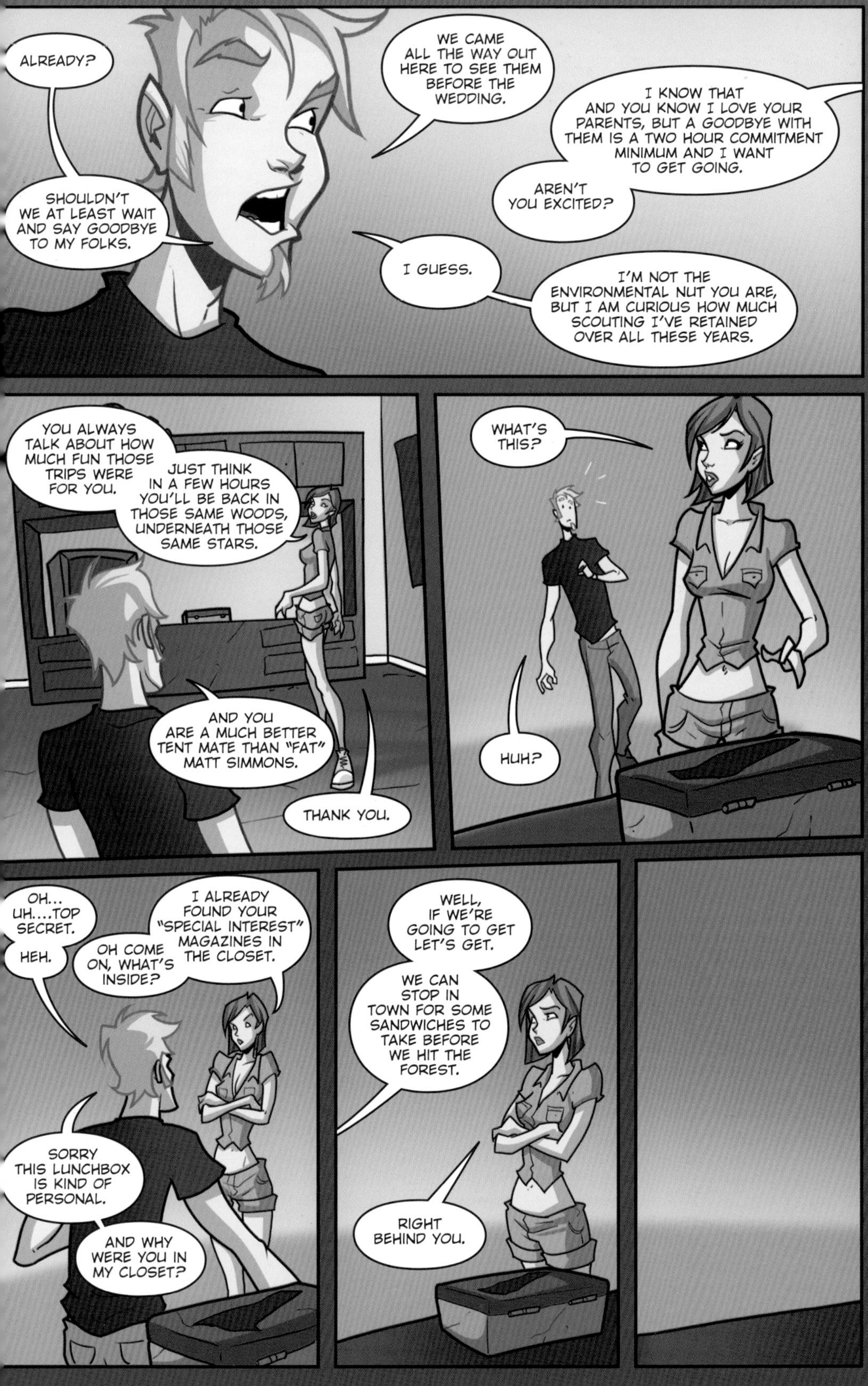
ALREADY?
SHOULDN'T WE AT LEAST WAIT AND SAY GOODBYE TO MY FOLKS.
WE CAME ALL THE WAY OUT HERE TO SEE THEM BEFORE THE WEDDING.
I KNOW THAT AND YOU KNOW I LOVE YOUR PARENTS, BUT A GOODBYE WITH THEM IS A TWO HOUR COMMITMENT MINIMUM AND I WANT TO GET GOING.
AREN'T YOU EXCITED?
I GUESS.
I'M NOT THE ENVIRONMENTAL NUT YOU ARE, BUT I AM CURIOUS HOW MUCH SCOUTING I'VE RETAINED OVER ALL THESE YEARS.
YOU ALWAYS TALK ABOUT HOW MUCH FUN THOSE TRIPS WERE FOR YOU.
JUST THINK IN A FEW HOURS YOU'LL BE BACK IN THOSE SAME WOODS, UNDERNEATH THOSE SAME STARS.
AND YOU ARE A MUCH BETTER TENT MATE THAN "FAT" MATT SIMMONS.
THANK YOU.
WHAT'S THIS?
HUH?
OH... UH....TOP SECRET.
HEH.
I ALREADY FOUND YOUR "SPECIAL INTEREST" MAGAZINES IN THE CLOSET.
OH COME ON, WHAT'S INSIDE?
SORRY THIS LUNCHBOX IS KIND OF PERSONAL.
AND WHY WERE YOU IN MY CLOSET?
WELL, IF WE'RE GOING TO GET LET'S GET.
WE CAN STOP IN TOWN FOR SOME SANDWICHES TO TAKE BEFORE WE HIT THE FOREST.
RIGHT BEHIND YOU.

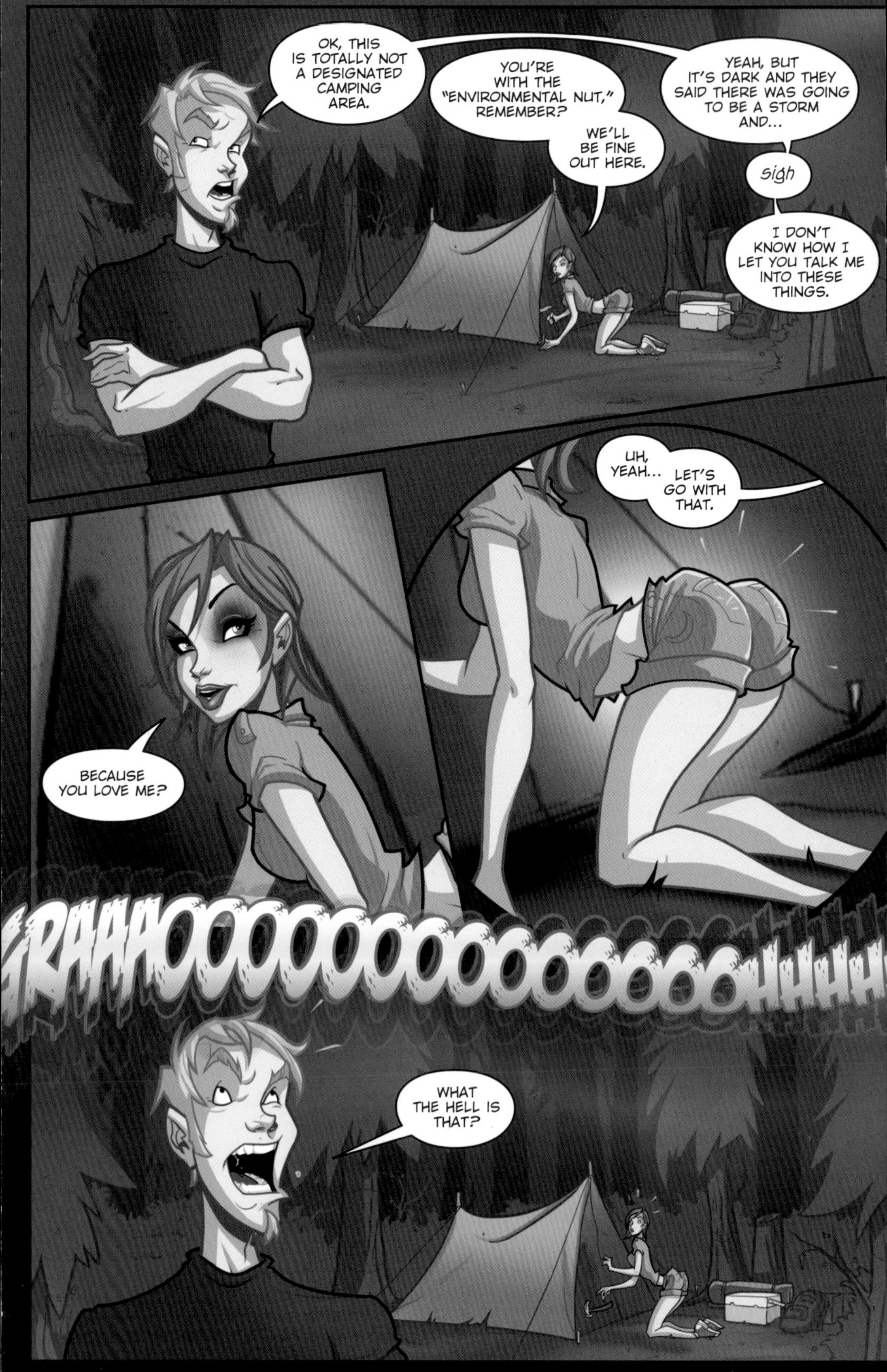
OK, THIS IS TOTALLY NOT A DESIGNATED CAMPING AREA.
YOU'RE WITH THE "ENVIRONMENTAL NUT," REMEMBER?
WE'LL BE FINE OUT HERE.
YEAH, BUT IT'S DARK AND THEY SAID THERE WAS GOING TO BE A STORM AND...
sigh
I DON'T KNOW HOW I LET YOU TALK ME INTO THESE THINGS.
BECAUSE YOU LOVE ME?
UH, YEAH... LET'S GO WITH THAT.
GRAAAOOOOOOOOOOOOOOOHHHHH
WHAT THE HELL IS THAT?

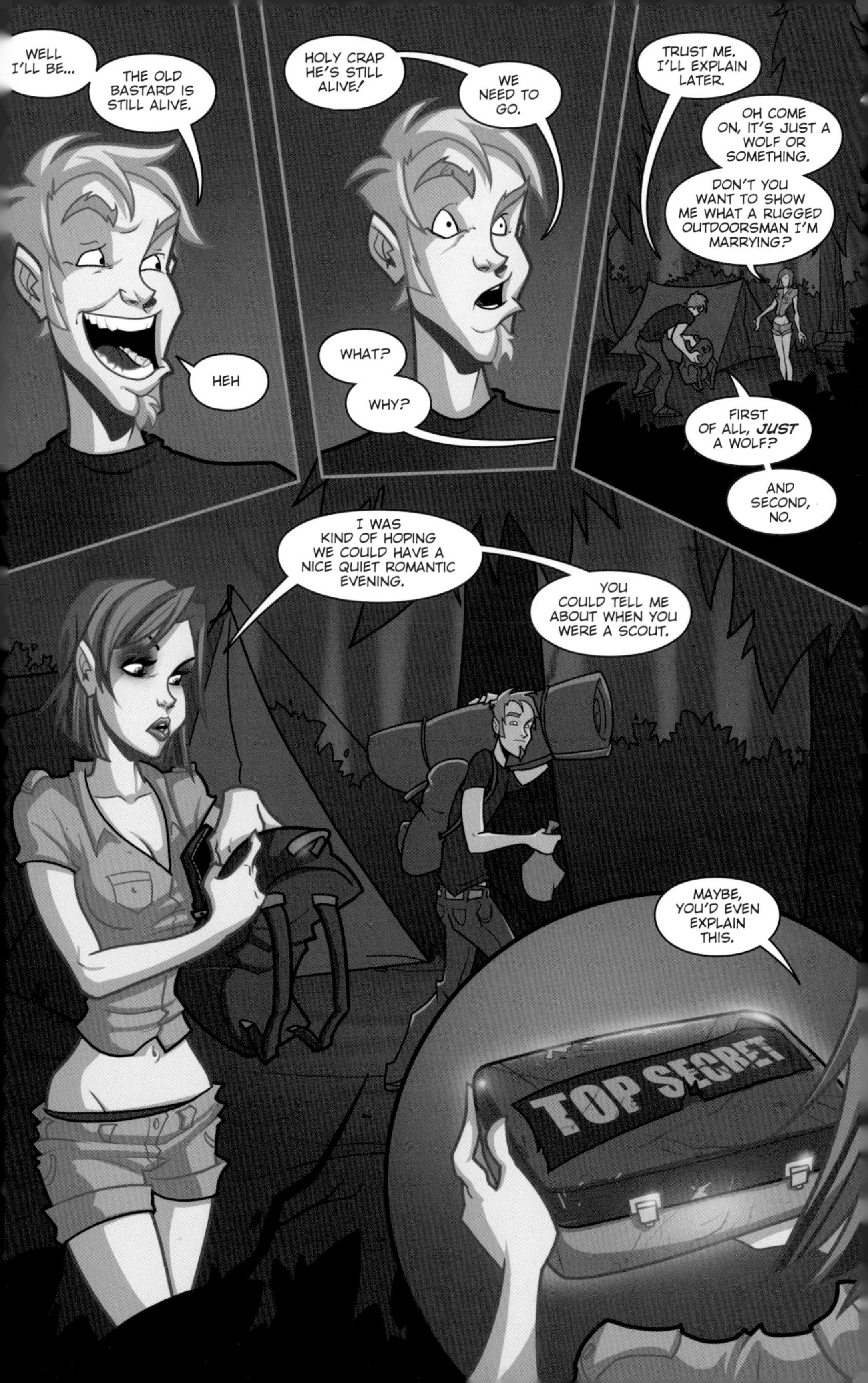
WELL I'LL BE...
THE OLD BASTARD IS STILL ALIVE.
HEH
HOLY CRAP HE'S STILL ALIVE!
WE NEED TO GO.
WHAT?
WHY?
TRUST ME. I'LL EXPLAIN LATER.
OH COME ON, IT'S JUST A WOLF OR SOMETHING.
DON'T YOU WANT TO SHOW ME WHAT A RUGGED OUTDOORSMAN I'M MARRYING?
FIRST OF ALL, ***JUST*** A WOLF?
AND SECOND, NO.
I WAS KIND OF HOPING WE COULD HAVE A NICE QUIET ROMANTIC EVENING.
YOU COULD TELL ME ABOUT WHEN YOU WERE A SCOUT.
MAYBE, YOU'D EVEN EXPLAIN THIS.
TOP SECRET

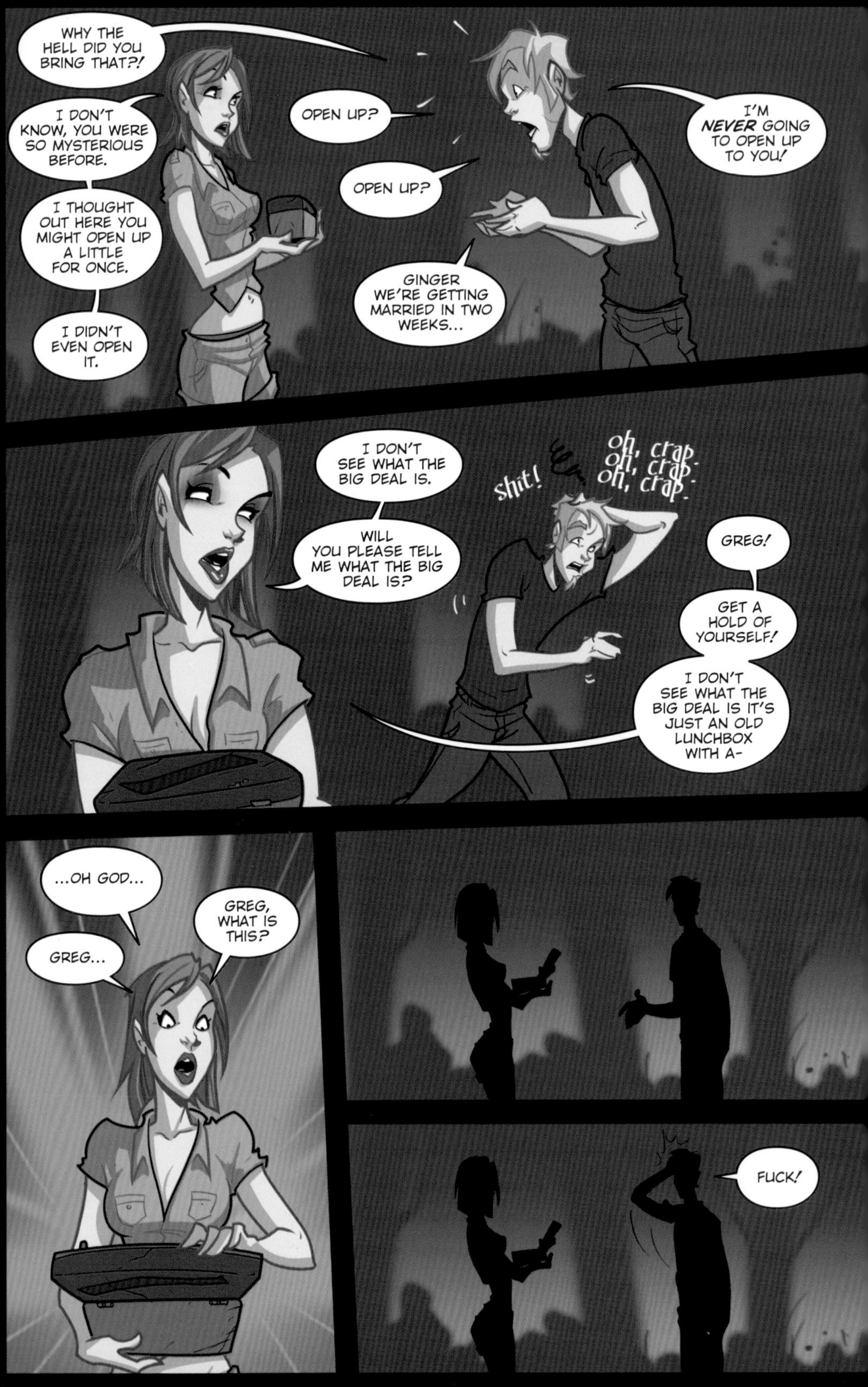
WHY THE HELL DID YOU BRING THAT?!
I DON'T KNOW, YOU WERE SO MYSTERIOUS BEFORE.
I THOUGHT OUT HERE YOU MIGHT OPEN UP A LITTLE FOR ONCE.
I DIDN'T EVEN OPEN IT.
OPEN UP?
OPEN UP?
GINGER WE'RE GETTING MARRIED IN TWO WEEKS...
I'M **NEVER** GOING TO OPEN UP TO YOU!
I DON'T SEE WHAT THE BIG DEAL IS.
WILL YOU PLEASE TELL ME WHAT THE BIG DEAL IS?
shit!
oh, crap. oh, crap. oh, crap.
GREG!
GET A HOLD OF YOURSELF!
I DON'T SEE WHAT THE BIG DEAL IS IT'S JUST AN OLD LUNCHBOX WITH A-
...OH GOD...
GREG...
GREG, WHAT IS THIS?
FUCK!

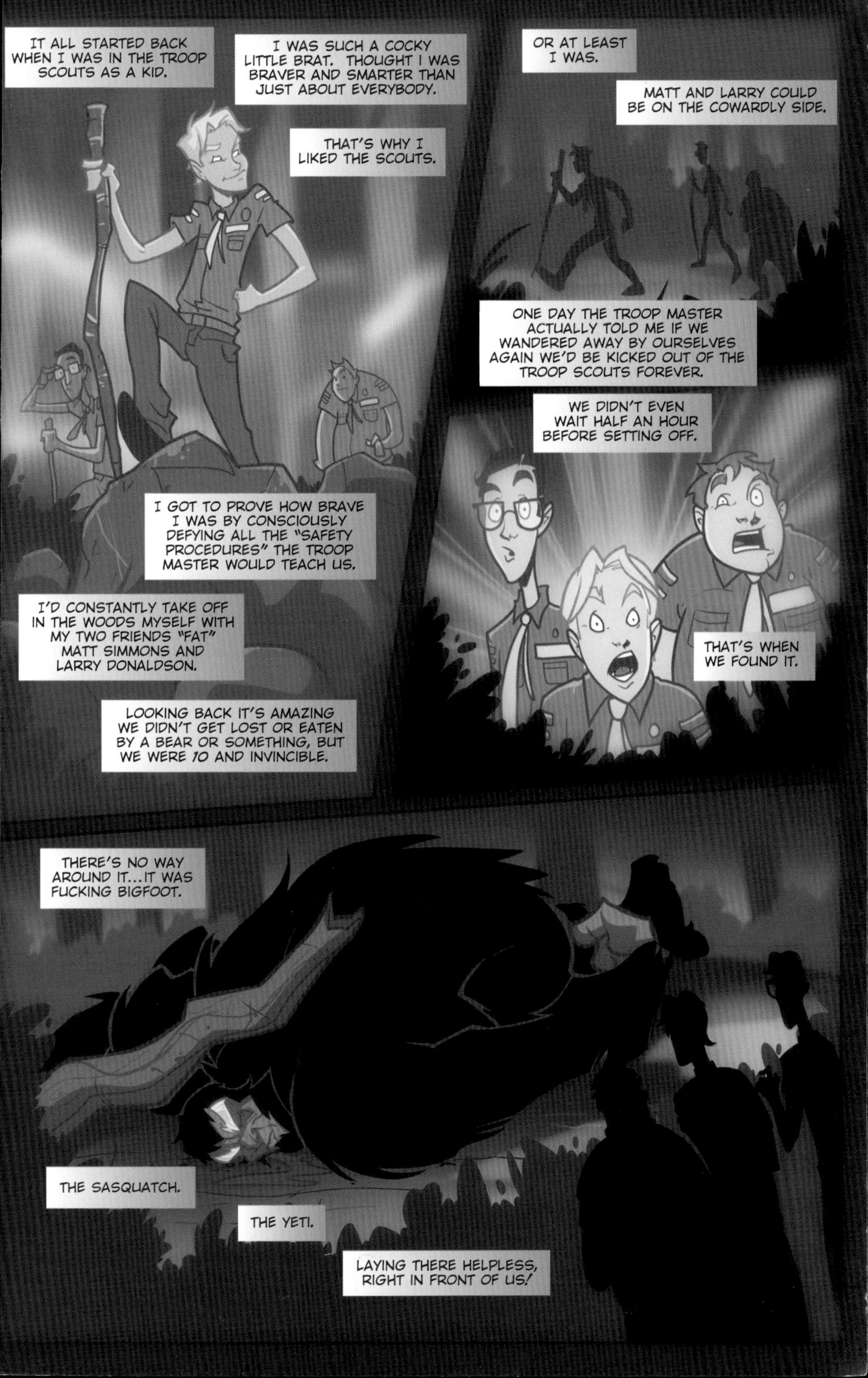
IT ALL STARTED BACK WHEN I WAS IN THE TROOP SCOUTS AS A KID.
I WAS SUCH A COCKY LITTLE BRAT. THOUGHT I WAS BRAVER AND SMARTER THAN JUST ABOUT EVERYBODY.
THAT'S WHY I LIKED THE SCOUTS.
I GOT TO PROVE HOW BRAVE I WAS BY CONSCIOUSLY DEFYING ALL THE "SAFETY PROCEDURES" THE TROOP MASTER WOULD TEACH US.
I'D CONSTANTLY TAKE OFF IN THE WOODS MYSELF WITH MY TWO FRIENDS "FAT" MATT SIMMONS AND LARRY DONALDSON.
LOOKING BACK IT'S AMAZING WE DIDN'T GET LOST OR EATEN BY A BEAR OR SOMETHING, BUT WE WERE *10* AND INVINCIBLE.
OR AT LEAST I WAS.
MATT AND LARRY COULD BE ON THE COWARDLY SIDE.
ONE DAY THE TROOP MASTER ACTUALLY TOLD ME IF WE WANDERED AWAY BY OURSELVES AGAIN WE'D BE KICKED OUT OF THE TROOP SCOUTS FOREVER.
WE DIDN'T EVEN WAIT HALF AN HOUR BEFORE SETTING OFF.
THAT'S WHEN WE FOUND IT.
THERE'S NO WAY AROUND IT...IT WAS FUCKING BIGFOOT.
THE SASQUATCH.
THE YETI.
LAYING THERE HELPLESS, RIGHT IN FRONT OF US!

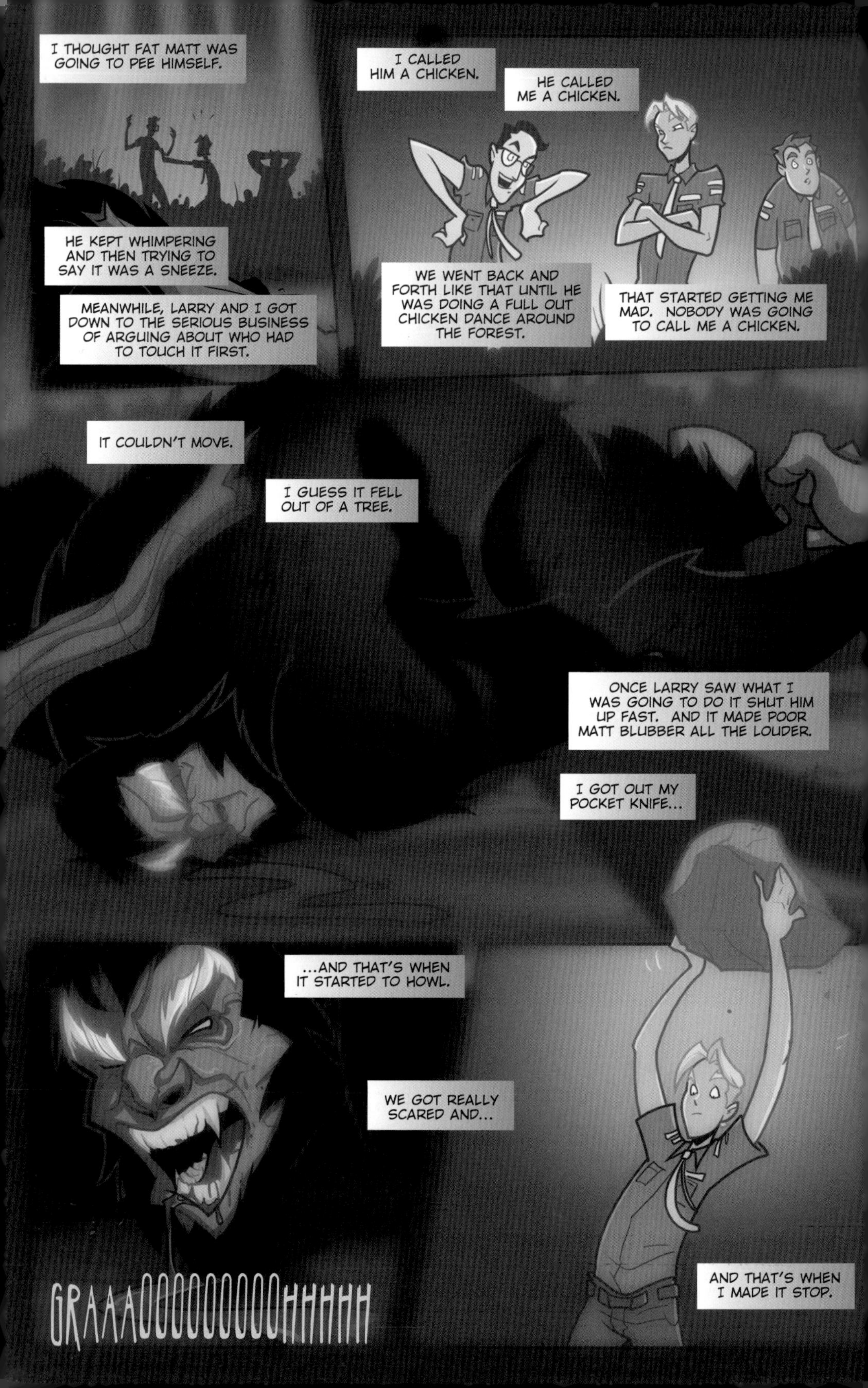
I THOUGHT FAT MATT WAS GOING TO PEE HIMSELF.
HE KEPT WHIMPERING AND THEN TRYING TO SAY IT WAS A SNEEZE.
MEANWHILE, LARRY AND I GOT DOWN TO THE SERIOUS BUSINESS OF ARGUING ABOUT WHO HAD TO TOUCH IT FIRST.
I CALLED HIM A CHICKEN.
HE CALLED ME A CHICKEN.
WE WENT BACK AND FORTH LIKE THAT UNTIL HE WAS DOING A FULL OUT CHICKEN DANCE AROUND THE FOREST.
THAT STARTED GETTING ME MAD. NOBODY WAS GOING TO CALL ME A CHICKEN.
IT COULDN'T MOVE.
I GUESS IT FELL OUT OF A TREE.
ONCE LARRY SAW WHAT I WAS GOING TO DO IT SHUT HIM UP FAST. AND IT MADE POOR MATT BLUBBER ALL THE LOUDER.
I GOT OUT MY POCKET KNIFE...
...AND THAT'S WHEN IT STARTED TO HOWL.
WE GOT REALLY SCARED AND...
GRAAAOOOOOOOOOHHHHH
AND THAT'S WHEN I MADE IT STOP.

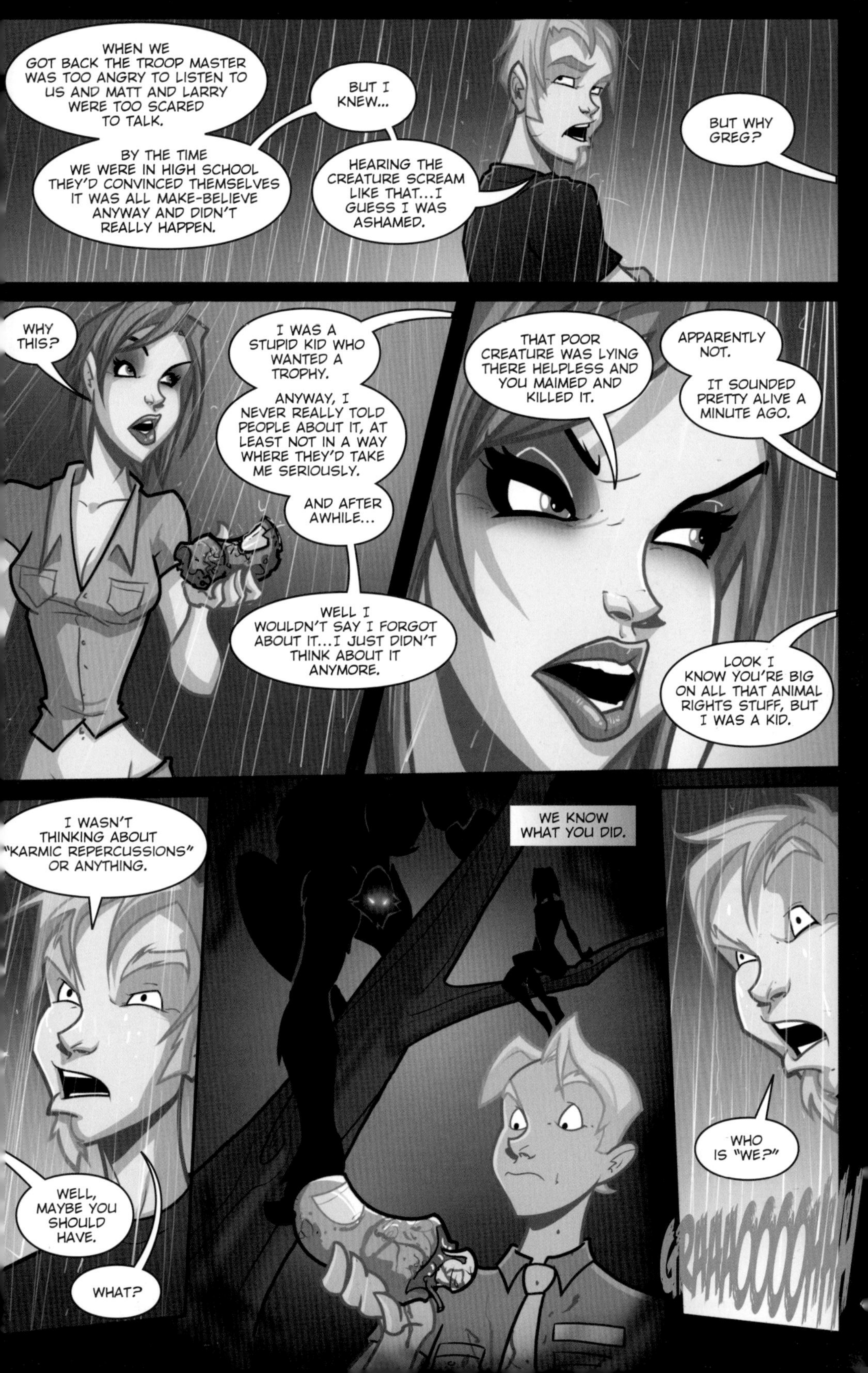
WHEN WE GOT BACK THE TROOP MASTER WAS TOO ANGRY TO LISTEN TO US AND MATT AND LARRY WERE TOO SCARED TO TALK.
BY THE TIME WE WERE IN HIGH SCHOOL THEY'D CONVINCED THEMSELVES IT WAS ALL MAKE-BELIEVE ANYWAY AND DIDN'T REALLY HAPPEN.
BUT I KNEW...
HEARING THE CREATURE SCREAM LIKE THAT...I GUESS I WAS ASHAMED.
BUT WHY GREG?
WHY THIS?
I WAS A STUPID KID WHO WANTED A TROPHY.
ANYWAY, I NEVER REALLY TOLD PEOPLE ABOUT IT, AT LEAST NOT IN A WAY WHERE THEY'D TAKE ME SERIOUSLY.
AND AFTER AWHILE...
WELL I WOULDN'T SAY I FORGOT ABOUT IT...I JUST DIDN'T THINK ABOUT IT ANYMORE.
THAT POOR CREATURE WAS LYING THERE HELPLESS AND YOU MAIMED AND KILLED IT.
APPARENTLY NOT.
IT SOUNDED PRETTY ALIVE A MINUTE AGO.
LOOK I KNOW YOU'RE BIG ON ALL THAT ANIMAL RIGHTS STUFF, BUT I WAS A KID.
I WASN'T THINKING ABOUT "KARMIC REPERCUSSIONS" OR ANYTHING.
WELL, MAYBE YOU SHOULD HAVE.
WHAT?
WE KNOW WHAT YOU DID.
WHO IS "WE?"
GRAAOOOOHH

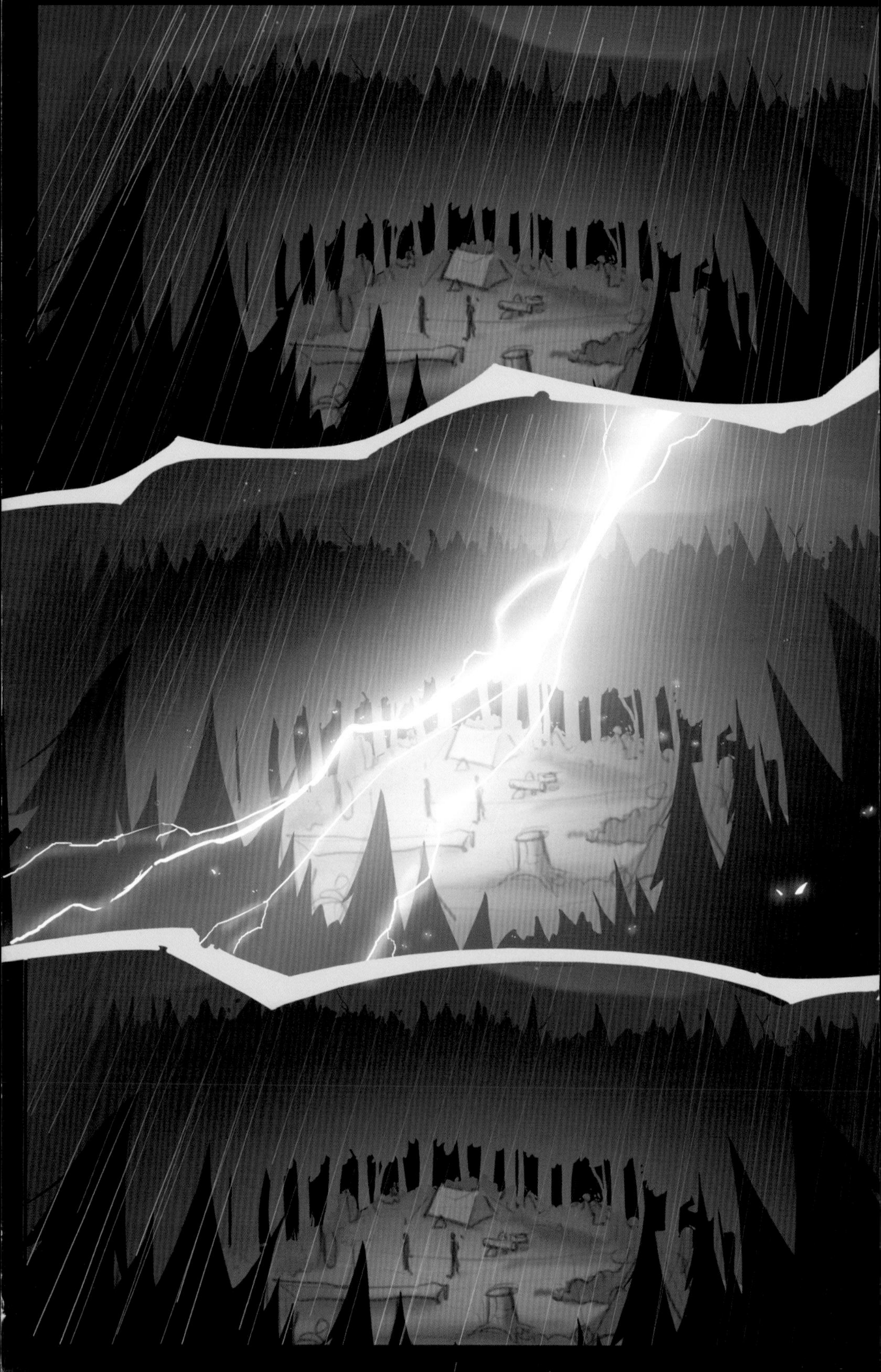

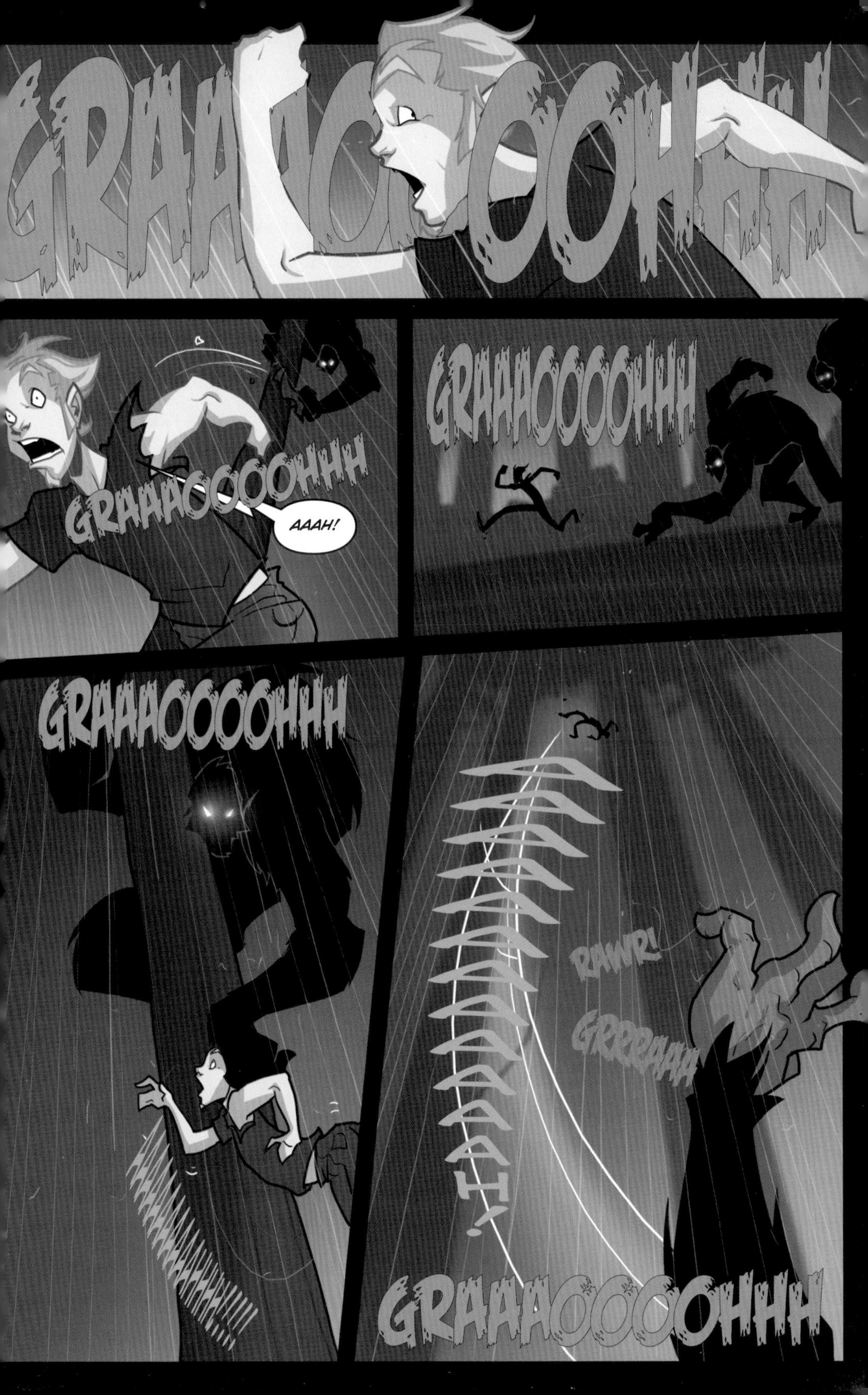
GRAAOOOOHHH
GRAAAOOOOHHH
AAAH!
GRAAAOOOOHHH
GRAAAOOOOHHH
AAAAAAAAAAAAAH!
RAWR!
GRRRAAAH
GRAAAOOOOHHH

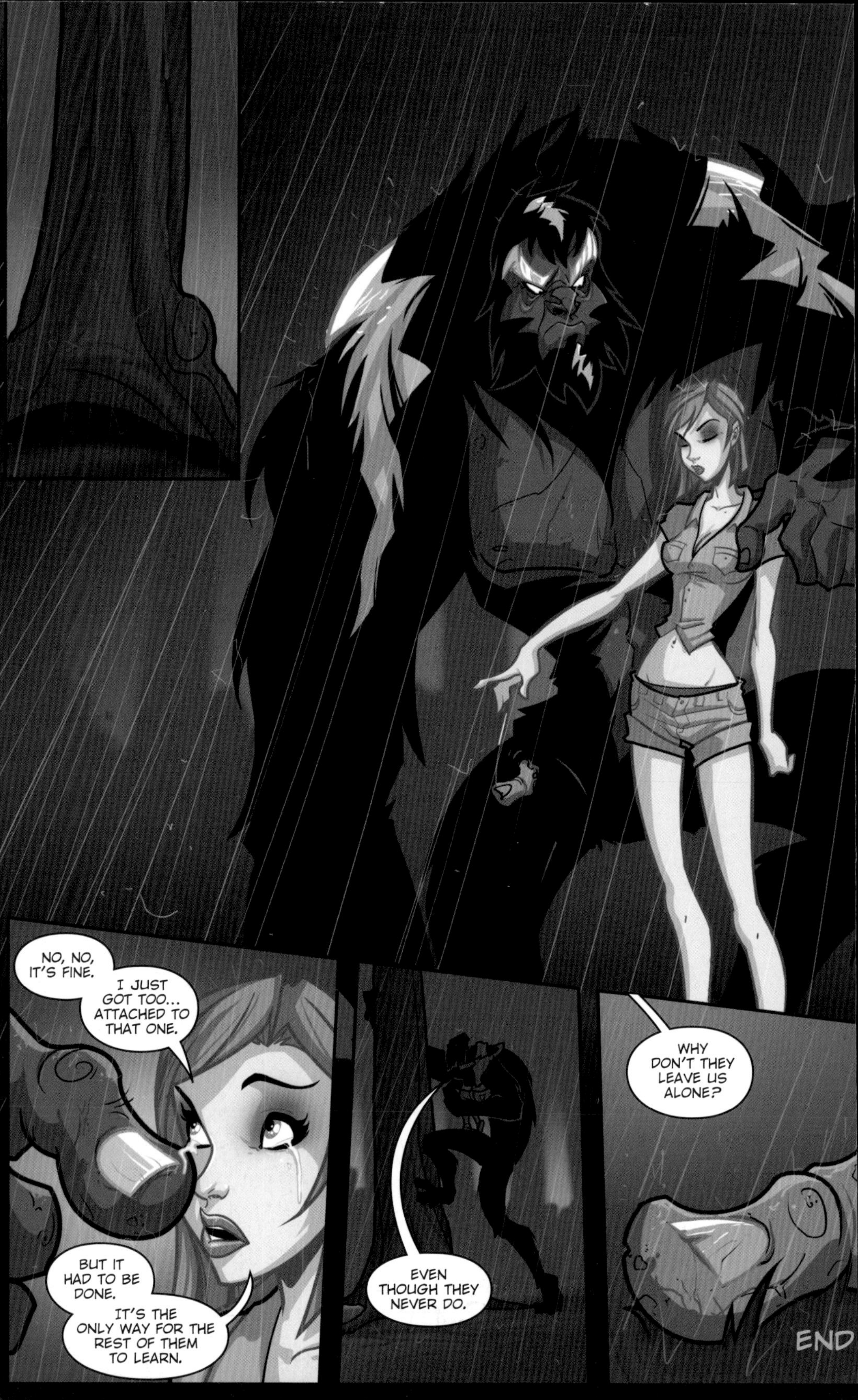
NO, NO, IT'S FINE.
I JUST GOT TOO... ATTACHED TO THAT ONE.
BUT IT HAD TO BE DONE.
IT'S THE ONLY WAY FOR THE REST OF THEM TO LEARN.
EVEN THOUGH THEY NEVER DO.
WHY DON'T THEY LEAVE US ALONE?
END

THE SASQUATCH CREW

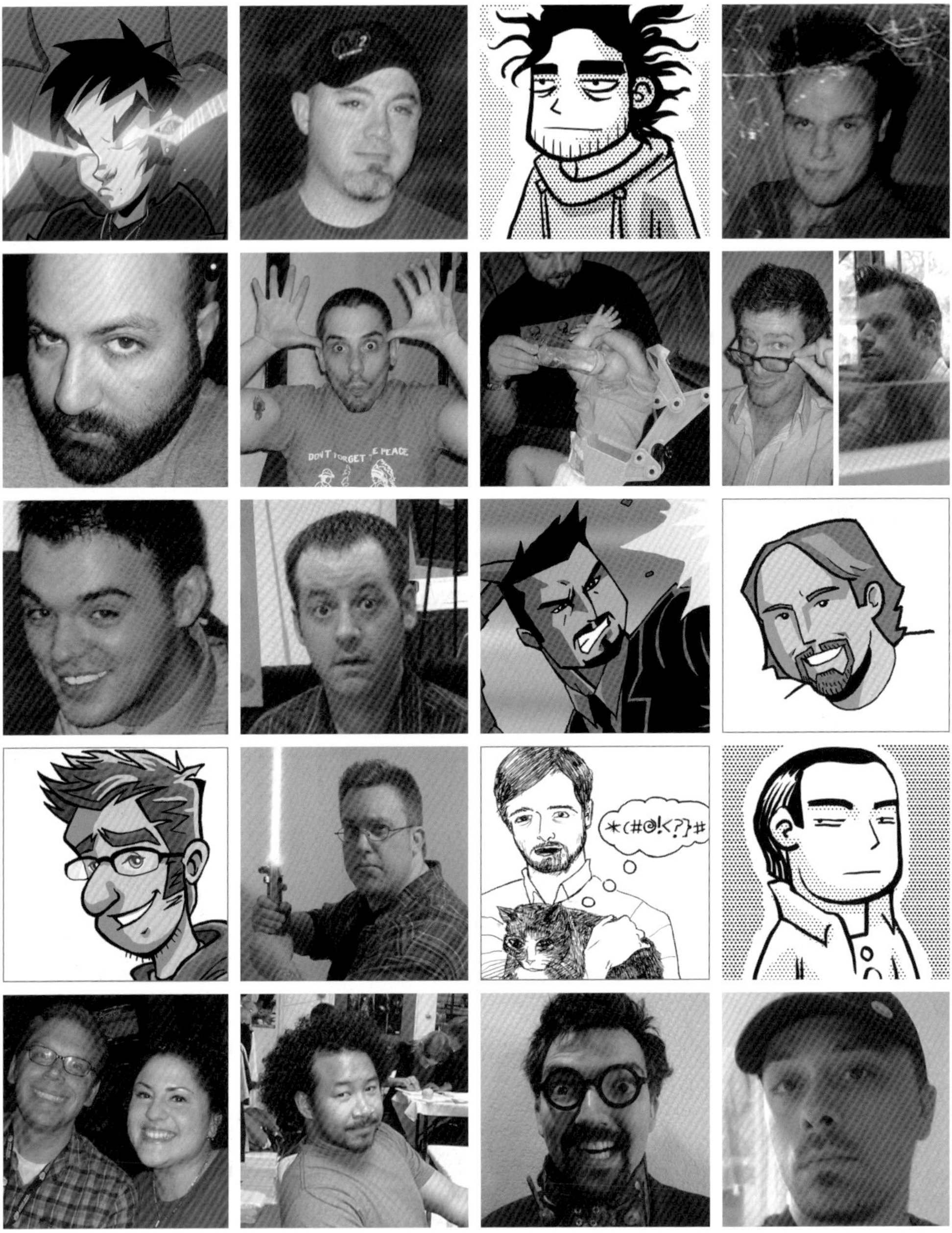
*(#@!<?}#

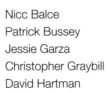

Martin Abel
Mykal Adyms
Nicc Balce
Bryan Baugh
Josh Boulet
Jason M. Burns
Patrick Bussey
Robin & Lawrence Etherington
Brant Fowler
Otis Frampton
Jessie Garza
Greg Gatlin
Andy "ND!" Genen
Grant Gould
Christopher Graybill
Andrew Gualberto
Benjamin & Marlena Hall
Paul Harmon
David Hartman
Josh Howard

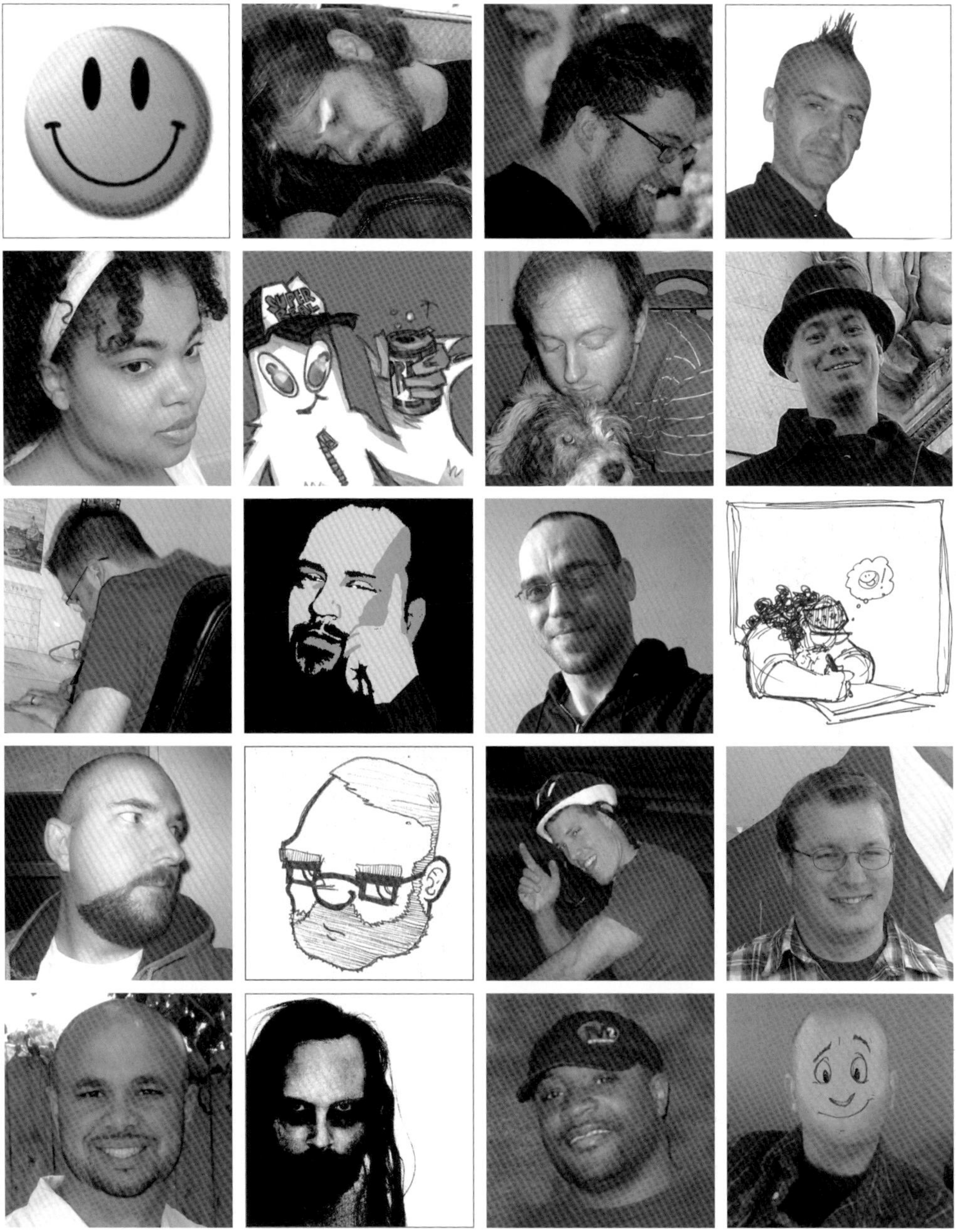

Courtney Huddleston
P.J. Kryfko
Tom Kurzanski
Guy Lemay
Frances Liddell
Jason Martin
Jeff McClelland
Matthew McClean
Wes Molebash
Alex Ness
Duane Redhead
Tone Rodriguez
Justin Stewart
Brian Thompson
Neil Thompson
Sean Thornton
William Wilson
Christopher C. Wolf
Mario Wytch
Scott Zirkel

Currently living all the way down in Australia, **Martin Abel** is an illustrator mostly working for magazines such as *Official Xbox Magazine* and *Maximum PC*. He enjoys caffeine a lot more than he should, likes the mysteries of life and even once dated a Sasquatch. Check out more of Martin's work at www.martinabel.com.

Mykal Adyms is co-founder of M2 Studio based in Moore, Oklahoma. He is a colorist/creator of *BattleGrounds*, M2 Studio's debut book. He has worked coloring various covers for such titles as *Ezra/Muse*, *Superstar* and colored the *Angel Quest* posters that appeared on HBO's *Entourage* season 2 episode 9. His art can be seen at www.m-2studio.com.

Nicc Balce began drawing by tracing mecha from old japanese magazines and doodling on walls and furniture while watching *Back to the Future* or *Star Wars* on vhs back in the 80's. Little did he know that over two decades later, his own comic *Random Encounter* and freelance illustration gig would occupy most of his time and keep him from going back to tracing mecha and doodling on walls and furniture. That said, he still watches *Star Wars* and *Back to the future*. More of Nicc's work can be seen at www.the-null.com.

Bryan Baugh regularly works as a storyboard artist in the animation industry. He has worked for Disney Animation, Warner Bros., Sony Television Animation, and other companies. His credits include shows such as *The Batman*, *Jackie Chan Adventures*, *Roughnecks: The Starship Troopers Chronicles*, *Teenage Mutant Ninja Turtles*, *Harold and the Purple Crayon*, *Men in Black*, *Masters of the Universe*, and *My Friends Tigger and Pooh*. He illustrated the graphic novel *The Expendable One* for Viper Comics, and also writes and illustrates his own comic book creation, *Wulf and Batsy*. He lives in Thousand Oaks, California, with his lovely wife, Monica, and three bloodthirsty killer cats. You can view more of his work at his website, www.cryptlogic.net.

Josh Boulet eats meat, drinks beer, and draws comic books.

Born and raised in Massachusetts where he began his writing career as an entertainment journalist, **Jason M. Burns** made the leap into comic books in 2004, quickly establishing himself as a unique talent with his first graphic novel, *The Expendable One*, as well as the critically acclaimed series *A Dummy's Guide to Danger*. Refusing to slow down, Burns is scheduled to release more than ten titles throughout 2007 and 2008, while also continuing to work in the film and television industry where he will direct his first feature later this year.

Patrick Bussey lives in Texas with his wife and daughter, where he plays with toys, draws dumb stuff, and likes to eat Little Caesar's Pizza. Pat also graduated from the Art Institute of Dallas with Brian Thompson, but some how still managed to get a job afterward.

Robin and **Lawrence Etherington: Studio Blink Twice** was founded in 2003 with a single goal: to breathe excitement and fun into paper and pixels. Having established their reputation with the Eagle-Award nominated (Favourite British Black and White Comicbook) *Malcolm Magic* 12-issue series, the Etheringtons are now working full time on their premier full-colour title, *MOON!*, which is scheduled for an international release in January 2008. People seem to like them because they are polite and are rarely late. Visit www.studioblinktwice.com to check more of their work.

Brant W. Fowler is a freelance writer and letterer currently residing in Kentucky. Brant is also EIC of www.silverbulletcomics.com, an internet columnist, a former Editor-In-Chief of two small comic companies, and regular blogger. Throughout most of the internet he is known as "Gonzogoose" or simply "Gonzo" for reasons he declines to comment on.

Otis Frampton is a 34 year old writer and illustrator best known for creating the Viper Comics series *Oddly Normal*. His illustration credits include work for such clients as Lucasfilm, Marvel Comics, Topps Trading Card Company, New Line Cinema and DC Comics. He is currently working on a new graphic novel as well as the sequels to *Oddly Normal*. You can learn more about Otis and his work by visiting otisframpton.com.

Jessie Garza is the president of Viper Comics and lives in Dallas, Texas with his wife, Aurora, and his biggest fan (his daughter) Caitlin Garza. To this day he hasn't broken the news to her that he does not draw or write comics.

After being chosen to be Arnold's replacement in a new series of *Terminator* movies and then being summarily fired for defiling Maria's private bath, **Greg Gatlin** set out on a soul searching trek across America. Through random selection, he was recruited by the Astrological Badger's Association (a secretive government homeowners association) and was taught all known forms of marital arts for the right side of his body and the art of deep sea origami for the left. Now possessing a lifetime supply of licorice sticks, Greg uses his powers to make comics.

He really should have learned something serious instead, but no he didn't want to listen... so now the Luxemburgish born **Andy "ND!" Genen** lives in Brussels where he works as a freelance comic-book-artist/illustrator. Duh! Well, at least he got his graphic novel *De leschte Ritter* printed in Luxemburg in November 2005 and now really hopes for more to come! See more of his work at scoundreldaze.deviantart.com.

Grant Gould is a Minnesota based illustrator who's worked for Lucasfilm (StarWars.com Kids Features, Celebration IV Artwork), Topps (*Star Wars, Episode III: Revenge of the Sith*, *Star Wars 30th Anniversary*, *The Lord of the Rings: Evolution*, and *The Lord of the Rings: Masterpieces*), Rittenhouse Archives (*Marvel Heroes: The Complete Avengers*, *DC Comics: Heroes and Villains*), Green Ronin Publishing (*Mutants & Masterminds* RPG), and more. Grant's also done some comic pin-up work for IDW's *Wormwood: Gentleman Corpse* and Viper Comics' *Oddly Normal*. Check out his website at GrantGould.com.

Christopher Graybill's soul has struggled strenuously to adapt to this chaotic planet. It finds most relief in drawing funny pictures about stuff. It currently resides in San Francisco working on a project called zebratron.com.

Andrew Gualberto is somewhat unique, almost interested at doing anything. His talent for writing eventually began during grade school when he and Nicc Balce joined a club to write for the school paper. After a few years, he was introduced to *Random Encounter* which Nicc created and asked to make any comments or suggestions. Inspired by the ideas Drew came up with, Nicc invited him to become a co-writer on *Random Encounter* and other future works.

Benjamin and **Marlena Hall** have been working together in comics since 2003. Their first book together was *Knights of the Dinner Table: Everknights #7* and they've continued on to do several short stories and the 3 issue series *Dead@17: Protectorate*. They are married and live in Texas. Visit them online at www. blueskycomics.com.

Paul Harmon lives in Los Angeles and works in comics and animation. His comic work includes *Mora*, *Sea of Red*, *Flight* and *Welcome to Falling Oaks*. Check out his website at www.dogmeatsausage.com.

David Hartman has worked in the animation industry for almost a decade as everything from a storyboard artist to Character designer to an Emmy nominated Director and everything in-between. His credits include *MTV'S Spiderman, Roughnecks: The Starship Troopers Chronicles, Astro Boy, Jackie Chan Adventures, Winnie the Pooh* and many more. He also does horror illustration work for comic books and magazines, makes short films about freaks and monsters and was the Visual FX supervisor on the cult film *Bubba Ho-Tep*. He recently directed two blood-soaked, animated music videos for Rob Zombie. You can see more of his stuff at his website www.sideshowmonkey.com

Josh Howard is the creator of *Dead@17*, and was recently named as one of the top 7 biggest icons in indie comics by *Wizard Magazine*. His other works include *Black Harvest* (Devil's Due) and *The Lost Books of Eve* (Viper Comics) and the upcoming *Clubbing* from DC/Minx. Josh lives in Arlington, Texas with his wife and two children. More of his work can be seen at www.joshhoward.net.

Little is known about **Courtney Huddleston**. What we do know is that he's from Mississippi, and that he is indeed a guy. When he's not trying to teach himself how to draw, he's usually spending time playing Dad, significant other, or some other silly game. See more of his work at www. courtneyhuddleston.com.

Though this is **P.J. Kryfko's** first written comic work he's been working the field for several years as an editor, journalist, and critic. You can visit him on-line at myspace.com/pjkryfko.

Tom Kurzanski is an illustrator and writer in New York City whose artistic body of work includes an adaptation of *Antigone*, *Karma Incorporated*, *Legends of the Middle-Man: the League of Professional Jealousy*, and *the Comic Book Project* from Dark Horse and Columbia Teachers College. He is currently at work on the first in a series of self-published children's books entitled *the Liar of Orpheus*, and collaborating on an original graphic novel for Viper. In his spare time, he is a fighter pilot in the movie: *Top Gun*. Visit his site at www.tomkurzanski.com.

Guy LeMay is a man of many talents. After shattering his punk rock dreams as a guitarist, he jumped into the field of comic book arts. After all, this may have been his true calling. He is an avid collector of comics and an aspiring artist since the age of 8. Guy has illustrated such comics as Gone South, *The Sparrow* - featured in *Dead@17,Rough Cut*: Vol.2 as well as various pin ups featured in many comic books. Be on the lookout for his latest project... *RABID*. He is very passionate about his art and hopes to continue to be successful with it.

Frances Olivia Liddell was born in 1978 in Jackson, Mississippi. She now resides in San Francisco, California where she is completing a Master of Fine Arts in Graphic Design at the Academy of Art University. Frances is a skilled designer, illustrator and loves working within the comics medium. Current projects include pencils for a new graphic novel written by Jason M. Burns, *Confessions* and her own graphic novel, *Grey*.

An active camper living and raised in the great northwest, **Jason Martin** can tell you firsthand that Bigfoot is real, and he likes to drink beer. So, if you're ever pitching a tent in Sasquatch country, be sure and stock your coolers with PBR, 'cuz Harry's developed a taste for the regions multitude of micro brews, and won't trash your camp for the cheap stuff. When Jason's not sharing brewskis with Bigfoot, he likes to work on his comic, *Super Real*. Be sure to checkout his site at SuperRealGraphics.com.

Jeff McClelland once lived in an apartment complex that actually served as the setting for a 1997 Bigfoot sighting (http://www.bfro.net/GDB/show_report.asp?id=5262). He believes the hype. You can read more of Jeff's work in *Strip Search* from Dark Horse Comics and the upcoming *Battle Grounds* series from 01 Comics and M2 Studio. Contact the man himself at andromedajonesart@yahoo.com.

Matthew McLean lives in beautiful Colorado. He is currently operating under the delusion that he is a writer. Additional works of his can be found at madbastard.hypersites.com.

Wes Molebash is the creator of the webcomic, *You'll Have That*, which is published by Viper Comics. Wes lives in Southern Ohio with his hot wife, Tricia, and their two cats, Sophie and Stella. When he's not drawing comics, Wes is playing videogames, watching movies, and avoiding household chores. His webcomic can be read at www.yhtcomic.com.

Alex Ness is a writer who has spent most of his life reading comics. He has also spent many years being educated in the field of history, working in comic stores, and shoveling snow in his beloved state of Minnesota. He has written poetry as well as prose for over 35 years and has written online about comics across the internet and at his own website PopThought.com since 2002.

Duane Redhead. Artist: *Teddy and the Yeti*, *Onyx Cross*, *2000AD*, Games Workshop.

Tone Rodriguez works out of "NORTH HOLLYWOOD," his family estate in Los Angeles, CA and comes from a long line of comic artists, his grandfather created *Dirty Debbie's Dollhouse* (the book was banned in most retail outlets back in 1962, and probably was responsible for his untimely death). Enough about that, Tone has drawn *Violent Messiahs*, *Snake Plisskin*, *The Simpson's Treehouse Of Horror*, *The Covenant*, *The U.T.F.* and a whole bunch of other stuff, including a short story in the HERO Initiative book due out in march, titled *The Unusual Suspects*, and covers and short story's for Ape Entertainment's *Bizarre New World*... but his all time favorite short story ever, ever, ever is something he's done for Viper Comics... he thinks that Bigfoot was in it, maybe?

Justin Stewart lives in Lexington, Kentucky. He's like to draw stuff, but mostly colors and letters other folks' stuff using his computer. His weekly webcomic can be found at www.poppedculture.net, along with said stuff he's done for himself and others.

Brian Thompson attended the Art Institute of Dallas with a full scholarship thanks to Abe Lincoln's head. Afterwards he left Dallas to live in the wilderness, eating only bugs and fast food, where he still remains to this day.

Neil Thompson is a man of many talents, but after discovering that those talents mostly revolved around grunt labor and head-butting, he decided to try his hand at football, basketball, bagpipes, running taco kiosks, hand-puppetry, and deep-sea snorkeling. Coming up short on those as well, he pursued Will Wilson's real passion of comic books. Today, he splits his time between Santa Monica and a Hyundai Accent.

Sean Thornton who? Mid-western born and raised, slightly overweight, under height fan-boy, artist wannabe. Yes, that sums him up nicely. Formally educated in Graphic Design at Illinois State University, Sean works in the field of graphic design at Osborn & Delong, located in Bloomington, IL, where he resides with his lovely wife Angela and "metro" feline, (as my boss refers to him) Louie.

William Wilson started his career writing an animated feature for John Carpenter and followed that up by writing his first comic book, a *G.I. Joe Frontline* one shot. Currently, he is writing a super hero epic *Born And Bred* with his writing partner and personal bodyguard, Neil Thompson and his spiritual comic book guru Tone Rodriguez. Married to his beautiful wife Tiffany, William lives in Los Angeles where he one day longs to discover his superpowers.

Writer and creator **Christopher H. Wolf** enjoys working on webcomics and online games, both of which can be found on his homepage at doompuppet.com. A long-time lover of comics, he's also developed online resources for other creators to use as well. He's also been mistaken for a Sasquatch on several occasions, leading to zany hijinks.

Mario Wytch is co-founder of M2 Studio based in Moore, Oklahoma. He is a penciler/inker/creator of *BattleGrounds*, M2 Studio's debut title. He has worked on such projects as *Myth*, *Armor EV*, and various projects for Quest comics. His work can be seen at www.m-2studio.com.

A few quick facts about **Scott Zirkel**... He's the author of *A Bit Haywire*. He lives in the Texas Hill Country with his wife and two children. And, while he never actually ran for office, was once elected president of the Republic of Kirabati on accident. To this day, he is still considered a national hero of the island nation. You can visit him at www.scottzirkel.com.

YAGN Jos
Josh Howard presents
Sasquatch /

ALSO AVAILABLE FROM VIPER COMICS

DEAD AT 17: THE COMPLETE FIRST SERIES (REPRINT)
ISBN: 0-9754193-0-7

DEAD AT 17: BLOOD OF SAINTS
ISBN: 0-9754193-1-5

DEAD AT 17: REVOLUTION
ISBN: 0-9754193-3-1

DAISY KUTTER: THE LAST TRAIN
ISBN: 0-9754193-2-3

RANDOM ENCOUNTER: VOLUME 1
ISBN: 0-9754193-8-2

ODDLY NORMAL: VOLUME 1
ISBN: 0-9777883-0-X

EMILY EDISON
ISBN: 0-9777883-2-6

THE MIDDLEMAN: THE TRADE PAPERBACK IMPERATIVE
ISBN: 0-9754193-7-4

THE MIDDLEMAN: THE SECOND VOLUME INEVITABILITY
ISBN: 0-9777883-4-2

THE EXPENDABLE ONE
ISBN: 0-9754193-9-0

MOSH GIRLS + MONSTERS: THE ART OF JOSH HOWARD, VOL. 2
ISBN:0-9777883-3-4

A BIT HAYWIRE
ISBN: 0-9777883-5-0

YOU'LL HAVE THAT: VOLUME 1
ISBN: 0-9777883-1-8

YOU'LL HAVE THAT: VOLUME 2
ISBN 10: 0-9777883-6-9 / ISBN 13: 978-0-9777883-6-1

VILLAINS
ISBN 10: 0-9777883-7-7 / ISBN 13: 978-0-9777883-7-8

AVAILABLE ONLINE AT WWW.VIPERCOMICS.COM